WISDOM IN THE FACE OF MODERNITY

Faith and Reason: Studies in Catholic Theology and Philosophy

The series aims at publishing scholarly studies that serve the project of "faith seeking understanding." We hope to assist in making available in English valuable work being done by theologians and philosophers abroad; in this regard we recognize a special place for the ongoing renaissance in French-language Thomistic theology and philosophy. In addition to translations, we intend to publish collections of essays and monographs from a range of perspectives, united by their common commitment to the ecclesial and sapiential work of "faith seeking understanding" so as to build up the Church and proclaim the Gospel afresh.

Editor-in-Chief
Roger W. Nutt, *Ave Maria University*

Co-editors
Michael Dauphinais, *Ave Maria University*
Reinhard Hütter, *Duke University Divinity School*
Matthew Levering, *Mundelein Seminary*

Advisory Board
Romanus Cessario, OP, *St. John's Seminary*
Gilles Emery, OP, *University of Fribourg*
Joseph Koterski, SJ, *Fordham University*
Matthew L. Lamb, *Ave Maria University*
Steven A. Long, *Ave Maria University*
Guy Mansini, OSB, *Saint Meinrad Seminary*
Bruce Marshall, *Southern Methodist University*
Charles Morerod, OP, *Diocese of Lausanne*
Francesca Aran Murphy, *University of Notre Dame*
John O'Callaghan, *University of Notre Dame*
R. R. Reno, *Creighton University*
Richard Schenk, OP, *Catholic University of Eichstätt-Ingolstadt*

Published Volumes
Serge-Thomas Bonino, OP, ed., *Surnaturel: Reflections on Nature and Grace*
Gilles Emery, OP, *Trinity, Church, and the Human Person: Thomistic Essays*
Lawrence Feingold, *The Natural Desire to See God*
Matthew L. Lamb, ed., *Catholicism and America: Challenges and Prospects*
Matthew L. Lamb, *Eternity, Time, and the Life of Wisdom*
Guy Mansini, OSB, *The Word Has Dwelt Among Us*
Adrian J. Reimers, *Truth about the Good: John Paul II on Moral Norms*
Daria Spezzano, *The Glory of God's Grace: Deification According to St. Thomas Aquinas*
Thomas G. Weinandy, OFM, Cap., *Jesus: Essays in Christology*
Lawrence J. Welch, *The Presence of Christ in the Church*
Thomas Joseph White, OP, *Wisdom in the Face of Modernity*

WISDOM IN THE FACE OF MODERNITY

A STUDY IN THOMISTIC NATURAL THEOLOGY

Second Edition

Thomas Joseph White, OP

 SAPIENTIA PRESS
OF AVE MARIA UNIVERSITY

Sapientia Press
of Ave Maria University
5050 Ave Maria Blvd.
Ave Maria, FL 34142
800-537-5487

Cover Design: Eloise Anagnost

Cover Image: Suspended angel and architectural sketch, c. 1600 (red chalk on paper) by Bernardino Barbatelli Poccetti (1542/8–1612) Hamburger Kunsthalle, Hamburg, Germany/The Bridgeman Art Library

Printed in the United States of America.

Library of Congress Control Number: 2015946323

ISBN: 978-1-932589-77-1

Ad Sedes Sapientiae

Midwinter spring is its own season
Sempiternal though sodden towards sundown
Suspended in time, between pole and tropic.
When the short day is brightest, with frost and fire,
The brief sun flames the ice, on pond and ditches,
In windless cold that is the heart's heat,
Reflecting in a watery mirror
A glare that is blindness in the early afternoon.

—T. S. ELIOT, Little Gidding

Melius enim est in via claudicare, quam praeter viam fortiter ambulare.

—ST. THOMAS AQUINAS

Contents

CHAPTER **6**
The Human Person as a Being-toward-Truth: The Case of Karl Rahner

PART **IV**

CHAPTER **7**
From Omega to Alpha: Toward a General Order of Metaphysical Inquiry

Acknowledgments

FOR ASSISTANCE in writing this book, my first debt of gratitude is to the Dominican Order, and principally to my brethren in the St. Joseph Province. Throughout the time of my work on this project, their fraternal support and encouragement (as well as patience) have been constant, just as their respect and friendship have been a great gift.

A number of people helped me think more seriously about this subject at earlier periods of the research: Joseph d'Amécourt O.P., John Miguel-Garrigues O.P., Fergus Kerr O.P., Mark J. Edwards, and John Saward. Many of them offered detailed comments on earlier drafts of the material. Michel Bastit has had a great influence on this book, especially upon the way in which I approach the thought of Aristotle. His kind encouragement and advice have been helpful throughout, and he was kind enough to read the entire manuscript twice. Matthew Levering and Reinhard Hütter offered their very helpful advice and encouragement in the editing process, and Diane Eriksen of Sapientia Press offered invaluable service as an editor. Sr. Susan Heinemann O.P. kindly read a number of chapters, and made numerous suggestions for improvement of the text. Stephen Brock and Reinhard Hütter offered trenchant and thoughtful remarks on particular chapters of the book, which helped greatly to improve its content. R. Trent Pomplun read the entire manuscript carefully and challenged numerous assumptions, inviting a variety of clarifications. Despite all of this assistance, however, none of the above-mentioned persons can be held accountable for the defects of my argument or presentation, which remain entirely my own.

Things would be remiss if I did not seek to thank especially my parents, Stephen and Charlotte White, whose love and support have always been unwavering. "Autem, Deo gratias qui dedit nobis victoriam per Dominum nostrum Iesum Christum" (1 Cor 15:57).

Abbreviations of Works
by St. Thomas Aquinas

Comp. Theol.	*Compendium theologiae ad fratrem Reginaldum socium suum carissimum*
Credo	*Collationes super Credo in Deum*
De ente	*De ente et essentia*
De spirit. creat.	*De spiritualibus creaturis*
De sub. sep.	*De substatiis separatis*
De ver.	*De veritate*
ELP	*Expositio libri Posteriorum*
ELPH	*Expositio libri Peryermenias*
Expos. de Trin.	*Expositio super librum Boethii de Trinitate*
In de Anima	*Sententia super De anima*
In de Causis	*In librum de causis expositio*
In de Div. Nom.	*In librum beati Dionysii de divinis nominibus expositio*
In Ethic.	*Sententia libri Ethicorum*
In de Heb.	*Super Boetium de Hebdomadibus*
In Ioan.	*Lectura super Ioannem*
In Meta.	*In duodecim libros Metaphysicorum Aristotelis expositio*
In Phys.	*In octo libros Physicorum Aristotelis expositio*
Sent.	*Scriptum super libros Sententiarum magistri Petri Lombardi episcopi Parisiensis*
ScG	*Summa contra Gentiles*
ST	*Summa theologiae*

Translations

Unless otherwise indicated, all English translations for texts of Thomas Aquinas are taken from the following works:

Comp. Theol.: Compendium of Theology, trans. C. Vollert (London: B. Herder, 1955).

De ente: Thomas Aquinas: Selected Writings, trans. R. McInerny (London: Penguin Books, 1998).

De potentia Dei: On the Power of God, trans. English Dominican Province (Westminster, MD: Newman, 1952).

De ver.: Truth, trans. R. Schmidt (Chicago: Henry Regnery, 1954).

Expos. de Trin.: Faith, Reason and Theology, trans. A. Maurer (Toronto: PIMS, 1987); *The Division and Methods of the Sciences: Questions V and VI of his Commentary on the De Trinitate of Boethius*, trans. A. Maurer (Toronto: PIMS, 1986).

In de Causis: Commentary on the Book of Causes, trans. V. Guagliardo, C. Hess, R. Taylor (Washington, DC: The Catholic University of America Press, 1996).

In Ethic.: Commentary on the Nicomachean Ethics, trans. C. I. Lintzinger (Chicago: Henry Regnery, 1964).

In Ioan.: Commentary on the Gospel of St. John, vol. 1, trans. J. Weisheipl (Albany, NY: Magi Press, 1980); vol. 2, trans. J. Weisheipl (Petersham, MA: St. Bede's Publications, 2000).

In Meta.: Commentary on Aristotle's Metaphysics, trans. J. P. Rowan (Notre Dame, IN: Dumb Ox Books, 1995).

In Phys.: Commentary on Aristotle's Physics, trans. J. P. Rowan (Notre Dame, IN: Dumb Ox Books, 1999).

ScG I: *Summa contra Gentiles* I, trans. A. Pegis (Garden City, NY: Doubleday, 1955).

ScG II: *Summa contra Gentiles* II, vol. 1 and 2, trans. J. Anderson (Garden City, NY: Doubleday, 1956).

ScG III: *Summa contra Gentiles* III, vol. 1 and 2, trans. V. J. Burke (Garden City, NY: Doubleday, 1956).

ST: Summa theologica, trans. English Dominican Province, 1920 (New York: Benzinger Brothers, 1947).

Preface

T. S. ELIOT'S poem "Little Gidding" begins with the image of a "midwinter spring" in which the unquenchable light of the sun shows forth even in the midst of a cold winter's day. This imagery contrasts with Eliot's earlier characterization of April as "the cruelest month" in "The Waste Land," the spring harbinger announcing yet another year of bewildering historical existence. Here, rather, the poet employs a Platonic image of the sun, not representative of heat, but rather of light, so as (arguably) to recall the beauty and undiminishable presence of God, and of the divine light, even in the winter season of modernity. Yet, this presence is discernable only amidst and in a world without thaw, still cold, and unconsoling. Is our historical age such a time? As regards the natural knowledge of God, and the promise of metaphysical reasoning, it would seem so. Certainly the promise of a springtime of rational thought concerning God looms always near, since the human person is perennially capable of metaphysical reflection about God. Nevertheless, the historical time we inhabit is also characterized by vivid disagreements about the capacity of philosophical reason to determine a meaning for human existence and to act as a vehicle for cultural renewal and unification. The possibility of a renewal of natural, philosophical theology remains questionable, therefore, thwarted by the impasses of a modern culture in which such aspirations are seen as irremediably difficult, as impossible, or as somehow politically infelicitous.

In a world in which great confusion reigns concerning the questions of the transcendent meaning of human existence and final ethical purposes, it is easy to believe that a given religious tradition might be the sole locus wherein one can find answers to ultimate questions. In Christian theology this has led to the claim (represented especially by Kierkegaard and Barth, in two different ways) that natural knowledge of God is not an

xviii   WISDOM IN THE FACE OF MODERNITY

authentic foundation for understanding human life with God, that philosophical interest in such a natural aspiration is in fact morally problematic,
and that, more basically, such knowledge is not possible. All true knowledge of God must occur through recourse to the loci of divine revelation.

In one sense, of course, such a thesis is radically opposed to the most
areligious themes of Enlightenment modernity, since it seeks to reassert
the epistemological primacy of divine revelation. In essence, however, the
Christian theological claim that human beings are incapable of natural
knowledge of God rejoins the modern Kantian, and post-Heideggerian,
prohibition on a philosophical, demonstrative approach to the mystery of
God. For in both these cases, the human being is naturally deprived of the
rational capacity to reason toward God by its own powers. One might
wish to emphasize the reality of revelation's gratuitous givenness and the
poverty of human possession by claiming the inaccessibility of the divine
"outside" of the historical event of God's Incarnation and crucifixion in
Christ. However, the parallel price to pay for this decision is very high.
The revelation of Christ must be projected upon a backdrop in which
modern human beings are intrinsically secular, and radically incapable of
ameliorating the areligiosity of their culture. Their being is traversed in
arbitrary fashion by a set of conflicting religious and anti-religious desires
that are incapable of any positive resolution or of any resolution in which
philosophical reason might play a role.

To this we must respond with the dictum of the Lord: "For those who
have not, even what they have will be taken from them" (Mk 4:25). The
graced actualization of the human person in an authentic response to
divine revelation is possible only if the human person is naturally capable of
knowledge of God. A true response to a "secular" anthropology of human
beings enclosed in themselves (*incurvatus in se*) cannot be found, then, by
appealing uniquely to the activity of grace in persons (though this is of
course fundamental). Such a response must also attain to knowledge of the
natural presuppositions of that activity, knowledge of the natural human
capacity for God. A theology that cannot articulate in philosophical terms
the rational creature's natural capacity for a return toward God cannot in
fact render intelligible the possibility of the encounter with God by grace
even as it occurs within divine revelation. Any total prohibition of natural
theology is implicitly radically secularizing. What is required in the face of
modernity's Kantian, Heideggerian, and Barthian impasses to natural theology, then, is a renewed consideration of the natural human orientation
toward the transcendence of God, and the ways in which this natural order
is awakened by and implicitly made active within the agency of grace.

It is the conviction and argument of this book that the modern philosophical and theological dismissal of medieval and classical metaphysics in

modernity was not something that was justified philosophically in any definitive and determinate way. On the contrary, precisely to resolve some of the crises generated by the secularization of reason in a modern, religiously indifferent culture, we should consider the alternative resources that are present in a less reductive, and more profound, tradition: that of classical and medieval metaphysics. This tradition receives its most insightful and forceful expression in the thought of Thomas Aquinas. Here, in fact, we will find determinate resources to help us rethink in an authentic fashion the relationship between creaturely autonomy and divine causality, such that we are not obliged to choose between a religious and sapiential vision of creation on the one hand, and a historical, scientific, and personalist vision on the other. The created order is invested with intrinsic meaning and purpose that modernity has in a variety of ways sought to uncover and render valuable. However, this same creation finds its own completion ultimately in God alone, its primary source and final end. Without the theocentric aspiration toward transcendence, all "lesser" meanings we might glean eventually pale and lose their deepest significance. This is especially the case for those meanings pertaining to the activities of human rationality and personal freedom themselves, activities to which modernity aspires to give primary value. The Thomistic pursuit of natural knowledge of God offers a much needed perspective not only on God, but also on the purpose of human existence in particular, and of created existence more generally.

The pursuit of natural knowledge of God, then, is a task that promises in a contemporary setting to be quite difficult and perhaps greatly misunderstood. Yet this task is also deeply meaningful and even necessary; for it is concerned with the truth about God and the truth about the human person, who can find happiness ultimately only in God himself. If the argument of this book is correct, then this is not the case simply for a given kind of human being or the human community of a given time and place. Rather, this is the case for all persons at all times, even for those persons who account themselves secularized, inhabiting a (more or less) post-religious culture. If we can come to know by natural reason that God exists, and that in his incomprehensible perfection he is what is greatest in the order of truth and happiness (or spiritual joy), then the capacity for such knowledge in us is genuinely perennial. Ultimately, then, it concerns the eschatological orientation of each human being, wherein we are ordered beyond all history, toward God himself. Understood in this light, the pursuit of this philosophical understanding is too important to forget or ignore in any given historical age. For this reason we must obey the Socratic injunction to pursue wisdom, even in the face of indifference or adversity, since the pursuit of wisdom ultimately concerns the true good of all of "the city," and not simply of a few. And, therefore, by way of analogy, we should confidently pursue a Thomistic renewal of understanding of the natural knowledge of God, the God whose light shines even in an age of metaphysical winter; indeed, the God whose perennial light as Creator shines even in the face of modernity.

Introduction

THIS BOOK is about natural theology as understood within the Thomistic tradition. Natural theology is of importance for Christian dogmatic theology insofar as it touches directly upon questions of the unity in God's works of creation and redemption. What do the works of creation tell us about the being and nature of God? How is this relation exemplified in a particularly important way in the relationship between philosophy and faith? What role should metaphysics play within Christian theology?

To claim that philosophical aspirations to natural knowledge of God have a place within dogmatic theology is, of course, characteristic of Catholic thought, which has consistently drawn upon the resources of classical metaphysics. Luther's reserve concerning natural theology, meanwhile, has been vigorously reformulated in modernity by Søren Kierkegaard.[1] Philosophical difficulties for natural theology have been compounded by the secularist philosophical project of Immanuel Kant. These two strands (Lutheran theological epistemology and Kantian critical epistemology) were fused together powerfully in the modern Reformed theology of Karl Barth.[2]

---

[1] For a contemporary appeal to Kierkegaard's work in this respect, see Alan Torrance, "*Auditus Fidei*: Where and How Does God Speak? Faith, Reason and the Question of Criteria," in *Reason and the Reasons of Faith*, ed. P. Griffiths and R. Hütter (New York and London: T&T Clark, 2005), 27–52. For an interpretation of Kierkegaard that suggests some presence of natural knowledge of God in his work, see Arnold B. Come, *Kierkegaard as Humanist: Discovering My Self* (Montreal: McGill-Queen's University Press, 1995), 182–86, 281–323.

[2] Kantian and classical Protestant influences upon the genesis of Barth's thought are helpfully examined by Bruce McCormack in his *Karl Barth's Critically Realistic Dialectical Theology* (Oxford: Clarendon Press, 1995).

Despite the influence of the Barthian project, recent theological literature defending the importance of philosophical theology, and of metaphysical reflection more generally, has not been lacking.[3] However, in the wake of the conundrums characteristic of Enlightenment theism (and its subsequent critics), many who emphasize the role of ontology in Christian theology are also critical of any attempt to make too sharp a distinction between doctrinal theology and a distinctly philosophical monotheism.[4] The question of the possibility or necessity of natural theology therefore continues to be a significant and potentially divisive issue in discussions between Christian theologians.[5]

Philosophical "theism," of course, also continues to be a characteristic topic of controversy between those modern philosophers who are intellectually disposed to theism and those who disavow the rationality of any such belief. The very notion of natural theology as a moral and metaphysical compass for the human person is highly contested within the context of modern thought and culture. Modern philosophers since Descartes have commonly given methodological primacy to the examination of the epistemological and moral dimensions of man, often in self-conscious distinction from, or in reaction to, the metaphysics of classical philosophy. The study of human interior life has become a central concern for philosophy, while the physical world is approached especially through the experimental sciences. It is a truism to note the tendency among many of the most influential modern philosophers to substitute for the classical ques-

---

3 See, for example, the exceptional works of Norman Kretzmann, *The Metaphysics of Theism* (Oxford: Clarendon Press, 1997), esp. 1–53; John Wippel, *The Metaphysical Thought of Thomas Aquinas* (Washington, DC: The Catholic University of America Press, 2000); Eleonore Stump, *Aquinas* (New York: Routledge, 2003); Denys Turner, *Faith, Reason and the Existence of God* (Cambridge: Cambridge University Press, 2004); Benedict Ashley, *The Way toward Wisdom* (Notre Dame: Notre Dame University Press, 2006), and Ralph McInerny, *Praeambula Fidei: Thomism and the God of the Philosophers* (Washington, DC: The Catholic University of America Press, 2006).

4 Consider in this respect, the very different (sometimes mutually opposed) but generically related theological reflections of John Milbank and Catherine Pitstock, *Truth in Aquinas* (New York and London: Routledge, 2001); David Bentley Hart, *The Beauty of the Infinite* (Grand Rapids: Eerdmans, 2003), esp. 1–34; John Betz, "Beyond the Sublime: The Aesthetics of the Analogy of Being," *Modern Theology* 21, no. 3, and 22, no. 1 (2005 and 2006): 367–411 and 1–50.

5 See the suggestive reflections of Charles Morerod on the ecumenical significance of philosophical differences in his *Ecumenism and Philosophy: Philosophical Questions for a Renewal of Dialogue* (Naples, FL: Sapientia Press, 2006), and the accompanying volume on the communal role of propositional truth claims: *Tradition et Unité des Chrétiens: Le Dogma Comme Condition de Possibilité de l'Oecuménisme* (Paris: Parole et Silence, 2005).

tions of being, goodness, and unity, questions concerning the philosophy of mind, or the possible meaning and uses of human freedom.

Coupled with this tendency are the various problems posed to classical metaphysics by the critiques of Kant, empiricist philosophy, and Heideggerian postmodernism, respectively. Philosophies critical of the kinds of aspirations to objective knowledge found in classical metaphysics have given rise to crises of foundations in epistemology, ethics, and ontology. Thus with the advent of modernity and postmodernity acute questions have been posed concerning the possible existence of a universal truth or that of an essence of human nature transcending the flux of history.[6] Questions about the ultimate sense of human existence, absolute moral principles, or the legitimacy of any form of religious aspiration in man all follow subsequently. Such a context influences profoundly the way the question is raised of whether or not the human person is a being naturally open to and ordered toward the true and the good, and toward God, questions that often receive critically hesitant or negative responses.

In this book I will be arguing from within a modern Thomistic tradition that confesses the inherent capacities of human nature for knowledge of God. The participants of this tradition understand this capacity of the creature as an important instance of the intrinsic meaning and goodness of creation. They also believe that this natural dimension of the human person plays an intrinsic role in his or her response to the dynamic activity of grace. The denial of the existence of the natural human aspiration toward God, then, is thought to lead not only to a serious misunderstanding of the nature of man but also to a problematic understanding of the human

---

[6] Despite their selective character, the remarks of George Cottier, "Thomisme et Modernité," in *Saint Thomas au XXe Siècle*, ed. S. Bonino (Paris: Éditions St.-Paul, 1994), 355–56, are suggestive: "The emergence of modernity as a 'principle' was progressive and took on diverse forms. I will briefly indicate some of these. The first form is the Cartesian *cogito* which posited the foundational primacy of the thinking subject, and from which modern philosophy derived a heritage. The second is represented by the diverse forms of empiricism, concomitant with the rise of the natural sciences, and by the interpretation that August Comte gave to them in his famous 'law' of the three ages of man. The third, which follows upon the Kantian *Critique*, is historicism. ('Spirit is time': this dictum of the young Hegel has its foundation in the Kantian theory of time as an *a priori* intuition of the sensations, which in turn conditions all of our knowledge. One is well aware what influence this thesis exerted upon Heidegger.) Knowledge is always 'situational,' that is to say, intrinsically marked by its spacio-temporal coordinates. The human intelligence cannot transcend time, but rather is enclosed within time. It is always 'perspectival.' . . . Thus, referring explicitly to Kant, one can decree, as Habermas does, that any return to metaphysics today is illusory, because we are, whether we wish it or not, in the epoch of *post-metaphysical thought*." [Translations from French in this book are my own unless otherwise specified.]

person's response to the demands of grace, and indeed, to a problematic articulation of Christian theology.

However, modern Thomistic thinkers, as I hope to show, have also tended to be sensitive to the importance of the philosophical oppositions to natural theology articulated in modern thought and are interested in responding to these difficulties on a variety of fronts.[7] The divergences between the intellectual orientations of modernity and the philosophical and theological heritage of Thomism, however, are often intense and profound.

An example of a central classical theme of Aristotelian and Thomistic philosophy that has frequently been ignored in modernity is that of "wisdom" (*sophia* or *sapientia*). Wisdom, in the thought of both Aristotle and Aquinas, implies at least two important properties. First, it is a "scientific" knowledge of the primary cause(s) of all things. Therefore, it gives an ultimate *explicative* theory of meaning for the realities we experience understood in relation to their transcendent origin: God. Extracting from Aquinas's work, one could say that when philosophy becomes *sapientia* it reflects on creatures in the light of God, as effects of God's own transcendent goodness and wisdom, in whom they participate, albeit in a finite way. Second, such reflection is the activity of the mind (the intellectual virtue) that perfects human activity teleologically. Natural theology implies an ethical knowledge concerning the final end of man that is directive of practical action. The capacity for such wisdom is characteristic of being human: it denotes something specific to the rational creature, a purpose for which we are made.[8]

In speaking of "natural theology" within this tradition, then, I do not mean to denote a discipline that would attempt to construct an understanding of God in separation from Christian theology so as to judge the latter according to the criteria of knowledge of the former. Rather, I mean a discipline that inquires into the distinctly natural or intrinsic capacity of the human mind to come to some real knowledge of the existence and nature of God by philosophical means, even though this knowledge is mediate and analogical. This capacity, in turn, is implicitly called upon when the human community is addressed by the Judeo-Christian revelation itself and becomes a constitutive element of man's response to God

---

[7] I am presuming here a broad definition of the Thomistic tradition, which responds in differing ways to the modern concerns of the natural sciences, continental philosophical atheism, or the debates characteristic of the analytical tradition.

[8] *ST* I, q. 1, a. 6: "For since it is the part of a wise man to arrange and to judge and since lesser matters should be judged in the light of some higher principle, he is said to be wise in any one order who considers the highest principle in that order. . . . Again, in the order of all human life, the prudent man is called wise, inasmuch as he directs his acts to a fitting end. . . . Therefore he who considers absolutely the highest cause of the whole universe, namely God, is most of all called wise."

under the working of grace. It also forms a part of subsequent doctrinal theological reflection. To claim that this dimension of the human person is natural, therefore, need not entail the belief that it achieves its own best realization outside the realm of Christian theological belief and practice.[9] In principle, it need not entail that such a non-Christian realization of natural knowledge of God even occurs at all (although, like Aquinas, I consider this point of view to be mistaken).[10] Even less is it a claim that this natural dimension of the person in the fallen state must or can be awakened without the work of grace. Grace can be given, after all, even to heal "merely" natural capacities afflicted by ignorance or the disorders of the will and the emotions. Perhaps in the fallen order, then, divine agency is necessary (either all or most of the time) to liberate persons for such reflection. Furthermore, if this is the case, such grace can also be refused by its recipients. To claim that such a natural capacity is latently present in all persons is perfectly compatible with the belief that the natural desire for knowledge of God is frequently suppressed, ignored, or gravely misinterpreted within a variety of religious and secular cultures.

The argument that natural theology is possible, however, entails an engagement with its objectors. And the claim that natural theology is possible

---

[9] When considering the question of "Christian philosophy," it is helpful to distinguish various effects of grace on the one hand (upon human intellection in the apprehension of revealed principles, the eliciting of intellectual desire for natural knowledge of God, or the quelling of sinful tendencies of cupidity) from the human natural capacity for knowledge of God and the specific structure of natural philosophical reasoning, on the other. The former effects of grace affect the healthy *exercise* of the latter "natural capacity for God" (since this capacity is wounded by sin, even to the point of ceasing to function in the absence of grace). However, grace does so without altering the specifically natural character, or *structure*, of the human capacity for God. Philosophical knowledge of God remains an intrinsic power of human nature, even when that natural power is hindered in its concrete historical exercise by sin. See the helpful studies on this topic by Jacques Maritain, *De la philosophie chrétienne* (1932), and *Science et Sagesse* (1935), in his *Oeuvres Completes*, vols. 5 and 6 (Fribourg and Paris: Éditions Universitaires de Fribourg et Éditions St. Paul, 1982 and 1984); John Wippel, *Metaphysical Themes in Thomas Aquinas* (Washington, DC: The Catholic University of America Press, 1984), 1–33; and Jean-Miguel Garrigues, "Autonomie Spécifique et Ouverture Personelle de la Raison à la Foi," *Nova et Vetera* (French edition) 98, no. 3 (1998): 95–106.

[10] Aquinas himself argues that for fallen human beings natural knowledge of God is difficult, time-consuming, and usually admixed with errors, but not impossible (*ScG* I, c. 4; *ST* I, q. 1, a. 1; q. I–II, q. 109, a. 1). However, because of the admixture of errors, the affirmation that human beings acquire true knowledge of God independently of Christian revelation is also an ambiguous one (*In Ioan.* XVII, lec. 2, 2195; lec. 6, 2265). See the helpful commentary on the relation between grace and natural knowledge of God in Aquinas by Santiago Ramirez, *De Gratia Dei* (Salamanca: Editorial San Esteban, 1992), 61–107.

in modernity must be stated against at least two formidable modern objections. One of these is philosophical: knowledge of God is not possible for human reason acting within a right acknowledgment of its boundaries. This claim is represented in a variety of forms in modernity, not least typically by recourse to empiricist philosophies. There is a widespread belief that modern science has exposed the groundlessness of ontological discourse concerning physical reality, simply rendering such discourse irrelevant. However, in its more typical form this thesis is represented by Kant and his spiritual inheritors. A central tenet of Kant's critical philosophy is that natural theology (real rational knowledge of the existence and nature of God) is impossible due to the fact that ontological claims are mere regulatory notions of reason. All claims to knowledge of God are implicitly and necessarily based upon a priori concepts, themselves derived merely from immanent constructions of human reason (which Kant terms "ontotheology").

The second objection is theological and in fact predates the first. It is the claim, originating in particular with Martin Luther, that a right use of natural knowledge of God is impossible for human beings due to the fallen character of human reason and the cupidity of the human will. In the economy of the fallen state of man, speculative metaphysical theology (which Luther terms *theologia gloriae*) amounts to a rival account of the divine that is set up over and against that which is offered in revelation (*theologia crucis*).[11] This would be the case, for Luther, even if such philosophies were able to facilitate some true knowledge of the transcendent identity of God.[12] Insofar as human beings would seek to find evidences of the Creator apart

---

[11] This view point is particularly manifest in Luther's *Heidelberg Disputation*. "That person is not rightly called a theologian who looks upon the invisible things of God as though they were clearly perceptible through things that have actually happened. . . . He deserves to be called a theologian who understands the visible and manifest things of God seen through suffering and the Cross. A theology of glory calls evil good and good evil. A theology of the Cross calls the thing what it actually is. That wisdom which sees the invisible things of God in works as perceived by man is completely puffed up, blinded, and hardened" (*Luther's Works*, ed. J. Pelikan [vols. 1–30] and H. Lehmann [vols. 31–55] [Philadelphia: Fortress Press, 1955–], 25:167; hereafter *LW*). This aspect of Luther's thought became a subject of renewed interest in the early twentieth century. See the representative and influential study by Walther von Loewenich, *Luther's Theology of the Cross* (Belfast: Christian Journals, 1976).

[12] In his *Commentary on Romans*, with respect to Romans 1:20 ("Since the creation of the world, his invisible nature, namely his eternal power and deity, has been clearly perceived in the things that have been made"), Luther does not deny that St. Paul refers to a capacity for natural knowledge of God, but claims that such knowledge is used only toward religiously disordered ends. *LW*, 25:157–58: "All those who set up idols and worship them and call them 'gods' or even 'God,' believing that God is immortal, that is eternal, powerful, and able to render help, clearly indicate that they

from the revelation of God in Jesus Christ, they are motivated by a pretension to understanding that is not distinct from the vice of idolatry. Of course, Karl Barth reworked these perspectives creatively in his own even more radical criticism of natural theology and the doctrine of analogical knowledge of God, which he initially termed (under the auspices of the *analogia entis*) "the invention of the anti-Christ."[13]

Against these two claims a person interested in the continuing project of natural theology is required to argue on a variety of fronts, and evidently some of these are strictly theological in kind. Does the desire to speak rationally of God in philosophical discourse necessarily stem from the effects of sin in the human person or not? Do the vices of the fallen self mitigate irrevocably against the valid exercise of any kind of natural theology? Is such philosophical discourse extrinsic to the revelatory claims of Christian scripture, or does the latter in fact entail and facilitate the former? Could one speak realistically and coherently of the God revealed in the Incarnation by grace without recourse to an ontology that would relate in some way to the ordinary (natural) experience of human beings? These questions are certainly important and, as regards the broader scope of the debate, unavoidable.[14]

However, this study seeks to look at another equally important set of questions directly related to the philosophical side of the equation. And in a more specific sense at one particular problem among others: namely, is true natural knowledge of God possible that does not in fact presuppose its object a priori? Is there such a thing as a "natural theology" that is not "ontotheological" in the senses given that word by Kant and subsequently by Heidegger? Second, if there is in fact the possibility of such knowledge, does this not wed us inextricably to some of the problems raised by Karl Barth in his criticisms of the *analogia entis* of Catholic theology? Are we in fact attempting to lay hold of God conceptually in the most illegitimate of ways when we claim to be able to understand something of God the Creator analogically? If natural theology is possible, it must also manifest against its

---

have a knowledge of divinity in their hearts . . . a knowledge or notion of divinity which undoubtedly came to them from God, as our text tells us. This was their error, that they did not worship this divinity untouched but changed and adjusted it to their desires and needs."

13 See especially Karl Barth's 1932 treatment of natural theology in *Church Dogmatics* I, 1 (London and New York: T&T Clark, 2004), xiii, 125–32, 162–86. On Luther's distinction between a *theologia gloriae* and a *theologia crucis* as applied to the possibility of natural theology, see 178–79.

14 See theological treatments of these issues by Turner, *Faith, Reason and the Existence of God*, 3–47; Reinhard Hütter, "The Directedness of Reasoning and the Metaphysics of Creation," in *Reason and the Reasons of Faith*, ed. P. Griffiths and R. Hütter (New York and London: T&T Clark, 2005), 160–93, and Betz, "Beyond the Sublime."

theological detractors a deep recognition of the transcendence and even the incomprehensibility of God. However, to do this *on its own terms*, it must do so through a distinctly philosophical form of theological apophaticism.[15]

The thesis of this book is that the metaphysics of Thomas Aquinas presents a pathway to true natural knowledge of God that is immune to the core criticisms of Kantian skepticism concerning knowledge of God, but one that simultaneously defends itself successfully against the charge of being an overly rationalist instantiation of natural theology or a form of "conceptual idolatry."[16] In itself, this is not an atypical claim, even if it remains a controversial one.[17] This book in fact examines various paradigmatic instantiations of modern Thomistic natural theology developed by persons who themselves made this argument in the wake of the Kantian and Heideggerian criticisms of natural theology (Étienne Gilson, Jacques Maritain, Karl Rahner). However, I will argue that there is an essential resource for the reading of Aquinas that has been neglected by these previous interpreters: the causal metaphysics of Aristotle. Or more to the point, certain Aristotelian dimensions of Aquinas's thought pertaining to the progressive analysis of the "causes of being" are of importance for Thomists seeking to speak truly and rightly about God. An Aristotelian analysis of causes allows one to do so in such a way as to avoid both the Scylla of an agnostic philosophical episte-

---

15 It should be noted here that while some Barthian critics claim that natural theology constructs a conceptually anthropomorphic account of God that obstructs reception of the true, positive content of the revealed knowledge of God, Eberhard Jüngel (*God as the Mystery of the World* [Grand Rapids: Eerdmans, 1983], 276–82) has argued that Aquinas's apophaticism necessarily banishes God from the creation, by a kind of metaphysical agnosticism, and therefore renders obscure the human presence of God revealed in Christ. Jüngel's reading of Aquinas on analogy and apophaticism is problematic, however. See the criticisms by Philip A. Rolnick, *Analogical Possibilities: How Words Refer to God* (Atlanta: Scholars Press, 1993), 189–284. Some have also leveled against Jüngel a theological response: in the absence of a theory of the *analogia entis* his theology suffers from an insufficient recognition of divine transcendence (via an apophatic theology). This in turn leads to a problematic mischaracterization of the immanent life of God that fails to distinguish God sufficiently from intra-worldly history. See in this respect David Bentley Hart, "No Shadow of Turning: On Divine Impassibility," *Pro Ecclesia* 11 (2002): 184–206.

16 The notion of "conceptual idolatry" by means of a "pretension to representation" of God comes from the French Heideggerian thinker Jean-Luc Marion. See his "De la 'mort de Dieu' au noms divines: l'itinéraire théologique de la métaphysique," in *l'Être et Dieu*, ed. D. Bourg (Paris: Cerf, 1986), 113.

17 Similar claims are made in the exceptional recent studies of Gregory Rocca, *Speaking the Incomprehensible God: Thomas Aquinas on the Interplay of Positive and Negative Theology* (Washington, DC: The Catholic University of America Press, 2004), and Thierry-Dominique Humbrecht, *Théologie Négative et Noms Divins chez Saint Thomas d'Aquin* (Paris: J. Vrin, 2005).

mology and the Charybdis of a philosophical discourse concerning God that would claim to know what God is, either by appeal to a priori concepts or by the articulation of an overly ambitious form of rationalist theism.

Furthermore, I will argue that such a causal analysis is necessary for a right interpretation of Aquinas's complex views on the subject of the analogical predication of being. For if Aquinas himself discusses several forms of analogical predication (analogy of proportionality, analogy *multa ad unum*—from the many to the one, and analogy *ad alterum*—toward the other), these analogies need to be understood by reference to their ontological grounding in the reality signified. In each of the interpreters previously mentioned there exists an imbalanced dependency on one of these three forms of analogical discourse to the near exclusion of the two others. This imbalance is due in each case to a neglect of the causal analysis of being that is characteristic of Aquinas's own thought. In essence a causal study of metaphysics as presented by Aquinas permits us to ascertain how we can pass from an initial analogical knowledge of beings we experience to an eventual, indirect, and analogical knowledge of the Creator. The central investigation of this book, then, concerns the possibility of Thomistic natural theology in the era after the Kantian and Heideggerian criticisms of metaphysics and the resources that the Aristotelianism of Aquinas provides for us within that setting.

The book is divided into four parts and eight chapters. Part I comprises chapter 1 and begins with observations concerning the renewal of modern Thomistic studies that was launched by the efforts of Pope Leo XIII in his encyclical letter *Aeterni Patris* (1879). I argue that the modern search for a Thomistic philosophical wisdom, or natural theology, is especially affected by two historical conditions. One is the fact that Aquinas's reflections derive from a medieval *theological* context. Aquinas himself distinguishes between a philosophical *via inventionis*, or way of inquiry, by which the intellect proceeds from initial, self-evident principles to scientific conclusions, and the *via judicii*, by which the intellect judges in the light of its more ultimate discoveries the initial principles from which it began. The first *via* concerns the genetic order of discovery of things as known for us (*quoad nos*), while the second concerns the order of nature, or perfection, concerning things as they are in themselves (*per se*).[18] Yet Aquinas himself did not seek to present a purely philosophical order of discovery, or *via inventionis*, even for many of the metaphysical principles that he invokes within the context of his Christian theological writings. A modern development of a Thomistic natural theology requires, then, an interpretation concerning the distinctly philosophical characteristics of Aquinas's metaphysics and their order of exposition. This study must

---

[18] *ST* I, q. 79, a. 8.

include a metaphysical analysis of human personhood if it wishes to speak analogically about the "personal" nature of God. Only if it does so can it hope to demonstrate in what real sense God can be said to be "wisdom," and consequently in what sense the pursuit of knowledge of God is a natural goal for the human person *qua* rational and free.[19]

Second, the Thomistic task of delineating any such order of inquiry in modernity should take into account the modern Kantian and Heideggerian critiques of metaphysical natural theology as ontotheology, as purely immanent constructions of reason that are heuristic at best and genuinely misleading at worst. Here I note a number of characteristics of ontotheological reasoning as these thinkers describe it. My basic point will be to identify in what way the kind of Enlightenment philosophical project they object to is in fact quite distinct from the metaphysical project undertaken by Aquinas. These criticisms challenge us, however, to identify a natural theology that does not presuppose implicitly that which it seeks to attain by rational argument. Therefore, the task I set out to reflect upon is the valid articulation of a Thomistic *via inventionis*, or path of discovery of God, that is not implicitly "ontotheological" in kind.

Part II of the book comprises chapters 2 and 3 and concerns the theme of wisdom in Aristotle's and Aquinas's thought, respectively. Attention is given to the concrete historical circumstances in which the authors wrote, precisely in order to argue that a permanently valid metaphysics and natural theology can be extracted from their writings that is based upon a progressive causal analysis of being (as substance and accident, and as actuality and potentiality). This form of thought begins from natural human experience. By reflection on the ontological conditions of possibility for the real beings that exist, it can arrive by way of a posteriori demonstrative arguments at the affirmation of the necessary existence of a transcendent origin of "created" beings, who is God. This structure of reasoning does not pre-

---

[19] See the suggestive remarks of Pope John Paul II to this effect in his encyclical *Fides et Ratio*, §83. The pope speaks about "the need for a philosophy of *genuinely metaphysical* range, capable, that is, of transcending empirical data in order to attain something absolute, ultimate and foundational in its search for truth. This requirement is implicit in sapiential and analytical knowledge alike; and in particular it is a requirement for knowing the moral good, which has its ultimate foundation in the Supreme Good, God himself. . . . [Here] I want only to state that reality and truth do transcend the factual and the empirical, and to vindicate the human being's capacity to know this transcendent and metaphysical dimension in a way that is true and certain, albeit imperfect and analogical. In this sense, metaphysics should not be seen as an alternative to anthropology, since it is metaphysics which makes it possible to ground the concept of personal dignity in virtue of [the human being's] spiritual nature. In a special way, the person constitutes a privileged locus for the encounter with being, and hence with metaphysical enquiry."

suppose logically either the given principles of revealed faith or an aprioristic concept of God. It escapes, in fact, the designate characteristics of ontotheology as they have been demarcated with reference to Kant and Heidegger in chapter 1.

Part III of the book (chapters 4 through 6) examines the efforts of three noteworthy representatives of the Thomistic tradition in modernity: Étienne Gilson, Jacques Maritain, and Karl Rahner. The goal is to evaluate the efforts of these thinkers to construct a *via inventionis* for Thomistic metaphysical natural theology in the wake of modern criticisms of classical metaphysics. Certainly other representatives of modern Thomism could have been chosen (Cornelio Fabro, Fernand Van Steenberghen, Charles De Koninck, Gustav Siewerth, Norman Kretzmann, and a host of others). However, the three aforementioned thinkers are noteworthy both for their widespread influence and for the acuity with which they each attempted to reinterpret Aquinas's work in a modern vein, particularly in response to the aforementioned objectors. For Gilson, this reinterpretation centers around Aquinas's metaphysics of existence and the real distinction in creatures between existence (*esse*) and essence. Correspondingly, he relies in an acute way upon Aquinas's analogy *ad alterum* as a means of understanding the analogical character of our knowledge of being. For Jacques Maritain, an analogical study of the transcendentals (properties coextensive with being, such as unity, goodness, and truth) stands at the heart of the metaphysical science of being. His theory favors the use of the analogy of proper proportionality. Karl Rahner, meanwhile, reinterprets Aquinas more radically in light of Kant's philosophy in an attempt to develop a metaphysics of the inner life of the human person and the spiritual operations of knowledge. His analogical thought depends almost entirely upon Aquinas's theory of the analogy *multa ad unum*.

My own claim in these chapters will be that in each of these thinkers essential elements of a Thomistic natural theology are presented concerning the metaphysics of *esse*, the problem of analogy and the transcendentals, and with respect to the metaphysics of personal spiritual operations. These elements can contribute to the constitution of a non-ontotheological form of natural theological reasoning. However, there are also some significant traces of aprioristic natural theology in their respective works. This is due in each case to the neglect of some dimension of Aquinas's causal study of being, a study that in fact derives from his Aristotelianism. Correspondingly, there are one-sided preferences concerning analogical predication in each of these modern thinkers because of a neglect of this same causal study. In these chapters, then, I seek to illustrate why a more acute attention to the Aristotelianism of Aquinas's ontology is quite helpful precisely in order to avoid such impasses. These chapters discuss classical Thomistic topics like the real distinction, the analogical understanding of being, the transcendentals, and the metaphysics of personal actions while setting these in relation to Aquinas's use of the Aristotelian notions of substance and accident, actuality and potentiality.

Part IV is presented in the last two chapters of the book. In chapter 7, I offer my own proposal of a Thomistic order of metaphysical inquiry (*via inventionis*) that passes from beings we experience to God. I argue that this reflection upon natural theology avoids the difficulties of undue aprioristic claims to knowledge of God, thereby circumventing the Kantian and Heideggerian criticisms of ontotheology. In doing so, I advocate for a harmonization between key elements of Aristotle's ontology as appropriated by Aquinas, on the one hand, and original elements of Aquinas's own thought, on the other. The latter are interpreted in homogeneous continuity with the former. In other words, I treat Aquinas primarily as an Aristotelian, yet without denying the original character of his metaphysics.

In chapter 8, I address from a philosophical angle the dual concerns that either natural theology allows us in fact to know nothing of what God is in himself, or it attempts to "know too much of God," even if it is non-aprioristic and despite all its epistemological precautions. Here the book examines the role the Aristotelianism of Aquinas plays in his interpretation of Dionysius the Areopagite's apophaticism. In what way does the causal knowledge of God as pure actuality render analogical names of God possible, and to what extent does the identity of God transcend all conceptual comprehension? In dialogue with what I take to be excessively apophatic conceptions of Aquinas's metaphysics, I argue that the knowledge offered by natural theological reasoning makes use of the *via negationis*, or negative way, primarily as a means of acknowledging God's transcendence and perfection, and that this procedure ultimately leads in fact to a positive form of knowledge. Even while the pure actuality of God transcends all experience and the mode of signification proper to our finite conceptual understanding, God can truly be known, albeit indirectly, mediately, and by recourse to analogical predication. Natural theology can therefore rightly be interpreted as a true form of wisdom due to the real knowledge of God to which it attains. However, philosophical wisdom is simultaneously intrinsically imperfect, since it fails to attain *immediate* knowledge of the transcendent God. Natural reason, for example, can only affirm "in darkness" that God is eminently good, wise, and personal, since God (in his own personal goodness and wisdom) remains utterly unknown in himself. Consequently, natural reason can identify *philosophically* that it is intrinsically (structurally) open to the *possibility* of collaboration with divine revelation from God, which alone can remedy its imperfection.

Perhaps what Aristotle says about ethics should apply to metaphysics as well: people should not attempt to write books on this topic until they have studied the subject for the better part of a lifetime.[20] In the case of metaphysics, this would stem not from the effects of the passions, but from the historical complexities, conceptual subtleties, and nobility of the questions entailed. Of course Aquinas's composition of the *De ente et essentia* at age twenty-five stands as a rare anomaly that proves the rule. Metaphysics is for the wise, and wisdom is acquired with age. Nevertheless, the patience and forbearance of the reader is urged. For if God exists and can be known to natural reason, then what Aquinas has said himself about this question is also true: that it is better in this life to know a little of the greatest things than to know much of those things that are inferior.[21] The desire to know something of God philosophically is a noble one, even when it is carried out in imperfect ways. For as the principal thesis of this book suggests, the mind is ultimately made for the knowledge of God. In thinking about God as carefully and truthfully as possible, we are in fact engaging in something proper to our dignity as rational creatures. And if providence is real, as indeed it is, then human beings should seek wisdom despite their imperfections, for in so doing they can hope to find mercy and forbearance from one who is infinitely wise. In the words of Aquinas (paraphrasing Augustine): "Melius enim est in via claudicare, quam praeter viam fortiter ambulare." "It is better to hobble along in the true way, than to walk forcefully in the wrong direction."[22]

---

[20] *Nic. Ethics* I, 3, 1095a2–11.

[21] *ScG* III, c. 25: "However slight the amount of divine knowledge that the human intellect may be able to attain, that will be for the intellect, as regards its ultimate end, much more than the perfect knowledge of lower objects of understanding."

[22] *In Ioan.* XIV, lec. 2, 1870.

PART I

CHAPTER 1

Identifying the Challenge: The Problem
of Ontotheology and the *Via Inventionis*
for a Modern Thomistic Natural Theology

T HE VERY IDEA of natural theology (or theological philosophy)
arouses suspicion on a variety of fronts within modern culture. It
is contested as a reasonable discipline, for example, by numerous
practitioners of modern Christian theology, within broad swaths of contemporary academic philosophy (especially in its most postmodern of realizations), and among many in the modern scientific community. Is the pursuit
of natural theology possible in the wake of the cultural inertia that derives
from these historically well-enrooted tendencies? In this opening chapter I
will seek to determine some of the basic historical conditions that affect modern Thomistic attempts to identify a natural capacity for knowledge of God.
To arrive at this end, I wish to consider briefly some particularly important
aspects of the intellectual environment within the Catholic Church in western Europe after the First Vatican Council, in interaction with post-Enlightenment philosophical traditions. This background framework is needed to
explain certain aspirations and challenges common to the Thomistic thinkers
under consideration in this book. What is the proper order of inquiry for a
philosophical theology that would seek to avoid the twin dangers of a-meta-
physical, theoretical agnosticism, on the one hand, and an overly confident
metaphysical apriorism (ontotheology), on the other? With respect to both
these extremes, the principal interlocutors of modern Thomism within the
continental tradition have been Immanuel Kant and Martin Heidegger.

Natural Theology as a Problem in Modernity

As the development of modern theology was in so many ways framed around
the questions of the Reformation (and the Catholic reaction to them), so

3

contemporary theology still bears the profound imprint of Martin Luther's moral criticisms of any possible natural demonstration of God's existence or distinctly philosophical reflection on God's attributes. His attempt to break with what he perceived as the customary medieval practice of dogmatic Christian theology in this respect stemmed from the conviction (in reaction to the scholastic tradition) that distinctly metaphysical philosophical argumentation and Aristotelian demonstration rendered obscure the mystery of the Cross of Christ as the unique locus of revelation.[1] The human capacity for knowledge of God is so deeply affected by sin that humanity can acquire knowledge of God in its fallen state uniquely by recourse to Christian revelation.[2] Man's desire for a *theologia gloriae*, a metaphysical study of the truth about God, stems not from an authentic love of God but from a morally problematic, and ultimately epistemologically inefficacious, intellectual cupidity. No likeness between God and the world is discernable except in light of the Incarnation, in wake of the initiative of God's self-manifestation.[3]

Such theological speculations seem quite alien to the concerns that animate the modern university, of course, and it is important to recall that they were in fact reinterpreted or even explicitly rejected not only by other members of the Reformation but also by later proponents of Lutheran scholasticism.[4] In the emergence of the modern German university there was a significant degree of cultural homogeneity between the places where

---

[1] Luther's invectives against Aristotelianism and Scholastic method more generally are notorious. See his *Disputation against Scholastic Theology*. "Thesis 50: Briefly, the whole Aristotle is to theology as darkness is to light. This in opposition to the scholastics" (*LW*, 31, 12). For a portrayal of Luther's theological method emphasizing his break with medieval practices, see Ingolf Dalferth, *Theology and Philosophy* (Oxford: Blackwell, 1988), 71–88. For a recent reappraisal of Luther's "Aristotelianism" that notes ways in which Luther appreciated and appropriated thought from the Stagirite, see Theodor Dieter, *Der junge Luther und Aristoteles; Eine historisch-systematische Untersuchung zum Verhältnis von Theologie und Philosophie* (Berlin and New York: De Gruyter, 2001). Bruce Marshall, "Faith and Reason Reconsidered: Aquinas and Luther on Deciding What Is True," *Thomist* 63 (1999): 1–48, has argued in favor of a high degree of likeness between Aquinas and Luther on questions of faith and reason. Not withstanding Marshall's very pertinent observations, it seems to me that on the question of the natural philosophical capacity to name God analogically, by way of metaphysical reflection, the two stand in stark relief to one another.

[2] *Lectures on Romans* 1:17–23 (*LW*, 25, 151–60).

[3] *Heidelberg Disputation*, §20–22 (*LW*, 31, 52–54).

[4] On development of philosophical reflection within the context of Lutheran orthodoxy, one may profitably consult Max Wundt, *Die deutsche Schulmetaphysik des 17. Jahhunderts* (Tübingen: Mohr Siebeck, 1939), and more recently Kenneth Appold, *Orthodoxie als Konsensbildung: Das theologische Disputationswesen an der Universität Wittenberg zwischen 1570 und 1710* (Tübingen: Mohr Siebeck, 2004).

baroque theological reflection left off and modern Enlightenment philosophical theism began. Leibniz, for example, was greatly influenced by the rational speculations about God in the manuals of medieval thinkers. Likewise, in seventeenth-century France, the emergence of Descartes's philosophical method, for all its radicality and originality, suggests numerous influences of late medieval scholasticism, bearing the imprint at multiple points of William of Ockham's epistemology, and Francisco Suarez's metaphysics and anthropology.[5]

At the same time, however, the emergence of modern philosophy in the seventeenth century rendered the medieval practice of philosophical speculation about God problematic in at least two ways. First, in practice, the theistic philosophical speculation of Enlightenment thinkers frequently had a distinctly political and religious goal: to establish autonomous natural norms of religious belief over and against the dictates of medieval Christian faith, theological doctrine, and traditional religious practice. Philosophical theism could amount to an exercise in rational "foundationalism" conducted in purposeful separation from revelation, over and against it, and not merely in distinction from it.[6] Or by contrast, such speculation could attempt to absorb revelation into itself, albeit in a radically reinterpreted, post-Christian form.[7] Second, more radical Enlightenment thinkers deepened the break with the tradition of Christian theological reflection, not only by attempting (however indirectly) to diminish the influence of revelation in public and academic culture, but also by questioning the very capacity of the human intellect to acquire knowledge of God.[8] Elements of Luther's thought, as Karl Barth saw quite well, had secular analogies in the modern

---

5 On this period, see for example Roger Ariew, "Descartes and Scholasticism: The Intellectual Background of Descartes' Thought," in *The Cambridge Companion to Descartes*, ed. J. Cottingham (Cambridge: Cambridge University Press, 1992), 580–90; Dennis Des Chene, *Physiologia: Natural Philosophy in Late Aristotelian and Cartesian Thought* (Ithaca and London: Cornell University Press, 1996); Étienne Gilson, *Index Scholastico–cartésien* (Paris: Alcan, 1913) and *Études sur le rôle de la pensée médiéval dans la formation du système cartésien* (Paris: J. Vrin, 1984).

6 One might consider John Locke's theism as a case in point. See the study by Nicolas Wolterstorff, *John Locke and the Ethics of Belief* (Cambridge: Cambridge University Press, 1996).

7 Hegel, for example, famously attempted to integrate into his own dialectical metaphysics of history both an appeal to Anselm's ontological argument and a self-consciously Lutheran understanding of the uniquely Christological character of all knowledge of God. See G. W. F. Hegel, *Lectures on the Philosophy of Religion*, vol. 3, trans. R. Brown, P. Hodgson, J. Stewart (Berkeley and Los Angeles: University of California Press, 1985), 275–359.

8 See Jonathan Israel, *Radical Enlightenment* (Oxford: Oxford University Press, 2001). Arguably the two most important works in this regard are Benedict de Spinoza's *Theological-Political Treatise*, trans. M. Silverthorne and J. Israel (Cambridge:

academy, and most especially in the skeptical philosophy of Hume and the critical philosophy of Kant. Contemporaneous with the rise of a thorough skepticism concerning the possibility of an authentic metaphysics, the modern sciences from the seventeenth century on increasingly presented themselves as the normative and certain mode of assuring true knowledge of reality. Where religious skepticism prevailed among Enlightenment philosophers, the respect for empiricist methods and the modern sciences tended to augment acutely. The eighteenth century American and French Revolutions (in differing ways) sought to create the possibility of a distinctly secular sphere of public culture deeply indebted to the sciences but free from any necessary influences of revealed religion (the political separation of church and state). The Reformation emphasis on personal knowledge of God in faith was recast in post-Enlightenment modernity as a political conviction about religious knowledge: it concerns a uniquely private belief that must not affect the realm of public culture directly. In the wake of the momentous effects of secularizing philosophies upon eighteenth- and nineteenth-century European and American culture, the theological claim that no certain knowledge of God is possible apart from that provided by faith, therefore, has seemed to many (from a cultural vantage point at least) quite plausible.

Vatican I and *Aeterni Patris*

It was in response to the philosophical and cultural situation briefly alluded to above that the Catholic Church in the nineteenth century sought self-consciously to retrieve and renew a tradition of scholastic and Thomistic philosophical speculation within the context of modern Christian religious culture. This Catholic interest in the renewal of scholastic studies was given great impetus by the affirmations of the dogmatic constitution *Dei Filius*, at the First Vatican Council (1870). In response to perceived errors of modern philosophical and religious thought, this document affirmed in unambiguous terms that man is able by the natural light of his reason to know with certitude of the existence of God, who is the transcendent origin and end of all things.[9] There is an irreducibly double order of knowledge, distinguished by two respective origins and objects. One springs from natural

---

Cambridge University Press, 2007), and Immanuel Kant's *Religion within the Boundaries of Mere Reason*, trans. A. Wood and G. Di Giovanni (Cambridge: Cambridge University Press, 1998).

9 "The same Holy Mother Church teaches that God, the source and end of all things, can be known with certainty from the consideration of created things, by the natural power of human reason (Rom. 1:20). . . . If anyone says that the one, true God, our Creator and Lord, cannot be known with certainty from the things that have been made, by the natural light of human reason, let him be anathema."

reason and reflects upon the objects of experience; the other stems from divine faith and considers the objects of revelation.[10] Such affirmations were intended to counter diverse modern philosophical positions: naturalism, materialism, rationalism. The council announced as a new priority the refutation of atheism and of skeptically critical agnosticism by philosophical means in order to affirm a truth not only about the existence of God but also about the nature of the human person and his or her capacities to know the truth about God, Creator of all things. The affirmation of two orders of knowledge, the natural and the revealed, aimed to demonstrate the limits of any "rationalistic" pretension to a merely human measure of truth without reference to revelation, which might be used to judge the latter by its own principles. This affirmation crystallized the Catholic distinction between natural and revealed theology, and obliged the renaissance of the former not only as a means of discovering ultimate philosophical truths about God and man, but also as a service to Christian theology, since the operations of grace evoke and make use of the activities of nature, which they presuppose. Therefore, the council also revoked as "fideist" certain theological positions that would reject the cooperation of the human intellect with revelation within the activity of faith, especially that cooperation enabled by the reflections of philosophical theology.[11]

The ambitions of the council, however, confronted serious difficulties. Throughout the nineteenth century, the Catholic Church's intellectual tradition was experiencing a renewal of vitality and creativity in both the scholastic and the historical branches of study. Nevertheless, the experience of previous centuries had not prepared it adequately for the challenges presented

---

Dei Filius, chap. 2, and first anathema (*Decrees of the Ecumenical Councils*, trans. N. Tanner [London and Washington, DC: Sheed and Ward and Georgetown University Press, 1990].)

10 *Dei Filius*, chap. 4: "The perpetual agreement of the Catholic Church has maintained and maintains this too: that there is a twofold order of knowledge [*duplicem ordinem cognitionis*], distinct not only as regards its source, but also as regards its object. With regard to the source, we know at the one level by natural reason, at the other level by divine faith. With regard to the object, besides those things to which natural reason can attain, there are proposed for our belief mysteries hidden in God which, unless they are divinely revealed, are incapable of being known."

11 *Dei Filius*, chap. 4: "Now reason, if it is enlightened by faith, does indeed when it seeks persistently, piously and soberly, achieve by God's gift some understanding, and that most profitable, of the mysteries, whether by analogy from what it knows naturally, or from the connection of these mysteries with one another and with the final end of humanity. . . . Not only can faith and reason never be at odds with one another but they mutually support each other, for on the one hand right reason demonstrates the foundations of the faith and, illumined by its light, develops the science of divine things; on the other hand, faith delivers reason from errors and protects and furnishes it with knowledge of many kinds" [translation slightly altered].

by the advent of modernity. A host of new intellectual and cultural factors had been introduced both by the ambitious efforts of modern thinkers such as Descartes, Hume, and Kant to rearticulate the bases of philosophy and also by the changes in knowledge wrought by the rise of the modern sciences. The Enlightenment tradition affirmed a radical discontinuity between the demands of tradition and the demands of reason. Modern man had evolved beyond the obscurantism of former times. Man then should live according to reason alone. Paradoxically, this kind of thinking could be strengthened by the historical claim that the ecclesiastical affirmation of an autonomous rational order proper to philosophy is itself a modern development. One could object that the very notion of such an autonomous rational order did not exist in the thought of either Aristotle or Aquinas.[12]

By its sharp distinction between the order of reason and that of reve-lation, the council, therefore, raised an acute question of the existence of a perennial philosophy of being, identifiable in the works of classical philos-ophy, and retrievable in the modern era. A coherent confrontation with the modern denial of man's metaphysical knowledge of God would need to respond to the new questions—both historical and philosophical—posed concerning the viability of such assertions. Would this in turn require a radical reevaluation of certain classical scholastic opinions? A host of thinkers within the Church would respond to this question affir-matively within the coming decades, in what has come to be termed the "modernist movement."[13]

---

[12] Such affirmations have not been lacking among modern scholars. Richard Bodéüs (*Aristote et la théologie des vivants immortels* [Paris: St. Laurent, 1992]) has argued that Aristotle's metaphysics is an attempt to place the efforts of philosophical ontology at the service of the theological explanations of reality given by the reli-gious cosmology of his time. "Aristotelian metaphysics is not the moment in his-tory where philosophy sought to discover the true nature of the gods over and against the obscurantism of Greek traditions, but where on the contrary the lights of the Greek theological tradition are imagined to have enlightened the obscurity which philosophy entered into when it sought to reflect upon first principles" (300). Meanwhile, Henri de Lubac, in *Surnaturel* (Paris: Éditions Montaigne, 1946), has argued at length that the notion of a "purely natural order" is absent from Aquinas's Christian theological vision of man. John Milbank (*The Suspended Middle: Henri de Lubac and the Debate Concerning the Supernatural* [Grand Rapids: Eerdmans, 2005]) has extended this line of thinking in order to argue in favor of a virtual non-distinction between theological and philosophical reflection. While my own interpretations of Aristotle and Aquinas will be markedly different from those of these thinkers, the notation of their positions marks out the exis-tence of an interpretive quandary.

[13] An informative historical treatment of the rise of the modernist crisis in France is provided by Pierre Colin, *L'Audace et le Soupçon: la crise du modernisme dans le catholicisme français 1893–1914* (Paris: Desclée de Brouwer, 1997).

In 1879, Pope Leo XIII would provide his own proposal for an intellectual renewal by the instigation to "Christian philosophy" contained in
his encyclical letter *Aeterni Patris*. This work summoned Christian
thinkers to a renewal of scholastic philosophy, and particularly the
thought of Aquinas. The document stresses especially the capacity of philosophy to attain real knowledge of God, his truth and perfections, and
also to discern rational evidences of the truth of revelation from exterior
signs, such as miracles. Philosophy provides, therefore, *praeambula fidei*,
that is, discernment of the truth of those revealed teachings that are attainable by the natural powers of human reason. In sacred doctrine, the intelligent service of divine revelation provided by methods obtained from
natural knowledge gives theology demonstrative coherence and order.
Meanwhile, objections of philosophies impeding the right cooperation of
the intellect with divine revelation can be shown to be erroneous from
premises of natural reason.[14]

The recommendations of the encyclical have their origins in the
Thomistic renewal that began in the mid-nineteenth century, a movement
that influenced deeply Gioacchino Pecci (the later Leo XIII), as a student.
At this time such thought was present especially within the Roman schools
of theology. It was to be elevated by *Aeterni Patris* to the status of a quasi-
official orthodoxy in ecclesiastical houses of formation in Italy, France, Ger-
many, and Belgium.[15] Nevertheless, as Alasdair MacIntyre has observed,
precisely because of the ferment of international research that the movement initiated, a valuable multiplicity of Thomistic orientations were to
develop within the twentieth century that would contribute to a much
more intricate understanding of Aquinas and diverse explications of his
thought.[16] Thus, in diverse ways, new historical studies were initiated (by
thinkers such as Mandonnet, Chenu, Gilson, Fabro, Van Steenberghen,
etc.) in parallel with attempts to rethink the classical Thomistic heritage in
confrontation with contemporary ideas (Maritain and Journet, Maréchal,
Rahner, and Lonergan). It is within this extended context that the tradition
examined in this book developed, in attempting to rethink historically,
philosophically, and culturally the uses of Thomistic philosophy for the
renewal of natural theology and the relation of the latter to Christian faith.

---

[14] *Aeterni Patris*, in the *Summa theologica*, vol. 1, trans. English Dominicans (Westminster, MD: Christian Classics, 1981), x–xi.

[15] On the effects of *Aeterni Patris* on the spread of Thomistic teaching in France at
the turn of the century, see Colin, *L'Audace et le Soupçon*, 172–85.

[16] Alasdair MacIntyre, *Three Rival Versions of Moral Enquiry* (Notre Dame: University of Notre Dame Press, 1990), 58–81.

Challenges for Post-Kantian Thomism

Chief among the challenges posed to post-conciliar Catholic thinkers was that of Kant's influential philosophical work. Kant's radical reinterpretation of the historical project of metaphysics was perceived as especially threatening to the aims of classical philosophy,[17] as it advanced the idea that all metaphysical notions are the results of a priori synthetic judgments and are pure concepts of understanding. Notions such as "substance," "causality," and "teleology" pertain immediately to the way in which the thinking subject organizes sensations internally and logically, but not immediately to the order of reality in itself.[18] Metaphysical "science," then, is explained in terms of a necessary transcendental "illusion" of pure reason permitting a theoretically coherent ordering of the subject's sensible experience.

Such theories not only prohibited classical interpretations of the study of being, but shifted the meaning of metaphysics from being an explanation of the structure of the real to explaining the immanent nature of human, transempirical reason.[19] Metaphysics, even in its classical representations, was now interpreted through the grid of an anthropological epistemology. Meanwhile, Kant's theory of natural theology as ontotheology denied the possibility of any objective, demonstrative knowledge of God. Kant affirmed the usefulness of the concept of God merely as a regulative notion of reason permitting the construction of systematic knowledge based upon experience, ordering it in reference to an ideal first principle that stimulates the deepening of human research. This unavoidable dimension of reason reveals the dissatisfaction of reason with the realities experienced empirically and its higher aim at systemization and explanation.[20]

---

[17] See "Le Kantisme interdit," in Colin, *L'Audace et le Soupçon*, 199–239. The letter *Depuis le Jour*, from Pope Leo XIII to French clergy (Sept. 8, 1899) deplored the influence of philosophical opinions denying the capacity of natural reason to know of "the existence of God, the spirituality and immortality of the soul, and the objective reality of the exterior world." Kant's moral and political thinking were perceived within French culture at large as giving justification to Republican ideals, and to the nineteenth-century movements for political secularization.

[18] *Critique of Pure Reason*, I, I, 2, trans. N. Smith (London: Macmillan, 1990), 120ff.; II, I, 1, esp. 368ff.

[19] *Prolegomena to Any Future Metaphysics*, trans. P. Carus and J. Ellington (Indianapolis and Cambridge: Hackett Publishing, 1977), §56: "As the psychological, cosmological, and theological ideas are nothing but pure concepts of reason, which cannot be given in any experience, the questions which reason asks us about them are put to us, not by the objects, but by mere maxims of our reason for the sake of its own satisfaction." See also §36, and §40.

[20] The appearance of this notion of ontotheology can be seen in *Critique of Pure Reason*, II, III, 7. This ultimate dimension of human reason has a positive and regulative function for the orientation of all human thinking: II, III, appendix, "The Final Purpose of the Natural Dialectic of Human Reason," 550–51: "This, indeed,

Kant claims to detect the inner mechanism of ontotheology in the mind's natural appeal to the so-called Ontological argument. The latter seeks to prove the existence of God from the notion of God itself, independently of reference to experience, in distinction from "cosmotheology," which refers to the experience of exterior realities deemed to have a necessary transcendent cause for their existence. Cosmotheology is impossible because the attribution of "causality" to anything that stands outside the order of immediate sensitive entities implies intrinsic contradiction (conceptual antinomies) or equivocity (radical non-intelligibility).[21] Analogical reflection on causality by non-sensible realities such as God (but also angelic beings, the Incarnate Word, grace, sacraments, etc.) transgresses the limits of pure reason, which is analytically bound—by a kind of univocal form of reflection—to the realm of the sensible. As is well known, then, Kant understands the Ontological argument to be at the base of all theistic speculative argumentation, such as that found in the cosmological argument (taken from the contingency of creatures), or the physio-theological argument (based upon the presence of teleology in creatures).[22] The latter are simply extended instantiations of the mind's attempt to organize all experience

---

is the transcendental deduction of all ideas of speculative reason, not as *constitutive* principles for the extension of our knowledge to more objects than experience can give, but as *regulative* principles of the systematic unity of the manifold of empirical knowledge in general, whereby this empirical knowledge is more adequately secured within its own limits and more effectively improved than would be possible, in the absence of such ideas, through the employment merely of the principles of the understanding. . . . In the domain of theology, we must view everything that can belong to the context of possible experience *as if* this experience formed an absolute but at the same time completely dependent and *sensibly* conditioned unity, and yet also at the same time *as if* the sum of all appearances (the sensible world itself) had a single, highest and all-sufficient ground beyond itself, namely, a self-subsistent, original, creative reason." See also *Prolegomena,* §57, on the constructions of ontotheology as an effect of the dissatisfaction of human reason with empirical experience: "And who does not feel himself compelled, notwithstanding all interdictions against losing himself in transcendent ideas, to seek rest and contentment, beyond all the concepts which he can vindicate by experience, in the concept of a being, the possibility of which cannot be conceived but at the same time cannot be refuted, because it relates to a mere being of the understanding and without it reason must needs remain forever dissatisfied?"

21 *Critique of Pure Reason,* A 609/B 637, 511: "We find [in the cosmological argument] the transcendental principle whereby from the contingent we infer a cause. This principle is applicable only in the sensible world; outside that world it has no meaning whatsoever. For the mere intellectual concept of the contingent cannot give rise to any synthetic proposition, such as that of causality. The principle of causality has no meaning and no criterion for its application save only in the sensible world."

22 *Critique of Pure Reason,* II, III, 5; II, III, 6, 507–24.

from within its own immanent notion of an ideal first principle.[23] Consequently, all natural theology is implicitly ontotheology.

While my reflections here are not intended as a detailed analysis of the Kantian critique, the question that it has raised for twentieth-century Thomists is the following: does Aquinas's project of metaphysical argumentation for the existence of God follow after the pattern of ontotheology as described by Kant, and to what extent? Or does Aquinas's thought offer an alternative form of argumentation that is immune to the Kantian criticisms of natural theology? Of relevance here is the identification of essential features of "ontotheology" as it persists across time, and can be attributed to various thinkers. Olivier Boulnois, a contemporary Scotist metaphysician, has identified four major components of Kant's ontotheological metaphysics that were in fact inherited from previous Enlightenment thinkers. However, he also argues that none of these are compatible with Aquinas's presuppositions and arguments.[24] The four elements are:

1. The affirmation that the most general notion of being, or *ens*, as a concept is capable of being attributed to anything that can be conceptually signified, whether a real being, a possible being, or a being of reason (a mental notion), such that the concept of "being," in the most general sense, applies *as much* to possibles or to mental intentions as it does to realities.[25]

2. The understanding that the notion of being commonly attributed to these diverse subjects is univocal at its core, and can be applied to both the finite and the infinite. It therefore contains within itself a scope of intelligibility capable of signifying anything from beings of reason (purely mental ideas) to the infinite being of God. This transcendental range of being (common to all categories of being, and to finite and infinite being) forms the subject of metaphysics. Since metaphysics studies all that to which the notion of being is applicable, there can be a "general metaphysics" of being according to its "common" intelligibility (common to all instances of being), and a "special

---

[23] *Critique of Pure Reason,* II, III, 7, 525–32.

[24] See Olivier Boulnois, *l'Être et représentation* (Paris: Presses Universitaires de France, 1999), especially 457–515; "La destruction de l'analogie et l'instauration de la métaphysique," in *Sur la connaissance de Dieu et l'univocité de l'étant,* texts of John Duns Scotus (Paris: Presses Universitaires de France, 1988), 11–81, and "Quand commence l'ontothéologie? Aristote, Thomas d'Aquin et Duns Scot," *Revue Thomiste* 95 (1995): 85–105.

[25] For an unambiguous indication of this way of thinking, see *Critique of Pure Reason,* A 290–93/B 347–9, 294ff.

metaphysics" concerning a particular being, for example, the infinite being of God.[26]

3. The idea that God is therefore signified by our most common notion of being and is understood by an additional difference added to this most general concept (such as the attribute of omnipotence, infinity, etc.). As known by our human thinking, therefore, God is a subcategory of the broader "science" of being, even as the notion of God refers to that which is the condition of possibility for all being (the ultimate explanation of reality). Ultimately the notion of infinite being is the epistemological condition of possibility for the notion of possible, finite being, since the latter includes within it the idea of "derivation from another."[27]

4. The definition of God's essence is construed a priori from the mind's metaphysical concepts. His existence can be postulated from a posteriori experiential-based arguments (arguing from "effects" to his existence as their transcendent cause) based *only* on the knowledge given by this a priori definition.

Taken in themselves, these four postulates are not original to the philosophy of Kant. As Boulnois and others have shown, all of them have precedents in the Enlightenment rational theologies of Leibniz, Wolff, and Baumgarten, from whom Kant inherited them directly.[28] His originality,

---

[26] See evidences for such views in *Critique of Pure Reason*, A 845–46/B 873–74, 661ff. As Eberhard Jüngel has pointed out (*God as the Mystery of the World*, 261–66) Kant does examine the grounds for the very possibility of human thinking about God by an appeal to some form of analogical predication in *Prolegomena to Any Future Metaphysics*, §57–60. He employs here a theory of predicamental analogy (analogy of proper proportionality) as the unique means to speak about any possible similitude between the world and God. His conception of analogical predication, however, is not incompatible with the logical univocity theory that Boulnois identifies in Kant's *Critique*. The latter could be understood as the necessary condition for the right exercise of the former.

[27] *Critique of Pure Reason*, A 578/B 606, 606: "The sum of all possible objects of our knowledge appears to us to be a plane, with an apparent horizon—namely, that which comprehends all within its sweep . . . the idea of an unconditioned totality [infinite being]."

[28] Boulnois himself makes the controversial (and disputed) claim that each of these four features has its original source in the medieval ontology of Scotus and is particularly indebted to the metaphysics of Suarez. In *l'Être et représentation*, Boulnois argues at length that the classical rationalist Enlightenment structure of metaphysics originated in the thought of Avicenna and Henry of Ghent and was given its basic framework by the original synthesis of Scotus. He attempts to document its transmission to modernity (Leibniz, Wolff, Baumgarten) through the philosophy of Suarez, and claims that

then, was not to have formulated the structure of such metaphysical thinking, but to have fundamentally reinterpreted it from the point of view of
the knowing subject's constructions of reason. The above-mentioned primary element (inherited from previous Enlightenment thinkers) was made
possible because of Kant's thematic disjuncture placed between the rational
concept of *ens* and the knowledge of real beings (the *noumena*, or things in
themselves). In what may be interpreted as a continuation of the Cartesian
turn from the things in themselves to the knowing subject, Kant transforms
the systematic knowledge of being into a study of the interior "grid"
through which reason interprets empirical experience, without a necessary
reference to the structure of reality itself. "Being" is a notion useful for
ordered thinking concerning any possible experience. The transcendental
science of being (the structure of reality itself) becomes the study of the
transcendental subject (the structure of human reasoning), and this study is

---

the presence of the four above-mentioned postulates were inherited from this tradition by Kant, who then reinterpreted them as truths concerned uniquely with the
pure constructions of reason in the transcendental subject. For the first of these elements, Boulnois appeals to Scotus, *Quaestiones subtilissimae super libros Metaphysicorum Aristotelis*, I, 1, 38–43, and Suarez, *Disputationes Metaphysicae* LIV, 1, 8–9, as
compared with *Critique of Pure Reason*, A 290–93/B 347–49. On the second point,
see Scotus, *Ordinatio*, I, d. 3, q. 2; III, a. 1–5 on the univocal concept of being and
the inclusion of the notion of God as infinite being within the "subject" of the study
of metaphysics. In *Disputationes Metaphysicae* I, 1, 19, Suarez affirms that God is
included within the study of "common being," and in I, 1, 26, concerning metaphysics: "ostendum est enim obiectum adaequatum huius scientiae debere compre-
hendere Deum." In II, 2, 36, he affirms with Scotus a certain univocity in the concept
of being. According to Boulnois, Kant reproduces this structure of reasoning in the
Critique of Pure Reason, A 845–46/B 873–74, in which the study of possible objects
in general is considered as the logically prior foundation for both the study of empirical, natural realities and the special studies of transempirical concepts such as the cosmos, the soul, and God. A compatible account of the history of ontotheology is
offered by Jean François Courtine in his work *Suarez et le système de la métaphysique*
(Paris: Presses Universitaires de France, 1990). See also the complementary recent
study by Vincent Carraud, *Causa sive ratio: La raison de la cause, de Suarez à Leibniz*
(Paris: Presses Universitaires de France, 2002).

One might object that Boulnois's thesis concerning Kant and the medievals
imposes in far too succinct a fashion a Heideggerian meta-narrative upon what is
in fact a quite philosophically heterogeneous body of material. For an alternative
account of Scotus's metaphysics (which defends him against the charge of Kantian
and Heideggerian "ontotheology"), see Gérard Sondag, *Duns Scot* (Paris: J. Vrin,
2005). My point here is not to take sides in this intramural debate between expert
Scotists, but only to underline the fact that one may in no way presuppose that
Kant's theories of metaphysics and natural theology that he inherited from preceding Enlightenment theists can apply rightly to Aquinas's own way of construing
the science of metaphysics.

teleologically ordered toward the notion of God. This latter notion is virtually contained in the initial notion of being as its absolute realization and ultimate organizing principle. Without this principle, the unity of human thought cannot be adequately maintained. However, both the notions of being and of God are *merely* products of human reason by which it orders itself toward its own systematic self-realization.[29]

Kant's ambitious theories about the nature of human knowledge and the structure of metaphysics clearly differ in noteworthy ways from the epistemological presuppositions and mode of metaphysical reasoning represented by the Thomistic tradition (a point that will become clearer in subsequent chapters). It is unsurprising, then, that Thomists reacted critically to Kantianism, claiming that his criticisms of metaphysics did not adequately apply to Aquinas's own theories of metaphysics and natural theology. However, Thomists also rightly perceived that Kant's perspective on the subject matter required them to reflect anew upon the foundations of realistic knowing of existents, as implicit in the philosophies of Aristotle and Aquinas, and to relate this to the critical positions of Kant. How can it be shown that one does know realistically and immediately the existences and natures of realities experienced? Can the notion of causality be legitimately extended beyond the phenomena of immediate sensible experience? What role does analogical thinking about God play in this process? Here the Thomistic tradition perceived the necessity to identify from experience (in contradistinction to Kant) properly metaphysical points of departure for a true knowledge of being, and to identify how such knowledge could lead to properly analogical knowledge of God, with concepts drawn from the experience of realities that are God's effects. In other words, how can the existence of God be demonstrated through reflection on the existents we know immediately if he transcends the field of empirical phenomena? How do the beings of realities we experience permit us to

---

[29] It is significant to note that in Kant's "pre-critical" work of 1763, *The Only Possible Argument in Support of a Demonstration of the Existence of God*, I, 2, 4–I, 4, 4, he develops a form of the Ontological argument that passes from the mere *logical possibility* of *any* existent reality to the necessary existence of a real, infinite primary being. The continuity between logical possibility and ontological possibility and necessity is, therefore, absolute and is bridged by the intellectual concept of being and its essential requisitions. Because we can conceive of the possibility of a being, such an existent has an essential structure, and this can be the case only because a primary necessary being exists as the source of such structure. It is comprehensible that Kant later came to interpret this ontotheological structure of reasoning as a merely immanent construction of reason. On this form of argumentation in Kant's early work, see Martin Schönfeld, *The Philosophy of the Young Kant* (Oxford: Oxford University Press, 2000), esp. 183–208.

speak in real terms and in an accurate way of the God who is, and not merely to speak of him as an a priori transcendental ideal of pure reason?

At the beginning of the twentieth century, such questions were discussed polemically by a number of Thomistic thinkers whose writings were to have an influential role during the Modernist Crisis of the 1910s.[30] One influential member of this group of thinkers was the Dominican Reginald Garrigou-Lagrange, appointed to the faculty of the Angelicum in 1909, whose version of Roman Thomism would act as an influential force of theological conservatism (which the Dominican himself tended to identify with Catholic orthodoxy itself) up until the Second Vatican Council.[31] Garrigou-Lagrange's writings represent one of the most serious efforts of this period to rethink the articulation of Thomistic natural theology in conformity with the theological intentions of Vatican I, and in critical confrontation with the Kantian critique. They are important for this study because they were to influence deeply French Thomism, and especially the thought of Jacques Maritain. They also represented the interpretation of Aquinas's thought that Étienne Gilson reacted against most vigorously.

In his work of 1910, *Les Preuves de Dieu*, the Dominican philosopher sets out to articulate the diverse a posteriori metaphysical demonstrations that pass from the examination of beings we know directly to the discovery of the necessary existence of God, and that can be presented in such a way as to refute what the author sees as the irrationality of Kantian skepticism. The key aims of the book are to show that our thinking is necessarily ontologically realistic (we know the beings of realities themselves), that the notion of causality is ontological and can have applications to that which transcends the sensible, and that our understanding of reality requires of us to explain the ultimate reason for the existence of series of essentially subordinated or interdependent realities by recourse to theism. Significantly, however, this anti-Kantian and anti-empiricist approach to metaphysics is based entirely upon an epistemological examination of the primary principles of intelligibility that are extracted pre-reflexively by the mind in its confrontation with experience, and that are said to be presupposed for any form of thinking whatsoever. In contra-distinction to Kant, who confined intuition to the sensible faculties, Garrigou-Lagrange insists

---

[30] See Henri Donneaud, "La *Revue Thomiste* et la Crise Moderniste," in *Saint Thomas au XXe Siécle*, ed. S. Bonino, 76–94, on such French thinkers as Pègues, Schwalm, Gardeil, and Sentroul. Thomistic "critical realism" was pursued in response to Kant at Louvain by Mercier, Noël, and Maréchal.

[31] On the role of Garrigou-Lagrange in the politics of theological orthodoxy in the twentieth century, see Étienne Fouilloux, *Une Église en Quête de Liberté: la Pensée Catholique Française entre Modernisme et Vatican II, 1914–1962* (Paris: Desclée de Brouwer, 1998), 47–48, 112–19, 283–87.

on a properly intellectual intuition of the primary principles of being.[32] From these "common sense" epistemological principles we derive rationally the structures of the reality they implicitly reflect, so as to know the laws of reality itself. To deny the applicability of such fundamental principles to the reality in itself is not only to deny the epistemological realism of our common sense, and practical activities, but also to confine speculative reason itself to absurdity, by the necessary violation of the principle of non-contradiction.

These principles are "perceived spontaneously in being, and our philosophical reason attributes them analytically to being."[33] They are six in number: the principles of identity, non-contradiction, substance, sufficient reason, causality, and finality. The principle of identity has being for its subject, and affirms that "each being is something determined," "each being has its own nature." Coinciding with this affirmation as its negative expression is the principle of non-contradiction: "a being cannot be both what it is and what it is not."[34] The third principle is that of the substance:

> The substance is nothing other than the primary determination of being, necessary in order to render intelligible as being a phenomenological group that presents itself as autonomous. From the first moment of the presentation of a sensible object of whatever kind, like the sheets in which a child is enveloped . . . as the vision grasps the color of this object, and touch grasps its form and its resistance, the intelligence in a confused way knows its *being*, as "something that exists." This primary object known by the intelligence becomes

---

[32] In the transcendental aesthetic, *Critique of Pure Reason*, I, I, 1, 65, Kant writes: "Objects are *given* to us by means of sensibility, and it alone yields us *intuitions*; they are *thought* through the understanding, and from the understanding arise *concepts*. But all thought must directly or indirectly, by way of certain characters, relate ultimately to intuitions, and therefore, with us, to sensibility, because in no other way can an object be given to us." In *Les Preuves de Dieu* (Paris: Beauchesne, 1910), 60–61, Garrigou-Lagrange states: "This fundamental objection to the demonstrability of the existence of God is based most especially upon the negation of the *intuition of the intelligible*, or the objective value of concepts. The concept is reduced by the nominalist to a composite image accompanied by a common name. It is reduced by Kant to being nothing more than an *a priori* form of thought destined to be related to the phenomena [of sensible experience]. We will briefly recall the insolvable difficulties into which both the empiricists and Kant immersed themselves by negating the abstractive intuition of the intelligible per se. Second, we will establish the existence of this intuition and its ontological value, and consequently, the value of the principle of causality as a law of being. Finally, we will demonstrate the transcendent and analogical value of this same principle."

[33] *Les Preuves de Dieu*, 70.

[34] *Les Preuves de Dieu*, 71–72.

in a precise way the *unique and permanent subject* (substance) once the intelligence notes the multiplicity of these phenomena and their changes. The multiple, in effect, is only intelligible in reference to unity, and the transitory only in reference to the permanent, or the identical. . . . *To say that a being is a substance is to say that it is one and the same in and through its multiple phenomena and changes.* The principle of substance, then, occurs as a further determination of the principle of identity, and the idea of substance as a further determination of the idea of being.[35]

A fourth principle, that of sufficient reason, also follows from that of identity: each reality has its intelligible reasons for being as it is, and such reasons can be discerned either as intrinsic, according to the nature of the reality, or as extrinsic, due to the activity of others. Garrigou-Lagrange insists that this principle is "analytic"; it enters into the initial apprehensions we make of the realities we experience. Thus this principle leads to an insight into the other two principles explaining the reason for the being of a thing: that of causality and of finality. Nothing is the cause of itself. Therefore, every being that can be or not be needs an extrinsic cause. To explain composite and changing beings it is necessary to posit such extrinsic causes. All beings, in their change and activity, are ordered toward a certain actuality, or end.[36] They are characterized by a teleological nature.

This critical method of reflection, which seeks to extract from the necessary laws of the intellect a reflection of the necessary laws of the real, points the intelligence toward the formulation of properly analogical concepts of God developed from the notion of being. These are applicable to God indirectly, insofar as he is discovered as the primary, necessary, and transcendent cause of the interdependent realities we experience directly (those existing in movement, caused by others, existing in contingency, having diverse degrees of perfection, acting toward a final end not determined by themselves, etc.).[37] The purification of our notions from all that derives from limitations proper to secondary, ontologically dependent realities permits notions of being, personhood, spirit, intelligence, and will to become properly applicable to God.

Garrigou-Lagrange's philosophy was an important attempt to develop a "critical realism" in the wake of Kant that could sustain a natural theol-

---

[35] *Les Preuves de Dieu*, 81–82.

[36] *Les Preuves de Dieu*, 84–95. See 95: "These are the metaphysical principles of the proofs of the existence of God. In and through sensible objects, the abstractive intuition of the human intellect attains being and its primary principles. All of these are connected back to the principle of identity, which itself expresses what pertains to being most fundamentally."

[37] *Les Preuves de Dieu*, IIIième partie.

ogy. His efforts would set the stage for much Thomistic thinking in France in the twentieth century. This was partly due to the fact that he acknowledged the need for a modern, start-to-finish interpretation of Aquinas's metaphysics, leading from initial principles to knowledge of God, established through a dialectical refutation of alternative philosophical traditions, and placed in the service of faith. Yet his work was also important because of its potential insufficiencies. In fact, his philosophical approach shared some of the presuppositions of the rationalist ontologies criticized by Kant, and eventually Heidegger.

This is apparent, for example, in his attempt to prove metaphysical realism by the epistemological examination of the primary principles of human reasoning. Aristotle and Aquinas do appeal to the aforementioned principles against skeptics as means of illustrating how the mind *necessarily* works in its encounter with reality. However, they do not derive the laws of that reality itself from an examination of the logically necessary use of the principles. Garrigou-Lagrange argues that our initial analytical notions achieve an intelligibility and coherence only through the application of the principles to reality, and *therefore* reflect the laws of this reality. By making the study of reality itself dependent upon a prior examination of the critical principles of reason, one makes the affirmation of efficient causality in the world the condition of possibility for final causality (or purpose) in human thinking.

This choice to begin metaphysics with epistemology is clearly post-Cartesian. Of Boulnois's four elements of Kantian ontotheology, this seems to resemble the first one: the study of being includes in one common structure of intelligibility both mental being (beings of reason) and real beings. The study of the former unveils the structure of the latter. Étienne Gilson has suggested that Garrigou-Lagrange's method based upon critical principles resembles in significant ways the philosophies of Leibniz and of Christian Wolff, who were both forebears of Kant's critical philosophy on the multiple points of metaphysical reasoning mentioned above.[38]

---

[38] See Étienne Gilson, *L'Être et l'Essence*, 2nd Edition (Paris: J. Vrin, 1972), 166–72, esp. 171n1. Ralph McInerny (*Praeambula Fidei*, 121–25) has recently suggested that Gilson's claims were politically motivated and have little historical plausibility, noting that Garrigou-Lagrange was not directly influenced by Wolff. While I am generally sympathetic to McInerny's criticisms of Gilson, I think that on this issue the French Thomist has a substantive point, even if it is in need of greater historical clarification. Vincent Carraud's study of Leibniz's interpretation of the principle of causality (*Causa sive ratio*, 391–495) suggests numerous points of contact with the argumentation of *Les Preuves de Dieu* offered above, and Garrigou-Lagrange was in fact an admirer of Leibniz. The idea that this structure of thinking could have been adopted and transmitted (in modified form) through the mediation of nineteenth- and early-twentieth-century Roman scholasticism is by no means implausible, and merits further study.

Whether this is the case or not, his work raises the question: can a properly philosophical point of departure for metaphysics be extracted from Aquinas's writings that avoids the solipsistic turns represented by modern thought, and yet identifies an experiential basis for the study of being?

Another related question raised by Garrigou-Lagrange's work concerns his analogical understanding of being, especially as it is applied to God through the mediation of the rational demonstrations mentioned above. The Dominican thinker invokes an interpretation of proportional, four-term analogy (*A* is to *B* as *C* is to *D*) that he inherited from Cajetan, in order to speak about the relation between creatures and God. In doing so, however, he seemingly substitutes a theory of logical predication for a reflection on ontological similitude.[39] He thus invokes the same notion of "being" to speak about *ens* (the object of the principle of identity), about substance, and about God, analogically, through a series of mental comparisons. But he does not sufficiently justify in what way this logical structure of comparison is derived from (or related to) the ontological structure of causality by which creatures in themselves really resemble one another, or resemble God. In this respect, his thinking clearly contains parallels to the second and third elements of ontotheology mentioned above. His portrayal of analogy risks treating God as a subject within the study of being, and adapts the notion of being "proportionally" to be able to define the nature of God. This proportional adjustment of signification ascribed to "being" (said of accidents, finite substance, and infinite substance, respectively) closely resembles the idea of a common science of being that embraces both perfect and imperfect existents. This way of thinking, however, results from the fact that he makes no reference to the *ad unum* analogy of being, which is also of central importance for Aristotle and Aquinas, and which is based upon a metaphysical analysis of causal dependency.[40] The multiple cate-

---

[39] Some have argued that Cajetan's understanding of proportional analogy substitutes a mental schema of logical attribution for an adequate study of the ontologically analogical nature of the real, reducing the latter to what is in fact an inadequate account of the former. On this point see Leo Elders, *The Metaphysics of Being of St. Thomas Aquinas in a Historical Perspective* (Leiden: Brill, 1993), 45–46. For interesting suggestions as to how Cajetan's account of Aquinas was in fact previously formulated by Thomas Sutton, and how Cajetan in turn rearticulated this view in reaction to Duns Scotus and Antoninus Trombetta, see Jean François Courtine, *Inventio analogiae Métaphysique et ontothéologie* (Paris: J. Vrin, 2005), 283–90, 337–57.

[40] According to Aristotle and Aquinas, the multiplicity of determinations represented by each of the ten Aristotelian categories are different, yet each is related to the substance as "toward one" common ontological foundation. *Metaphysics Γ*, 2 (1003a33–1003b10); *In IV Meta.*, lec. 1, 537–39. However, Cajetan's attribution of the notion of being to both substance and accidents according to a certain proportion (which Garrigou-Lagrange adopts) does not make use of this *multa ad unum* analogy for the understanding of being as substance and accidents.

gories of being (the diverse accidents) are understood by Aristotle analogically in reference to the one substance in which they inhere "formally," and
by which they are caused to be. The diverse genera of substance are understood by Aquinas analogically as dependent upon the unique transcendent
causality of God. (I will return to these points in subsequent chapters.) The
vulnerabilities to the charge of ontotheology that are implied by the argumentation of Garrigou-Lagrange were to be exposed in a keener way by the
development of the Heideggerian critique of ontotheology, which deepened yet further the problems posed to classical metaphysics.

Heideggerian Ontotheology and Thomistic Analogy

The Heideggerian deconstruction of the western metaphysical tradition,
undertaken especially in *Being and Time* (1927), and developed in subsequent works in a variety of ways, was to exert as profound an influence
upon modern Thomistic philosophy as the *Critique* of Kant, deepening,
in some sense, the effect of the latter. This influence was due particularly
to Heidegger's criticisms of ontotheology (even as Kantian regulatory theory), which were in turn related to his insistence upon the necessary philosophical bracketing of faith.

Heidegger's critique of metaphysical theology presupposes his understanding of the history of western metaphysics as consisting in a "forgetfulness of Being" (*Seinsvergessenheit*), presided over instead by a history of the
study of entities (*seiendes*).[41] The study of ontic determinations, formulated
by the use of the most general of all concepts (*to on, ens*) and expressed in
Aristotle's categories, has obscured the true problem of being: "why is there
something rather than nothing?" This latter question deals with something
more problematic than the simple attribution of existence to the entities we
experience, or a discussion of their essential determinations. It confronts the
enigmatic, singular "given-ness" and temporality of existents, as well as the
possible nothingness of the entities we know. Through the attentiveness to
the latter, the "ontic-ontological difference" becomes manifest: the divide

---

[41] *Being and Time*, trans. J. Macquarrie and E. Robinson (Oxford: Blackwells, 2000),
§6, 26: "The Being (*Sein*) of entities 'is' not itself an entity. If we are to understand
the problem of Being, our first philosophical step consists in not . . . 'telling a
story'—that is to say, in not defining entities as entities by tracing them back in
their origin to some other entities, as if Being had the character of some possible
entity. Hence, Being, as that which is asked about must be exhibited in a way of its
own essentially different from the way in which entities are discovered." The
obscuring of the problem of Being by the notion of entities, and the teleological
extension of the later notion to the project of a theology of the supreme entity is,
for Heidegger, a common characteristic of western thought from Aristotle to Hegel.

between these beings and Being itself.[42] What is unique to man (*dasein*) is that he is a being who questions Being, who is "capable of the ontological."[43]

The true meaning of the notion of "being" for Heidegger (as contrasted with entities) is (in)famously difficult to interpret. It has overtones of Scotist *haecceitas* (interpreted by Heidegger as a singularity of historical existence distinct from categories or transcendental notions), Spinozist monism (in and from which all things emanate), Hegelian identification of the absolute with unfolding temporality (being unveiled only by and with nonbeing), and a kind of "secularized" Christian mysticism (phenomenological descriptions of the self derived from Meister Eckhart and Lutheran Pietism).[44] Yet, however one interprets it, the ontic-ontological difference between entities and being, for Heidegger, definitely excludes the possibility of a classical philosophical theology.

The development of Heidegger's criticisms of natural theology as ontotheology is complex and suggests a variety of stages, sometimes overlapping. In his early Lutheran period he purposefully eschews any attempt to think philosophically about God as something contrary to a worthwhile ontology, and attempts to trace an initial history of erroneous thinking of God in terms of "being" from Plato and Aristotle to Aquinas and Suarez.[45] Here the theological influences of his study of Luther are explicit, and are joined with a critical stance toward scholastic theology and the *analogia*

---

[42] See *Introduction to Metaphysics*, trans. G. Fried and R. Polt (New Haven and London: Yale University Press, 2000), 34: "Why are there beings at all instead of nothing? . . . What are we really asking? Why beings as such are. We are asking about the ground for the fact that beings *are* and are what they *are*, and that there is not nothing instead. . . . We are interrogating beings in regards to their Being."

[43] *Being and Time*, §12, 32: "Dasein is an entity which does not just occur among other entities. Rather it is ontically distinguished by the fact that, in its very Being, that Being is an *issue* for it. . . . It is peculiar to this entity that with and through its Being, this Being is disclosed to it. *Understanding of Being is itself a definite characteristic of Dasein's Being.* Dasein is ontically distinctive in that it is ontological."

[44] Consider, for example, the various interpretations of Joseph Kockelmans, *On the Truth of Being* (Bloomington: Indiana University Press, 1984); Theodore Kisiel, *The Genesis of Heidegger's Being in Time* (Berkeley and Los Angeles: University of California Press, 1993); Herman Philipse, *Heidegger's Philosophy of Being* (Princeton: Princeton University Press, 1998); Julian Young, *Heidegger's Later Philosophy* (Cambridge: Cambridge University Press, 2002); S. J. McGrath, *The Early Heidegger and Medieval Philosophy: Phenomenology for the Godforsaken* (Washington, DC: The Catholic University of America Press, 2006).

[45] Although it is arguably only at the very end of this period, Heidegger's treatment of the metaphysics of God in his 1929 lecture course *The Fundamental Concepts of Metaphysics: World, Finitude, Solitude* (trans. W. McNeill and N. Walker [Bloomington: Indiana University Press, 2001], 41–57) lays the foundations for what he would subsequently say concerning ontotheology.

entis.[46] In writings from his subsequent atheistic period, there are clear affirmations that Christian faith is itself an obstacle to right thinking about the question of being, and must be suspended as a condition for the practice of philosophy. The certitude of the believer necessarily imposes a goal to such reflection in terms that hide the problem of being behind the notions of a supreme entity.[47] However, in later writings from his post-war period, ontotheology is given a more precise description, applicable not to any and every possible form of natural theology but to a particular form of reasoning Heidegger seeks to delineate as being philosophically inauthentic.[48]

Consistently over these various periods, ontotheology is criticized particularly for its attempts to describe God metaphysically in terms of an entity (*ens*) like others, differing primarily as the causal explanation of the latter, by means of the principle of sufficient reason (whatever is not the cause of itself must be caused by another). The explanation of finite entities is conceived of in terms of one's universal, most general notion of entity, itself intelligible ultimately only in reference to the notion of a supreme entity. This primary being, meanwhile, is *causa sui* and serves as a condition of possibility for the existence and intelligibility of *any possible series of entities* that depend upon him. However, he is also conceived of by recourse to them and in terms of them, portrayed as their archetypal instantiation. Thus, any possible being implies the existence of God. "Caused beings" are studied metaphysically by recourse to a theory of univocal predication that is constructed teleologically in view of the edification of the theology of the supreme being who is their cause. Meanwhile, reflection on the aforementioned "caused beings" is the condition of possibility for the very notion of the supreme being.[49] A system of logical discourse (*logos*) results that is

---

[46] S. J. McGrath (*The Early Heidegger and Medieval Philosophy*, esp. 151–84) has offered a very interesting and well-argued account of the ways in which the study of Luther's theology directly influenced Heidegger's early philosophy. See also the study by Kisiel, *The Genesis of Heidegger's Being in Time*, 149–219.

[47] See *Introduction to Metaphysics*, 7–8 (which dates originally to 1935). Heidegger affirms that any reference to Christian faith or to "Christian philosophy" is antithetical to true philosophical and ontological research.

[48] See in particular "The Onto-theo-logical Constitution of Metaphysics," in *Identity and Difference*, trans. J. Staumbaugh (New York: Harper and Row, 1969), 42–74.

[49] Metaphysical theology attempts to reconcile the irremediable difference of being and entities within a common logic. "The Onto-theo-logical Constitution of Metaphysics," in *Identity and Difference* (70–72): "Because Being appears as ground, beings are what is grounded; the highest being, however, is what accounts in the sense of giving the first cause. When metaphysics thinks of being with respect to the ground that is common to all beings as such, then it is logic as onto-logic. When metaphysics thinks of beings as such as a whole, that is, with respect to the highest being which accounts for everything, then it is logic as theo-logic. . . . The

comprehensive, coherent, and circular. It necessarily applies to anything that might be, and relates this being to God. Metaphysics is therefore "always, already" on its way toward God, as soon as it "thinks" any "being" (as finite and dependent), yet obscures the problem of Being itself (*Sein*), literally making it unthinkable. The true confrontation of man with himself as a being who *questions* Being becomes impossible.

Whatever one may make of the German philosopher's history of metaphysics, and brooding, quasi-mystical ontology, there is no question that Heidegger's vision moves us from Kant's definition of ontotheology into a postmodern format well known today. Metaphysical thinking about God for Heidegger pertains no longer to Kant's *necessary structure* of the thinking subject (even as illusory but unavoidable), but rather to the arbitrary and *unnecessary constructions* of the thinking subject. The human being is distinct (as *dasein*) because his irreducible, existential singularity escapes the natural determinations (categories) of being, *and* can be aware of itself precisely in its historical singularity in time. This also allows it to understand itself as given being ("thrown" in the world), and as a being in time *toward* nothingness. Metaphysics is a self-constructed system, an ontological narrative project of world interpretation that fabricates arbitrary logical structures for the organization of life in the factical world. As an attempt to master reality as comprehensively as possible, medieval metaphysics is artificial by nature (an artifact of man) and attains its historical culmination in the culture of modern technology, which seeks to master reality. Yet no "explanation" of existence is possible, and no teleological purpose to human existence is now discernable. Recourse to the notion of a supreme being even as a hypothesis is an attempt to hide from the facticity of being-toward-nothingness. Neither modern technological culture nor classical metaphysics provides an authentic interpretation of the meaning of the

---

onto-theological constitution of metaphysics stems from the prevalence of that difference which keeps Being as the ground, and beings as what is grounded and what gives account, apart from and related to each other; and by this keeping, perdurance is achieved. . . . The deity enters into philosophy through the perdurance . . . the perdurance results in and gives Being as the generative ground. This ground itself needs to be properly accounted for by that for which it accounts, that is, by the causation through the supremely original matter—and that is the cause as *causa sui*. This is the right name for the god of philosophy. Man can neither pray nor sacrifice to this god. Before the *causa sui*, man can neither fall to his knees in awe, nor can he play music and dance before this god. The god-less thinking which must abandon the god of philosophy, god as causa sui, is thus perhaps closer to the divine God. Here this means only: god-less thinking is more open to Him than onto-theo-logic would like to admit."

temporality of man's being, and the mystery of Being. Nor do they permit a true intellectual confrontation with one's own temporal finitude.[50] Whatever the merits of his critique, and however insightful (or obscure) his own notions of being, it is clear that Heidegger's description of western metaphysics as ontotheology in the terms described above cannot have a universal applicability.[51] In effect, Heidegger's portrayal of ontotheology presupposes that there exists in this "tradition" of western European metaphysics an ongoing attempt to understand God as the supreme being by an invocation derived from our ordinary notions of common being (*ens*). It does so by constructing a transcendental science of metaphysics, which would include both God and created realities under

---

[50] On the unique character of the human being, see, for example, *Being and Time*, §12–15, 42–45, 53–59; pp. 32–35, 67–71, 78–90.

[51] Heidegger claimed that his criticisms were pertinent for thinkers from Aristotle to Hegel. A number of influential contemporary medieval scholars argue, meanwhile, that historically many of the attributes of such thinking began to develop implicitly only with Scotus's rearticulation of Avicennian metaphysics. Concerning ontotheology, the medieval historian Alain de Libera writes: "For a medievalist this characterization of the essence of 'Aristotelian' metaphysics holds true principally for *one* of the Latin interpretations of Avicenna which was formulated within the medieval schools, and which by the bias of nineteenth century neoscholasticism, decisively informed Heidegger's vision of metaphysics, namely: Scotism. In fact, it is with Duns Scotus that metaphysics is presented as a science which has as its common object being and as its eminent object God. This thesis is supported by a certain number of principles of 'Avicennian' origin, transposing the theory of the 'indifference of essence' onto the 'level' of the concept of *ens*." *La Philosophie Médiévale* (Paris: Presses Universitaires de France, 1989), 72–73. Similarly, Olivier Boulnois ("Quand commence l'onto-théologie? Aristote, Thomas d'Aquin et Duns Scot") discusses Heidegger's own hesitations in labeling Aristotle's thought a form of ontotheology, and criticizes as problematic his characterization of Aquinas's *Prologue* to the commentary on the *Metaphysics*. Boulnois himself claims that both these thinkers stand outside the boundaries of the appellation. See also, Jean-Luc Marion, "Saint Thomas d'Aquin et l'onto-théo-logie," *Revue Thomiste* 95 (1995): 31–66, and Jean François Courtine, "Métaphysique et ontothéologie," in *La Métaphysique*, ed. J. M. Narbonne and L. Langlois (Paris and Quebec: J. Vrin and Les Presses de l'Université de Laval, 1999), 137–58, whose arguments agree in this respect. For an interpretation of Scotus contrasting on several points with that of Boulnois and these other authors, see Richard Cross, "Where the Angels Fear to Tread: Duns Scotus and Radical Orthodoxy," *Antonianum* 76, no. 1 (2001): 7–41. Cross rightly notes that Scotus distinguishes clearly a logical and semantic theory of "being" (including intentional or possible beings) from the metaphysics of real beings. His univocity theory of logical predication does not imply an ontology of "univocal assimilation" of the notion of primary being to that of common being. Cross's arguments suggest that a number of the characteristics of ontotheology as described by Heidegger might also be inapplicable to the Subtle Doctor's work as well.

a common subject of study. This science can invoke the notion of possible being as a means to reflect on the necessary conditions for any being whatsoever. The demonstration of God in this system is dependent upon the a priori (non-experiential) appeal to epistemological principles of causality and of sufficient reason. The intellect, then, explains all possible being to itself by positing the notion of a first necessary entity that gives intelligibility to secondary entities, even as this primary entity is itself explained in terms of them. The connection between this system of entities (both possible and real, finite and infinite) is guaranteed by a set of mentally immanent laws (such as the "principle of causality," "sufficient reason," etc.) that are accessible a priori, as soon as the thinking subject reflects upon the conditions for his or her own thought.[52]

The metaphysics of both Aristotle and Aquinas, meanwhile, insist that all true metaphysical reflection begins from knowledge of real existents, and can in no way begin from a theory of possible being. They seek to determine the structure of reality, not by recourse to a mentally immanent system of laws of thinking, but by recourse to a study of the intrinsic and extrinsic causes of beings. In doing so, both thinkers appeal to an analogical understanding of the predication of "existence" that avoids any appeal to a logical theory of univocal concepts. They cannot, therefore, be easily charged with the assimilation of the notion of the primary being to that of common being.[53] Only the latter is the immediate object of metaphysics, while the former transcends per se the scope of metaphysical science. (I will return to this point subsequently.) Their philosophies can of course be described as ontotheological insofar as the knowledge of God is their ultimate teleological aim. Yet the integral examination of the beings we experience directly need not be compromised by this teleology, nor must an essential definition of God follow necessarily from a conceptual grasp of the problem of "being." On the contrary, an experiential, analogical study of the very structure of the beings we know immediately could be said to lead naturally to the ultimate question of the existence of a transcendent, primary cause of being. The God in question, however, is not *causa sui* (a Cartesian appellation, in no way found in Aristotle or Aquinas), but in fact transcends entirely the realm of causality. Correspondingly, this study cannot presuppose a priori either the concept or the existence of such a transcendent reality, but must demonstrate the exis-

---

[52] Vincent Carraud, in his dense and well-documented work *Causa sive ratio*, has argued that these are all attributes of Enlightenment metaphysics that Kant, and post-Kantian philosophers, inherited from Leibniz and Wolff.

[53] The sign of which is that Scotists who defend such a "univocal core" of predication of the concept of "being" to both creatures and God commonly accuse Thomists of using *equivocal* speech concerning God and creatures, such that the two cannot adequately be related logically.

tence of God uniquely by a posteriori modes of argumentation, based on experience of existence in the realities around us.

Observations such as these would form the basis for the contention of modern Thomists: the failures of modern ontology can be seen as the opportunity to rediscover the true insights of Aquinas's natural theology. The case for this claim has to be made, however; and as I will argue in successive chapters, it has not been established so simply. Heidegger's critique not only intensifies the post-Kantian question of how the mind attains being in the first place but also requires a treatment of the analogical discovery of the structures of being (its principles and causes), which leads in turn to another analogical form of questioning concerning the relation of these realities to the transcendent first cause of being. The Thomistic thinkers considered in this book were extremely sensitized to the difficulties of such an enterprise, and their efforts collaborate toward an integral solution.

The Metaphysical Problem of the Person

A final issue that needs to be mentioned in this context is that of the human person. Kant introduced into modern philosophy the notion of the dignity of the human person as a subject of ethics in the *Groundwork for the Metaphysics of Morals* (1785) and *The Metaphysics of Morals* (1787). The person is discussed strictly in the ethical domain, without reference to the ontological structure of the acting subject. (The acting subject is treated "ontologically" in the *Critique of Pure Reason* uniquely in terms of the structure of the transcendental ego.) His attempts to speak of human personhood are related to his metaphysical understanding of man in practical terms, through the study of human freedom, ethics, and the categorical imperative. The Kantian descriptions and prescriptions relative to human liberty and ethics were to inspire in the twentieth century diverse personalist schools of thought, such as that of the French neo-Kantian Renouvier, or that of the phenomenologist Max Scheler, whose work would react against certain ethical notions from Kant's anthropology. With these one must also note Maurice Nédoncelle and Emmanuel Mounier.[54] Heidegger's philosophy of the *dasein* and of the existential

---

[54] Max Scheler, *Le Formalism en Ethique et l'Ethique Matèrièle des Valeurs* (Paris: Seuil, 1955; first ed., 1916) insists upon an understanding of the person that considers emotional values, corporeality, and inter-personal reciprocity, so as not to reduce man to a self-regulating, rational, voluntary actor. The person is the summit of all ethical values: "It is a mistake of antipersonalistic ethics to assume that the person's directedness *beyond* himself, essential for any ethically positive posture, and the *absence* of his intending his own value would contradict the fact that the person realizes his value *in* precisely this posture and that the values of the person are above all other values in terms of rank. . . . The value of the person is the highest value

structures of the human being did not, of course, form part of the person-alist movement. It did, however, attempt to speak of ontology particularly with regard to man, as the being who questions Being, and therefore as the privileged locus for the study of ontology.

These diverse movements presented modern Thomists with a number of philosophical challenges. Confrontation with modernity meant consid-ering the human person in metaphysical terms, and this in part so as to restore intelligibility to human existence in post-Christian cultures in which the absence of any true human end was commonly affirmed. How could a rearticulation of Thomistic metaphysics treat the subject of the human person ontologically, while respecting the phenomenological com-plexity of man's experience and his human activity? Could the latter con-tribute in some way to deepening the understanding of the former, and vice versa? Furthermore, if, as Aquinas claims, the knowledge of the good is dependent upon the knowledge of being, then a realistic ontology would seem necessary for a correct ethical understanding of human activ-ity (ordered toward the good), and conversely, examination of the moral activity of man might permit Thomistic metaphysics to treat anew the metaphysics of the good. Heidegger had proposed to study the *dasein* as the most revealing subject for the study of being. For Thomists, then, could the human person, as both body and spiritual soul, reveal the struc-ture and causes of being in an exceptional way? And could this knowledge be especially helpful for the development of natural theology?

Via Inventionis for a Thomistic Theological Metaphysics

I have mentioned above in the introduction that the chief consideration of this book is the right articulation of an appropriate way of progressive dis-covery for Thomistic metaphysics in the wake of the Kantian and Heideg-gerian accusations that all natural theology amounts to ontotheology. I have suggested above why such accusations are problematic and have alluded in passing to resources that exist in Aristotelian and Thomistic

---

level; and it is superior to all values of things and of feeling-states. The 'willing' of the person can never be better or worse than the person in question. . . . And simi-larly, his value is a unique value. . . . Accordingly in addition to the universally valid good (and the content of oughtness resulting from it), there is for every person an *individually valid* good that is not less objective and evidential." (*Formalism in Ethics and Non-Formal Ethics of Values*, trans. M. Frings and R. Funk [Evanston, IL: Northeastern University Press, 1973], 507–9.) His thought was to influence Mounier, in works such as *Le Personnalisme* (Paris: Presses Universitaires de France, 1949), which incited discussion among Christian intellectuals: see Fouilloux, *Une Église en Quête de Liberté*, 164–69.

thought for a distinctly alternative account of natural knowledge of God. Precisely because it eschews any systematic schema of all beings, including divine being, based upon aprioristic conditions for understanding, Thomistic metaphysics falls outside the scope of the criticisms of Kant and Heidegger. Instead, it is committed to the progressive unveiling of the philosophical affirmation of God based upon a study of the structures of intra-worldly being. In what remains of this chapter I would like to identify briefly five elements that must be present in any valid Thomistic account of the natural knowledge of God of this kind. Subsequent chapters will seek to delineate what proper form such elements should take and how they might be rightly understood in relation to one another.

First, if the Kantian *Critique* presupposes that all knowledge of being is constructed by appeal to regulatory concepts of the transcendental subject, Thomism insists on the realistic ascription of existence and goodness to the very being of things. Therefore, a basic question concerns the entry way or point of departure for a Thomistic metaphysics. How is it that human beings have a natural capacity to know that which exists and to pose ontological questions that in turn call for metaphysical reflection, ultimately permitting the opportunity to construct a natural theology?

Second, what role does the analogical understanding of being play, and how is it related to an Aristotelian-Thomistic study of the causes of being? If this tradition rejects the possibility of the formation of any aprioristic concept of God, it nevertheless insists upon the possibility of the eventual construction of an analogical understanding of being, goodness, truth, and unity (the transcendentals) as well as causality and teleological operations. Notions extracted from the ordinary "folds" of reality can be properly ascribed to the divine and transcendent source of all finite secondary existence, even if imperfectly. This requires, however, that the immanent causes of the interdependent beings we experience are duly analyzed for their own sake as a prelude to the discussion of God.

Third, it is clear that no proper understanding of the natural knowledge of God can take place unless demonstrative reasoning concerning God is possible. The Thomistic claim—entirely at odds with both Kant and Heidegger—is that the right form such thinking should take is a posteriori in nature, proceeding from the realities we perceive and know, considered as dependent and caused, to an indirect and mediate understanding of their transcendent source. How do the "Five Ways" of Aquinas, for example, function as representative arguments of this kind? In what way does the causal nature of his argumentation render possible the distinctly analogical ascription of created perfections (being, goodness, etc.) to the primary being? How are such ways of thinking utterly different from the characterizations of natural theology as ontotheology in the modern tradition?

Fourth, what is the role that an ontological analysis of personal actions or operations should play in the development of a natural theology? More specifically, in what sense does the analogical ascription of personal goodness to God depend upon the prior analysis of human personal goodness as teleological in character? How do the aforementioned causal analysis and a posteriori monotheistic argumentations of Thomism render possible a reflection upon God as pure actuality and therefore as personal goodness? This latter question is essential for determining in what way natural theology may rightfully claim to be sapiential, that is to say, to be concerned with the highest good, to which the human person should naturally aspire as a rational, free agent.

Lastly, if there is the possibility of genuine knowledge of God, then in what sense is the pursuit of this knowledge open to the charge of "conceptual idolatry"? In what way do safeguards against the pretension to theological rationalism emerge *from within* the philosophical consideration of creatures, and causal-analogical reflection on God? Here the simultaneous truth and imperfection of a posteriori, causal argumentation are of great significance. For natural knowledge of God emerges as the expression of an inward inclination or tendency of the human mind to wish to know most perfectly the first and final cause of all things, God. Yet this same knowledge, by its indirect and imperfect character, also bespeaks a radical incompleteness, so that just as it has some kind of true form and perfection in the order of nature, it also suggests a radical imperfection and potentiality as regards the creature's intimacy with God. This dual-truth is very significant theologically, even if it emerges from within the optic of a distinctly philosophical horizon. It has great implications for the Christian theology of grace as well as for one's understanding of the intrinsically eschatological purpose of all revelation.

A conversation about the innate human possibility of natural theology touches directly upon the question of whether true knowledge of God has ever emerged outside the realm of human reflection on religious revelation (Christian theology). This takes us back to the conversation between Aquinas and the Reformation. Does such knowledge exist in a distinctly "philosophical" vein? In search of evidence in this regard, it is reasonable to begin with a consideration of the non-Christian philosopher who most influenced Aquinas, and who most revolted Luther. Can we delineate in Aristotle's writings the shape of a natural reasoning that leads to God, one that is not explicitly based upon revelation? Does this form of philosophical theology fall prey to the criticisms developed by Kant and Heidegger, or is it in fact the expression of a genuinely human, natural knowledge of God?

PART **II**

CHAPTER **2**

Knowledge of God as Wisdom according to Aristotle

I
T HAS BECOME nearly programmatic in modern theology to refer to
Aristotle's theology as a foil against which Christian conceptions are
considered in their originality. God is portrayed by Aristotle in
metaphysical terms as eternal, impassible, self-thinking thought, and this,
we are told, is mistaken.[1] This God is imprisoned in a world of solipsistic
ignorance of other realities, incapable of interpersonal reciprocity or true
love of others.[2] Such metaphysical theism is far removed from the Creator
of the Old and New Testament, who is engaged in the history of salvation.[3]
Slightly more mild, Thomistic criticisms are launched against Aristotle's

---

[1] Consider Robert Jenson, *Systematic Theology*, vol. I, *The Triune God* (Oxford: Oxford University Press, 1997), 94: "Greece identified deity by metaphysical predicates. Basic among them is timelessness: immunity to time's contingencies and particularly to death, by which temporality is enforced. . . . In this discourse, deity is a quality, which may be analyzed as immunity to time plus whatever are its necessary conditions . . . the hardly surpassable results of this reflection are Aristotle's sheer undistracted Self-consciousness and Plotinus' One above even the plurality of being something." Jenson argues against these perspectives from what he considers to be biblical premises. See, for example, 138ff.

[2] Emil Brunner, *The Christian Doctrine of God*, trans. O. Wyon (Philadelphia: Westminster, 1950), 152: "The God of Aristotle is neither a 'Lord-God' nor a Creator, neither the One who freely elects, nor the One who stoops down to man."

[3] Walter Kasper, *Jesus the Christ*, trans. V. Green (Tunbridge Wells, UK: Burns and Oates, 1993), 175: "In Greek metaphysics . . . freedom from suffering and passion (*apatheia*) were always regarded as supreme attributes of the divine. The God of the Old Testament on the other hand is known as God of the way and of guidance, as God of history, etc."

"essentialism" (his metaphysics of substance), which is said to obscure a true knowledge of being (as *esse*) and which insufficiently reflects on the transcendent efficient causality that is proper to a Christian metaphysics of creation.[4] As will become clear in subsequent chapters, I do not think that all these reflections are entirely false. However, it is also the case that Aristotle's philosophical theology contains resources for responding to the modern and contemporary concern with the ontotheological critique of an aprioristic metaphysics. Furthermore, far from being entirely surpassed by Aquinas's biblical and metaphysical monotheism, Aristotle's reasoning contributes a number of key elements that are central to the right articulation of Thomistic theological reasoning.

In this chapter and the next, then, I wish to study the question of knowledge of God in the thought of Aristotle and Aquinas, examining each one separately, yet underlining important points of contact between the two. In neither section do I intend to present an exhaustive investigation of the theology of the two thinkers.[5] However, a focused inquiry is necessary in order to identify the particular contexts and forms of the theological aspirations of Aristotle and Aquinas, respectively. My goal is twofold. First, I wish to explain elements of the historical contexts in which Aristotle and Aquinas developed their understanding of wisdom. Second, I wish to identify the structure of an analogical causal analysis of being that can be identified within and extracted from their historically conditioned works. I will argue that such an analysis has a perennially valid truthfulness: it is a manner of thinking about the structure of being that remains true in each historical age, including our own. Concerning Aristotle, then, my specific inquiry will concern the theme of wisdom (*sophia*) as a scientific knowledge of the causes of being, and concerning Aquinas, I will treat the question of the twofold knowledge of God, that is to say both natural and revealed knowledge, and their relation. This brief study, in turn, will permit us to identify better the historically distinctive challenges posed to metaphysicians in modernity, as well as to discern where the possibilities have lain for the articulation of an enduring form of ontological thinking across time.

---

[4] See, most notably, Étienne Gilson, *Being and Some Philosophers* (Toronto: PIMS, 1952), 70–72. I will return to Gilson's views below in chapter 4.

[5] Important recent defenses of the rationality of Aristotle's natural theology have been offered by Michel Bastit, *Le Quatre Causes De L'Être Selon La Philosophie Première D'Aristote* (Louvain: Éditions Peeters, 2002), esp. 349–82, and McInerny, *Praeambula Fidei*, esp. 245–82. As will become clear in the discussions below, my own perspectives are particularly indebted to those of Bastit.

The Platonic Background of Aristotle's Protreptic Aspirations

Aristotle, as a fourth-century B.C. thinker, did not approach theology with the same questions as Descartes and Kant. He did not consider the divine nature first and foremost with a view toward "proving" God's existence irrefutably to atheists, or with the ambition to show the necessary a priori conditions for a knowledge of God. This knowledge, on the contrary, is in a certain sense presupposed. Aristotle believes that *some* kind of knowledge of the divine is the *unique* form of knowledge that man has never lost because it has been preserved constantly throughout the ages.[6] His efforts to shed light philosophically (and somewhat correctively) on such traditional religious beliefs is conceived in terms of wisdom, and the relation of wisdom to God. Such knowledge is an ultimate speculative science that entails knowledge through causes, and provides an ultimate principle for practical action and civic virtue.[7] This framework of thought was inherited from Plato, such that the theme of wisdom perhaps established the deepest continuity between the two thinkers, and yet it is a topic significantly altered by the disciple.[8] Concerning the relation of wisdom to God, therefore, first I will discuss the Platonic background conception and Aristotle's alteration of key aspects, and second I will map out structural elements for the philosophical approach to God as presented by Aristotle in the *Metaphysics*. These considerations will permit us to retrace summarily but precisely central elements of Aristotelian thought that were to be assimilated in turn by Aquinas.

The theme of wisdom (*phronesis* or *sophia*) in Plato's thought is as problematic as it is central. It is central because it can be seen as a continual thread throughout his work from the *Apology* to the *Epinomis*, and no theme, except the closely related theme of education, seems to be so unifying to all of his *corpus*.[9] Yet it is also problematic because it is a progressively evolving theme, of which Plato struggles to give a satisfactory account, and in which it could be argued that he fails. I will outline three problems that

---

6 *Metaphysics* Λ, 8, 1074b8–14. Aquinas interprets this as an affirmation of the culturally universal belief in the existence of immaterial substances. *In XII Meta.*, lec. 10, 2597.

7 *Metaphysics* Λ, 1, 981b26–982a2.

8 See Marie-Dominique Philippe, "La Sagesse selon Aristote," *Nova et Vetera* (French ed.) 20, no. 4 (1945): 325–74.

9 See, for example, *Apology*, 20d, 23a; *Euthydemus*, 278e3–284e6, 288d5–293a6; *Phaedo*, 68b7–69d5; *Republic* VII, 532b, 537c, 540a; *Laws* X, 897c; *Epinomis*, 980c7–986a7. All English translations are taken from *Plato: Complete Works*, ed. J. M. Cooper and D. S. Hutchinson (Indianapolis and Cambridge: Hackett Publishing, 1997). A number of these passages are analyzed in detail by A. J. Festugière, *Les Trois Protreptiques de Platon* (Paris: Vrin, 1973), with respect to the theme of wisdom. I will refer repeatedly to his study below.

Plato's work gave rise to concerning wisdom, from three successive periods of his philosophical career, and I will then discuss how Aristotle rearticulated these questions in a different way to unknot the problems. The first such problem, found in the earlier period and exemplified in the *Euthydemus*, concerns a circular definition of the object of practical wisdom. The second, found in the *Phaedo* and *Republic*, concerns wisdom as the contemplation of the ideal forms and of the good. The third, found in the *Epinomis*, understands the good and wisdom in terms of a state liturgy offered to the order of the heavens. These proposals prepare more adequate Aristotelian solutions: wisdom will be seen as the science of the primary cause of being, and as a final end of human activity and of civic education.

Plato's philosophical efforts have as their background the teaching and example of Socrates, whose instruction suggested the need for a reform of the state in accordance with true virtue, itself considered as a form of wisdom. (This wisdom was initially announced by the oracle at Delphi, and eventually embraced by Socrates himself as a service to the divinity.)[10] The themes of virtue, true piety, wisdom, and reform of the state are intertwined in Socrates' discourse in the *Apology*, as they will be (in other, diverse forms) in Plato's later works.[11] Consequently, in the Socratic dialogue, the *Euthydemus*, the theme of wisdom initially surfaces as related to the problem of the government of the state, in the search for a science that provides political virtue.[12] This wisdom must be a uniquely interior good of the soul, since the possession of exterior goods, in the absence of this good, will not benefit us. Material goods will be of no avail to the provision of happiness without a knowledge of how to use them.[13] "Wisdom is the only existing thing which makes a man happy and fortunate."[14] Nevertheless, as Festugière shows, Plato reveals himself to be perplexed concerning the exact nature of such wisdom. His eventual explanations of the good accorded by political knowledge entail an endless circularity. The "royal art" he is seeking is the science of making men good, but this goodness is what? It is the accomplishment of this very activity that is the science of making men good. So the good of each

---

[10] *Apology*, 20d–e, 23a, 25a–b, 29a–b, 36d–e, 38c.
[11] Festugière, *Les Trois Protreptiques de Platon*, 10–11: "The idea of wisdom, and the theme of the exhortation to wisdom are in a sense the entirety of Plato. The ultimate goal of his efforts is the reform of the state. The state will not be restored unless the citizens practice virtue. They will not practice virtue unless they know what true virtue is. Virtue, therefore, is founded upon a knowledge of the absolute Truth, that is to say, knowledge of true Being and the veritable Good. Virtue, then, is a science, the true name of which is 'wisdom.'"
[12] *Euthy.*, 278e3–284e6; 288d5–293a6.
[13] *Euthy.*, 281b5–d7.
[14] *Euthy.*, 282c8.

man is to make others good, and so on.[15] This same problem will arise concerning later attempts to identify the good with either the useful or the beautiful.[16] Both imply means to or effects of something that is sought for its own sake, and thus fail to provide a fully satisfactory account of wisdom.[17]

Wisdom as civic virtue will be reintroduced in the *Republic* VI, 505c2–4, and this time the problem will be rethought in light of the doctrine of the forms and the virtue of contemplation. This doctrine has appeared in the *Phaedo*, where philosophy is considered as a preparation for death and the contemplative life of the immortal soul.[18] (It has also appeared in the *Symposium* as regards the ultimate good and beauty.)[19] In the *Republic* the doctrine of the forms and of immutable being and goodness will be introduced in relation to the contemplative life as a way of resolving the question of what wisdom is. It is by governing in accordance with this ultimate form of knowledge that the guardians can establish true justice in the city, conceived primarily as a participation of each citizen in the form of the good according to his particular task and rank.[20] Knowledge of this form is knowledge of the immutable beauty and goodness that truly is (507b7), and is the object of thought but not of sight (507b10). Consequently, this wisdom is a "knowledge according to the whole."[21] It is precisely the task of dialectics (the equivalent to Aristotle's speculative sciences) to yield an account of the whole of things, in the light of the first principle (which is the immutable good) so as to be able to order all else.[22]

---

[15] *Euthy.*, 288d5–293a6. Plato admits his confusion in 292d1–e6: "Socrates, you seem to have got yourselves into a frightful tangle." See the commentary of Festugière, *Les Trois Protreptiques de Platon*, 29–31.

[16] *Protagoras*, 356b3–c2; *Gorgias*, 470d5 and following.

[17] *Les Trois Protreptiques*, 47–53.

[18] *Phaedo*, 67e5–69b8.

[19] *Symp.*, 205e1–206a2, 210b8–211a4.

[20] *Rep.* VI, 505a2–507b10. 505a2: "[T]he form of the good is the most important thing to learn about and [the fact] that it's by their relation to it that just things and the others become useful and beneficial." This responds to the problem introduced in Book *a* (357b and following) concerning the philosophical quest for an interior justice that is a wisdom pursued for its own sake (presumably following the example of Socrates, whose interior justice and wisdom were goods more important than any exterior good, even including the life of the body).

[21] *Rep.*, 537c7: "For anyone who can achieve a unified vision is dialectical, and anyone who can't isn't." 537d6: Dialectic permits one to "[go] on with the help of truth to that which by itself is."

[22] *Rep.*, 511b3–e, 533b–c, 541a, in 540a he writes: "Then, at the age of fifty those [guardians] who've survived the tests and have been successful both in practical matters and in the sciences must be led to the goal and must be compelled to lift up the radiant light of their souls to what itself provides light for everything. And once they've seen the good itself, they must each in turn put the city, its citizens, and themselves in order, taking it as their model."

Yet in the *Republic* Plato's protreptic ambitions also face grave difficulties. He cannot in fact identify directly what the good is.[23] It is something beyond subsistence and existence, and can be spoken about only by images, as representational comparisons.[24] Furthermore, as a universal form, the good is conceived in a strictly univocal fashion. Unsurprisingly, then, the corresponding problem of how human beings participate in the immutable good contemplated by the philosopher remains a largely unresolved question.[25]

In response to these problems, Plato evolves yet again in his later works in a final attempt to address the question of wisdom and its relation to the good, through his doctrine of the mediation of the divinity by the visible heavens, and the related civic worship of the immortal deities of the heavens (in *Laws* X and the *Epinomis*). Here we see Plato backing away from earlier (Hericlitean) affirmations of the non-intelligibility of the sensible world, developing instead an argued affirmation of the universal primacy of soul over body, and thus of the animation of the heavens by a living principle.[26] (This is accompanied by his interest in astronomy

---

23 *Rep.*, 506d2–e5. "[L]et us abandon the quest for what is the good itself for the time being . . . [for] it is too big a topic. . . . But I am willing to tell you about what is apparently an offspring of the good and most like it."

24 *Rep.*, 508b10–c2: "What the good itself is in the intelligible realm, in relation to understanding and intelligible things, the sun is in the visible realm, in relation to sight and visible things." 508e4–6: "In the visible realm, light and sight are rightly considered sunlike, but it is wrong to think that they are the sun, so here it is right to think of knowledge and truth as goodlike but wrong to think that either of them is the good—for the good is yet more prized."

25 As Giovanni Reale points out (*Toward a New Interpretation of Plato*, trans. J. Catan [Washington, DC: The Catholic University of America Press, 1997], 203), there are three enigmatic points concerning the good in the *Republic* that remain unresolved: (1) the essence of the good itself remains unknowable, (2) the causal and explanatory role of the good for justice and knowledge is affirmed but not explained, (3) the good is said to be the cause of being and essence, but this is not explained. (One may readily agree with this accurate description even if one is reserved about Reale's ambitious appeal to the "unwritten doctrines" of Plato as a way of resolving the enigmas.) The acuteness of the problem of how beings are related to the forms and to the good becomes particularly evident in the *Parmenides*, where a critical turn toward the theory of the forms is manifest. See the study of Plato's self-criticism on this point by Kenneth Sayre, *Plato's Late Ontology: A Riddle Resolved* (Princeton: Princeton University Press, 1983), esp. 18–186.

26 See *Laws* X, 893b–896e. Plato argues that an ordered series of moved movers requires an initial self-moving mover who is alive and a soul animating the changes and order of the heavens. 897c: "If, my fine fellow, the whole course and movement of the heavens and all that is in them reflect the motion and revolution and calculation of reason, and operate in a corresponding fashion, then clearly we have to admit that it is the best kind of soul that cares for the entire universe and directs

under the influence of Eudoxus, through which he had become sensitive to the mathematical intelligibility of the physical world and its corresponding order.)[27] This permits him to develop a visual, representational paradigm of the divine in terms of the cosmos. The movements of the stars represent to us the stability of the heavenly beings, who move always in the same way in accordance with the good, and wisdom for us is accorded through the contemplation of these movements.[28] Thus, the heavens (considered as a reflection of the divine) provide a certain sensible and temporal communication of divine wisdom, and consequently permit a civic piety and imitation of these divine beings, such that the city is brought into harmony with the sacred order of the world, which is willed by the first mover, who is the ultimate principle of deity.[29] The just wisdom of the city is to live in accordance with the divine, through the mediation of civic worship offered to the heavens. It is in this way that the good is obtained.

Aristotle's early *protrepticus, On Philosophy*, contains a doctrine very close to that of the late Plato (so much so that certain scholars have attributed the *Epinomis* to Aristotle). He clearly affirms here the representational paradigm of the celestial bodies as examples of wisdom.[30] In *On the Heavens*, Book α, chapter 12, we also see Aristotle propounding a theory of the heavens as imitating the divine goodness to differing degrees, by movements of a circular nature that are eternal, simple, and stable. They are thought to be alive and moved by superior, contemplative intelligences. Meanwhile,

---

it along the best path." The circular motion of the stars, immobile at the center, reflects the revolution of intelligence, that is to say, by a single movement, law, regularity, and uniformity (898a–b).

[27] *Les Trois Protreptiques*, 13. On the emergence of a teleological conception of nature as demiurgic art in the later works of Plato, see also James Lennox, "Plato's Unnatural Teleology," in *Platonic Investigations*, ed. D. O'Meara (Washington, DC: The Catholic University of America Press, 1985), 195–218.

[28] *Epin.,* 980c7–986a7.

[29] *Epin.,* 989a1–b2; 988a1–e4: "No Greek ought to fear that being mortal we should never concern ourselves with the divine. We should have quite the opposite thought; the divine (i.e., the cosmos) is never without intelligence nor is it at all ignorant of human nature, but it knows that if it teaches we will follow along and learn what we are taught. And of course it knows that the very thing that it teaches us and that we learn is number and how to count. . . . Therefore, since we now claim soul is the cause of the whole cosmos, and all good things have causes that are good . . . it is no wonder that soul is the cause of every orbit and motion, and the best kind of soul causes orbits and motions that tend toward the good."

[30] See *On Philosophy*, fragments B9, B17–19, B28–9, B48–50, B93. In B49 he writes: "[T]o the philosopher alone among craftsmen belong laws that are stable and actions that are right and noble. For he alone lives by looking at nature and the divine. Like a good helmsman he moors his life to that which is eternal and unchanging." (All translations of Aristotle are taken from *The Complete Works of Aristotle*, 2 vols., ed. J. Barnes, [Princeton: Princeton University Press, 1984].)

inferior beings, such as man, are complex and can attain their perfection (contemplation of the divine) only through a multiple set of actions.[31]

Despite these similarities, progressive developments in Aristotle's own thinking led to critical reevalutations of his teacher's work, and a thoroughgoing attempt to rearticulate an understanding of wisdom, the good, and virtue. This entails certain significant relativizations of the place of celestial bodies in his theology, and the development of a non-representational, purely metaphysical conceptualization of the divine and its relation to secondary beings. (However, Aristotle does retain an important role for the celestial beings in his cosmology and understanding of intermediary causation.) In discussing this, I will first note three important philosophical problems in Plato's protreptic philosophy that Aristotle discerned and to which he proposed novel and significant solutions, particularly in the *Nicomachean Ethics*. These permitted him to restructure Plato's aspirations upon new foundations. Having mentioned these, I will then discuss ways in which Aristotle sought to articulate a speculative understanding of wisdom in the *Metaphysics*.

Aristotelian Rearticulation of the Platonic Aspirations

A primary Platonic aporia that has already been mentioned in the *Euthydemus* concerns the problem of the nature of wisdom as a good that is a virtue. Plato tries to identify this good successively with "the royal art," pleasure, beauty, the contemplation of the forms and of the good, and, finally, with a sapiential philosophy of nature and a corresponding civic piety. What, then, is this virtue or excellence sought by the soul for its own sake, proper to man, and upon which his ultimate moral realization depends? Aristotle's *Nicomachean Ethics* seeks to re-situate the problem of wisdom and virtue, of the good and political reform, by first reconsidering the good not in the line of stable and unchanging forms, but as an end (*telos*). Furthermore, the diverse ends pursued by man take place in the form of activities. Thus the good is thought to be that in view of which man acts in his diverse activities.[32] The complete end is the best activity

---

[31] *On the Heavens* II, 12, 292a19–24: "We think of the stars as mere bodies, and as units with a serial order indeed but entirely inanimate; but we should rather conceive them as enjoying life and action. On this view the facts cease to appear surprising. For it is plausible that the best-conditioned of all things should have its good without action, that that which is nearest to it should achieve it by little and simple action, and that that which is farthest removed by a complexity of actions."

[32] These affirmations are made on the basis of observational facts. *Nic. Ethics* I:1, 1094a1–4: "Every art and every inquiry, and similarly every action and choice, is thought to aim at some good; and for this reason the good has rightly been declared to be that at which all things aim. But a certain difference is found among ends; some are activities, others are products apart from the activities that produce them."

that he can accomplish, in accordance with his highest excellence (or virtue), and thus in accordance with his own proper "function," as a being endowed with a rational nature.[33] This end, in Book X, will of course be identified with wisdom (*sophia*), which is a knowledge of the first principles of all things, and a contemplation of truth and of the divine.[34] (I will return to the virtue of wisdom below).

In these texts, then, one sees Aristotle drawing together a number of new ideas that are of great consequence in his thought: he affirms that the good implies the notion of a final causality (of the *ratio finis*, as Aquinas would say), and therefore can be understood fully only in terms of this causality. The final cause, in turn, must be understood in terms of activity (or actuality) and potentiality, and not only formally.[35]

A second problem with Plato's notions of wisdom during his middle period (of the *Phaedo*, and *Republic*) is revealed by the criticisms Aristotle formulates in *Nicomachean Ethics*, Book I, 6, concerning his univocal notion of the good. I have noted above that Plato's quest for wisdom implies an identification of this wisdom with the form of the good, and entails a corresponding problem of how all things participate in this universal (univocal) form. He will eventually attempt to resolve the moral dimensions of this problem through the notion of heavenly motion as a medium for the communication of the good. Aristotle, however, demonstrates that God (or the divine) cannot be the formal cause of the goodness of things (which are good *through their own acts*). Correspondingly, "the good" is expressed in different things or properties in irreducibly proportional (or analogical) ways. This diversity is analyzed according to diverse "categories" of being, and as related "focally" to the substance as first among the categories.

These categories refer to the inherent complexity of beings we experience, and are (for Aristotle) tenfold: those of substantial being (e.g., a human being, a horse, or a tree), quantity, quality, relations, time, place, being in a position, having, acting, and being acted upon (or capacity).[36] Goodness or the lack thereof "divides" along the lines of this inherent

---

33 *Nic. Ethics* I, 7, 1097a27–30, 35: "Clearly not all ends are complete ends; but the chief good is evidently something complete. Therefore, if there is only one complete end, this will be what we are seeking. . . . We call complete without qualification that which is always desirable in itself and never for the sake of something else." 10981a16–18: "[The] human good turns out to be activity of soul in conformity with excellence, and if there is more than one excellence, in conformity with the best and most complete."

34 *Nic. Ethics* X, 7–8, 1177a11–1178b32. See also Book *K*, 7, 1141a9–19.

35 These notions are exploited here in ethics, but also have already been employed importantly in the study of nature in *Physics* II, 7–III, 2.

36 See the helpful study of interpretative problems concerning the categories by Paul Studtmann, "Aristotle's Categories" in the electronic *Stanford Encyclopedia of*

ontological complexity, as does unity. In other words, the human goodness of a moral virtue (a quality of the soul attained through habitual activity) is understood differently from the goodness of a person's height (the goodness of his or her quantity) or family history (the goodness of his or her relations), and the like. And all of these analogical senses of "goodness" (without being reducible to one another) depend upon the substantial goodness of a wholistic reality, for example, the substantial goodness of a human being.[37] It is one human being who is virtuous, tall, and athletic, of good upbringing, and so on. Likewise, goodness must also be interpreted in terms of actuality and potentiality. Within any of the categorical modes of being there is a real distinction between the "potentiality for" versus the "actuality of" goodness. The substantial goodness of a human being, for example, may be only potential (there is goodness in potentially conceiving a child), or it may be actual (the conceived child is intrinsically good), and likewise for the goodness of moral virtue in a human being (which may have yet to develop or may already exist in act), the best height for competing in athletics, the ideal family surroundings, and so on.[38] These are goods that can "come into being." (These are points I will return to below). A major consequence of Aristotle's argument (along with the critique of the Platonic forms in general) is to separate the question of the being and goodness of realities we experience, on the one hand, from the question of the being and goodness of God, who is now considered only as their transcendent efficient and final cause, but not their formal cause.

The third rearticulation of Plato's discussion of wisdom and the good is prepared by these two, in reaction to a third problem appearing in the

---

Philosophy at http://plato.stanford.edu/entries/aristotle-categories/. An excellent defense of the realism of the categories has recently been offered by Benedict Ashley in his *The Way toward Wisdom*, 61–91.

37 *Nic. Ethics* I, 6, 1196a23–29: "Further, since things are said to be good in as many ways as they are said to be (for things are called good both in the category of substance, as God and reason, and in quality, e.g. the virtues, and in quantity, e.g. that which is moderate, and in relation, e.g. the useful, and in time, e.g. the right opportunity, and in place, e.g. the right locality and the like), clearly the good cannot be something universally present in all cases and single; for then it would not have been predicated in all the categories but in one only." 1196b24–26, 27–28: "But of honor, wisdom, and pleasure, just in respect of their goodness, the accounts are distinct and diverse, the good, therefore, is not something common answering to one Idea. . . . Are goods one, then, by being derived from one good or by all contributing to one good, or are they rather one by analogy?"

38 *Nic. Ethics*, 1096b29–31. As sight is to the eye so reason is to the soul. This proportional comparison will be explored in terms of being in act and being in potentiality in *Metaphysics* Θ, 6 and applied to goodness in chapter 9. This suggests that goodness, like being, is understood in analogically diverse ways as substance and accident, act and potentiality. I will return to this point further on.

later works, especially in the *Epinomis*. Plato proposed at the end of his life a form of wisdom that involved a practice of piety in the service of heavenly movements, themselves seen to be reflections of divine wisdom. But is this form of mediation real or imaginative? What is the necessary relationship between watching the heavens turn (their order and beauty granted) and knowledge of God's wisdom? Aristotle introduced in the *Physics* an alteration of the Platonic notion of God as a soul animating the universe, stressing instead the absolute transcendence of God with respect to all physical realities, in his demonstration of the *unmoved* first mover.[39] This was completed in the *Metaphysics* through his identification of God as pure actuality. These conceptions allowed him to develop a non-representational, conceptually analogical and metaphysical notion of God's transcendence, as one who cannot be confused with any being undergoing movement or change. Wisdom, then, for Aristotle, will be a search for the first cause of beings, itself unmoved, necessary and separate. Before I move on to a discussion of this study, the unifying conclusion of the three above-mentioned points should be stated: Aristotle in his criticisms of Plato permits a way of thinking about God as a *transcendent horizon*, the knowledge of whom is attained through an *activity proper* to man. This activity is the virtue through which man attains his *end*. God's wisdom and goodness are formally separate from that of man, and yet man becomes good and wise by activities of the *nous*, by which he comes to know something of the first cause.[40] Thus, the end of man is the virtuous

---

39 *Physics* VIII, 5, 257a32–257b26, 258a5–8, 258b4–9. *Generation of Animals*, IV, 3, 768b17–19. There must be a first cause of movement. Even if this is a self-moving mover (implying a composition of act and potentiality) this mover requires in turn a primary unmoved mover without potentiality. The uniqueness of this philosophical position in comparison to Plato's primary self-mover is brought out well (in the context of Thomistic discussions on the *ScG* I, q. 13), by Norman Kretzmann, *The Metaphysics of Theism*, 81–82. Compare *Laws* X, 893c2–896c3, which argues for the necessity of a primary self-moving mover, a soul that animates the heavens.

40 I will not treat here the question of whether the agent intellect described in *On the Soul* III, 5 may be identified with the pure actuality of God. Michael Frede has recently argued for the plausibility of this interpretation, in "La Théorie Aristotélicienne de l'Intellect Agent," in *Corps et Âme*, ed. R. Dherbey (Paris: J. Vrin, 1996), 377–90. Given the aporia that surround Aristotle's discussions on the immortal soul, it is perhaps difficult to determine with certitude his views of the relation of the *nous* to God. Nevertheless, what is certain is that God's state of contemplation is eternal, while man's is present only for a short period of time (*Metaphysics* Λ, 9, 1071b14–31), and that man's intellect passes from potentiality to actuality, while God's intellect has no potentiality in it whatsoever (1074b15–27). Furthermore, as Aquinas points out (*In de Anima* III, lec. X, 734ff.), *for Aristotle*, (1) the capacity for active extraction of intelligible contents from phantasms is a power *of the human soul*, (2) this power necessarily coexists within the soul with the *potentiality*

activity of wisdom (philosophical contemplation), through which he attains knowledge of the transcendent first cause, God.[41]

Aristotle does leave a place in his ethics for more imperfect human activities, pertaining to civic and moral virtue, and exemplified particularly in friendship.[42] This has given rise in modern scholarship to great debate as to whether Aristotle's conception of the good is "inclusive" or "exclusive."[43] While Aristotle's early work *On Philosophy* seems to posit wisdom and contemplation as the sole human good, the *Nicomachean Ethics* contains passages asserting that inferior goods, such as the moral virtues and friendship, are essential to human happiness.[44] It is not unreasonable, therefore, to interpret Aristotle as affirming the necessity of moral goodness both for a happy life (its intrinsic value), and for a life of contemplation (its instrumental value), even while maintaining its essential incompleteness without

---

of that same soul to receive intelligible concepts, and (3) all composition of actuality and potentiality is absent from God. It is possible to argue, therefore, that for Aristotle the agent intellect pertains per se to the human soul and not to God.

[41] It is important in this respect to note Aristotle's dissociation of *phronesis*, or practical wisdom, from *sophia*, which is speculative knowledge of the first principles of being, the separated substances (for example, in *Nic. Ethics* VI, 5, 7). Nevertheless, the question of the political teleology of the city is treated in terms of wisdom, since through education, wisdom can be favored as the final end of the citizens for which the laws of the government should provide prudentially. Thus wisdom is *specifically* theoretical but provides ultimate practical orientation to human activity, through its influence upon the *exercise* of prudence. (I, 13, 1102a5–10; X, 9, 1179b32–1180b30). This interpretation is illustrated with a detailed commentary on Aristotle's texts by Denis Bradley, *Aquinas on the Twofold Human Good* (Washington, DC: The Catholic University of America Press, 1997), 369–77.

[42] *Nic. Ethics* I, 13, 1103a4–10; X, 8, 1178a9, 20–25.

[43] A study of this dispute is offered by Bradley, *Aquinas on the Twofold Human Good*, 377–95, who himself argues that Aristotle holds an inclusive account of inferior activities with regards to *sophia*, activities that provide an imperfect but intrinsic *eudaimonia*.

[44] *Nic. Ethics* X, 7 (see 1177a12–18; 1178b24–25) maintains firmly that theoretical wisdom is the sole human activity providing complete happiness, and that this activity is self-sufficient. It actuates that which is "divine" in the human soul, and contemplation is the activity that most resembles God. X, 8 (see 1178b20–29): Happiness extends therefore just as far as contemplation, and animals have no share in it (while moral virtues pertain to man's hylomorphic composition). (Compare this to *On Philosophy*, frag. B29.) At the same time, however, friendship and moral virtues are not merely instrumental to the stability and augmentation of contemplative life. X, 6, 1176b5–8: "Now those activities are desirable in themselves from which nothing is sought beyond the activity. And of this nature excellent actions are thought to be; for to do noble and good deeds is a thing desirable for its own sake." VIII, 1, 1155a5: "Without friends no one would choose to live, though he had all other goods."

the contemplative virtues.[45] The knowledge of God, then, is the true final end of the human being, who is made for wisdom, according to Aristotle. Yet this truth need not diminish one's rational appreciation of certain necessary yet lesser goods of human existence.

Wisdom in the *Metaphysics*

I will now move to the second of the two points concerning Aristotle that I mentioned at the beginning of this chapter, that of wisdom considered as knowledge of God, and the theme of wisdom as it is present in the *Metaphysics*.

As has already been stated, the notion of the good as a final cause, the notions of act and potentiality, and the understanding of being (as well as the one and the good) as attributed proportionally to the diverse ten categories, are all discoveries of major importance in Aristotle's thought. These appear already in *Physics* I and II, where Aristotle develops his account of the diverse ways in which things may be said to be "causes" (these being four). All physical substances can be understood to be composed of form and matter. They are moved by others as efficient causes, while moving in accordance with their own principles toward final ends (these ends are the final causes of their regular movements). This causal analysis permits an authentic philosophical science of nature (*physis*). The nature of each thing is determined by its form, which gives definition to its internal material components. The activity of movement can in turn be understood in terms of potentiality and actuality (another Aristotelian innovation). The actuality of the natural form of each thing is understood best by the end it pursues (every form is in act toward a natural end), while the potentiality of a thing for physical transformation derives from its matter. This potentiality of matter allows every physical being to be altered by another physical being.

All of the discoveries of this particular study present an immense subject in themselves. Yet they are related to the theme of wisdom precisely because Aristotle's initial causal analysis of beings-in-movement (in *Physics*, Book *A*:7 to Book *B*:1) provides him with the key structures to which all physical realities are reducible (or so he believes), and this permits him to argue in Books VII and especially VIII, 1–6, for the necessary existence of a primary immobile first mover. This means that the ultimate aspiration of the *Physics* concerns wisdom, or knowledge of God as the first moving

---

[45] *Physics* II, 8, 199a9: "[W]here there is an end, all the preceding steps are for the sake of that." The rational activities of moral virtue may be sine qua non means that are themselves a primary participation in contemplative happiness, since the latter implies a complete blossoming of reason, which presupposes the former, like the flowers of a plant presupposing the stem.

cause of secondary realities. By his study of movement, then, Aristotle is more concerned than Plato to take seriously the attempts of the natural philosophers to study the universe scientifically.[46] At the same time he is also interested (perhaps as Plato was at the end of his life) to orient his study toward the demonstration of an immobile and necessary first being, free from any material change or becoming. He concludes, however, that the divine is utterly separate from the cosmos and cannot be represented in relation to the world in terms of the soul/body distinction or the celestial motions. God is unlike these realities, and transcendent of such representations. Consequently, Aristotle will approach the question of the nature of God through his study of being.

In analyzing Aristotle's *Metaphysics* in terms of the theme of wisdom, and of the access to knowledge of God, a common thread of argument emerges, from Book *A* to Book *Λ*, passing by key intermediary stages in Books *E*, *Z*, and *Θ*. The study of the *Metaphysics* is a vast work, yet the specific theme of wisdom (as related to final causality) can be seen in key passages throughout, permitting an interesting form of unifying interpretation. Therefore, I will briefly pass through the various books, from *A* to *Λ*, illustrating this theme from precise texts. I hope to show a triple unity in Aristotle's thought between the notions of (1) the causal study of being as the most universal science, (2) the place within this science of the final cause, which alone permits wisdom and a knowledge of the good, and (3) the analogical knowledge of being that this causal study implies, permitting an analogical metaphysics and sapiential theology. In illustrating these interrelated themes I will also mention the important role played by the study of the actuation of the qualities of the soul specific to the *nous*, such that precise analogies for God's perfect actuality can be properly identified from human rational acts. These themes will in turn be rearticulated by Aquinas, as I hope to show. They form a foundation for the studies of the modern thinkers to be considered in turn.[47]

---

[46] See Edward Halper, "Aristotle on Knowledge of Nature," *Review of Metaphysics* 37 (1984): 811–35, who shows that Aristotle retains from Plato the notion that science is of the universal and necessary, but at the same time discovers that nature, because it is the source of stability, order, and teleology, which is "always, or for the most part" the same, can be known scientifically.

[47] In attempting to focus on a unifying theme of the *Metaphysics*, it cannot be ignored that since Werner Jaeger's *Aristotle: Fundamentals of the History of His Development* (first German edition, 1912; English edition, Oxford: Clarendon Press, 1948), a genealogical approach to this book has become common, which deciphers therein a heterogeneity of tractates of differing points of view, some earlier works and some later. Criticisms of Jaeger's interpretations have not been lacking. A particularly convincing one is found in Ralph McInerny's "Ontology and Theology in the *Metaphysics* of Aristotle," in *Being and Predication* (Washington, DC:

Book *A* defines the state of the question concerning a universal science to which all others are subordinated, and which concerns the primary principles and causes of all things. Just as it is a fact of experience that all actions are ordered to ends, so also we see that "all men by nature desire to know" (Book *A*, 1, 979a22). Knowledge is an end pursued for its own sake. Just as the artist differs from the man of experience by his knowledge of causes, so theoretical science also implies knowledge according to causes. "The theoretical kinds of knowledge [are] more of the nature of wisdom than the productive. Clearly then wisdom is knowledge about certain causes and principles" (981b32–982a2). In other words, among the hierarchy of sciences, the productive are subordinate to the theoretical, and if there is an ultimate science among the latter, it is of the ultimate principles and causes of things.

The overarching key to Aristotle's vision of metaphysics is given, then, in chapter 2 of Book *A*. Wisdom, as the science of the causes of all things, is the *most universal* science. The wise man "has in the highest degree universal knowledge, for he knows in a sense all the subordinate objects," not individually, but by means of causality, and analogically (982a8, 22–23). Aristotle, therefore, is working toward a more universal science than that of physical beings in motion: one that pertains also (and especially) to separate, non-material being.[48] Because physical beings are more immediately known by us, but ultimately explained by separate substance, theology is ultimately required for a complete etiological study of being. The realities that are the most intelligible in themselves are the hardest for man to know, and require the most effort (982b1–4). Thus wisdom is an ascent (by the study of being and its causes) to the knowledge of God as the ultimate cause of all things. It is God, then, who is the ultimate principle of this science, and who is ultimately himself the wisdom in question (983a6–8).[49]

The Catholic University of America Press, 1986), 59–66. Though the genealogical approach still finds many adherents (see, for example, Bertrand Dumoulin, *Analyse Génétique de la Métaphysique d'Aristote* [Paris: Les Belles Lettres, 1986]), acceptance of the conceptual homogeneity of the *Metaphysics* has been considerably aided by the masterful work of Giovanni Reale, *The Concept of First Philosophy and the Unity of the Metaphysics of Aristotle* (first Italian edition, 1961); translated into English by J. Catan (Albany: State University of New York Press, 1980). Reale demonstrates the continuity of the etiological, ousiological, and theological themes throughout the diverse books. Thus ontology, causality, and theology are intrinsically related in Aristotle's intention. My own perspective, however, as will become clear, places slightly more emphasis than Reale upon the *final* cause of being and the importance of *actuality* as a principle and cause of being in addition to that of the *ousia-substance*. The texts that I will cite will hopefully justify this point of emphasis. They will also help illustrate important points of continuity between Aquinas's metaphysics and Aristotle's.

48 See, for instance, Books *A*, 3, 995a15–20; *B*, 2, 996b1–14, 997a15; *E*, 1.

49 As will become progressively clear from my analysis, I do not wish to endorse the view that God is the genetic first principle of intelligibility that gives ultimate explanation

As I have mentioned above as my second point, this study of being is also a study of the *final* cause of all things, which is the ultimate good: "And the science which knows to what end each thing must be done is the most authoritative of the sciences. . . . And this end is the good in each class, and in general the supreme good in the whole of nature. Judged by all the tests . . . this must be a science which investigates the first principles and causes; for the good, i.e., that for the sake of which, is one of the causes" (982b5–10). This science of the principles of being is not only ultimately a theological one, but also a study of the good that is the final cause of things. Wisdom, then, as in Plato's thought, aspires to the knowledge of the good, but here in terms of teleology. This permits, as I will mention below, the affirmation of a separate, transcendent principle of being who is substantial goodness, without the affirmation that this principle is the form of the good for all secondary realities.

In what remains of Book *A*, Aristotle will pursue an examination of the knowledge of causes as it existed in the thinkers previous to himself, noting the fact that the formal cause has been discovered only very imper-

---

to metaphysics as a science for Aristotle. This perspective has been articulated by Michael Frede, for whom the intelligibility of secondary substances *qua* substance can only be had once we understand what substance is in its most perfect realization (in separate substance, God). (See *Essays in Ancient Philosophy* [Oxford: Clarendon Press, 1987], 81–95). An exemplary hierarchy of forms is affirmed, wherein the knowledge of the first gives intelligibility to the inferiors (88–89). Thus the knowledge of God is an (intuitive?) a priori which permits *in turn* a scientific analysis of substance. In this case, God's existence is demonstrated only in an improper sense, by dialectical argument (94–95). I will make two assertions which differ from this account: One is that the study of being is genetically grounded in experience and pertains to sensible substances, according to their *own intrinsic principles*, which are twofold, those of substance and accidental properties, and those of act and potentiality. Only afterward is the separate substance of God analyzed, in comparison with beings which are more well known *to us*. Thus, if the divine is eventually discovered to have an *ontological and etiological* priority with regards to secondary beings, it does not have a *logical* priority in the formulation of our initial concepts of being and substance. Second, the relation between realities we experience and God is established in terms of *causality* and not exemplarity. Argumentation is based on the principles of things themselves, and therefore presupposes knowledge of them, leading progressively to God as a lesser known, transcendent cause and principle of all things. This requires that our initial concepts must be "stretched" analogically to speak imperfectly of God. A number of these points have recently been brought to light by Enrico Berti, in his analysis of Frede's work in "Multiplicity and Unity of Being in Aristotle," *The Aristotelian Society* 101, part 2 (2001): 185–207. Frede's interpretation, which Berti claims is strongly Platonic, seems to embroil Aristotelian metaphysics in all the ambiguities which open ontology to the Kantian criticisms of ontotheology as a self-referentially founded, logically circular science.

fectly (by the Platonic notion of forms, which he criticizes).[50] Meanwhile, no one hitherto has in fact discovered the final cause:

> *That-for-the-sake-of-which* actions and changes and movements take place, they assert to be a cause in a way, but not in this way, i.e., not in the way in which it is its nature to be a cause. For those [Anaxagoras and Empedocles] who speak of reason or friendship class these causes as goods; *they do not speak, however, as if anything that exists either existed or came into being for the sake of these* but as if movements started from these. In the same way, those [the Platonists] who say the One or the existent is the good, say that it is the cause of substance, *but not that substance either is or comes to be for the sake of this.* Therefore, it turns out that in a sense they both say and do not say the good is a cause; for they do not call it a cause *qua* good but only incidentally.[51]

The natural philosophers have said something about the good in terms of efficient causality, and the Platonists in terms of formal causality, as a cause of substance, but no one has understood the good according to its nature, as final causality, and as the final cause of the existence, and of the coming to be of the substance of things. Aristotle's *Metaphysics* will set out to do just this, achieving this study in the final chapter of Book *Λ*.[52]

In Book *α*, Aristotle restates the question of causality introduced in Book *A*, this time not in a historical perspective, but in a properly philosophical mode, arguing critically that the four notions of causality are intrinsic to our way of understanding realities we experience, and that causality is limited. Appeal to the notion of a regression to the infinite leads our thinking into absurdity or contradiction. Book *B* is an exploration of the aporia associated with this science, of which Aristotle discusses fifteen.

The third theme I have mentioned (the analogical nature of our knowledge of being) becomes more apparent in Book *Γ*. Here Aristotle establishes the subject of this science: it concerns being *qua* being (and not insofar as it is quantifiable, or in motion, etc.). Aristotle is preparing a study of the principles and causes of being (*Γ*, 1–2, 1003a26–34), and it is in this context that an analogical way of identifying this subject (being = *to on*) is now introduced. "There are many senses in which a thing may be

---

[50] *Meta. Λ*, 7, 988a35–988b1.

[51] *Meta. Λ*, 7, 988b6–15 (emphasis added).

[52] It is significant that just after studying the goodness of God and of other things in relation to God, Aristotle repeats the same complaint about the absence of a study of final causes—and, therefore, of the good—in the natural philosophers and Platonists, in *Λ*, 10, 1075b2–24. Aquinas, as I will show, will pick up upon these very criticisms in order to rearticulate the notion of the good as described by Dionysius and Augustine.

said to 'be' but they are related to one central point, one definite thing, and are not homonymous" (1003a32–34). He gives seven examples of this with regard to things said to "be," yet notes that they are all said with particular reference to the substance as the primary referent.[53] Differing significations of the word "being" can be understood as "toward one" (*pros hen*) common foundation—the substance—and thus in a sense according to a common notion of "being," though it be analogical.[54]

---

[53] *Meta. Γ* 2, 1003b5–11: "So, too, there are many senses in which a thing is said to be, but all refer to one starting-point; some things are said to be because they are substances, others because they are affections of substance, others because they are a process towards substance, or destructions or privations or qualities of substance, or productive or generative of substance, or of things which are relative to substance, or negations of some of these things or of substance itself."

[54] Aristotle compares the notion of being to that of health: "Everything which is healthy is related to health, one thing in the sense that it preserves health, another in the sense that it produces it, another in the sense that it is a symptom of health, another because it is capable of it" (1003a35–37). This theory of a multiplicity of senses of a word referred to one referent (*pros hen*) has given rise to a series of interpretive problems. As Pierre Aubenque has made clear (*Le Problème de l'Être chez Aristote* [Paris: Presses Universitaires de France, 1972], 190–205), Aristotle does not invoke here a theory of the "analogy of being." Analogy (or proportion) for Aristotle concerns primarily a mode of logical predication, while the *explicit* notion of analogical *structures of being* has its foundations in Aquinas's interpretations of these passages (see *In IV Meta.*, lec. 1, 534–43), and in later scholastic commentary.

Nevertheless, two points can be mentioned in support of the later Thomistic interpretation. The first concerns the "Parminidean triangle" in Aristotle's method, of a relation between language, concepts, and realities. The study of what we say about reality provides a genetic disposition to realize what we *think* and this reflects something already assimilated from the reality *itself* in what it *is*. (See *On Interpretation*, I, 1.) Thus the study of language in Aristotle, due to his epistemological realism and method of study, implies that there is a correspondence to the ontological differences and natures of things. (This interpretation is developed by Marc Balmes, *Peri Hermeneias. Essai de réflexion, du point du vue de la philosophie première, sur le problème de l'interprétation* [Fribourg: Ed. Univ. de Fribourg, 1984], 211–38.) Second, Aristotle himself unambiguously refers to the ontological foundations for his analogical theory of being in Book *Λ*, chapters 4 and 5, where he interprets universal *ontological causality* in analogical terms: "The causes and the principles of different things are in a sense different, but in a sense, if one speaks universally and analogically, they are the same for all" (*Λ*, 4, 1070a31–32). It is therefore reasonable to speak of an analogical knowledge of being in Aristotle, according to diverse principles and causes, which will end, as I will argue, in an analogical knowledge of the primary being, God.

A second problem concerns the affirmation in Book *Γ*, 1, 1003b34–35 that we are searching for a science which is "generically one." This affirmation concerns the identification of a characteristic common to every science: it studies a given genus of beings. Therefore a few lines later (1004a5), when Aristotle repeats that being is not in a genus, but common to every genus, we can understand that it is an exceptional

Aristotle will eventually apply this theory of "focal meaning" to the substance in relation to the other categories (e.g., the quantity of a substantial being, its qualities, relations, etc.) in Book *Z*. First, however (in *Γ* 3–8) he studies the critical axioms of knowledge (such as the principles of non-contradiction and identity), which are the foundations of all science and which imply an ontological realism. They have already been introduced as a problem in the second aporia of Book *B* (996b26–997a15). (It is by the critical examination of these principles, of course, that Garrigou-Lagrange sought an entry into metaphysics, as I have mentioned above.) Book *Δ* is a collection of definitions that Aristotle's study clearly presupposes (see *Z*, 1, 1028a10–11; *Θ*, 5, 1046a5), and that was added at this point (perhaps by an editor).

Book *E*, meanwhile, which normally followed *Γ*, formulates the search for *causes* now strictly in relation to its subject "being *qua* being," established in Book *Γ* as a complex notion. "We are seeking the principles and the causes of the things that are, and obviously of things *qua* being . . . but all sciences mark off some particular being—some genus, and inquire into this, but not into being simply nor *qua* being" (*E*, 1, 1025b1–2). Aristotle is concerned with a study of being that is applicable to both beings in motion and (possibly) separate, immaterial being. The latter, however, can be known only through a *causal study* of being that begins with the beings that we experience directly.

At this point, then, it is very significant that Aristotle reintroduces in Book *E*, 2, four meanings that being is said to have. (These have already been stated initially in Book *Δ*, 7.) They are: (1) being as chance events or "accidental," (2) being as true and false, (3) being as understood according to the diverse "categories" (as substance and its corresponding properties), (4) being as actuality and potentiality.[55] These notions are meant to establish an

---

science because it touches upon the universal causes of all things, across the diverse genera of substance. (See *B*, 4, 1001a4–29; *E*, 1, 1026a24–32; *Λ*, 4, 1070b1–3, 5–10; 5, 1071a24–36.) My understanding differs, then, from that of scholars who claim that Aristotle is affirming a common genus of being (for example, "substance") to which all other meanings must be attributed and which is included in every sense of the attribution "to be." This is the perspective of Frede in *Essays in Ancient Philosophy*, 84–85, and of Leo Elders, "Aristote et l'objet de la Métaphysique," *Autour de Saint Thomas d'Aquin* (Paris: FAC eds., 1987), 147-66. A more detailed defense of the interpretation I invoke can be found in Berti, "Multiplicity and Unity of Being in Aristotle," 193–204.

55 ". . .'being' has several meanings, of which one was seen to be the accidental, and another the true (non-being being the false), while besides these there are the figures of predication, e.g. the 'what', quality, quantity, place, time, and any similar meanings which 'being' may have; and besides all these there is that which is potentially or actually . . ." (*E*, 2, 1026a34–1026b2). The terminology here can be confusing. "Accidental" when used by Aristotle in this text refers to characteristics of being

analogical conception of being and prepare the diverse study of causes that is to occupy the rest of Aristotle's work, until Book Λ. Aristotle goes on to demonstrate in Book E, 2–4 why the first mode of being (accidental chance compositions and occurrences) cannot be a subject of scientific analysis. This leaves three other senses of being. That of the categories (substance and properties) concerns the *formal cause* of being *qua* being, to be studied in Book Z. That of potentiality and actuality concerns the *final cause* of being *qua* being, to be studied in Book Θ. The problem of "truth" in fact pertains to the question of the human intellect thinking about that which exists. It can be treated only after this (analogical) causal study of being, since truth (all that the mind can affirm about reality) is coextensive with that-which-is. Once we have studied the principles of being, we can talk about what is true. The theme of truth will reappear, therefore, at the end of Book Θ, after a study of being in actuality and being in potentiality. It is the study of the final causality of being as actuality that will yield an ultimate causal intelligibility concerning both substance and truth, and will prepare the way to the ultimate causal study of Book Λ, concerning separate being.

In Book Z, the first and third theme I have mentioned above (the search for causes of being and the analogical knowledge of being) come directly into union to establish the substance (*ousia*) as the "cause according to the form" of being. Aristotle is concerned here, of course, with immanent formal causality (the cause of a thing *being* what it is) rather than with transcendent exemplary forms (Platonic ideas). In Book Z, chapter 1, then, Aristotle now articulates his theory of "being which is said many ways" from Book Γ in terms of the ten categories, all of which are understood in reference to the substance. The quantity of a person exists, as do his qualities, relations, and so on, yet these all exist in dependence upon his being as a distinct substance.[56] If the substance unifies the

---

resulting from their irreducibly singular material individuality, and from chance events. These are dimensions of being not subject to formal explanation by the study of the causes of being, and yet they exist. Meanwhile, the properties of a substance (denoted by the categories) are sometimes also called "accidents" insofar as they depend upon the substance for their being. However, the two uses of the word "accident" are in fact unrelated.

56 *Meta. Z*, 1, 1028a10–31. This interpretation of an analogical manner of signifying being (from Book Γ) now applied to the substance and its properties (or "accidents"), according to a *pros hen* mode of signification, has generally gained scholarly consensus. It is articulated by G. E. L. Owen ("Logic and Metaphysics in some Earlier Works of Aristotle," in *Logic, Science and Dialectic* [Ithaca: Cornell University Press, 1986], 180–99), in terms of a theory of "focal meaning" by which the significations of the categories as "being" are only complete in reference to the substance. This relationship of signification, however, does not mean that the ontological priority of the substance implies logical priority as well, such that "being" be understood uniquely as substance. (On the contrary, see Δ, 11, 1019a1–6: the

diverse determinations of being ontologically, the question, then, is, what is "substance"? To name this determination, Aristotle develops his own expression: *to ti ein einai*, literally, "that which is in that which was," or "that which endures in a thing essentially in and through the changes it undergoes," from which the medievals derived the Latin term of *quidditas*, or quiddity.[57] After lengthy examinations of substance as subject, essence (*to ti ein einai*), universal, and genera, excluding various hypotheses, Aristotle affirms a causal solution to the problem in the final chapter of the book. Aristotle's examples show that the singular being alone exists (corresponding to what he call "first substance" in the *Categories*), but that it implies in its singular being an essential determination or nature (the *Categories'* "second substance"). The substance is therefore the immanent formal cause of the singular reality in both its unique existence as a being and its essential determination as a given kind of reality. Each substance has (or is) a "core" that remains through time, and that accounts for the reality's holistic, permanent identity under both these aspects.[58]

The third theme I have mentioned above is that of the final cause. The problem of act and potentiality, and therefore of final causality, begins to be introduced by Aristotle in Book *H* in view of an explanation of physical substances in movement, which undergo change. How do the form and matter constitute one substance (*H*, 1)? This question will be resolved especially in chapter 6 in terms of the principles of act and potentiality. Actuality is the end toward which the substantial form tends, while the matter of the reality is source of potentiality.[59] Aristotle is seeking a

---

ontological priority of substance is not a priority of genus.) Each of the categorial determinations retains its ontological uniqueness, according to this theory. Qualities (such as kindness or musical skill) really exist as distinct properties of a substantial being (such as a person). This is why it is essential to note the fact that even amidst the unity of categories in relation to substance an *analogy of proper proportionality is the basis for their common intelligibility*: *A* is to *B* as *C* is to *D*, or "being" is to quality as "being" is to quantity, and so on. The common notion of being extends across the ten categories in a "proportional way" and attains it signification only amidst the irreducible diversity of these determinations. Only after this is this notion attributed to the substance *pros hen*, when we affirm that the being of the properties depends upon substantial being. Therefore, the being of the substance does not destroy the real diversity of being among the accidents. This point will clearly become important in Book *Λ*.

57 Short for the Latin equivalent of *to ti ein einai: quid quod erat esse*.

58 *Meta. Z*, 17, 1041b4–8. My understanding of the Aristotelian substance is as a singular entity implying an essential determination. For a similar point of view, see Charlotte Witt, *Substance and Essence in Aristotle* (Ithaca and London: Cornell University Press, 1989), esp. 112–21.

59 This interpretation of Book *H* as providing a point of transition from the problem of form and matter to the problem of actuality and potentiality (of Book *Θ*) is offered

scientific understanding of movement in physical beings, much as he has already in *Physics* III, 1, in terms of potentiality and act. Here, however, he is searching for the proper principles of being *qua* being, and his study of the being of movements will have for its eventual interest the articulation of an analogical way of speaking about separate substances. This will become apparent in the treatment of the final cause in Book *Θ*.

In Book *Θ*, after beginning with a study of potentiality, Aristotle considers being in act in chapter 6. He seems to identify two different modes (*poion ti*) of actuality and potentiality: one that characterizes the substance-in-actuality and the other that concerns the operations and movements (or exercise) of the substance in its change in being "toward" a state of perfection.[60] The first form of actuality, then, would concern the coming into being of substance (substantial becoming) or its being in act, and the latter the attaining of perfection through operation. With regards to such operations, he distinguishes between operations having an end in themselves (immanent acts) like knowing and loving and "movements," which do not imply an end in themselves (transitive acts) but which terminates in the alteration of a separate extrinsic reality. The latter kind of operations are called "actualities" only in an imperfect sense, while the former are more properly said to be being in act.[61] Thus in chapter 6 we clearly see Aristotle moving toward an understanding of actuality exemplified by *living* beings.[62] Living beings exemplify being-in-actuality in a double way: both by the actuality of the substance of a living being (its formal determinations subsisting in being that derive from the living soul, informing the matter of the body), and by the perfection, or actuation, of the vital operations that have their ends in themselves *through their activity* (immanent operative acts of the living being).[63]

---

by Theodore Scaltsas, "Substantial Holism," in *Unity, Identity and Explanation in Aristotle's Metaphysics*, ed. T. Scaltsas, D. Charles, and M. L. Gill (Oxford: Clarendon Press, 1994), 107–28.

60 *Θ*, 6, 1048a26: ". . . let us discuss actuality, what (*ti esti*) and what sort of thing (*poion ti*) it is." 1048b6–9: "But all things are not said in the *same sense* to exist actually, but only by analogy —as *A* is in *B* or to *B*, *C* is in *D* or to *D*; for some are as movement to (*pros*) potentiality, and the others as substance to (*en*) some sort of matter." See also chapter 8, 1050b2: ". . . substance or form is actuality."

61 *Meta. Θ*, 6, 1048b28–35.

62 Physical movement implies an actuality of the matter, and therefore is an act only in an imperfect and temporary sense, as "the act of that which is in potentiality insofar as it is in potentiality." See *Physics* III, 1, 201a9 and following.

63 This analysis of actuality as substance and as operation can be seen also in *On the Soul* II, 1, 412a20–26, in which two forms of actuality (*entelecheia*) are mentioned: that proper to the soul as the substance of the living body, and that proper to the operations of the same living being. This has been analyzed in relation to Book *Θ* by Aryeh Kosman, "The Activity of Being in Aristotle's *Metaphysics*," in

He thus introduces an analogical mode of identifying actuality, through a "synthetic and analogical induction," by comparing between diverse kinds of actuality even within a given substance.[64] Being in act (*energeia*) and being in potentiality are understood by proportional analogy, atrributed *either* to actuation of potential substances or to operations and movements of such substances. What I wish to underline here, then, is the fact that actuality is analyzed (analogically) as the final cause of potency, yet it assumes within itself the previous (analogical) division of substance and the diverse categories.[65] So, for example, Socrates as a child may exist in act as a substantial human being, yet his moral teaching, or the adult shape of his facial features, exists only in potentiality. The potentiality or actuality of Socrates' being pertains, then, not only to his substantial form, but in another way to his qualities, quantities, and so on, *respecting each one in their uniqueness and proportional intelligibility as being*. Each of these determinations takes on a new and more profound intelligibility when considered in light of act and potentiality, revealing the tendency toward the final cause of being. Being in act is the immanent end of the very being of each of the genera of determinate reality. To come into being as such, to become a physiologically mature adult, or a philosopher, or a father, or a being who prays, are all teleological perfections, yet they are not actuations of being reducible to one another.

In chapter 8 of Book *Θ* Aristotle demonstrates the primacy of act over potentiality for the substance of each reality (as well as for its rational intelligibility, and its being in time). Here he is approaching the heart of his metaphysical enterprise, and by his notion of the final cause of being *qua* being is preparing directly for a theological aspiration to wisdom concerning the transcendent first cause, God. His demonstration of the primacy of actuality with regards to substance will again focus not only on the metaphysical understanding of substantial becoming, but also on the end attained through teleological operations.[66] In an ordered series of physical

---

Unity, Identity, and Explanation in Aristotle's Metaphysics, 195–215, who argues that the Aristotelian notion of actuality is thereby analogical and known through these diverse forms. It presupposes the former distinction of substance and accidental properties, and applies analogically to each.

[64] *Meta. Θ*, 6, 1048a30–1048b9.

[65] See, for example, *Metaphysics Θ*, 8, 1050b12–16, and *Physics* III, 1, 201a10–14, where physical movement as actuality (*entelecheia*) is understood by a fourfold analogy, according to quality, quantity, substance and place.

[66] *Meta. Θ*, 8, 1050a4–16: "But [actuality] is . . . prior in form and in substance, e.g. man is prior to boy and human being to seed; for the one already has its form, and the other has not. Secondly, because everything that comes to be moves towards a principle, i.e. an end. For that for the sake of which a thing is, is its principle, and the becoming is for the sake of the end; and the actuality is the end, and it is for the sake

beings, then, the substantial being of a new thing necessarily depends upon previously existent realities in act. Furthermore, that which comes to be comes to be in view of an operational end, in accordance with its nature. Therefore, this actuation toward an end, which is inscribed in the nature of each thing, is also received from another via the nature received. Only insofar as a thing is actuated toward its own natural end can it in turn act as an efficient cause upon other realities, and so every efficient cause depends in turn upon a previous actuality that precedes it and actuates it.[67] This means that any reality being or having been in some way in potentiality (substantially, or under an accidental aspect) and belonging to an ordered causal series of such agents is necessarily dependent upon others for its actuation. Such a series cannot be infinite. This principle of the primacy of actuality (with regard to both substance and operation) will require the necessary existence of a first substantial actuality without potentiality, which is prior to the causal series.[68] This is particularly evident with regard to corruptible beings, whose relative necessity can be accounted for only by appeal to separate, necessary, and incorruptible beings.[69] This understanding of the primacy of actuality will prepare a theological metaphysics, therefore, of separate being, by means of a *causal* understanding of God as the first mover, understood in terms of pure actuality (as the primary actuality and final cause of secondary beings). It will permit a properly analogical manner of speaking about God, based on the effects of his being upon secondary beings, those that we experience directly.

---

of this that the potentiality is acquired. For animals do not see in order that they may have sight, but they have sight that they may see. And similarly men have the art of building that they may build, and theoretical science that they may theorize; but they do not theorize that they may have theoretical science, except those who are learning by practice; and those do not theorize except in a limited state, or else they have no need to theorize. Further, matter exists in a potential state, just because it may attain to its form; and when it exists *actually*, then it is in its form." The primacy of actuality is next applied to movements as well (1050a17–23). It is applicable therefore to both transitive and immanent activities (1050a24–9).

67 *Meta. Θ*, 8, 1050a30–34. Efficient operational causality then is a result of a teleological orientation in a thing, and depends in turn upon the realities which actuate that thing. Here we find the deepest truth of the principle of causality: nothing is the cause of itself.

68 *Meta. Θ*, 8, 1050b3–6: "From this argument it is obvious that actuality is prior in substance to potentiality; and as we have said, one actuality always precedes another in time right back to the actuality of the eternal prime mover." A helpful commentary on the theological implications of this thinking for Aristotle is offered by Bastit, *Le Quatre Causes De L' Être*, 332–35, 358–61.

69 See *Meta. Θ*, 8, 1050b7–27. Lines 17–19: "Imperishable things, then, exist actually. Nor can anything which is of *necessity* be potential; yet these things are primary; for if these did not exist, nothing would exist."

Having established the primacy of actuality as the final cause of being in Book Θ, 8, Aristotle is now prepared to speak about the good (which implies the notion of "final end"), as he promised in Book A, chapters 2 and 7. It is the operations of substances that permit them to attain their end and become "good." Such operations perfect the form. They are what *On the Soul* has called "secondary acts" because they are not necessary for the fundamental subsistence of the reality. Rather, they must be "accidental" actuations of the substance: its qualities, habits, relations, and so on.[70] Because they are accidental, they are capable of contrary states, that is to say, good or evil.[71] (Moral evil, for example, results from a defective use of the human operation of rational choice). Operations permit imperfect substances to *become* good or evil, even while remaining in their being accidental to the substance. Nevertheless, for Aristotle, as shall be seen, they reveal something *as actuality*, analogically attributable to separate being *substantially*. This is because separate substance (i.e., God) is pure actuality, and therefore his substance and operation are one and the same. Consequently, he is all good in both substance and operation, and is incapable of evil.[72] It is interesting to note, then, that by briefly analyzing operative acts such as *qualities* (he gives the examples of the activity of building, and of health, which qualify vital operations), Aristotle prepares a way of attributing goodness analogically to separate realities. I will show below the importance of this for Aquinas.

It is not surprising, therefore, to find Aristotle also treating intellectual truth just afterward, in chapter 10. He has promised to discuss truth as one of the four ways of "saying being" (in Book E, 2), and since truth is coextensive with being, and he has now analyzed the principles of being; he can now speak of truth. Here he distinguishes between truth as a quality of the intellect versus the "ontological truth" of realities, which is the measure of the former.[73] In understanding intellectual truth-in-act in relation to being-in-act he is also preparing ways of speaking of God as subsistent contemplation, in whom intellectual truth and ontological truth are identical (in Book A, chapters 7 and 9). In chapters 6–10, then, the categories of substance (as singular being in act), essence, and quality are now reconsidered analogically in terms of actuality and potentiality. They are being discussed "ontologically" in order to be attributed analogically to the transcendent causality of God, who is substantial act, theoretical knowing, and goodness (in whom substance, essence, and operation are identical). Both the human qualities of operational goodness and the intellectual quality of truth (concerning the

---

[70] *Meta. Θ*, 9, 1051a4–17.
[71] *Meta. Θ*, 9, 1051a11–17.
[72] *Meta. Θ*, 9, 1051a18–21.
[73] *Meta. Θ*, 10, 1051a34–1051b17.

essences of beings) reveal something of being that is eventually applicable to the substantial actuality of the first mover, who knows and loves himself.

Aristotle's Book *I* treats the problem of the one and the multiple. Because unity is coextensive with being, it is now comprehensible in light of the discovery of the principles of being. Book *K* can be interpreted as a notebook, with a recapitulation of themes from earlier books.

In Book *Λ*, Aristotle returns to his initial aspiration, announced in Book *A*, of a universal science of the primary cause of all things. This knowledge is wisdom, and concerns the separate substances, and the being of the unmoved first mover, that is to say, God. It permits us to treat the question of the eternal, subsistent goodness of God and thus the final cause with respect to the divine. Aristotle has already posited the existence of separated substance in Book *E*, 1. In Book *Λ*, however, his scientific reflection concerning God does not presuppose the existence of God, but rather develops organically out of the study of the principles of being in Books *Z* and *Θ* (as substance/accidents, act/potentiality). It is following from the causal, analogical knowledge of being *qua* being as attained in sensible beings that Aristotle will now offer a demonstration of the ontological necessity of God as the primary cause of all beings. This argumentation is based upon the ontological primacy of actuality over potentiality, and allows in turn for the development of properly analogical thinking about God as a primary, transcendent, universal cause, who is pure actuality.

At the end of his discussion of the three kinds of substances in chapters 1 to 3, then, Aristotle offers a mini-treatise on the causes and principles of sensible beings in chapters 4 to 5.[74] Here he identifies a universally applicable, analogical notion of causality (pertaining to "being *qua* being") permitting him to situate each singular being within a common, universal science.[75] Form, matter, and privation (and the moving cause, which is the form of one thing acting upon another) can be said of each of the ten categories analogically, respecting the singularity of each. So, for example, a substance has a determinate form, matter, and capacity for privation (allowing it to be acted on by another), but so does a given quantity, a physical quality, and the like. Causality in the order of being, therefore, is universal according to an analogy of proper proportionality, where the cause in question (such as the form/matter composition) is applied to each

---

[74] A helpful commentary on these two chapters is offered by Michel Bastit, "Etiologie et Théologie," in *Essais sur la Théologie d'Aristote*, ed. M. Bastit and J. Follon (Louvain: Éditions Peeters, 1998), 51–68.

[75] *Meta. Λ*, 4, 1070a31–2: "The causes and the principles of different things are in a sense different, but in a sense, if one speaks universally and analogically, they are the same for all."

category in a unique way.[76] This universal application of the causes of form and matter to each category must also be understood in terms of potentiality and actuality. The substance can exist in act or in potentiality, but so can a given quantity, quality, relation, and so on.[77]

Second, these universal principles that apply to each category also apply to each singular reality in question only by mode of an analogy of proper proportionality. What exists in act is the singular alone. A given thing's nature or determination that it holds in common with others is known universally, by a kind of univocal concept. But this nature exists only within a set of singular realities, and we know these singular existents only by way of an analogical comparison. So, for example, the formal nature of Socrates and Plato is the same ("man," "rational animal"). But the being in act of Socrates is distinct from the being in act of Plato, such that "man" *exists-in-act* in each one in a proportional and analogical way.[78]

Third, the substances themselves are said to be relative universally to the primary cause of substance. Even though the being in act of each substance is ontologically unique, nevertheless, each substance enters into an analogous relation to the primary cause of its existence (God). This relation of dependence affects necessarily all other categories of being since these depend upon the substantial being of individual realities, which themselves ultimately depend upon God.[79]

Aristotle, then, has introduced a notion of the universality of the causality of substance (as form/matter) and actuality that respects (1) the fact that these principles are understood analogically across the diverse categories of being and (2) the fact that these principles are universally applicable to all beings, but are instantiated as such only within individual, singular realities in act. Finally, (3) these realities in act are substances that are universally intelligible in accordance with their transcendent primary cause. Universal ontological science is established, therefore, without recourse to the Platonic forms. It must study only singular realities in act,

---

[76] *Meta. Λ*, 4, 1070b17–20: "All things have not the same elements, but analogically they have; i.e. one might say that there are three principles—the form, the privation, and the matter. But each of these is different for each class." I do not think this should be read in contradiction to the earlier assertion of the substance as the formal cause of being with regard to the categories. Formal determination is proper to substance in a particular way, but the substance as form also necessarily implies the irreducible multiplicity of the diverse categorical properties that it unifies.

[77] *Meta. Λ*, 5, 1071a4–17.

[78] *Meta. Λ*, 1071a18–21: "The primary principles of all things are the actual primary 'this' and another thing which exists potentially. The universal causes, then, of which we spoke do not *exist*. For the *individual* is the source of the individuals. For while man is the cause of man universally, there is no universal man."

[79] *Meta. Λ*, 5, 1071a33–6.

respecting the diversity of determinations within them without reducing them to an intellectual universal or transcendental notion (such as "being," "oneness," etc.). The key to this universal science not only is the comparison of the causes of being proper to each thing according to proportionate analogy, but also ultimately comes from the demonstration of a necessary primary and separate substance that is actuality, and is the universal cause of all secondary beings *qua* being.

Aristotle's affirmation of the necessary existence of separate substance(s) in Book Λ, chapter 6, presupposes as a given the eternity of movement in the physical world, and claims that the first rotation of the circular heaven must be actuated by another eternally, who is immaterial, and who is always in act.[80] I will not analyze his argumentation here because it is beyond the scope of my study.[81] I wish to note, however, that underlying the ancient Greek cosmological setting for the Stagirite's argumentation, the principles he explicitly invokes are metaphysical: the ontological primacy of substance with regard to accidents and the primacy of actuality over potentiality. These assertions entail a third one: that of the primacy of separate substances over physical ones, the latter depending causally upon the former. The separate substances, meanwhile, are both substantial actuality and operation.[82] If there were no operative and substantial first cause of movement that was itself beyond all potentiality (and thus all movement), there could be no suc-

---

[80] *Meta. Λ*, 6, 1071b5–22.

[81] A detailed analysis of Aristotle's argumentation is offered by Enrico Berti, "Unmoved Mover(s) as Efficient Cause(s) in *Metaphysics L*, 6," in *Aristotle's Metaphysics Lambda*, ed. M. Frede and D. Charles (Oxford: Clarendon Press, 2000), 181–206. Berti claims that Aristotle makes two confusions, identifying continuity of movement in the physical world with *eternity* of movement, and identifying the eternity of the world's existence with the eternity of its *actual* order (194).

Aristotle attributes significant roles to the living stars and to the separate substances with respect to the primary unmoved mover. (See, for example, Λ, 8.) Nevertheless there are important differences between them. Unlike God, living stars remain in potentiality with respect to place (Θ, 8, 1050b19–28; Λ, 1, 1069a30–1060b1). The separate substances, meanwhile, have a cosmological role of assistance, but do not move the first heaven (this is the role of the prime mover) (Λ, 8, 1074a31–39). Furthermore, they are not the final cause of all movements. This is reserved to God's goodness alone, as will be seen below.

[82] *Meta. Λ*, 6, 1071b5–6: "For substances are the first of existing things, and if they are all destructible, all things are destructible." 1071b13–20: "But if there is something which is capable of moving things or acting on them, but is not actually doing so, there will not be movement; *for that which has a capacity need not exercise it.* . . . Even if it acts this will not be enough, if its *substance is potentiality*; for there will not be *eternal* movement; for that which is in potentiality may possibly not be" (emphasis added). Aristotle clearly attributes to the separate first mover(s) the actuality both of operation and of substance, in what will soon be shown to be one unique and simple act of existence (see Λ, 7, 1072a31–2).

cessive actuation in the interdependent series of moved movers. In this sense, the underlying philosophy of nature and the metaphysics of Book *Λ*, 6 are the same as what has already been articulated in Book *Θ*, 8, and in the notion of the necessary existence of a primary mover in *Physics* VIII, 5.[83]

---

[83] It is clear from Aristotle's analysis that he sees God as the primary *final* cause of being *qua* being, that all lesser beings in some way imitate. There is a great deal of interpretive dispute concerning the question of how or in what way God is seen by Aristotle as the source of the efficient causality of being. A robust affirmation of the separate first mover as the primary *efficient* cause of actuation of the being in movement and substantial generation of secondary beings has recently been rethought by certain Aristotelian scholars. See, for example, Enrico Berti, "Unmoved Mover(s) as Efficient Cause(s) in *Metaphysics L*, 6," in *Aristotle's Metaphysics Lambda*, and "De qui est fin le moteur immobile?," *Essais sur la Théologie d'Aristote*, 5–28). Berti's reading challenges the traditional understanding of the text (followed, for example, by Aquinas) in which the first separate efficient cause of physical movement is seen to be a moving mover (a living intelligence) itself relative to the primary immobile mover as a final cause who acts on secondary beings primarily through the desire he inspires in the latter (see *Λ*, 7, 1071a21–28). Instead, Berti argues that one can affirm that the primary, immobile mover, who is pure act, is the first efficient cause of the actuation of other realities' substantial becoming, and movement, but that this form of efficient causality is transcendent, different from physical efficiency. This causality is also teleological insofar as its efficiency with respect to others is the effect of God knowing and loving *himself* as final cause (*Λ*, 10, 1075b8–11). Yet even if this interpretation is correct, the primacy of act over potentiality (as the final cause of being) is the key to Aristotle's understanding of both the actuation of secondary beings and the self-fulfillment and joy of the primary being.

Despite the ingenious character of Berti's argumentation, I find the traditional reading more plausible. (See, for example, the analysis of W. D. Ross, *Aristotle's Metaphysics* [Oxford: Clarendon Press, 1924], cxxxff. and more recently Michel Bastit, "La Science Théologique d'Aristote," *Revue Thomiste*, 93, 1 [1993]: 26–49). According to this interpretation, the unmoved mover of Aristotle's "first heaven," through his attraction over all others as final cause, is the source of the *efficiency* of the first moved mover, who acts *instrumentally* upon all others. This results in the production of the beings of this world. "On such a principle, then, depend the heavens and the world of nature" (1072b13). As Aquinas rightly notes, all beings thereby depend substantially upon the pure actuality of the being of God: "Hence it is on this principle, i.e., the first mover viewed as an end, that the heavens depend both for the eternality of their substance and the eternality of their motion. Consequently, the whole of nature depends on such a principle, because all natural things depend on the heavens and on such motion as they possess. It should also be noted that Aristotle says here that the necessity of the first motion is not absolute necessity, but necessity from the end, and the end is the principle which he later calls God inasmuch as things are assimilated to God through motion. Now assimilation to a being that wills and understands (as he shows God to be) is in the line of will and understanding just as things made by art are assimilated to the artist inasmuch as his will is fulfilled in them. This being so, it follows that the necessity of the first motion is totally subject to the will of God" (*In Meta. XII*, lec. 7, 2534–35). There

Aristotle develops, then, a philosophical theory that *implicitly* functions in relative independence from the cosmological, representational paradigm inherited from Plato. Every being in movement in the series of beings we experience depends upon another who moves the physical reality from potentiality to act (for instance, through substantial generation), and actuality of substance is primary with regard to the actuality of the other categories, which refer to accidental determinations. The substantial and accidental ontological dependencies present in moving beings (themselves both in act and potentiality) imply, therefore, the necessary existence of a transcendent unmoved first mover who is without potentiality, being pure actuality and necessarily subsistent. The first mover not only is substantial act but through his operation is ultimately responsible for the movement of the world. Thus, not only the attribute of substantial *entelecheia* is attributable to him analogically, but also the qualities of secondary *entelecheia*, those of immanent vital acts.[84] In the primary being "first act" and "second act" are identical: he is not only substance but also operation. His pure actuality is thus not only immaterial, simple, perfect, and unchanging; it also implies perfectly actuated *nous*, and is good. It is precisely as such that he is the first absolute and universal cause of all things.[85] In God's imma-

---

are, of course, differing ways of being subject to the will of God. The former interpretation of Berti would entail the necessary affirmation that God knows the world and wills its good, acting upon it (like the general upon the army, or a doctor upon a patient, metaphors employed by Aristotle for God in Book *Λ*, chapter 10) based upon his own contemplation and love of himself. Meanwhile, Aquinas is clearly suggesting here that God according to Aristotle does know the world, even as he is the final cause of all that depends upon him. I will not try to resolve the (infamously debated) question of whether God, for Aristotle, does in fact know the world. Instead, I will return to the question of the theological significance of Aquinas's *own appropriation* of Aristotle on this point in chapter 8.

[84] Aristotle refers to God as primary in respect to *entelecheia* in *Meta. Λ*, 5, 1071a35–36, and identifies the substance of God with his *entelecheia* in *Λ*, 8, 1074a35–36. Compare this with the notion of first and second acts (*entelecheia*) in *On the Soul* I, 2, 412a17–26.

[85] *Meta. Λ*, 7, 1072b1–11: "That that for the sake of which is found among the unmovables is shown by making a distinction; for that for the sake of which is both that *for* which and that *towards* which, and of these the one is unmovable and the other is not. Thus it produces motion by being loved, and it moves the other moving things. Now if something is moved it is capable of being otherwise than it is. Therefore if the actuality of the heavens is primary motion, then insofar as they are in motion, in *this* respect they are capable of being otherwise—in place, even if not in substance. But since there is something which moves while itself unmoved, existing actually, this can in no way be otherwise than as it is. For motion in space is the first of the kinds of change, and motion in a circle the first kind of spatial motion; and insofar as it is necessary, it is good, and in this sense a first principle." Aristotle affirms here the uniqueness of God as the primary unmoved mover with regard to

nent operations of knowledge and appetitive delight in the good, then, he is his own object of knowledge and love. Consequently, these operations are identical to his eternal, living being.[86] God is subsistent contemplation.[87] In his actuality he is therefore his own final end, and he is this perfect realization of being substantially and simply.

Though I do not wish to analyze here the attributes of the first mover according to Aristotle (in chapters 6 to 10), I will complete this study by mentioning uniquely the place of the good in chapter 10. Aristotle began his study of wisdom by seeking the first, universal causes of all beings *qua* being, and he associated this aspiration with a knowledge of the final cause, of the good, and of the divine. These orientations come together in

---

the celestial beings, who change with respect to place. In Λ, 8 Aristotle discusses the hypothesis of fifty-five separate substances that are responsible for the movements of the stars. (In effect, Aristotle is concerned with contemporary cosmology as well as the Greek polytheistic heritage.) Extensive discussion exists over whether or how Aristotle understands the separate substances of Λ, 8, to relate to God, the prime mover of the first heaven and (by extension) of all things, who is discussed in Λ, 6–7, and 9–10. Many interpreters see Λ, 8, as a later text that has been introduced into the *Metaphysics*. (See, for example, Leo Elders, *Aristotle's Theology* [Assen: Van Gorcum, 1972], 57–68.) Ross (*Aristotle's Metaphysics*, cxxxix–cxl) examines the interpretive difficulties and claims that there must be in the separate substances some kind of spiritual potency (or even spiritual matter) that renders them ontologically inferior to God. He hypothesizes—quite reasonably—that the latter substances might be moved in a spiritual fashion by desire for the primary being, so as to act in accord with his wisdom over all other beings. Other thinkers claim that there are simply fifty-five gods for Aristotle, and that the characteristics of Λ, 9, apply to each of them. (See Joseph Owens, *The Doctrine of Being in the Aristotelian Metaphysics* [Toronto: PIMS, 1978], 438–54.) Yet it is not clear on this reading what to do with Λ, 8, 1074a31–38, as well as other texts mentioned below. As G. E. R. Lloyd points out ("*Metaphysics Λ, 8*," in *Aristotle's Metaphysics Lambda*, 245–74, esp. 267), there is no reading that manages to alleviate all of the interpretative difficulties. Basically, Aristotle does not clarify fully the relation between God the prime mover and the other separate substances so as to offer us a total explanation. Yet, three truths do stand out from the texts that seem to give us some orientation. First, God the prime mover of the first heaven, who is pure actuality, is also the first cause of the movement of all things, which are in turn hierarchically subordinated movements. He is therefore the principle upon whom the universe depends ontologically (1073a23–30). Second, there is a single ruler of the universe, by whom it is governed (1070b34, 1072b13, 1076a5). Finally, God alone is the first good and final cause of the whole universe (1076a3–4). In following the analysis of David Sedley on these matters ("*Metaphysics Λ, 10*," in *Aristotle's Metaphysics Lambda*, 327–50, esp. 333 n. 11), we can cite Aristotle's remark from *De Gen. et Corr.* II, 10, 337a21–22: "If there is a plurality of movers, they must somehow be under a single mover."

[86] *Meta. Λ*, 1072b14–25.
[87] *Meta. Λ*, 1072b25–31.

the final chapter of Book Λ, in Aristotle's analysis of the divine goodness, seen both as the transcendent principle of causality (identical with God in himself), and as the immanent principle of order and change for secondary realities.[88] The latter act in view of a goodness proper to each one (through its own operation and final end), yet in doing so, these realities aid one another to attain the respective ends of each other (as members of a household).[89] In doing so, they simultaneously imitate the transcendent goodness of God by their own being in act.[90] All, then, are seemingly ordered to God as a final end, in and through a vast hierarchical structure.

From these reflections, one can see how Aristotle's study resolves the problem of wisdom. God is understood not only as the primary being who is the universal cause of all other beings but also as the primary good. All secondary beings attain a certain goodness through their operational acts, by which they implicitly come to resemble in some way the primary goodness and eternity of God. For the human being, this is attained through the intellectual knowledge of God and the consideration of other realities in relation to him. Man attains his end by the virtue of wisdom, by which he considers all things in the light of their highest cause. He becomes wise in considering the wisdom and goodness of God as manifested in his effects.

Aristotelian Theology and Ontotheology

After this consideration of the theme of wisdom in Aristotle's *Metaphysics*, as related to the themes of causality, finality, and analogy, brief observations can be made as concerns the Kantian and Heideggerian criticisms of ontotheology that I discussed above. First, God's ontological priority as it is understood by Aristotle does not entail a *logical* priority of the notion of God (as, say, "substance") in a way that would determine his theological enterprise in an aprioristic fashion. On the contrary, the beings we experience are at the origin of a metaphysical knowledge that can in turn permit indirect and imperfect but real knowledge of God in comparative terms.[91]

---

88 *Meta. Λ*, 10, 1075a11–14. "For the good is found both in the order and in the leader, and more in the latter; for he does not depend on the order but it depends upon him."

89 *Meta. Λ*, 1075b15–24. 18: "For all are ordered together to one end."

90 This is affirmed most clearly in *Meta. Θ*, 8, 1050b19–34. On imitation in *Metaphysics Θ* as applied to this chapter of Book Λ, see David Sedley, "*Metaphysics Λ*, 10," 333ff.

91 As I have mentioned above, my understanding differs from Michael Frede's assertion that God acts as a logical principle of understanding for Aristotle's notion of substance from the beginning of the *Metaphysics* (*Essays in Ancient Philosophy*, 79). I also disagree, therefore, with his application of the *pros hen* analogy of attribution to all secondary beings as related to the primary being as their exemplary cause

Analogies for the divine are drawn from secondary realities and "purified" in order to be attributed to God, while respecting God's absolute difference as pure actuality.[92] In other words, Aristotelian *sophia*, at least as I understand it, is not susceptible to Kant's critique of ontotheology, since it does not presuppose its teleological object (God) in the foundation of its immediate scientific object (being). The study of the latter does not necessarily entail the discovery of the former, and the knowledge of the divine is dependent upon the previous knowledge of secondary beings and is conceived (analogically) in terms of them, as their transcendent cause, and not them in terms of the divine. In locating the true point of conflict between Aristotle and Kant, then, the real question is not whether argumentation for God necessarily presupposes an aprioristic conception of the existence of God (since it does not), but whether or not we are naturally capable of true knowledge of beings and their intrinsic and extrinsic causes *qua being*, or whether such claims to knowledge are in fact merely the a priori constructions of reason. If the former is the case, then Aristotle's theological method is sound.

Second, Aristotle's metaphysical theology also resists the Heideggerian designation of ontotheology as an a priori theistic orientation for philosophy that renders obscure both the problem of being as such and the study of beings that are more immediately evident to us. Aristotle's study of the causes of being, far from beginning with God, studies first the substance, actuality, and potentiality of physical realities, respecting by a complex articulation of proportional analogies the singularity of each being, the diversity of each of the genera of the categories, the uniqueness of each species within a given genus, and the uniqueness of each substance in act with regard to all others. It is difficult to see, then, how one could rightfully claim that the singularity of being is ignored by Aristotle. The universal principles of causality do not exist in themselves, but only according to a proportional comparison of singular realities in act. In continuity with this attentiveness to the singular character of existence, Aristotle's account of act and potency allows him to take seriously the historical character of individual beings that exist in becoming, while simultaneously maintaining that this ontological becoming is profoundly intelligible, because it has a causal structure. When realities we experience are studied according to their causal intelligibility, they in turn suggest to the philosopher the necessity of a transcendent causal horizon, since they are also shown by this same historical structure to be derived or "given" being by another.

(84–95). This interpretation does not seem to me to have a very strong foundation either in Book *Γ* or Book *Λ*.

[92] For a suggestive discussion of this theme see André de Muralt, "Analogie et Négation dans la Théorie Aristotélicienne," in *Comment Dire l'Être* (Paris: J. Vrin, 1985), 109–12.

Third, then, God for Aristotle does not enter into philosophy as an extrinsic imposition of religion upon philosophy, but is approached through questions that derive intrinsically from the study of beings we experience. The goodness of God is not the formal cause of the goodness of other realities (as it threatens to be for Plato), and likewise cannot be configured with them under a common "transcendental science" of being. Rather, each reality in act attains goodness through its own progressive activity, in interdependence upon the others. God's goodness is known only because he is the primary efficient and final cause of this hierarchically ordered causal series, which exists in distinction from him. God is not immediately disclosed to human intuition. Rather, he is known only mediately and analogically as the transcendent wisdom upon whom all others depend. Nor is God "contained" within the horizon of ontical being, as if he could be conceived as one in a series of secondary, dependent beings, or as an extension of these. Instead, he is known only as the transcendent cause of these beings, and by an analogical attribution of names that respects his absolute difference as pure actuality.[93]

Finally, Aristotle's conceptual metaphysics of substance and act, teleology and goodness, permits him to articulate a contemplative understanding of God's nature without recourse to Plato's imagistic representational models. Therefore his thought aspires to a form of ontological thinking that is not reducible to the conventions of a given culture's scientific cosmology or examples derived from technological (artistic) causality. Metaphysical causation transcends all technological or cosmological models. In contrast to Heidegger's characterization of ontotheology, then, the *logos* of Aristotelian metaphysics is not reducible to the *techne* of rhetoric—a discourse constructed for merely instrumental and political ends. Rather, it is concerned with the perennial truth about the structure of reality itself, the existence of God and the final purposes of human beings. Aquinas, as we shall see, will preserve much of Aristotle's structure of thinking concerning these discoveries.

---

[93] One could ask in turn if it is not Heidegger who has failed to respect the truly ultimate "ontological difference" between historical beings in act, and the transcendent, pure actuality of God? Is the transcendence of God still "thinkable" for Heidegger, given his conception of being? Or has he in fact "banished" the pure actuality of God (in his wholly other, non-composite simplicity) from the possibility of being thought? See the interesting arguments to this effect by David Bentley Hart in "The Offering of Names: Metaphysics, Nihilism, and Analogy," in *Reason and the Reasons of Faith*, 255–94.

3

Context and Elements of Aquinas's Natural Theology

IN THE PREVIOUS CHAPTER I discussed the Aristotelian understanding of knowledge of God as wisdom, and the way that the philosopher's metaphysical understanding of God developed out of a certain framework of reflection received from Plato. I have suggested that even if Aristotle's theology remains closely related to a particular cosmological conception of the universe (allowing an important role for the primary moved movers who are the living celestial beings), nevertheless, his philosophy explores conceptually analogical ways of speaking about God that are at least *implicitly* dissociable from these received representational paradigms. (This was, at any rate, the judgment of Aquinas, who sought to extricate these elements and to develop his analyses making use of them.) Furthermore, I have argued that the causal analysis of being and theology in Aristotle's *Metaphysics* escapes the criticisms launched against ontotheology that were discussed in chapter 1.

In this chapter, I will seek to show two things: First, that Aquinas purposefully appropriated Aristotle's causal analysis of being, but within a different historical context, that of medieval Christian theology. Second, that in appropriating this metaphysical philosophy, he also transformed it—both in light of the philosophy of his age and in order to speak about topics proper to his Christian intellectual environment. Thus, the Aristotelian causal analysis of being is used by Aquinas as a theologian to articulate a metaphysics of "creation," to develop an explicit theory of analogical predication with regard to God, and to speak about God as "personal" in rigorously analogical terms. To treat Aquinas's appropriation and transformation of Aristotelian wisdom, then, I will consider briefly the context of Aquinas's intellectual project, as a Christian theologian interested in bringing into harmony the "pagan" wisdom of the gentiles, and especially the Aristotelian philosophical sciences, with the wisdom of revelation. Having identified elements of this interpretative stance, I will first attempt to show how Aquinas adopts into his own thinking much (if not all) of the natural theology theory of Aristotelian physics and metaphysics, while purposefully dissociating this theory from the hierarchical cosmos of the living stars (placing man, instead, at the summit of the visible creation). Second, I will discuss how he attempts to understand the universal relation of the world to God, not only in terms of movement and substantial change (generation and corruption), but also in terms of *creation*, founded upon the *esse*/essence distinction in all creatures. This latter distinction does not do away with the Aristotelian understanding of the structure of being, but "assumes" it. Significantly, Aquinas even extends the application of Aristotelian concepts, by speaking of this distinction in terms of actuality and potentiality, and in terms of causality. This metaphysical way of speaking about the creation will allow Aquinas to develop explicitly an understanding of the analogical predication of perfections of creatures to God that is both proper and apophatic, by a new use of the "analogy of attribution" *ad alterum*. Finally, having discussed these matters, I will make mention of how the *immanent operations* of personal *creatures*, as "secondary acts," are important for Aquinas, as they were for Aristotle, for attributing to God analogically in proper terms the attributes of personhood: intelligence and will.

The study of these elements of Aquinas's thought will permit a better understanding of the challenges presented to the modern Thomistic authors under examination in the following chapters. Even if Aquinas's Aristotelian-inspired metaphysics avoids an ontotheological turn (as I shall argue), nevertheless, this metaphysics was developed within the context of a medieval *theology*. Therefore, a properly philosophical order of investigation into metaphysical principles is not developed for its own sake. (In a sense, such a concern is distinctly modern.) Is it possible, then, that a Thomistic "natural theology" concerning God, creation, analogy, and so on, be extracted from Aquinas's theological work? That is to say, how can his proper metaphysics of creation be derived from a specifically philosophical order of investigation (*via inventionis*), and within a modern philosophical climate? Furthermore, how can such an investigation treat metaphysically the problem of the human person, and eventually arrive at clarifying in analogical terms the personal nature of the first cause? As I hope to show, these questions received very different responses from the diverse modern authors who will be studied in the third section of this book.

The Christian Theological Context of Aquinas's Natural Theological Reflections

Aquinas's theological work was situated within the context of the thirteenth-century debate over the possible integration of the Aristotelian sciences (and philosophical theology) by Christian thinkers in the medieval university. The debate was greatly affected by the influential interpretations and commentaries of the Aristotelian *corpus* effectuated by Avicenna and Averroes, which presented diverse points of compatibility or incongruity with the confession of the Catholic faith. Avicennian ontology (as a synthesis of neo-Platonism with Aristotelian elements) and Averroest interpretations of Aristotelian texts deeply influenced the Latin scholastic doctors, especially as the latter were attempting to clarify the nature of conceptual predication concerning God, in relation to a metaphysical theology of creation (a tradition that had already developed from the time of Boethius). Meanwhile, thinkers associated with the movement that has been called Latin Averroeism defended interpretations of the Stagirite that threatened to contradict faith in the name of philosophical reason.[1]

Amidst the Latin reception of Aristotle, however, at stake on a deeper level was the question of the exclusivity of the classical Augustinian theological heritage as a paradigm for Christian thought, now faced with a differing conception of wisdom and science attained by observational study and natural powers in the Aristotelian tradition.[2] The Augustinian hierarchy of

---

[1] For example, among the doctrines associated with heterodox Aristotelianism mentioned in the bishop of Paris's condemnation of thirteen errors, on December 10, 1270, were the affirmation of the eternity of the world, the unicity of the human intellect, the determinism of moral acts based upon knowledge alone, and the denial of providence (due to the fact that God does not know anything other than himself). See Fernand Van Steenberghen, *Maître Siger de Brabant* (Louvain: Éditions Peeters, 1977), 74–75, and following, on the thought of Siger and other Latin Aristotelians in relation to such condemnations.

[2] Reception of Aristotelian science was progressive throughout the thirteenth century in both Paris and Oxford until the crisis of the Paris condemnations of 1277. Christian Augustinian thinkers of the 1230s and 1240s attempted to consolidate Aristotelian discoveries within a larger framework of theological reflection, largely with the mediating aid of Avicenna's philosophy. Such was the case for thinkers such as Richard Kilwardby and Robert Grosseteste, who foreshadowed the efforts of Albert the Great and Bonaventure. On this initial Aristotelian ecclecticism see Fernand Van Steenberghen, *La Philosophie au XIIIe Siècle* (Louvain: Éditions Peeters, 1991), 109–76. The author suggests that neo-Augustinianism as a *distinct philosophy* was explicitly constituted only after the condemnations of 1277, as an alternative to Thomism and heterodox forms of Aristotelianism (406–11). On some of the implicit tensions between Augustinianism and Aristotelianism see Alasdair MacIntyre's *Three Rival Versions of Moral Inquiry* (Notre Dame: University of Notre Dame Press, 1990), 82–126.

disciplines had been encoded in the twelfth century within the framework of the interpretation of the senses of scripture, such that history, mathematics, and the liberal arts were to have their place within the all-encompassing illuminative science of the Christian faith, itself subordinated to sacred scripture.[3] This preserved the Pauline identification of the Christian gospel as the authentic form of divine wisdom, as compared to pagan folly.[4] Consequently, the *unique* sapiential perspective unifying all learning was that of theological reflection within faith.[5] Aristotelianism posed the question, therefore, *theologically* as well as philosophically, of what place the independent human knowledge of the nature of things in themselves (according to their respective causes and principles) could have with regard to Christian revelation (and Augustinian theology). This question was particularly pointed concerning Aristotelian theology and metaphysics when considered in relation to a Christian understanding of creation.

The Christian tradition, however, was not a stranger to the role played by reason in the affirmation of the existence of God. The patristic tradition had been concerned to emphasize the rationality of belief in God, and had sought a conceptual precision for speaking about God in proper terms in

---

3 This teaching finds a basis in Augustine's affirmations of the place of secular learning with regard to biblical interpretation in *De Doctrina Christiana* II–IV. In the twelfth century at the university of Paris, Hugh of St. Victor had attempted a return to the organization of studies based on these theories, as expressed in his *Didascalion: de Studio Legendi*. (On this point see Beryl Smalley, *The Study of the Bible in the Middle Ages* [Notre Dame: Notre Dame Press, 1970], 86–87.) The Augustinian notion of theological wisdom as unifying all study is related to the epistemological theory of direct divine illumination as a basis for all human knowledge, itself being teleologically ordered toward graced knowledge of the Divine Word as the Interior Teacher. (See, for example, *De Magistro, De Trinitate* IV, 2; VIII, 2; IX, 7; *De Vera Religione*, 31; *de Genesi. ad Litteram.*, XII.) Augustine seems to deny the existence of an agent intellect in *Civitate Dei*, X, 2; parallel doctrines can be found in Plotinus, *Enneads*, V, 1, 10, 10–13 and 6, 4, 19–22, who also opposes this Aristotelian theory. On Augustine's epistemology as related to his textual interpretation see Richard Markum, *Signs and Meanings* (Liverpool: Liverpool University Press, 1996), 79–101.
4 See 1 Cor 1:17, 21–25; 2:6; 3:19; 12:8; Rom 11:33–36; 16:27.
5 This is the perspective, for example, of Bonaventure in his *Collationes in Hexaemeron* of 1273, which defends the unity of Christian wisdom, against the idea of an independent philosophy, by an explanation of seven degrees of illumination, ranging from that of the natural philosophical sciences to those of faith, sacred scripture, contemplation, visions, prophecy, mystical rapture, and, finally, the beatific vision. Philosophical knowledge, therefore, is intrinsically teleologically ordered toward the beatific vision. See the analysis of Van Steenberghen, *La Philosophie au XIIIe Siècle*, 180–203.

great dependence upon the Greek, pagan philosophical heritage.[6] Augustine himself—who criticized pagan wisdom in favor of the unique wisdom of Christ—clearly not only showed an intense respect for the role of reason within faith but also affirmed certain non-banal powers of philosophical argumentation and discovery, operative in distinction from reflections on Christian faith and revelation.[7] More fundamentally, though, the possibility of natural knowledge of God was clearly affirmed in scripture itself.[8]

Within this larger context Aquinas set out to rearticulate the relations of faith and reason in terms of two complementary forms of wisdom (each having its own object and origins), while affirming the mutual cooperation of the two. This perspective is most clearly expressed in his incomplete work, *Expositio super librum Boethii de trinitate*, written around 1257–1258, just a year before embarking upon the *Summa contra Gentiles*. There we find him affirming a twofold knowledge of the divine. The first is philosophical, natural to man, and indirect, that is to say, attained by means of philosophical reflection upon creatures, considered as effects of God. This is the pagan wisdom of "first philosophy," which permits the articulation of a hierarchy of sciences.[9] The other knowledge is *that which God has of himself,* and which comes to human beings by means of grace, revealed in Christian doctrine. Faith in this revelation permits the beginning of a participation in the

---

6 See, for example, John of Damascus, *De Fide Orthodoxa,* I, c. 1 and 3, whose thought is indicative of the Byzantine tradition, and who directly influenced Aquinas (*ScG* I, c. 13; *ST* I, q. 2, a. 1, ad 1).

7 He offers rational arguments for the existence of God based upon the order of the world (*Serm.* CXLI, 2) and on the necessity of an unchanging principle (*Confessionum* X, 6, 4), and from the existence of immutable truth (*De Libero Arbitrio* II, 7–33; *Confessionum* VII, 10, 16), as well as arguments for the spirituality and immortality of the soul (*De Immortalitate Animae*, VI, 10).

8 See, for example, Wisdom 13:5, which affirms this possibility. Significantly, chapter 13 condemns those who mistake the heavenly bodies for divine (v. 2), yet with less severity (v. 6) than is attributed to idolaters, in chapter 14:8–21. These passages form a background for the well-known Pauline affirmations of Romans 1:19–20. Aquinas comments on these passages in his *Super Epistola ad Romanos,* I, lec. 6, in affirming that man cannot know in this life the essence of God, but by his natural powers can come to know God by his *sensible* effects, through the threefold Dionysian reflection on causality, on super-eminence, and by negation. In the *Expos. de Trin.*, q. 1, a. 2, he cites these Pauline verses as a primary *auctoritas* for the acceptation of Aristotelian wisdom as a natural theological knowledge distinct from revelation (in q. 2, a. 2).

9 Aquinas retains Hugh of St. Victor's sevenfold liberal arts of the Augustinian tradition, resituating them within the Aristotelian hierarchy of sciences. See *Expos. de Trin.*, q. 5, a. 1, ad 3. A helpful commentary is offered by Ralph McInerny in "Beyond the Liberal Arts," in *Being and Predication*, 25–47.

knowledge of God in himself directly. It attains its fulfillment in the eternal life to come for which faith is a preparation.

> The nature of science consists in this, that from things already known conclusions about other matters follow of necessity. Seeing that this is possible in the case of divine realities, clearly there can be a science about them. Now the knowledge of divine things can be interpreted in two ways. First, from our standpoint, and then they are knowable to us only through creatures, the knowledge of which we derive from the senses. Second, from the nature of divine realities themselves, and although we do not know them in their own way, this is how they are known by God and the blessed. Accordingly, there are two kinds of science concerning the divine. One follows our way of knowing, which uses the principles of sensible things in order to make the Godhead known. This is the way the philosophers handed down a science of the divine, calling the primary science "divine science." The other follows the mode of divine realities themselves, so that they are apprehended in themselves. We cannot perfectly possess this way of knowing in the present life, but there arises here and now in us a certain sharing in, and a likeness to, the divine knowledge, to the extent that through the faith implanted in us we firmly grasp the primary Truth itself for its own sake.[10]

The knowledge that God has of himself is related to Christian doctrine by Aquinas in terms of an analogy taken from Aristotelian science, between a principle and a subordinated science.[11] The principles of divine science revealed in sacred doctrine, and subsequently identified with the twelve articles of the creed, yield real knowledge of the divine nature as it is, but proportioned to man according to a discursive mode proper to his intellect within his pilgrim state, a state in which he does not yet see God. (Consequently, these are principles that man must accept to receive in faith.) Furthermore, this knowledge of God through revelation appeals to the human being's natural orientation toward God as the first truth. It can therefore

---

10 *Expos. de Trin.*, q. 2, a. 2.
11 *ST* I, q. 1, a. 2. Doctrinal revelation contains a necessary and scientific element not from its philosophical character, but because it is subordinated proportionally to the knowledge God has of himself (the science of God), which is shared in by the blessed. The notion of subordinated science is taken from *Posterior Analytics* I, 7 (75a38–b20), and is quite obviously used here by analogy in a way proper to the mystery of faith, to express the real continuity between the eternal vision of God and the doctrinal knowledge of God in earthly life, while fully respecting the difference with regard to the manner of knowing the divine that is proper to each. On the notion of sacred doctrine as subordinated science, see James Weisheipl, "The Meaning of *Sacra Doctrina* in *Summa theologiae* I, q. 1," *Thomist* 38 (1974): 49–80.

assume and redirect any natural knowledge of God that is present within the human subject, under the auspices of a greater end. In the life of the human person a cooperation results in which the natural intellectual orientation toward God as the primary truth is taken up into the search to understand the deposit of Christian faith. This cooperation permits the theologian not only to adopt the discoveries of philosophy (and, thus, for Aquinas, a large part of Aristotelian doctrine) but also eventually to bring such *philosophical* argumentation into the study of God's self-revelation (i.e., into *sacra doctrina*).

> The gifts of grace are added to nature in such a way that they do not destroy it, but rather perfect it. So too the light of faith, which is imparted to us as a gift, does not do away with the light of natural reason given to us by God. . . . Accordingly we can use philosophy in sacred doctrine in three ways. First, in order to demonstrate the preambles of faith, which we must necessarily know in [the act of] faith. Such are the truths about God that are proved by natural reason, for example, that God exists, that he is one, and other truths of this sort about God or creatures proved in philosophy and presupposed by faith. Second, by throwing light on the contents of faith by analogies, as Augustine uses many analogies drawn from philosophical doctrines in order to elucidate the Trinity. Third, in order to refute assertions contrary to the faith, either by showing them to be false or lacking in necessity.[12]

Even within the domain of revealed knowledge the determinations of created nature are respected so that the investigations of philosophical objects have their own specific character, and their own natural order of discovery (or *via inventionis*). Their study implies, therefore, the existence of scientific

---

[12] *Expos. de Trin.*, q. 2, a. 3 (Leon. L, 98–99): "Dicendum, quod dona gratiarum hoc modo nature adduntur, quod eam non tollunt set magis perficiunt; unde et lumen fidei, quod nobis gratis infunditur, non destruit lumen naturalis rationis diuinitus nobis inditum. . . . Sic ergo in sacra doctrina philosophia possumus tripliciter uti: primo ad demonstrandum ea que sunt preambula fidei, que necesse est in fide scire, ut *ea que naturalibus rationibus de Deo probantur, ut Deum esse, Deum esse unum, et alia huiusmodi uel de Deo uel de creaturis in philosophia probata, que fides supponit*; secundo ad notificandum, per aliquas similitudines ea que sunt fidei, sicut Agustinus in libro De Trinitate utitur multis similitudinibus ex doctrinis philosophicis sumptis ad manifestandum trinitatem; tertio ad resistendum his que contra fidem dicuntur, siue ostendendo ea esse falsa, siue ostendendo ea non esse necessaria" (emphasis added). An insightful commentary on this threefold exercise of philosophy in theology is given by Leo Elders, "Le Rôle de la Philosophie en Théologie," *Nova et Vetera* (French edition) 72, no. 2 (1997): 34–68. (Unless stated otherwise, all Latin citations of Aquinas in this book will be taken from the Leonine edition of his works, with the volume and page number indicated prior to the citation.)

disciplines distinct from that of theology, each with a relative degree of inherent integrity, *even when they are used within theology.* This is the perspective one encounters also in Aquinas's later works, such as the *Summa contra Gentiles* and the *Summa theologiae*:

> But any things concerning creatures that are considered in common by the philosopher and the believer are conveyed through different principles in each case. For the philosopher takes his argument from the proper causes of things; the believer, from the first cause—for such reasons as that a thing has been handed down in this manner by God, or that this conduces to God's glory, or that God's power is infinite. Hence, also [the doctrine of the faith] ought to be called the highest wisdom, since it treats the highest cause. . . . And, therefore, human philosophy serves her as the first wisdom. Accordingly, divine wisdom sometimes argues from principles of human philosophy. For among philosophers, too, the first philosophy utilizes the teachings of all the sciences in order to realize its objectives. Hence again, the two kinds of teaching do not follow the same order. For in the teaching of philosophy, which considers creatures in themselves and leads us from them to the knowledge of God, the first consideration is about creatures; the last of God. But in the teaching of faith, which considers creatures only in their relation to God, the consideration of God comes first, that of creatures afterwards. And thus the doctrine of faith is more perfect, as being more like the knowledge possessed by God, who, in knowing Himself, immediately knows all things.[13]

Because of the interdependence between grace and nature implied by this position, the discoveries of philosophy, and particularly of metaphysical theology, become of essential importance for a correct cooperation of reason with revelation, and for an intellectual reflection concerning the

---

[13] *ScG* II, 4. See likewise, *ST* I, q. 1, a. 6, ad 2, "The principles of other sciences [than *sacra doctrina*] either are evident and cannot be proved or are proved by natural reason through some other science. But the knowledge proper to this science comes through revelation, and not through natural reason. Therefore it does not pertain to it to prove the principles of other sciences. [*Et ideo non pertinet ad eam probare principia aliarum scientiarum*] but only to judge of them. Whatsoever is found in other sciences contrary to any truth of this science must be condemned as false." This statement entails no fideistic denigration of natural reason. We have already seen in the citation from the uses of philosophy in theology that the refutation of philosophical errors also belongs to the task of philosophy. The demonstration of scientific conclusions derived from principles and the dialectical refutation of errors of natural reason are the work of philosophy, even in the context of sacred doctrine. For a longer discussion on this point, see Bradley, *Aquinas on the Twofold Human Good*, 84–88.

nature of God and his relation to creation. Without such reflection, the theologian cannot speak in a sufficient way of the relation between the creation and God. An ambiguity will result concerning that which can be said properly (analogically) of God in his transcendence of creation, versus that which is attributed to God by way of metaphor.[14]

Simultaneously, as mentioned above, the revelation of sacred doctrine is understood to assume man's natural intellectual capacity for God, elevating this capacity to a new, graced form of knowledge (through faith) that requires the cooperation of man's nature. A new synergy between nature and grace, philosophy and revelation, is thus elaborated in which human thinking is applied to the mystery of God revealed in sacred doctrine. This is exemplified by the use Aquinas makes of philosophical concepts to speak analogically of the properly revealed mysteries of Catholic faith, such as the Trinity, the Hypostatic Union, or the Eucharist.[15] Aquinas, therefore, both maintains the specificity of a natural order of philosophical scientific investigation and simultaneously claims that philosophical knowledge can and must be placed in the service of revelation. The latter process presupposes that there is a given intelligibility within scriptural revelation, but makes use of philosophical analogies to illuminate the inner sense of this revelation. At the same time, paradoxically, to serve the theological truth of the revelation—and in light of its message— Aquinas also modifies and develops his understanding of the specifically natural truths of the philosophical order, including those inherited from Aristotle and other non-Christian thinkers.

---

[14] On metaphorical as opposed to properly analogical predication, see *ST* I, q. 13, a. 6. Aquinas believes that scriptural metaphors have a supremacy as a form of divine communication in human language, since they better convey to corporeal persons the affective truths of divine love, and since they both reveal and conceal a deeper nexus or concentration of divine mysteries. However, interpretation of scriptural metaphors requires reference to proper analogies that are also conveyed by Scripture, and subject to confirmation and clarification by philosophical reason. One cannot understand expressions of "the wrath of God" or "the strong arm" of God without considering God's transcendent justice and power, which are identical with his incorporeal goodness and wisdom.

[15] This is the case, for example, in his Trinitarian concept of "subsistent relations" (*ST* I, q. 40), the Hypostatic Union conceived of as two natures united hypostatically in the unique *esse* of Christ (*ST* III, q. 17), or in his Eucharistic doctrines of "transubstantiation" and of "conversion of substance" (*ST* III, q. 75, a. 4). These doctrines make use of the clarity of diverse philosophical concepts to speak in an analogical way of the supernatural mysteries of faith, which can be known (imperfectly) only in faith. The theological formulations of these concepts (such as that of a "subsistent relation") denote something irreducible to any of our natural experiences, yet they imply no intrinsic contradiction or irrationality. Moreover, they are "adequate" in some real way to the mystery they signify.

Aquinas's Christian Reinterpretation of Aristotelian Physics and Metaphysics

St. Thomas's critical evaluations and use of the Aristotelian *corpus* (and other ancient and medieval philosophical authors) are influenced by his theological perspective in important ways that seek to adapt the insights of philosophical science to the truths of revelation. I have already suggested in the previous chapter how Aristotle's philosophical principles developed in a certain kind of implicit independence from the cosmological representation that formed the background of his thought. Aquinas was explicitly concerned to identify more clearly the philosophical core of Aristotelian insights in separation from pagan cosmological elements that were in contradiction to Christian doctrine. He accomplishes this in a twofold way with respect to his interpretation of Aristotelian physics: first, he denies the immortal life of the celestial bodies,[16] and second, he argues that the eternity of the (created) universe cannot be demonstrated philosophically, contrary to what Aristotle claims.[17]

The first of these claims has for its context the Christian affirmation that the human person is the summit of God's visible creation, and that the immortal spiritual soul of man is the unique spiritual principle ontologically united with the material world. Aquinas thus distances himself from the intermediary moved-movers of Aristotelian physics. (He maintains a possible role, however, for the angels as the *separate* primary movers of the physical cosmos, thereby respecting what he takes to be the scientific insights of classical astronomy, bringing these into relation to biblical notions of the providence of angels.)[18] Aquinas will extract from Aristotle, therefore, only the versions of the first-mover argument that he believes to be philosophically sustainable based on the principles of moving beings (the four causes), and that necessitate a primary, unmoved mover. He will couple this philosophical discovery of immaterial substance with the other similar discovery of Aristotelian philosophy of nature: that of the immateriality

---

[16] See, for example, *In VII Phys.*, lec. 21, 1050–58. *In XII Meta.*, lec. 10, 2586–89.

[17] For a criticism of Aristotle's argument in *Physics* VIII (250b10–253a21), see *In XII Meta.*, lec. 5, 2497–99. Aquinas defends, however, the presence of a notion of providence in Aristotle's thought (*In II Phys.*, lec. 7, 206; lec. 14, 268). As mentioned before, Aquinas defends the notion that God can be said to know the world and will its good, according to Aristotle (*In XII Meta.*, lec. 7, 2535; lec. 11, 2614). He attributes a doctrine of creation to both Aristotle and Plato (see, for example, *De sub. sep.*, 9), understanding by "creation" a complete ontological dependence of secondary realities upon God for all that they are. In this light, he also claims that the Aristotelian affirmation of the imperishability of primary matter does not exclude its creation by God (*In I Phys.*, lec. 15, 139).

[18] See the remarks of Leo Elders, "St. Thomas Aquinas' Commentary on the *Metaphysics* of Aristotle," in *Autour de St. Thomas d'Aquin* (Paris: FAC Éditions, 1987), 134–38.

(and for Aquinas, the incorruptibility) of the human soul, as demonstrable by natural reason.[19] He will combine these two discoveries with the Aristotelian understanding of final causality implicit in the natural inclinations of all things, which he will claim both denotes and requires a universal providence.[20] The combination of these three doctrines permits Aquinas to argue *in distinctly Aristotelian, philosophical terms*, that the first mover must govern the movements of the physical universe *in view of* the good of the most noble inhabitant of this universe, the one having a spiritual soul as the form of his body. Therefore, man is seen as the teleological end of the physical creation, in view of which God governs all that is.[21] It is precisely this creature, who is made in the image of God, who can "return" to God as his natural end, by contemplation (as Aristotle noted), assisted by God's grace.[22] Philosophy of nature, therefore, is a form of wisdom for Aquinas as it was for Aristotle, even while being reinterpreted in conformity with biblical revelation.[23]

Despite these affirmations, Aquinas does not substitute for the immortal celestial beings the human person as a visible paradigm of the divine present in our world. Instead he is interested to understand how all things are strictly relative to God. This relativity is not necessarily temporal, since Aquinas does not think that creation in time can be proven (or disproven) philosophically.[24] Rather, it is manifested principally on two levels: one concerns the dependence of all physical things upon the first mover, indicated through their substantial becoming. (They come to be and cease to be through physical change, and not all beings can be like this.) The second, a more universal level of ontological dependence, concerns the being of *all* created realities in relation to God as Creator (including non-physical realities, such as angels). Aquinas will attempt to relate these two in his conception of metaphysics.

---

[19] See, for example, *ScG* I, c. 13, on the first mover, and *ScG* II, c. 63–79, on the immateriality of the soul of man.

[20] *ScG* III, c. 21–24.

[21] See *ScG* III, c. 22, where he concludes: "So, if the motion of the heavens is ordered to generation, and if the whole of generation is ordered to man as a last end with this genus, it is clear that the end of celestial motion is ordered to man, as to an ultimate end in the genus of generable and mobile beings. Hence the statement of Deuteronomy (4:19) that God made celestial bodies, '*for the service of all people.*' "

[22] *ScG* III, c. 25, 37, 51–53.

[23] The sapiential aspiration of the *Physics* is affirmed, for example, in *In II Phys.*, lec. 6, 196.

[24] *De aeternitate mundi, contra murmurantes.* See the analysis of John Wippel, "Thomas Aquinas on the Possibility of Eternal Creation," in *Metaphysical Themes in Thomas Aquinas* (Washington, DC: The Catholic University of America Press, 1993), 191–214.

In pursuing this metaphysical reflection, Aquinas will take up a middle way between Avicenna and Averroes. Avicenna had included the "necessary being" of God within the study of being as an element of its subject. Consequently, the study of God as the ultimate cause of created substances is an object of special science within the general subject of metaphysics.[25] God is necessary being and the backdrop against which possible being (of essences given *esse*) is understood.[26] Averroes reacted against this conception of metaphysics, which begins by giving itself its own ultimate object (God) and instead claims (in a more empiricist vein) that the philosophy of nature, which proves the existence of immobile, immaterial substance, gives metaphysics (the study of separate substances) the knowledge of its object.[27]

Aquinas will articulate metaphysical science in Aristotelian terms as a study of the ultimate causes and principles of being, as the most universal science, and as that which hierarchically orders all other forms of speculative and practical knowledge. In the prologue to his *Sententia super Metaphysicam* (his commentary on the *Metaphysics*), he carefully develops differing definitions of this science, affirming that it is called "metaphysics" insofar as its subject transcends the diverse genera of being and has for its object "common being." Insofar as it seeks out the primary, ultimate causes of being *qua* being, it can rightfully be called "first philosophy." Meanwhile, this science can be called "theology" because it can attain knowledge of God and the separate substances, *but only insofar as they are the ultimate causes of its subject, being.*[28] The first and last of these three points are especially sig-

---

25 *Avicenna Latinus, Liber de Philosophia Prima sive Scientia Divina*, ed. S. Van Riet (Leyden and Louvain: Brill and Éditions Peeters, 1977), I, c. 2, n. 12 and 14 (vol. 1, p. 11, 14): "Manifestum est igitur quod haec omnia cadunt in scientiam quae profitetur id cuius constitutio non pendet ex sensibilibus. Sed non potest poni eis subiectum commune, ut illorum omnium sint dispositiones et accidentalia communia, nisi esse. . . . Sequitur ergo necessario ut haec scientia dividatur in partes, quarum quaedam inquirunt causas ultimas, inquantum sunt causae omnis esse causati inquantum est esse; et aliae inquirunt causam primam ex qua fluit omne esse causatum inquantum est esse causatum, non inquantum est esse mobile vel quantitativum." See the examination of Avicenna on this point by Albert Zimmermann, *Ontologie oder Metaphysik?* (Louvain: Peeters, 1998), 144–52.

26 In *Liber de Philosophia Prima sive Scientia Divina*, I, c. 5, Avicenna treats the first principles of this science, among which are necessary being and possible being. In chapter 6 he will define necessary being as uncaused being, in the light of whom all other being receives its relative intelligibility as caused and as having possible existence (37): "Dicemus igitur quod necesse esse per se non habet causam et quod possibile esse per se habet causam."

27 Averroes, *In II Phys.*, 26, v. 59. An analysis of Averroes's reaction to Avicenna is offered by Michel Bastit, *Les Principes des Choses en Ontologie Médiévale* (Bordeaux: Éditions Bière, 1997), 23–25, and Zimmermann, *Ontologie oder Metaphysik?* 152–54.

28 *In Meta.*, prologue.

nificant. In affirming that the "subject" of metaphysics is "common being," Aquinas accepts the Avicennian interpretation of the proper object of metaphysics as being *qua* being, and not separate substances, as Averroes affirmed. The metaphysical knowledge of being does not presuppose the knowledge of the unmoved mover. On the contrary, knowledge of being is implicitly present at the start of all the other sciences, including physics.[29] Yet Aquinas maintains the theological orientation of "first philosophy" in keeping with the search for proper causes of being, while dissociating God from the *subject* of this science as such. The primary being and cause of others is not himself located within the genus of "common being," in contradistinction from the thought of Avicenna.[30] This means that, for Aquinas, God is approached through metaphysical theology only indirectly. God does not fall within the study of that which is caused by God ("common being"), and is not comprehended within the conceptual idioms of created being. This also means that the experiential study of the proper principles of being does not presuppose the notion of God in order to give intelligibility to those beings, even if knowledge of God is an intrinsic teleological effect of this investigation.[31] In both these senses, Aquinas's thought seems

---

29 Hence metaphysics does not receive its principles from another science, as, for example, from the demonstration in philosophy of nature of the existence of separate substances, as Averroes thinks. See *In IV Meta.*, lec. 1, 1149–51; XI, lec. 1, 2151. It is metaphysics, rather, that gives the first principles of understanding to all the other sciences (see *Expos. de Trin.*, q. 5, a.1, ad 9). This perspective is arguable in strictly Aristotelian terms, as Aristotle's *Physics* clearly presupposes the notions of substance, act, and potentiality, the ten categories, being and unity, as well as the axiom of non-contradiction, most of which are employed in the first few chapters of that work. (See, for example, *Physics* I, 2, 184b27–185a4; 185a27–185b7.) Nevertheless, Aquinas does think that if the philosophy of nature does presuppose a foundational metaphysical realism in its first principles, the demonstration of the unmoved mover disposes to the posterior, complete study of a metaphysical science. See *In II Physics*, lec. 4, 175, and *Expos. de Trin.*, q. 5, a. 1, ad 9. I will return to the interpretation of these issues in chapter 7.

30 *In Meta.*, prologue: "From this it is evident that, although this science [i.e., metaphysics or first philosophy] studies the three classes of things mentioned above [i.e., God, the intellectual substances, and being in general], it does not investigate any one of them as its subject, but only being in general. For the subject of a science is the genus whose causes and properties we seek, and not the causes themselves of the particular genus studied, because a knowledge of the causes of some genus is the goal [*finis*] to which the investigation of a science attains." It should be noted that Aquinas is speaking loosely of a "genus" of being here, as he holds, like Aristotle, that being is not in a genus, and is known only by proportional analogy, across the diverse genera. See *In III Meta.*, lec. 8, 433.

31 For Aquinas, God is philosophically intelligible only indirectly—as a transcendent, unknown origin of being (based upon a posteriori *quia* demonstrations that pass

quite consistent with Aristotle's, and avoids entirely the form of reasoning that Heidegger terms ontotheology. If the latter in fact exists at all in the medieval tradition (which is highly disputable), then it would have to be located in the form of thought initiated by Avicenna and the subsequent interpretations of Scotus and Suarez, who understand God as coming under the subject of metaphysics.[32]

Aquinas's motivations for his own interpretation of the subject of metaphysics are not only philosophical, however. By the articulation of the intrinsically apophatic character of natural theology, he is showing the "space" created nature itself offers for the revelation of the Trinity, a revelation that can be given only by God, supernaturally.[33] In this way Aquinas seeks to resolve the ambiguity present in Aristotle's texts concerning the nature of philosophical wisdom, which, because it is knowledge of the wisdom God has of himself, is seemingly a "divine" form of knowledge.[34] For Aquinas, this is wisdom insofar as it offers *mediated* knowledge of God as the transcendent cause of being.[35] Only *sacra doctrina* permits man to have knowledge of God as an *immediate* subject (by virtue of a divine revelation), and correspondingly inaugurates a higher science of God and the blessed.

---

from effects to causes). This viewpoint harmonizes with his apophatic conception of analogical attribution to God, which I will return to below.

32 Scotus reinterprets Avicenna's thought with the help of his own appeal to a univocal concept of being, explaining how both God, as infinite and necessary being, and creatures, as finite, possible being, can be thought of in related terms by the use of this common concept. By then articulating the cosmological and ontological arguments in terms of the notions of necessary and possible being, he establishes an argumentation in which God must be thought of as necessary being once there is sufficient examination of the notion of contingent and possible creatures. The concept of being as it is derived from the latter provides a notion that can be used to conceptualize God's existence so that God's attributes may be signified by means of common transcendental concepts. Meanwhile finite beings are themselves explained by appeal to the perfect instantiation of being in God as the necessary ontological condition for the possibility of creatures. Nevertheless, for Scotus, the fact that we possess a notion of being potentially attributable to God is not sufficient to warrant the ontological affirmation of God's existence. See on these issues Richard Cross, *Duns Scotus* (Oxford: Oxford University Press, 1999), 16–41, 139 n. 35; *Duns Scotus on God* (Aldershot and Burlington: Ashgate, 2005), 36–37, 258; Courtine, *Suarez et le Système de la Métaphysique*, 137–54.

33 See *Expos. de Trin.*, q. 1, a. 4: "The Trinity of persons cannot be known from the divine causality itself, because causality belongs in common to the whole Trinity. Neither is it expressed in negative terms. Consequently it is absolutely impossible to give a demonstrative proof that God is threefold and one."

34 *Metaphysics A*, 2, 983a8–10; *Λ*, 7, 1072b15, 25.

35 See *In I Meta.*, lec. 3, 64.

The *Esse*/Essence Distinction and the Metaphysics of Creation

In a certain sense, St. Thomas's study of created being takes on a fundamentally Aristotelian form. He accepts the fourfold causality common to the hylomorphic composition present in all physical beings, and he establishes a science of the causes of being principally in terms of substance (as the formal cause of being) and of actuality and potentiality (which concern the final cause of being *qua* being).[36] Substantial forms exist only as singular beings (there are no separate universals).[37] The study of substances is analogical insofar as the unity of substance does not dissolve the diversity of categories, which are said to "be" according to proportional analogy.[38] Actuality and potentiality are also said of the ten categories, and thus of accidents as well as substances: operations can exist in act or in potentiality, as can substantial beings. Therefore, the "primary act" of the substance is distinguished from the "secondary acts" of the operations.[39] All singular existing beings are ontologically composed of actuality and potency, and are therefore not caused by themselves, but must be studied in their causal dependencies in relation to the transcendent primary cause.[40] Being is therefore known analogically, as is God, the ultimate object attained by the study of metaphysics.

On the other hand, however, Aquinas's interpretations of Aristotle's concepts and terms stand in a complex relationship to his own metaphysics of *esse* and essence, which he developed in an original way.[41] In

---

[36] On the substance as the formal cause of being *qua* being see *In VII Meta.*, lec. 17, 1648–49, 1678; on actuality as a principle and cause, IX, lec. 1, 1769.

[37] *In V Meta.*, lec. 9–10; *ST* I, q. 29, a. 1.

[38] *In VII Meta.*, lec. 1, 1246–51. The being of a substance is really distinguishable from the being of its quantity, qualities, relations, etc., even if the latter depend for their being upon the former. For example, the quantity of a thing can change, even while it remains substantially the same being.

[39] *In IX Meta.*, lec. 5, 1828.; lec. 9, 1870.

[40] *In XII Meta.*, lec. 4, 2484–86.

[41] The history of the *esse*/essence distinction previous to Aquinas is complex. Avicenna first employs the distinction in a programmatic way within medieval philosophy, attributing existence (*esse*) to created realities as an accident of their essence. God creates the world through the mediation of a series of subordinated separate intelligences, uniting such possible essences with their existence. These essential forms take on a kind of eternal necessity alongside God as the conditions of possibility for the emanation-into-existence that characterizes this understanding of creation. William of Auvergne rearticulated the distinction as a Christian theologian placing emphasis on the absolute liberty of God to give existence to the essential natures he wished to create by his all-powerfulness, thus breaking with Avicenna's emanationist schema, and subordinating all created forms to the absolute liberty and intelligence of God. Aquinas's approach resembles that of William but transforms

affirming a real distinction (or composition) of essence and existence in all created things, Thomas does not deny the Aristotelian structural principles of matter and form, substance and accidents, act and potentiality, as constituting the physical realities we experience. He introduces into such substances, however, a more fundamental distinction between the reality's essential determination (as, in the case of physical creatures, composed of matter and form of a particular kind), and the existence, or being in act of the reality (which Aquinas called its "act of existence," or *actus essendi*).[42] This composition obtains not in only all physical substances, but in all created substances, and is therefore common to all creatures, including separated intelligences (the angels).

> [Separated] intellectual substances are not composed of matter and form; rather, in them the form itself is a subsisting substance; so that form here is that which is and being itself [*esse*] is act and *that by which* the substance is. And on this account there is in such substances but one composition of act and potency, namely the composition of substance and being [*substantia et esse*]. . . . On the other hand, in substances composed of matter and form there is a twofold composition of act and potentiality: the first of the substance itself which is composed of matter and form; the second, of the substance thus composed, and being [*esse*]. . . . It is therefore clear that composition of act and potentiality has greater extension than that of form and matter. Matter and form divide natural substance, while potentiality and act divide common being.[43]

Such thinking permits Aquinas to articulate three important tenets of his doctrine of creation. First, it permits him to explain a common divi-

---

the distinction in two ways. First, he articulates the distinction in terms of actuality and potentiality, by an analogical extension of these Aristotelian transcendental principles that are applicable to all categories. *Esse* is not an accident of essence, but instead founds it as its actuality, and applies to all accidents as well. Second, he identifies this distinction with Boethius's claim that in creatures there is a real distinction between *esse* and *id quod est*. In his *Super Boetium de Hebdomadibus*, Aquinas therefore rearticulates Boethius's notions of *participated* being in creatures in terms of the *esse*/essence distinction. For an analysis of this historical background, see Aimé Forest, *La Structure Métaphysique du Concret* (Paris: J. Vrin, 1931), 133–66.

42 *De ente et essentia*, c. 2 and 5.

43 *ScG* II: 54. In his diverse texts Aquinas offers four sorts of justification for the real distinction between the essential determination and the existence in every created being: the incapacity of essence to account for existence; the divine simplicity as opposed to the real composition in creatures; the participation of diverse realities in existence, which is not itself common to any genera of being; the limitation of the perfection of existence by essence. See, for example, *De ente*, c. 4; *De ver.*, q. 10–12; *In de Heb.*, 2; *De potentia Dei*, q. 7, aa. 1–2.

sion between *esse* and essence in all created realities, such that the being (*ens*) of each one is composed of an "essence having existence" (*essentia habens esse*).[44] Only in God alone is there a being (*ens*) in whom *esse* and essence are identical. Thus the *ens* of God alone is identical with his existence (*esse*).[45] Second, this doctrine not only permits Aquinas to articulate a composition common to physical and purely spiritual creatures, but also gives him a way to theorize as to how primary matter (the pure potentiality present in all material things) is entirely dependent ontologically upon the creative act of God (through the *esse* of its essential form, which gives existence to the materiality of the created substance).[46] All created reality is therefore embraced by the distinction, from immaterial angels to primary matter. Third, by recourse to the Neoplatonic axiom that *esse* in a creature is limited by its particular essence, as related to the transcendent *causality* of God as subsistent *esse*, Aquinas is able to articulate an original theory of participated being in creatures, as received by causation from the first being. All that exists participates in existence because it *receives* its existence from the primary cause, who is himself subsistent being (*ipsum esse subsistens*).[47]

Participation theory in Aquinas, however, does retain some distinctly Aristotelian characteristics. Because Aquinas articulates the *esse*/essence distinction in terms of actuality and potentiality (with existence as the actuation

---

[44] The acknowledgment of Aquinas's affirmation of the real *composition* of *esse* and essence in each created being has sometimes been obscured in twentieth-century scholarship by the tendency to reify or hypostasize *esse* as a self-subsisting entity independent of or above all essential determinations. Étienne Gilson, in *Being and Some Philosophers*, 190–204, argues that there is no concept of *esse* as such, implying that it is distinct from and lies beyond essence. Yet Aquinas teaches that "essence is said of that by which and in which being has existence" ("Essentia dicitur secundum quod per eam et in ea ens habet esse"), in *De ente*, c. 1 (ed. Marietti, 1954). See also *ELPH* I, lec. 5, 70 (Leon. I, 27): "Ipsum ens est fons et origo esse." *ScG* III, c. 66 (Leon. XIV, 188): "Nihil enim dat esse nisi inquantum est ens actu." For a detailed criticism of the assertions of Gilson, see McInerny, *Being and Predication*, 173–89. On the composition of *esse* and essence in every *ens*, see Michel Bastit, "Le Thomisme est-il un Aristotélisme?" *Revue Thomiste* 101 (2001): 101–16. I will return to related topics in the following chapter.

[45] On the non-distinction of *esse* and essence in God, see *De ente*, c. 4; *ScG* I, c. 22; *ST* I, q. 3, a. 4 (Leon. IV, 42): "Est igitur Deus suum esse et non solum sua essentia." On the identity of *ens* and essence in God, *ScG* II, c. 53 (Leon. XIII, 391): "Solus Deus est essentialiter ens."

[46] *ST* I. q. 44, aa. 1–2.

[47] *ST* I, q. 61, a. 1: "God alone is his own existence; while in everything else the essence differs from the existence. . . . From this it is clear that God alone exists of his own essence: while all other things have their existence by participation. Now whatever exists by participation is caused by what exists essentially." See also *ST* I, q. 44, a. 1.

of essence), he is able to understand the limited act of each being as a participation received from and existing in-view-of the pure actuality of God. In
other words, participation as actuality must be understood by reference to
the transcendent efficient and final causality of God.[48] This permits him to
avoid an emanationist, Platonic understanding of God as in some way formal cause of either the creature's being or its goodness.[49] Instead, as pure act,
in whom *esse* and essence are identical, God remains utterly transcendent
with regard to the creature, whose ontological frailty is exemplified by the
real composition within it of *esse* and essence.[50] Nevertheless, because *esse* in

---

[48] *ST* I, q. 3, a. 8: "It is not possible for God to enter into the composition of anything, either as a formal or a material principle. First, because God is the first efficient cause. Now the efficient cause is not identical numerically with the form of
the thing caused, but only specifically: for man begets man. But primary matter
can be neither numerically nor specifically identical with an efficient cause for the
former is merely potential, while the latter is actual. Secondly, because, since God
is the first efficient cause, to act belongs to Him primarily and essentially. But that
which enters into composition with anything does not act primarily and essentially, but rather the composite so acts. . . . Thirdly, because no part of a compound can be absolutely primary among beings—not even matter, nor form,
though they are the primal parts of every compound. . . . Now it has been proved
that God [as pure actuality] is absolutely primal being."

[49] Aquinas follows Aristotle in understanding goodness primarily in terms of final
causality, and notes the criticisms in *Metaphysics A*, 7, 988b6–15, of Empedocles and
Plato, who understood goodness in terms of efficient and formal causality, respectively. (See *In I Meta.*, lec. 11, 177–79.) In *ST* I, q. 5, a. 4, ad 1–3, he uses the same
principle to reinterpret the Dionysian and Augustinian notions of God's goodness as
(respectively) a formal cause (as beauty) or an efficient cause (the good diffusive of
itself). The good is the final cause of the existence of things (q. 5, a. 2, ad 1): "Goodness as a cause is prior to being, as is the end to the form." In *De ver.*, q. 21, a. 4,
Aquinas criticizes the Platonist notion that God is the formal cause of goodness in
participated beings, based on Aristotelian principles of act and potentiality. In a. 5,
Aquinas treats the goodness of God in a twofold way. First, with Aristotle in *Metaphysics Θ*, 9, he affirms that the distinction of substance and accident does not exist in
God and that since God's act of being implies an identification of "first act" (of the
substance) and "second act" (of what are in creatures the accidents) he is necessarily
subsistent goodness. Second, however, Aquinas introduces the *esse*/essence distinction. The creature's nature is not good essentially, but only in so far as it has existence,
received from God: "Even granted that absolute goodness were attributed to a creature because of its substantial existence, nevertheless the fact would still remain that it
has goodness by participation, just as it has a participated existence. But God is goodness essentially inasmuch as his essence is his existence. . . . Goodness has the character of a final cause. But God has this, since he is the ultimate end of all beings just as
he is their first principle. From this it follows that any other end has the status or character of an end only in relation to the first cause." See also *ScG* I, c. 37.

[50] Michel Bastit, *Les Principes des Choses*, 181–82, lists a number of important reasons
one should hesitate before ascribing to Aquinas's doctrine of *esse* a Neoplatonic

creatures is received from God, its singular actuality *imitates* imperfectly God's transcendent being. This fact allows Aquinas to speak of God as not only the transcendent efficient, and final cause of the being of each reality, but also as its exemplary cause. All participated existents are modeled in some way upon the pure actuality of the Creator.[51] There is a participatory structure present at the heart of each created being due to its causal composition: the *esse* of each one manifests something of the transcendent wisdom and goodness of God.

Aquinas's main presentations of the demonstrative knowledge we can have of God do not appeal explicitly to the real distinction in creatures between *esse* and essence as a way of discovery of the existence of God.[52] His preferred arguments have their basis in Aristotelian physics and metaphysics, and repose especially upon the notion of the primacy of actuality over potentiality in any series of essentially ordered, ontologically interdependent causes. (He explores, however, such ordered causal series in different senses, according to material, efficient, formal, exemplary, or final causality.) At the term of such causal demonstrations, Aquinas employs his so-called eliminative method, or *via reductionis*, to remove from his understanding of the first, uncreated cause all notions of being that are proper to creatures as such.[53] Significantly, we find him here eliminating the real

---

character: *esse* and essence are distinguished by Aquinas, but only within one composite *ens*. This affirmation does not do away with the proper principles of secondary causes, and Aquinas rejects any univocal causality in the order of being. *Esse* is never conceived of as having "infinite or finite modes," and the theory of Platonic, separate ideas is rejected. Substances are identical with individual subjects, and are understood in terms of form and actuality. Consequently, it is the form that gives existence to the reality. See also, Rudi Te Velde, *Participation and Substantiality in Thomas Aquinas* (Leiden: Brill, 1995), 256 and following: "[T]he Neoplatonic concept of participation undergoes a fundamental transformation in Aquinas." For Aquinas's affirmation of the transcendence of God vis-à-vis any form of emanationist pantheism, see *In de Causis*, prop. 24, lec. 24, and prop. 3, lec. 3. For criticisms of Platonic notions of causality, see *In de Causis*, prop. 6, lec. 6, and *In de Div. Nom.*, V, lec. 1. For criticisms of the Platonic forms, see *De ver.*, q. 10, a. 6; *ScG* II, c. 26; III, c. 24, 69; *In de Div. Nom.* V, lec. 2.

51 *ST* I, q. 44, aa. 1–4.

52 For instance, in *ScG* I, q. 15; *ST* I, q. 2, a. 3; or in the *Comp. Theol.*, c. 3–4. This statement is, I think, not controversial. John Wippel, *Metaphysical Themes in Thomas Aquinas*, 133–61, notes that almost all Aquinas's analyses of the real distinction presume knowledge of the first cause. I am not dealing here with the more controversial question of whether the distinction can be used as a basis for the reinterpretation of the "five ways," or presents itself a way in which to approach the question of the existence of God, though I will discuss these questions in subsequent chapters.

53 In the *ST* the order of identification of attributes follows an order of reflection comparable to Aristotle's in Book Λ, chapters 7 and 9, in that Aquinas first discusses God's substance or essence as pure actuality, and then his immanent operations. Q. 3

composition of existence and essence in creatures when discussing the necessary being of God.[54] This means that at the term of his Aristotelian-inspired arguments for the existence of God, Aquinas develops an understanding of God not only as pure actuality, in whom substance and actuality are identical, and in whom there is no accident (as is the case for Aristotle), but also as subsistent *esse*, who is his essence and who is necessary per se. Consequently, the first being whose existence is proved is the transcendent Creator who causes being in all things (as an efficient cause), and from whom all receive their finite and participated existence and goodness. An important effect of this mode of argumentation is that it allows Aquinas to make use of the Aristotelian causal method of demonstration of God's existence (by indirect means, a posteriori, passing from effects to their cause), and his intrinsically related use of analogical predication, in order to speak now about God as the transcendent *Creator* of *being*. Thus he develops a unique theory of analogical predication of attributes to God, using key elements from both Aristotle and the metaphysics of *esse*, in relation to the Christian understanding of God as a Creator who is known imperfectly from his created effects.[55]

The Perfection of the Primary Cause

Of particular importance for this theory of theological predication is Aquinas's notion of the perfection of God as related to creatures. The perfection of God is discussed in both the *ScG* and the *ST* immediately after a series of reductions used to eliminate compositions and dependencies that are not present in the uncaused and simple being of God. It thus fol-

---

concerns God's essence, and through a series of negations of imperfections affirms the divine simplicity. Q. 4–6 treat God's actuality and therefore his perfection and goodness. Q. 7–11 negate from God the imperfections proper to physical beings: spatial finitude, mutability, temporality, or multiplicity, so as to further our understanding of God's actuality. In q. 14 Aquinas will treat the immanent operations of God (as intellect and will). The *ScG* follows a different order, which places all of the eliminative negations after the demonstration of the first being (in c. 14–28) and prior to positive attributes such as perfection and goodness. The immanent operations of intelligence and love, however, are similarly placed afterward (c. 44 and following). For an analysis of this approach through eliminative reduction, see Kretzmann, *The Metaphysics of Theism*, 113–38. I will return to the question of analogical naming of God according to Aquinas in chapter 8.

54 *ScG* I, c. 22; *ST* I, q. 3, a. 4; *Comp. Theol.*, c. 11.

55 I am not concerned here to justify Aquinas's use of Aristotelian-based principles and arguments to prove the existence of God as the Creator of every being in its *esse*. However, the questions raised by this methodological stance will be a concern for the majority of thinkers whose work I will examine below.

lows as a final result therefrom.[56] Aquinas argues for absolute divine perfection based upon several factors: the non-existence of potentiality in God (his pure actuality), the non-composite form of God's being (divine simplicity), and the fact that he is the efficient cause of all other beings (who cannot enter into composition with them but is the source of all their formal, perfecting determinations). St. Thomas makes use, then, of both the Aristotelian affirmation of the non-distinction between substance and perfecting operation in the primary being who is pure actuality (from *Metaphysics* Λ, 7), and also the affirmation of the identity of *esse* and essence in God. Because God is pure actuality, he precedes and is the cause of all the operative perfections found in the diverse genera of substances, even while his own substance and operation are identical. Because he is his own existence and the source of existence for all others, he is the universal cause of being, and of all the perfections found in diverse modes of being proper to each kind of creature.[57] Consequently, since created effects must bear some resemblance to their transcendent cause, the existent perfections of all things must be said to resemble God in some way. Aquinas will conduct a clarification of God's attributes by analogical predication, especially through an examination of the perfective operations of the intelligence and will. It is the "secondary actuality" of the operations of human reason that Aquinas, following Aristotle (Λ, 7 and 9), will attribute analogically to the essence (and primary actuality) of God. Furthermore, Aquinas will identify such operations in God with his very subsistent *esse*, which is his essence. Before I analyze this point, however, I will briefly discuss Aquinas's important understanding of analogical attribution of names with regard to God.

---

[56] This is especially clear in the *ScG* I, in which c. 28 on perfection follows after thirteen eliminations, but also in *ST* I, q. 4, which follows after the six eliminations of q. 3, aa. 1–6.

[57] *ScG* I, c. 28: "Every excellence in any given thing belongs to it according to its being [*esse*]. . . . Hence, the mode of a thing's excellence is according to the mode of its being. For a thing is said to be more or less excellent according as its being is limited to a certain greater or lesser mode of excellence. Therefore, if there is something to which the whole power of being belongs, it can lack no excellence that is proper to some thing. But for a thing that is its own being it is proper to be according to the whole power of being. . . . God therefore, who is his being, has being according to the whole power of being itself. Hence, he cannot lack any excellence that belongs to any given thing. . . . Again, each thing is perfect according as it is in act, and imperfect according as it is in potency and lacking act. Hence, that which is in no way in potency, but is pure act, must be most perfect. Such, however, is God. God is, therefore, most perfect."

Analogical Predication of Names to God

As I have shown in the previous chapter, the theory of an analogical under-standing of being was already developed to a certain extent by Aristotle. The Stagirite initially distinguished between univocal terms and equivocal terms, with the latter being those that can be applied differently to diverse realities, while signifying a common aspect.[58] In later works, Aristotle will develop *diverse senses* of equivocal predication. He uses these especially as related to the problem of being, oneness, and the good. So, for example, as I have mentioned previously, he develops a proportional form of attribution in *Nicomachean Ethics* I, 6, to speak analogically about the good. Goodness is said by proportional analogy (*A* is to *B* as *C* is to *D*) of the diverse categor-ial modes of being: the "goodness" (*A*) of a quality (*B*) (such as a virtue) is different from the "goodness" (*C*) of a quantity (*D*) (such as the right amount).[59] Aristotle will consider in the same way "being" and the "one," as proportionally analogical terms attributed in different ways to each categor-ial mode of being.[60] He also uses this "analogy of proper proportionality" to speak of the analogical way in which "being" is ascribed to diverse sub-stances. Each singular substance is said to "be" in an absolutely unique way, yet one can make an analogical comparison between them in ascribing "being" to each one proportionally.[61] This form of analogical predication is also used to compare actuality and potentiality across its different modes of realization, whether they be substantial, operational, or related to move-ment.[62] "Actuality" and "potentiality" are said in proportionally analogical ways of the substance, of an operation, or of a movement.

Aristotle develops a second form of equivocal predication, however, in his discussions of the unity of the science of being and the problem of the substance. In *Metaphysics Γ*, 2, for example, he introduces a *pros hen* form of analogy, giving the famous examples of "health" and of "the medical art."

---

[58] *Categories*, 1, 1a1–15. Aristotle distinguishes between *synonymous*, or univocal, terms and *derivative*, or equivocal, terms. An example of the former is "animal" as ascribed to either man or beast. An example of the latter is "grammarian" as com-pared to "grammar." The grammarian receives his name from the grammar he knows, and therefore there is a causal relation between the two. An analogical understanding of things related to the art of grammar follows from this.

[59] See *Nic. Ethics* I, 6, 1096a12–29: "Clearly the good cannot be something univer-sally present in all cases and single; for then it would not have been predicated in all the categories but in one only."

[60] So, for instance, "being" or "oneness" is said of a substance in a different way than it is said of a given quality, quantity, relation, etc. See *Metaphysics B*, 4, and *Λ*, 5, where this is intimated. I will return to Aquinas's commentaries on these passages in later chapters.

[61] *Meta. Λ*, 5, 1071a18–24.

[62] *Meta. Θ*, 6, 1048a25–1048b9.

Everything which is healthy is related to health, one thing in the sense that it preserves health, another in the sense that it produces it, another in the sense that it is a symptom of health, another because it is capable of it. And that which is medical is relative to the medical art, one thing in the sense that it possesses it, another in the sense that it is naturally adapted to it, another in the sense that it is a function of the medical art. . . . So, too there are many senses in which a thing is said to be, but all refer to one [*pros hen*] starting-point; some things are said to be because they are substances, others because they are affections of substance, others because they are a process towards substance.[63]

Aristotle's point is that "being" can be ascribed in analogical ways to the multiple aspects of a reality, but is ascribed particularly to that which is said to "be" in the primary sense, as that *toward which* or *because of which* the others exist. In Book *Z*, 1, he will use this theory of a *pros hen* analogy to speak about the substance, as the formal cause of the other determinations of being. It is the substance in particular that is said to "be," and the other categorial modes of being are said to exist only in dependence upon (*pros hen*) this one, primary mode of being.

Aquinas adopts these diverse forms of analogical predication of being and, like Aristotle, relates them to the causal analysis of being (in terms of the diverse categorial modes of being, substance and accidents, actuality and potentiality). How, exactly, these diverse analogies are related to a causal study of being is a question treated in diverse ways by the modern Thomists considered in the next section of this book, and I will return at length to these problems below.[65] My main interest at this point, however, is to note how Aquinas not only adopted a certain kind of Aristotelian

---

[63] *Meta. Γ*, 2, 1003a35–1003b8.

[64] *Meta. Z*, 1, 1028a10–30.

[65] For much of my understanding of Aquinas's theory of analogy, which will become evident progressively, I am indebted to the study of Michel Bastit, *Les Principes des Choses*, 55–64, as well as John Wippel, *The Metaphysical Thought of Thomas Aquinas*, 73–93. A number of modern Thomistic thinkers (Ralph McInerny, David Burrell, Gregory Rocca) have sought to interpret analogy theory in Aquinas as primarily concerned with the relations of intentional logical predication rather than real ontological similitude between creatures and God. See most characteristically Ralph McInerny, *Aquinas and Analogy* (Washington, DC: The Catholic University of America Press, 1996). It is not my intention in this work to deal with the questions this form of thought raises, important though they may be. For a helpful critical reflection on this line of thinking and a convincing defense of the ontological basis of analogy in Aquinas's thought, see Lawrence Dewan, "St. Thomas and Analogy: The Logician and the Metaphysician," in *Form and Being: Studies in Thomistic Metaphysics* (Washington, DC: The Catholic University of America Press, 2006), 81–95.

theory of analogy, but also developed out of it a different form of analogical predication in the light of his metaphysics of creation, in order to speak of the perfections that one can attribute to God as the Creator. This form of analogical predication is related in particular to the metaphysics of the *esse*/essence distinction, which reveals the dependence of creatures upon the transcendent actuality of God.

St. Thomas, like Aristotle, distinguishes between an analogical predication according to proper proportionality (*A* is to *B* as *C* is to *D*), and a *pros hen* form of predication, in which a multiplicity of terms are referred in particular to one that is primary. This latter form of analogy is commonly called an "analogy of attribution."[66] In further developing Aristotle's thought, however, Aquinas, in turn, *distinguishes two types* of analogy of attribution. One he entitles a *multa ad unum* analogy of attribution, and the other an *ad alterum* analogy of attribution. The former corresponds to Aristotle's *pros hen* analogy of Book *Γ*, 2, and Book *Z*, 1. "Healthy" can be ascribed to a multiplicity of treatments, or symptoms, but principally to the healthy reality itself. Metaphysically speaking, "being" can be ascribed to the accidents (such as qualities or relations), but is ascribed principally to the substance. It is essential to note in this context that *Aquinas wishes to exclude definitively the use of this form of analogy* to speak about the relation between creatures and God. This is precisely because it would make both God and creatures fall under a common heading, *multa ad unum*, that of "being." This would include both God and creatures under a unique subject of study, that of "common being."[67]

---

66 Aquinas himself tends to use the term *proportio* to express the notion of the reference of one to another who is first, or of a multitude to a first (a *pros hen* analogy). Cajetan entitled these forms "analogies of attribution." A similitude between two different relations (*A* is to *B* as *C* is to *D*) Aquinas calls *proportionalitas*, and Cajetan named these "analogies of proper proportionality." The terms from Cajetan tend to be employed constantly in Thomistic as well as Aristotelian scholarship, and so I use them also to designate these two kinds of analogy found in both thinkers' work.

67 We see Aquinas clearly distinguishing these two kinds of analogy of attribution in *ST* I, q. 13, a. 5, and stating that *only* the *ad alterum* attribution is valid for the creature/God relation. This is also the case in *ScG* I, c. 34, and in *De potentia Dei*, q. 7, a. 7: "Now this kind of predication is twofold. The first is when one thing is predicated of two with respect to a third: thus being is predicated of quantity and quality with respect to substance. The other is when a thing is predicated of two by reason of a relationship between these two: thus being is predicated of substance and quantity. In the first kind of predication the two things must be preceded by something to which each of them bears some relation: thus substance has a respect to quantity and quality: whereas in the second kind of predication this is not necessary, but one of the two must precede the other. Wherefore since nothing precedes God, but he precedes the creature, the second kind of analogical predication

The *ad alterum* analogy of attribution, meanwhile, is based on the relation of "one to another." Aquinas gives the example of a quantity that is said to "be" because of its relation to the being of the substance of a reality. The quantity is ontologically dependent upon that to which it is related etiologically. He also gives the entirely different example of the relation of creatures to the Creator. The former are said to exist because of the relation to another, the primary being, who causes their existence and their perfections.[68]

Two things should be noted concerning this particular form of analogy. The first is that it is based upon the causality of creation. It is because God is the transcendent, primary cause of being that all secondary realities exist in a relation of ontological dependence upon him. Therefore, it is not surprising to find Aquinas indicating a profound relationship between the real distinction of *esse* and essence in creatures and their analogy *ad alterum* in relation to the Creator. The fact that each singular being in act is caused by God and resembles God's subsistent being in its own singular act of being means that all bear some likeness to their transcendent cause as the "other" from whom they receive their existence. Consequently, for Aquinas the most perfect name attributable to God is that of "He Who Is" (Ex 3:14), signifying his perfection and uniqueness in existence.[69] It follows from this that certain perfections of creatures can be attributed to the

---

is applicable to him but not the first." Clearly Aquinas wishes to exclude the possibility of God and creatures being understood under a common analogical term that includes both, such as "being," "truth," and so on. Whether this is a legitimate concern or not, his view clearly differs from the Scotist notion of the transcendentals and the recourse to a theory of univocity (the logical core of a concept of "ens" as potentially applicable to both finite and infinite being). It also differs from Suarez's *analogia entis*. The latter understands both God and created being within one subject matter in analogical fashion (according to a *multa ad unum* analogy, in which God is the unique *ens* in reference to which the *multa* of all creatures are understood). I will return to this structure of thought in examining the metaphysics of Karl Rahner.

68 *ST* I, q. 13, a. 5: "Therefore it must be said that these names are said of God and creatures in an analogous sense, that is, according to proportion. Now names are thus used in two ways: either according as many things are proportionate to one [*multa habent proportionem ad unum*], thus for example *healthy* is predicated of medicine and urine in relation and in proportion to health of a body, of which the former is the sign and the latter the cause: or according as one thing is proportionate to another [*unum habet proportionem ad alterum*], thus *healthy* is said of medicine and animal, since medicine is the cause of health in the animal body. And in this way some things are said of God and creatures analogically, and not in a purely equivocal or in a purely univocal sense. For we can name God only from creatures. Thus, whatever is said of God and creatures is said according to the relation of a creature to God as its principle and cause, wherein all perfections of things pre-exist excellently."

69 *ST* I, q. 13, a. 11.

Creator analogically *ad alterum*, as to the one from whom they receive these perfections, and who possesses them in a supereminent way.[70]

---

[70] A number of twentieth-century scholars have argued that the *ad alterum* form of analogical thought predominates exclusively in Aquinas's mature thought. See especially Bernard Montagnes, *La doctrine de l'analogie de l'être d'aprés saint Thomas d'Aquin* (Louvain: Éditions Peeters, 1963); but also Étienne Gilson, *Le Thomisme*, 6th edition (Paris: J. Vrin, 1965), 123–25; Forest, *La Structure Métaphysique du Concret*, 10–23. Montagnes, for example (*La doctrine*, 81–114) noted that Aquinas designates analogical attribution to God in terms of proportional analogy in *De ver.*, q. 11, a. 2 (a work written between 1256 and 1259), and that later he uses instead the *ad alterum* analogy consistently (in texts such as *ST* I, q. 13, a. 5). He develops from such an analysis an evolutionary thesis concerning Aquinas's metaphysical thought, which he claims moves from a more Aristotelian conception of being to a development of more Neoplatonic elements in light of the real distinction.

    The context for such claims is related to a reaction against the predominating use of the analogy of proper proportionality in anterior scholastic thought, as exemplified by Cajetan and reproduced in the thought of Garrigou-Lagrange, which I discussed in chapter 1 of this study. Garrigou-Lagrange attributes, for example, "being" to accidents, to substance, and to God in a proportional way, without sufficient mediation by recourse to the analogy of attribution for understanding either the relation of the accidents to the substance (*multa ad unum*) or the actuality of created being to the transcendent being (*ad alterum*). He defends the primacy of the analogy of proper proportionality in *Dieu, Son Existence et Sa Nature* (Paris: Beuschesne, 1914), 530–31. For a similar argument, see also Jacques Maritain, *Les Degrés du Savoir* (Paris: Désclée de Brouwer, 1932), 821–25.

    As Leo Elders has pointed out, however ("St. Thomas Aquinas' Commentary on the *Metaphysics* of Aristotle," 129–31), the analogy of proper proportionality is frequently discussed favorably by Aquinas in his Aristotelian commentaries written near the end of his life. Therefore it is clearly erroneous to think of him as rejecting its use altogether, even if he does not employ it to discuss the similitude between the world and God. Aquinas even uses the proportional analogy alongside both kinds of analogy of attribution in his *In I Ethic.*, lec. 6–7, especially paragraphs 94–95, where he follows Aristotle's rejection of the Platonic notion of a universal, univocal good and formal cause of all participated goods, and assents to the divisions of goodness according to the analogical divisions of the categories, the diverse forms of substance and the diverse actuations of operations. This would suggest that the right use of this analogy permits one to understand creatures in their likenesses to one another, and consequently is a precondition for understanding these creatures in turn as analogically similar (*ad alterum*) to the Creator. The two forms of analogy therefore "interlock" and complement each other in Aquinas's mature thought. Furthermore, the discontinuity between *De ver.*, q. 11, a. 2, and later texts should not be exaggerated: in both kinds of texts he is reacting against the use of a *multa ad unum* analogy to speak of creatures and God in relation to common being (as we have seen in Avicenna, and later in Suarez), and is seeking another way of expressing analogy. This intention was progressively clarified through recourse to the *ad alterum* analogy.

Second, however, for Aquinas, this primary cause is known only very imperfectly. He distinguishes between univocal causes, which produce their own natural form in another (for example, through biological reproduction of like by like), and equivocal causes, in which some determination present in a form is transmitted by effect upon another (such as the sun causing heat in earthly bodies).[71] In the first form of causality, the cause and effect share a common *ratio* (i.e., the same essential characteristics, determination, or intelligibility). So a human being begets human beings, trees spawn saplings, and so on. In the second form of causality, however, the cause and effect do not share a common *ratio*: the sun causes man and plants to be, but does not share in their specific natures. Aquinas says that God is a unique kind of equivocal cause. In addition to not sharing a common nature with creatures, God is not in a common genus, species, or category with any created being.[72] God is not even a participant of the "common being" present in all things. Thus, as an equivocal cause of creation, he is utterly transcendent with respect to his effects and is not directly namable by any genus. Consequently, the philosophical ascent from effects to their transcendent cause cannot be made by means of univocal forms of predication (the identification of properties somehow common to both God and creatures). God is not in a common *ratio* with creatures—even one of a transcendental property of being (i.e., *esse*, goodness, unity, or truth).[73]

Because God transcends infinitely his effects that we experience, his perfections cannot be apprehended intuitively, nor can created perfections be attributed to him in univocal terms. How, then, does God resemble his effects? Aquinas bases his affirmation of a likeness between God's perfection and those perfections of the creatures that are his effects on the principle that effects resemble the forms that cause them: "The form of an effect, therefore, is certainly found in some measure in a transcending cause, but according to another mode and another way."[74] While all of the perfections proper to creatures can be found in God as their transcendent

---

[71] *ScG* I, c. 29, 31; *ST* I, q. 13, a. 2.

[72] *ScG* I, c. 23–25, 32; see the commentary by Kretzmann, *The Metaphysics of Theism*, 147–57.

[73] *ST* I, q. 13, a. 2: "Now since our intellect knows God from creatures, it knows him as far as creatures represent him. Now it was shown above that God prepossesses in himself all the perfections of creatures, being himself simply and universally perfect. Hence every creature represents him, and is like him so far as it possesses some perfection: yet it represents him not as something of the same species or genus, but as the excelling principle of whose form the effects fall short, although they derive some kind of likeness thereto, even as the forms of inferior bodies represent the power of the sun."

[74] *ScG* I, c. 29.

cause in some way, such perfections *as we know them* are proper to creatures. Perfections in color, physical strength, memory, and the like reveal
something of God's being in his virtual power and goodness (since he created them), but their qualities or natures are not attributable to God
except metaphorically. Other perfections unqualifiably designate a perfection without defect and are potentially attributable to God *per se*, such as
goodness, wisdom, and being (*esse*).[75] Even in these cases, however, such
proper attributions of names are possible only either through the negation
of properties found in temporal, imperfect beings (such as when we say
God is immutable, or infinite) or because they express a relation of causal
dependence, as when we say that God is the "highest good," "subsistent
being," "the first truth," and so on. The *mode* of the existence of these
properties in God, therefore, must be other than in creatures and cannot
be apprehended per se or represented by knowledge drawn from secondary beings.[76] Nevertheless, such perfections must simultaneously be attributed to God in a positive and supereminent way. Aquinas's natural
theology, therefore, is profoundly apophatic yet only in a qualified way.[77]

Personal Operations Attributed to God

At the beginning of this chapter I mentioned the important part that the personal operations of intelligence and will play for Aquinas in his clarification
of the analogical names of God. It is important to note that Aquinas does not
attempt to prove God's existence from the metaphysical examination of
human personal acts. (This point will be of consequence for my examination
of Karl Rahner, in particular.) Nevertheless, he does note himself that Aristotle in *Metaphysics*, Book *Λ*, has demonstrated that God, who is primary substance and actuality, is also intellectual operation having himself as his
primary intellectual object, and that this contemplative life *is* God's subsistent

---

[75] *ScG* I, c. 30.

[76] *ScG* I, c. 30.

[77] Aquinas clearly differs from Maimonides, who affirmed that the only natural
knowledge of God is equivocal and apophatic, such that when we say God is living, for example, we mean only that he is the cause of living beings and is not like
any inanimate thing. Instead Aquinas thinks we can speak about God's relation
toward creatures as giving the perfections that we discover in them as his effects.
Consequently, even if we do not know per se the mode in which such perfections
exist in the first cause, we can attribute them supereminently to him as having
them (positively) in a primary sense. See *ST* I, q. 13, a. 2: "So when we say, *God is
good*, the meaning is not, *God is the cause of goodness*, or, *God is not evil*; but the
meaning is, *Whatever good we attribute to creatures, pre-exists in God*, and in a more
excellent and higher way. Hence it does not follow that God is good, because He
causes goodness; rather, on the contrary, He causes goodness in things because He
is good." I will return to these issues in chapter 8.

being.[78] Aquinas will attempt to flesh out this demonstration of the personal nature of the first cause *after* his demonstrations of God's existence and after his eliminations of imperfections proper to created substance and actuality.[79] He will treat at length, then, the immanent operation of divine life, not by studying analogies from substance and actuality, essence and *esse*, but instead by examining "secondary acts" (i.e., what Aristotle has called operational acts), the operations of intellect and will that are proper to the rational soul. Without treating his dense argumentations at length, I simply wish to note here that Aquinas's strongest argumentation is based upon the previously established points: the necessary existence of an analogy between the perfections of creatures and the transcendent being of God, who is the universal author of perfection. Aquinas develops this point by employing one of the Aristotelian principles from Book Θ, 8, mentioned in the previous chapter: the actuality of operations of a given nature depends upon the substance in actuality. If this substantial actuality is dependent upon another, then the actuality of its operations also depends upon the other. For Aquinas, this is, of course, true of all things particularly in relation to God the Creator as the primary being in actuality and cause of the being in act of all others. Therefore, St. Thomas reasons, the perfections proper to the forms of created things are received from their transcendent source, in whom such perfections exist in a higher state, separated from the imperfections implicit within creaturely existence.[80] Why, though, should intellect (and with intellect, will and personhood) be attributed to God's perfection in a proper way? Here Aquinas makes use of an argument from the perfection of the intellectual faculty as that which is most noble among creatures (and thus most perfect). The intellect is capable in a certain way of becoming all things through knowledge of

---

[78] *ST* I, q. 14, a. 4.

[79] *ST* I, q. 14, prologue: "Having considered what belongs to the divine substance, we have now to treat of God's operation. And since one kind of operation is immanent, and another kind of operation proceeds to the exterior effect, we treat first of knowledge and of will (for understanding abides in the intelligent agent, and will is in the one who wills); and afterwards of the power of God, the principle of the divine operation as proceeding to the exterior effect." Aquinas thus follows precisely the order of Metaphysics Θ, 8. After treating the primacy of actuality with regard to the substance as regards God, he will now treat the primacy of actuality as regards operation (or secondary *entelecheia*). Movement, meanwhile, was considered by Aristotle an imperfect form of operation (transitive acts, as opposed to immanent acts), and Aquinas will transform the notion of transitive operation analogically to speak of God's creative power, having for its exterior effect the giving of being, as well as divine providence.

[80] *ScG* I, c. 44; *ST* I, q. 14, a. 1, ad 1: Aquinas notes that the perfections of God cannot be qualities, but must be his substance. This corresponds closely with Metaphysics Θ, 9, 1051a4–21 and Λ, 6, 1071b13–25, on the identification of quality and substance, and second and first *entelecheia*, in the perfect actuality of separate substance.

them: it contains a capacity for universality, and is therefore immaterial. This
gives the intellect a kind of potentially universal power (for knowing all
things), and it permits the soul to attain a teleological end *within itself*
(through the immanent operations of knowing and of contemplation).[81]
Immateriality, universality, and spiritual power are perfections of the intellect
that are not limited uniquely to the mode of being proper to creatures. They
can be attributed analogically to the first cause. God, insofar as he is the universal cause of all beings and is himself without potentiality or matter, must
be said to be immaterial. Insofar as he is perfect, he must be said to contain
his perfection within himself through his own operation (of self-contemplation and love), and insofar as he is the universal cause of all beings, he must
be said to know such beings universally, and to give being to them through
his own power, which is proper to divine understanding.

Aquinas therefore affirms, like Aristotle, that God is wisdom and that
this wisdom is his very substance and actuality.[82] This analogical form of
predication will also allow Aquinas to develop a theory of God's will, love,
and personal nature.[83] He will ultimately complete his treatment of the
analogical nature of the relationship between God and creation in terms of
an artistic analogy. God creates the beings whose essential determinations
he has thought, in accord with his own wisdom and self-contemplation,
giving them being by the power of his creative act.[84]

Aquinas and Ontotheology

The Kantian and Heideggerian objections to natural knowledge of God
were considered in chapter 1: natural theology is inevitably ontotheological
because it attempts to study the conditions of existence for any possible
being. To do so it must have recourse to a consideration of the immanent

---

[81] See *ScG* I, c. 44; *ST* I, q. 14, a. 1.

[82] *ST* I, q. 14, a. 1, ad 2: "Whatever is divided and multiplied in creatures exists in
God simply and unitedly. Now man has different kinds of knowledge, according
to the different objects of his knowledge. He has *intelligence* as regards the knowledge of principles; he has *science* as regards knowledge of conclusions; he has *wisdom*, according as he knows the highest cause; he has *counsel* or *prudence*,
according as he knows what is to be done. But God knows all these by one simple
act of knowledge. . . . Hence the simple knowledge of God can be named by all
these names; in such a way, however, that there must be removed from each of
them, so far as they enter into the divine predication, everything that savors of
imperfection; and everything that expresses perfection is to be retained in them."
In *ScG* I, c. 45, and *ST* I, q. 14, a. 4, Aquinas offers arguments to demonstrate
that God's act of understanding is his absolutely simple being. A detailed study of
this argumentation is offered by Kretzmann, *The Metaphysics of Theism*, 169–96.

[83] *ScG* I, c. 72–80; *ST* I, q. 19, 20, 29.

[84] *ST* I, q. 15, a. 2.

laws of human systematic thinking (i.e., principles of causality and sufficient reason) that are employed when metaphysicians attempt to explain
sensible reality. The use of these principles eventually requires (or invites)
the invocation of an aprioristic concept of God in order to explain the sum
total of all possible knowledge and experience. This structure of thinking
places God at the summit of the science of metaphysics and simultaneously
makes him the ultimate explanatory principle of human understanding.
God is thereby assimilated by natural theology into its own systematic representation of "being," and in this process the divine is inevitably conceived
according to a quasi-univocal logic (i.e., in terms of dependent beings), as
the "supreme being" who alone is self-caused (*causa sui*).

By these standards of measure, however, Aquinas's methodological
procedure cannot be characterized as ontotheological.[85] His reflections
begin not from a consideration of possible beings, but from the analysis of
beings that exist. As he adopts from Aristotle a causal analysis of being that
is based on an analogical understanding of the principles of being, his
metaphysics leads not to a consideration of the immanent laws of human
understanding, but to an analysis of the metaphysical structure of concrete
beings, in terms of substance and accidents, actuality and potency. The
notion of God is not virtually implicit within this initial study of *ens*, and
God is not included within the subject of metaphysics. Thomistic philosophical approaches to God, then, do not depend upon aprioristic conceptions of the divine. Instead, God's existence must be demonstrated
uniquely by a posteriori, causal arguments based upon the consideration of
effects, which require an extrinsic, transcendent cause.

Furthermore, it is not clear in what way one might coherently argue
that Aquinas's methodology assimilates God to the logic of intra-worldly
being. On the contrary, analogical reflection concerning beings we experience paves the way for a more ultimate analogical reflection about God
that respects the divine transcendence and incomprehensibility. The discovery of God's causality of existence in creatures permits an analogical
attribution of perfections to God *ad alterum*, which implies no apprehension of God's essence or nature. The being and perfections of God are not
included within a common *ratio* alongside those of creatures. God for
Aquinas is not *causa sui*—nor could he be—because the latter notion
implies composition, and God escapes all real composition of *esse* and
essence: his transcendent being is entirely simple.[86] Personal attributes of
intellect and will can and should be predicated of God, but only while

---

85 For a more detailed expression of this argument concerning Aquinas's thought, see
    the analysis of Boulnois, *l'Être et représentation*, 457–62.
86 On this last point, see the interesting line of argument by Jean-Luc Marion in his
    "Saint Thomas d'Aquin et l'onto-théo-logie," 31–66.

affirming simultaneously that we do not know the personal nature of the Godhead per se, as it transcends infinitely its created effects.

A Restatement of the Problems

In spite of the great clarity of the metaphysical and theological reflections of Aquinas, there are many difficulties that result from any attempt to articulate a Thomistic philosophical metaphysics within a modern context. In briefly discussing five of these puzzles, I will also recapitulate themes mentioned in previous chapters of this book. Because these are all issues reflected upon by the modern Thomists under consideration in the next section of this book, the clarification of these difficulties will introduce the study that follows.

First, I have mentioned St. Thomas's firm affirmations that specifically philosophical discoveries are natural (proper to our created capacity for natural understanding), and have their own principles even when they are articulated within the context of *sacra doctrina*. Such is presumably the case, therefore, for the metaphysical themes that I have described above, which Aquinas claims unambiguously are discoveries of reason (such as that of the *esse*/essence distinction, the philosophical discovery of creation, the metaphysics of participated being, the attribution of personal perfections to God). Nevertheless, such theories are articulated within a medieval cultural context in which a distinctly theological mode of investigation prevails; it is no secret that Aquinas does not give us a specifically philosophical *via inventionis* for many of his key metaphysical affirmations. (This arguably is the case even for the *esse*/essence distinction, which was articulated within the context of a Christian theological study of creation.) Much of Aquinas's metaphysics, therefore, is developed, as Norman Kretzmann has stated, from the top down: in reflecting on creation as seen in light of its relation to God the Creator. Modern thinkers attempting to rearticulate Thomistic metaphysics in the wake of Kant and Heidegger have been very sensitive to this fact. Is it in fact possible to develop a monotheistic metaphysics philosophically without logical dependency upon the theological presuppositions of *sacra doctrina*? If so, in what way? If not, is there any possibility of a distinctly natural knowledge of God?

Second, I have discussed the fact that Aquinas adopts (and reworks) the Aristotelian causal study of being as substance and accidents, actuality and potentiality. Yet how is this study related to the metaphysical developments proper to Aquinas (which I have just listed) that are clearly absent from Aristotle's thought? Can an Aristotelian *via inventionis* for philosophical theology be made (or altered?) to account for the metaphysics of the *esse*/essence distinction, or of participated being? Or is the inverse necessary? Does the

Aristotelianism of Aquinas need to be radically reinterpreted in light of his "Christian metaphysics" of created, participated *esse*? Are these two options truly opposed? Is there a clearly identifiable homogeneity within the metaphysical thought of Aquinas in this respect?

Third, I have noted above that Aquinas not only adopts the Aristotelian theory of the equivocal signification of the notion of being, but also develops this theory in unique ways. He adopts from Aristotle the analogy of proper proportionality and the analogy of attribution *multa ad unum* or *pros hen*, but simultaneously construes in a very original way a third analogy (*ad alterum*) in order to speak about the analogical relation between a created reality and its transcendent, creative cause. How, then, are these diverse analogical ways of thinking about being related to one another? Can they be ordered within a unified causal analysis of being (of substance/accidents and actuality/potentiality), such as that which Aquinas adopted from Aristotle? But if this is so, how is this causal analysis of Aristotle related to the metaphysics of creation, in terms of the *esse*/essence distinction? If a response to these questions can be found, surely this will permit us to clarify how *ad alterum* analogical predication (itself based upon knowledge of God's equivocal creative causality) is conceptually related to Aquinas's own evident use of a causal analysis of being.

The treatment of these previous issues prepares the response to a fourth question: how can a Thomist attain demonstrative knowledge of God that is analogical, based upon a causal study of the beings we experience? Fifth, how may the operations proper to the human person (acts of intelligence and will) tell us something about being that is eventually applicable to the transcendent being of God, analogically? Only the answer to such questions permits one to affirm absolutely the existence of a philosophical *wisdom*, because it permits the justification of the affirmation of the transcendent truth and goodness of God. If the living stars no longer play an intermediary role for the articulation of this understanding, could the human person have this role instead? If man is the only personal being of which we have a direct philosophical experience, how can he reveal something of being (through his spiritual operations), analogically attributable to God's subsistent being in a proper way?

In the next three chapters I will examine how three modern Thomists, Gilson, Maritain, and Rahner, all sought to respond in various ways to the issues mentioned above. Each of them examines topics that lie at the heart of any integral response to the modern critique of natural theology, and each contributes partial solutions to the problem. However, I also hope to show that each neglects in some fashion important dimensions of Aquinas's causal metaphysics. Correspondingly, each makes use of one of the three forms of analogical predication from Aquinas in ways that discriminate unnecessarily

against the other two. For Gilson, a theologically inspired metaphysical doctrine of creation is substituted, in some respects, for an Aristotelian analysis
of causes, and this leads to an exclusive emphasis on the *ad alterum* analogical thought of Aquinas. This usage threatens to impose a Christian theology
of creation upon the metaphysical study of being, such that all secondary
beings are conceived from the beginning of metaphysics as participated *esse*
in relation to a primary notion of unparticipated, pure *esse*. For Maritain,
the idea of an "intuition of being" yields transcendental notions that substitute for a causal analysis of being. This leads to an exclusive use of the
analogy of proper proportionality (as I have argued in chapter 1 for Garrigou-Lagrange). This usage threatens to found a notion of the divine
within a quasi-univocal understanding of being, attributed to accidents, to
substance, and to divine being in proportionally analogical ways. The passage to predication of attributes to God is based no longer on a causal
demonstration of the Creator, but on a logical extension of concepts. For
Rahner, an aprioristic "pre-apprehension" of the infinite *esse* of God acts as
a kind of substitute for an a posteriori causal demonstration of God's existence. This leads to an exclusive use of the *multa ad unum* analogy, which
in turn threatens to engulf God and creatures within a common science of
transcendentals (not entirely unlike what Aquinas warned against). Such
thinking makes God identical with the greatest possible metaphysical truth
that man can conceive of. Each of these imbalances implies something akin
to the metaphysical impasse of ontotheology as denoted by Kant and then
Heidegger. Avoiding such constructions, however, can be achieved by
rethinking the relation of the Thomistic analogical discourse concerning
being with respect to Aquinas's Aristotelian-inspired causal study of being.
This is the possibility I will explore in chapter 7.

PART III

CHAPTER 4

Exodus 3:14, the Real Distinction, and Theo-ontology: The Case of Étienne Gilson

A QUINAS CLAIMS unambiguously that there is a rational, natural basis for the affirmation of the existence of God. He simultaneously holds that this God who is known indirectly by reason is the very God in whom Christians believe (otherwise) by faith. If St. Thomas's metaphysical reflection is conducted under the illumining light of revelation, then, it nevertheless has its own natural structure of reflection and *via inventionis,* or way of progressive discovery. Thus, while Aquinas does not attempt to construct a natural theology separated from theological faith, he nevertheless does provide distinctly metaphysical argumentations for monotheism from within the purview of Christian theology. What, then, is the possibility of our identifying a structure of natural theological reasoning that moves from beings that are creatures to God? And how does this mode of reflection alert us to the truth of Aquinas's affirmation of a composition in created being: one constituted by the real distinction between essence and existence?

Étienne Gilson is a thinker of central importance for these questions, not only because of his great contribution to the renewal of medieval studies in the twentieth century, but because he was acutely sensitive to (and fascinated by) the paradox of a Christian metaphysics, which unfolds under the influences of revelation, but which is formally distinct from the latter. Moreover, he developed such a notion in explicit reaction to the intellectual work of Kant and Heidegger, with their prohibitions on any form of natural theology as ontotheology. In attempting to interpret natural knowledge of God according to Aquinas in terms of the real distinction between existence and essence, he insisted on the qualitatively distinct character of St. Thomas's metaphysics in comparison to that of Aristotle,

103

and believed that this understanding of metaphysics could respond effectively to the criticisms of Kant and Heidegger. However, he also moved
progressively throughout his life toward a properly theological notion of
Christian metaphysics, or toward what I, following Yves Floucat, will call
a "Theo-ontology."[1] The latter is a metaphysical view of God and the
world accessible *only in faith and by means of revelation*, toward which
philosophical reason can in turn tend, and which it can approximate, but
which it cannot procure on its own. Theology becomes, in this vision of
metaphysics, the lodestar toward which philosophical wisdom may orient
itself, but without which the latter is rendered inefficacious.

In this chapter I set out to do two things. In the first part of the chapter I will examine Gilson's thought concerning natural rational access to the
discovery of existence in beings we experience (by means of the judgment
of existence) in contra-distinction to what he took to be the "essentialism"
of Aristotle. I will discuss his corresponding emphasis on the importance of
the real distinction between essence and existence, and its place in the discovery of God by means of rational demonstration. This form of thinking
is particularly indebted to recourse to the *ad alterum* analogy for understanding the relation between creatures and God. I will especially underscore the crisis of foundations that this form of argumentation underwent
for Gilson from 1950 onward, and explain how this led to his own particular form of Theo-ontological thinking later in life. In the second part of
the chapter I will evaluate critically several of the standpoints Gilson takes
as given. On the one hand, I will discuss why I think that Gilson's notion
of the judgment of existence as an entry point into metaphysical realism
does provide an important response to concerns raised by Kantian philosophy. Most especially, however, I will argue that there is a philosophy of existence in Aristotle, and that it is reflected in Aquinas's conscious
interpretations of Aristotle. While this Aristotelian philosophy is not the
immediate source of real distinction metaphysics of Aquinas, there are ways
in which Aristotle's thought, at least as it is read by Aquinas, can be seen to
open from the interior toward the heights of Thomistic thinking on *esse*
and essence, and created being. This latter point is particularly important.
For if the causal thinking of Aristotle can potentially be seen as being in
organic logical continuity with Aquinas's metaphysics of creation, then the
Theo-ontological option of the later Gilson (in which revelation in some
real sense provides the principles of metaphysical understanding) is not
necessary, nor desirable. Instead, an organic Thomistic causal metaphysics
must be articulated that encompasses both the discoveries of the Aristotelian distinctions and the Thomistic metaphysics of creation.

---

[1] See the study of Yves Floucat, "Étienne Gilson et la métaphysique thomiste de
l'acte d'être," *Revue Thomiste* 94 (1994): 360–95.

Existence and the Critique of Essentialist Metaphysics

The French philosopher and historian Étienne Gilson (1884–1978) is a figure of central importance for modern Thomistic studies. As a Roman Catholic layman and medieval historian in the secularized Sorbonne of the first half of the twentieth century, he was confronted with the challenges of post-Kantian and -Heideggerian thought in a particularly demanding way. While Gilson was deeply influenced by the spirit of *Aeterni Patris*, he maintained a very critical stance with regard to scholastic intellectual circles, and his destructive project with regard to much in the Thomistic tradition was part of an attempt to reconstruct a new point of departure for understanding Aquinas's metaphysics. In distancing himself from both the ecclesiastical Thomists of his age and the secular rationalism of the French university, he found a certain support for his rereading of the history of metaphysics in Heidegger's thought, and sought a way to transcend the Kantian impasses of the critique of metaphysics based upon the Thomistic doctrine of *esse*. Before treating his metaphysical proposals, however, I will briefly discuss his critical stance toward classical ontology.

Gilson's critique of classical and Enlightenment metaphysics is many-sided, both historically and philosophically. In diverse ways, he concentrates on the obscuring of the awareness of being as an effect of conceptualist essentialism. This latter term denotes a kind of rationalization of the real, by which the analysis of mental constructs derived from reality is substituted for an authentic, or sufficiently profound, encounter with the world in its unthematizable existence.[2] Such thought parallels in many ways Heidegger's theory that the study of *seiendes* or *ens* in the western metaphysical tradition has hidden the problem of *Sein*. Gilson differs from Heidegger, however, on the meaning he assigns such words and on

---

[2] Gilson's most important examinations of the history of metaphysics are *Being and Some Philosophers*, 1949, and especially *l'Être et l'Essence*, 1st ed. 1948, 2nd ed. 1972. In the latter work he studies the prefigurations of modern rationalist ontologies in the thought of Plato, Aristotle, Avicenna, and Scotus, which took form in Suarez's philosophy, and which culminated in the essentialisms of Descartes, Leibniz, and Wolff. These in turn stimulated the critique of Kant and the subsequent death of metaphysics in modernity. In his analysis of Suarez, Gilson sees "a complete and definitive affirmation of essence free from any non-conceivable element that reason would be incapable of assimilating integrally. . . . It is [from Suarez onward] that, in some sense reacting against the moderate teaching of Thomism itself, the philosophy of the European schools became 'essentialized,' taking the form of a tentative to deduce the real analytically from a catalogue of essences, defined once and for all. . . . However, for this to transpire, it is first necessary that metaphysics assign to itself as its proper object essence alone, to the exclusion of this 'unknown' which is always suspect to reason: the act of existence" (152).

the content of the metaphysics of being as *esse*.[3] Here I will mention only three elements of Gilson's critique of essentialism, which have an important bearing upon the issues discussed above.

First, Gilson famously insists on a fundamental differentiation between the metaphysics of Aristotle and the thought of Aquinas. The former thinker understood being as substance (*ousia*) and therefore as a formal determination (a species of essentialism). "The de-existentialized *ousia* of Aristotle does not permit one to resolve the problem of existence; it does not even permit one to offer an adequate interpretation of this kind of causality."[4] Because Aristotle's philosophy does not permit one to acknowledge existence in its singularity, beyond all essential determinations, it cannot adequately understand the efficient causality of *esse* as such. By the same measure, creation—that form of causation exerted by God as Creator of existent being—is literally unthinkable for Aristotle. Aquinas, by contrast, was able to consider the problem of existence as the central problem of metaphysics. This insight came from his unique understanding of the *esse*/essence distinction, and was related to his Christian conception of the creation of being.

Second (and analogously), Gilson criticized the modern rationalist ontologies he claimed were derived from Suarez due to their conceptualization of being, which implied a loss of contact with sensitive experience of the inassimilable brute existence of reality. In the place of an experiential inquiry concerning the being of that which exists, this tradition had substituted a metaphysics of possible being structured by axioms of understanding, such as the principles of non-contradiction, identity, causality, and sufficient reason. He noted what he took to be the infiltration that such rationalist idealism had made into nineteenth- and twentieth-century Thomistic scholasticism, under the title of "critical realism." Such Thomistic

---

3 Gilson admired in Heidegger's thought his original search for being, in critical distantiation from post-Cartesian rationalism. He discusses his admiration for and identification with Heidegger under certain aspects (as well as certain differences) in *l'Être et l'Essence*, 2nd ed., 350–78, and in the essays of *Constantes Philosophiques de l'Être*, ed. Monique Couratier (Paris: J. Vrin, 1983), 168–230. 204: "It is true that, for the most part, traditional metaphysics was characterized by a kind of constant flight from being, and by a marked preference for 'entity': *ens in quantum ens*. It is almost always here, in fact, that metaphysics locates its own object [of investigation]. To the extent that this is the case, the Heideggerian revindication of the rights of being is well-founded, and the common-place metaphysics of 'entity' must be surpassed." This passage echoes the introduction of *Being and Time*, written in 1929. Pierre Aubenque, "Étienne Gilson et la Question de l'Être," in *Étienne Gilson et Nous* (Paris: J. Vrin, 1980), 79–92, has shown the influence of Heidegger upon Gilson as early as 1941, in the fourth edition of *Le Thomisme*, in which the author began to form the mature positions that characterized his later thought.

4 *L'Être et l'Essence*, 65. On Aristotle, see 49–65.

strategies of defense against Descartes's skepticism and Kant's critiques, he argued, made use of the same starting points for ontology as the thinkers who contributed to the discrediting of metaphysics.[5]

Third, therefore, Gilson accused the two principal ecclesiastical schools of Thomistic studies (Rome and Louvain) of holding to principles foreign to and incompatible with Aquinas's thought. He affirmed that Garrigou-Lagrange of the Roman school maintained a conception of the analogy of being between God and the world uniquely in terms of proper proportionality (following the Cajetanian tradition) and that this transformed analogical predication to God into a form of quasi-univocal Scotism (for Gilson, also a form of essentialism).[6] Instead, he would insist on the necessity of recourse to the analogy of attribution *ad alterum* in order to speak of God, as is manifest in texts of Aquinas. He also distanced himself from the Louvain school, because of its interest in critical epistemology as a means of defending metaphysical realism, and he rejected the ambition of Cardinal Mercier and his disciples to articulate a philosophical order of Thomistic studies completely independently of the *theological* order of inquiry present in the two *Summas* of Aquinas. Instead, Gilson wished to propose an order of metaphysics developed within the context of the Christian philosophy of Aquinas, which maintained the theological teleology of such inquiry, in contra-distinction to the modern (Suarezian) ontological study of being as indifferent to either God or creatures. It is Christian theology, Gilson claims, that gave Aquinas the *philosophical* order of inquiry that we find in his writings. In the *Summa theologiae*, for example, St. Thomas passes from the study of being immediately to the study of God, and in relation to God, to the study of creation, human beings, human acts, and so on. This is the order of inquiry that should serve as a model for Christian metaphysics.[7]

---

5 In this respect see the study *Réalisme Thomiste et Critique de la Connaissance* (1939). Gilson did not reject the existence of such critical principles of metaphysical reasoning (most of which are explicit or implicit in Aquinas's writings), but in an noteworthy article in the *Revue Thomiste* 52 (1952), "Les Principes et les Causes," which was reedited and republished in *Constantes Philosophiques*, 53–84, he argues that the principles of non-contradiction, identity, and causality are critical axioms common to all acts of understanding, but actuated only through experiential contact with existent reality, which is given through the judgment of existence. This latter activity initially brings us into contact with being, and permits the formation of the critical axioms through reflection upon experience. Gilson studies the history of these axioms in modern thought and affirms that the principle of sufficient reason originates with Leibniz and not Aquinas. He thinks it can be defended, however, as a "Thomistic" principle, if it is understood as a modification of the principle of causality.

6 *Introduction à la Philosophie Chrétienne* (Paris: J. Vrin, 1960), 142.

7 *Le Thomisme*, 5th edition (Paris: J. Vrin, 1948), 16: "The theology of St. Thomas is that of a philosopher, but his philosophy is that of a saint. . . . Because of this one sees why it is natural to expound the philosophy of St. Thomas according to

Gilson's virulent criticisms of diverse non-Thomistic metaphysical traditions reveal a desire to search out a new point of departure for the study
of metaphysics and a new *via inventionis* that one might uncover directly
from the texts of Aquinas himself, without recourse to the subsequent
scholastic tradition. Gilson maintained that the theological order of metaphysical inquiry in the *Summa contra Gentiles* and *Summa theologiae* did
not constrain the philosophical character of Aquinas's enterprise, but
instead enhanced it. The effects of grace upon nature were to restore a
proper order to philosophical reflection manifest in these works, permitting an ontological reflection free from any anthropocentric rationalist
idealism.[8] This theological order of inquiry, however, is not that of
Aquinas in his statements concerning philosophy, and the *via inventionis*
proposed by Gilson does meet with certain difficulties, which I will mention below, as a result of his understanding of Christian philosophy and
theocentric metaphysics.[9]

---

the order of his theological reflection. . . . To extract from his theological works the
philosophical truths that they contain, and then to reconstruct them in an order
that is designated by philosophy, this would be to believe that Aquinas wished to
construct his philosophy in view of purely philosophical ends, not in view of the
ends that are proper to this Doctor of the Church." To develop a Thomist philosophy independent of this order, abstracting from Christian faith, would be to
"present a *philosophia ad mentem santi Thomae* as if it were a *philosophia ad mentem
Cartesii*" (26n3). "In a word, the true object of metaphysics is God" (28).

[8] Gilson defends this approach by invoking Aquinas's notion of the *revelabile*, that
is, of that content of revelation which can in theory be discovered naturally by
man, such as the existence and attributes of God, the immateriality of the soul,
etc. (See *ST* I, q.1, a. 3, ad 2.) His desire is to extract from Aquinas's study of *sacra
doctrina* the implicit philosophical *revelabilia* as they appear within the order of
Aquinas's reflection. Thus, this reflection will be specifically philosophical, but
ordered by superior theological influences. See *Le Thomisme*, 5th ed., 23–28.

[9] This order, which appeared already in the second edition of *Le Thomisme* (1924),
was criticized by the Dominican Pierre Mandonnet, in *Bulletin thomiste* 1 (1924):
133–36, as incompatible with Aquinas's own teaching. Mandonnet cites *ScG* II, c.
4 (as I have done in the preceding chapter), on the distinction between the philosophical and theological orders of investigation. In addition, I will only note here
that Gilson's affirmation that God is the "object" of metaphysics for Aquinas
stands in some real tension with Aquinas's own distantiation from Avicenna in his
prologue to the *Metaphysics*. Furthermore, Aquinas frequently speaks in favor of an
Aristotelian order for the study of sciences: first, logic, mathematics, natural philosophy, ethics, then metaphysics. See, for example, *Expos. de Trin.*, q. 5, a. 1; *In de
Causis, prooem.*; *In VI Ethics*, lec. 7, 1211. This order clearly contrasts with Gilson's
theological starting point for philosophy. I will examine consequences of Gilson's
via inventionis below.

The Judgment of Existence and the *Esse*/Essence Distinction

Gilson proposes a way of entry into metaphysical investigation that is experiential, based upon the intellectual apprehension of the existence, or being
in act (*esse*), of singular beings through sensible experience. In doing so, he
wishes to distance himself from Enlightenment ontology, which (to his
mind) is based upon the Scotist or Suarezian universal concept of being
(*ens*), including possible being, infinite being, and beings of reason. The
"judgment of existence" is precisely the intellectual experience that permits
the intelligence to gain contact with extrinsic, existent reality so as to be
"measured" by it, beyond all immanent logical or conceptual constructions.

> We have a concept of being [*ens*], but not of existence [*esse*]. . . .
> Saint Thomas distinguishes between two operations of understand-
> ing. The first is that which Aristotle calls the intellection of simple
> essences (*intelligentia indivisibilium*), and which consists in the
> apprehension of the essence as an indivisible. The second is that
> which consists in either a composition or a dissociation of essences in
> forming propositions. This second operation, which Saint Thomas
> calls *compositio*, is that which today we call "judgment." Both of
> these operations aim toward knowing reality, but they do not equally
> penetrate it to the same depth. Apprehension attains the essence,
> which is formulated by a definition, while judgment attains to the
> very act of existence: *prima operatio respicit quidditatem rei, secunda
> respicit esse ipsius.* (*Sent.* I, d. 19, q. 5, a. 1, ad 7). . . . That which first
> enters human understanding is, therefore, essential being, or the
> nature, but not existence. . . . That which is offered to our thought,
> when we say "exists," is the very act of existence, that is to say this
> absolute actuality that is actual existence.[10]

This judgment takes place in and through experience, presupposing
our sensible receptivity to realities, as well as the continuity of operation
between sensation and intellect. However, it attains *through* sensation the
being as such of realities experienced.

> The intellect can "see" being in the sensible things we perceive. The
> continuity between intelligence and sensation in the knowing subject
> permits this. . . . When the concept of being [*être*] is . . . abstracted
> from a concrete existent perceived by the senses, the judgment that
> predicates being of this existent, attributes it as the intellect has con-
> ceived of it, that is to say, as "seen" within the sensible reality from

---

[10] *Le Thomisme*, 5th ed., 61–62.

which it was abstracted. . . . By the same measure, the intellect appre-hends within its object, that which is most profound in it: *actus essendi*.[11]

Gilson's point is simple: the intellect operating in ordinary sensible experi-ence of reality can come to know other existent realities, each in their respective singularity, alterity, and transcendence, as existing. When we experience that a person is tall, plays the piano, laughs, is a man, can die, is rational, and so on, we also always experience that this person is, and our knowledge of the existence of the reality transcends that which we can assimilate conceptually of the essence of the person in his or her diverse qualities, measurements, relations, and the like. Such experience implies knowing something unique in each reality. Yet the awareness of the exis-tence of each being that we experience provides the possibility of universal metaphysical inquiry into the ontological construction of reality by means of analogy. The judgment of existence thus permits the application of the notion of being to all created realities, according to proper proportionality. Each singular reality is said to "be" in a unique way, according to anal-ogy.[12] This approach is not empiricist insofar as it affirms that a distinctly metaphysical reflection is necessary for a comprehension of concrete reali-ties experienced. Gilson insists, however, that the *sensible*, transconceptual, singular reality is the initial source of metaphysical knowledge. He aspires, therefore, to an experiential metaphysical realism.

Gilson's reflection passes directly from this initial experience of being to the insight into the *esse*/essence distinction. He has affirmed that the judgment of existence permits the person to attain ontological experience of the existence of the singular reality beyond all conceptual assimilations

---

11 *Réalisme Thomiste et Critique de la Connaissance*, 225–26. Clearly this text (written in 1939) differs from the one previously cited (from 1948) since here Gilson speaks of a conceptual apprehension of *esse*, whereas there he denies the existence of such a concept: *esse* is attained only in a judgment. He also denies the possibil-ity of a concept of existence in a letter to Maritain written in 1947; see *Correspon-dance 1923–1971*, ed. G. Prouvost (Paris: J. Vrin, 1991), n. 68, 166. Yet in later works, such as *Constantes Philosophiques de l'Être*, 42, 148–49, 153, 156, 166, he speaks of a conceptual intuition of *esse* mediated through sensible experience. I will return below to a discussion of the concept of *esse*.

12 Gilson does not deny the use of the analogy of proper proportionality for compar-isons between creatures, but for comparisons between creatures and God. See his "Eléments d'une métaphysique thomiste de l'être," *Autour de St. Thomas* (Paris: J. Vrin, 1983), 103: "The presence, in each substance, of an act of *esse* that is proper to it, is that which irreducibly separates Thomistic ontology from Scotist ontology. Because each being has its own *esse*, distinct from all others, 'being' cannot be predicated of two substances except analogically." See *ScG* I, c. 22 (Leon. XIII, 68): "unumquodque est per *suum* esse" (emphasis added).

of essential determinations. He also affirms, however, that this same experience permits one to attain *in the reality* something beyond the essence *of the reality*, by which it exists in act (the *actus essendi*), which Aquinas names the *esse*. In other words, in attaining to the non-assimilated, non-quidditative, extra-mental existence of the reality, one is also grasping a real distinction in the reality itself between its essence and its existence.

> If Thomistic ontology truly includes . . . [the ontology] of Aristotle, then it must truly recognize within the structure of each real being the presence of a cause of being that can be grasped by a concept, and which is the essence. But if Thomistic ontology also implies an effort to surpass the thinking of Aristotle, in identifying over and above essence an act of this same essence, then it is obliged to recognize the actuality that is proper to *esse*, which, because it transcends the essence, also transcends all concepts. . . .[13] In the doctrine of St. Thomas, the truth of judgment is based less upon the essence of things than upon their *esse*. Truth consists of the adequation of the intelligence with reality, and this finds its complete expression in the operation of the intellect which, surpassing the simple apprehension of the quiddity of a being, attains the act that causes it, because it *exists*.[14]

The judgment of existence, therefore, permits a metaphysical discovery of the real distinction in every being (*ens*) of the essential determination of the reality (*essentia*) and its existence (*esse*). It is the *esse* that provides the dynamic actuality of being to the essence such that each reality has a singularity and uniqueness, even while possessing inherent determinations that can be found in others. The awareness of the real distinction between essence and *esse* in each of the beings we experience (and in ourselves) leads Gilson to pose immediately a more ultimate question: if the existence of each reality cannot be accounted for by *what* the

---

13 *L'Être et l'Essence*, 113. Gilson problematically asserts the identity of the Thomistic essence with the Aristotelian substance, and denies knowledge of existence in Aristotle. I will return to these claims below.

14 *L'Être et l'Essence*, 122–23. Compare Aquinas, *Commentarum Sententiarium*, I, d. 19, q. 5, a. 1, *solutio*, ed. Mandonnet (Paris: P. Letheilleux, 1929), 1:486: "Cum autem in re sit quidditas ejus et suum esse, veritas fundatur in esse rei magis quam in quidditate, sicut et nomen entis ab esse imponitur; et in ipsa operatione intellectus accipientis esse rei sicut est per quamdam similationem ad ipsum, completur ratio adaequationis, in qua consistit ratio veritatis." "While, in a thing, there is its quiddity and its own existence, truth is founded more in the existence of the thing than in its quiddity, just as the name of 'being' derives from existence. And in this operation [of judgment] the intellect receives the existence of the thing as if through a certain likeness to it. By this order of adequation is attained, and it is in this that the order of truth consists" (trans. mine).

reality is essentially, and if all such realities imply an existential contingency actually (because they can be or not be) then our metaphysical awareness of their composite nature orientates us toward the question of a transcendent cause who is necessary being and who is the cause of the existence of all others:

> [This distinction] expresses the fact that a being in which the essence is not the existence does not have by itself [essentially] that which is necessary in order to exist. . . . That such beings do exist, we know by experience, because in fact we know directly only such beings as these. . . . So long as they exist, they remain beings for which the existence finds no justification from appeal to what they are essentially. This is what the distinction of essence and existence is, and it is because it is profoundly real that it obliges one to pose the problem of the cause of finite existences, which is the problem of the existence of God.[15]

Before I discuss Gilson's interpretation of Aquinas's natural theology, I will note here briefly three problems raised by his assertion that the judgment of existence attains immediately the knowledge of the real distinction above-mentioned. These are problems I will return to below. First, one must raise the question of the difference between the quidditative concept of the form of the reality and that form itself. If we only know the essential determinations of things in themselves *partially and progressively* by our quidditative concepts, then the real "essence" of the reality escapes also any absolutizing, complete intellectual assimilation. Second, is the knowledge of existence, which we attain in the most simple judgments (for example, "Paul exists"), the same as the profound metaphysical knowledge of *esse* as *actus essendi* in each reality? This would seem to require that every judgment of existence implies a profound theological perception of reality. If this is not the case, is there instead a progressive deepening of the initial awareness of existence—through a causal analysis of being—leading to the latter understanding? Otherwise stated, what role should the Aristotelian principles of substance and of actuality play in metaphysical investigation concerning being? These principles are present in Aquinas's work, but do not form part of Gilson's *via inventionis*. Aquinas's texts habitually employ the real distinction within a theological context in which the demonstrative knowledge of God is *presupposed*. Do we need to employ the principles of a causal analysis in order to demonstrate the existence of God? Perhaps it is *only then* that we can understand most radically what it means to say being is created, and that each thing

---

[15] *Le Thomisme*, 5th ed., 53.

receives its *actus essendi* from God. A third question results from these two: can the logical distinction between *esse* and essence be understood merely as a distinction of two complementary concepts corresponding diversely to one *ens*? If *ens* is understood by Aquinas as *id quod est habens esse*, then this could be suggested. *Essentia* and *esse* both designate different aspects of the *same* reality (*ens*). Therefore, one can ask, does this initial *conceptual* distinction in our way of apprehending being necessarily entail the *onto-logical* distinction between essence and existence in a given reality? As I will show below, Gilson's awareness of this latter question was to lead him to significant alterations of his thought after 1950.

An Existential Interpretation of the Five Ways

In his works written between 1940 and 1950, Gilson approaches the Five Ways of Aquinas in a twofold way: historically, with a consideration of their origins, and philosophically, based on the presupposition of the knowledge of the real distinction.[16] His historical considerations of the diverse original senses of these five ways are somewhat incidental, yet telling, for his interpretation of Thomas's treatment of them. In effect, Gilson wishes to show how Aquinas reinterpreted all five of these diverse and seemingly incompatible arguments from previous thinkers (Aristotle, Avicenna, John of Damascus) in light of his own understanding of the distinction between essence and existence. The arguments of both the *Summa contra Gentiles* and the *Summa theologiae* are thus best understood when reread in light of Thomas's early work *De ente et essentia*, and of the arguments found therein.[17] Thus Gilson is going to offer a demonstration of the existence of God based upon the discovery of *esse* as distinct from essence, a discovery that he certainly thinks is unique to Aquinas.

Gilson rejects all a priori knowledge of God, departing from ideas or preconceived understandings of the "essence" of God, such as in the case of the Ontological argument. Knowledge of that which exists begins with the objects of our sensible experience, as the measure of our true thinking. It is in the being of these realities, attained by the judgment of existence, that we must seek evidence of the necessary existence of a primary being upon which they depend.

> Because all objects of experience require God as their cause, one can begin from them in order to demonstrate that God exists, but because the existence that is given to us is not that of God, one absolutely must demonstrate [that God exists]. . . . To not see the essence of God

---

16 See most indicatively *Le Thomisme*, 5th ed. (1948), 119, and following.
17 *Le Thomisme*, 5th ed., 120.

is to not have any proper concept of God; and the latter would be necessary in order to have an [a priori] certitude of his existence. Therefore the only recourse left to man "here below" is to ascend to God by reflection, based upon the sensible knowledge we have of his effects. . . . This requires us to pass from the given existences of beings we experience to the inferred existence of their cause.[18]

He wishes to show that the real distinction between what the reality is (its essence) and its being in act (its *esse*) reveals that the reality itself cannot explain or account for its own real existence. The fact that I am a human person (with all of the acts or capacities that are herein entailed) cannot account for the fact that I am. On the contrary, my existence is something given to me that in turn permits me to be the human person that I am. The Five Ways will be reread, subsequently, as five ways of demonstrating experientially that the essence of any reality we can experience is limited existentially. It is dependent upon an act of being by which it exists, and that the essence of that thing cannot account for.

> One must then necessarily admit that the Thomistic proofs for the existence of God develop immediately upon an existential plane, as demonstrations that there exists a first cause of the existence of movements and of the beings that flow therefrom; a first existential cause of all the causes and their efficient effects; a first necessary exis-tent, cause of the actuation of all the possibles; a first term in the orders of Being, the Good and the True, cause of all that participate in these orders; a Final End, the existence of which is the "why" of all "why something exists."[19]

The limited act of being present in each reality requires in turn the neces-sary existence of a first being as its efficient cause, who is himself necessary existence, and in whom there is no real distinction between essence and existence.

> From this point of view, the proofs of the existence of God consist in connecting back in all these various orders, in the name of the princi-ple of causality, all the beings which are *ab alio* to the only being that is *a se*. The beings that are from another, which do not have in them-selves that by which they exist, are exactly these beings of which we say that the essence is in them distinct from their existence, by opposition to being per se, of which the very essence is to exist. One can say, then, that all the Thomistic proofs of the existence of God are at base the

---

[18] *Le Thomisme*, 5th ed., 84, 87.
[19] *Le Thomisme*, 5th ed., 119.

search, over and above the existences that do not suffice for themselves, for an existence that does suffice for itself, and because it suffices, can be the primary cause of all the others.[20]

The distinction between essence and existence thus appears "the work horse of all the proofs. It is not a sixth way; it is rather the metaphysical core of the five others, purged of their abstract relations of existentiality."[21] The philosopher can affirm that the essence of this primary being thus discovered is to exist. He is necessary being, and a pure act of existing (*Ipsum esse subsistens*). Consequently, he is the cause of existence for all secondary realities, which depend directly and uniquely upon him for their act of being. His existence can know no change, potentiality, participation, or dependence upon another. He is, and his unique existence suffices to itself.

In light of this natural theology, Gilson will articulate the likeness between created beings and the transcendent *esse* of God in terms of the analogy of attribution *ad alterum*. Just as the singularity of each created *esse* in relation to all others is articulated by recourse to the analogy of proper proportionality, so each one of these is in turn related by a similitude *ad alterum* to the Creator. God in his existence contains preeminently the perfections of his creatures, which resemble him as his effects.[22] Nevertheless, Gilson insists that with Aquinas there is no *ratio* common to creatures and Creator, due to the uniquely transcendent form of causality implied by creation.[23] Gilson's use of the analogies of proportionality and of attribution *ad alterum* are both centered upon the *esse*/essence distinction. One is applied horizontally, in attributing *esse* analogically to diverse created realities. The other is applied vertically, in ascribing *esse* to each reality insofar as it is relative to a primary transcendent cause of existence, from which it receives *esse*. This leaves open the question of the order between the two analogies. As I will argue below, a causal analysis of substance and actuality permits the resolution of this problem. In the absence

---

[20] *Le Thomisme*, 5th ed., 119–20. Compare *De ente*, c. IV: "Therefore it is necessary that each thing whose existence is other than its nature has its existence from another. And because whatever is from another is reduced to what is per se as its first cause, there must be some thing which is the cause of the being of all things by the fact that it is existence alone, otherwise there would be an infinite regress in causes, since everything which is not existence alone has a cause of its existence, as has been said. It is evident then that an intelligence [i.e., an angel] is form and existence, and that it has existence from the first being who is existence alone, and that this is the first cause, God."

[21] *Le Thomisme*, 5th ed., 120.

[22] *Le Thomisme*, 5th ed., 150–59.

[23] *Le Thomisme*, 5th ed., 153. This is why Gilson affirms that we can have no concept of God, but only a judgment of his existence. See also *Le Thomisme*, 6th ed., 113–29.

of such an analysis, Gilson's thought will adopt a primarily theological perspective on analogy (interpreted in light of creation), and therefore tend
toward an unbalanced insistence upon the *ad alterum* analogy.

Problems with the *Esse*/Essence Distinction

Averroes, Duns Scotus, and Suarez all criticized (in different ways) the
assertion of a real distinction between existence and essence in created
realities. Gilson was never ignorant of these positions. On the contrary, he
argued in *l'Être et l'Essence* (1948) that the incomprehension concerning
Aquinas's discovery of the *esse*/essence distinction (by Scotus and Suarez)
led to modern metaphysical "essentialism" and the loss of an authentic
philosophy of being. Throughout his life, Gilson was never to abandon
the *esse*/essence distinction and its centrality, nor this general historical
account. In 1950, however, after completing his extensive study of Duns
Scotus,[24] he began to raise questions concerning its philosophical demonstrability. From this date onward, one begins to see in his writings the
search for a new foundation for this distinction other than that of the
experience of the judgment of existence, which he had claimed attained
being in act, over and above the reality's essence. Gilson expressed his difficulties in a letter to the Dominican theologian Michel Labourdette, in
July 1950.

> I have just finished a big book on Duns Scotus. . . . Philosophically,
> how can I demonstrate that being is not *essentia realis*, but *habens esse*?
> Personally, I do not know of a demonstration [for the real distinction]
> that does not implicitly postulate the notion of *actus essendi*, and there-
> fore which is not circular. . . . I believe, meanwhile, that the notion of
> *esse* is included in that of *ens* as its principle. One either sees it, this
> principle, or one does not see it. . . . I think like you, that there exists
> a Christian metaphysics permitting the development of a scientific the-
> ology; I *know* that it is that of St. Thomas; however, because I cannot
> demonstrate it to Scotists, I ask myself how, *in fact*, a certain kind of
> theological relativism is avoidable?[25]

Significantly, one finds in public writings subsequent to this letter the
admission of the philosophical indemonstrability of a real distinction of
essence and *esse* based upon direct, sensible experience. This admission is

---

[24] Published as *Jean Duns Scot, introduction à ses positions fundamentales* (Paris: J.
Vrin, 1952).

[25] "Correspondance Étienne Gilson–Michel Labourdette," ed. H. Donneaud, *Revue
Thomiste* 94 (1994): 482–84.

made in reference to the opinions of Duns Scotus and Suarez.[26] As a consequence, Gilson was to embark upon a new foundation for this distinction that is specifically theological, and that was to characterize his philosophy as "Christian" in a unique way.

Exodus 3:14 and Theo-ontology

As Gilson's letter to Labourdette makes clear, *esse* is a notion that, for him, is both genetically and absolutely primary in philosophical reflection, and that illuminates the ultimate signification of *ens*. In other words, the right metaphysical understanding of a singular being can be grasped only when one attains its act of being as what is ultimate in that reality. This attaining of *esse* as distinct from essence, however, is henceforth suspected by Gilson of being indemonstrable from the point of view of a distinctly philosophical *via inventionis*. Gilson will claim instead that its discovery presupposes "already" a certain notion of a pure act of being, which in turn permits the experiential insight of a real distinction in the realities we experience between essence and the act of existing. Where, then, does this notion of being as *esse*, as pure existence, originate? In his later period of writing, Gilson's argument will be that it comes from Exodus 3:14, interpreted within Christian tradition as: "I am He Who Is." It is the scriptural word of God itself that reveals the notion of existence as pure act (*esse*), attributable to God alone, and that permits the intelligence, informed by the purity of this notion, to see retrospectively, in natural, *philosophical* experience, a necessary real distinction between existence and essence in all finite realities.

> How did Thomas Aquinas achieve the awareness of the very possibility of this notion? It certainly results from a supreme effort of abstraction, since, in order to form it, the intellect must conceive, apart from the condition of being an existent, the act owing to which the existent finds itself in this condition. . . . Now obviously, to abstract this notion from that of substance and to distinguish it from the notion of essence was precisely to create it. How did St. Thomas come by this new notion? . . . [He] may well have first conceived the notion of an act of being [*esse*] in connection with God and then starting from God, made use of it in his analysis of the metaphysical structure of composite substances. . . . This is a good time to remember the curious remark made by Thomas himself at the end of the *Summa contra gentiles* I, chapter 22, where, after establishing that God's essence is His very *esse*, the theologian adds that "this sublime

---

26 See *Introduction à la Philosophie Chrétienne*, 55; *Elements of Christian Philosophy* (Garden City, NY: Doubleday, 1960), 130–31; *Le Thomisme*, 6th ed., 97n85.

truth Moses was taught by our Lord." Now, Moses could not learn
this sublime truth from our Lord without at the same time learning
from him the notion of what it is to be a pure existential act. This
invites us to admit that, according to Thomas himself, the notion of
esse can be learned from the very words of God.[27]

The intelligence, instructed by revelation, achieves a correct *philosophical*
outlook upon reality. The nature of the intelligence is thus restored by
grace to its original metaphysical capacities.

> Scripture itself . . . says that the proper name of God is: He Who Is.
> Because it says it, I believe it, and while I adhere thus to the object of
> faith, my understanding is enlightened by this more penetrating contact
> of the intellect with the primary notion of being. In one and the same
> movement, then, the mind discovers, on a philosophical level, a pri-
> mary principle of unexpected depth, attained through a sort of intellec-
> tual apprehension—imperfect but true—of the object of faith itself.[28]

Gilson does not wish to affirm that this interpretation of Exodus 3:14
manifests the exhaustive theological meaning of the word of God, nor
does he see the natural restoration of the human intelligence as revelation's
unique or even primary purpose. Nevertheless, the consequences of his
position are weighty: henceforth it must be admitted that a realistic metaphysical knowledge of being and of God is possible for the human person
only in cooperation with revelation. True philosophy must be conducted
under the illuminating influence of Christian faith.

Subsequent to the articulation of this position, the shape the "proofs
for the existence of God" take (in the sixth edition of *Le Thomisme*, for
example) is distinctly Theo-ontological. That is to say, the activity of
Christian philosophy is conducted in light of the revealed knowledge of
God as "He Who Is." The latter notion is an essential element of the *via
inventionis* of philosophy.[29] The monotheistic "demonstrations" of Aristotle, Avicenna, or John Damascene, when employed by Aquinas, are only
seen to *approximate* the understanding of God as Creator that is provided
by the metaphysics of the real distinction, and the understanding of God
as *Ipsum esse subsistens*. They approach this God otherwise known by faith

---

[27] *Elements of Christian Philosophy*, 131–32.
[28] *Introduction à la Philosophie Chrétienne*, 58.
[29] *Thomism; The Philosophy of Thomas Aquinas*, 6th ed., trans. L. Shook and A. Maurer (Toronto: PIMS, 1992), 95: "Note well that for Thomas Aquinas this revelation of the identity of essence and existence in God was equivalent to a revelation
of the distinction between essence and existence in creatures."

asymptotically, through a systematic inquiry organized *by theology* itself.[30] The metaphysics of the real distinction is henceforth demonstrable for Gilson only *in light of* the demonstration of the existence of God as the unique necessary being.[31] Furthermore, this ultimate demonstration itself into the created character of being presupposes (in the existential order of history) the illumination of revelation (i.e., the biblical understanding of

---

[30] *Thomism*, 6th ed., 75–83. Pages 76, 77, 81, 82, 83: "[T]he proofs of the existence of God . . . are the work of a theologian pursuing a theological end. . . . The all-too-real disagreements about the meaning of the proofs arise first of all from the fact that *they have been treated as philosophical proofs*. . . . The question is tied to the possibility of a theological view of *philosophy*. . . . For this . . . to be possible without the whole enterprise being reduced to the level of a convenient eclecticism, it is first and foremost necessary that the theologian not commit *the error of making a philosophical synthesis out of philosophies*. . . . Sacred doctrine is not physics . . . or metaphysics. . . . But it can know about all these kinds of knowledge in a single higher light that is truly of *another order*. . . . None of the five ways makes use of the properly metaphysical notion of being as Aquinas himself—going beyond Aristotle—conceived it. Nowhere in all his work has he proved the existence of God, the pure act of being, starting from the properties of beings [*esse* and *essentia*]. However, even while laboriously collecting the proofs for the existence of God bequeathed by his predecessors, he cannot not have had in mind the new notion of *esse* that is going to enable him to transcend, even in the purely philosophical order, the perspective of his most illustrious predecessors. *Theological* reflection opens out with philosophical elucidations, as though natural reason were becoming conscious of resources she knew nothing about until she became involved more completely in the theologian's sacred science. This fact is so surprising that even among Aquinas's most famous disciples many have lacked the courage to follow him. Descending *from theology to bare philosophy*, they have watched *sacra doctrina* break up *and metaphysics itself crumble in their hands*" (emphasis added).

[31] See *Thomism*, 6th ed., 83n85, where Gilson retracts his earlier position of the fifth edition of *Le Thomisme*. On 93–94 he offers three arguments for the non-composition of *esse* and essence in God, based upon God's being the cause of all other being. As Ralph McInerny points out, however, this leads to a logical contradiction, in that the real distinction of *esse* and essence is now established at the term of metaphysical reflection, even while Gilson presupposes the real distinction as the initial proper object of Aquinas's metaphysics. Otherwise, how would we be able (on Gilson's terms) to distinguish Aquinas's work from that of "essentialism" (*Praeambula Fidei*, 305)? Interestingly, in an essay written in 1973, Gilson returned to a variant of his earlier interpretation of Aquinas: the real distinction can be discerned through genuine philosophical analysis of beings we experience. Subsequently, the discovery of God's existence by means of the real distinction can be understood as a "sixth way," never explicitly developed by Aquinas himself, who seems primarily to have discussed the topic in the light of the knowledge of God's existence and simplicity. See *Autour de Saint Thomas*, 106–7, in comparison to *Thomism*, 6th ed., 84–97. A study of the evolution of Gilson's thought is offered by Floucat, "Enjeux et Actualité d'une Approche Thomiste de La Personne," 375–80.

creation), which it depends upon.[32] The metaphysics of the real distinction takes on its theoretical "necessary," then, primarily as a facet of Aquinas's Christian *theology*.

Evidently, such reflections place great (perhaps excessive) emphasis on the properly Christian theological dimensions of Aquinas's metaphysical writings. They simultaneously suggest a foreshadowing of a postmodern theology that would locate the principle justifications of Christian philosophical metaphysics within the objects of divine faith alone. It is indeed permissible to wonder whether such thinking is perfectly compatible with the teaching of the First Vatican Council, or with that of Aquinas himself.

Critical Reflections

I wish to raise three critical points with regard to Gilson's interpretation of Aquinas's metaphysics. First, I will attempt to discuss more fully an understanding of the judgment of existence as a point of departure for the study of metaphysics, and I will suggest why I think a *concept* of *esse* is a necessary element of this experience. Because conceptual, abstract knowledge is imperfect, the elucidation of the initial notions of "*esse*" and "essence" requires a step-by-step investigation into the problem of being. Second, I will discuss problems stemming from Gilson's misinterpretations of Aristotelianism as an essentialism, and his neglect of the presence of Aristotelian principles and causes in Aquinas's metaphysical thought. Understanding how the latter principles permit a *progressively enriched* understanding of existence for both Aristotle and Aquinas helps us propose solutions to some of Gilson's difficulties, particularly concerning Aquinas's understanding of the real distinction, and the understanding of God as *Ipsum esse subsistens*. Third, having made such suggestions, I will briefly attempt to note some tensions that exist between Gilson's notion of a revealed concept of being and Aquinas's theological teaching. This former theory risks fusing or confusing the specific objects of the natural and supernatural intellectual acts, and in this sense even suggests a kind of fideistic form of thought. Ironically, because of this, one can argue that a kind of grace-nature extrinsicism results, in which the natural metaphysical aspirations of the intellect are not intrinsically capable of arriving at the terminus that the revealed metaphysics of creation would require from them. This is exemplified by a seemingly ontotheological use of the *ad alterum* analogy of attribution, in which all beings are understood a priori in relation to a primary, unparticipated being. Each of these problems is in some way related to Gilson's order of philosophy (extracted from *sacra doctrina*) that I have noted above.

---

[32] *Thomism*, 6th ed., 95–97.

The Judgment of Existence and Realistic Knowing

If Gilson's criticism of Garrigou-Lagrange's study of the principles of critical reason as a starting point for metaphysics does have merit, nevertheless, the Dominican thinker did correctly identify the key point of conflict and divergence between Kantian and Thomistic thought on the question of metaphysical thought: can we have true knowledge of extra-mental being, considered specifically as being, or is all intuition of singulars distinctly sensible? A principal strength of Gilson's reappropriation of Aquinas lies in his insistence upon the primacy of the judgment of existence. In effect, Gilson's starting point for metaphysics does develop an aspect of Garrigou-Lagrange's thinking in order to respond effectively to the Kantian critique. In reaction to modern philosophical method since Descartes and Kant, in which epistemology precedes ontology, Gilson's desire is to identify a genetically primary point of contact with realities, through sensations, in which the intelligence can have a "naive" experience of singular existents, which is also specifically intellectual, and not merely sensible. This intellectual experience of the *existence* of things permits the human person to maintain contact with realities over and above the intentional interiority of our memories, concepts, reasonings, and so on, and provides a genuine starting point for metaphysical reflection.

To perceive the nature of this epistemological activity better, I will attempt to list briefly a number of elements that characterize this operation, according to Aquinas's analysis.[33] Aquinas asserts that the primary operation of the intellect functioning through sensitive experience is that of apprehension, by which the mind assimilates conceptually (though progressively and imperfectly) the essential determinations proper to the realities experienced. *Coinciding with* such experiential apprehensions is the production of a fundamental, most general concept—that of being (*ens*)—since the mind perceives (however dimly), in all its experiences, that "there are beings."[34] This conceptual formation presupposes the capacities of the sensitive powers that are themselves continually in contact with actually existing physical beings. These capacities assimilate "intentionally" the individual physical determinations of the realities known. The representational unification of sensitive forms by the "common sense" faculty provides the

---

[33] These reflections will be based partly upon the study of Aquinas's thought by Leo Elders, "La connaissance de l'être et l'entrée en métaphysique," *Revue Thomiste* 80 (1980): 533–48. For a more detailed, and slightly different, account see Wippel, *The Metaphysical Thought of Thomas Aquinas*, 23–43.

[34] *De ver.*, q. 1, a. 1 (Leon. XXII.1, 5): "Illud autem quod primo intellectus concipit quasi notissimum et in quod conceptiones omnes resoluit, est ens." *De potentia Dei*, q. 9, a. 7, ad 15 (ed. Marietti, 76): "Primum quod in intellectum cadit, est ens." See also, *De ente*, prologue; *ST* I, q. 11, a. 2, ad 4.

imaginative "phantasms" from which the agent intellect can extract the *intelligible, quidditative form* implicit within them, corresponding incompletely but really to what the reality is ontologically.[35] We can know, therefore, what realities are ontologically, but only through an experience of their sensible "accidents," and by mode of abstraction. The importance of this Thomistic understanding of human epistemology for the point I am considering is that it entails necessarily the notion of an abstract concept of *ens*, extracted by the agent intellect from the complex process of exterior and interior sensitive experiences and representations. Therefore, our minds do attain true knowledge of the beings we experience sensibly.

Furthermore, Aquinas insists that all of our concepts attain the singular determinate reality only under the aspect of abstracted conceptual knowledge (implying the universal mode of the human concept).[36] This apprehension of the reality, however, is never absolutely severed from concrete experience, and permits a "return" to the reality through the second intellectual operation (called *compositio* by Aquinas), which Gilson calls the judgment. It transpires through sensible experiences, by use of the images drawn from experience, and attributes the universal determination to concrete singular subjects (e.g., "This is a human being").[37] But in doing so, the intelligence is confronted with a multiplicity of *entia* that are intrinsically diverse, and thus develops the ontological axiom that is genetically primary for its metaphysical development: "this being is not that being" (*quod hoc non est illud*).[38] In becoming aware of the irreducible *difference* between the beings experienced, the intellectual notion of being (*ens*) diversifies (by proper proportionality) and the mind comes to distinguish conceptually the singular existence (*esse*) proper to each being *as experienced through the judgment of singular realities*. This gives rise to a unique judicative concept, that of "existence" (*esse*). This concept, like that of *ens*, is abstract, but has its field of application within the judicative confrontation of the mind with the singular beings we encounter. It "looks" conceptually precisely at the ontological uniqueness of each one ("Peter *is* a human being." "Peter *exists*.").[39] The formation of this concept thus per-

---

35 *ST* I, q. 85, a. 1, especially ad 4; q. 84, a. 6.

36 *ST* I, q. 86, a. 3. This is why there is no science of chance happenings, or of singular future contingencies: *ST* I, q. 86, a. 4.

37 See *Sent.* II, d. 3, q. 3, a. 3, ad 1; and *ST* I, q. 87, a. 7. Aquinas calls this intellectual action a "return to the phantasm" (*conversio ad phantasmata*).

38 On the priority of the judgment of non-contradiction, formed in the light of the positive apprehension, see *In X Meta.*, lec. 4, 1997, and the article of Leo Elders, "Le premier principe de la vie intellective," *Revue Thomiste* 62 (1962): 571–86.

39 In *ELPH* I, lec. 5, 19–22, Aquinas employs unambiguously a concept of *esse* and ascribes the apprehension of such a concept to Aristotle himself (in relation to realistic logical predication in Aristotle's thought).

mits a *composite* conceptual approach to each being *qua* existing. Every *ens* is experienced by composite conceptual judgment as an *essentia habens esse*, or as an existing-being-of-a-given-determination.[40] In this sense, Gilson is right to emphasize the unique character of our thought regarding *esse*, since it concerns precisely the experience of the irreducible ontological uniqueness of each reality in its existence. Like *ens*, this notion is diversified analogically and proportionally to adapt to the intrinsic diversity of existents encountered by the judgment of existence.[41]

If these observations of Aquinas are correct, then they have consequences related to Gilson's theory of the entry-point into metaphysics. First, because the quidditative concept of a thing is abstracted from experiences of the sensible accidental properties of realities and has a universal mode, it is far from perfect; it can in no way *comprehensively* signify the real essence of a reality.[42] To think "Peter is a *man*" need not entail that one possess a distinctly metaphysical knowledge of what a man is (i.e., a philosophical understanding of the human essence in terms of body and spiritual soul). The danger of essentialism derives, therefore, first and foremost from an overestimation of the abstractive capacities of the intellect, and not from a forgetfulness of existence. In this sense, Gilson's suggestion that the conceptual powers of the intellect somehow attain immediately a metaphysical understanding of the essence of the reality resembles the thinking of Descartes more than it does that of Aquinas. Second, therefore, the initial concepts of "being" and of "existence" are related to simple apprehensions and judgments concerning existent realities at hand. They do not contain in themselves the conceptual depth and intensity of the notion of *esse* and essence as used to signify the real distinction and the metaphysics of creation. Correspondingly, they have a banal function in human discourse. If there is to be a more prolonged inquiry into metaphysical principles, initial intuitions will not suffice, and a more developed investigation is necessary.[43] Third, then, the notions of being and of existence diversify and are understood analogically in the light of the proper principles of being (such as substance and actuality), such that these concepts are *progressively*

---

[40] Aquinas notes the conceptually composite nature of the judgment of existence in *Expos. de Trin.*, q. 1, a. 3.

[41] As I will note in the next chapter, this notion of being is also diversified analogically by the diverse categorial modes of being *within* the substance (i.e., the *esse* of the quantity, qualities, relations, etc., of a given being).

[42] See Aquinas, *Credo*, prologue, 7.

[43] This line of argument was developed by Cornelio Fabro, *Participation et causalité selon saint Thomas d'Aquin* (Paris-Louvain: Publications Universitaires de Louvain, 1961), 74–85, 537–51, although Fabro himself proposes a less Aristotelian understanding of Aquinas's principles than the one I am advocating.

enriched by the causal study of metaphysics and a proper *via inventionis.* To develop this argument I will move on to my second point.

Existence and Essence in Aristotle and Aquinas

Despite the fact that Aquinas's division of the Aristotelian substance and accidents into the essential and the existential represents a certain kind of innovation, Gilson's remarks regarding Aristotelian essentialism are excessively one-sided, and therefore obscure the complexity of the problem.[44] In fact, as Susan Mansion has shown in response to Gilson, Aristotelian realism is based upon a certain notion of the judgment of existence.[45] Aristotle states in the *Posterior Analytics* that the knowledge of the sciences is indeed derived through an assimilation of the essential intelligibility of things. This intelligibility derives from real substances that imply in themselves formal determinations.[46] Such scientific study, however, always presupposes the experiential knowledge of the existence (*to einai*) of the realities that one comes to know, and that concerns singular individual existents. One cannot study what something is essentially (*ti esti*), unless one has first determined that it exists (*ei esti*). This is why, for Aristotle, one cannot even say what a fantastical creature such as a goatstag is, since such creatures simply do not exist.[47]

---

[44] A sign of this is the fact that in contrast to Gilson himself, Aquinas attributes to Aristotle a notion of creation (as the ontological dependence of all things upon the first cause, God, for their being), and clearly speaks of this as a dependence in the order of *esse*: *De potentia Dei*, q. 3, a. 5. See Mark Johnson, "Did St. Thomas Attribute a Doctrine of Creation to Aristotle?" *New Scholasticism* 63 (1989): 129–55, and Lawrence Dewan, "Thomas Aquinas, Creation and Two Historians," *Laval théologique et philosophique*, 50 (1994): 363–87.

[45] Susan Mansion, *Le Jugement d'Existence Chez Aristote* (Louvain: Centre De Wulf-Mansion, 1976).

[46] *Post. Analytics* I, 2, 71b9–16; I, 4, 73a21–74a3; II, 1, 89b21–90a34; *Metaphysics* Z, 1, 1028a36–b4.

[47] *Post. Analytics* II, 7, 92b5–12: "Again, how will you prove what a thing is [*ti esti*]? For it is necessary for anyone who knows what a man is or anything else is to know too *that* it is [*ei esti*] (for of that which is not, no one knows what it is—you may know what the account or the name signifies when I say goatstag, but it is impossible to know what a goatstag is). But if you are to prove what it is and that it is, how will you prove them by the same argument? For both the definition and the demonstration make one thing clear; but what a man is and that a man is are different. Next, we say it is necessary that everything that a thing is [*einai*] should be proved through demonstration, unless it is its substance. But existence [*to einai*] is not the substance of anything, for being [*to on*] is not in any genus" (translation slightly modified). As Mansion notes (*Le Jugement d'Existence*, 254 and following), Aristotle uses the terms *einai, to einai,* and *to on* synonymously here, in distinction from the "whatness" of the reality known. The epistemological order between the

Such thinking helps us to understand why Aristotle, in reaction to Platonism, created the term *to ti ein einai* to designate the substance of the reality. It is precisely in the concrete singular existence (*einai*) of individuals that the intelligence perceives inductively (and abstracts conceptually) the nature (*ti ein einai*) of the reality.[48] The affirmation of Aquinas in *Expos. de Trin.*, q. 5, a. 1, ad 9, that a certain knowledge of being is present at the origins of all of the sciences is, therefore, seemingly very compatible with Aristotle's understanding of *episteme*. Significantly, Aquinas in his mature commentaries on such Aristotelian texts attributes to the philosopher a knowledge of existence (*esse*) as preceding the possibility of any scientific knowledge of essence, and in his discussion of Aristotle's example of the "goatstag" seemingly opposes Avicennian positions he had defended in *De ente et essentia*, according to which the essence of a thing can be defined without knowledge of its existence. This suggests a possible evolution toward "Aristotelian existentialism" in Aquinas's thinking that Gilson does not sufficiently take into account.[49]

If, however, as I have mentioned, Aristotle equates *einai, to on*, and *to einai*, in the *Posterior Analytics*, why does "existence" play so little a role in the study of the *Metaphysics*, giving way instead to a study of the principles of being? The reason is that the concepts of "being" (*to on*) and of "the one" are not contained within any of the genera, but are common analogically to all of them. Consequently, we understand more precisely what existence or being or oneness is when we understand what the principles of the diverse categories are, that is, substance as the cause according to the form of being, and act and potentiality as the final cause. The problem of existence, therefore, is resolved by the study of the principles of being, which

---

two is clear. The essence cannot be known without experiential contact with the existence (thus the need for induction by the *nous* based on multiple sensible experiences of existent realities: 92a37).

Aristotle's realism in these passages poses a serious objection to the arguments the young Aquinas (influenced by Avicenna) uses in *De ente*, c. IV, to establish the *esse*/essence distinction. Here he claims a real distinction of the essence from the existence of a reality due to man's mental capacity to conceive of such an essence ("man" or "the sphinx") independently of knowing whether such things exist. We can conceive of a sphinx's essence without knowing if one exists. Aristotle asserts the opposite: we only know what a man is because we experience the existence of individual men, and we cannot know "what" the goatstag, or the sphinx, are, because they do not exist. The "sphinx" is a compound image.

[48] *Prior Analytics* I, 4, 73b26–27; *Metaphysics A*, 9, 991a12–14; *M*, 9, 1086a37–b5; *Z*, 13, 1038b11–12.

[49] See especially, *ELP* II, lec. 6; I, lec. 2; and also *ELPH* I, lec. 3 and 5. See also the study of Ralph McInerny, "Do Aristotelian Substances Exist?" *Sapientia* 54 (1999): 325–38.

clarify what being is.[50] Significantly, Aquinas sees well in his commentary on the *Metaphysics* that Aristotle wishes to resolve the problem of being (or existence) in terms of substance. He defends his interpretation against Avicenna's criticisms of Aristotle. The Muslim philosopher had claimed that existence (*esse*) was an *accident* of the essence of each reality, implying that it had to be understood similarly to the predicamental categories (accidents) that depend upon the substance. Aquinas, in contrast, affirms the trans-categorical nature of *esse* (it is not an accident, but pertains to the substance as well) *and* affirms his *own teaching* that *esse* has to be understood "according to the principles of essence."[51] This suggests that for Aquinas one must understand the existence of a multiplicity of accidents by reference to the being of the substance upon which they depend.[52] The existence of this substance will subsequently be understood in terms of its being in act and being in potentiality.[53] This is important because it sug-

---

50 F. X. Maquart, "Aristote n'a-t-il affirmé qu'une distinction logique entre l'essence et l'existence?" *Revue Thomiste* 26 (1926): 62–72, 267–76, shows that the Aristotelian concept of being (*to on*) in the *Metaphysics* as a participle ("be-ing") signifies existence (*einai*), as we see in the *Posterior Analytics*. (In this sense it is not translated well by the Latin *ens*.) As a substantive it signifies the essence ("a being"). Aristotle's Book *Z* poses the question of the unity of essence and existence, since the *ousia* consists of the singularly existing essence. Why is "this" existent here a *man*? This investigation follows the opposite order of Gilson's. The mind moves from the diversity of concepts (existence, essence) to their unifying ontological principle (the substance).

51 *In IV Meta.*, lec. 2, 558 (ed. Marietti, 155): "Sed in primo quidem [Avicenna] non videtur dixisse recte. Esse enim rei quamvis sit aliud ab eius essentia, non tamen est intelligendum quod sit aliquod superadditum ad modum accidentis, *sed quasi constituitur per principia essentiae. Et ideo hoc nomen Ens quod imponitur ab ipso esse, significat idem cum nomine quod imponitur ab ipsa essentia*" (emphasis added). "But in regard to the first point, [Avicenna] does not seem to be right; for even though a thing's existence is other than its essence, it should not be understood to be something added to its essence after the manner of an accident, but something established, as it were, by the principles of the essence. Hence the term being, which is applied to a thing by reason of its very existence, designates the same thing as the term which is applied to it by reason of its essence."

52 *In IV Meta.*, lec. 2, 561–63. Commenting upon the idea that being and unity are coextensive, transcategorial properties, Aquinas states (561): "Since being and unity signify the same thing, and the species of things that are the same are themselves the same, there must be as many species of being as there are of unity, and they must correspond to each other. For just as the parts of being are substance, quantity, quality, and so on, in a similar way the parts of unity are sameness, equality and likeness."

53 *In IX Meta.*, lec. 1, 1768–69. Beginning his commentary on Book *Θ*, Aquinas states (1768): "Having established the truth about being as divided into the ten categories, the Philosopher's aim here is to establish the truth about being as divided

gests that on some basic level, existence for Aquinas can be understood only by reference to a causal analysis of substance and accidents, act and potentiality. Thus Aquinas affirms the *esse*/essence distinction as a trans-categorical distinction (applicable to all the categories of being) *even while fully respecting* the causal structure of substance and accidents as understood by Aristotle: the substance is the ontological cause of the accidents of a being.

This is all the more significant insofar as for Aristotle, the trans-categorial principles of metaphysics are precisely those of act and potentiality (common to all the categories), which permit him ultimately to explain being, oneness, truth, and goodness (the so-called transcendentals). By presenting the *esse*/essence distinction as a trans-categorical distinction applying to all the categories analogically (in conscious contrast to Avicenna) *and* by articulating the distinction itself in terms of actuality and potentiality, Aquinas clearly approaches as closely as possible the Aristotelian understanding of the causes of being, even while reinterpreting the latter in terms of his own metaphysics of *esse*. He *extends* the application of the ultimate causes of Aristotle (those that are trans-categorial: act and potentiality) so as to articulate in a new way the causal dependence of created being upon the transcendent, pure actuality of the Creator.[54] By the same measure, however, this suggests that there are ways that *for Aquinas* the Aristotelian principles can be seen to open intrinsically from below toward "the metaphysics of Exodus," even as the latter descends from above. We see this most clearly in his commentary on Aristotle's study of the actuality and potentiality of substances in *Metaphysics Θ*, 8. Commenting on Aristotle's treatment of the dependency of all secondary beings upon God in the order of actuality and existence (*esse*, in Aquinas's Latin translation of the text), Aquinas does not hesitate to insist on Aristotle's insight into the potentiality of beings of a given nature to exist or not exist, and on their universal dependence upon

---

into potency and actuality." In 1769, Aquinas makes clear that he thinks that for Aristotle, substance and accidental categories, act and potency, are the two major "divisions" of being.

[54] Aristotle himself affirms in *Metaphysics Θ*, 8, 1050b6–13, that the eternal substance *exists* (*esti*) necessarily, while the perishable substances exist (*einai*) actually or potentially, and are capable individually of ceasing to be. Likewise, in *Λ*, 7, 1072a31–32, 1072b10, the primary mover, God, in whom actuality and substance are identical, exists necessarily and is absolutely simple. These passages would suggest that "actuality" and "existence" are at times coextensive terms for Aristotle, as they frequently are for Aquinas. This point will be of importance in subsequent chapters, where I will suggest that the transcendental properties of being (truth, oneness, goodness, etc.) can be understood in metaphysically scientific terms only through a causal analysis of being in act. Only actuality, for Aristotle, is a trans-categorial *cause* of being, and so only this principle explains in *causal* terms the transcendental structure of being. Such an understanding is necessary in order to eventually attribute goodness, truth, or oneness to the primary transcendent *cause*, who is pure actuality.

God, who alone necessarily exists in act.[55] Here, from within an Aristotelian purview, the transcendental metaphysical composition of nature
and existence necessarily arises. Even if it does not translate immediately
into a metaphysics of the real distinction, it does suggest a potential for logical continuity between Aquinas's Aristotelianism and his own distinct
metaphysics of *esse*, a continuity found within a distinctly *philosophical
order* of investigation.[56]

As I will argue below (in chapters 7 and 8), Aquinas's real distinction
is fully comprehensible only subsequent to *both* the investigation of substance and actuality *and* the demonstration of the existence of God as pure
actuality.[57] However, for the distinction to take on any intelligibility
within the scope of our natural reason, it needs to be discoverable (and
discovered) in creatures we experience immediately through the ordinary
powers of philosophical, metaphysical reflection. How can this take place?

Following my previous observations, three conclusions can be proposed, corresponding to three degrees of intelligibility for the *esse*/essence

---

[55] Aquinas commenting on *Metaphysics Θ*, 8, 1050b5–16, notes that actuality and
potentiality are applied to not only the existence of movement but also the existence (*esse*) of substance. *In IX Meta.*, lec. 9, 1869 (ed. Marietti, 450): "Sed id
quod possible est esse, contingit non esse in actu. Manifestum est ergo, quod illud
quod possibile est esse, contingit esse et non esse. Et sic potentia simul contradictio-
nis est, quia idem est in potentia ad esse et non esse." "But what is capable of existing may possibly not be actual. Hence it is evident that what is capable of existing
may either exist or not exist; and thus the potency is at one and the same time a
potency for opposite determinations, because the same thing is; in potency both to
existence and non-existence." (See also lec. 3, 1805; lec. 5; 1825, lec. 9, 1868–71.)
Consequently, Aquinas sees that for Aristotle the question of the actuality and
potentiality in the being of the substance reveals a capacity of an essentially determined being to exist or not exist, and it will eventually be seen that this leads us
back to a necessarily existent being in whom the substance and being in act (or
ousia and actuality) are absolutely one (*In XII Meta.*, lec. 5, 2494; lec. 7, 2524–27).

[56] This idea has been developed in greater detail in the study of Lawrence Dewan,
"Aristotle as a Source for St. Thomas' Doctrine of *esse*," currently published at
www.nd.edu/Departments/Maritain/ti00/schedule.htm.

[57] A survey of Aquinas's writings reveals that the *non-distinction* of existence and
essence in the primary being is generally affirmed only after the demonstration of
God's simplicity and pure actuality, suggesting that the ultimate philosophical perspective on the real distinction is attained only in light of the philosophical discovery of God. This is very clear in *ScG* I, c. 22, following I, c. 13–21, in *ST* I, q. 3,
a. 4, and in *Comp. Theol.*, I, c. 9, following c. 3. As James Weisheipl has noted, in
this respect, Aquinas follows exactly the Avicennian order of argumentation for the
non-distinction in God. See his *Friar Thomas d'Aquino* (Washington, DC: The
Catholic University of America Press, 1983), 132–33. In the *ScG* chapters 22, 25,
and 26, without citing him, Aquinas follows closely the argumentation of Avicenna's commentary on the *Metaphysics H*, 4.

distinction. First, for both Aquinas and Aristotle, it would seem that the initial concepts of "existence" and "essence" developed through experiential contact with sensible realities are realistic. Knowledge of being by the judgment of existence provides a point of entry to the study of "being *qua* being." However, it does not give us immediate access to the *esse*/essence distinction. Second, the discovery of the real distinction may be argued to be a legitimate *philosophical* discovery, but only through a series of metaphysical precisions concerning the proper principles and causes of being, in which the initial conceptual division of *esse* and essence takes on a deeper intelligibility, in the light of the understanding of act and potentiality. Here, for example, reflection on the contingency of beings we experience (their capacity to exist or not exist), as well as their unity and multiplicity in the order of being, can lead to exacting metaphysical arguments for the real distinction of essence and existence in beings we experience. These are arguments with a basis in Aquinas's texts themselves.[58] Third, the affirmation of the non-distinction in God between his existence and essence takes on its deepest intelligibility after the demonstration of the existence of God, and reflection on God's pure actuality, simplicity, and absolute perfection. In the light of this monotheistic perspective, a third level of intelligibility emerges concerning the initial distinction: all created beings can be seen to have an existence immediately received from God, who is himself existent being, and in whose uniquely necessary being they participate. The real distinction is the deepest dimension of their created dependence. If my proposals are correct, then, the real distinction is not, as Gilson affirms, a principle given by revelation that founds all metaphysical reflection, but on the contrary, it is an ultimate insight that is progressively deepened only in and through a prolonged philosophical investigation.

Theo-ontology and Specifically Philosophical Wisdom

By initially beginning his metaphysics from the perspective of creation with what he claimed was a theological order of inquiry received from *sacra doctrina*, Gilson united these three levels of intelligibility into one: the judgment of existence is expected to give us almost immediately the deepest principles of the reality (the distinction of *esse* and essence), which we see are characteristic of *created* being in relation to the unparticipated *esse* of the Creator. This is, of course, the metaphysical perspective of Aquinas in his *De ente et essentia*. But the latter text does not purport to establish a distinctly philosophical order of metaphysical investigation. Gilson affirms in

---

[58] See, for example, *ScG* I, c. 15, for an indication of the former; *De ver.*, q. 27, a. 1, ad 8, and *ScG* I, c. 21, for indications of the latter. I will return to this subject in chapter 7.

his letter to Labourdette that "the notion of *esse* is included in that of *ens* as its principle," and by this presupposes a notion of being in act as initiating the study of metaphysics, rather than as something to be discovered analogically, and progressively through experience. Consequently, when confronting opposing positions, Gilson was unable to justify the real distinction philosophically and instead formalized it *theologically*, affirming its origin by grace, which henceforth becomes a presupposition to all true metaphysical inquiry. The concept of *esse* is derived from a consideration of Exodus 3:14. Paradoxically, then, whereas Gilson was prone to deny any concept of existence on the natural level, he did in fact have recourse to such a concept within the order of grace, and employed this to make sense of his distinctly Christian understanding of philosophy.

This position attempts to make natural metaphysical reflection profoundly harmonious—even continuous—with the revelation given in faith. Ironically, however, it risks engendering a kind of extrinsicism between the grace of revealed metaphysical knowledge of the Creator as *Ipsum esse subsistens* and the natural philosophical capacities of the human mind. On the one hand, the revelation is meant to act as a guiding light for the human mind even within its properly *philosophical* order of knowing and way of investigation (which seems intrinsicist). However, the very necessity of such Theo-ontological reasoning suggests that the range of knowledge of our natural philosophical thinking is of questionable adequacy, especially as pertains to the metaphysics of creation. If the principles of metaphysics are distinctly theological, then one can ask without injustice if the metaphysics of Exodus is in fact something alien to the natural scope and ends of the human intellect. In that case, have we not come dangerously close to doing what Heidegger accused Christian philosophy of attempting? If the God of revelation is made the primary object and end of metaphysics as such, philosophy seems on account of faith either to be alienated from its true object, or simply void of any intrinsic purpose.

Of relevance here as well is Gilson's somewhat one-sided use of the *ad alterum* analogy of attribution, which is developed in relation to the notion of the creative activity of God. If all being is measured in the light of a *revealed understanding* of God as "He Who Is," that is to say, as pure *esse*, then each secondary being is also understood necessarily as a participated being reflecting imperfectly its transcendent source. This *ad alterum* likeness between creatures and Creator derives from God's subsistent being, due to the likeness between himself and his effects. In the absence of a *prior* Aristotelian causal analysis of created being in *via inventionis*, however, the intrinsic *causal basis* for the Creator/creature analogy is insufficiently developed. Gilson's metaphysics of created dependency, therefore, is open to the charge of being an extrinsic theological projection imposed upon philosophy, making pure *esse* (God) the a priori theological measure of the metaphysical analysis of beings we experience directly. Does this not resemble the ontotheological form of thought criticized by Heidegger, as one that substitutes a theology of creation in the place of an authentic philosophical reflection on the problem of being?

Lastly, then, one can raise the question of whether a kind of fideistic methodology has entered into Gilson's later thinking, since he seems to make the natural, philosophical specification of the human intelligence directly dependent upon the objects we know by the light of faith.[59] St. Thomas states quite clearly in *ST* I, q. 1, a. 6, ad 2, that the light of faith gives the believer a certain judgment concerning the conclusions of natural sciences in their respective compatibility with, or opposition to, Christian faith, but that it does not befit the faith to be itself at the source of the demonstration of the principles of these sciences.[60] In other words, the believer can judge in faith that certain philosophical conclusions are incompatible with the revealed truth to which he adheres, but in order to refute these errors, or to discover philosophical truths himself, he cannot avoid doing the work of philosophy. This requires an analysis of the *objects* of natural experience, *as attained by* the philosophical sciences, *even when* such analysis is placed in the service of the defense of Christian teaching *within theology*.[61]

Evidence of this perspective is also found in Aquinas's treatise on faith in the *Summa theologiae*, where he develops at length the affirmation that faith is not, properly speaking, an intellectual *habitus*. It does not qualify directly the intelligence according to its own natural inclinations and development.[62] If the habitual activity of faith provided the intelligence with new metaphysical concepts (and especially concepts of such central importance to the natural life of the intelligence as Gilson ascribes to *esse*), then it is difficult to see how Aquinas could affirm such a teaching. Clearly Aquinas does think that Scripture provides a unique and ultimate perspective on the mystery of God, human existence, and the order of creation. And certainly this perspective deeply influenced the historical evolution of

---

[59] For a critical reflection on Gilson's position in this regard that is gentler, but nevertheless quite clear, see the fine analysis by Serge-Thomas Bonino, "Pluralisme et théologisme," *Revue Thomiste* 94 (1994): 530–53.

[60] *ST* I, q. 1, a. 6, ad 2, "The principles of other sciences [than *sacra doctrina*] either are evident and cannot be proved or are proved by natural reason through some other science. But the knowledge proper to this science comes through revelation, and not through natural reason. Therefore it does not pertain to it to prove the principles of other sciences [*Et ideo non pertinet ad eam probare principia aliarum scientiarum*]."

[61] See *Expos. de Trin.*, q. 2, a. 3, on the third use of philosophy in *sacra doctrina*.

[62] See especially *ST* I–II, q. 62, a. 2; II–II, q. 1, aa. 1, 4; q. 2, aa. 1, 3, 4.

human philosophical reflection. However, Scripture itself does not provide any distinctively natural, philosophical concepts that the mind might not obtain (in theory) by its proper powers.[63] And clearly Aquinas thinks that the notion of *esse* is such a concept. Such philosophical notions are endemic to a distinctively philosophical mode of inquiry into reality, even when they harmonize felicitously with our understanding of the mystery of God derived from revelation. [64]

Conclusion

Gilson's study of existence in Aquinas contains helpful suggestions for a way of responding to Kantian and Heideggerian prohibitions on thinking concerning the transcendence of God. It also raises important methodological questions, and (I have argued) problems, which might be resolved, in part at least, by explicit recourse to some of the Aristotelian dimensions of Aquinas's thinking. The real distinction between *esse* and essence must be related to Aquinas's use of the Aristotelian causal analysis of being as substance and accidents, actuality and potentiality.

If this is the case, however, then the latter causal study of being must also must be related in some way to the medieval conception of the transcendental notions coextensive with *esse* (unity, truth, goodness). For Aquinas, the latter are employed to speak about God through the medium of analogical discourse, as we have seen in chapter 2. In the following chapter I will discuss, therefore, another influential modern proponent of Thomism, Jacques Maritain, and the way in which he treated the question of the transcendentals and analogical predication in his interpretation of Aquinas's philosophy of being. My concern here, too, will be to discern the success of his project in relation to the challenge of the ontotheological critique. As we shall see, the Aristotelian dimensions of St. Thomas's thinking, in this case as well, offer significant resources for the right consideration of central themes in Thomistic metaphysics.

---

[63] This is precisely what contrasts faith with the gift of intellectual prophecy, which does imply the reception of infused species. *ST* II–II, q. 171, a. 1; q. 173, a. 2.

[64] The historical parallel to this affirmation is the claim that Aquinas's metaphysics of *esse* builds on the efforts of his *philosophical* predecessors, even as he seeks to develop this philosophical tradition in order to better articulate the mystery of faith. A great deal of controversy surrounds the issue of ways in which both non-Christian and Christian Neoplatonists in late antiquity had themselves derived their own variant of a real distinction between existence and essence in order to speak of metaphysical composition in creatures. How did such thinking in turn influence Aquinas? For a helpful orientation to this topic, see Stephen Brock, "Harmonizing Plato and Aristotle on *Esse*: Thomas Aquinas and the *De hebdomadibus*," *Nova et Vetera* (English edition) 5, no. 3 (2007): 465–94.

5

The Transcendentals and the Analogy of Being: The Case of Jacques Maritain

I N THE PREVIOUS CHAPTER I have argued that the human mind is capable of attaining true knowledge of being (*ens*) and of existence (*esse*), and that this knowledge implies conceptual thinking about existence. I have also claimed that a progressively enriched understanding of both of these concepts requires, for Aquinas, a reflection on the intrinsic causes of being. The next question one might confront, however, relates to the so-called transcendental notions, those notions that for Aquinas are coextensive with being, namely: oneness, truth, and goodness. These too are analogical concepts that "transcend" the diverse categorical modes of being (substance, quantity, quality, relation, etc.) by applying to all of them. Like being and existence, they too may eventually be predicated analogically of God as the primary cause of created being, unity and multiplicity, goodness and truth. For God in himself exists in a uniquely eminent way, is absolutely one, subsistent truth, and supreme goodness. How, then, may the human mind arrive *in via inventionis* at the insight that these notions are rightly predicable of the divine nature, albeit in an utterly transcendent and supereminent way?

In this chapter, I will consider Jacques Maritain's answer to this question. My goal will be to analyze how Maritain develops a conceptual, analogical science of being *qua* being, based upon Gilson's Thomistic understanding of the judgment of existence. This science, for Maritain, is made possible by what he terms an "intuition of being." I will then proceed to examine how Maritain develops from such a starting point a metaphysical reflection upon the human person, and an interpretation of the Five Ways of Aquinas. This will allow us to consider how Maritain attributes transcendental notions analogically to the transcendent God.

My basic claims will be threefold. First, Maritain rightly underscores (against the objections of Kantianism) the fact that the mind must intuitively grasp, within ordinary experience of singular existents, certain basic structures of reality, from which we can derive first principles of metaphysical reasoning. The transcendental notions, like the categorical modes of being, denote this fore-theoretical ground of things which we "already know" implicitly through ordinary experience, and from which we can derive further knowledge. In this sense, Maritain's appeal to an intuition of being as an example of what Aquinas calls *intellectus*, or the "habit of first principles," is warranted. Second, however, Maritain makes this initial intuition of transcendental notions such as existence and goodness do too much work, because he goes on to identify it with another intellectual process that Aquinas terms *resolutio*. This term, in fact, signifies for Aquinas a twofold form of *reasoning* (not intuition) by which the human thinker reflects on the causes of things. It requires, therefore, a causal analysis. Third, Maritain's notion of this analogical intuition of the transcendentals leads to an absolute use of the analogy of proper proportionality in metaphysics (following Cajetan and Garrigou-Lagrange), to the exclusion of the other two types of analogy discussed in chapter 3. The structure of such thinking in fact risks introducing an a priori knowledge of God (derived through intuition) into any demonstration of the existence of God, as the precondition for the latter. Clearly such thinking would suggest an ontotheological structure of thought similar to that described by Kant, despite Maritain's desires to avoid the criticisms of the latter. This form of thought in Maritain in fact results from his neglect of the Aristotelian causal analysis of the transcendental notions, which we find in Aquinas's own thought. A correct interpretation of *resolutio* in St. Thomas's texts reveals the need for a study of intrinsic causes of being in order to ground a demonstration of a primary "extrinsic" cause of being, God. This study, in turn, allows one to ascribe transcendental attributes to God analogically, according to the analogy of attribution *ad alterum*, without any ontotheological presuppositions. Despite its setbacks, Maritain's metaphysical thought contains many constructive intuitions. At the end of this chapter I will propose amendments in order to rethink the valid insights of Maritain in relation to a causal analysis of being.[1]

---

[1] My analysis of the Five Ways as interpreted by Maritain will not include a historical inquiry concerning the adequacy of his interpretation of Aquinas's *ST* I, q. 2, a. 3. For such historical studies, see Fernand Van Steenberghen, *Le Problème de l'Existence de Dieu dans les Écrits de S. Thomas d'Aquin* (Louvain: ÉISP, 1980); Leo Elders, *The Philosophical Theology of Thomas Aquinas* (Leiden: Brill, 1993); Wippel, *The Metaphysical Thought of Thomas Aquinas*, 379–575. This study will not even concern itself per se with the philosophical adequacy of Maritain's arguments for God's existence. Instead, the primary question will be to examine the relation of

Jacques Maritain (1882–1973), like Étienne Gilson, was a Catholic layman, actively engaged in the renewal of Thomistic studies, particularly in France and North America. Unlike Gilson, however, he was a convert to Catholicism (a formerly agnostic disciple of Henri Bergson in the Sorbonne). He was not an academic writer, nor uniquely a metaphysician. His writings on culture, politics, art, morals, and theology sought to contribute to a wide-reaching renewal of Thomistic thought within modernity and touched on diverse questions. His approach to Thomist commentators was also noticeably different: he sought aid from Cajetan, John of St. Thomas, and his original Thomistic mentor, Reginald Garrigou-Lagrange. Maritain saw the commentary tradition as providing continually renewed interpretations of Aquinas's thought within each historical age. He was particularly interested in the theme of wisdom (*sapientia*) as an ultimate intellectual *habitus*, permitting the philosopher to attain, through natural theology, a "descending" outlook upon man's existence and activity from the perspective of the ultimate cause: God.[2] Maritain's main metaphysical writings are found in *Les Degrés du Savoir* (1932), *Sept Leçons sur l'Être* (1933), *Court Traité de l'Existence et de l'Existant* (1947), *Approches de Dieu* (1952), and in the article "Réflections sur la Nature Blessée," published in the *Revue Thomiste* in 1968, and reprinted in *Approches sans Entraves* (1973). The first two works, influenced by Garrigou-Lagrange, concentrate especially upon the content of the so-called intuition of being and the degrees of philosophical science. The third and fifth works attempt to rethink this intuition starting from the Gilsonian judgment of existence as an entry point for metaphysics. *Approches de Dieu* applies this synthetic understanding to the discovery of the existence of God, as demonstrated through the Five Ways.

Diverse Philosophical Approaches to Reality: The Degrees of Abstraction

Maritain's treatment of the manner in which one may approach and understand human experience philosophically is characterized in terms of the scholastic doctrine of the degrees of abstraction, which is itself an interpretation of the Aristotelian division of the speculative sciences. Aristotle, in a number of texts, distinguishes between the philosophy of physical nature, the study of mathematics, and the science of metaphysics, according to the subject studied by each one. The subject of the philosophy of physical

---

these "five ways" with the *via inventionis* of metaphysics articulated beforehand. The criticisms concerning this prior element of his thought will in turn be seen to touch directly upon the success of his arguments in philosophical theology.

2 See, for example, *Sagesse*, in *Oeuvres Complètes*, vol. 9 (Fribourg and Paris: Éditions Universitaires and Éditions St.–Paul, 1990), 1137–51.

nature is sensible, mobile being (since what is studied are precisely the causes of movement and change in nature). Mathematics is a science of quantities understood "separately," that is to say, by numerical abstractions taken from moving, sensible beings. However, as a study of quantity it concerns objects that do not exist in themselves apart from these singular sensible realities. (There are no ideal numbers existing in themselves.) Metaphysics, meanwhile, can be understood apart from the sensible singular reality, because it aspires ultimately to a knowledge of separate substances, which themselves really do exist apart from material being.[3]

In discussing this division of sciences, Aquinas will develop another aspect of their diversity: each kind of science not only considers reality under a different aspect but also implies a different *mode of knowing*. This idea is found in the *Expos. de Trin.*, qq. 5 and 6, where he is commenting on Boethius's use of the Aristotelian distinctions. Here, in q. 5, aa. 3 and 4, he will distinguish between three kinds of abstraction, corresponding to the "objects" of each respective science: *abstractio totius, abstractio formae*, and *separatio*.[4] The former considers the whole in relation to the parts and

---

3 See *Metaphysics E*, 1, 1026a13–17: "For natural science deals with things which are inseparable from matter but not immovable, and some parts of mathematics deal with things which are immovable, but probably not separable, but embodied in matter; while the first science deals with things which are both separable and immovable." Previously, Plato attempted to identify a hierarchy of the speculative sciences in the *Republic* VI, 509d–511c. There he distinguishes sense knowledge (concerning either objects of sense or artistic models) from the intelligible realm. The intelligible realm consists of two forms of knowledge. One is mathematical knowledge of the physical world (based upon hypothesis and illustrated by sensible models). The other is dialectic, which attains the separate forms, and is therefore based upon first principles. Aristotle's hierarchy of the sciences clearly differs. He attempts to develop an authentic study of the principles of physical nature in studying causes of becoming and change *immanent* to natural realities. This is a knowledge other than that which is based upon mathematical hypotheses (*Physics* I, 1; II, 2–3, 194b10–195a3). In addition, pure mathematics, for Aristotle, is a science distinct from the study of sensible nature (as it is also for Plato) but it does not consider separate forms. For Aristotle, mathematical entities are mentally abstracted from physical realities, and do not exist in themselves, contrary to what the Pythagoreans and Platonists affirm. (See *Metaphysics M*, especially 2, 1077b1–16.)

4 For considerations on Boethius's Aristotelianism in this text, see Ralph McInerny, "Boethius and St. Thomas Aquinas," in *Being and Predication*, 143–58. For other important texts of Aquinas concerning the speculative sciences and corresponding modes of abstraction, see: *In VI Meta.*, lec. 1; XI, lec. 7; *In I Phys.*, lec. 1; and *ST* I, q. 85, a. 1. Can this distinction of degrees of abstraction be founded upon the texts of Aristotle himself? *Physics* I, 1, 184a24–25, refers to the knowledge of nature as that of "a whole . . . comprehending many things within it." This offers a textual basis for the *abstractio totius* of Aquinas. For a study on this mode of abstraction as contrasted with quantitative abstraction in Aristotle, see Erico Berti,

abstracts the universal form from individual non-constitutive parts. It conceives of man, for example, as composed of flesh and bone, but not insofar as composed of *this* flesh and *these* bones. This "degree of abstraction" makes possible a universal investigation of the natures of physical, changing realities, leaving out the consideration of their individual particularities. The second type of abstraction considers a "formal" aspect of a reality (i.e., in mathematics, the quantitative aspect). Real quantities exist only in perceptible matter, but they are formalized conceptually by the mind for the sake of mathematical study. Aquinas says that the third intellectual operation (*separatio*) has for its subject determinations in existent reality such as "being, substance, actuality, potentiality," which both are found in physical beings and can exist separately from matter. They are therefore analogically applicable to the separate substances and the divine nature.[5] Maritain adopts this Thomistic teaching, and follows Cajetan and John of St. Thomas in speaking of these three modes of knowing as "degrees of abstraction."[6] The question then becomes, for Maritain, how does the mind naturally attain the "third degree" of abstraction and begin to reflect metaphysically? How does the mind recognize that such terms are potentially capable of naming God, and how does one come to speak rightly about God analogically?

Influenced by Gilson, Maritain accepted the starting point of metaphysics as the judgment of existence, and attempted to develop from this

---

"Reconsidérations sur l'Intellection des 'Indivisibles' selon Aristote, *De Anima* III, 6," in *Corps et Âme*, ed. Romeyer Dherbey (Paris: J. Vrin, 1996), 391–404.

[5] *Expos. de Trin.*, q. 5, a. 4: "Something can exist separate from matter and motion in two distinct ways: first, because by its nature the thing that is called separate in no way can exist in matter and motion, as God and the angels are said to be separate from matter and motion. Second, because by its nature it does not exist in matter and motion; but it can exist without them, though we sometimes find it with them. In this way being, substance, potency, and act are separate from matter and motion, because they do not depend on them for their existence, unlike the objects of mathematics, which can only exist in matter, though they can be understood without sensible matter."

[6] See, for example, *Les Degrés du Savoir*, 71–78, in reference to Cajetan, *Comm. In de Ente et Essentia*, prologue, q. 1; John of St. Thomas, *Curs. Phil.*, Log. II, q. 27, a. 1. This interpretation is not self-evident simply because *separatio* as a term does not necessarily imply the notion of abstraction. Subsequent scholarship has provided firm arguments in favor of Cajetan's interpretation of *separatio* as an abstractive activity. See Edward Simmons, "The Thomistic Doctrine of the Three Degrees of Formal Abstraction," *Thomist* 22 (1959): 37–67. Aquinas refers very clearly to the abstract character of the conceptualization of notions potentially applicable to separate realities in *ST*, q. 85, a. 1, c. and ad 2: "Some things *can be abstracted* even from common intelligible matter, such as *being, unity, power, act*, and the like, as is plain regarding immaterial things" (emphasis added).

his own philosophical assertion of an "intuition of being." According to Maritain, the human subject is capable of an intuition of being, given in ordinary experience of existents, which in turn permits one to attain the *separatio* mode of abstraction. The transcendental notions perceived by this intuition are analogical and can extend to all being, including the being of God. I will discuss each of these points below briefly.

The Judgment of Existence and the Intuition of Being

I have noted in the previous chapter that Gilson sought to avoid a conceptual "essentialism" with regard to being, and, therefore, even denied (in certain writings) the possibility of any concept of existence. Aquinas, meanwhile (at least as I have interpreted him) was shown to affirm that we do have a concept of *esse* and of *ens*, attained through the judgment of existence. How do such concepts come about, and to what do they correspond in reality? These are the questions Maritain sought to respond to with his notion of the intuition of being. The function of the intuition of being is precisely to permit the intelligence to perceive, within a judgment of existence, the being (*ens, esse*) of realities experienced, considered insofar *as being* (*ens secundum quod est ens*). It permits, consequently, a *separatio* abstraction, yielding objective knowledge of that which is potentially "separable" from material being, and therefore provides concepts that are attributable analogically to immaterial realities. It should be mentioned here that the idea of "intuition" (*intuitio*) appears infrequently in Aquinas's work.[7] For Maritain, the intuition of being implies an assimilative act of the intellect that precedes any deductive reflection. It is a form of intellectual knowledge acquired spontaneously in the course of the subject's contact with reality, through the experience of sensation. It corresponds to some extent, then, to the Aristotelian notion of the habit of first principles (the Aristotelian *nous*), which Aquinas calls the habit of *intellectus*.[8]

---

[7] *In Sent.* II, d. 9, q. 1, a. 8, ad 1: "The reasoning power arrives at a knowledge of the truth by inquiry, while the intellect sees [the truth] by a simple intuition of it [*intellectus simplici intuitu videt*]; hence reasoning reaches its completion in the [understanding of the] intellect; further, certitude in demonstrative proofs is achieved through a resolution to first principles, which pertains to the intellect." For Maritain, the idea of an intuition of being had its previous origins in the thought of Garrigou-Lagrange. See *Dieu, Son Existence et Sa Nature*, 107–10, which in turn refers to Cajetan's *intueri* in his commentary on *De ente et essentia*. It does not seem, therefore, that Maritain's notion can rightly be considered as Bergsonian, despite the latter's emphasis on intuition, since for Maritain such intuition is entirely conceptual and proper to the intelligence alone, while, as he himself claims, the Bergsonian intuition is the effect of a voluntary, affective sympathy. See *Sept Leçons sur l'Être*, 54.

[8] See *Nic. Ethics* VI, 6, 1140b31–1141a8; *In VI Ethic.*, lec. 3 and 5; *ST* I–II, q. 57, a. 2.

Intellectus, for Aquinas, certainly can denote a variety of intellectual activities.[9] Among them, however, is the activity of basic intellectual insight, by which the mind gains its initial and most fundamental conceptual starting points in a pre-theoretical way. Certain notions are simply given within experience as a precursor for all future thinking. Some of these are "categorial," such as the basic intuition that gradually emerges in human thinking (no matter how vaguely) that "there are substantial things," "they have these quantities," or "they have these qualities." However, others of these are transcendental and apply to all that exist and that we experience: basic notions such as "being," "oneness," or "goodness," which human language employs to speak about virtually all there is.[10] Although such names are employed in ordinary language in extremely complex and subtle ways in order to speak about the diversity of existents, their qualities, quantities, goodness, unity, and so on, these categorical and transcendental notions are also genetically primary, indispensable starting points for the gradual development of mature human thought.

In fact, Maritain does not hesitate to explain his own theory of intuition by recourse to Aquinas's notion of *intellectus*.[11] For Maritain, such intuition (or insight) apprehends being in a unique way with regard to the discovery of existence, differing from the ordinary apprehension of a quiddity (such as "man" or "plant"). Normally quidditative apprehension precedes the judgment of existence (as is the case when we identify by a judgment that "a plant is there" only because we have previously apprehended what a plant is, and now apply this universal knowledge to a new singular experience). Conceptualization of existence, for Maritain, however, occurs *within* the judgment of existence, and is *preceded by it*. Only the conscious intellectual experience of the singularity of the existence of individuals permits us to attain an analogical concept of *esse*. ("This plant

---

[9] See the classic study by Julien Peghaire, *Intellectus et Ratio selon St. Thomas d'Aquin* (Paris: J. Vrin, 1936), especially, 247–61, and Francois-Xavier Putallaz, *Le Sens de la Réflexion chez Thomas d'Aquin* (Paris: J. Vrin, 1991), 135–49.

[10] It is clear that for Aquinas the first principles of knowledge include a grasp of being (*ens*), and with it some notion of unity, the truth, and the good. However, these notions are applicable only to the world of substantial things, having formal determinations and accidents, so that some basic grasp of the categorical determinations of things needs to be included as a dimension of our basic intellectual insight. There is evidence for this view in *In V Meta.*, lec. 9, 889–94, which I will return to below. See also the study by Lawrence Dewan, "St. Thomas and the Seed of Metaphysics," in *Form and Being*, 35–46.

[11] Maritain at times relates the expression "intuition of being" directly to the Thomistic notion of *intellectus*. See, for example, *Sept Leçons*, 53; and the article "Pas de Savoir sans Intuitivité," in *Approches sans Entraves*, 940, where he refers to *intellectum* in *ST* II–II, q. 8, a. 1, ad 2, to explain "intuition."

exists.") This unique form of abstraction permits the consideration of the principles of being, considered *qua* being.

> In the instant that our senses experience a sensible existent, the concept of being and the judgment "this being exists" . . . come forth spontaneously from the intellect. . . . In this primary of all of our concepts that is considered for itself [*esse*], our metaphysical intelligence perceives being in its analogical extension, disengaged from its [initial] empirical conditions.[12]

Maritain theorizes an order of conceptual development in a way that is similar to Aquinas. The initial apprehension of *ens*, or of a *res*, is verified in the senses by a "return to the phantasm" wherein the judgment of existence exerts itself with regard to the real act of being of the reality in question. Only subsequently is a concept of existence formulated.

> In the awakening of the intellect and through a mutual reciprocity, the formulation of an *idea* ("this being") and of a *judgment* both take place in the same instant. The latter is composed by joining the object of thought with the act of existence. . . . "This thing exists" or "this being exists". . . . Conjoined with the first judgment of existence, the idea of being therefore springs up, of "that which exists or can exist." In this way, the intellect understands itself [its own process of judging], and makes the act of existence an object of thought. . . . Thus the mind derives a concept or notion of existence (*existentia ut significata*).[13]

The importance of this theory is that it permits us to explain in what way the intelligence "disengages" from experiential reality the ontological determinations proper to physical beings considered as existing, being, having unity, being good, and so on. These basic notions will, in turn, be capa-

---

[12] *Court Traité*, 35, note 13.

[13] Ibid. Maritain sees the "principle of identity" as being formed after the concept of *esse*, as an axiom expressing the content of the intelligence's assimilation. ("That which exists, exists.") This interpretation differs to some extent from my own offered at the end of the previous chapter (based on the studies of Leo Elders), since, according to that interpretation, the principle of identity is implicitly formulated with the initial apprehension of *ens* in the "first operation," and gives content to the first judgment (of non-contradiction): "This being is not that being." The judgment of existence and the concept of existence would arise only when one begins to reflect on the intellectual experience of the ontological singularity of beings as existing. For my understanding of Maritain on this point, I am indebted to Lawrence Dewan, "Jacques Maritain, St. Thomas, and the Birth of Metaphysics," *Études Maritainiennes/Maritain Studies* 13 (1997): 3–18.

ble of an (analogical) universal extension to all that which exists. Maritain's
theory clearly has a basis in Aquinas's texts, as Aquinas himself (1) thinks
that all human thinking begins from such basic concepts, and (2) relates
the *separatio* abstraction to the second operation of the intellect. It is seemingly within a judgment, for Aquinas, that this "degree of abstraction"
takes place.[14]

A question must be raised at this point, however. It should be noted that
the *separatio* concepts Aquinas actually mentions in *Expos. de Trin.*, q. 5, a. 4,
seem to be related directly to Aristotelian causal principles, since Aquinas
explicitly mentions concepts such as "being [*ens*], substance, actuality,
potentiality." These are not the same thing as the conceptualization of *esse*,
attained through the judgment of existence, nor the concepts of unity, truth,
and goodness. As I have argued in the previous chapter, for Aquinas, the initial notion of *esse* is understood more profoundly in the light of the causal
analysis of principles of being (as substance and actuality). If an initial conceptual understanding of *esse* occurs through judgment, further understanding requires a causal analysis of being, and following from this a causal
demonstration of the existence of God. This alone permits us to clarify how
we might attribute names to the "separate" reality of God. Maritain, however, does not engage in this kind of *via inventionis*, and this is largely related
to his understanding of the transcendentals as the object of metaphysics,
directly apprehended by the *intellectus* habit of the intuition of being.

The Transcendentals, *Intellectus*, and *Resolutio*

Maritain affirms that the transcendentals are the object of metaphysics.[15]
These are notions attained by the *separatio* degree of abstraction within the
intuition of being, which he claims can potentially be attributed analogically
to God. The study of transcendental notions evolved greatly in the context

---

[14] *ST* I, q. 85, a. 1, ad 1: "Abstraction may occur in two ways: first, by way of composition and division; thus we may understand that one thing does not exist [*esse*]
in some other, or that it is separate [*esse separatum*] therefrom. Secondly, by way of
simple and absolute consideration; thus we understand one thing without considering the other. Thus for the intellect to abstract one from another things which
are not really abstract from another, does, in the first mode of abstraction, imply
falsehood." The operation of "composition and division" in Aquinas's language
indicates the operation of judgment, in which intellectual truth or falsehood
occurs. The affirmation of a thing "existing separately" implies a conceptual "composition" between the quiddity and the concept of existence (*esse*), and therefore
makes the statement a truth claim, rather than a mere definition. See also *Expos. de
Trin.*, q. 5, a. 3, c.

[15] This is the approach particularly in his *Court Traité*, and in "Réflections sur la
Nature Blessée," in *Approches sans Entraves*, in *Oeuvres Complètes*, vol. 13 (Fribourg
and Paris: Éditions Universitaires and Éditions St.-Paul, 1992), 767–822.

of medieval philosophy.[16] For Aquinas, as for his predecessors, these are notions that are coextensive with being (such as *res, aliquid, unum, bonum, verum*). They signify in diverse ways the content of all that which is.[17] In *De ver.*, q. 1, a. 1, Aquinas specifies that these notions signify general modes of being, as distinct from the special modes of being proper to the ten categories. This is to say that they are not specific to one of the categories alone (such as quality, quantity, relations, etc.), but common to all and found in a unique way within each. Qualities, quantities, relations, places, and such all exist, are good, are one, and so on. It is in this sense that Aquinas himself understands such notions as "transcendent" with regard to the categories. *Res, aliquid, unum, bonum,* and *verum* are coextensive with *ens* and *esse*, and express the intelligible order and sense of being.[18]

---

[16] The study of notions "convertible" with being has its prehistory in the philosophies of Aristotle and Plato. (See, for example, *Republic* 507b; *Sophist*, 245c–255e, 260a; Metaphysics *Γ*, 2, 1003b23–1005a18; *K*, 3, 1061a15–17; *Nic. Ethics* I, 6, 1196a23–34.) Avicenna spoke in different places of being (*esse*) as *res, aliquid, bonum, verum,* and *unum* (*Metaphysics* I, c. 4, 27 and 30; c. 5, 31–34; c. 8, 55–56; IV, c. 3, 212). The first systematic treatment of the topic, however, was presented by Phillip the Chancellor in his *Summa de bono* (ca. 1225–28), at Paris, and the topic was subsequently explored by Alexander of Hales and Albert the Great. For studies on the transcendentals, see particularly Mark Jordan, "The Grammar of *Esse*: Re-reading Thomas on the Transcendentals," *Thomist* 44 (1980): 1–26; Jan Aertsen, *Medieval Philosophy and the Transcendentals* (Leiden: Brill, 1996). My intention here is not to produce a study of the transcendentals in Aquinas, but simply to evoke the context of Maritain's theories.

[17] See, for example, *Sent.* II, d. 27, q. 1, a. 2, obj. 2 (Mandonnet II, 698): "The good transcends the genus of quality, and is convertible with being." See also *De ver.*, q. 1, a. 1; q. 21, a. 3; *ST* I, q. 30, a. 3 c. and ad 1; *In X Meta.*, lec. 3, 1975; *In I Ethic.*, lec. 6, 81.

[18] The basic text on the transcendentals in Aquinas is *De ver.*, q. 1, a. 1, where he justifies the above-named fivefold distinction of terms coextensive with *ens* and *esse* through a series of "modes of differentiation." Being can be considered (1) either per se or with respect to another. If per se then (2) either positively (as *res* or "a determinate reality") or negatively (as *unum*. that which is indivisible), and if with respect to another then either (3) in distinction from it (as *aliquid* or "something other") or as fitted to it (*convenientia*). If the latter is the case, this can be with respect to appetite (*bonum*, all that is, is somehow good) or with respect to intellect (*verum*, all that is, is somehow true). See the helpful commentary by Jordan, "The Grammar of *Esse*," 13–21. (Jordan, however, attempts to interpret reductively *res, aliquid,* and *unum* as modes of *ens, verum,* and *bonum*. Yet if the notions of *res* and *aliquid* both denote something distinct, they presumably have their own content.) *Res* can perhaps best be interpreted as signifying the "essence" of each thing experienced, while *aliquid* seems related to the unique act of being proper to each reality. See the discussion by Wippel, *The Metaphysical Thought of Thomas Aquinas*, 192–94.

For Maritain, it is precisely the intuition of being (as an act of *intellectus*) that permits us to discover these transcendental notions from the beings we experience *through* the judgment of existence. These notions, therefore, will give *content to what we know of being qua being*, and therefore permit us to identify the object of the *separatio* abstraction, that is, *the object of the study of metaphysics.*

> The intuition of being is the intuition of both the character and analogical value of being. . . . One has to have . . . the intellectual perception of the inexhaustible and incomprehensible reality thus manifested as an object. This intuition makes one a metaphysician. . . . Thus each of the transcendentals is being itself considered under a certain aspect. . . . There is no real distinction between being and unity, between being and the truth, between being and goodness. These are notions convertible with being, but founded in the reality itself.[19]

As I will discuss below, this apprehension of the transcendentals, for Maritain, is analogical (according to an analogy of proper proportionality), and applies to both created and uncreated being. Before this is treated, however, a question must be raised.

Maritain's affirmation is that the transcendental notions are the object of the *intellectus* habit *and* the object of the science of metaphysics. The latter object is also known for Maritain by what Aquinas terms *resolutio*, or resolution, which Maritain equates with *intellectus.*[20] I would like to suggest briefly here why the second of these affirmations is problematic. Aquinas does affirm that the transcendental notions are assimilated by the intellect through the *intellectus* habit. This operation comes about experientially through sensation and precedes any form of demonstrative proof or deduction. While such knowledge is not innate, it is acquired in an intuitive and pre-reflexive fashion. Therefore, once we begin to think, we are always, already conceptually aware of being, unity, goodness, and truth, no matter how vaguely, when we begin to think and speak about what exists and to make definitions.[21] This habit, however, is different

---

19 *Sept Leçons*, 52, 76.
20 In *Sept Leçons*, 53–54, Maritain speaks of the intuition as the *intellectus* habit, while on p. 63 he identifies this with the *resolutio* to transcendental notions that Aquinas describes in *De ver.*, q. 1, a. 1. Likewise, *Court Traité de l'Existence et de l'Existent*, 22, relates "intuition" to *resolutio* in *De ver.*, q. 12, a. 3, ad 2 and 3.
21 Aquinas follows Aristotle (*Posterior Analytics* I, 3) in arguing that there cannot be a regression to the infinite in the order of demonstration. Certain principles and definitions are known per se by *intellectus* from the beginning and are necessary for demonstration (I, 6 and 9, 75b36–76a9). For Aquinas such notions include the transcendentals. *Expos. de Trin.*, q. 6, a. 4: "In the speculative sciences we always proceed from something previously known, both in demonstrating propositions

from what Aquinas calls *resolutio*. The latter is a *reflexive* process of philosophical investigation. That is to say, far from being immediately intuited,
it requires prolonged philosophical inquiry and rational reflection. Furthermore, as Jan Aertsen has made clear, this reasoning process of *resolutio*,
for Aquinas, can occur in two different ways. One can attempt to "resolve"
or "reduce" a thing into its first principles, so as to permit scientific deduc-
tions based upon first principles and causes, or one can attempt to
"resolve" one's definitions to the most fundamental notions they presuppose.[22] Both of these processes presuppose the most basic notions we are
given through our initial intuitions of reality, but are not identical with
the intuitive grasp of these notions. Rather, the first form of *resolutio* "goes
forward" from basic experience (and primary notions) to eventual scientific discoveries about the structure of reality. It employs resolution-based
reasoning in view of the study of principles and causes. Therefore, it
makes possible the movement *in via inventionis* that starts with things as
they manifest themselves to us initially, and eventually discerns more
deeply their structure as they exist in themselves. The latter form of *resolutio*, meanwhile, "goes backward" from basic experience to see what were
the initial starting-points of human knowledge. It is an epistemological
study, meant to discern the underlying archeology of all rational reflection,
the most basic concepts from which all laws of thought are derived. The
discovery of the transcendentals as the genetically primary notions common to all acts of understanding comes about, for Aquinas, through this
latter form of study. We can deduce, upon rational reflection, that there
are certain starting points to our thinking, that were always, already there,
even if we were not reflexively aware of them. Here we discover the pri-

---

and also in finding definitions. . . . Inquiry in all the speculative sciences works back
to something first given, which one does not have to learn or discover (otherwise he
would have to go on to infinity), but which he knows naturally. Such are the
indemonstrable principles of demonstration . . . to which all demonstrations of the
sciences are reducible. Such, too, are the first conceptions of the intellect (for example, being [*entis*], one and the like), to which all definitions must be reduced."

22 Aertsen, *Medieval Philosophy and the Transcendentals*, 73–79. This double form of
resolution is present in the text of *Expos. de Trin.*, q. 6, a. 4, just cited above, and
well as *De ver.*, q. 1, a. 1: "When investigating the nature of anything, one should
make the same kind of analysis [*reductionem*] as he makes when he reduces a
proposition to certain self-evident principles. Otherwise, *both types of knowledge*
become involved in an infinite regress. . . . That which the intellect first conceives
as . . . the most evident, and to which it reduces all its concepts, is being. Consequently, all the other conceptions of the intellect are had by additions to being"
(emphasis added). One finds a clear indication that resolution is meant to move
"forward" toward knowledge of causes in *Expos. de Trin.*, q. 5, a. 4, which I will
discuss below.

mary notions that are the basis for such axioms as the law of non-contradiction and the principle of identity.

This differentiation of terms leads to two important conclusions. The
first is that both forms of resolution (back to epistemological principles or
forward to causal principles in realities) *presuppose* the apprehension of the
special and general modes of being (signified by the categories and the transcendentals). We always, already know something of what qualities, quantity, time, place, or unity, goodness, being, are *before* we begin to reflect
critically upon *either* our initial principles of knowledge *or* the causes of the
beings we experience. Otherwise, any form of thinking would be impossible. By contrast, we do not simply grasp intuitively (by *intellectus*) the principles of being *known reflexively, and explicitly as such*. To come to know
such principles, a self-conscious causal analysis of reality is necessary. Second, the differentiation between two kinds of *resolutio* is important because
it shows that for Aquinas the resolution to transcendental concepts is *not* a
resolution to causes per se. The former is an epistemological reflection,
while the latter is a causal science. Perhaps, then, for Aquinas the first principles of metaphysical science are not the transcendentals, but the Aristotelian causes of being. This is why the notions he identifies as *separatio*
notions in *Expos. de Trin.*, q. 5, a. 4, are those of "being, substance, actuality and potentiality." Such notions *take on intelligible content only* within
the context of a causal analysis of being. Maritain, however, identifies the
epistemological *resolutio* to basic notions common to all definitions with
the *resolutio* to proper principles and causes, and sees both occurring in the
discovery of the transcendentals as the object of metaphysical science
through the intuition of being. This problematic understanding of metaphysics is integrally related to his understanding of the analogy of being.

The Analogy of Being: Proper Proportionality

Maritain affirms that the judgment of existence permits the intelligence to
attain knowledge of the singular existence in act of each reality experienced. Consequently, our metaphysical concepts (those of the transcendentals), are intuited in an intrinsically analogical mode, according to the
analogy of proper proportionality. Only this form of analogical realism
respects the primacy of the singular act of each reality with respect to the
universalizing conceptual capacity of the human mind.

> The form or abstraction that is proper to metaphysics does not pro-
> ceed from simple apprehension or from an eidetic visualization of a
> universal more universal than the others. It proceeds from the eidetic
> visualization of a transcendental which imbibes all that is, and which
> takes on an intelligibility of irreducible proportionality or analogy (*A* is

to its own existence as *B* is to its own existence). This is due to what our judgment [of existence] discovers: the actuation of a being by its act of existing, grasped as transcending the limits and conditions of empirical existence, and therefore understood in the unlimited extension of its intelligibility.[23]

Furthermore, the intuition of being *qua* being permits an implicit awareness of an *analogy of proper proportionality* between the realities we experience and God, the transcendent cause of all that is.

It is when an individual reality is grasped in its pure singularity that the intellectual intuition of being is produced. But at the same time, and in the same instant, one becomes aware of the mystery of being and of its horizon without limits, of the irreducible diversity in which it manifests itself to the mind in each existent. For in seeing that this rose *exists*, I see in the same instant that outside of myself *exists* as well, each in its own way, a great diversity of other things. This is why precisely through the intuition of being—I would say as something *formally* given to the intellect—one perceives the analogy of *esse* in the plenitude of its signification. I mean to say that one perceives, then, not only that the concept of being is of itself intrinsically analogous (analogy of proper proportionality), like that of all of the transcendentals, but also that the analogy of being is *the reason and key* to that of all the transcendentals, and that it crosses the threshold of the infinite. If each of the diverse existents is good in its own way, or one it is own way, it is *because* each one *exists*. . . . And ultimately, this is because there is an *Esse* that is self-subsistent, analogically known, although infinitely above our grasp, in which and with which all of the other transcendentals are realized as pure act, and are absolutely identical.[24]

---

[23] *Court Traité*, 38–39. Passages such as these (see also "Nature Blessé," 795) may suggest that the initial intuition of being not only attains being as it is present in physical beings, but "extracts" immediately the transcendental notions of being as it exists separately from material reality. In this case the mind would attain knowledge of separate reality intuitively directly from physical reality. A preferable way of interpreting the notion of *separatio* in Aquinas is to distinguish between the *via inventionis* and the *via iudicii* (*ST* I, q. 79, a. 9). In the "way of discovery" the mind attains the notion of being through experience of sensible existents, which permits it to identify a scientific problem for study. *After* the discovery of the causes of being and the demonstration of the necessary existence of the first being, and the precision of certain analogical concepts attributed rightly to the first being, one can see *in retrospect* (*in via judicii*) the notions initially apprehended, that are potentially attributable to God analogically. For an interpretation of Aquinas in this sense, see Lawrence Dewan, "St. Thomas, Physics, and the Principle of Metaphysics," in *Form and Being*, 47–60.

[24] "Nature Blessé," 796–97.

This important affirmation has a significant consequence: the infinite being of God is grouped with finite beings as signified adequately (in analogical ways) by the transcendentals.

> Like the notion of being, the notion of existence is of itself, essentially from the first instant, an analogical notion, validly applicable to the Uncreated just as it is to the created.[25]

Therefore, the intuition of being attains the transcendental attributes of being analogically in such a way as to extract intelligible content potentially applicable to the separate being of God. If we compare this analysis with the study of Aristotle and Aquinas made in the first two chapters of this book, two striking features of Maritain's thought should now be clear. First of all, Maritain correctly notes the analogical nature of the insight (or *intellectus*) into being. Transcendental notions are ascribed in analogical ways (according to proper proportionality) to diverse beings, or to diverse categorial modes of being. It is therefore reasonable to conclude that the mind apprehends these notions through an analogical comparison of realities and of the diverse modes of categorial being within a given reality. So for instance, we understand what the goodness of qualities are analogically by observing qualities in diverse beings (such as the colors of this plant versus the mathematical intelligence of this student). Or we understand what goodness is when comparing analogically the goodness of a given quality (a virtue) with the goodness of a given quantity (the right amount). Maritain's theory of the analogical perception of being embraces this side of Aristotelian realism, and founds such apprehensions (convincingly) within the prior experience of the judgment of existence.

Maritain's conception of the science of being, however, also permits that we obtain quasi-immediately (by the intuition of being) the object of this science (the transcendental dimensions of being). This knowledge prepares us directly to speak analogically of God. There is, therefore, no causal analysis of the proper causes of being *immanent* to the realities we experience (as substance and accident, actuality and potentiality) prior to the demonstration of God's existence and attributes. Rather, one can proceed directly from the analogical intuition of the transcendental properties of finite beings to the demonstration of a primary, infinite cause of being. Yet Aquinas, like Aristotle, affirms clearly that the science of being *qua* being studies the intrinsic causes of being in the realities we experience (rather than the transcendental notions).[26]

---

[25] *Approches de Dieu*, 23.

[26] *In VII Meta.*, lec. 1, 1245–46; lec. 17, 1648–49. The positing of the transcendentals as the object of metaphysics is an explicit teaching of Duns Scotus. (Duns Scotus,

Second, Maritain seems unaware of Aquinas's use of the *ad alterum* analogy to speak of the relation of creatures to God, but focuses exclusively on the analogy of proper proportionality to discuss this relation. These two points are no doubt related. In the absence of a resolution to intrinsic causes of beings we experience, we lose in turn the sufficient philosophical foundations for a second resolution to what Aquinas terms an extrinsic *equivocal* and *transcendent* cause of being, known by another form of analogical thinking. Instead, the analogical intuition of the transcendental dimensions of being seems to contain implicitly the notion of God within its initial object (as the infinite realization of the transcendental notions). These critical remarks can be further developed after consideration of Maritain's study of the human person and his discussion of the Five Ways.

The Being of the Human Person

Maritain was interested in developing a metaphysics of the human person as a response to what he considered the misguided absolutization of human subjectivity in modern continental philosophy. Yet he also recognized, perhaps more than Gilson, the necessity for such a development within the Thomistic tradition, as a way of considering a genuinely novel set of metaphysical questions: What is the being of a human person? How does the person reveal what being is in a unique way? At the same time, he also holds that the human subject is ultimately intelligible as a personal subject *only through* a metaphysical investigation. I wish here to note two elements of Maritain's thought on the person: the use of the distinction of first act and second acts, with application to human self-awareness, and his affirmation that perfective goodness is accidental in man, while it is substantial in God.

I have discussed in chapter 1 the Aristotelian study of substance and operations as first act and second acts (respectively) in *On the Soul* II, 1, and in *Metaphysics* Θ, 8–10. As previously mentioned, Aquinas also develops the notion of first act and second act.[27] For him first act is the substantial existence of the embodied soul and its powers (with its particular nature and accidents). The second acts are the operations of these powers

---

Ordinatio I.8.I.3, n. 115; see Cross, *Duns Scotus*, 147–48.) That it is the teaching of Aquinas, however, is at least highly disputed. Some Thomistic scholars do argue that the transcendentals can be interpreted as the proper object of metaphysics for Aquinas. (See Aertsen, *Medieval Philosophy and the Transcendentals*, 113–58.) However, this point of view is not universal: compare Wippel, *The Metaphysical Thought of Thomas Aquinas*, 23–93.

27 See, for example, *ST* I, q. 48, a. 5; q. 76, a. 4, ad 1; q. 105, a. 5; I–II, q. 3, a. 2; q. 49, a. 3, ad 1.

by which the soul attains its diverse ends and thus perfects itself.[28] Maritain develops these points so as to explain the human capacities for knowledge and love of self and of others in metaphysical terms. The first act of the human person must be understood by recourse to the metaphysics of *esse* and essence. Amidst our experiences of the existences of multiple singular human beings, the intellect can decrypt an essential structure of human nature and its operations (an essence common to all persons). The essential nature of man apprehended through experience, however, is simultaneously perceived (by the judgment of existence) as subsisting in a unique way in each person (due to the singularity of the *esse* of each one). The knowledge of the being and goodness of each person consequently implies a knowledge of *both* human nature (essence) *and* of the metaphysical uniqueness of each human being (his or her *esse*).[29]

The teleological fulfillment of the human person takes place through "second acts." Man's personal operations presuppose realism concerning both one's own being and the being of others. Both can be known by the human intellect for what they *are*, and consequently, the person can truly love himself and others realistically, by virtue of the goodness perceived in his own existent person and that of others.[30] Such operative actuation of the person occurs through self-giving love on behalf of others (for instance, in

---

28 *ST* I, q. 48, a. 5: "Act is twofold; first and second; The first act is the form and integrity of a thing; the second act is its operation." *ST* I, q. 105, a. 5: "For the less perfect is always for the sake of the more perfect: and consequently as the matter is for the sake of the form, so the form which is the first act, is for the sake of its operation, which is the second act; and thus operation is the end of the creature."

29 See *Les Degrés du Savoir*, appendix IV, in the second edition (in *Oeuvres Complètes*, vol. 4, 1045 and following): "And when the subject or the agent is a person . . . the body subsists by way of the subsistence of the spiritual soul [and this subsistence] brings with it a higher perfection, such that an active and autonomous state of exercise results. This [subsistent person] is a complete whole enveloping itself in the sense that the totality [the spiritual person] is in each of the parts. . . . Possessing itself, this "whole" makes its own . . . the operations that it exercises: they are not only from it, but also belong to it. . . . They are an integral part of the possession of self by oneself that is characteristic of the person. All of these traits . . . denote the ontological depths of our subjectivity. We have there the ontological foundation for the properties of the person in the moral order . . . the aspiration to a freedom of autonomy, and the rights of the person."

30 *Sept Leçons*, 125: "Being is the love of the good: for each being is the love of a good, which first and foremost is its action itself. . . . This good towards which each tends, one calls a final end; it is an end for the agent, and love of this end is the formal reason for the action of the agent." This affirmation needs to be qualified. The operative perfection of the person (through spiritual acts of intellect and will) remains "accidental" with regard to the substance. Its *esse* is only relative to the *esse* of the "primary act." Yet the substantial being of the person comes to fulfillment only by such accidental operations in accordance with its prescribed teleological end.

friendship), and thus perfects the spiritual nature of the human person.[31] While voluntary love and acts of intelligence fulfill the human person teleologically, these remain second acts having an accidental mode. They depend upon the substantial being of the embodied soul, and can happen or not happen. In God, however, this distinction between first and second acts does not exist. The perfections that are accidental in human persons have some kind of substantial mode in God, who is his intelligence and love.[32] Consequently, human spiritual acts should play a role for us in clarifying how we may rightfully characterize God's operative life (analogically).

Intuitions of a Primary Being and the Five Ways

Like Aristotle and Aquinas, Maritain does not attempt to demonstrate the existence of God directly from a study of the human person as such. Instead, in *Approches de Dieu* he interprets the Five Ways of the *Summa theologiae* in light of the intuition of being and the analogical knowledge of the transcendental structure of being.[33] His causal arguments for the existence of God presuppose this prior study. My goal in this brief presentation will be to show how Maritain uses the analogy of proper proportionality to establish his "intuition of a first being." Second, I will examine his interpretations of the Five Ways of Aquinas. My criticisms come at the end of this presentation, where I will show the consequences of the absence of a study of the intrinsic causes of being in Maritain's study. Without a study of such intrinsic causes, the a posteriori *causal* appeal to a primary, extrinsic, transcendent source of being is not adequately prepared for and justified rationally. Instead, one must substitute a kind of a priori intuition of the being of God, based on the analogical study of the transcendentals (an intuition that is in turn verified by argumentation).

Maritain begins his exposition of the Five Ways by insisting on the necessary common human experience of the intuition of being discovered in a personal manner (i.e., concerning *one's own* existence and that of realities experienced that are *other* than oneself in their being). This intuitive discovery of God implies three moments. First, I have the experience of

---

31 *Court Traité*, 84: "The spiritual existence of love is the supreme revelation of existence for the self. The self—being not only an individual matter, but also a spiritual person—possesses itself and 'takes itself in hand,' insofar as it is spiritual and free. And in view of what end does it possess itself and act as a self, if not for what is greater . . . in all truth, to give of itself to another?"

32 *Sept Leçons*, 123.

33 I will not examine here Maritain's controversial "sixth way" based upon personal consciousness (*Approches de Dieu*, 81–93) since it is not clear that it is a metaphysical argument. For a positive estimation of it, however, see Elders, *La Théologie Philosophique de Saint Thomas d'Aquin*, 217–18.

the alterity of the being of the other vis-à-vis my own; this leads immediately to a sense of my own contingency *as* a being, who exists actually, but who can cease to exist; and thus, third, I sense the necessary existence of a primary measure of the real beyond myself.

> Thus the primordial intuition of being is the intuition of the solidity and inexorability of existence and second, of the death and nothingness to which my existence is subject. Third, in the same bolt of intuition—which is nothing other than my becoming conscious of the intelligible value of being—I realize that this solid and inexorable existence perceived in everything I experience implies—I don't know yet under what form, perhaps in the things themselves, or perhaps separate from them—an existence that is absolute and irrefragable, completely free from nothingness and death. These three bonds by which the intellect encounters actual existence as affirming itself independently from the self . . . take place within one and the same intuition, that the philosophers would explain as being an intuitive perception of the essentially analogical content of the primary concept, the concept of being.[34]

Furthermore, I can clarify intuitively that the other physical contingent realities that I experience cannot themselves be the ontological measure and source of all that exists, and that they like myself are limited and depend in diverse ways upon others for their being. This kind of radical metaphysical dependence on another cannot extend on indefinitely. Thus there must be one who is first and beyond both myself and the universe I experience. This other can only be a transcendent source of existence, himself self-subsisting and necessary being, upon whom all others depend for their being.

> In the second stage . . . I see that my being, first of all, is subject to death, and second that it depends upon the entirety of nature, upon the universal whole of which I am a part. And this being-with-nothingness that is my own being, implies in order to be, being-without-nothingness, this absolute existence *that I first perceived in a confused fashion as contained within my primordial intuition of existence.* But whereas the universal whole of which I am a part is being-with-nothingness, by the very fact that I am a part, and then finally, because the universal whole does not exist by itself, so I see now that being-without-nothingness must really exist apart from this world. There is another All who is separate, another Being, transcendent and sufficing for himself, unknown in himself, and activating all beings, who is . . . self-subsistent being. And therefore *the internal dynamism of the intuition of existence, or of the*

---

[34] *Approches de Dieu,* 15–16.

intelligible value of being, allows me to see that absolute Existence or Being-without-nothingness, transcends the entirety of nature, and thus I am faced with the existence of God.[35]

Here we see the ultimate function of the analogy of proper proportionality for Maritain: the intuition of being grasps the "being" of myself, of the other contingent realities, and then of God. "Being" (like the other transcendentals) can be applied analogically to each reality, including God (*A* is to *B* as *C* is to *D* as *E* is to *F*): "being" is to myself as "being" is to another, as "being" is to God, and so on. In fact, the knowledge of the being of God seems to be, for Maritain, already implicitly contained within the intuition of finite being, as its most perfect and necessary realization. The medium for the attribution of being to God, therefore, is the intuition of a primary cause of being *qua* being for all of the contingent realities we experience. Within the intuition that the contingent beings we experience depend upon another, the proportionally analogical concept of "being" is naturally extended to God, understanding him as the uniquely transcendent, necessary being who is the cause of all others.[36]

The second part of Maritain's *Approches de Dieu* will be an attempt to develop scientifically all that is *implied* in this initial intuition of a necessary first being. The *quinque viae* will be interpreted as five ways of demonstrating, according to diverse causal orders, the last of the above-mentioned intuitions—that is, along with myself, the other realities I experience imply in themselves ontological dependence upon others, and cannot be the source of their own being. Thus, their actual existence can be explained only by appeal to one who himself is beyond any ontological order of dependency. This being implies in himself no imperfection or limit. Maritain affirms that these so-called proofs are really more like ways of discovery that give a mediated evidence, not through direct experience, but from the effects of God, so that we have "evidence of the fact that the divine existence must be affirmed."[37]

---

35 Ibid., 16–17 (emphasis added).

36 Maritain's approach resembles in certain ways that of Garrigou-Lagrange discussed in chapter 1. The intuitive knowledge of "what" a given thing is (the principle of identity), entails a simultaneous intuition of its dependence upon others (the principles of causality and sufficient reason). This suggests (for Maritain at least) that we can attain in a quasi-immediate way by our intellectual experience of beings the intuition of something that is absolute and a primary cause. Within our most fundamental intellectual experiences of reality there is embedded a presentiment of the existence of God. I explore in chapter 7 ways in which I think this less discursive natural sense of the existence of God can be understood by recourse to a causal analysis of being, rather than Maritain's intuition of being.

37 *Approches de Dieu*, 20–22.

Each of Maritain's five demonstrations reposes upon diverse causal orders of which we have a direct experience. These causal orders and all the realities by which they are constituted cannot explain themselves ontologically, but imply the necessary existence of one who is at their origin as the transcendent source of their determinations and being. At the heart of each of Maritain's five demonstrations will be the axiom of the impossibility of a regression to the infinite in any of the given causal orders. It is in light of the absurdity that results from a denial of a non-regression to the infinite that we can see that the only intelligible way to make sense of our experience, examined in a metaphysical way, is to posit a first cause of existence who is necessary being and pure act.

The first way, then, considers the existence of beings in movement. What we experience moves and changes, and all that is moved is moved by another. Considered metaphysically, physical realities are capable of receiving diverse existent determinations in and through movement. Yet movement implies that the potentiality to receive this or that physical determination is actuated by *another* who is the efficient source of the movement. The actualization of a being in movement, to be what it is, depends, then, on a whole series of others who act on one another, and who move it. Each reality considered thus implies both a potentiality in itself and an actuality that it receives from its diverse interactions with others. But if this is the case, no reality in movement can be explained ontologically in its *being* as a reality that is moved, without reference to another. To seek to explain these realities by an infinite series of such causes simply pushes back the question each time, since any reality in the order implies potentiality, and thus requires another who permits its actuality. If there is not something primary in the order of being, who is himself an unmoved mover and who accounts for the "whole," we can never explain what we do in fact experience directly: the existence of beings in movement.

> But if there was not a primary agent, the reason for the action of all the others would never be given existence; nothing would move nothing. One cannot ascend from agent to agent without end; it is necessary to stop at a primary agent. And because it is primary it is not itself moved by any other. . . . It is the absolutely unmoved Agent who actuates and moves all the rest.[38]

In his exposition of the second way, Maritain considers the diverse orders of efficient causes. The realities that we experience are acted upon by others, and these actions affect directly (in different ways) their existence and operations. This is also true, in turn, for the realities that are themselves

---

[38] Ibid., 29.

efficient causes. None of the realities we experience, therefore, are the cause of themselves in their being: they depend upon others that act upon them. Thus, each reality is dependent for its being upon a causal series of efficient agents. Can the existence of realities that act on each other be accounted for by appealing to an infinite series of interrelated causalities (of all types)? Maritain distinguishes between *homogeneous* causes and *heterogeneous* causes. The former imply an identity in nature between cause and effect, as a mother who feeds her child is identical in natural kind with her child: they are both human beings. The latter causality implies a diversity of natural kinds, as the sun that heats the earth's atmosphere permitting human life is of a different nature than the mother and her child. Maritain specifies that the notion of an infinite series of *homogeneous* causes implies in itself no inherent contradiction. So, for instance, human beings could beget human beings over an infinite time, without any necessary limit. The idea is not intrinsically absurd. However, a series of *heterogeneous* causes cannot go on to the infinite. Plants live and grow by the assimilation of carbon, which presupposes a physical environment of air and light upon the earth's surface, which in turn presupposes a relative position and movement of the earth with regard to the sun, and so forth. When one considers the existence of such a heterogeneous causal order, no reality, in its action, can explain its own existence without reference to another—itself in turn dependent upon another. These "lines of intelligibility" inscribed in the universe's causal orders call for an actual, first efficient cause of existence, which is absolutely necessary and thus above this causal order, as its transcendent source.

> Thus, while it is impossible that a thing be the efficient cause of itself (it would then precede its own existence), efficient causes are connected by complementarity, so that, in a vast diversity of ways, they condition each other and cause one another. And this interdependency between the causes extends in all directions. But it is not possible to extend to the infinite from cause to cause. In the universal scope of interactions . . . if there were not a first cause beyond all others, upon which all others depend, then whatever constellations [of interdependent causes] one considers . . . simply would not be. One must therefore acknowledge the existence of a primary uncreated cause that exists immutably by itself, over and above all the particular causes and their connections.[39]

The third way begins from the study of necessity and contingency in changing, physical beings. There is a relative degree of necessity in things we experience—even in physical things—because they retain certain properties through time, despite the change and becoming that they undergo.

---

[39] Ibid., 35–36.

This continuity presupposes certain essential structures that are inscribed in the order of reality. Yet these essential structures are not absolutely necessary because physical realities are also fundamentally contingent: they can exist or not exist.[40] What is more, they do not exist in and of themselves, but maintain their contingent existence only *from and with others.* The realities we experience are thus neither perfectly necessary nor entirely contingent; so the *existence* of necessity in and through contingency calls for a first, absolutely necessary existent, which exists by itself, from which all others are derived. If one attempts to posit, in the place of God, an infinite series of contingent realities alone, this would explain nothing. Each contingent reality implies, in the intelligibility of its being, an ontological dependence upon another to explain its *relative* necessity. Any series of contingent realities thus requires a first necessary being to create the series. To argue that a pure contingency stands at the origin of all things is to affirm in fact the primacy of nothingness, thereby negating all necessity and determination. And this idea obviously stands in contradiction to reality as we experience it.

The fourth demonstration examines the degrees of perfection in things according to the transcendental orders that are identified by the intuition of being. Goodness, beauty, life, knowledge, love, truth, and above all, being are found to exist according to differing degrees of perfection or of value, in the diverse realities we experience. Each of these orders is analogical and diverse, but also implies a unity. One person can possess a greater goodness or beauty than another, or can possess it differently. In either case, however, an underlying common order of goodness or beauty is implied, and every order implies a first term of perfection, by which that order is measured. Yet any reality that has these qualities and that is itself relative to other realities possessing these qualities differently, in a greater or lesser way, cannot be first. It is a member of the order, in which it participates, and consequently is not the cause of its own goodness, being, and so on.

> In other words, it is necessary that there exist somewhere a maximum or a supreme degree of goodness (and other transcendental values we have discussed). But this maximum or supreme degree, because it is the primary cause of all that is good in other things, is the summit *beyond* the infinite series of all the possible degrees of goodness in other things. It is a superior degree that is outside of the series. It is a transcendent primary cause, which is good in and of itself, and therefore which does not have goodness but which is goodness—itself subsistent Goodness.[41]

---

[40] Ibid., 41: "Generally speaking, a thing is contingent if its non-occurrence or its 'absence of position' in being is not an impossibility."

[41] Ibid., 46–47.

The author acknowledges that this demonstration depends upon the axiom: in any series in which there is a greater and a least, there must be something first that is greatest. Maritain affirms that this principle is necessary and evident in and of itself.

The final demonstration is based upon the governing of things toward an end. Amidst the diverse realities we experience, we can note certain stable and constant orientations present in beings without intelligence. The universe manifests a system of regular relations oriented in stably defined ways. The realities in nature imply, in their very natures, tendencies toward certain ends, and these tendencies are thus identical with their very ontological structures. All things are determined intrinsically by certain ends toward which they tend, and which therefore characterize what they are. But if teleology is inscribed ontologically in non-spiritual realities (other than artistic ones), these certainly do not come from the human intelligence, but neither from the realities themselves, which are, rather, constituted by such tendencies. Their existence thus depends upon a first intelligence and orderer, an author of these determinations who is both omnipresent and distinct from the things themselves. This being cannot, in turn, depend upon another for his teleological accomplishment, because this only prolongs the difficulty. We must affirm a first transcendent cause in which existence and intellect are the same, and whose own end is his own proper goodness.[42]

Due to the imperfect but real knowledge of God afforded by these demonstrations, Maritain concludes that the human intellect is naturally capable of knowing God. Such knowledge fulfills man's desire for understanding and meaning in a unique way. Consequently, one can detect the existence of a teleological inclination inscribed in human beings toward this knowledge as an end. The question of the natural desire for knowledge of God is of course a complex one. Here it suffices to note that for this philosopher, the existential development of the person (through "second acts" of intelligence and love) can be resolved only in relation to the truth and the goodness of being, and ultimately in relation to the primary being, truth, and goodness who is God. This truth and goodness of God's being is identical with God's wisdom. Therefore, the demonstration of the existence of God permits the philosopher to identify the contemplation of such wisdom as the natural end of man.

Critical Reflections

As I have mentioned above at several points, Maritain's philosophical exposition of metaphysics lacks a study of the *intrinsic* causes of being *qua* being,

---

[42] Ibid., 51–56.

meaning a study of the substance and actuality as the formal and final causes of a thing's existing. He substitutes for this instead a study of the transcendental notions. In order to reflect critically on his thought, therefore, I will discuss briefly Aquinas's position on resolution to proper causes, and will attempt to rethink the stages of Maritain's metaphysics in correspondence with what I take to be alternative aspects of Aquinas's approach.

Resolution and Causality

I have remarked above that Maritain's notion of an intuition of being seems to unite the activity Aquinas names "resolution" with the *intellectus* habit of the intellect (which grasps proper principles). However, Aquinas clearly affirms that *resolution* moves in two directions. One can move "backward" from our ordinary conceptions to seek the most fundamental notions present in our apprehension of the categorial modes of being. These are the general modes of being intrinsic to all the categories (the transcendentals). For Aquinas (following Aristotle), such study makes one aware of the irreducible first principles of *critical* reasoning: the principle of identity ("each being we experience exists") and that of non-contradiction ("something cannot both be and not be under the same aspect at the same time"). These principles are grasped as laws of ordinary thinking that accompany our most basic, pre-reflexive apprehensions and judgments.[43] Maritain, following Garrigou-Lagrange, begins metaphysics with the resolution to such principles, approaching being chiefly through the critical study of definitions, rather than through the study of causes. He identifies the primary transcendental notions of the intellect with the object of the *separatio* level of abstraction, and thus makes their study the subject of metaphysics.

However, Aquinas clearly thinks that resolution also moves "forward" from our initial, experiential apprehension of the categorial modes of being to the study of the causes and principles of being *qua* being.[44] Such

---

[43] *In IV Meta.*, lec. 6, 605: "In the first operation [apprehension] the first thing that the intellect conceives is *being*, and in this operation nothing else can be conceived unless being is understood. And because this principle—it is impossible for a thing both to be and not be at the same time—depends on the understanding of being . . . then this principle is by nature also the first in the second operation of the intellect, i.e., in the act of combining and separating [i.e., judgment]." For Aquinas, as for Aristotle, knowledge that external realities exist is self-evident and manifest to the senses (*In II Physics*, lec. 1, 148). If someone denies such knowledge, no direct refutation is possible, unless the skeptic is willing to affirm anything to exist or to truly be (*In XI Meta.*, lec. 5). (Aristotle notes, however, that the skeptic will still eat bread, even if he claims that he does not know if it exists: *Metaphysics K*, 6, 1063a28–35.)

[44] A very clear example of this is found in *Expos. de Trin.*, q. 5, a. 4: "Thus the principles of accidents are reducible to the principles of substance, and the principles of perishable substances are reducible to imperishable ones, with the result that all

resolution involves an analysis of reality such as we first encounter it, so as to discover the necessary per se causes of the reality as it is constituted in itself.[45] Aquinas affirms that this form of reduction can be of two kinds: that to intrinsic causes of the realities studied, and that to their extrinsic causes.[46] To understand better his affirmation, it is important to refer to a parallel text in Aquinas's commentary on *Metaphysics Λ*, 4 and 5. Here he states clearly that metaphysical science studies both the intrinsic causes being considered *qua* being and the extrinsic causes.[47] The ultimate transcendent cause studied in metaphysics is the primary being, as stated in the prologue of the *Metaphysics* and Book *E*, 1. The intrinsic causes, however, are explicitly affirmed to be the principles of substance (as form existing in matter), and actuality and potentiality.[48]

---

beings are reducible to certain principles in a definite graded order. And since the principle of the being of all things must be being in the highest degree, as the *Metaphysics* says [*A*, 2, 993b24–31], these principles must be most perfect and therefore supremely in act, so that they have no potentiality whatsoever . . . because act is prior to and more excellent than potentiality." On the *intellectus* of first principles as the source of a process of reasoning toward the discovery of further principles, see *ELP* I, c. 1, lec. 1; *ST* I, 79, a. 8. For Aquinas, the study of the logical structure of predication can offer a basis for reflection on causal, ontological foundations for our affirmations in the realities to which the predications are assigned. On this point see the studies of Jan Aertsen, *Nature and Creature* (Leiden: Brill, 1988), 54–91, and Michael Tavussi, "Aquinas on Resolution in Metaphysics," *Thomist* 55 (1991): 199–227.

45 *Expos. de Trin.*, q. 6, a. 1, c. 3: "Now reason . . . advances from one thing to another in the order of reality; for example, when a demonstration is made through external causes or effects: by synthesis when we go from causes to effects, by analysis [*resoluendo*] when we proceed from effects to causes."

46 *Expos. de Trin.*, q. 6, a. 1, c. 1 and 3.

47 *In XII Meta.*, lec. 4, 2468–69: "[N]ot only what is intrinsic is a cause, but also what is extrinsic, i.e., a mover. [Therefore] it is evident that principle and element differ. For principle in the strict sense means an extrinsic cause, as a mover, since it is from this that motion proceeds; whereas element in the strict sense means an intrinsic cause, of which a thing is composed. Yet both are called causes, i.e., both extrinsic principles and intrinsic ones. And in a sense principle is divided into these, i.e., into intrinsic and extrinsic causes. For there are certain intrinsic principles, as has been shown in Book *Δ* [paragraphs 755–56]; for example, the foundation of a house is a principle of it in the sense of matter, and a soul is the principle of a man in the sense of form."

48 *In XII Meta.*, lec. 4, 2475: "Now some beings (substances) are capable of separate existence, and others (accidents) are not, because modifications and motions and accidents of this kind cannot exist apart from substances. It is evident, then, that the first principles in the category of substance are also the causes of all the other categories. This applies not only to the first moving cause but also to intrinsic causes; for the matter and form of a substance are the causes of its accidents." 2477: "Then [Aristotle] gives a second way in which the principles of all things are proportionally the

This text needs to be placed alongside those of Aquinas's *Expos. de Trin.*, q. 5, a. 4, and q. 6, a. 1, ad 1 and 3. As I have mentioned above, in the first of these texts, Aquinas identifies the *separatio* degree of abstraction with the Aristotelian causal notions of "substance, actuality, and potentiality." These are notions potentially attributable to separate being. Both here and in the second text, he distinguishes resolution to intrinsic causes versus resolution to extrinsic causes. An Aristotelian interpretation of these diverse texts on resolution brings them into an intelligible unity: the resolution to intrinsic causes in metaphysics comes about through the study of substance and actuality as causes of beings *qua* being. Subsequently, due to the primacy of actuality over potentiality, the philosopher can consider a resolution to *extrinsic* causes upon which intrinsic causes depend. (Each substantial reality we experience is in some way actuated by another.) Through the consideration of causal dependencies (existing in causal series), one can arrive by this ultimate resolution at the affirmation of a necessary *primary* extrinsic and *transcendent* cause, which is God. Seen in this light, we can understand the content of the *separatio* degree of abstraction, which Aquinas says includes notions such as "substance, actuality and potentiality." These are *causal* notions derived initially from a study of intrinsic causes of being *qua* being and attributed subsequently, by analogy, to the being discovered as the transcendent extrinsic cause of being. This interpretation helps make sense of Aquinas's assertion in both *Expos. de Trin.*, q. 5, a. 4, and the prologue to his commentary on the *Metaphysics* that the subject of metaphysics is the being of realities we experience directly, and that God is approached by this science only as the cause of its subject. Discovery of the intrinsic causes resolves the study of being. Each being, however, is actuated by an extrinsic cause, and such beings exist in interdependent series of moved movers. Therefore, the mind is turned toward a more ultimate theological investigation concerning the primary extrinsic cause of being.[49] This interpretation harmonizes well with the *Metaphysics* of Aristotle (at least, as I have presented it in chapter 2). The primary being, for Aquinas, has an ontological priority with regard to all others, but *for us* this is discovered last.[50] The primary being, then, does not have a logical priority for the formation of our concept of being. There can be no quasi-immediate (virtually pre-experiential) intuition of the infinite being of God based upon the consideration of the transcendental

---

same. He says that the principles of all things are proportionally the same in another sense inasmuch as we say that actuality and potentiality are the principles of things."

[49] This assertion is also made in *In XII Meta.*, lec. 4, 2481. See the comments of Aertsen, *Medieval Philosophy and the Transcendentals*, 119–21, which interpret Aquinas in a similar sense.

[50] This is Aquinas's teaching in *Expos. de Trin.*, q. 6, a. 1, ad 1 and 3, citing Aristotle, *Physics* II, 1, 184a16–21.

dimensions of being. On the contrary, knowledge of God presupposes knowledge of being, substance, actuality, and potentiality in the realities we experience directly. Subsequently, an a posteriori causal demonstration of the real dependence of these realities upon a transcendent primary cause permits one, in turn, to extend notions of "being," "substance," and "actuality" analogically so as to attribute them to the first cause.

Analogical Study of the Causes of Being

How can Maritain's metaphysics of the human person and his demonstrations in natural theology be reevaluated from the viewpoint of an intrinsic causal analysis? To treat these topics here, I will briefly sketch out a reinterpretation of elements of Maritain's study, taking account of this missing aspect. (However, I will attempt to further develop such an approach in the following chapters.) In so doing, I will suggest how the diverse Thomistic analogies discussed in chapter 3 (the analogy of proper proportionality, the *pros hen* or *multa ad unum* analogy, and the *ad alterum* analogy) can be seen to be incorporated into this study, and related to causal knowledge of principles. This will be a corrective to Maritain's exclusive use of the first of these analogies. Once this solution has been proposed, I will evaluate briefly Maritain's metaphysics of the human person and his treatment of the *quinque viae*.

Aquinas, following Aristotle, notes that the study of being *qua* being begins from the initial experience of the categorial modes of being. This experience of *ens* is multiple (or "said in many ways"), and known in its oneness only proportionally.[51] The being of a quantity is understood distinctly from the being of a quality, and so on. Yet all the categories reveal something of being.[52] Second, then, because we understand being to be common (proportionally) to the diverse categories, we can also ask *why* there is this unity amidst the diversity? Why is being apprehended, not only in a proportional diversity, but also in a unity? This question leads into a reflection on the formal determination of being, of the substance as

---

51   *In VII Meta.*, lec. 1, 1331–34.

52   What is true of being is also true of oneness or goodness. On unity and being, see *In IV Meta.*, lec. 2, 561. On goodness, see *In I Ethic.*, lec. 6, 81: "Now good, like being with which it is convertible, is found in every category. Thus the *quodquidest* or substance, God, in whom there is no evil, is called good; the intellect, which is always true, is called good. In quality good is predicated of virtue, which makes its possessor good; in quantity, of the mean, which is the good in everything subject to measure. In relation, good is predicated of the useful which is good relative to a proper end. . . . The same may be said of the other categories. It is clear, therefore, that there is not some one good that is the idea or the common *ratio* of all goods. Otherwise good would not be found in every category but in one alone."

the principle of unity. In *Metaphysics Z*, 17, Aristotle resolves his study of the substance, now understood as the unifying ontological cause (according to the form) of the other categorial modes of being.[53] For Aquinas, substance, or the *quod quid erat esse*, implies both the singular existence of a given reality and its essential (or formal) determination.[54] In the light of the discovery of this cause, the other properties of being (denoted by the other categories) can be understood to exist only by the substance, and therefore can be called "accidents" of the substance.

As I have shown in chapter 3, the substance as a cause of the accidents is understood with the help of a second form of analogical reflection: the *multa ad unum* analogy. The resolution to the substance as a principle of unity comes about through insight into the cause of the unity amidst the analogical diversity of categorial modes of being.[55] It passes, then, from a multiplicity of effects (each understood as "being," in an analogically proportional way) to a unifying cause of being (*multa ad unum*). Therefore, if

---

[53] Though I am obliged in this brief presentation to skip steps, it should be noted here that Aristotle's study of the *ousia* in *Metaphysics Z* presupposes the study in *Physics* II of the principles of movement in sensible substances (form and matter), which have therefore already been understood as common to all the ten categories. In the *Metaphysics*, Aristotle is now asking why this material form (common to the categorial modes of being) *exists as a unity*. This is the question of the cause "according to the form" of being insofar as being. In his commentary on Book *Z* (*In VII Meta.*, lec. 17, 1648–69, 1678), Aquinas notes the importance of the "why" question for the discovery of causes in the *Posterior Analytics* II, 1–2, and its application to the question of the *ousia* as the formal cause of being at the end of Book *Z*, in chapter 17. This principle and cause resolves the problem of the multiple elements existing in a unity (paragraphs 1672–80). For an informative study on Aquinas's "scientific" approach to the substance, see Aertsen, *Nature and Creature*, chapters 1–3. However, Aertsen does not treat actuality as a cause of being in Aquinas's metaphysics, but instead interprets the "substance" as a (de-existentialized) essence, or nature, to be understood in turn by Aquinas relative to the Platonic predication of participated *esse*, common to each essence (see 80–91, 112–26). According to my interpretation, this would leave out the key role of the metaphysics of actuality as a bridge between the metaphysics of the substance, and that of the *esse*/essence distinction.

[54] *In VII Meta.*, lec. 16, 1636–39; *In VIII Meta.*, lec. 1, 1687.

[55] *In II Meta.*, lec. 1, 278: "Now there are two ways in which we attain knowledge of the truth. The first is the method of analysis [*resolutionis*], by which we go from what is complex to what is simple or from a whole to a part. . . . Now our knowledge of the truth is perfected by this method when we attain a distinct knowledge of the particular parts of a whole. The other method is that of synthesis [*compositionis*], by which we go from what is simple to what is complex; and we attain knowledge of truth by this method when we succeed in knowing a whole." Analystic insight into a principle of unity makes synthetic understanding possible in light of that principle.

the proportional analogy safeguards the initial discovery of the diversity of being, it also helps us see why the problem of unity arises, and opens the way to the causal resolution of the problem through the analysis of substance. The substance is the one "being" amidst the other multiple categories to which they are all referred *pros hen* (as the formal cause of their being).[56] The fact that the substance may have been considered initially as only one of the categorial modes of being among others (pre-reflexively, by the *intellectus* habit, according to Aquinas) does not entail its being apprehended initially as a *cause*. We can think very vaguely that there are things as well as properties (such as dimensional quantities) of these things. Yet to think metaphysically is to ask the question of *what* remains determinate and primary in this thing in question over time, such that it *exists* in its continued unity and identity. For this insight, a reflexive analysis of substantial being is necessary, attaining a resolution to the cause.[57] The substance, for Aquinas, is the formal cause of being.

The study of the final cause of being as being in potentiality ordered toward actuality can be applied analogically to the ten categorical modes of being, as I have mentioned in chapter 2. The actuality of a quality is different from the actuality of a substance. The study of actuality respects the distinction of substance and accidents, and, therefore, the understanding of the substance as the *cause* of the accidents. It presupposes, therefore, the above-mentioned *resolutio*. The substance/accident distinction permits us to see why Aristotle and Aquinas speak of different modes (*poion ti*) of being in act, attributable to the substance and to accidents respectively in

---

56 *In VII Meta.*, lec. 1, 1251: "From this it is clear that substance itself is said to be a being of itself, because terms which simply signify substance designate what this thing is. But other classes of things are said to be beings, not because they have a quiddity of themselves . . . but because 'they belong to such a being,' i.e., because they have some connection with substance, which is a being of itself."

57 Aquinas notes, however, the *implicit* awareness of the causal dimensions of being present even in the initial apprehension of the categorial modes, and contributing to the derivation of the categories (*In V Meta.*, lec. 9, 889–94: The initial perception of the substance and essence have to do with apprehending that the reality is unified in itself and something of what it is. The apprehension of qualities and quantity implies an initial knowledge of the form and the matter, respectively. Grasping relations implies the reference of the substance to something other than it. Time and place imply an exterior measure of the substance as a whole, while actions and passions reveal the substance as acting on or being acted upon by another. Habits are relations to extrinsic realities that do not determine the substance.) These affirmations suggest the importance of the judgment of existence in our initial contact with the realities experienced, through which we apprehend *inchoately* their intrinsic unity of being, and their intrinsic and extrinsic causes. For *explicitly developed* understanding of these, however, philosophical analysis is required.

an analogical way.[58] *It is only after making the distinction between substance and accidents by a causal analysis,* therefore, that we can understand the difference between primary actuality and secondary actuality, and the relation between the two. The secondary acts of personal operations, for example (qualities of the intellect and will) do indeed perfect the substantial being of the human person. In the light of such a causal analysis, however, such operations (secondary acts) are now understood as accidental.[59] They depend causally upon the primary actuality of the substance of the person (and its powers) which they perfect. (I will return to the importance of this point below.)

Because being in actuality is a cause that transcends the substance/accident distinction, it is therefore a *transcendental cause,* applying to all the categorial modes of being. This is significant, because it would suggest that if the transcendental properties of being (such as *bonum, unum, verum,* etc.) must be understood in the light of an Aristotelian causal analysis (as I have suggested), then they need to be interpreted in terms of actuality and potentiality. Only act and potentiality are principles that clarify *in causal terms* the nature of being *common to all* the categorial modes of being. Therefore, it is only after attaining knowledge of being in act and being in potentiality as the final cause of being *qua* being that a scientific clarification of the ontological meaning of the transcendental notions is possible.[60] For both Aquinas and Aristotle, for example, it is knowledge of being in act as the final cause of being that permits us to understand goodness: a thing is good to the extent that it is in act (either substantially or operationally).[61] Likewise with truth and unity: a thing is also more perfectly true, and more unified to the degree that it is in act. Potentiality, meanwhile, is related to what can be good, what can be true, or what can be one (and therefore with what

---

58 *In IX Meta.,* lec. 5, 1824 (on *Θ*, 6, 1048a25–30): Aquinas affirms categorically that while the notion of actuality is taken initially from physical motion, it applies also to actuality which is devoid of motion (for example, to the being in act of substances, and to that of immanent acts). This point will be of importance for showing a relation between act/potency and the *esse*/essence distinction.

59 As Aquinas affirms: see *De ver.,* q. 21, a. 5.

60 Aquinas follows this position and distances himself from Plato. The transcendentals should not be thought of as separate ideas, existing in themselves, but must be understood in causal terms. *In XII Meta.,* lec. 4, 2482–83: "The first principles which are understood to be most universal are actuality and potentiality, for these divide being as being. They are called universal principles because they are signified and understood in a universal way, not so that universals themselves are subsisting principles, as the Platonists claimed, because the principle of each singular thing can only be a singular thing. . . . For things which do not belong to the same genus, as colors, sounds, substance and quantity, have different causes and elements . . . even though these are proportionally the same for all things."

61 *ST* I, q. 6, a. 3.

is divisible). The potentiality for nonbeing can be seen to be at the source of an absence of goodness or an absence of truth.[62] The interpretation of the "content" of being, goodness, truth, and unity, then, requires recourse to the metaphysics of actuality and potentiality.

An important advantage of this *causal* interpretation of the transcendental notions (in terms of act and potentiality) is that it gives a foundation for the analogical attribution of transcendental notions to God based upon a causal demonstration of God as pure actuality. Such an approach, I would argue, also permits us to understand the use of the *ad alterum* analogy discussed in chapter 3. God discovered as pure actuality is wholly beyond the transcendental determinations of being that we experience in substances around us. However, as their primary cause, he must contain in himself the perfections of being in act (such as goodness, unity, and truth), in a wholly other and more perfect way. Such thinking avoids the dangers present at times in Maritain's way of speaking, where he seems to include the being of God within the transcendentals, supposedly apprehended by a kind of a priori intuition according to the analogy of proper proportionality.[63] I will attempt here to justify such reasoning briefly.

As I have indicated in chapter 2, *Metaphysics* Θ, 8–10, shows us Aristotle (after studying being in act) preparing conceptual notions of goodness, truth, and substance that will be analogically applicable to God (in Book Λ, 6–10). This attribution supposes the demonstration of God's necessary existence as the primary transcendent (extrinsic) cause of all beings, and as pure actuality. This demonstration is rooted in the discovery in Θ, 8, of the priority of actuality with regard to potentiality for substances. The substantial beings we experience are all actuated by one another within causal series, in which potentiality precedes act for the individual being (which comes to be and comes to act), but act precedes potentiality in the order of extrinsic causes.[64] Here one can identify where the need for a study of extrinsic causes appears: *it originates within the study of the intrinsic causes of beings, and the ontological dependencies upon others which they imply.* That which is actuated is actuated by another: thus

---

[62] *ST* I, q. 49, a. 1.

[63] Maritain, *Approches de Dieu*, 23: "Like the notion of being, the notion of existence is of itself, essentially from the first instant, an analogical notion, validly applicable to the Uncreated just as it is to the created."

[64] Aquinas comments (*In IX Meta.*, lec. 8, 1848): "For what exists potentially must always be brought to actuality by an agent, which is an actual being. Hence what is potentially a man becomes actually a man as a result of the man who generates him, who is an actual being; and similarly one who is potentially musical becomes actually musical by learning from a teacher who is actually musical. And thus in the case of anything potential there is always some first thing which moves it, and this mover is actual."

the need to "resolve" these causal dependencies to something primary, not in potentiality, which exists "separately," necessarily, and without potentiality.[65] One now begins to see how the first being can be known for Aquinas only as what he terms an "equivocal" cause: as pure actuality, God's being in act utterly transcends the effects by which we come to know him, since these limited beings are "composed" of act and potentiality.[66] Thus, this resolution to the primary extrinsic cause of being for Aquinas can be understood as a resolution *ad alterum* (and not by a comparison of proper proportionality, as Maritain affirms). The caused beings that are his effects denote his necessary existence by similitude, as one from whom they exist, who they must resemble. Nevertheless, from our consideration of creatures, we are capable of signifying what God is only very imperfectly. Consequently, God's pure actuality is not included in the transcendental range of human knowing.[67] Because he utterly transcends his effects, he remains unknown in "what" he his. Because God is pure actuality, however, he must possess (in an entirely transcendent and more perfect way) the perfections of being in act, perfections rightly denominated by transcendental notions such as unity, truth, and goodness.

---

65 *In IX Meta.*, IX, lec. 8, 1866: "[Actuality] is prior in time, as has been said above (1848), because the actuality whereby the generator or mover or maker is actual must always exist first before the other actuality by which the thing generated or produced becomes actual after being potential. And this goes on until one comes to the first mover, which is actuality alone; for whatever passes from potency to actuality requires a prior actuality in the agent, which brings it to actuality."

66 In *In IX Meta.*, lec. 7, 1849, Aquinas points out that equivocal generations imply some kind of likeness between the agent in prior actuality and its effect, and refers back to VII, lec. 8, 1444–47, where he discusses Aristotle's distinction between univocal causality and equivocal causality. He mentions there (para. 1445) a kind of causality that is partly equivocal and partly univocal—giving the example of the artist, who is an equivocal cause of his work, but whose artistic idea is a certain kind of univocal cause for the work produced. In the *ST* I, q. 13, a. 5, Aquinas will first discuss why the equivocal causality of God permits only an *ad alterum* analogy of attribution of names to God, as one who entirely transcends his effects. Subsequently, having discussed divine knowledge (I, q. 14, aa. 1–7), he will introduce the artistic analogy to discuss the activity of creation, which implies a kind of likeness between creation and God (I, q. 14, a. 8).

67 *In de Causis*, prop. 6: "For what the intellect first grasps is being [*ens*]. The intellect cannot apprehend that in which the character of being is not found. . . . But, according to the truth of the matter, the first cause is above being [*supra ens*] inasmuch as it is itself infinite *esse*. 'Being,' however, is called that which finitely participates in *esse*, and it is this which is proportioned to our intellect, whose object is the quiddity or 'that which is' [*quod quid est*]. . . . Hence our intellect can grasp only that which has a quiddity participating in *esse*. But the quiddity of God is itself *esse*. Thus it is above intellect" (translation slightly modified).

Personalist Metaphysics and Natural Theology

The analysis I have sketched out here will be treated more fully in the following chapters.[68] However, based on what has been said, a few brief comments can be made concerning Maritain's metaphysics. First, his study of the being of the human person seemingly contains many important insights.[69] One must contend, however, that the affirmation of the accidental nature of personal operations and their nature as second acts with reference to the primary act of the substance are not intuitive discoveries, but acquire their logical necessity only within the context of a causal analysis of being. This point is important for several reasons. It would seem that only such analysis will permit the human intellect to understand *itself* (its true purpose) by attaining absolutely true necessities (as is proper to causal knowledge alone). Only if the mind is actuated with regard to its teleological end can it in turn come to understand the full meaning of its own operation. Attaining the truth of causes (in philosophy but also in other sciences) permits one to justify the existential thirst for truth as a comprehensible and valid one. This theorization in turn permits one to begin to understand the teleological orientation of the person toward wisdom (as a knowledge of the primary, transcendent cause, who is God). Second, only such causal distinctions will permit us to distinguish posteriorly in what way the personal perfections of intellect and voluntary goodness (or love) can be attributed to God in himself. Such personal perfections in the human person are accidental properties, yet they are attributed to God in a substantial way by Aquinas. This can be made intelligible only if we have demonstrated through the causal series of substantial dependencies that God's substance (or essence) is actuality, and has no operations distinct from his essence. It also requires that we justify in causal terms the attribution of created perfections (such as intelligence) to the transcendent Creator.

My main criticism to be made here concerning Maritain's Five Ways is the absence of a rooting of these arguments in a study of intrinsic causes of being. In the absence of such a study, his examination of the nature of the dependencies implied by the five kinds of ordered causal series remains problematically unclear at points. This is particularly the case for the First, Second, and Fourth Ways. In the First and Second Ways, for example, he does not distinguish between per se (or essentially ordered) causes and accidental causes. For Aristotle and Aquinas, essentially ordered causes are *actual* causes,

---

[68] A key element I have intentionally omitted here is the place of the *esse*/essence distinction with respect to the discovery of the existence of God, and the articulation of the *ad alterum* analogy of God as Creator in relation to created, "participated being." I will return to these questions in chapter 7.

[69] On this subject, see Yves Floucat, "Enjeux et Actualité d'une Approche Thomiste de la Personne," *Revue Thomiste* 100 (2000): 384–407.

such as one's current dependence upon the oxygen in the atmosphere in order to exist, and the dependence of the atmosphere upon the agency of the sun in order to exist, and so on. Such simultaneous, interdependent causality cannot go on to the infinite; there must be something first in the series of such causes. Accidental causes are not actually existent, but are based upon dependence in the past or future. For example, parents remain accidental causes of their children's existence, even when the children no longer need to them to exist. A series of such causes can exist without end, then, as it does not require causation *in act* but only causation *in potentiality*, having been actuated in either the past or the future.[70] Indeed, according to Aristotle, an infinite series of accidentally ordered causes does exist because for him the world is eternal. Aquinas, meanwhile, affirms that philosophically speaking, this is not metaphysically impossible. Yet both thinkers repudiate the possibility of an essentially ordered, and actually existent, infinite causal series. The differentiation of the two forms of causality is indispensable.

Second, Maritain's arguments from movement and efficient causality (in the First and Second Way) do not distinguish between substantial change and accidental change. He appeals equally to operational changes as well as substantial ones as signs of ontological dependency. Yet it is necessary to distinguish between the two. Accidental changes do bear witness to the particular fragility of a being and its ontological dependence on others, but it is not clear that we can proceed directly from such changes to the existence of a first being. The reason is that accidental changes depend not only on one being acting upon another but also upon the substantial being in which they subsist. So, the more fundamental question is: how does one changing substance relate to another? Do we need something beyond all change to account for the existence of changing substances? To make complete sense of these arguments, therefore, there is a need to appeal to extrinsic causes of *substantial* generation and conservation, understood in terms of actuality and potentiality (in an essentially ordered causal series). Everything that *subsists* in act (or comes to be substantially) by another depends on that other (and subsequent beings) for its being in act.

It could be asked, then, whether all five ways in the *ST* depend upon causal interdependencies at the level of substantial being. Let us accept for

---

[70] On this frequently employed distinction, see *In VI Meta.*, lec. 3, 1202–22. Maritain speaks instead of homogeneous versus heterogeneous causes. This distinction does not overlap perfectly with the other. Homogeneous causes are not always accidental. A mother carrying a child in her womb is an actual (homogeneous) cause of existence. Furthermore, heterogeneous causes are not always essentially ordered. The oxygen a man breathed in yesterday was a heterogeneous cause of his existence then, but is not now. The examples Maritain gives in *Approches de Dieu*, 35, of heterogeneous causes, like the one just given, are not essentially ordered. This means they could potentially go on to the infinite.

the sake of argument the disputed claim that the Five Ways depend on the five Aristotelian causes: the First Way is based upon material causality, the Second on efficiency, the Third on the contingency of formal causes, the Fourth on exemplary causality, and the Fifth on teleology. In this case, one might suggest that each causal series examined implies ontological dependence on *both* the accidental and the substantial level. Material beings change accidentally and substantially, and their being in movement implies both forms of potentiality when they are "moved" by others. The efficient causality discussed in the Second Way applies to the efficient causes not only of accidental being but also of substantial being. It is more universal than the First Way, since it can apply not only to material but also to non-material beings that have an efficient cause. (God is the primary efficient cause of the being of separate substances.) The Third Way can be interpreted in reference to the capacity to be or not be substantially, and thus applies to everything that is not absolutely necessary. The Fourth Way can be understood causally in terms of degrees of perfection proper to being in act: that which is more perfectly in act implies greater goodness, truth, and nobility. Because the realities we experience are only imperfectly actuated (in both substance and operation), they indicate the necessary existence of a more perfect being who is pure actuality, goodness, and truth. Ostensibly the Fifth Way appeals only to accidental operations by which substances attain their teleological ends, but insofar as these operations are prescribed by the formal natures of the substances that possess them, they therefore raise the question of the first cause of the teleological order inscribed in these substances. In each of these cases, an examination of intrinsic causes of substance leads to the appeal to an extrinsic cause (from which and toward which all things exist).

Finally, there is the lack of appeal to causation in the Fourth Way of Maritain. He bases the demonstration on the supposedly self-evident axiom that in any series in which there is a greater and a least, there must be a first that is greatest. Aquinas does sometimes appeal to this Neoplatonic axiom as a seemingly self-evident principle.[71] However, besides the fact that the axiom is clearly not true for mathematics, in metaphysics it would seem to suggest that the notion of God as the greatest being is an innate, self-evident truth. Such a priori knowledge of God is clearly something that Aquinas wishes to deny in relation to Anselm's Ontological argument. From a Thomistic point of view, an a posteriori demonstration by degrees of perfection will certainly need a grounding in extrinsic causal dependencies. Since the exemplary cause in itself implies only a mentally immanent standard of measure and not a direct extrinsic cause, appeal to it will need to somehow be related to one of the other causes.[72]

---

[71] See *ScG* I, c. 13.
[72] See the discussion by Wippel, *The Metaphysical Thought of Thomas Aquinas*, 474–75.

Conclusion

In conclusion it can be said that Maritain's metaphysical science rightly affirms a relation between the judgment of existence, the conceptual intuition of being, and the *separatio* degree of abstraction. He claims insightfully that the perception of being afforded by this intuition is analogical, and he attempts to relate this analogical science of being to the metaphysics of the human person and the articulation of a causal demonstration of God in natural theology. I have attempted to show where an analysis of the intrinsic causes of the beings we experience requires a rethinking of several of these positive elements. In the next chapter I will study the question of how the human person might be brought to the forefront within modern Thomistic studies. A key question will be how an emphasis upon the being of man should be related to such a causal study.

6

The Human Person as a Being-toward-Truth: The Case of Karl Rahner

I F THE JUDGMENT of existence, the transcendental notions, and the analogical study of causes must all play some role in a Thomistic sapiential philosophy, they cannot do so without a sufficient treatment of the being of the human person. Among the transcendental notions mentioned in *De veritate*, q. 1, a. 1, Aquinas discusses the true and the good as general modes of *ens*. Truth and goodness are modes of being as it stands "in relation to another," that is to say, in relation to the cognitive and appetitive powers of the human soul.[1] Analysis of these terms, then, manifests a profound harmony between being and the intellect and will, respectively. On the one hand, our personal life of reflection and choice is dependent for its development upon our interactions with extra-mental reality in its transcendental dimensions: we consider the

---

[1] *De ver.*, q. 1, a. 1: "Some [terms] are said to add to being because the mode they express is one that is common, and consequent upon every being. This mode can be taken in two ways: first, insofar as it follows upon every being considered absolutely; Second, insofar as it follows upon every being considered in relation to another. . . . If the mode of being is taken in the second way—according to the relation of one being to another—we find a twofold use. The first is based on the distinction of one being from another. . . . The second is based on the correspondence one being has with another. This is possible only if there is something which is such that it agrees with every being. Such a being is the soul, which as is said in *On the Soul* [III, 8, 431b21], 'in some way is all things.' The soul, however, has both knowing and appetitive powers. *Good* expresses the correspondence of being to the appetitive power, for, so we note in the *Ethics* [I, 1, 1094a2], the good is 'that which all desire.' . . . *True* expresses the correspondence of being to the knowing power, for all knowing is produced by an assimilation of the knower to the thing known."

truth of things, and attempt to choose what is genuinely good. In this sense, the soul can "become all things" by knowledge and by love, to follow the expression of Aristotle and Aquinas. Yet, inversely, precisely because the human person tends toward the truth, and has a deliberate appetite for the good (by spiritual love), personal operations themselves reveal something unique about being.

A correspondence exists, then, between the gradual development of the "subjectivity" of the person (in his or her spiritual operations) and the general modes of being common to all that exists. To speak in Kantian and Thomistic terms simultaneously, there is a parallel relationship between the transcendental modes of being and man's transcendental subjectivity. Similarly, a point of contact with Aquinas can be seen in Heidegger's understanding of human being as *dasein*, as the place of the greatest unveiling of being (*Sein*).[2] Being is perceived as true and as good only within the operative acts of the person. Therefore, something ontologically unique is disclosed in and through man's awareness of being. What is the intrinsic relationship, then, between the development of the transcendental subject of man, and the transcendent structure of being? How do both of these terminate in the transcendent wisdom of God? Evidently, such questions touch directly upon the issue of a philosophical wisdom toward which the human person naturally aspires.

Such questions were also at the center of the early writings of the famous German Jesuit Karl Rahner (1904–1984). During the decades following the modernist crisis, while Garrigou-Lagrange was expositing his own "classical" interpretation of Aquinas in Rome, Rahner was attempting to reevaluate the legacy of Thomism in light of the critical project of Kant and the Heideggerian critique of classical ontology. After his entry with the Jesuits in 1922, he studied closely the writings of Aquinas, Kant, and Joseph Maréchal (the initiator of "transcendental Thomism") from 1924 to 1927 and followed the lectures of Heidegger between 1934 and 1936.[3]

---

[2] *Being and Time*, §14, 34–35. "Thomas is engaged in the task of deriving the 'tran-scendentia'—those characters of Being which lie beyond every possible way in which an entity may be classified as coming under some generic kind of subject matter (every *modus specialis entis*), and which belong necessarily to anything, whatever it may be. Thomas has to demonstrate that the *verum* is such a *transcendens*. He does this by invoking an entity which, in accordance with its very manner of Being, is properly suited to 'come together with' entities of any sort whatever. This distinctive entity . . . is the soul. . . . Here the priority of 'Dasein' over all other entities emerges, although it has not been ontologically clarified. . . . By indicating Dasein's ontico-ontological priority in this provisional manner, we have grounded our demonstration that the question of Being is ontico-ontologically distinctive."

[3] For a brief biography, see William V. Dych, *Karl Rahner* (Collegeville, MN: Liturgical Press, 1992), 4–17.

In his early theological work, he sought to provide an interpretation of Aquinas in affinity with the anthropological metaphysics of both Kant and Heidegger.[4] My goal in this chapter, then, will be to examine Rahner's philosophical theology, in particular with respect to his metaphysics of the human person.

Rahner's work stands in interesting juxtaposition to the two previously considered Thomistic thinkers. Unlike Gilson and Maritain, he attempts to reinterpret Aquinas's metaphysics of the human person and natural theology from within an all-encompassing study of the phenomenology of human subjectivity, with particular attention given to epistemology. This approach is unmistakably Kantian in many respects, and it has received criticism from some as a form of anthropocentric metaphysical reductionism.[5] However, Rahner's metaphysics is grounded in the study of the judgment of existence and is in turn related to the analogy of being, by which he attempts to speak metaphysically of God. In addition, his reflection on the being of the human person touches upon central questions that remain largely unresolved: how does the distinctive being of the human person allow us to say something metaphysically about God? If his solutions to the problem of a modern Thomistic metaphysics remain inimically problematic, study of his analysis can also illustrate the location of outstanding difficulties, and possibilities.

Here, I will consider briefly the background of Rahner's thought as reflected in the doctrine of metaphysical analogy delineated by Joseph Maréchal. I will then expose briefly Rahner's argumentation for the existence of God from operative acts of the intellect as developed in his principal philosophical work, *Spirit in the World*. I will then discuss his positions critically on two counts: (1) with regard to its inadequate response to the impasse to metaphysics as formulated by the Kantian critique, and (2) by looking at some of the consequences of the absence of a

---

4 See in particular, Karl Rahner, *Geist in Welt: Zur Metaphysik der endlichen Erkenntnis bei Thomas von Aquin* (first German edition: Innsbruck, 1939), *Spirit in the World*, English trans. W. Dych (London: Sheed and Ward, 1968), which is in turn influenced greatly by Joseph Maréchal, *Le Point de Départ de la Métaphysique*, Cahier I–V (Paris: Félix Alcan, 1926). Unless otherwise stated, I will refer uniquely to the first edition of the latter work, as that is the edition by which Rahner was influenced in the composition of his own work.

5 Most famously by Hans Urs von Balthasar in his *Cordula oder der Ernstfall* (Einsiedeln: Johannes, 1966), English trans. R. Beckley, *The Moment of Christian Witness* (San Francisco: Ignatius, 1994). See also Rowan Williams, "Balthasar and Rahner," in *The Analogy of Beauty: The Theology of Hans Urs von Balthasar*, ed. John Riches (Edinburgh: T&T Clark, 1986), 11–34. See the measured analysis of Rahner's thought by J. A. Di Noia, "Karl Rahner," in *The Modern Theologians*, ed. David F. Ford (Oxford: Blackwells, 1997), 118–33.

causal analysis of being with respect to the consideration of human personal being as operative truth and goodness. Among these consequences is the fact that Rahner's conception of the *analogia entis*, taken from Maréchal (and Suarez), introduces elements of ontologism (the claim to aprioristic knowledge of God) worthy of the Heideggerian appellation of "ontotheology." The latter criticism suggests the need for an alternative reflection in which a causal analysis of the principles of being can in turn permit an understanding of the operative agency of the human person *qua* being, and an analogical attribution of personal properties to God as the transcendent origin of personal being.

Analogia Entis in Maréchal

The Belgian Jesuit Joseph Maréchal (1878–1944), who taught Thomistic metaphysics at Louvain in the first third of the twentieth century, sought to respond to the Kantian critique of classical metaphysics by reinterpreting the "transcendental subjectivity" of the human person in Thomistic terms. The human subject is constituted a priori (prior to all thematic reflection on our given experience) by a dynamic teleological order toward the transcendental "structure" of being.[6] Like Maritain, Maréchal interprets the Thomistic object of metaphysical science to be the transcendentals, and he considers these to be the primary principles for the understanding of being. He also affirms that these primary notions are discovered intuitively within the judgment of *esse*, or existence, as the starting point of metaphysics.[7] However, from the experience of judgment he does not proceed to the study of being *qua* being by an analysis of the existents

---

6 This point is stated with remarkable clarity in the second volume of *Le Point de Départ de la Métaphysique* V (Paris: Desclée de Brouwer, 1949), 68–70: "The initial requirement of any 'critique' is an object present to our consciousness which is submitted as such to a reflective examination. . . . The ancient critique [of classical metaphysics, which 'critiqued' objects by studying their causes] posited from the first an object that was ontological, and included within this object the transcendental subject. The modern critique [of philosophy after Descartes and Kant] begins from the transcendental subject and postulates an ontological object. It is the thesis of this work that the *ontological critique and the transcendental critique*— despite the difference of the point of view from which they initially envisage the object—both converge by right upon a single final result: a dynamic metaphysics. If this is the case, then the conclusion imposes itself upon us: there must exist fundamental correspondences between the two critiques, permitting us to treat each one as the simple transposition of the other. But what will be the key to this transposition? . . . *the metaphysics of the knowing subject*."

7 *Le Point de Départ* V, 221: "The possession of the truth—or the grasp of the object—which occurs within the synthetic judgment (*compositio aut divisio*), expresses itself through the mode of affirmation or negation. This possession of the

experienced. Instead, he analyzes the a priori conditions that are necessarily implicit within the *immanent intellectual* act of affirming *esse* of the sensible phenomena experienced.[8] Here he will analyze the grasp of transcendental notions as a cognitive condition for the development of any knowing subject. It is the study of the activity of the intellect affirming knowledge of being that allows us to discover an inevitable tendency toward universal metaphysical science immanent to the intellect, itself ordered dynamically and teleologically toward God. An anticipatory, "pre-apprehensive" knowledge of the primary and infinite *esse* of God is implicit within each apprehending judgment concerning limited, finite *esse*, and makes possible our thinking regarding being.[9] In this way, Maréchal seeks to establish a point of unity between a scholastic understanding of being (*esse*) as a *constitutive* transcendental found in all that is in reality, and Kant's understanding of transcendental *regulative* notions (such as that of "God," "the soul," "the cosmos"), as explained, for example, in his transcendental theology in the *Critique of Pure Reason*.[10] The a priori dynamisms of intellect imply a necessary reference to the ontological determinations of being discovered through experience. Gradual knowledge of real being is the condition of possibility for the development of the thinking subject.[11] Likewise, the ontological determinations we

truth is connected formally, for St. Thomas, to a quasi-intuitive principle, that is to say, to the activity of *intellectus . . .* of simple apprehension."

8 *Le Point de Départ* V, 42–43, 199–201: The initial principle of understanding is the principle of identity (clarified through judgment), which has a transcendental structure, including the notions of *esse, unum, bonum, aliquid*, which form the subject of metaphysics. Rahner also makes the transcendentals the subject of metaphysics, in *Spirit in the World*, 188. Both thinkers refer to *Expos. de Trin.*, qq. 5 and 6, as a proof text, in the same way as Maritain. (I have argued above that this constitutes a misreading of Aquinas's text.) Yet for Maréchal (unlike Maritain), these notions at the point of departure characterize only the operative structure of *the intellect's manner of construing* the external phenomena. Only subsequently will he set out to demonstrate their necessary ontological foundation in the phenomena perceived.

9 See *Le Point de Départ* V, 233–327. I will examine Rahner's version of the argument below.

10 See especially within the "Second Division: Transcendental Dialectic," chapter 3, section 7, "Critique of All Theology Based upon Speculative Principles of Reason," in the *Critique of Pure Reason*, 525–31.

11 Maréchal argues that the intellect's judgments of phenomena as "being" have a necessarily ontological foundation. This is based upon the resolution of an apparent contradiction in the Kantian affirmation of phenomena without recourse to affirmation of the *noumena*. *Le Point de Départ* V, 42: "The relationship to truth is inherent in objective thought, for, once it is denied, it emerges within the negation itself. The moment in which you say: 'There is no truth,' you affirm implicitly the accord of your thought in general with reality. That is to say, you affirm the existence

reflect on a posteriori (in light of experience) also manifest to us the structure of the a priori orientations of the human mind. The dynamism of human thinking is ordered by its desire of infinite *esse*, in the light of which the intellect grasps all finite being experientially. This tendency toward the infinite makes the potential range of our human thought coextensive with all that is, or all that is possible. An implicit knowledge of God is, therefore, regulative of all other thinking concerning being.

The analogy of being is understood in this context as the key to the a priori structure of human understanding and provides the ultimate explanation of the abstractive knowledge of being occasioned by the agent intellect. First, for Maréchal, not only do the transcendental modes of being form the object of metaphysics, but these modes find their most perfect realization in the infinite being who is God. God is considered, then, as included within the subject of metaphysics: the scientific range of the transcendentals.[12] Second, analogical comparison with infinite *esse* enters into the very act by which we know and judge that any finite being exists. An analysis of the agent intellect (which I will return to below) permits the discovery of an a priori orientation of the human mind toward infinite *esse* implicit in each act of judgment. Maréchal reinterprets Aquinas's thought in conformity with this epistemology. St. Thomas's Augustinian affirmations that the mind always judges a given truth in the light of the primary truth who is God are now understood to mean that the mind's transcendental orientation toward God is the precondition for the formulation of all transcendental concepts.[13] Similar interpretations are given of Aquinas's citations of Dionysius affirming that the intellect "participates" in each act in the transcendent truth of God's intellectual light.[14] It is due to the tele-

---

of a relationship to truth in the very act by which you attempt to deny this relationship universally." The affirmation of a strictly phenomenal object is shown to be self-contradictory, because it entails an ontological truth claim about the nature of human knowing. Because of this, one must seek a new affirmation that transcends this contradiction. An examination of our a priori structure of reasoning seeks to demonstrate, then, that the mind is ordered toward being and is potentially coextensive with all possible being. Intellect is potentially coextensive, then, with all that might derive from infinite being. As Denis Bradley has shown, the movement of such argumentation resembles greatly Hegelian reasoning in *Lectures on the Philosophy of Religion*, vol. 1. See Denis Bradley, "Transcendental Critique and Realist Metaphysics," *Thomist* 39 (1975): 631–67.

[12] See, for example, *Le Point de Départ* V, 176–77.

[13] See, for example, *De ver.*, q. 1, a. 4, ad 5, as related to *De Trinitate* IX, 7, and *De vera religione*, 31.

[14] See *ST* I, q. 88, a. 3, c. On the Dionysian theme of intellect as a "participated power" in Aquinas, see Eduard-Henri Wéber, *La Personne Humaine au XIIIe Siècle* (Paris: J. Vrin, 1991), 426–36. John Knasas has shown in "Transcendental Thomism and the Thomistic Texts," *Thomist* 54 (1990): 81–95, the problematic character of

ological dynamism that orders all knowledge toward God that the human person can receive knowledge of diverse existents.

The diversity of existents that we judge to "exist," therefore, are seen ultimately to exist *themselves* in reference *pros hen*, or *multa ad unum*, to the one transcendent and absolute (infinite) *esse, in the light of which* we understand all others.[15] If we recall here that for Maréchal, the infinite *ens* of

Maréchal's interpretations of the texts of Aquinas on these points, since St. Thomas does not identify the theological affirmations of man's knowledge "in light of the first truth who is God" or concerning knowledge as "participated truth," with the genetic starting-point of knowledge. (On the contrary, see *De ver.*, q. 1, a. 4, ad 6; *ST* I, q. 16, a. 6, ad 1; q. 88, a. 3, c.: knowledge begins from the senses.) The former propositions are more ultimate affirmations made after the discovery of the existence of God, reflection on his transcendent nature, and the identification of the spiritual nature of the intellectual soul. This clearly differs from Aquinas's contemporary, Bonaventure. See *Itinerarium Mentis in Deum*, V, 4, in *Works of St. Bonaventure*, vol. 2, ed. P. Boehmer and Z. Hayes (New York: Franciscan Institute Publication, 2002), 115: "How remarkable, then, is the blindness of the intellect which does not take note of that which it sees first [divine being], and without which it can know nothing. But just as the eye, when it is concerned with the variety of colors, does not see the light through which it sees other things, or if it sees it, pays no attention to it, so the eye of our mind, intent as it is on particular and universal beings, pays no attention to that being which is beyond every genus even though it is that which first comes to the mind, and it is through this that all other things are known." Maréchal has fused together the way of progressive discovery of principles and the act of ultimate judgment in light of first principles. While the approach bears some resemblance to the medieval Augustinian tradition, it is clearly very different from that of Aquinas.

15 *Le Point de Départ* V, 177: "Between pure actuality and the most diffusive potentiality, there are intercalated, under the name of 'beings,' graded participations between these two extremes. . . . And these mixed appellations offer this in particular: that they are all ordered *in subordination to one supreme unity* . . . for [to quote Aquinas, *In IV Meta.*, lec. 1] 'the Philosopher says that although being [*ens*] is said in multiple senses, it is not predicated equivocally, but with respect to one thing; not to one thing which is one merely in meaning [*ratione*], but to one which is one according to a given nature,' and which therefore has for the human spirit the real value of an object."

This commentary on Aquinas's commentary on *Metaphysics Γ*, 1, is striking. Maréchal orders all finite beings *pros hen* toward the infinite being of God. Rahner will do the same in *Spirit in the World*, 172–73. The reading is entirely out of context, however, since neither Aristotle nor Aquinas is speaking theologically here of the relation of secondary beings to the first being. Indeed, in the next chapter of the *Metaphysics* (Γ, 2), Aristotle will show that the attribution of being across the ten categories (by proper proportionality) may be resolved through the study of substance as that unity toward which the multiplicity of determinations tend. If we apply the same analogy to the creature/God relation (which neither Aristotle nor Aquinas does) then we get an application of analogy very like that which is rejected by Aquinas in *ScG* I, 34; *De potentia Dei*, q. 7, a. 7; and *ST* I, q. 13, a. 5,

God is included within the subject of metaphysics, it seems clear that there is a Suarezian interpretation of Aquinas's doctrine of analogy at work in his theory of the transcendental knowledge of being. Both God and creatures are understood in common terms, with the divine *esse* as the positive pole and ultimate term of analogical predication of being, in relation to which all others (as finite beings) are related and in terms of which they must be understood.[16] Being is perfectly "realized" only in the absolute being of

since it groups God and the creature together under a common heading, in reference to a third ("being"), which gives a unifying intelligibility. This schema corresponds closely, however, with the Suarezian interpretation of the object of metaphysics as God and finite being, analogically compared. On the inclusion of God within the "subject of metaphysics," see *Disputationes Metaphysicae* I, 1, 19, and the commentary by J. F. Courtine, *Suarez et le système de la métaphysique*, 206–27. On the analogical concept of *ens* as simultaneously equally applicable to finite and infinite being, see, for example, *Disp. Meta.* II, 2, 8: "I affirm, therefore, in the first place, that there corresponds to the formal concept of being, adequately and immediately, an objective concept that signifies explicitly neither substance nor accident, neither God nor creature, but all of these by mode of oneness [*per modum unius*], insofar as all of these things are in a certain way similar to one another and they all pertain to being." On Suarez's use of the analogy of attribution in order to understand the multiplicity of all created beings as ordered toward the being of God, see *Disp. Meta.* XXVIII, 3, 10, and the comments of Courtine in *Inventio analogiae: Métaphysique et ontothéologie*, 291–336.

16 Suarez, *Disp. Meta.* XXVIII, 3, 16: "This analogy [of intrinsic attribution] or relation that the creature, by reason of its being, can have with respect to God . . . is founded in its intrinsic being, bearing within it a reference to or essential dependence upon God. . . . The creature is, in its essence, being [*ens*] by participation from this being that is in God by essence . . . as if from its universal and primary source, from which all others flow by a certain participation. *For in effect every creature is being by some reference to God, insofar as it participates from or it imitates in some manner the being of God. And, insofar as it has being, it depends essentially upon God, much more still than an accident depends upon the substance. It is thus that we say of the creature that it is being by reference or relation to God*" (emphasis added).

Courtine notes that: "The question of the existence of God is envisaged by Suarez in a quasi-deductive perspective, and the problem poses itself uniquely within the context procured by an analysis of the concept of 'being' taken as a [common] name. Being taken as a name furnishes the least common denominator for all that which is, from mere possibles all the way to God, pure act, and it acts as a middle term permitting one to pass from one extreme to the other. . . . With this one would naturally contrast the Thomist procedure, that examines the question of the existence of God within a wholly other context. Basing itself upon beings precisely insofar as they exist effectively, such that each of them is different and yet they are proportionately identical . . . the proofs lead to God even as they show that he exceeds the sphere of being. . . . With Suarez by contrast . . . the movement of the proof is absolutely different, and in a certain sense, the final destination is already present in and from the point of departure." *Suarez et le système de la métaphysique*, 244–45.

God, while intellect is directed toward this supreme *esse* in each act of limited judgment. In God transcendental intellect and transcendental being are identical: the transcendental subjectivity of man and the transcendental modes of being *both* attain their fulfillment in the absolute *esse* of God.[17] I will return to some of the consequences of this use of analogy after I have briefly considered Rahner's philosophical argumentation for this teleological structure of human knowing, and for the existence of God.

Rahnerian Method

Rahner's analysis in *Spirit in the World* resembles Maréchal's. He attempts to analyze the structure of the *operation* of knowing, particularly in the knowledge of beings attained through the judgment of existence, and implying the abstractive dynamism of the agent intellect.[18] His lengthy reflections follow a set methodological pattern of investigation. First, he will describe a given act of knowing (be it sensible or intellectual, or both). Second, he will identify the diverse, a priori conditions for the possibility of this activity. Third, he will deduce, by an examination of such elements in their intrinsic structure, the non-evident yet necessary dynamisms of these immanent, intellectual, and sensible acts, such that they might function as they do. Fourth, he will defend by dialectical arguments (arguments of retorsion) the truth of the structure of human knowing that he has deduced. If we do not accept the given structures he has concluded to be in operation, we contradict ourselves, since we necessarily employ such operations in our affirmative negation of them. Rahner will pursue this method successively at deeper and deeper "archaeological" levels of the knower so as to clarify more fully what personal being is, as a dynamic spiritual reality seeking to know being in and through sensible experiences, and thus as "spirit in the world." Epistemological activity is considered ontologically.[19] Ultimately, the method is used to detect a teleological orientation of the

---

[17] Despite parallels with Hegel, Maréchal clearly maintains an absolute differentiation between the divine and the created intellect. See *Le Point de Départ* V, 306–15.

[18] Rahner's study begins with a commentary on *ST* I, q. 84, a. 7, on the "return to the phantasm" implicit in every act of judgment (pp. 3–54). Aquinas is studying in this context an operative power of the soul, the activity of which is a "second act" with regard to the "first act" of the embodied soul and its preconstituted faculties.

[19] "A transcendental argument is one that starts with the undeniable existence of some state of affairs and argues from the fact to the *a priori* condition(s) for the very possibility and intelligibility of such a state of affairs. Rahner argues from our experience of subjectivity and particularly of knowing and willing, to what must be the *a priori* condition(s) for the very possibility of what we do all the time." Fergus Kerr, *Immortal Longings: Versions of Transcending Humanity* (London: SPCK, 1997), 173.

human intellect toward God (infinite *esse*) as the a priori condition for the possibility of every act of knowing. In this investigation, I will approach Rahner's central line of argument with a particular concern to establish only the essential components of his arguments for such a natural theology.

Presence in the World, Doubt, and Human Sensibility

Rahner, taking up a Heideggerian treatment of Cartesian doubt, characterizes man first and foremost as a being who questions being. The condition of possibility for doubt concerning what exists is the presence of the knower to the world of existents.[20] Questioning being, therefore, has a double sense. It reveals something of the transcendental a priori structure of the subject who questions, and it implies a being-in-the-world of *universal scope*: open to all that is insofar as it is.[21] Presence to oneself in the act of questioning presupposes the presence of the being of the sensibly given other (through the "return to the phantasm") as the condition for its possibility.[22] Therefore, as for Maréchal, the a priori transcendental structure of the person and the a posteriori science of the transcendental attributes of being are intrinsically related and inseparable. The transcendental notion of truth (or knowability) is affirmed as an ultimate principle unifying from within these two transcendental structures:

> If being able to know and knowability are thus intrinsic characteristics of being itself, then an actual, individual knowing cannot be

---

[20] See *Being and Time*, §53–59, 78–86, on *dasein* as being-in-the-world, as related to the experience of doubt.

[21] *Spirit in the World*, 58–59: "The metaphysical question as transcendental question is this pervasive question about being itself raised to conceptual form. In actually asking the metaphysical question man becomes aware of what he is in the ground of his essence: he who must ask about being." Rahner adopts the Heideggerian characterization of the transcendental subject of the *dasein* as the being "transcending" all categorial modes of being. (See *Being and Time*, §10, 30–31; §219, 261–63.) Yet he differs notably in relating this a priori transcendental structure in man to the total possible extension of existent beings. In this latter respect he clearly adopts a Thomistic realism as regards epistemological truth, as well as a Suarezian understanding of the potential extension of the intellect in accordance with the *analogia entis*. I will return to these points below.

[22] This affirmation is defended critically. If I doubt its truth, I demonstrate that I necessarily know something of the sensible reality I question or doubt, because the problem of its being is a question for *me*, which characterizes my own intellectual presence to myself. If "my" being-in-thinking is itself inseparable from the *problem* of the being of the sensible other, then my knowledge of myself is inseparable from a certain knowledge of the other. Nevertheless, this is not to say that we have an a priori, thematic concept of "being." The problem of that-which-is, in ourselves and in others, is posed precisely as a question. See Rahner, *Spirit in the World*, 57–65.

definitively conceived in its metaphysical essence if it is understood merely as the relationship of a knower to an object different from him, as intentionality. The fundamental and first point of departure for a metaphysically correct understanding of what knowledge is must rather be seen in the fact that being is of itself knowing and being known, that being is being-present-to-self.[23]

From this description of the fundamental and unavoidable human activity of knowing-in-questioning, what can be identified as the irreducible elements constituent of the person? This is the problem of the a priori conditions for the "return to the phantasm," since our manner of knowing is always situated within sensitive experience of the world, represented through our imaginative use of sensations.[24] This activity implies three elements: sensation, the judgment of existence (with the corresponding question of the ontological content of its object), and abstraction. I myself am a knower present to myself in and through the act of knowing the being of the other in sensible experience, and this implies abstraction: an intellectually immanent grasp of "what" a thing is.[25]

Rahner argues that the activity of sensation must presuppose a direct contact with the material and sensible other, not mediated by any objectification or intentionality. ("Intentionality" here signifies the sensible and conceptual forms of our internal knowledge through which we know and experience reality.) We must have a sensible receptivity to the other in the being of its reality, as the condition for the possibility of our knowing. This must be because our sensation is experienced only within the context of a critical question concerning being, which permits sensible realities to become a question for us. Thus, through sensation, we necessarily attain being. Were this not the case, our knowing "would remain in its fundamental act an intuition of its own intensity of being, and would not be a receptive intuition of another, of something objective in its own self."[26] If we doubt that we have sensible experience of realities other than ourselves, the very formulation of this question presupposes a certain *intellectual* knowledge of the other, and this can be the case only if we already really have "contact" with others in our sensations by an intuition of being. Metaphysical realism is the a priori condition for the possibility of human sensation.[27] Consequently, this sensation

---

23 *Spirit in the World*, 69–70. See also 72–73.

24 Ibid., 78–81.

25 Ibid., 117–19.

26 Ibid., 79.

27 Rahner wishes to maintain the Thomistic affirmation of the realism of sensation. Sensible forms contain "materially" the quidditative forms, which are in turn abstracted by the agent intellect, such that abstract concepts are realistic in content (*Spirit in the World*, 79). Nevertheless, he founds the realism of sensation upon its

is always, already structured from within by its role of mediation for our judgments of existence and our abstractions. This means that a study of sensation leads necessarily to a study of these intellectual operations.

Abstraction within the Judgment of Existence

The heart of Rahner's argument lies within his characterization of the necessary conditions of the act of conceptual abstraction, itself both presupposing and ordered toward a judicative realism concerning the being of reality. The dynamism of abstraction, founded in the activity of the agent intellect, can eventually be seen to carry in itself an a priori (non-thematic, non-conceptual) orientation toward absolute being (*esse*). This permits us to identify a natural orientation of the human person toward the absolute, who is God, implicit within every ordinary act of human knowing.

The argument begins with the differentiation between sense and abstractive intellect. Sensible experience alone cannot account for the objectification of our experience of others as different from ourselves, and the reciprocal, corresponding notion of ourselves as "subjects," since sensible knowledge is immediately receptive to the sensible qualities and quantities of others, and does not imply any noetic appreciation of ontological "distance" or differentiation.[28] Since both abstraction and complex judgments imply the immanent qualification of the intelligence, the examination of them is what occupies the greater part of the analysis of *Spirit in the World*. It is within the examination of the first activity, abstraction, that the key to Rahner's natural theology is discovered.

---

a priori functioning within our "intuitions of being," in the judgment of existence. The argument implies a circularity since the judgment of existence and the abstractive knowledge of being also presuppose real sensible experience of existents. Aquinas, by contrast, affirms in *In II Phys.*, lec. 1, 148, that sensible realities are self-evident. To question their existence or to question whether we have sensations of them is a sign of a lack of discernment between what can be questioned philosophically and what can be understood as evident. "To wish to demonstrate the obvious by what is not obvious is the mark of a man who cannot judge what is known in itself and what is not known in itself."

28 *Spirit in the World*, 117–26: Rahner's argument is based upon the Thomistic theme of reflectivity (*reflexio*). (See *ScG* IV, c. 11.) Intellect differs from sense in its capacity to situate the other as being another in relation to itself. This implies a self-reflective awareness of which sensation is incapable. The universal is the sine qua non condition for this dissociation of the intellect from the singular sensible, by which the mind can objectify the other through a mode in accordance with its own spiritual nature (by abstracting from material individuality). However, such universal abstractions arise and are employed only in conceptual judgments concerning sensibly known beings. Rahner does not respond to either Platonist or Nominalist objections to this Thomistic theory for the origin of universals.

Abstractions have three a priori constituent dimensions, according to Rahner. First, they have a universal mode, but always refer back to a singular subject. They refer, in normal use, to a "this." There is then an intrinsic unity between the universal concept and the "conversion to the phantasm." The former has a concrete reference point through the latter process.[29] Second, this reference of the universal to a singular subject occurs only within a judgment of existence, and such judgments can be understood in a twofold manner. They imply a "concretizing synthesis," joining an object and a predicate (similarly to Kant's a posteriori synthetic judgments), but also they involve an "*affirmative* synthesis" that targets that-which-is, per se.[30] "Looked at correctly, objective knowledge is not reached until the affirmative synthesis, or expressed in another way: *a concretizing synthesis occurs in real thought only as an affirmative synthesis.* Objective knowledge is given only when a knower relates a universal, known intelligibility to a supposite existing in itself."[31] Third, abstraction-in-judgment thus implies a quality of adequacy or inadequacy with regard to the nature and reality of that-which-is, otherwise said, of truth or falsehood. Truth, as a necessary a priori constituent factor in the activity of abstraction, appears as the adequacy of our conceptual judgments in accordance with reality. Here we see the theme of the coextensive character of intellect and being beginning to emerge, as the coextensive relation between the transcendental subject and the transcendental structure of being *qua* being.[32]

---

29 *Spirit in the World*, 121: "The Thomistic thesis that intellectually there are only universal concepts, and that the universal concept is known only in a conversion to the phantasm, are the two descriptions of this one structure of any and all of our knowledge, and they must be kept together." Rahner, following Aquinas, calls such synthetic judgments the process of *concretio*, outside of which, he says, abstraction does not occur.

30 Here is Rahner's use of Maréchal's "transcendental Thomistic" resolution of what is perceived as an inherent contradiction in Kant's thought. Bradley, "Transcendental Critique and Realist Metaphysics," 640–41: "Kant's account of the objectivity of knowledge Maréchal regarded as an error originating in a self-contradictory doctrine of phenomenality. The transcendental deduction of the 'affirmation ontologique' is designed to expose this contradiction and to supply a true account of the ontological ground for the noetic object. The linchpin in Maréchal's deduction is the concept of final causality, for it enabled him to appropriate the principal conclusion of traditional theory: that all agents must have some final end or terminus for their activity." See *Le Point de Départ* V, 375.

31 *Spirit in the World*, 125. The final cause of intellectual activity is the affirmation of being, without which the transcendental activity of the subject is unintelligible and its study self-contradictory. Rahner will give an argument from retorsion for this principle, as will be seen below.

32 Ibid., 125–26.

For Rahner, then, conceptualization according to its very a priori structures can be understood only as intrinsically ordered toward a knowledge of being, of the reality of things in themselves. Following Maréchal, he seeks to adopt Kant's critical epistemological turn while insisting on its immanent completion through the subject's intrinsic orientation toward metaphysical realism. We should note, however, that Rahner has not yet told us where this objective knowledge of being-in-itself originates, even if it is supposedly intrinsic to our acts of knowing. His defense of the irreducibility of this characterization of human thinking makes appeal to a dialectical argument from retorsion. If we doubt or deny this metaphysically realist orientation to our conceptual judgments, that suspension or negation itself implies an operative judgment making a claim as to what is not-true or true concerning the real nature of our intellectual acts.

> Such a reference [*Hinbeziehung*] is essential to human knowing. Insofar as thought necessarily thinks objectively, there is no thought without the affirmation of an in-itself. Man always thinks something of another something and thus always supposes something which is in itself [*Ansichseiendes*]. Even if he doubts or denies that he reaches this in-itself in his knowledge, that his thinking is true of something which is in itself, he supposes such an in-itself. For doubt or denial of such an in-itself constitutes one anew: the "that such a thing is not to be reached," the "that we are able to decide nothing about such a possibility," all of this presupposes something which is thought of independently of the actual process of this thinking, hence an in-itself. . . . The elimination of an in-itself explicitly realized in thought implicitly establishes one again.[33]

Having posed these three elements as necessary to any act of abstraction, Rahner's next step is to seek to unveil the necessity of positing the "agent intellect" as the operative, vital intellectual function permitting the process of abstraction. How is this done? On the one hand, it has been established that universal concepts have their origin in sensible experience of the real, yet exist in the intelligence according to a universal mode. On the other hand, these concepts are realistic in orientation, that is, they imply an orientation toward reality as it truly is. Consequently, their signification must have its *origin* in the experience of a sensible reality through which the conceptual "quiddity" of this given reality is discovered, even while being secreted by the intelligence itself, which alone can account for the universal mode of the concept (since universals do not appear in the singular reality that we judge to exist). Consequently, we can affirm a two-

---

[33] Ibid., 131–32.

fold dimension to the intellect: as "possible" in its receptivity to "what" realities are, and as an activity, as "agent," in grasping conceptually the determination of the sensible reality experienced.[34] This argument corresponds closely to that of Aquinas. The universal mode of the concept allows one to affirm the immaterial character of human abstraction, and the human intellect, and therefore, ultimately, the immaterial nature of the human soul.[35] However, the activity of the agent intellect is interpreted by Rahner in a unique way (following Maréchal),[36] as a grasping of the *limited* character of the sensible realization of the universal form, *by comparison* with the unlimited. It is this process to which I will now turn.

Pre-apprehension, Natural Theology, and the *Analogia Entis*

The key to understanding Rahner's natural theology comes from what follows. Having established, by what we might consider an a posteriori argument based on effects, that there is something called an "agent intellect" responsible for our acts of abstraction, Rahner will go on to clarify how this vital act of the intelligence functions. Importantly, he rejects traditional Thomistic descriptions of the agent intellect. Aquinas presents sensible phantasms as "material causes" upon which the agent intellect must act as a kind of efficient cause, so as to assimilate the implicitly intellectual determinations "carried within" these sensations and form a universal concept based upon them. Instead, Rahner sees the agent intellect as acting upon sensible experiences *negatively*, recognizing their existent forms in the material precisely by the fact that they are *limited*.[37] Singulars limit the

---

[34] Ibid., 135–41.

[35] See, for example, *ST* I, q. 75, aa. 2 and 6; q. 79, aa. 1–4; q. 85, a. 1.

[36] See *Le Point de Départ* V, 148–55.

[37] *Spirit in the World*, 142: "[T]he agent intellect . . . is not the power to imprint on the possible intellect a spiritual image of what has been sensibly intuited. It is precisely in this way that the intelligible species cannot be understood. The agent intellect is rather the capacity to know the sensibly intuited as limited, as a realized concretion, and only to that extent does it 'universalize' the form possessed sensibly, only to that extent does it liberate the form from its material concretion." Both Aristotle and Aquinas distinguish clearly between sensible images and intelligible species, or forms, despite Rahner's suggestion to the contrary. Compare *ST* I, q. 85, a. 1, ad 3: "But phantasms, since they are images of individuals, and exist in corporeal organs, have not the same mode of existence as the human intellect, and therefore have not the power of themselves to make an impression on the passive intellect. This is done by the power of the active intellect which by turning toward the phantasm produces in the passive intellect a certain likeness which represents, as to its specific conditions only, the thing reflected in the phantasm. It is thus that the intelligible species is said to be abstracted from the phantasm; not that the identical form which previously

application of the universal scope of the concept, and particularly of the concept of being. The realities we experience are understood in the act of abstraction as being limitations of *esse*—itself limited in and by each given form-in-matter, or essence, in which one experiences it.

> We must therefore ask how the agent intellect is to be understood so that it can know as limited, confined, and thus as of itself embracing further possibilities. Obviously this is possible only if, antecedent to and in addition to apprehending the individual form, it comprehends of itself the whole field of these possibilities and thus, in the sensibly concretized form, experiences the concreteness as limitation of these possibilities, whereby it knows the form itself as able to be multiplied in this field. This transcending apprehension of further possibilities, through which the form possessed in a concretion in sensibility is apprehended as limited and so is abstracted, we call "preapprehension" ("Vorgriff"). . . . So our task will be to determine the breadth of the horizon comprehended *a priori*, which horizon, apprehended as such in the pre-apprehension, offers the possibility of experiencing the forms of sensibility as limited, of differentiating them from the ground of their limitedness, the sensible "this," and thus of creating for knowing the possibility of a complete return [i.e., of abstraction].[38]

The pre-apprehension (*vorgriff*) that Rahner describes in this passage results from a process of insatiable intellectual drive present in the agent intellect and ordered toward *esse*. It is at the origins of each act of abstraction. These acts occur, in effect, by means of a pre-apprehensive comparison between a given material realization of *esse* (i.e., in a concrete being) and a non-conceptual, "unthematized," but possible absolute realization of being. Indeed, such a comparison is the very condition for knowing the limited beings we experience sensibly.

---

was in the phantasm is subsequently in the passive intellect, as a body is transferred from one place to another." For a similar teaching, see *ST* I, q. 86, a. 1.

38 *Spirit in the World*, 142–43. Note that the concept of *esse* is more than the concrete entity for Rahner because its universal mode is indicative of not only its abstract character but also its transcendent order to the total *possible* realization of being. Behind this view of abstraction is the affirmation of the a priori tendency of the mind to the total possible realization of *ens*, be it infinite or finite, real or possible. This implies a dependence upon Suarez's theory of possible being as related to the *analogia entis*. All *possible* realizations of created being are contained within the analogy of being and ultimately referred *multa ad unum* to the absolute *esse* of God. (See *Disp. Meta.* II, 4, 3, and Courtine, *Suarez et le Système de la métaphysique*, 293–321; Boulnois, *l'Être et représentation*, 439–43.)

Thomas knows essences only as the limiting potency of *esse*, as the real ground and expression of the fact that *esse* in the individual "this" is not given in its unlimited fullness. . . . *Esse* is determining, fulfilling, not determinable and fulfillable. Therefore, it cannot really be determined by another. . . . Form, species, and so on, limit *esse* only as every potency limits its act.[39]

If this is the case, what is the positive pole toward which the intellect is always, already ordered in this very act of comparison, concerning *esse* in-itself and the fullness of the possible realization of *esse*? The awareness that a given quidditative form is limited by its singular existence is possible only if one has a logically prior pre-apprehensive grasp of unlimited being. Only an intellectual orientation toward *being that is infinite* can account for our capacity to reflect comparatively upon any possible finite being as limited. What emerges, then, is the ultimate a priori condition for all intellectual knowledge: the pre-apprehension of infinite *esse*.

This discovery enables Rahner to reflect in turn on what it means to attribute *esse* analogically to the diverse finite realities we experience sensibly, and secondly, to consider the intrinsic range of application of this notion of *esse* purified of its limited realizations as we discover them in the experience of material, sensible realities. What he describes in this reflection is a system of objects, each participating in *esse* to a varying degree, according to an analogy of similitude, each one reflecting intrinsically in its own way something of an infinite act of plenitude.

Esse is not a "genus," but appears rather as intrinsically variable, not as statically definable, but oscillating, as it were, between nothing and infinity. The essences are only the expression of the limitation of their *esse*, which is limitless in itself, to a definite degree of the intensity of being in this or that definitive "being." Thus the essences no longer stand unrelated one after the other, but are all related to the one *esse*. And *esse* is not the emptiest, but the fullest concept.[40]

This structure of analogical thinking, like that of Maréchal, posits a notion of *esse* applicable *multa ad unum* to creatures and God, respectively. The being of the former realities (when considered apart from its limited conditions in which we experience it) finds its fulfillment in the being of God. We can discover that a priori, in our apprehensions and judgments concerning that-which-is-in-itself in any given reality we experience, we are able to judge that it exists precisely because our intelligence is always ordered already toward an absolute *esse* and unthematized pure act. Likewise, that

[39] *Spirit in the World*, 160–61.
[40] Ibid., 162.

which we judge to exist in a finite way is simultaneously understood to be relative to an unparticipated, infinite source of existence, who is God. A structure of analogical resemblance characterizes, then, not only the tendencies of man's transcendental subject (through his comparisons of beings with unlimited being) but also the transcendental structure of being itself.

> For *esse* appeared as the inner ground which holds together in its unity the determinations of an existent as its own, and lets them separate out as different from each other in such a way that they always still remain those of a single existent in its in-itself and can be related to this in-itself. So the *esse* of an individual being appears first of all at least as the intrinsic, sustaining ground of all the determinations which can possibly belong to the existent in question. But it is also in itself the fullness of all possible determinations absolutely. For in every judgment it is the same to-be-in-itself that is pre-apprehended. . . . *But it follows from this that* esse *in itself must be the absolute ground of all possible determinations: it is in itself "of all things the most perfect," fuller than anything else that can be thought of as reality with a particular determination.* It is in itself "the actuality of every form," "the actuality of every thing," the unified, generative ground of every conceivable quidditative determination. . . . *Its infinity is . . . that of the already and always possessed fullness of all conceivable determinations.* . . . The judgment which ascribes certain quidditative determinations to something which exists in itself, to the exclusion of other possible determinations, is implicitly and precisely a judgment that *esse* does not belong in all its fullness to this thing which exists in itself. But this also means that the real objects of our judgments are not distinguished perhaps merely by their quidditative determination, but precisely by their *esse* as the ground of these latter. Thus, every judgment is precisely a critique of the object, an evaluation of the measure of *esse* to what is judged.[41]

A number of interesting features present in this passage should be noted. First, the transcendent pole of all knowledge (God, as infinite *esse*) is judged to exist in an implicit way *in every act* of judgment. Second, this judgment can occur only against the background of a consideration of "all possible determinations" of finite being, and the question of an absolute

---

[41] Ibid., 177–79 (emphasis added). Citations from *De potentia Dei*, q. 7, a. 2, ad 9; *ST* I, q. 4, a. 1, ad 3; q. 3, a. 4, c.; and q. 5, a. 1, c., respectively. It is significant that these passages from Aquinas on participated *esse* presuppose the philosophical discovery of the existence of God, and examine creatures in reference to the God who has been discovered, while Rahner bases the apprehension of being as "participated" upon the a priori teleological determination of the agent intellect logically prior to all a posteriori demonstrative argument.

realization of being that transcends all that has been or could be experienced. In other words, we can and must conceive of God against the backdrop of possible being as "the absolute ground" of all possible determinations. Third, God as infinite *esse* is understood as the most perfect being conceivable, "fuller than anything else that *can be thought of* as reality with a particular determination." Despite Rahner's attempt to ground his metaphysics in a judicative realism, then, his argument for God's existence, like the Ontological argument, clearly passes from the order of thought (consideration of the possible, and the notion of infinite being) to the order of being (affirmation of the existence of God). The experience of limited determinations leads to the insight that "any conceivable determination" requires a being that is beyond all finite determinations, that is greater than anything that can possibly be thought. Seen in this way, sensible experiences become the occasions for an illumination by the intelligence (in the light of its own order toward a pre-apprehended absolute being), in which it estimates the limited character of the sensible reality relative to its own absolute end, infinite being. However, the end itself, God, is not demonstrated by means of arguments derived from the causal structure of the sensible realities themselves.

Spirit in the World, and Theological Reflections on the Person

Despite the problems which Rahner's philosophical work raises (and to which I will return shortly), numerous theological intuitions develop in continuity with these reflections, and are of importance here. First of all, Rahner's "epistemological" natural theology presents the human person as a paradoxical being. In his transcendental subjectivity, man is dynamically oriented toward God, who is absolute being, and this is reflected in the most intimate of his intelligence, in his most ordinary acts. A desire for God animates his very being-toward-truth. Yet simultaneously, precisely because his knowledge of truth is exercised uniquely within the boundaries of sensible experience, which of itself can yield no natural knowledge of God, God remains naturally unknown to the human person in categorical terms.[42] Philosophy ends in apophaticism, a natural, negative theology. Consequently, man is a spiritual being-in-the-world developing dynamically in history, yet constantly awaiting a thematized, or sensible and conceptually intelligible, knowledge of who God is. The structure of human subjectivity also anticipates internally an absolute, immediate, non-thematic, and intuitive intimacy with God. Man's natural philosophical quest is precisely, in another

---

[42] See *Spirit in the World*, 187 and 191, where Rahner affirms that the sensible world as such can give us no necessary knowledge of transcendent being.

sense, a recognition of the need for a gratuitous revelation from God, and is even the a priori condition for this recognition. God is discovered philosophically as an unknown mystery. Intimate knowledge of his identity is made possible, then, only if he communicates such knowledge freely through the medium of divine self-revelation. The person can thus be seen theologically, in light of the Christian "answer," to be in a sense "naturally" disposed to a sensible and conceptual revelation of God in history, as well as a transcendental immediacy with God by grace, one that can be achieved only beyond history, in the immediacy of the divine presence and life.[43]

Critical Reflections

Because Rahner has followed Maréchal methodologically in avoiding the study of ontological causality as a means to approach God, he is obliged instead to make use of an argument that passes from the order of thought to the being of God. Rahner's metaphysics unites a diversity of elements that have been discussed in previous chapters: the judgment of existence, the analogical knowledge of being, the study of spiritual operations to clarify analogies for God, and the demonstration of God's existence. Yet notably absent is a causal analysis of being, and as a substitute for such an analysis there is the study of the immanent structure of the transcendental subject, emerging through the act of doubt and the unavoidable affirmation of existence in each judgment. The operative "second acts" of knowledge studied from within form the basis for this ontology, without reference to a study of being as substance and accidents, actuality and potentiality, existence and essence. Here I would like to make two criticisms. The first is to suggest that Rahner and Maréchal introduce ontological presuppositions into their presentation of the transcendental deduction of the a priori conditions for the act of knowledge that are not warranted *if* one wishes to adhere strictly to the presuppositions of Kantian methodology. Their analysis, therefore, does not adequately respond to the Kantian impasse to metaphysical realism. Meanwhile their epistemology, by beginning from a suspension of certitude concerning the ontological content of the judgment of *esse*, does not really provide a basis for reclaiming a Thomistic realism, and therefore, a realistic *discovery* of the teleological orientation of the mind. Second, in the absence of a causal analysis of substance and actuality, one cannot adequately situate the relation of "first actuality" and "second actuality," and consequently the problem of spiritual operations as accidents with regard to the substantial form of the

---

[43] These themes are explored in depth in Rahner's *Hörer des Wortes*, German original, 1941; English trans. Joseph Donceel, *Hearer of the Word: Laying the Foundation for a Philosophy of Religion* (New York: Continuum, 1994).

embodied, spiritual soul. Without such a distinction there is not an adequate base of support for a causal demonstration of God's existence as the primary being and first mover of the human intellect. In fact, Rahner's analysis seems to *presuppose* what it sets out to demonstrate: the a priori (unthematized) apprehension of infinite *esse*. The means for articulating this presupposition come from Rahner's use of the *multa ad unum* analogy. Both finite and infinite being are always, already understood in relation to a common concept of *esse*, itself perfectly realized in God. Consequently, Rahner's interpretation of the *analogia entis* depends implicitly upon a variation of the Ontological argument for the existence of God, and as a structure of argumentation is not immune to the Kantian and Heideggerian criticisms of ontotheology.

Realist Presuppositions within a Transcendental Deduction

Both Maréchal and Rahner propose to alleviate an intrinsic contradiction within Kantian thought after having first adopted the presuppositions of Kant's epistemological method. They distinguish, then, between the interior activity of the apprehension of sensible phenomena construed conceptually as "being" and the ontological reality of the external world (the *noumena*). The examination of the internal life of the mind in its transcendental dynamism, however, permits us to see its necessarily teleological order toward that which truly exists. So, for instance, the act of doubt, when examined by this transcendental method, reveals as a condition of possibility for the act of doubt the affirmation of some really existing being, and doubt about sensation implies the intellectual judgment of the existence of the sensible reality in question. From a Kantian starting point, an internal contradiction is exposed and resolved by recourse to Thomistic epistemological realism. However, this method itself can be seen to be self-contradictory in many ways. First of all, is there a necessity to pass from the inevitable regulatory notion of "being" in each judgment to an ontological content for this concept within the phenomena? In the methodological context of Rahner's argument, the recourse to Thomistic realism is uncritical.[44] Such a tendency is manifest in another way in the Rahnerian replacement of what Kant considers to be the "critical faculties" of the intellectual life by Thomist "psychological faculties" or faculties of the soul—a view that, in turn, presupposes ontology, causality, and finality. Thus the simple a priori regulative *conditions* of knowing (of Kant) are indeed *presupposed* from the beginning to reclaim a priori *constitutive* faculties, causes, and tendencies. If the critique is

---

[44] For a development on this point, see Denis Bradley, "Rahner's *Spirit in the World*, Aquinas or Hegel?" *Thomist* 41 (1977): 167–99.

posed loyally, however, the existence of such given "structures" becomes precisely a problematic issue.[45]

On the other hand, one could quite arguably read Rahner's philosophy as merely running parallel to that of Kant. His critical analysis of the a priori constituent factors of the judgment of existence is not, then, intended as a transformation of Kantian thought, but rather as an alternative, more realistic account of human epistemology. Even self-referential knowing always implies an orientation toward that-which-is, and therein toward the truth. This interpretation would also be consistent with Rahner's acceptance of Heideggerian arguments against Cartesian solipsism. Yet even if this is the case, a second set of problems arises because this realism of Aquinas that Rahner wishes to present seems to be jeopardized by the initial methodological suspension of realism. If the initial apprehension of real beings is questioned, can it be reestablished by recourse to a deductive argument? Aristotle, or course, thinks not. "It is evident too that if some perception is wanting, it is necessary for some understanding to be wanting too—which it is impossible to get if we learn either by induction or by deduction, and demonstration depends on universals, and induction on particulars, and it is impossible to consider universals except through induction."[46] First principles of human thought (such as the knowledge of the existence of the world) cannot be deduced but only induced through experience.[47] It is only after the principles of existent realities have come to be known (inductively and by resolution) that they can be defended critically by dialectical arguments (such as those that employ the principle of non-contradiction). He who denies such principles contradicts himself in doing so. However, if we bracket methodically experiential knowledge of existents (*noumena*) from the beginning in order to examine only the transcendental subject, is even an inductive knowledge of beings still possible? Based upon the principles of Aristotelian realism, deduction could never establish the foundations for such knowledge, per se.

A third, related problem arises in Rahner's use of critically defensive arguments as sufficient demonstrations. If we do not accept that our judgments are ordered a priori toward an ontologically realistic knowledge, we

---

[45] On this point see Étienne Gilson, *Réalisme Thomiste et Critique de la Connaissance* (Paris: J. Vrin, 1939), 131–37. Bradley, "Transcendental Critique and Realist Metaphysics," 640–47, has shown in what ways Maréchal's work presupposes such "pre-critical" postulates in its critique of Kant.

[46] *Post. Analytics* I, 18, 81a38–81b8.

[47] *Nic. Ethics* VI, 3, 1139b28–31: "Now induction is of first principles and of the universal and deduction proceeds *from* universals. There are therefore principles from which deduction proceeds, which are not reached by deduction; it is therefore by induction that they are acquired." (See also, Aquinas, *In VI Ethics*, lec. 3, 1147–49.)

hereby contradict ourselves, since we must employ a judgment of existence in *affirming* that it *is* possible that our intellectual life *is* not realistic. Such arguments do show that we are indeed bound to think in realistic terms and to measure our thoughts by certain notions of being, truth, progress, and realism. They do not necessarily show that such notions permit us to know reality in itself, and that they are anything more that regulative notions of human reason.[48] In other words, the question of a true confrontation and comparison between Aquinas and Kant needs to take place on a more fundamental level: the examination of what we mean by "experience," and that of our conceptual judgments' adequacy to that experience. Are our abstract concepts constructed by the intelligence as an addition to the "phenomena" of experience, or do such concepts assimilate something of the existent natures of realities experienced, of *what* they *are*? Seemingly, Gilson is right to insist upon the necessity of true knowledge of existence not only as the starting point for realistic metaphysics, but also as a starting point for the analysis of human epistemology. Understanding our epistemological capacities for realism is possible only in light of metaphysical analysis, and not the inverse.[49]

It can be argued that Rahner's project fails to establish the teleological order of the mind toward being precisely because of the methodological suspension of epistemological realism chosen as a starting point. Aquinas asserts that sensible experience (and not the analysis of the transcendental subject) is the starting point for human knowledge, and necessarily precedes the intellect's self-awareness and self-analysis (which follow from it as a consequence).[50] If this is the case, then the mind discovers its own teleological orientation toward truth only as a consequence of its realistic study of the natures and structures of the reality it experiences. It is the being in act of the world that actuates the potentiality of the mind, and this in turn permits the mind to know itself by reflecting upon its own acquisitions of conceptual knowledge. This is particularly the case when the mind discovers the ontological principles and causes that structure reality itself, and most especially when it begins to know something of the primary, transcendent cause,

---

48 For a further development of this criticism, see John Knasas, *The Preface to Thomistic Metaphysics* (New York: Peter Lang, 1990), 52–64.

49 See Gilson, *Réalisme Thomiste*, 213–39.

50 See *ST* I, q. 78, a. 4. This is empirically verifiable in the development of knowledge with children, who first study others and learn to imagine and conceptualize objects which they react to emotionally before they formulate rationally their own feelings and thoughts, and this process is reflected in linguistic development. Otherwise, children would begin with Cartesian doubt and proceed to a transcendental deduction in order to establish the a priori conditions of possibility for the affirmation of the reasonableness of their desire for food, attention, objects, and so on, and this would be reflected in the way they spoke.

God. In this case, the Aristotelian and Thomistic study of wisdom, as a study of first causes, does indeed permit the teleological fulfillment of man's transcendental subject, but only because the mind has studied from experience the principles of existent realities.

Causal Analysis and Secondary Acts

Another consequence of Rahner's method is the absence of the study of substantial and accidental being, as well as actuality and potentiality, as causal dimensions of being. This means that there is no metaphysical causal study of the human being. This has serious philosophical consequences. Only the inductive (or resolutive) knowledge of the substance as the "cause according to the form" of the categorial modes of being permits one to distinguish the substance from its accidents. Consequently, one can distinguish between the modality of act and potentiality proper to the substantial being (first act) and the operations of that same substance that are accidental modes of actuality (secondary acts). Rahner's metaphysics seeks to establish an anchoring point within the operations of man's spiritual activities as a basis for ontological analysis. However, if these operations imply something "accidental" by their dependence upon the substantial being in act of the person, can they form the adequate point of departure for a direct route to the demonstration of the existence of a transcendent, primary being?

Such a claim is problematic in three ways: First, it is not obvious how the "accidental being" of man's spiritual operations is related to his bodily, material being. The latter is more self-evident to our immediate sensible experience. Therefore, it would seem that the existence of the spiritual soul must be demonstrated as a precursor to thinking about the relation of *immediate* dependency of human intellectual operations upon God. Can the uniquely spiritual character of the human intellectual operations be demonstrated without the prior philosophical analysis of natural bodies and of diverse living things as compared with the human person? The study of human operations of the *nous* for Aristotle is conducted by analogy with the sensible faculties of animal life and logically presupposes this analysis.[51] Second, can we understand the content of the judgment of *esse* without an examination of the intrinsic principles of being? Otherwise, what content does the concept of "being" have?[52] And without this knowledge, can we even begin to pose

---

[51] See the helpful study of Charles Kahn, "Aristotle on Thinking," in *Essays on Aristotle's De Anima*, ed. M. Nussbaum and A. Rorty (Oxford: Clarendon Press, 1992), 359–79, especially on the study of *aisthesis* in Aristotle. Under this heading in *On the Soul* are included initially both the sensitive powers and the operations of *nous*, and Aristotle progressively distinguishes the latter as powers possessing no physical organ.

[52] Rahner, like Maritain, makes the transcendental notions the subject of metaphysics, and thus can be questioned on the same point elaborated in the last chapter. For

realistically the question of the causal relation between beings we experience and an extrinsic, primary, infinite being to whom the others are referred ontologically? As I have noted in chapter 3, Aquinas in his Five Ways seems to argue for the existence of God based upon various forms of *substantial* as well as accidental dependence in the order of being. In fact, it is not obvious how accidental being taken alone can refer immediately to the transcendent being of God as its cause, since it implies for us *in via inventionis* a more obvious immediate dependency upon the being of the substance in which it inheres, or the efficient operations of other substances. For Aristotle (and, I think, Aquinas) it is by the diverse ontological dependencies of the substantial beings that we are in turn referred necessarily to extrinsic causes. Third, then, if one does wish to argue that God must exist as a prime mover of man's spiritual acts of intellect and will, (1) one must establish the metaphysical irreducibility of these faculties to physical being, and (2) one must analyze their development in terms of the causal notions of potentiality and actuality.[53] Yet even in this case, only the principle of the priority of actuality over potentiality permits one to demonstrate the necessary recourse to an extrinsic prime mover of human spiritual operations. This principle for Aristotle and Aquinas can be established (rather than presupposed) only through a metaphysical analysis of the principles of being *qua* being.[54]

In the absence of the causal analysis proper either to the philosophy of nature or to metaphysics, Rahner centers his argument around the intrinsic

---

Aristotle, "oneness," "being," "goodness," etc., are intelligible only analogically in reference to the categorial modes of being in which they are apprehended. Rahner seeks to locate their "universal extension" not in relation to the causes of the categorial modes of being (substance and act), but in the a priori universal range of extension of the agent intellect, ordered toward all possible being.

[53] Aquinas offers an argument for the necessity to pose a first extrinsic mover of the intellect for the passage from potentiality to actuality in the activity of human thinking in *ST* I, q. 79, a. 4. However, this argument presupposes the demonstration of the immaterial nature of intellectual operations (I, q. 75, aa. 2 and 6). In *ST* I–II, q. 9, aa. 3 and 4, he argues that there must be a primary extrinsic mover of the will on similar grounds (with reference to *Eudemian Ethics* VII, 14, 1248a16–45). This argument also appears in *De malo*, q. 6. Strictly speaking, the causality referred to is not a creative causality, but rather a *moving* cause, causing potentiality to pass to actuality in man's spiritual operations. However, Aquinas refers to this first mover as God, and in the context of the *Summa theologiae*, this presupposes the prior demonstrations of God's existence, attributes, and creative activity. Whether such an argument could be extracted out of this theological context and developed independently by a philosopher is a question that the texts do not resolve.

[54] Aquinas studies Aristotle's discovery of this principle in *In IX Meta.*, lec. 7–8 (see paragraph 1866), and refers back to it as the basis of Aristotle's demonstration of the primary mover who is pure actuality in *In XII Meta.*, lec. 5, 2499, and lec. 6, 2506, 2518.

orientation of the human mind toward God, as implicitly pre-apprehended by the agent intellect in every intellectual act of abstractive judgment. Given his initial methodological suspension of a realistic epistemology, however, his account of abstraction is based not upon the capacity of the mind to assimilate the formal determinations of realities experienced, but upon the negation of their limits, conceived in relation to the a priori finality of the human mind: infinite being. This introduces a very original understanding of abstraction precisely as (1) comparison with pure *esse*, (2) the determination of a limited *esse* in sensible beings, and (3) conceptualization of such beings through a critical negation of their limits. Thus, instead of a study of the principles of being in realities we experience, this metaphysical science is structured by a mentally immanent system of comparison. Every abstraction is accomplished by relating any given sensible being to the pre-apprehended notion of infinite *esse*.[55] Quidditative concepts are determined negatively by the intelligence subsequent to a comparison with the mind's own immanent *telos*. However, it is difficult to see how the negation of a limit found in any given sensible form can come to constitute a positive knowledge of that being in itself, since such a limit is construed by a *relation of reason* fabricated by the intelligence to measure two things comparatively; and likewise, a negation exists as a "being of reason" only in the intelligence itself.

Within his characterization of abstraction, Rahner seems to *presuppose* a system of participation of all beings in *esse*, an *esse* toward which the intelligence is simultaneously, always, already directed in all its encounters. But this, too, hardly seems to be immediately experientially justified, nor can it be necessitated simply by the fact that one can attribute "being" to all the realities one experiences by the judgment of existence. It seems rather to rest on an artistic analogy of similitude *multa ad unum*—Rahner's *analogia entis*—by which all *esse* is considered a priori according to an exemplar, absolute *esse*. The absolute "type" is the common, standard measure of all others.[56]

---

[55] Rahner follows Aquinas (*ST* I, q. 7) in distinguishing between an "infinite of privation" proper to matter and a "negative infinite" proper to God, according to his pure perfection that transcends the limitations of all secondary beings. (See *Spirit in the World*, 185.) In a sense, Rahner's metaphysical system unfolds between these two infinites as between "a below" and "an above." Sensible beings, on the one hand, in their material indeterminacy are "below" the intellect's proper object. The mind naturally moves upward through the negation of the limits we experience in them. This direction "upward" occurs, meanwhile, by means of an immanently conceived ideal—a pre-apprehension of infinite *esse*—so as to formulate an a priori teleological term for all thinking. Yet we never grasp God in himself. What seems to result is a mentally immanent movement between the imperfect beings experienced and the transcendental ideal to which the mind aspires.

[56] Boulnois, *l'Être et représentation*, 351–72, has argued that historically it is with the thought of Henry of Ghent that there is the unification of the a priori demonstration of God's existence from immanent mental acts with the transcendental attribution of

This leads to a second point concerning absolute *esse* as the *telos* of human knowing. It is difficult to see how one can pass from the affirmation of the non-limited character of human knowing, and from the a priori openness to all the horizons of possible realization of being, to the affirmation of a necessary positive finality in such acts of knowledge. The former characteristics are negative and invoke the indetermination and restlessness of the intelligence in its experience of sensible objects. The latter affirmation posits a necessary, positive, and infinite term. Surely one can invoke the former philosophical discovery as a *sign* that points to the *question* of an absolute being, who alone can satisfy the human intellectual dynamism. It is quite another thing, however, to pass from this problem to the necessity of God's existence as a reality. Is this not the passage from the idea of a possible reality to that reality's being, which is characteristic of the Ontological argument?[57] And if this is the case, then in fact we have not really transcended the difficulties elaborated by Kant and Heidegger in their criticisms of metaphysics. For the characteristic of the ontotheological form of thought par excellence is the centralization of all conceptions of being (as possible or real) around the aprioristic notion of the divine being, with the latter as that which regulates all metaphysical thinking from the beginning.

---

being to all that exists. Consequently, the notion of being attains its plenitude in God as primary *ens*. (The medieval thinker self-consciously seeks to reappropriate Avicennian metaphysics in this respect.) For Henry of Ghent (as for Rahner) the a priori demonstration presupposes a posteriori knowledge of sensible realities and abstraction of concepts of being, goodness, and so on. Such experience, however, is not the sufficient condition for the transcendental subject's orientation toward the perfect exemplarity of these conceptual entities. *Summa questionum ordinariarum*, 22, 5 (134 E): "From the truth and goodness of creatures we conceive of the absolute truth and goodness. In effect, if in abstracting from this good here or that good there we can think of the good and of truth taken absolutely, not as it is in this one and that one, but as permanent, in this we are conceiving of God." Boulnois, ibid., 359: "In reality, the perfection of creatures cannot be thought if we do not already know the divine perfection as the condition of possibility [of created perfection]. The representation of God is the transcendental condition of any and all representation."

57 This is the conclusion of the Kantian critique of Rahner's thought offered by Wilfred G. Phillips, "Rahner's *Vorgriff*," *Thomist* 56 (1992), 257–90, who claims that Rahner's arguments amount at most to the demonstration of the idea of infinite being as an ontotheological "regulatory notion" implicit to all judgments. See also Bradley, "Rahner's *Spirit in the World*," 198: "[E]ven if we assume that judgment affirms finite *esse naturale*, we cannot infer that the Infinite Being which is the condition of possibility for judgment of finite *esse naturale* is, for that reason, also the condition of possibility for finite *esse naturale*. The latter condition can only be established by an argument from efficient causality or by means of the Ontological argument."

Conclusion

The above-mentioned criticisms suggest that Rahner has not entirely succeeded in rearticulating a Thomistic natural theology that responds adequately to the Kantian and Heideggerian reserves with regard to
ontotheology. However, in contrast to Étienne Gilson, he finds the study
of human spiritual operations essential for the articulation of an analogical
science of being permitting realistic discourse about God. My arguments
suggest that the absence of a causal analysis *prior to* the elaboration of such
a study is a hindrance to its correct development. In the absence of such
an analysis, the use of the distinction of substance and accidents drops
out, along with a corresponding use of the analogy of proper proportionality as a way of thinking about diversity and universality in created being.
This absence of the substance/accident distinction in turn allows Rahner
to portray the intentional life of the intellect as something potentially coextensive with all being without a sufficient acknowledgment of its merely
accidental character, with respect to human being. A non-causal, ontotheological form of thinking results, in which thought—once it becomes sufficiently aware of its ontological presuppositions—understands its own
essence *as being* to be realized most perfectly in God's being. Therefore,
suggestive as Rahner's thought is, it leaves unresolved the question of in
what way really (if at all) human spiritual acts of knowledge and love are
analogous to the transcendent wisdom and love of God. In chapter 8 of
this book I will consider how personal properties can be attributed analogically to God in light of philosophical arguments for the existence of God.
These arguments must be themselves based upon causal demonstrations,
the subject to which I will now turn.

PART IV

7

From Omega to Alpha: Toward a General Order of Metaphysical Inquiry

THE PURPOSE of this book has been to investigate the grounds for an authentic Thomistic natural theology, one that is immune to the modern criticisms of ontotheology as posed by Kant and Heidegger. Their objections were considered in chapter 1: natural theology is inevitably ontotheological because it attempts to study the conditions of existence for any possible being. To do so it must have recourse to a consideration of the immanent system of human laws of thinking (i.e., principles of causality and sufficient reason) that are employed when metaphysicians attempt to explain sensible reality. The use of these principles eventually requires the invocation of an aprioristic concept of God in order to explain the sum total of all other possible knowledge. This structure of thinking places God at the summit of the science of metaphysics and simultaneously makes him the ultimate explanatory principle of human understanding. God is thereby assimilated by natural theology into its own systematic portrayal of "being" such that the divine is conceived according to a quasi-univocal logic (i.e., in terms of dependent beings), as the "supreme being." For Kant such a notion of God is a transcendental illusion of pure reason that allows us to organize all other possible knowledge, but there are no grounds in our sensible experience for affirming that such a being exists. For Heidegger, by contrast, this ontotheological concept of God converts into an absolute a merely ontic determination of being. Theism is a delusion that springs forth from our existential inauthenticity, and that prohibits us from wrestling in truth with the real questions of being and nothingness.

Thomistic metaphysics, however, affirms something entirely different. The claim of chapters 2 and 3 was that an alternative form of thinking can be found in Aquinas's Aristotelian methodology. Metaphysical science begins not from a consideration of possible beings but from the experiential knowledge of that which exists. This leads not to a consideration of the immanent laws of human understanding but to an analysis of the metaphysical structure of concrete beings, in terms of substance and accidents, actuality and potency. Truly philosophical approaches to God are not based upon aprioristic conceptions of the divine, but upon a posteriori argumentation. The latter does not assimilate God to the logic of intraworldly being but begins from study of beings in the world in order to come progressively to the affirmation of a transcendent cause of all that exists. An analogical reflection concerning beings we experience paves the way for a more ultimate analogical reflection about God that respects the divine transcendence and incomprehensibility.

Chapters 4, 5, and 6 examined ways in which three noteworthy modern thinkers attempted to extract profound truths from Aquinas's work in order to explain the way the mind ascends philosophically toward God by its own natural powers. These efforts were discussed critically in light of the principles of Thomistic methodology mentioned above. In the case of each of the thinkers considered, traces of thinking reminiscent of ontotheology were noted and were explained by the absence of some aspect or aspects of this methodology. Correspondingly, each of these thinkers was seen to have problematically identified a particular form of Thomistic analogical predication (*ad alterum*, proper proportionality, *multa ad unum*, respectively) as characteristic of Aquinas's metaphysical thought in general. My claim up until this point, then, has been that it is necessary for Thomistic natural theology—after Kant and Heidegger—to recover an Aristotelian order of inquiry that passes from a consideration of the intrinsic formal cause of being (as the substance) to the final cause of being (as actuality) to the eventual affirmation of God who is subsistent being-in-act. An understanding of the order between Aquinas's various uses of analogical predication is deeply interrelated to an understanding of his study of the causes of being.

What remains for the final section of this study, then, is to consider a proper order of investigation (or *via inventionis*) for the progressive discovery of the existence of God, from a Thomistic perspective. How can the mind inquire rightly into the structure of reality as known metaphysically, and come by way of this inquiry to the eventual affirmation of the existence of God, as the uniquely transcendent cause of all else that exists? Of course, any attempt to think succinctly about such a vast subject cannot pretend to be comprehensive. My goal here, however, is quite focused, as I wish to present four basic "building blocks" of a progressive metaphysical inquiry that leads to natural knowledge of the existence of God. Why are these elements paradigmatically important for a Thomistic metaphysics that is immune to the charge of ontotheology? How do each of these elements fit together? How does Aquinas's understanding of analogical predication find its root and explanation within this order of inquiry? The metaphysical arguments that I will give in each of these sections are necessarily cursory, given the limited scope of the inquiry under consideration.[1] However, the presentation of the arguments is intended primarily not to demonstrate the validity of each aspect of Aquinas's metaphysics mentioned against all foreseen objections, but to demonstrate how the causal analysis of each section of the *via inventionis* under consideration either follows from or renders possible the causal reasoning of the proximate sections.

The primary issue that a metaphysical science must be concerned with is the claim that metaphysical study does in fact attain to true knowledge of the existence and structure of things in themselves. The first section of this chapter, then, deals with the important question of the point of departure for metaphysical science: presuming that we can come to an authentic knowledge of existence (by the judgment of existence), how does this knowledge give rise to a scientific (i.e., causal) reflection on being? Only if such a causal study is possible in the first place can one respond effectively to the objection that all such thinking is based upon immanently mental constructions, rather than real knowledge of existents.

A second issue concerns the order of inquiry into the structure of beings, and the way this study itself opens naturally to an eventual argumentation for the existence of God. The second section, therefore, examines the order of a Thomistic causal study of being (conducted in terms of substance and accidents, and act and potentiality), and the analogical knowledge of being that it permits. The analysis of the intrinsic and extrinsic causes in realities we know immediately will form the basis for eventual demonstrations of the necessity of a transcendent cause of existence. It also permits the elaboration of an analogical conception of being that makes use of both the analogy of proper proportionality and the analogy *multa ad unum*. This causal study will eventually allow one to speak truthfully about God in analogical terms (by means of the analogy *ad alterum*), even while respecting the divine transcendence.

The third issue concerns the relationship between an Aristotelian causal analysis of being and Aquinas's metaphysics of the real distinction between *esse* and essence. If a progressive study of the principles of being is conducted in terms of the principles of substance and actuality, how does this relate, then, to the distinctly Thomistic metaphysics of the real distinction? Can an understanding of the latter be derived from distinctly philosophical

---

[1] For this reason I have alluded throughout this chapter to secondary scholarship on Aquinas that complements or qualifies the arguments and affirmations I make.

premises, or is it something that is intelligible only from within the context of Christian revelation regarding creation? The third section of this chapter attempts to shows that from within this antecedent causal study one may derive a set of questions that leads to the philosophical discovery of the Thomistic real distinction. One can invoke the latter, then, without depending upon any kind of a priori theological presupposition. Consequently, both the principles of Aristotelian causality (substance, actuality) and the Thomistic principles of existence and essence can be integrated into a distinctly philosophical science of being. This study in turn permits one to articulate a set of a posteriori arguments for the existence of God.

If genuine philosophical knowledge of God is derived not from aprioristic intuitions but from a posteriori demonstrations, then there must exist a continuity between the examination of the metaphysical principles of being and the demonstration of God's existence. The fourth section shows how from *both* the antecedent causal study of being (as substance and accidents, act and potentiality) *and* the consideration of the real distinction (*esse* and essence) one can derive genuine a posteriori arguments for the existence of God. This form of argumentation provides the basis for a genuinely natural knowledge of God, yet one that, by its analogical nature, fully respects the divine transcendence and incomprehensibility.

In the fifth and final section of this chapter, I will consider an important objection: if genuine philosophical knowledge of God depends upon a cultivated practice of metaphysical analysis and reasoning, how is it possible that it could have any importance for the vast majority of human persons, who do not have either the time or energy (and in some cases, the natural gifts) to pursue such reflection? Here I will focus on the human capacity for natural knowledge of God identified by philosophical reasoning. How does this natural dimension of the human being manifest itself in persons who do not undertake an explicit, philosophical reflection of the kind under discussion? In the absence of a "scientific" philosophical reflection on God, how can the question of the existence of God still arise readily, in a natural way, for all human beings?

Points of Departure: Physics, Metaphysics, and the Proper Object of Metaphysics

The first question that naturally arises concerns the entry way into properly metaphysical inquiry about the structure of reality as we experience it. I have argued above in chapter 4 that Étienne Gilson rightly identified the point of initial divergence between Kantian epistemological skepticism and Thomistic metaphysical realism. It is because *within* the sensations one can come truly to know the being, unity, and goodness of things that there exists a question, or legitimate interrogation, concerning the causes of their existence, their unity, and their goodness. It is because one can come to know that realities are interdependent as existents that the affirmation of causality as ontologically real is entirely justified. It is, moreover, because the attributes of beings are in some sense initially self-evident to the mind that we can inquire more profoundly into the "shape" or foundations of these attributes within the reality itself. Consequently, the Thomist need not feel obliged to demonstrate deductively the existence of singular beings of diverse natural kinds, with their various categorical properties, such as their qualities, discrete quantities and shape, or their relations. Furthermore, the various habits, actions, receptivities, locations, positions, and environments of beings we experience all derive in some way from their qualities, quantities, and relations. In short, these various modes of being (denoted by the Aristotelian categories) are always, already given as the fore-theoretical ground that in turn makes philosophical thought possible. The *defense* of realism in confrontation with skepticism is not identical with philosophical analysis of reality as such, but instead is comprised of critical, dialectical arguments. If one refuses the basic realism of categorical and transcendental concepts, then the natural life of the intelligence is inevitably sterilized, and the capacity for in-depth reflection on the order and meaning of reality is thwarted in advance.[2]

Even if we bracket in this context the important debate with skepticism, however, the advocate of Aristotelian methodology might naturally hesitate in perplexity as to how metaphysical inquiry should proceed. For despite all I have said above in favor of Gilson's theories of metaphysical realism and the judgment of existence, we are not obliged to follow Gilson and Maritain in pursuing the way of "existential Thomism," that is to say, of a philosophical reflection that would consider *esse* almost immediately in its deepest and most momentous of senses: as the act of being that is derived from a unique, transcendent source—God. For, as I have pointed out in chapter 4, if all our knowledge implies some basic understanding of being and existence (and corresponding concepts of *ens* and *esse*, for Aquinas), nevertheless the initial knowledge of being functions at a rather

---

[2] This does not mean, of course, that critical arguments in favor of realism and causality are not warranted, but only that realism is not produced as the result of such arguments. For helpful reflections on causal realism in response to empiricist and analytic criticisms, see Elizabeth Anscombe, "Causality and Determination," *Causation*, ed. E. Sosa and M. Tooley (Oxford: Oxford University Press, 1993), 88–104; Alfred J. Freddoso, in his introduction to Francesco Suarez's *On Creation, Conservation and Concurrence: Metaphysical Disputations*, 20–22 (South Bend, IN: St. Augustine's Press, 2002), xliii–lxxiii; Lawrence Dewan, "St. Thomas and the Principle of Causality," in *Form and Being*, 61–80.

banal level, in our ordinary awareness of the given world, in which we function practically and learn progressively without necessarily undertaking a more elevated exercise of philosophical reflection. Furthermore, as I have made clear regarding Aristotelian epistemology, some knowledge of what *exists* is required for any authentic science, or form of knowledge. In other words, knowledge of beings and of existence (as well as of unity, the true, and the good) stands at the forefront of our inquiry into sciences and arts as diverse as geometry, ethics, carpentry, modern physics, and medicine. So in what way might these *other* forms of practical and speculative reflection *necessarily precede* ontological considerations, and perhaps offer us ways of entry into the more elevated and ultimate form of philosophical reflection represented by metaphysics and natural theology?[3]

The reason that this question is so important is that a Thomistic response to the ontotheological challenge must be able to show that we have the capacity from our initial knowledge of existents to construct a distinctly metaphysical science of the *causes* of beings *in this world* (intrinsic and extrinsic causes of beings) as a prelude to a posterior causal and analogical discussion of the mystery of God. Only then will we be able to clarify how it is that our notions of existence, or goodness derived from things that we know directly, can eventually be attributed analogically to God, as the primary *cause* of those realities. If our mind cannot "gain purchase" directly in realities we know for a properly metaphysical consideration of the causes of being, then this task is not feasible.

However, a number of Thomistic scholars—among them such prominent thinkers as Benedict Ashley and Ralph McInerny—concur in claiming that this kind of metaphysical study of causes is not immediately

---

3 This question is related to the problem of subordinated sciences. The speculative sciences, for Aristotle, seem to be ordered hierarchically based on the respective universality, penetration, and simplicity of explanation of each. A superior science is more universal, profound in its penetration of the causes of reality, and simple in its causal explanations. Thus the observational sciences named in *Post. Analytics* I, 13 (such as optics, mechanics, harmonics, nautical astronomy) are based upon *particular* sensible facts, but seem to be subordinated to mathematical principles (which come from the science of quantity—common to *all* physical beings), for the precision of observational methods. Likewise, they are subordinated to a more universal and explanatory science of the principles and causes of moving beings *qua* having a principle of motion and rest, that of the *Physics*. (See *Physics* II, 1–2.) Physics, in turn, is subordinated to metaphysics, which studies the same beings, not *qua* moved, but *qua* being. This science also extends universally to both sensible and "separate" being (*Metaphysics E*, 1), and understands all beings with regard to their ultimate first cause, God, or the divine (*Λ*, 6–10). Though the diversity of sciences is based upon their respective subjects, and not upon their respective degrees of abstraction, one might argue with Maritain that a diversity of philosophical abstractions does indeed *result from* the diversity of scientific principles induced.

attainable.[4] They argue instead (based in part upon the very texts of Aristotle and Aquinas) that any true causal study of being *qua* being itself *presupposes* a knowledge of immaterial realities (beings such as God or the immaterial human soul). This knowledge is provided not by metaphysics (nor by a priori presuppositions) but by the philosophical study of the causes of natural movement (the subject of Aristotle's *Physics*).[5] The latter science terminates in the argumentative demonstration of a first unmoved mover, of a being without physical characteristics, that is the source of movement for all others. *In light of* this discovery of immaterial being, it is possible to proceed with the metaphysical study of being in both its material and immaterial modes. A decisive philosophical reflection on nature, then, must necessarily precede any scientific elaboration of Thomistic natural theology. An exhaustive consideration of the textual and philosophical basis for this viewpoint exceeds the scope of my inquiry, but I will note here some of the more salient arguments of these interpreters, and afterward attempt to respond to them.

First, the natural object of our mind's consideration is surely the reality we experience through sensation. Thus while it is clear that we do come to know realistically the being, natures, and "categorial" characteristics of the realities we experience, these realities are themselves subject to movement. They are beings immersed in change, such that one might argue that the primary (genetic) object of the human intelligence is *ens mobile*, or being in movement.[6] Should a primary consideration of beings not concern itself, therefore, above all with the speculative understanding of the sources of change and movement in the physical realities that we experience naturally? Should we not first of all study material forms, and ask what matter is and if all that exists is material? This is, after all, more in keeping with the empirical scientific realism that characterizes our concrete form of ordinary understanding and that informs modern scientific study of the physical universe.[7]

---

[4] See in particular the recent arguments to this effect by Benedict Ashley, *The Way toward Wisdom*, 61–169, and Ralph McInerny, *Praeambula Fidei*, 188–218.

[5] "Movement" in this Aristotelian perspective is a broad term, denoting something like physical change.

[6] See Ashley, *The Way toward Wisdom*, 61–72, esp. 62; McInerny, *Praeambula Fidei*, 169–73, 189–91. McInerny (190) claims that this interpretation of Aquinas is found already in Cajetan's discussion of the mind's commensurate object in his *In De ente et essentiae D. Thomae Aquinatis*, ed. M.-H. Laurent (Turin, 1934), 4–20. "Ens concretum quiditati sensibili est primum cognitum cognitione confuse actuali." For a similar definition in Aquinas, see *ST* I, q. 88, a. 3. Note, however, that in neither of these texts is there a mention of *ens mobile*, or changing being per se.

[7] Ashley, *The Way toward Wisdom*, 162–63: "The Aristotelian position does not expect from natural science more than to prove the existence of some causes that are not material. It leaves to Metascience [metaphysics] the positive discussion of the nature of these causes. . . . The real question, of course, is not what Aquinas held the

If we begin immediately from a consideration of beings *qua* being, do we not run the risk of flight into a conceptual world of reified abstraction?

Second, both Aristotle and Aquinas unambiguously affirm that the ordinary order of speculative inquiry is to begin from realities better known to us, so as to proceed to the knowledge of realities that are more evident and ultimate in themselves.[8] The normal order of inquiry for the physical beings that we experience should be first to consider them in their constitutive structure as physical, changing beings, so as progressively to arrive at the knowledge of immaterial, non-physical reality. So Aristotle will inquire into the nature of sensation in *On the Soul* so as progressively to determine that the life of human, abstractive reason is not reducible to sensation but instead implies something immaterial transcending the world of physical forms.[9] And in *Physics* VIII, on the basis of the previously demonstrated principles of physical change (form, matter, actuality, and potentiality in the order of movement, extrinsic series of efficient causes), the philosopher will argue that *to make integral sense* of the changing, physical world, it is rationally necessary to have recourse to the affirmation of something that is not physical, and ultimately to something immaterial that is not subject to change by another.[10] In this way, from empirical starting points, the Aristotelian student passes from a consideration of the intrinsic causes of physical being to the more ultimate consid-

---

subject of Metascience to be or how it is to be discovered or validated, but whether in view of modern science his position remains true. Though so many Thomists want to bypass this question, while at the same time accepting Aquinas' Aristotelian epistemology, it must be frankly faced. The purely logical coherence of Aquinas' demonstration of the existence of immaterial substances has never been refuted. . . . The premise of the argument that asserts the impossibility of an infinite regress in efficient causes whose efficiency depends on another agent can be refuted only at the expense of denying, as Hume did, the principle of causality on which all natural science depends."

[8] See, for example, Aquinas, *Expos. de Trin.*, q. 5, a. 1, ad 9: "Although divine science [metaphysics] is by nature the first of all the sciences, with respect to us the other sciences come before it. For, as Avicenna says, the position of this science is that it be learned after the natural sciences, which explain many things used by metaphysics, such as generation, corruption, motion, and the like. . . . Moreover, the sensible effects on which the demonstrations of natural science are based are more evident to us in the beginning. But when we come to know the first causes through them, these causes will reveal to us the reason for the effects, from which they were proved by a demonstration *quia* [from effects to causes]. In this way natural science also contributes something to divine science, and nevertheless it is divine science that explains its principles."

[9] See the transition in *On the Soul* III, 3–4, 427a17–430a9.

[10] *Physics* VIII, 4–5, 254b8–258b9. See Ashley's rearticulations of the Aristotelian and Thomistic arguments for the immateriality of the intellect and of the prime mover in *The Way toward Wisdom*, 92–114.

eration of immaterial, transcendent being. The passage from one to the other, however, is facilitated by the aforementioned demonstrations (of immaterial intellect and the unmoved first mover), which are included in the science of the philosophy of nature.

Third, there is a textual argument. Both Aristotle and Aquinas seem to say quite clearly that in the absence of natural philosophical demonstrations of the existence of "separate, immaterial being," the rational grounds for metaphysical inquiry are absent.[11] Following the conditions of the *Posterior Analytics* for the establishment of a true science it is necessary to know first that an object exists in order to inquire into what the object is.[12] In order, then, for the study of metaphysics to be justified, we must first demonstrate the need for a study that stretches beyond the consideration of physical beings alone. This is accomplished only when *through the principles of natural philosophy* one demonstrates that there exists separate, immaterial being (whether that of the immaterial human intellect, potentially separable from the body at death, or the transcendent, primary unmoved mover). Consequently, philosophy of nature provides knowledge of the subject of metaphysics: *both* immaterial and material beings considered *qua* being. Only once we know rationally that there are beings that are immaterial is the study of metaphysics justified as a science, because *only then* are we capable of identifying the proper subject of this science.[13] Its purpose is to consider beings, both material and immaterial, insofar as they have being, insofar as they exist. And existence, like the other transcendentals (goodness, unity, truth, etc.) can then be understood to be in no way limited to the material realizations in which we encounter

---

[11] Aristotle seems to say as much in *Metaphysics E*, 1, 1026a27–32: "If there is no substance other than those which are formed by nature, natural science will be the first science; but if there is an immovable substance, the science of this must be prior and must be first philosophy, and universal in this way, because it is first." Commenting upon this in *In VI Meta.*, lec. 1, 1170, Aquinas writes: "If there is no substance other than those which exist in the way that natural substances do, with which the philosophy of nature deals, the philosophy of nature will be the first science. But if there is some immobile substance, this will be prior to natural substance; and therefore the philosophy of nature, which considers this kind of substance, will be first philosophy. And since it is first, it will be universal; and it will be its function to study being as being, both what being is and what the attributes are that belong to being as being." See also *In XI Meta.*, lec. 7, 2267, and *In III Meta.*, lec. 6, 398. McInerny (*Praeambula Fidei*, 193) comments: "Any one of these passages would suffice to make the point but their cumulative effect shows it to be inescapable that, for St. Thomas, metaphysics as a science of being as being, where being has more reach than sensible being, depends upon knowing that there are immaterial beings."

[12] *Posterior Analytics* II, 1, 89b23–35.

[13] See the application of this epistemic criteria to the debate in question by Ashley in *The Way toward Wisdom*, 61–64.

it. These transcendental characteristics of being are capable of transcendent realizations, discovered precisely in the immaterial beings that are
beyond ("separated from") the realm of physical matter.[14] This is why the
study of the causes of being in the *Metaphysics* of Aristotle (substance and
accidents, actuality and potentiality) is a study of being in the world we
experience as a preparation for speaking analogically about the higher
realm of separate being that is characteristic of human souls after death,
separate substances (Aquinas's angels), and, especially, the transcendent,
primary cause of existence, who is God.

There is much in such a viewpoint that is reasonable. Furthermore,
this understanding of Aristotle and Aquinas appeals accurately to many
elements of their own respective texts on these subjects. Without disagree-
ing entirely, then, with such an interpretation, I will offer here six reasons
for why I think it is insufficient or problematic.

First, there is a textual consideration of significance. The claim that *ens
mobile* (changing being) is the natural primary object of the human intellect
is not sufficiently grounded in Aquinas's thought.[15] On the contrary, their
affirmations in this regard are quite explicit: the natural object of the human
intellect is being *tout court. Quod primo cadit in intellectu est ens.*[16] For
Aquinas, as for Aristotle, all basic realism is implicitly *metaphysical,* and *on
this account* potentially ordered toward knowledge of God.[17] In the fore-the-

---

[14] McInerny, *Praeambula Fidei,* 194–214, argues that Aquinas's judgment of *separatio,* which attains to the knowledge proper to metaphysics, is based upon the judgment that there exist immaterial beings. 210: "The judgment of separation that
establishes the possibility that there is a science beyond natural science and mathematics is the judgment that something exists apart from matter and motion." In
this way, the demonstrative arguments of natural philosophy establish the basis for
(or principles of) metaphysics as a science.

[15] This point has been helpfully underscored by Lawrence Dewan in his "St.
Thomas, Physics and the Principles of Metaphysics," *Form and Being,* 47–60, esp.
55–56. The arguments in the following pages are heavily indebted to the perspectives of this essay.

[16] *ST* I, q. 5, a. 2: "The first thing conceived by the intellect is being; because everything is knowable only inasmuch as it is in actuality, as is said in *Metaphysics* IX
(1051a31). Hence, being is the proper object of the intellect, and is that which is
primarily intelligible, just as sound is that which is first audible." One might note
that the idea here is that knowledge of actuality (being in act) as identified in
Metaphysics Θ is the primary kind of knowledge, and that this *precedes* any possible knowledge of natural philosophy. This contrasts with Ashley's affirmation
(*The Way toward Wisdom,* 134) that the metaphysical notion of actuality depends
upon the study of the philosophy of nature.

[17] In *ST* I, q. 87, a. 3, ad 1, Aquinas claims that the connatural object of the human
intellect is "ens vel verum, consideratum in rebus materialibus." He affirms in numerous texts that the sense of *ens* here is metaphysical, alluding to the analogical knowledge of *ens* as substance and accidents in *Metaphysics* Γ, as that which is implicitly

oretical ground of the world that we encounter in every act of authentic human knowing, there is a genuine intellectual perception of being, as well as of unity, truth, and even, at least in an implicit way, ontological goodness.[18] Furthermore, the *metaphysical* notions of the substance, accidental properties (such as those of qualities, quantities, and relations), as well as notions of actuality and potentiality are all grasped in a vague, embryonic way, even from the time of our initial intellectual experiences of the world.[19]

Second, then, far from *establishing* a basis for such distinctly metaphysical notions as being, substance, act, and potency, the study of nature as physical beings in motion *presupposes and depends upon* such notions. In this sense, the realistic study of the causes of physical identity and change through time in the philosophy of natural movement is itself subordinated to and dependent upon a more basic ontological realism.[20] It is true that by reasoning about matter and the causes of material being, the arguments of

---

known in our initial understanding of reality. This most basic form of realism can preexist prior to any kind of natural philosophy, and yet is a seed of the highest form of wisdom. See, for example, *In VI Ethic.*, lec. 5, 1181: "We judge that some people are wise unqualifiedly, i.e., as regards the entire domain of beings. . . . Such unqualified wisdom is the most certain of all sciences, inasmuch as it attains to the first principles of beings, which just in themselves are most known, though some of them, viz. the immaterial [things], are less known to us. Nevertheless, the most universal principles are more known even to us, such as those which pertain to being inasmuch as it is being: knowledge of which [principles] pertains to wisdom, in that unqualified sense of the word; as is clear in *Metaphysics* 4." ("St. Thomas, Physics and the Principles of Metaphysics," trans. Dewan, *Form and Being*, 55 n. 19.)

18 *ST* I, q. 16, a. 4, ad 2: "Intellectus autem per prius apprehendit ipsum ens; et secundario apprehendit se intelligere ens; et tertio apprehendit se appetere ens. Unde primo est ratio entis, secundo ratio veri, tertio ratio boni, licet bonum sit in rebus." "The intellect apprehends primarily being itself; secondly it apprehends that it understands being; and thirdly, it apprehends that it desires being. Hence the idea of being is first, that of truth second, and the idea of good third, though the good is in things."

19 In his commentary on *Metaphysics Δ* (*In V Meta.*, lec. 9, 889–92), Aquinas offers a metaphysical theory for the derivation of the categories. His analysis of predication suggests that even prior to a causal analysis of substances, the mind grasps the categorical modes of being as different dimensions of the substance, so that a person knows in an embryonic, initial way the diverse "folds" of reality even before he or she philosophizes. Our attributions of quiddities to things signify "what" a thing is, while the subject signifies the particular substance in its singularity. The predicate of quantity signifies properties derived from the matter of the substance; the qualities signify those properties that derive from it on account of its form; relations signify something not in the subject absolutely, but by reference to another.

20 *In III Phys.*, lec. 3, 285: "And so it is altogether impossible to define motion by what is prior and better known other than as the Philosopher here defines it. For it has been said that each genus is divided by potency and act. Now since potency and act pertain to the first differences in being [*de primis differentiis entis*] they are naturally

natural philosophy can counter the mistaken presuppositions of reductivist, materialistic empiricism, especially by the demonstrations of immaterial reality. Nevertheless, this task is distinct from the burden of responding to a more (epistemologically) fundamental problem: that of ontological skepticism. It is one thing to think everything is material; it is another, and a greater error, to consider that we cannot have true knowledge of the natures, structures, and causes of realities we experience. This is why in his commentary on *Metaphysics* Γ Aquinas recognizes that the primary principles of philosophical reasoning are metaphysical, and that they are so fundamental that they can be defended only by recourse to dialectical argumentation (the axioms of non-contradiction, identity, and causality). These principles are based upon our most fundamental perceptions of being. Only once such perceptions are acknowledged as our already given starting points is *any* constitutive theoretical science possible, including a study that concerns itself with physical change, and the principles of change as form and matter.[21]

---

prior to motion. And the Philosopher uses these to define motion." This is an unambiguous statement of the dependence of natural philosophy upon metaphysical realism and even an implicit grasp of properly metaphysical notions.

[21] Already in *The Sophist* 247–57, Plato clearly seeks to refute the Eleatic philosophers' denial of a plurality of beings by a study of change and becoming based in fundamental metaphysical principles of "being" (*to on*), difference and sameness, as well as potentiality (in 247e). Significantly, we find Aristotle in *Physics* I, 1–3, refuting the Eleatic denial of beings-in-becoming by distinguishing the problem of the one and the multiple (treated by Parmenides) from the problem of the proper principles of becoming. However, to do so, he appeals to categorial modes of being (substance, quantity, etc.), to the metaphysical principle of non-contradiction, and to notions of potentiality and actuality. On the ontological foundations of the science of nature, see Lambros Couloubaritsis, *La Physique d'Aristote* (Bruxelles: Éditions Ousia, 1997), 93–162. Aquinas, meanwhile, states explicitly in *ELP* I, lec. 5 (trans. Dewan, "St. Thomas, Physics and the Principles of Metaphysics," *Form and Being*, 56, emphasis added): "But of some propositions the terms are such that they are in the knowledge of all, such as 'a being,' 'something one' and the others which pertain to a being precisely as a being: for 'a being' is the first conception of the intellect. Hence, it is necessary that such propositions not only in themselves, but even relative to everyone, stand as known by virtue of themselves: for example that it does not happen that the same thing be and not be, and that a whole is greater than its own part, and the like. Hence such principles *all sciences receive from metaphysics*, to which it belongs to consider being, just in itself [*ens simpliciter*], and those things which belong to being." Ashley (*The Way toward Wisdom*, 66) insists that for Aristotle and Aquinas "no discipline proves the existence of its own subject" but must receive its principles from others, and therefore metaphysics receives its principles from physics. However, on just this point, Aquinas insists that the primary principles of *all sciences* are not demonstrated, but rather *received* through our primary metaphysical insights into reality. These insights *in turn* make possible the "special sciences" of particular aspects of being (such as the study of movement). See also *In IV Meta.*, lec. 1, 547.

One sign of this dependency of philosophy of nature upon metaphysics is the fact that all "natural philosophy" Thomists of the kind under consideration presuppose the terminology of the categories ("substances," "qualities," etc.) and even notions of actuality and potentiality in order to study the causes of physical change.[22] While the study of physical beings helps clarify the content of these notions, it does not provide grounds for them, as they are derived from more basic *ontological* experiences.

Third, the proposal that the object of metaphysics is provided by natural philosophy, insofar as the latter yields a demonstration of immaterial substance, flies in the face of Aquinas's explicit proposals. On the contrary, St. Thomas, in consistency with the ideas examined in chapters 3 and 5, claims both in his commentary on Boethius's *De Trinitate* and in the prologue to his commentary on the *Metaphysics* that metaphysics as a science is concerned with beings *qua* being and with the intrinsic causes of beings we experience directly. Only derivatively is it then capable of speaking of the transcendent, extrinsic cause of all secondary beings, God the Creator.[23] Therefore, God *does not fall under the subject of metaphysics* for Aquinas except as the transcendent cause of the subject of this science.[24] However, if physics were to demonstrate the existence of the immaterial first mover (who is in fact God, for Aquinas),[25] and if then this demonstration provided the subject of metaphysics, then it is obvious that God would come under the *subject* of metaphysics, which would concern itself with material and immaterial being (and in a sense, then, with finite and infinite being). Here we are most certainly close to Averroes's point of view but far from that of Aquinas, who purposefully distanced himself from Averroes on just this issue, as I have noted in chapter 3.[26]

---

[22] See, for example, Ashley, *The Way toward Wisdom*, 72–85, who studies the principles of non-contradiction and causality, as well as the categorical modes of being, as first principles of natural science. Meanwhile, McInerny, in *Praeambula Fidei*, 215–18, claims that the natural philosophy demonstration of immaterial being allows us to grasp the most universal notions of being as being, one and multiple, act and potency, which are in turn applicable to all beings, whether material or immaterial. Both these viewpoints seem to differ from Aquinas's own views.

[23] See, in particular, *Expos. de Trin.*, q. 5, a. 4.

[24] I follow here in large part the analysis of Aquinas on this point by John Wippel, in his articles "Aquinas and Avicenna on the Relationship between First Philosophy and the Other Theoretical Sciences (*In De Trin.*, q. 5, a. 1, ad 9)" and " 'First Philosophy' according to Thomas Aquinas," in *Metaphysical Themes in Thomas Aquinas*, 37–57.

[25] See the reasonable arguments to this effect by Anton Pegis, "St. Thomas and the Coherence of the Aristotelian Theology," *Medieval Studies* 35 (1973): 67–117.

[26] And at any rate, it is problematic to argue that a philosophical demonstration of the existence of God as the immobile first mover is needed as a precondition to think philosophically about "separate being." "Pre-philosophical" religious traditions are the authentic cultural vehicle for such an idea and transmit to us at the

Fourth, no proper analogy for transcendent being is possible if there is not initially some knowledge of being as a proper object given in common human experience. While an argument from physical motion may have the capacity to demonstrate the existence of immaterial substance that itself transcends the physical, nevertheless, for such argumentation to have an intelligible meaning, it must demonstrate that such immaterial substance *exists*. In other words, knowledge of the *existence* of mobile beings is presupposed at the beginning of such argumentation, and the capacity to think about the immaterial analogically in its "substantiality," "actuality," and "potentiality" is a necessary pre-condition for the coherence and meaning of such argumentation. As Aristotle's own argumentation in *Physics* VIII shows, the move from material movers to immaterial movers (who arguably have immaterial potency to move themselves) and the subsequent move to a primary, immaterial first mover who is pure actuality both require the capacity to cross from physical notions of movement, subsistence, actuality, and potency to notions that denote the immaterial.[27] This means that, at the very least, these notions as they are employed in the *Physics* are already *implicitly* metaphysical, and become in some sense explicitly so even at the term of the argumentation of Aristotle's (and Aquinas's) natural philosophy. If this were not the case, not only would the final primary mover of Aristotle's *Physics* literally be unthinkable, but also any possible metaphysics of God would disseminate into unintelligible polysemy. From terms taken from the physical world, we could derive only a purely equivocal language for the divine.

---

very least the conceptual hypothesis of the existence of God. This would suffice to ask the question of whether or in what way potential analogies of what God truly is are found in the consideration of beings in this world. To think otherwise is to presume an existential religious neutrality or hostility that is not typically characteristic of human beings. As I mentioned in chapter 2, Aristotle believes that some kind of knowledge of the divine is the *unique* form of knowledge that man has never lost because it has been constantly preserved throughout the ages (*Metaphysics* Λ, 8, 1074b8–14). Aquinas interprets this as an affirmation of the culturally universal belief in the existence of immaterial substances (*In XII Meta.*, lec. 10, 2597).

27 Consider, for example, the implicitly metaphysical analogies in the following statement, which discusses (1) contingent, physically moved being; then (2) perennial, immaterial, self-moving being; and finally (3) immaterial, unmoved pure actuality. (*Physics* VIII, 5, 256b21–27): "Now we see the last things, which have the capacity of being in motion, but do not contain a motive principle, and also things which are in motion but are moved by themselves and not by anything else: it is reasonable, therefore, not to say necessary, to suppose the existence of a third term also, that which causes motion but is itself unmoved. So, too, Anaxagoras is right when he says that Mind is impassive and unmixed, since he makes it the principle of motion; for it could cause motion in this way only be being itself unmoved, and have control only by being unmixed."

Fifth, if some object is given in ordinary experience (as it must be) that is eventually analogically applicable to the divine (albeit through the mediation of a causal analysis of being) then there is given to immediate experience the knowledge of being as a proper object of study. And if this is the case, then a true science of being *qua* being is possible without recourse to the demonstration of immaterial substance in the philosophy of natural change. Quite simply, following the canons for science from the *Posterior Analytics*, we experience beings that *exist*, are *one*, are *good*, and so on, and therefore we can think about being as an immediate subject of study ("what is existence? unity? goodness?").[28] Any argumentation to the contrary (in the name of metaphysical science) is quite dangerous, because if we cannot know being conceptually from the start based upon direct experiences, we never will come to know this object through purely mediate and non-experiential philosophical demonstrations.[29]

Sixth, the textual citations of Aquinas to the effect that without demonstrations of immaterial substance natural philosophy would "be first philosophy" are not entirely transparent.[30] Equally reasonable alternative interpretations of these passages exist.[31] However, in any event, this

---

[28] *In VI Meta.*, lec. 1, 1147: "All these particular sciences which have just been mentioned are about one particular class of being, for example, number, continuous quantity or something of this kind; and each confines its investigations to 'its subject genus,' i.e., dealing with this class and not with another; for example, the science which deals with number does not deal with continuous quantity. For no one of the sciences deals with 'being in an unqualified sense,' i.e., with being in general, *or even with any particular being as being*; for example, arithmetic does not deal with number as being but as number. *For to consider each being as being is proper to metaphysics*" (emphasis added). See also the analysis of Dewan, "St. Thomas, Physics and the Principles of Metaphysics," *Form and Being*, 54.

[29] This is why, for example, Aquinas will insist (*ELP* I, lec. 21, on Aristotle at 77b3–5) that metaphysics gives the principles for all other sciences, giving here the example of mathematics, insofar as it permits us to attain to the *existence* of the objects studied in these sciences.

[30] As mentioned in the citations above, Aristotle argues this way in *Metaphysics E*, 1, 1026a27–32. In *In VI Meta.*, lec. 1, 1170, Aquinas comments: "If there is no substance other than those which exist in the way that natural substances do, with which the philosophy of nature deals, the philosophy of nature will be the first science."

[31] Dewan, for example ("St. Thomas, Physics and the Principles of Metaphysics," *Form and Being*, 51–53) argues that "first philosophy" in Aristotle's Book *E*, 1, and Aquinas's usage could simply designate "universal science" and "metaphysics," rather than "the philosophy that is first," meaning that in the absence of a demonstration of immaterial substance, only a *metaphysics* of the physical world is possible (and a philosophy of nature remains indistinguishable from metaphysics). Only if one knows of the existence of separate substances is natural philosophy understood as a distinct study of the intra-worldly causes of physical change alone as differentiated from the more universal study of being *qua* being, which considers all that

particular idea of Aristotle commented upon by Aquinas is not absolutely compelling as the basis for a total interpretation of the object of metaphysics. Citations from other textual loci suggest quite clearly why for Aquinas metaphysics is a causal science originating from basic human experience, which advances progressively from the consideration of beings in this world as substances in act, and as composed of essence and *esse*, to the eventual consideration of *arguments for* the existence of God. Such distinctly metaphysical arguments do not logically presuppose the previous knowledge of God's existence. One can still *inquire into* the question of immaterial reality while thinking metaphysically about reality.[32]

In conclusion, I would hold that metaphysics as a causal science is possible based upon immediate experiences of beings in the world, without *necessary* recourse to demonstrations of immaterial being derived from the philosophy of natural movement. Aquinas—following Aristotle's order of the sciences—does presuppose that the metaphysician has had the opportunity to ponder the truth of the science of physical change (the study of natural forms, material potency, teleological change, and the study of physical movement). Aquinas says quite clearly that metaphysics as a science should normally proceed chronologically after the philosophical consideration of physical nature. However, the two sciences begin from distinct experiential objects (physical realities considered as changing, or beings considered as being) and arrive at distinct ends (the immobile first mover, or the primary being in act of God, who is subsistent contemplation). Properly metaphysical study of causality (consideration of intrinsic and extrinsic causes of being *qua* being) must be possible, as a distinct *experiential* subject of study. Otherwise, transcendental notions cannot be understood in terms that are connatural to our ordinary form of human knowing, that can be attributed to God as the primary cause of being. Consequently, they would not be capable of being used progressively to speak of God analogically.

---

exists, including the world of immaterial beings. John Wippel, meanwhile (*The Metaphysical Thought of Thomas Aquinas*, 55–62) simply argues (perhaps less satisfyingly) that on this point Aquinas may simply be discretely commenting upon Aristotle's view, while differing from him in fact.

[32] As Dewan points out ("St. Thomas, Physics and the Principles of Metaphysics," *Form and Being*, 54) in *In VII Meta.*, lec. 11, 1525–27, Aquinas sees Aristotle considering sensible substances with a view to *trying to determine* if there exist substances separate from matter, immaterial numbers, Platonic forms, and the like. This logically presupposes, evidently, the *question* of the existence of separate beings, rather than their prior demonstration. Examples such as this one abound in the commentary on the *Metaphysics*.

Analogical and Causal Study of Being: Substance and Accidents, Actuality and Potentiality

How, then, does our experience lead us to the analysis of a causal structure of concrete being? And how in turn does this analysis "open from within" toward the discovery of the real distinction between *esse* and essence, as well as the gradual discovery of grounds for the arguments for the existence of God? To come to these later arguments, it is first necessary to delineate the basis in our experience for a causal analysis of being, first as substance and accidents, and subsequently as actuality and potentiality.

The world as we experience it confronts us with an irreducible diversity of natural kinds. The beings we experience are identifiably distinct and are composed of characteristic properties. By the latter we may come to know the constitutive features of beings as essentially distinct from one another. So, for example, we can clearly identify differences between human beings (such as Socrates, Paul, or Catherine) and other living beings (such as horses, trees, or a single living cell); nonliving being (such as stars, stones, or water molecules); and artifacts (such as wooden bowls, microscopes, or motor vehicles). The world is a world of kinds. And these kinds are themselves comprised of individuals, each having a multiplicity of properties: a given size and weight, material component parts, various sensible qualities, characteristic actions, habits, or potential capacities, and so on. The list of categorical attributes fills out the content of what we mean when we say that things "exist," that they are existents. A consideration of the genera of attributes (qualities, quantities, relations, habits, capacities, etc.) helps us understand the various configurations that existence takes on around us. "Being is said in multiple ways," and as we have seen in chapters 1 and 2; this means that "being" can and must be attributed to individual beings in analogical fashion (according to the analogy of proper proportionality), since the existence of each one is unique. Likewise, the being of a given quality (such as Socrates' being clever) is distinct from Socrates' being a father (a relation governed by a habit), or his weighing 150 pounds (a quantity), and so on. Consequently existence takes on an analogical shape in each given reality itself (denoted according to the analogy of proper proportionality), due to the multiplicity of "categorial determinations" or properties, of which it is composed. In the words of Aquinas:

> Being cannot be narrowed down to some definite thing in the way in which a genus is narrowed down to a species by means of differences. For since a difference does not participate in a genus, it lies outside the essence of a genus. But there could be nothing outside the essence of being which could constitute a particular species of being by adding to being, for what is outside of being is nothing, and this

cannot be a difference. Hence the Philosopher proved that being cannot be a genus. Being must then be narrowed down to diverse genera on the basis of a different mode of predication, which flows from a different mode of being; for "being is signified," i.e., something is signified to be, "in just as many ways" (or in just as many senses) as we can make predications. And for this reason the classes into which being is first divided are called predicaments, because they are distinguished on the basis of different ways of predicating. Therefore, since some predicates signify what (i.e., substance); some, of what kind; some, how much, and so on; there must be a mode of being corresponding to each type of predication. For example, when it is said that a man is an animal, is signified substance; and when it is said that a man is white, is signified quality; and so on.[33]

What has been said here for being can also be said of goodness or unity. These two "decline" according to the categorical determinations of reality. There is a certain goodness to Socrates' intellectual insight (a quality of his) that is distinct from the goodness of his being a father, or husband (relations governed by habits). And it is possible, therefore, that he could be an insightful metaphysician, but a mediocre husband, since these are truly distinct dimensions of his being. Likewise, there is a unity to his quantity that is distinct from the unity of his nature, or the unity of his thought. The description of what exists in the beings around us, then, necessarily leads us toward an analogical description of existence, goodness, and unity, according to an analogy of proper proportionality. "Being," "goodness," and "unity" are ascribed in multiple ways to the multiplicity of categorical determinations of being. No mode can be entirely reduced to another, as if all were quantity, or relation, or quality, or substance.

Mere description of reality is not enough, however, insofar as the multiplicity of attributes we confront within existents, and the multiplicity of existents themselves, leads us to inquire into the sources (or causes) of unity in things. For even amidst multiplicity there is some fundamental unity, already signified by the fact that being, unity, and goodness are *common* to all the categorical modes of being. If Socrates is a human being, snub-nosed, articulate, of such a weight and height, a husband, a conscientious objector, and so on, then these diverse characteristics all really *exist* in him in distinct ways, as constituent of the being that he is. Yet surely he is also *one* being. Just as the properties of being and oneness are coextensive for

<hr/>

[33] Aquinas, *In V Meta.*, lec. 9, 889–90. For contemporary theoretical discussion on ways in which ordinary language discloses the categorical modes of being, one can consult with profit the essays in *Categories: Historical and Systematic Essays*, ed. M. Gorman and J. J. Sanford (Washington, DC: The Catholic University of America Press, 2004).

Aristotle and Aquinas, so too the *henological* question about the origins of unity and multiplicity ("why is Socrates one?") is also an *etiological* and *ontological* question about the causes of being. "Why does Socrates exist as one?" And consequently, the question of what gives unity to his being amidst this multiplicity of attributes is also the question of the cause of his being this being here, a being of this kind (a human, rational animal). In other words, what is the "formal cause" of Socrates' being, *qua* being?[34]

Here one can begin to understand the metaphysics of the substance as the study of the formal cause of the existence of a being. The analysis of this subject by Aquinas presupposes much that has been studied in Aristotle's *Physics* in terms of the dual principles of form and matter in all existent, physical beings.[35] It also presupposes the analyses of living forms (animate beings) from *On the Soul*, and their vital operations.[36] The key to

---

34 This confluence of themes is evident in Aquinas's treatment of substance as the formal cause of being, and the way in which the question of the cause of unity in beings leads us to the "scientific" knowledge of the substance, in *In VII Meta.*, lec. 16–17, esp., 1639–40, 1649–52, 1676–80. *In VII Meta.*, lec. 16, 1637: "Unity is predicated of things in the same way that being is, since they are interchangeable, and unity is predicated of a thing because of its substance. For a thing has one substance, and those things are numerically one whose substance is numerically one. And it is also evident that a thing is called a being because of its own substance." Lec. 17, 1650: "Whatever is such that one does not ask *why* it is, but is that to which the other things under investigation are reduced, must be a principle and cause; for the question why is a question about a cause. But the substance in the sense of essence is a thing of this kind; for one does not ask why man is man, but why man is something else [for example, intellectual, i.e., because of his soul]; and it is the same in other cases. Therefore the substance of a thing in the sense of its essence is a principle and cause." On the "henological" themes in Aristotle's metaphysics more generally, see Couloubaritsis, *La Physique d'Aristote*, 103–22. Similarly, on this theme in Aquinas's metaphysics, see Aertsen, *Nature and Creature*, 230–78.

35 Every natural being we experience has an intrinsic formal determination and a certain persistent physical identity over time, which we can call a nature. It also has certain material component parts at progressively "descending" levels (in Socrates' case, the physical organs, cells, molecules, atoms, etc.). Furthermore, the beings we experience are radically generable or corruptible, in the sense that they can come to be or cease to be (through substantial change). Socrates can die, and the matter of his body can be progressively "re-assimilated" to the natural environment. Consequently, as there is in each being a true capacity for transformation into other beings of differing kinds, so there must be a principle in each physical being that is susceptible to substantial alteration, and which we can term "matter" or "material potentiality." See the arguments to this effect in Aquinas, *In VII Meta.*, lec. 2, 1285–89.

36 This analysis leads to a non-reductivist account of the essential causes of organic, living beings. The essential cause of life (even in completely perishable, living beings such as trees and house pets) cannot be any particular element (i.e., a physical organ) or merely a material structure (i.e., a set of relations). Rather, all living beings have an essential unity as animate beings, and therefore a different form of

a distinctly *metaphysical* analysis, however, is based not on a consideration of beings as subject to physical change, nor upon an understanding of living beings as organic, self-organizing forms. Rather, it is based on three key dimensions of an existent considered *as being*: (1) its *singular unity* as an existent, (2) its natural characteristics as a given *kind* of thing, and (3) its *persistence of identity* through time.

The first of these dimensions of substantial being is understood through the insight that the multiplicity of properties of a given existent *inhere within* a more fundamental unity. What is the cause of the unity of a being amidst its plurality of characteristics and material parts? This ontological unity is caused by the substance. The substance is that which exists in and by itself, giving ontological unity to the whole and consequently to all its parts and properties.[37] Because substances are something primary in our understanding of reality, they cannot be "proven" to exist by recourse to something more fundamental. Rather, their existence can be defended only dialectically. Without the affirmation of such a principle, the acceptance of any real ontological unity becomes an impossibility, and so the unity of beings (at whatever microscopic, macroscopic, or experiential level we might like to consider "ultimately real") in fact is ultimately illusory.[38] Furthermore, the very thinking of distinct "things" is rendered unintelligible. The reason for this is that denial of this principle in turn undermines the other two dimensions of substance aforementioned: that of natural kind and persistence in identity. If things do exist each having a distinct unity, then they have a unity of kind and a persistence in being that characterize them as well. However, if they do not exist as distinct substances, then these other characteristics of being are in fact also non-existent. Both the

---

being from nonliving ones. This life principle is the source of the unity, organization, and dynamic interactions of the material elements. For a brief, but helpful, contemporary defense of this understanding, see Norman Kretzmann, *The Metaphysics of Creation* (Oxford: Clarendon Press, 1999), 296–99.

37 *In VII Meta.*, lec. 1, 1248: "In every class of things that which exists of itself and is a being in an unqualified sense is prior to that which exists by reason of something else and is a being in a qualified sense. But substance is a being in an unqualified sense and exists of itself, whereas all classes of beings other than substance are beings in a qualified sense and exist by reason of substance. Therefore substance is the primary kind of being."

38 Aquinas argues to this effect in *In VII Meta.*, lec. 17, 1676: "For if [the substance] is an element, the same argument will apply again both to this and to other elements, because it will have to be numbered with the others [i.e., it will be a substance]. . . . And since it has already been proved that in every composite which is one there must be something in addition to its elements, the same question will then apply to this something else. . . . Hence in this way there will be an infinite regress; but this is absurd."

admission of unitary beings and the search for intelligibility necessarily require (at least implicitly) recourse to a metaphysics of substance.

Second, that by which a thing is *what* it is, is also the source of its unity as a given *kind* of thing. Natural identity informs the totality of a unity of being and characterizes its ontological unity. This is the principle that Aquinas calls the "quiddity" and that designates the essence or nature of a thing. For example, Paul is one because Paul is a *human being* in all that he is. In every thing that we discover in him (i.e., his thinking, writing, walking, etc.) this essential determination is present. Therefore, the unity of singular existence in a thing and the unity of essence *both* derive from the same ontological principle. The substance is the source of this essential determination of each being, which gives an order to its parts and properties. That is to say, the substance is at the origins of our saying both these kinds of statements: "Paul is *this* man here (not that one)." "All the natural determinations that we find in Paul are manifestations of the *kind* of being he is, a human being, having the same nature as Peter."[39] Consequently, the substance is the *formal cause* of a being, the source of its various natural determinations, and its concrete singularity.[40] Without recourse to the notion of the substance as a cause of the determination of a given being, the unifying essence is ontologically inexplicable. The search for definitions in this case would become absurd. By contrast, then, the search for definitions implies an implicit recourse to the metaphysics of substance.

Third, this unity is perceptible in and through change, as the substance is that which permits a continuity of identity of the whole being through time, as *this* being and as *this kind* of being. Certain properties come and go in a given existent, yet we can continue to identify it as one identical being through time. This is due to the fact that something in the reality is not subject to alteration, despite the "accidental" changes that a reality undergoes. The substance, as the cause of the formal identity of a singular being, is also that which is itself not subject to alteration through time. It is *because* Paul is a substance that he is this singular being, this human being that endures as one, even though he changes in various secondary, accidental ways.[41]

---

[39] *ST* I, q. 29, a. 2: "According to the Philosopher (*Metaphysics* V, 1017b23), substance is twofold. In one sense it means the quiddity of a thing, signified by its definition, and thus we say that the definition means the substance of a thing. . . . In another sense substance means a subject of *suppositum*, which subsists in the genus of substance. . . . For, as it exists in itself and not in another, it is called subsistence. . . . As it underlies some common nature, it is called a thing of nature [*res naturae*]." See also *In VII Meta.*, lec. 10, 1490; *De potentia Dei*, q. 9, a. 1.

[40] See Aquinas's analysis to this effect in *In III Meta.*, lec. 4, 384.

[41] Aquinas, *In VIII Meta.*, lec. 1, 1687–90, discusses this continued existence in time by substantial material forms. He does so in the context of a discussion that

The discovery of this causal structure of being allows us to understand the passage from the use of the analogy of proper proportionality to the use of the *pros hen* or *multa ad unum* analogy by Aristotle and Aquinas. The former mode of attributing being, unity, and goodness was employed to safeguard the true diversity of the categorical modes of being. It preceded and gave rise to a reflection on the causes of unity in a substance, amidst its multiplicity. The latter mode of attributing being takes into account the analysis of the substance as a cause of being of the other categorical modes of being. It therefore signifies properties as *accidents*, which are dependent upon the substance as regards their manner of existing. The multiple determinations of beings that we know proportionately as each existing (such as Paul's qualities, quantitative size, various relations to others, etc.), are reconceived in light of our study of the substance as the cause of being. They are now considered *pros hen* or *multa ad unum* with regard to the source of their unity.[42] All that exists in Paul (in its irreducible diversity) exists because of his substance, or rather, *within* his substance. Because he is this human being here—a concrete, living, material form— he has properties (such as his various qualities, quantity, friendly relations, etc.) which depend for their existence upon his substantial being, that is, his being alive as this kind of being. The substance is the cause of unity and being of these properties (now understood as accidents). It is the substance "in which" they inhere and "to which" they must be attributed.

The study of the substance in turn opens up "from within" to the question of the actuality and potentiality of being. This is the case because substantial beings not only exist. They also come and go. Not only do their accidents change (like the change of Descartes from a fleshy color to a pale color, or his loss of twenty pounds), but they themselves also change substantially (i.e., the death of Descartes). How, then, to account for the process of change, from a distinctly metaphysical point of view? Here Aristotle and Aquinas introduce three distinct modes of actuality and potentiality to account for the capacity to change and the act of change, respectively.[43]

The first basic mode of potentiality and actuality applies to physical changes (movements of quantitative or qualitative alteration, or change of place). Changes of these sorts affect the accidents of beings, which when changing continue, nonetheless, to inhere in the substance of a given being. If we gain or lose weight, change color slightly, move to a different city, and so on, we still remain the same existent as before.

distinguishes such accidental change from the substantial change that characterizes the generation and corruption of substances.

[42] See clear statements to this effect in *In V Meta.*, lec. 9, 885; VII, lec. 1, 1247; *De potentia Dei*, q. 7, a. 7; *ST* I, q. 13, a. 5.

[43] Cf. *Metaphysics* Θ, 3, 1047a30–b2; 6, 1048a25–b9; *In IX Meta.*, lec. 3, 1805 and lec. 5, 1824–31.

More profound, however, is that "mode" of being in act and potency that pertains to the substance. We can be or not be. We have the potential to exist or not exist, and this capacity is the metaphysical trace of our contingency, one that underlies all of our historical existence. There was once when we were not, and there will be a time again that we will not be (at least not as we are now, as physical beings). And so there is also in us this mode of being in act that is substantial, which Aquinas terms "first act" or the act of the substance, which can be potentially or actually.[44]

Lastly, there is the mode of actuality and potentiality that is proper to our teleological operations. We are beings who become more perfect through time. This occurs, in living beings, through the operations of vital activities (from respiration, nutrition, and sensation to growth and reproduction). In human beings, these teleological acts take on a distinct form of perfection in the rational operations of intellect and will. We are beings who reason, intuit, learn, desire, love, and choose, building up (potentially at least) the "habits" of the intellectual and moral life within us.

Here it is important to make two points. First, these teleological operations that perfect living beings are themselves "accidents" as regards living substances. If Socrates finally manages to find a good definition of piety or justice, and if Descartes derives the mathematical principles of calculus, then each of them will become more perfect in a given order of intellectual inquiry. But if they do not manage to accomplish these remarkable feats, they will still remain *substantially* the same living beings, admittedly, in a far less *qualified* state of being. Second, the metaphysical distinction of actuality and potentiality, therefore, applies "transcendentally" to all the "categorial modes of being." The two philosophers may exist as substances in act, but they may also potentially cease to exist. And they might develop as *actually existent* qualities a habitual knowledge of the ethics of piety or the mathematics of calculus. Actuality and potency—as teleological perfections of being *qua* being—are realized in analogical ways, substantially or accidentally.[45] However, this also suggests that those transcendental notions

---

[44] *In XI Meta.*, lec. 9, 1870: "What may possibly not be is corruptible either absolutely or in a qualified sense inasmuch as it is said to be possible for it not to be. For example, if it is possible for some body not to be in a place, that body is corruptible as far as place is concerned; and the same applies to quantity and quality. But that is corruptible in an absolute sense which is *capable of not existing substantially*. Therefore it follows that everything potential inasmuch as it is potential is corruptible" (emphasis added). See likewise Aquinas's claim in *De potentia Dei*, q. 3, a. 8, ad 12: "Actuality and potentiality are not different accidental modes of being, such as go to make an alteration: they are substantial modes of being. For even substance is divided by potentiality and act, like any other genus."

[45] *In IX Meta.*, lec. 5, 1826–29: Aquinas follows Aristotle in distinguishing between the actuality of substance and the actuality of operations. He defends Aristotle's

that are common to all the categories, and therefore are coextensive with being (such as existence, unity, goodness, and truth) also can and should be thought of in terms of the notions of actuality and potentiality. Like existence, actuality is not reducible to a quidditative or essential realization of being.[46] Rather, a thing exists, is one, and is good, by the fact that it exists in act. Teleological operations also qualify the ways in which beings exist, are one, or become good.[47] To the extent that something exists in act, is one, and is good, it is also knowable, and therefore can inform the truth content of our affirmations about reality.[48] Being in act, then, is a *transcendental cause* applicable to all the categorical modes of being. It is the final cause of being as being, and therefore allows us to think about the transcendental notions *etiologically*, in a most ultimate light.

Why is this "transcendental extension" of our notions of being in act and being in potentiality so important? Here I will note three reasons that will in turn announce the next stages of argumentation in the metaphysical order of inquiry I am proposing. First, if actuality is a transcendental feature of being (applicable to all the categories) then it bears intrinsic resemblances to the Thomistic notion of *esse* as a transcendental that is

---

"proportional and analogical" induction of actuality in *Metaphysics* Θ, 6, 1048a35–b9. Because being in act exists only in these intrinsically diverse modes, it can be known only through analogical comparisons, and consequently, "actuality is one of those first simple notions. Therefore it cannot be defined [i.e., by recourse to a more fundamental notion]."

[46] *In IX Meta.*, lec. 7, 1846: Aquinas makes this clear while discussing Aristotle's argument that actuality precedes potentiality "with respect to definition" or "intelligibility." Every natural kind must first exist in act in order to be understood. Actuality, however, does not enter into the essential definition of any particular kind of being, but rather is common to every kind of being that exists in act. Therefore, it cannot be grasped "quidditatively" through an essential definition, but must be made known analogically (as something present in all beings and categories in a proportionate way).

[47] Aquinas shows how the resolution of the metaphysical problem of goodness is treated by Aristotle in light of the distinction of actuality and potentiality in *In IX Meta.*, lec. 10; similarly, truth is treated in lec. 11, and oneness just after, in Book *I*, lec. 1.

[48] *In IX Meta.*, lec. 11, 1903, 1912: "Now truth follows being because the structure of things in being and in truth is the same. Hence those things which are not similar in being are not similar in truth. . . . Therefore, since truth consists chiefly in actuality, it is unfitting that there should be error or falsity in all those things which are actual only and are what something truly is, since they are quiddities and forms; but they must either be understood if they are grasped by the intellect, or not be understood at all if they are not grasped by the intellect." Aquinas is saying here that beings in act—to the extent that they are in act—have an essential content or intelligible structure, containing an intrinsic ontological truth for the intellect, whether they in fact are known or not.

also common to all the categories. But being in act is also a fundamental feature of Aristotle's and Aquinas's *causal* metaphysics. Therefore, if Aquinas's real distinction between *esse* and essence can be employed to explain the being in act and being in potency of substances (and vice versa: if the *esse*/essence distinction must be understood in terms of act and potency), then Aquinas's "real distinction" is itself a causal principle, that is intelligible *in continuity with* the framework of a metaphysical science of substance and actuality *as a more ultimate discovery within this science*. Second, a causal metaphysics of being in act and being in potency makes manifest the intrinsically composite character of all the beings in this world, and their ontological dependencies. This in turn leads organically to the ultimate question of the existence of a transcendent cause of all dependent beings. Third, the causal analysis of actuality and potentiality in creatures provides a metaphysical basis for understanding why God must be said to be pure actuality, and therefore permits the ascription of analogical names to God. Each of these points needs to be discussed. It is toward the first of these successive tasks that I will now turn.

The Real Distinction between Existence and Essence

As of yet, I have presented a sketch of Aquinas's interpretation of Aristotle's metaphysics (or perhaps, inversely, an Aristotelian sketch of Aquinas's ontology).[49] The goal has been to identify how basic knowledge of existents might give rise to a progressive, analogical, and causal understanding of being in terms of substance and accidents, actuality and potentiality. However, this reflection does not resolve the questions raised in chapters 3 and 4 concerning the rational basis for Aquinas's metaphysics of *esse* and essence (the real distinction of these two principles in all creatures). Nor has it touched upon Aquinas's use of the famous *ad alterum* analogy to discuss the likeness between creatures and God, *Ipsum esse subsistens*. Here, then, I would like briefly to present arguments by which the previously discussed metaphysics of substance and accident, actuality and potentiality, can be seen to open organically "from within" toward the more ontologically fundamental distinction between *esse* and essence as understood by Aquinas. The goal of each argument is to show how the Aristotelian form/matter composite (as understood by Aquinas) cannot account for its own existence in act, and therefore cannot be identical with its existence. "Essence" here denotes a form/matter composite of a given kind, with the potency to exist in act. *"Esse"* is the *actus essendi*, the act of being of a singular being,

---

[49] For a similar "Aristotelian" view of Aquinas (and Thomistic view of Aristotle), see the argumentation of Ralph McInerny in his *Praeambula Fidei*, 283–306.

or existent (*ens*) by which it exists.[50] By appeal to such arguments, I hope to suggest ways of deriving the latter (distinctly Thomistic) distinction logically out of the former causal analysis. This will in turn permit a discussion of the *ad alterum* analogy in the following chapter.[51]

Where might we find places of continuity between Aquinas's Aristotelian metaphysics of substance and actuality and the Thomistic meta-

---

[50] For the purposes of the discussion below, I am conceiving of "essence" as pertaining to a form/matter composite of a given kind. In doing so, I am appealing to a distinctly "Thomistic" account of essence, reminiscent of the *De ente et essentia*, and not to Aristotle's *to ti ein einei* of *Metaphysics Z*, which most Aristotelian scholars associate with the form of the substance. However, at times I refer to "essential form," rather than "essence," insofar as the essential determination of the form/matter composite is given to the matter by the form. On this latter point, Aquinas and Aristotle, I take it, agree.

[51] In one sense, this seems like the wrong sort of approach. As I have discussed in chapter 3, Aquinas reinterpreted Aristotelian hylomorphism and act/potency composition in light of the Christian metaphysics of creation, the *esse-essentia* distinction, and his own variant of participation theory. Noteworthy modern and contemporary scholars have warned against ambitious assimilations of the metaphysical thinking of the two figures, and have emphasized the distinctively medieval, Christian, and Neoplatonic origins of many of Aquinas's own ideas. This is the case particularly in his way of conceiving of the form/matter composite as an "essence" (inspired by Avicenna), as well as in his understanding of "intensive *esse*" and his interpretation of transcendental notions such as existence and goodness in light of the concept of participation. (See on these topics, for example, Fabro, *Participation et Causalité selon S. Thomas D'Aquin*, 179–207; John Wippel, "Thomas Aquinas's Commentary on Aristotle's *Metaphysics*" and "Platonism and Aristotelianism in Aquinas," *Metaphysical Themes* 2 [Washington, DC: The Catholic University of America Press, 2007], 240–89.) Therefore to think of these notions (essence, *esse*) in light of the Aristotelianism of Aquinas seems to invert the order of reflection of Aquinas himself, and to cut against the grain of the historical process by which the Christian metaphysics of Aquinas was derived in its medieval philosophical and theological context.

While discussion of the many historical issues involved exceeds the scope of my inquiry in this study, it is important to realize that in the context of my own discussion below, I am employing notions of essence, *esse*, and participation in a distinctly Thomistic sense, based upon what I take to be Aquinas's own thought, not that of Aristotle. My presupposition, however, is that the Aristotelian principles adopted by Aquinas are to be understood in logical and ontological continuity with his own distinctly Thomistic theses. Therefore, it is not odd to find Aquinas trying to identify precedents or grounds within his "Aristotelianism" for a leap to a more ultimate level of reflection. This is why I am particularly interested in Aquinas's *own interpretation* of Aristotle's *Metaphysics*, where we often find him claiming a basis in Aristotle's reflections for his own notions of *esse* and essence. Furthermore, as I have also mentioned in chapter 3, Aquinas did discuss his notions of *esse* and essence in terms of actuality and potency. Therefore, his theory of participation, while implying a distinctly Platonic understanding of exemplarity, is also based in

physics of creation, construed in terms of *esse* and essence? Here I would like to explore briefly three such venues.[52] The first is based upon the Aristotelian doctrine of the substantial generation of beings by one another. The second stems from the Aristotelian understanding that neither form nor matter, nor the teleological operations of a substance, accounts comprehensively for the being of that substance (for "why" the substance exists). The third is based upon the important Aristotelian affirmation that being is not in a genus (that it is not "divisible") because it is common to every genus, species, accident, and individual. From each of these distinctively Aristotelian metaphysical starting points, one can find arguments for affirming a real distinction between the nature of a being and its existence. Consequently, form/matter composites can be understood as potential kinds of beings (essences), which are not being per se, but rather which *have* being. The essence of any such composite reality is distinct from its existence. None of these arguments logically presupposes prior intuitive or demonstrative knowledge of the existence of God.

The first argument begins from the Aristotelian metaphysical analysis of substantial generation.[53] Contrary to what some thinkers (such as Gilson) have affirmed, Aristotle clearly teaches that the capacity to exist or not exist pertains not only to the properties of a being but also to that being as a substance. A substance can exist or not exist.[54] And material beings always come into existence through substantial generation, in dependence upon others who act as extrinsic causes of their coming into

---

significant ways upon creative reappropriations of Aristotelian accounts of efficient causality, perfecting teleology, and pure actuality. To participate in *esse* is to receive limited existence from a uniquely transcendent, efficient cause who is pure actuality. Likewise, participated *esse* is a source of teleological perfection in creatures. Creatures participate in goodness by their existence in act, and in their own intrinsic teleological activities imitate the transcendent perfection of God's pure actuality. (With respect to the latter points, see the arguments of Aimé Forest, *La Structure Métaphysique du Concret*, 128–65, 307, and Leo Elders, *The Metaphysics of St. Thomas Aquinas in a Historical Perspective*, 218–30.)

[52] The arguments offered below are necessarily somewhat cursory, and I have referred in footnotes to places where they are developed at further length. In addition to the arguments I have given, see the very insightful treatment of this issue in Steven Brock, "On Whether Aquinas's *Ipsum Esse* is 'Platonism,'" *Review of Metaphysics* 60 (2006): 723–57.

[53] For this first argument, my views are indebted in part to the argumentation of Lawrence Dewan in "St. Thomas and the Distinction between Form and Esse in Caused Things," in *Form and Being*, 188–204.

[54] On existence as pertaining to substantial beings that come into being in act, and can potentially exist or not exist, see *Physics* I, 7, 190a32; *Metaphysics Z*, 8, 1033b19–29; *H*, 1, 1042a25–b8; *Θ*, 8, 1050a4–b6.

being.[55] Therefore, if Aquinas, following Aristotle, affirms that the being of the accidents depends upon the being of the substance, this does not mean that "substance" signifies the same thing as "existence." For a given substance is also *given existence* by and through others, and can be or not be.[56]

From this Thomistic starting point, we can then move to the observation that there exists in nature a hierarchy of forms: the forms of beings we experience are ontologically dependent in that they receive existence through the activity of "superior" forms. For the sake of this argument, hierarchy can be determined strictly in accord with nonreciprocal ontological independence: the higher is higher because it can exist without the lower, while the contrary is not the case. Consequently the former in some respect exists more perfectly in act. For example, the parents who engender a child can exist without the child and do not depend upon it for their existence, while the inverse is not the case. The child has its substantial generation (its coming into being) from the parents. Likewise, the living substances on the earth depend for their coming into being upon the sun's

---

[55] Aquinas points out that this "caused" dimension of beings enters into their very composition, ontologically. *In VIII Meta.*, lec. 1, 1687: "It must be noted that in one sense substance means matter, and in another sense form, and in still another the thing composed of these. For matter is called substance, *not as though it were a being considered to have actual existence in itself, but as something capable of being actual* (and this is said of a particular thing). And form, which is also termed the intelligible structure because the intelligible structure of the species is derived from it, is called substance *inasmuch as it is something actual,* and inasmuch as it is separable from matter in thought but not in reality. And the thing composed of these is called substance inasmuch as it is something 'separable in an absolute sense,' i.e., *capable of existing separately by itself in reality; and it alone is subject to generation and corruption*" (emphasis added).

[56] In a series of parallel texts, Aquinas insists on the fact that only God is the direct cause of the "absolute existence" of created beings. (See for example *ScG* III, c. 44, 65, 67; *De potentia Dei*, q. 5, a. 1; *ST* I, q. 104, a. 1.) However, in order to distinguish his position from that of Avicenna, who posited the immediate creation of forms in matter from an immaterial source, Aquinas claims that created forms really do beget one another as composite forms. Significantly, he appeals to Aristotle's *Metaphysics* Z, 8, in this respect. In doing so he argues that created beings all receive their existence from God, and yet can act as causes of each other's *becoming*, and therefore even each other's *coming into existence* as substantial beings. See *De potentia Dei*, q. 5, a. 1, obj. 5 and ad 5, where he writes: "If with Aristotle we hold substantial forms to be educed from the potentiality of matter, natural agents will dispose not only matter but also the substantial form into actual existence, only however, in regard to its eduction from the [preexistent] potentiality of matter. . . . In this way, they will be principles of existence as concerns beginning to be, but not concerning existence absolutely [*essendi principia quantum ad inchoationem ad esse et non quantum ad ipsum esse absolute*]." See Dewan's analysis of this text in "The Importance of Substance," *Form and Being*, 111–13.

activity and its proximity to earth, insofar as the sun is responsible for the warmth of the climate in which living beings may exist. Yet the existence of the sun does not depend upon living beings.[57]

Cases such as these entail that the inferior form (or generated substance) receives existence due to the prior efficient activity of the superior one, or superior ones. And this implies then that the inferior imperfectly partakes of, or participates in, the *perfection* of existence that pertains to the superior being, due to the activity of the latter. Without being our parents, the atmosphere, the sun, and so on, we receive existence from and because of these causes. However, if a generated natural form and its existence were really ontologically identical, it would be impossible for that being to receive existence from and through another. By this I do not mean to deny that the substance of a thing is the "formal cause" of its existence, as Aquinas says it is.[58] A thing has existence "by its form." Nor do I mean to deny that in receiving one's natural form, one receives existence. However, the natural form of a thing is not the efficient cause of its own existence, and the forms of things we experience can exist or not exist. Existence is something each form has, not something it is. If the child existed "due to her nature alone," she would not be able to receive her existence from her parents since this existence would pertain by right to her natural form. Nor would she be a contingent being, who could one day cease to exist. Likewise, a given kind of living being would be unable to be maintained in existence by the environmental system of the sun, water, atmosphere, and the rest, since the existence of this living being would be identical with its nature. It could not be contingent as regards its existence. In sum, existence would be incommunicable across singulars of a same kind, or across natures of different kinds, if singular beings possessed existence by nature. Therefore, if we were to affirm an identity of existence and nature in material beings, it would be impossible to acknowledge the metaphysical truth of substantial generation.[59]

---

[57] *De potentia Dei*, q. 5, a. 1, ad 7.

[58] See, for example, *In VII Meta.*, lec. 6, 1388.

[59] In *De potentia Dei*, q. 5, a. 1, Aquinas argues from this observation that every being that is generated depends for its being on others, and consequently no generated form can be the direct and absolute source of its own existence. Therefore, the existence that is common to all such beings cannot be accounted for by recourse to material beings, but must have a transcendent source. "The existence of a thing made depends on its efficient cause inasmuch as it depends on the form of the thing made. Now there can be an efficient cause on which the form of the thing made does not depend directly and considered as a form, but only indirectly: thus the form of a generated fire does not depend on the generating fire directly and by reason of its species, seeing that it occupies the same degree in the order of things, and the form of fire is in the same way in both the generated and

To admit substantial generation, then, is also to acknowledge that while the actuality of a substantial form stems from its existence, natural forms are not identical with their existence. This requires in turn, that we affirm an ontological composition in all such generated beings between their natural form (which can be or not be) and their being in act, or *esse*. Generated substances have existence in themselves uniquely due to the activity of hierarchically superior substantial forms, from and through which their coming-into-existence occurs, through which they receive existence. The latter is communicated to them as essentially determined beings (forms-in-matter) that can be or not be. This existence, while intrinsic to them as substances, is also truly distinct from their essential forms. Therefore, there is a distinction in substances between their existence and their essence, as generated form-matter composites of a given kind. [60]

A second vein of argumentation is based upon the essential natures of beings we experience. The formal kinds of things we know (including the things that we are as human beings) cannot procure their own existence.[61] They cannot do this either (1) by their formal natures, (2) by their material component parts and material potentiality, nor (3) by their teleological operations and activities. The formal nature of a thing is not identical with its existence because the existence of a substantial form depends not only upon the form itself but also upon the material component parts that are

---

in the generating fire, and is distinguished therefrom only by a material distinction, through being seated in another matter. Hence since the generated fire has its form from some cause, this same form must depend on some higher principle, that is the cause of that form directly and in respect of its very species. Now seeing that properly speaking the existence of a form in matter implies no movement or change except accidentally, and since no bodies act unless moved, as the Philosopher shows, it follows of necessity that the principle on which the form depends directly [i.e., for its existence, as an efficient cause] must be something incorporeal, for the effect depends on its active cause through the action of a principle. And if a corporeal principle be in some way the cause of a form, this is due to its acting by virtue of an incorporeal principle and as its instrument." See also *De potentia Dei*, q. 7, a. 2; *In de Causis*, lec. 18; *In VIII Phys.*, lec. 2, 987; *De sub. sep.*, c. 9.

[60] Thus, Aquinas remarks succinctly in *ScG* II, c. 52: "The substance of each and every thing belongs to it through itself and not through another. Thus, it does not pertain to the substance of air to be actually luminous, since this quality it acquires through something else. But every created [i.e., caused] thing has its being through another; otherwise, it would not be caused. Therefore, the being of no created substance is that substance." A more extensive analysis is offered by Dewan in "Form and *Esse* in Caused Things," *Form and Being*, 201–2.

[61] A parallel, more extensive form of this argument is found in David Twetten, "Come distinguere realemente tra esse ed essenza in Tommaso d'Aquino: Qualche aiuto de Aristotele," in *Tommaso D'Aquino e l'oggetto della Metaphisica*, ed. Steven Brock (Rome: Armando, 2004), and recently rearticulated in McInerny, *Praeambula Fidei*, 303 n. 18.

informed by this nature, and radically, upon the material potentiality as well. Form alone then does not suffice for existence in material things due to the reality of matter.[62] The same can be said of the matter: what a thing is made of, its parts, and potentiality for change as an individual subject, do not alone account for its existence. For this we have to appeal to the formal nature that gives unity, internal organization, and teleological order to the material components. Finally, the teleological operations themselves of composite material substances (such as living things) are only accidents of these substances. Therefore, they do not cause the substance to exist. Whether one thinks or does not think, sees or does not see, walks or does not walk, does not account for whether one has existence.[63] Consequently, existence is not identical with either the formal nature of a thing, its material components and potentiality, or its teleological operations. The essence of a thing, for Aquinas, however, is equivalent to its determination as a form-matter composite of a particular kind, tending toward particular ends. Yet, in a given reality, if none of these *essential* aspects of a physical thing *is being*, all three of these *have existence*. In such an existent, then, existence is not identical with essence.

Last, there is the question of a universal participation in being. Participation is not a word used by Aristotle to discuss metaphysical composition.[64] However, Aristotle does affirm that "being is not in a genus," because it is common to every genus, species, accident, and individual.[65] In

---

[62] If forms existed without matter, there could be no substantial generation of composite beings, in which forms come into being by being educed from matter. *De potentia Dei*, q. 3, a. 8: "For being is not predicated univocally of the form and the thing generated. *A generated natural thing is said to be per se and properly, as having being and subsisting in that being: whereas the form is not thus said to be, for it does not subsist, nor has it being per se* [i.e., independently of matter]. . . . Consequently, it is not correct to say that the form is made in matter, rather should we say that it is educed from the potentiality of matter. And from this principle that the composite [of form and matter] and not the form is made, the Philosopher (*Metaphysics Z*, 8) proves that forms result from natural agents [rather than separate forms]" (emphasis added). Aquinas makes clear here that he is in full agreement with what he takes to be Aristotle's own doctrine on the subject, while simultaneously claiming that form and being are really distinct in created beings. See also *In VII Meta.*, lec. 7, where he makes similar arguments.

[63] *De potentia Dei*, q. 3, a. 8: "Accidents are described as beings, because by them a substance is qualified or quantified, but not as though by them it is simply, as it is by the substantial form. Hence it is more correct to say that an accident is of something than that it is something." See, likewise, *In VII Meta.*, lec. 1.

[64] He is critical of Plato in this respect, insofar as the Platonic notions of participation implied participation in the separate forms, and therefore a theory of separate ideas (*Metaphysics A*, 6, 987a29–988a16).

[65] *Metaphysics B*, 3, 998a20–999a22.

a series of what are often complex and profound arguments, Aquinas shows that this truth has a metaphysical foundation in the real distinction between *esse* and essence. The fact that existence is common to every genus implies that there is a real distinction or composition between nature and existence in all things we experience.[66] In a summary fashion, one can consider the argument in quite an Aristotelian fashion by beginning from the individual and working toward greater universality. No individual we experience can be considered coextensive with all that exists, because we experience a multiplicity of individuals, each of which exists. Existence is common to each. However, there also is no identity between any accident (such as a quality or quantity) and existence, because diverse accidents exist, and each exists in dependence upon a substance in which it inheres. No species of substance is coextensive with existence, as it is proper to every specific kind of substance to exist. (That is to say, existence is not divided by species, but rather, is common to every species.) Finally, being is not particular to a given genus, as every genus of being *exists*. Yet this means that existence as such is not per se either an individual, an accident, a specific kind of reality, or a genus. And consequently, no individual substance of a specific kind, pertaining to a given genus, is identical with its being. Rather, this substance *has* being. Every limited substance we experience of a given kind in fact participates in existence, but is not itself coextensive with existence, or identical with existence. It is necessary, then, to consider the nature of such substances truly distinct from their existence.[67]

---

[66] Relevant texts include: *Sent.* I, d. 8, q. 4, a. 2; *De ver.*, q. 27, a. 1, ad 8; *ScG* I, c. 25; *De potentia Dei*, q. 7, a. 3; *ST* I, q. 3, a. 5, *Comp. Theol.*, c. 14. See the helpful discussion of this form of argumentation in Wippel, *The Metaphysical Thought of Thomas Aquinas*, 157–61.

[67] Do we not run the risk here of reifying a concept of being, one that is in fact simply the most general notion, a kind of ideal form, common to all beings? And in this case, have we not departed from Aristotle's thought altogether, and launched into an illusory idealism? In fact, in what is an astonishing argumentation, Aquinas claims (see *In de Heb.* II; *In VIII Phys.*, lec. 10, 1053–54; *ST* I, q. 3, a. 6, c. and ad 2) that *even if* Plato were correct and there were common *forms* that were participated in by the others, in this case the *Aristotelian* theory of actuality and potentiality would apply to them. Insofar as they themselves were distinct from the beings that participated in them, they would exist separately, and their existence would therefore be differentiated from that of the realities that participated in them (like the form of whiteness as distinct from white things). And in this case, the forms would themselves be specifically distinct from one another as well (like the form of the horse and that of man). Therefore, there would exist *in the forms themselves* a real distinction between existence and essence, since existence would not be reducible to any one form. So on the hypothesis of a reified Platonic generic notion (which Aquinas does not believe in) we still return to the necessity of a real distinction in all *singular* beings of essence and existence, due to

Hypothetically speaking, *if there were* to be a being in which essence and existence were identical, then (1) it could not be identical with any limited, finite existent.[68] A being in which existence and essence were identical could not be a member in a series of finite beings. (2) Consequently, all other existents would have to receive existence from this being as their primary cause. It would be the origin of the participated existence of all others. (3) This being would have to transcend in its perfection the limitations of all distinct species and genera, all accidents and individuating matter. The reason for this is that it could have no limiting characteristics by which to differentiate it from others merely generically, specifically, accidentally, or individually. Were it to have such features, then it would be a being alongside others, and consequently would participate in existence as one in a series of finite beings. (4) This being would have to contain within itself (in a higher way) all the perfections of existence and nature that are found in limited, finite creatures. Therefore, it would have to be the unique being in which existence was perfect. This being the case, then, there could only be one such being.[69]

Note that the order of reasoning here is in fact the inverse of that attributed to natural theology according to Kant, that is to say, as ontotheology. The reason is that for Kant, the proofs of the existence of God presuppose the prior formulation of the idea of God. Any a posteriori argumentation for God's existence is in fact dependent upon an a priori conception of God. The idea of God is an organizing principle of transcendental reason, in light of which all other real or possible existents may be conceived hypothetically as a dependent totality. In the Thomistic case that has just been considered, however, we have begun from compositions present in all realities experienced so as to conceive of the possibility of a reality that is not composite and thus limited. In this case the way of proceeding is truly a posteriori insofar as (1) it is only by working negatively

---

Aristotelian presuppositions. Being cannot be the most generic notion. Existence is always singular. Furthermore, if there is some one being that is existence by nature, he is the source of all existence, but is not in a genus of "being." See in this respect Aquinas's discussion in *De sub. sep.*, c. 3, 4, and 9, where he emphasizes that the notion of participation should be interpreted in light of the Aristotelian distinction of actuality and potentiality, with criticism of Plato's theory of forms.

68 This "hypothetical" kind of thinking about the possibility of only one first being in which existence and essence are identical is present in Aquinas's thought. See, for example, *De ente*, c. 4; *ScG* II, 52, second argument; *In VIII Phys.*, lec. 10, 1053–54; and the analysis of Wippel, *The Metaphysical Thought of Thomas Aquinas*, 150–57.

69 Relevant for thinking about these three points is *ST* I, q. 4, aa. 2–3, on the repercussions of God's not being in any genera or species, as related to his absolute perfection and transcendence of creatures.

from individuals, accidents, species, and genera that one conceives of participated existence as something truly distinct from substances and their essential natures. This in turn provides for the hypothetical possibility of conceiving of God from realities we experience as one whose essence is to exist—indirectly and by analogy. (2) The existence of this transcendent cause of being is not demonstrated from the metaphysics of the real distinction as we have considered it here, but is only hypothesized. Consequently, one can understand the real distinction in creatures *without* this either presupposing or necessitating as a consequence the intuitive or demonstrative knowledge of the existence of God. The real distinction of *esse* and existence can thus be analyzed as a metaphysical composition of actuality and potentiality in realities we know *in via inventionis* prior to the demonstrative arguments for the existence of God. It forms a stage, then, in a causal analysis of the structure of reality, leading to the eventual affirmation of the existence of God. It is toward this last stage of argumentation that I will now turn.

Ways toward God: A Posteriori Demonstrations

In turning toward the central topic of this chapter, the demonstrative knowledge of the existence of God, it is necessary to reemphasize what exactly is under consideration in this study. Here I will not try to reproduce a comprehensive presentation and defense of the Five Ways of Aquinas's *ST* I, q. 2, a. 3, or any similarly important Thomistic text. A technical and historical discussion of Aquinas's own forms of argumentation vastly exceeds the purpose of this study. Furthermore, an intricate and robust account of the natural demonstrations for God's existence must inevitably seek to answer to a whole series of important philosophical and scientific objections on such controversial subjects as movement and inertia, cosmology and belief in causality, teleology in nature, degrees of being, and so on. This conversation of Thomistic metaphysics *ad extra* is certainly necessary. My aim here, however, is rather to examine the logical continuity between a causal analysis of being and the articulation of a posteriori arguments that are impervious to the accusations of ontotheology. How do the answers to previous questions concerning the structure of being prepare us to think rightly about an a posteriori demonstrative knowledge of God, like that elaborated by Aquinas in his rational arguments for the existence of God?

For this purpose, I will consider here four arguments for the existence of God, each based upon the causal structures of being discussed in this and previous chapters. The first three derive from the three modes of being in act and being in potency studied in Book Θ of Aristotle's *Meta-*

physics: those pertaining to movement, substantial existence, and teleological operations, respectively. The fourth way is derived from the real distinction between *esse* and essence in all beings we experience. The first of these arguments corresponds roughly to the First Way of Aquinas's *ST* I, q. 2, a. 3, and is based upon the being in act and being in potency of movement. The second is quite similar to the argument from contingency in *ScG* I, c. 15, and is based upon the potency to exist or not exist in substances. The third resembles the Fifth Way of the *ST*, q. 2, a. 3, read in a distinctly metaphysical fashion. It is based upon the being in act and potency of teleological operations. The fourth combines elements from both the argumentation of *De ente et essentia*, chapter 4, and the Fourth Way of the *ST* I, q. 2, a. 3. It is based upon the *esse*/essence distinction as an ultimate form of act/potency composition.[70]

In each case I will attempt to show: (1) that the argumentation in question begins from real ontological compositions and interdependencies of beings this world (intrinsic compositions denoting the necessity of extrinsic causes), which exist in all the beings we can come to know through human experience; (2) that each of these ways depends upon the insight that actuality precedes potentiality in the order of being, such that realities composed of potentiality of some kind depend in turn upon beings in act; and (3) that each of these ways depends uniquely upon an a posteriori form of causal demonstration, in which the explanation of all secondary

---

[70] For the purposes of economy of presentation, I would like to mention here some interpretive presuppositions at play in my presentation of Aquinas's arguments. My attempt in the following pages is to show how a causal argument for the existence of God can build upon a causal inquiry into the beings we encounter directly, as previously presented. The first way I offer below is essentially a metaphysical reading of the First Way from *ST* I, q. 2, a. 3, based upon the act/potency distinction in beings subject to change. The second way is an argument from contingency, based upon the act/potency distinction in beings at the level of their substantial being. I take this form of argument from *ScG* I, c. 15, *rather than* the Third Way of the *ST* because the latter argument employs recourse to the idea that were there no non-contingent cause (i.e., if God did not exist), there necessarily would have been a time that nothing existed. And therefore nothing would exist now. This complex form of argumentation raises numerous interesting philosophical questions that I do not wish to treat here and that the simpler argument from the *ScG* conveniently avoids. The third argument I give is basically the teleological argument, the Fifth Way from the *ST*. I interpret this argument in distinctly metaphysical terms by appealing to the act/potency distinction at the level of operations in beings we experience, and to what this reveals about the natures of the beings in question. The fourth argument I offer (from the real distinction in dependent beings) is taken directly from the *De ente*, c. 4. I then use it in turn to "interpret" the Fourth Way from the *ST* (the argument from the hierarchy of perfections) in a way that Aquinas himself did not do, but that I think is consistent with his metaphysical principles.

realities is possible only by recourse to something beyond any causal series of interdependent beings. In other words, each way in question ends by requiring us to "exit" from the world of limited, dependent beings, finding God as the reason why this world exists at all.

The first argument is from motion.[71] It is derived from that modality of being in act and being in potentiality that Aristotle and Aquinas note exists in all material beings: all such beings are subject to movement and change. This is particularly evident in accidental properties of substances we experience. For example, such realities change their weight or size, undergo transformations of color, capacity, skill or health, and move or are moved from one position to another. In short, there are changes of quantity, changes of quality, and changes in location that characterize all physical beings. On a broader level, we might consider changes of a substantial kind as a form of physical movement as well (changes of substantial generation or corruption). Things change from being only potentially to being actually, or from being actually to ceasing to exist.[72] In all of these cases motion or change denotes potentiality in a substance. For "nothing can be undergoing change unless it is in potentiality to that toward which it is undergoing change."[73] Furthermore, a thing undergoing change cannot both be in actuality and potentiality under the same aspect at the same instant. A given reality can be changing others even while it is changed by another, but it cannot simultaneously be both changing and being changed under the same aspect.

To this first claim, we must add a second. That which exists in potentiality can be moved to actuality (thus undergoing alteration or change) only by something that is already in actuality. We see this in the world of inanimate and animate physical beings that we experience. Each being is moved (from potency to actuality) due to the activity or operation of

---

[71] For further reflection on this argument, see in particular Elders, *The Philosophical Theology of St. Thomas Aquinas*, 89–96; Scott MacDonald, "Aquinas' Parasitic Argument," *Medieval Philosophy and Theology* 1 (1991): 119–55; Rudi Te Velde, *Aquinas on God* (Aldershot: Ashgate, 2006), 48–60; Van Steenberghen, *Le Problème de l'Existence de Dieu dans les Écrits de S. Thomas d'Aquin*, 113–22 and 165–80; James Weisheipl, "Galileo and the Principle of Inertia," and "The Principle *Omne quod movetur ab alio movetur* in Medieval Physics" in *Nature and Motion in the Middle Ages*, ed. William Carroll (Washington, DC: The Catholic University of America Press, 1985), 49–63, 75–97; John Wippel, *The Metaphysical Thought of Thomas Aquinas*, 444–59.

[72] Aquinas commonly distinguishes three kinds of accidental, non-substantial change: that which is based upon change of place, quantitative growth or diminution, and qualitative alteration. He distinguishes these from substantial change, which pertains to the generation or corruption of substances. See, for example, *In VIII Meta.*, lec. 1, 1688.

[73] *ST* I, q. 2, a. 3.

another. In the case of any being that undergoes qualitative, quantitative, positional, or substantial change, there is necessary recourse to an extrinsic cause in act, which accounts for the "movement" from potentiality to actuality that such change entails. Every being we experience exists as this kind of being, not only as one having been subject to ontological alteration of some sort in the past, but also as one *being* altered in some way, *and* as one *capable* of further alteration due to the sort of being that it is. Therefore, in its very manner of existing, each being subject to change is characterized by being in potentiality.

This leads us to consider the existence of actual change in the physical world we experience as derived necessarily from an essentially ordered series of interdependent beings. In the series (or "web") of changing realities we experience, each is moved from potentiality to actuality by others.[74] If we consider the *actually existent* (rather than historical) series of such beings undergoing change, no such being can account fully for its own existence as a being that is moved. Each existent that undergoes change is in turn subject to actual transformation by another, and this one to another, and so on. Therefore, the existence of each being that is subject to change is explained only by recourse to another. Of course, we could envisage the multiplication of such a series of imperfect, interdependent beings to the infinite. However, this would do nothing to explain ultimately how or why this series of interdependent beings should exist, since it would not permit us to render a final, sufficient reason for the being in act of *any* of the members of the series, let alone all of them. Confronted with such an impasse, the human intellect may rightly ascertain that there exists necessarily a first, unmoved mover who transcends the world of potentiality and change. As one who is pure actuality, he is the origin and cause of the movement and change of all secondary beings. Without appeal to this transcendent cause, the movements from potency to act in the limited beings we experience are inexplicable.[75]

---

[74] To cite Aquinas's pithy phrase, "that which is moved is moved by another." *ST* I, q. 2, a. 3.

[75] This argumentation can be expanded so as to apply even to spiritual creatures, both human beings and separate substances (if they exist) who might change themselves by actions of intellect and will. Aquinas offers argumentations to this effect concerning the spiritual activities of the human soul. (See for example *ST* I–II, q. 9.) In doing so, one can also appeal to the principle "every thing that moves is moved by another." Insofar as they are self-moving movers, changing spiritual beings have a *potentiality of intellect and will* to "move themselves" intrinsically toward a more perfect state. This in turn requires a transcendent cause who is the "extrinsic" source or origin for their intellectual and voluntary movement from potency to act, and who sustains the latter in being. For a helpful discussion of this topic see, Wippel, *The Metaphysical Thought of Thomas Aquinas*, 449–53. On the question of

The second way I will consider here begins from the second mode of being in act discussed by Aristotle in *Metaphysics* Θ, that pertaining to the being in act and being in potentiality of contingent substances. This form of argumentation is more succinct and vertiginous. As I have mentioned in chapter 4, Aquinas and Aristotle both observe that substances in the physical world can exist or not exist. This fundamental contingency with respect to existence derives from the fact that every such material existent is substantially generated by others and is in turn capable of substantial corruption. This capacity for being or not being can be conceived of, then, in terms of being in act or being in potentiality. All contingent material substances have the potential to exist in act, or to cease to exist in act.[76]

It follows from this that in the actual world order of physical substances, each contingent being is a caused reality. It is dependent upon others for its existence. In this case, then, no essentially contingent cause can account for its own existence. However, the positing of an actual, infinite chain of dependent, contingent beings would not allow us to explain why there exist such beings, since each would in turn be caused by another or others. To makes sense of the actual world of physically contingent beings that exists, then, we need to posit a transcendent being that exists necessarily. Aquinas puts it in this way:

> We find in the world certain beings, those namely that are subject to generation and corruption, which can be or not be. But what can exist [*quod est possible esse*] has a cause because, since it is equally related to two contraries, namely being and non-being, it must be owing to some cause that being accrues to it. Now, as we have proved by the reasoning of Aristotle, one cannot proceed to infinity among

---

God's transcendent causality and the simultaneous existence of free will, see Bernard Lonergan, *Grace and Freedom and Gratia Operans*, in vol. 1 of *The Collected Works of Bernard Lonergan* (Toronto: University of Toronto Press, 2000); David Burrell, *Freedom and Creation in Three Traditions* (Notre Dame: University of Notre Dame Press, 1993); Brian Shanley, "Divine Causation and Human Freedom in Aquinas," *American Catholic Philosophical Quarterly* 72, no. 1 (1998): 99–122.

76 Aquinas, commenting upon *Metaphysics* Z, 7 (1032a20–22), writes (*In VII Meta.*, lec. 6, 1388): "Everything that is generated by nature or by art is capable both of being and of not being. For since generation is a change from non-being to being, the thing generated must at one time be and at another not be, and this would be true only if it were possible for it both to be and not be. Now the potential element which each thing has both for being and not being is matter; for it is in potentiality to the forms by which things have being, and to the privations by which they have non-being, as is clear from what was said above." Aquinas specifically refers to this understanding of existence and substantial generation in Aristotle in his argumentation from contingency for the existence of God in *ScG* II, c. 15. See on this point, Wippel, *The Metaphysical Thought of Thomas Aquinas*, 439n105.

causes. We must therefore posit something that is a necessary being. Every necessary being, however, either has the cause of its necessity in an outside source or, if it does not, it is necessary through itself. But one cannot proceed to infinity among necessary beings the cause of whose necessity lies in an outside source. We must therefore post a first necessary being, which is necessary through itself.[77]

Of course, one might conjecture, as Aquinas does in this text, about the possibility of a multiplicity of immaterial, necessary beings upon whom the contingent world we experience depends. Is it possible that the argument from contingency might allow us to ascertain that there exists some immaterial being or beings, but leaves open the question of whether or not there exists a unique, necessary being? As Aquinas rightly notes, if there are a multiplicity of "necessary" beings that are not subject to material corruption (take Aristotle's fifty-five unmoved-movers from *Λ*, 8, or Aquinas's angels, for example), then these beings are themselves differentiated in some way from one another.[78] Otherwise they would be ontologically indistinguishable. If they are not distinguished by the fact that one is absolutely necessary and the cause of all the others, then they are distinguished by either differentiation of essence or accidental differentiating characteristic perfections.

If the former is the case (differentiation according to essence),[79] then in each of the beings in question, the essence will not be coextensive with all that exists (i.e., considering the existence of the other necessary beings of a differentiated essence). But in this case, the arguments mentioned above apply: there must be a real distinction in such existents between essence and existence, since existence is not appropriated exclusively to a given genera or species. And realities that are composites of essence and existence are caused realities, since none of them can account for its own existence through the principles of its essence. Therefore all such secondary, immaterial realities must be caused by a being that is uniquely necessary.

However, these immaterial realities might be thought to somehow differ only according to their accidental perfections. If this is the case, then each of these beings is composed of a substance of a given kind and accidents. To the extent that this is true of each of these necessary non-contingent beings, then each is composed of actuality and potency, since some accidental perfections exist in act in each one that do not exist in the others. None of them can account for the being in act of the others, and consequently we must

---

[77] *ScG* I, c. 15. Translation slightly modified.

[78] *ScG* I, c. 42.

[79] Aristotle himself argues that each separated substance must have a distinct species, or essence, in *Metaphysics Λ*, 8, 1074a31–39, a view Aquinas will adopt in his own argumentation concerning angels.

have recourse to a primary transcendent cause, who is pure actuality, and who contains in a higher way the perfections of each. In this way we come eventually to the necessary affirmation of a unique cause of all that exists, one that is absolutely necessary, and cause of existence in all others.[80]

The third way begins from the consideration of the third mode of being in act in *Metaphysics Θ*, that of teleological operations. Here, one might well begin an argument for God's existence based upon efficient causality, since it is the operation-in-act of a given substance that accounts for its action upon another. Because operations of existents account for the coming into being, or conservation in being, of other existents, one could employ the dependencies signaled by such operations in order to "ascend" back up to a unique and universal source of existence. Indeed, Aristotle seems to allude to the idea in *Metaphysics Θ* (while discussing this subject) that there must exist something primary in the order of efficient causality, and this argumentation in turn closely resembles Aquinas's Second Way in the *ST* I, q. 2, a. 3.[81] At the same time, however, this mode of being in act and being in potentiality is employed to account for the perfections and imperfections in beings that tend naturally toward a given end.[82] Therefore, such operations also allude

---

[80] The above paragraph is a modified form of Aquinas's argumentation in *ScG* I, c. 42, argument eight. For a more extensive consideration of this text, see the analysis by Kretzmann in *The Metaphysics of Theism*, 160–65.

[81] *Metaphysics Θ*, 8, 1050a30–b5: "Where, then, the result is something apart from the exercise [through transitive rather than immanent operational action], the actuality is in the thing that is being made, e.g., the act of building is in the thing that is being built and that of weaving in the thing that is being woven, and similarly in all other cases, and in general the movement is in the thing that is being moved; but when there is no product apart from the actuality [i.e., as in immanent, operational action], the actuality is in the agents, e.g., the act of seeing is in the seeing subject and that of theorizing in the theorizing subject, and the act of life is in the soul. . . . Obviously, therefore, the substance or form is actuality. From this argument it is obvious that actuality is prior in substance to potentiality; and as we have said, one actuality always precedes another in time right back to the actuality of the eternal prime mover." Aristotle probably is referring here to the first moved-mover of the heavens who in turn is moved through contemplation of the primary unmoved mover. See Aquinas's remarks in *In IX Meta.*, lec. 8, especially paragraph 1866, which make clear that he thinks this passage refers us to the causal primacy of act over potency in the order of efficient causality, whereby an argument ultimately can be derived for the dependency of all beings upon the pure actuality of God as the primary cause.

[82] Aquinas discusses operational activities as the metaphysical principles of perfection at length in *In IX Meta.*, lec. 7–8. In lec. 8, 1865, he discusses immanent acts of perfection as follows: "But when nothing else is produced in addition to the activity of the potency, the actuality then exists in the agent as its perfection and does not pass over into something external in order to perfect it. For example, the act of seeing is in the one seeing as his perfection, and the act of speculating is in

to the possible existence of a primary cause of the order-toward-an-end that is ontologically inscribed in things.

The argument begins from a metaphysical reflection on teleological operations.[83] Just as formal natures come to be and operate in view of immanent purposes or natural extrinsic effects, so too this teleological tendency is inscribed in their very beings *as being*. In other words, teleological operation tells us something about the potentiality of a thing to become actuated in a certain way, in view of its natural perfections. This is true, in a certain sense, at every level of nature as we experience it. The human person is characterized by an intellectual tendency toward truth, and a voluntary desire for the good, and for happiness. The animated living thing is characterized by a set of operations in view of its own good and the good of its own species (survival, self-nourishment, growth, reproduction). This tendency is mirrored in analogous ways in turn in the organs and cells of living things, and their dynamic operations in view of identifiable, normative ends. Inanimate beings are characterized above all by a set of intrinsic habitual actions or dispositions that come together in a predictable pattern of behavior (denoted by what we might call laws of nature).[84] To note all this is to say nothing for or against an "argument from design" regarding God as transcendent intellect.[85] Rather, it is to say that in their activities and operations, the beings we experience habitually tend intrinsically toward certain ends, and that these tendencies are constitutive of what they are. They are composed of the potency for such actions in their very manner of being.

---

the one speculating. . . . [Likewise,] happiness is a good of the one who is happy, namely, his perfect life. . . . Thus it is evident that happiness does not consist either in building or in any activity of the kind which passes over into something external, but consists in understanding and willing." For a clear indication of the principle deployed in Aquinas's own argumentation, see *ScG* III, c. 24–25.

83 The following paragraphs are partially indebted to the reflections of M. D. Philippe in vol. 3 of *De l'Être à Dieu. De la philosophie première à la sagesse* (Paris: Tèqui, 1977), 344–48, 362–66.

84 This hierarchy of degrees of teleological realization that I have listed is discussed by Aquinas in *ScG* III, c. 22–23. See also *ST* I, q. 59, a. 1.

85 In his *In I Meta.*, lec. 11, 177, Aquinas discusses the fact that the final cause was understood by Aristotle as an intrinsic principle of order within nature. He claims that this was an advance over pre-Socratic theories of nature, since Anaxagoras had previously considered teleology uniquely as an extrinsic principle of intellectual, efficient causality by mind (intended purpose) exerted *upon* the form and becoming of things. The distinction between these two kinds of final causality (intrinsic/natural versus extrinsic/intellectual) seems to be lacking in much of the modern discourse *pro et contra* concerning intelligent design. I am indebted to Dewan, "The Importance of Substance," *Form and Being*, 106n28, for the application of this text to the contemporary debate.

The next stage in this argument derives from the realization that this tendency-toward-actuation is not something that any of the aforementioned beings (human, sensate, or inanimate) can of themselves choose or determine. Such inscribed purposes or teleological determinations are characteristics of *what* they are *essentially*.[86] That is to say, these essential patterns of behavior are not decided upon—or realized by one's own operational determination—but are ontologically inherited, or given in being. The essence of a being that tends only potentially toward a given end, then, is necessarily not the cause of itself, but depends upon another (or others) for the kind of being that it is to be.[87] However, in this case there is a sense in which the order toward perfection of some sort inscribed in each thing denotes causation by another who is not himself composed of potentiality and actuality.[88] Were this not the case, we would be obliged to seek the source of the teleological order of our very nature in another cause of the same kind, that did not itself determine its own order-toward-actuality, and that cause would in turn depend upon another, and so on. Again, recourse to the infinite in a series of imperfect beings composed of potentiality and actuality would not explain sufficiently how or why this series of interdependent beings exists. Therefore, there must exist some being who is pure actuality, who transcends the world of beings in poten-

---

[86] *ST* I, q. 5, a. 5: "Everything is said to be good so far as it is perfect. . . . Now a thing is said to be perfect if it lacks nothing according to the mode of its perfections. But since everything is what it is by its form (and since the form presupposes certain things, and from the form certain things necessarily follow), in order for a thing to be perfect and good it must have a form, together with all that precedes and follows upon that form. Now the form presupposes determination or commensuration of its principles, whether material or efficient. . . . Further, upon the form follows an inclination to the end, or to an action . . . for everything, in so far as it is in act, acts and tends towards that which is in accordance with its form." This is not to deny that such operations are accidents of substances, but to say that in them a given kind of substance finds its plenary realization as the kind of being that it is. See in this respect *De ver.*, q. 21, a. 1; *ScG* I, c. 38; III, c. 20; *ST* I, q. 6, a. 3.

[87] This is, it seems to me, a distinctly metaphysical way of thinking about the Fifth Way, in *ST* I, q. 2, a. 3. Such argumentation requires that the inclination toward an end be understood as something intrinsic to the being of a thing, rather than extrinsic. Nevertheless, this intrinsic "order-toward" is not accounted for by the thing itself. See in this respect the reflections of Aquinas in *De ver.*, q. 5, a. 2; q. 25, a. 1.; *ScG* III, c. 2; 20, *ST* I, q. 5, a. 4; I–II, q. 1, a. 2.

[88] *ScG* I, c. 28: "Everything that is imperfect must be preceded by something perfect. Thus, the seed is from the animal or the plant. The first being must, therefore, be most perfect. . . . Again, each thing is perfect according as it is in act, and imperfect according as it is in potency, and lacking act. Hence, that which is in no way in potency, but is pure act, must be most perfect."

tiality. In him subsistence and teleological perfection are identical, such that his nature is his perfect operation. As the cause of the tendency toward perfection in all others, he is necessarily the supreme good who is imitated only imperfectly in secondary beings.[89]

The fourth way is based upon the real distinction or composition between *esse* and essence in each of the realities we experience. As Étienne Gilson saw rightly, the argument is simple *once* we have discovered the rational grounds for the real distinction. No being in which essence and existence are truly distinct is the cause of its own existence. For a thing that cannot procure its own existence through the principles of its essence must be dependent upon others in order to exist. This is characteristic of every being we experience: it receives its existence from another, or others. To cite Aquinas: "Existence cannot be caused by the form or quiddity of a thing—[that is] as an efficient cause—because in this way a thing would be a cause of itself and produce itself in existence, which is impossible. Therefore it is necessary that each thing whose existence is other than its nature has its existence from another."[90] Evidently, this dependency in the order of existence cannot go on infinitely, and so there must exist a being in whom existence and essence are identical that is the cause of all others.

Another way of articulating this argument can be derived from consideration of the participation of all things in the varying degrees of perfection.[91] In all the beings in which existence and essence are distinct, there are perfections of greater or lesser degree. The essences of beings we experience exist in varying ways and in varying degrees of perfection, and these are manifest through their teleological operations. This explains, for example, why there is a hierarchy of goodness among things. Beings such as persons are of a more noble essence than non-rational animals, or non-sentient beings, and among human beings, some have acquired more goodness through their various rational and voluntary operations than others. But where there exists a more or less perfect in the order of existence, there is *the possibility* of a first existent in which the essence is most

---

[89] Aquinas offers an explanation of creatures' likenesses in goodness to God in *ScG* III, c. 19, 20, 25. 19 and 25: "Everything tends through its motion or action towards a good, as its end. Now, a thing participates in the good precisely to the same extent that it becomes like the first goodness, which is God. So, all things tend through their movements and actions towards the divine likeness, as towards their ultimate end. . . . Since all creatures, even those devoid of understanding, are ordered to God as to an ultimate end, all achieve this end to the extent that they participate somewhat in his likeness. Intellectual creatures attain it in a more special way, that is, through their proper operation of understanding him. Hence, this must be the end of the intellectual creature, namely, to understand God."

[90] *De ente*, c. 4.

[91] I am referring here to Aquinas's Fourth Way in *ST* I, q. 2, a. 3.

perfect.[92] Now since those things that participate in existence but are not their own existence depend upon others for their existence, they necessarily *receive their perfection from another*. But this cannot go on to the infinite. Therefore, there must exist some being that is the giver of all such perfections, one in whom existence and essence are one, and in whom perfections such as being, nobility, and goodness are not limited.[93]

This primary being exists necessarily. It has no differentiations that accrue to it from genera, species, accidents, or individuation. Consequently, it is not identical with "common being" since the latter is itself divided by the diversity of genera and species, substances and accidents.[94] Nor can we then think of God as a substance among other substances (as a designation such as "supreme being" would seem to suggest), because this would entail that we think of him as a being of a given kind *having* existence (from another).[95] Rather, the primary existent is himself subsistent

---

[92] In stating things this way, I am avoiding Aquinas's appeal in the Fourth Way to the axiom, "Where there exists a greater and a lesser, there must be something first that is greatest." I have raised questions about the use of this axiom in chapter 5. Instead, I am following the suggestion of John Wippel (*The Metaphysical Thought of Thomas Aquinas*, 469–79) of employing the real distinction in order to interpret the degrees of perfection, as Aquinas does at times in the *ScG*. This renders the appeal to exemplary causality (degrees of perfection) relative to an appeal to efficient causality (the transcendent source of *esse*).

[93] Based upon the real distinction, Aquinas presupposes a heterogeneity and hierarchy of kinds of realities that each participate in goodness, as they do in *esse*. In *ScG* I, c. 38, he states the argument for God's existence this way: "Each good thing that is not its goodness is called good by participation. But that which is named by participation has something prior to it from which it receives the character of goodness. This cannot proceed to infinity, since among final causes there is no regress to infinity. . . . We must, therefore reach some first good, that is not by participation good through an order towards some other good, but is good through its essence." On the relation between participation, goodness, and perfection, see the helpful analysis of Rudi Te Velde, *Participation and Substantiality in Thomas Aquinas*, 21–34, and on the causal argument for a primary source of participated perfection, Leo Elders, *The Philosophical Theology of St. Thomas Aquinas*, 110–20.

[94] See *De ente*, c. 5; *ScG* I, c. 23–27; *ST* I, q. 3, aa. 5–6.

[95] *De potentia Dei*, q. 7, a. 3, ad 4: "Substance is not rightly defined as a self-subsisting being: for being cannot be the genus of a thing according to the Philosopher, because nothing can be added to being that has not a share of being, and a difference should not be a part of the genus. If, however, substance can be defined notwithstanding that it is the most universal of genera, its definition will be 'a thing whose quiddity is competent to have being not in a subject.' Hence the definition of substance cannot be applied to God, whose quiddity is not distinct from his being. Wherefore God is not contained in the genus of substance, but is above all substance."

existence (*Ipsum esse subsistens*) and pure actuality.[96] His essence is his existence. All other beings receive their being from him, and can therefore participate in existence uniquely because he causes them to exist as Creator. Because creatures are effects of God that resemble their Creator, we can reflect on the mystery of God analogically, deriving names for God from creatures. In chapter 8 I will undertake a consideration of analogical language concerning God derived from creatures. Prior to this, however, I will first consider an important objection to the aforementioned arguments.

The Human Person as Being toward Ontological Truth and Goodness

Discussion of a rational structure of monotheistic argumentation should not permit us to overlook the personalistic context in which the topic of God is evoked. The question of the existence of God does not derive merely from an indifferently rational investigation of the world, but arises from a deeper existential orientation of the human person toward ultimate questions of truth and moral meaning. For Aquinas, this orientation has its roots in the spiritual faculties of the human person, the intellect and will, which are themselves oriented toward the true and the good in all of their universality.[97]

Here, however, an objection can be raised. Natural philosophical human knowledge of God, as Aquinas himself admits, is not only rare. It is also difficult and often contaminated with error.[98] Given this fact, one

---

[96] *ST* I, q. 3, a. 4; q. 4, a. 2.

[97] *ST* I, q. 78, a. 1; q. 80, a. 2; q. 105, a. 4: "The potentiality of the will extends to the universal good; just as the object of the intellect is universal being." As I have mentioned in earlier chapters, the human capacity for conceptual abstraction (which pertains to the universal and therefore transcends material individuality) denotes for St. Thomas that the human intellectual faculty is immaterial. It therefore functions as a sign of the incorruptibility of the human soul. (See, for example, *ScG* II, c. 79–81; *ST* I, q. 75, aa. 2, 6; *In de Anima* III, lec. 7.) Similar Thomistic arguments for the immateriality of the soul are made based upon human self-reflexivity and choice, arguments that aspire to demonstrate that the self-awareness and deliberative willing of human beings are not ontologically reducible to the material body or sensible psychology (*ScG* II, c. 47–49). They are "second acts" enrooted in the "primary act" of personal subsistence. *ST* I, q. 77, a. 1: "For the soul by its very essence is an act. Therefore if the very essence of the soul were the immediate principle of operation, whatever has a soul would always have actual vital actions, as that which has a soul is always an actually living thing. . . . So the soul itself is called first act, with a further relation to the second act. Now we observe that what has a soul is not always actual with respect to its vital operations . . . the potentiality of which, however, does not exclude the soul. Therefore it follows that the essence of the soul is not its power. For nothing is in potentiality by reason of an act, as act."

[98] *ScG* I, c. 4–5; *ST* I, q. 1, a. 1.

might pose the following objection: the capacity for rigorous metaphysical argumentation concerning the natural knowledge of God is exercised very rarely. Therefore, human beings do not manifest a marked tendency to seek to know that God exists naturally, by means of rational deliberation. Even if such philosophical knowledge of God exists, in fact it is something culturally marginal and existentially irrelevant for the vast majority of human beings.

To respond to this objection briefly, I would like to appeal to Aquinas's understanding of the way in which the universal human capacity to ask why or if God exists arises naturally in most persons. We can phrase the question in this way: if the human person by his or her very nature tends toward asking the question of the existence of God, and if most human beings do not employ complex philosophical modes of reasoning, then how does this tendency manifest itself readily in common ways in all human beings?

The first thing that needs to be considered is the question of a priori knowledge of God. I have argued in chapter 6 that Karl Rahner's notion of a "pre-apprehension" of being as a characteristic of all human knowledge is intrinsically problematic insofar as it introduces a kind of aprioristic dynamism into human epistemology, and correspondingly advances a tacitly Anselmian argumentation for the existence of God (the Ontological argument). Nevertheless, if human beings question the meaning of their own personal subjectivity in confrontation with the transcendental characteristics of reality, then it is possible that the structure of reality itself raises the question of the existence of God for the human person. The question of the meaning of our natural appetite for truth and for the good, for example, can be deepened by the question of the existence of God, even as the structure of reality itself proposes to us the question of the necessity of God's existence.[99] In this sense, reality itself can yield intuitions of a transcendent God that affect us in the depths of our person. Can we affirm this, however, without falling back into the claim that there exists an intuitive, pre-theoretical knowledge of God (as Maritain does)? More to the point, how can we be sure to avoid the idea that logical certitude of the

---

[99] Aquinas makes analogous claims in *ScG* III, c. 25. There he repeatedly relates the desire for truth to the causal inquiry into the origins of being, and argues that the human being can be fulfilled only by knowledge of God: "There is naturally present in all men the desire to know the causes of whatever things are observed. Hence, because of wondering about things that were seen but whose causes were hidden, men first began to think philosophically; when they found the cause, they were satisfied. But the search did not stop until it reached the first cause, for 'then do we think that we know perfectly, when we know the first cause' (*Metaphysics A*, 3, 983a25). Therefore, man naturally desires, as his ultimate end, to know the first cause. . . . So the ultimate end of man is the knowledge of God."

existence of God can be rightly derived merely from the content of an a priori intuition (i.e., the Ontological argument)?

Aquinas addresses this latter question in his famous consideration of the Ontological argument in *ST* I, q. 2, a. 1, ad 1 and 2. Here he claims that "to know that God exists in a general and confused way is implanted in us by nature." However, this stems not from an innate idea of God, but from the transcendent orientation of the human desire for the good, "inasmuch as God is man's beatitude." The natural desire for happiness orients the rational creature toward the supreme goodness of God in an implicit way, yet, "this is not to know absolutely that God exists, just as to know that someone is approaching is not the same as to know that Peter is approaching." And consequently, "there are many who imagine that man's perfect good which is happiness, consists in riches, and other pleasures, etc." Clearly, then, while the human person is made for God as the supreme good, according to Aquinas, the inner movement of the human person toward God must transpire intellectually through understanding acquired from the knowledge of existents and goods we experience immediately. Consequently, as he goes on to explain, it is not self-evident to all that when we say the word "God," we mean to denote Anselm's idea of God as "something than which nothing greater can be thought," since some have thought, for example, that God was a body. "Yet granted [for the sake of argument] that a person understands by this word 'God' is signified something than which nothing greater can be thought, nevertheless, it does not therefore follow that he or she understands that what the word signifies exists actually, but only that it exists mentally." In short, our impressions of what God is, or might be, are drawn from this world, so that even as we are personally meant to know God as the unique source of our ultimate happiness, we also must do so in terms that are consistent with our limited nature, itself characterized by nonintuitive understanding of God derived from creatures.[100]

While the consideration of human happiness does locate the desire to question the existence of God within a decidedly existential human context, it does not resolve the question of how a majority of human beings might arrive at thinking about God intelligibly by natural reason, in the

---

[100] The rapport between the desire for happiness and the capacity to conceptualize a primary being and truth is clearly underscored in *ScG* III, c. 25: "For each effect that he knows, man naturally desires to know the cause. Now the human intellect knows universal being. So, he naturally desires to know its cause, which is God alone. Now, a person has not attained his ultimate end until natural desire comes to rest. Therefore, for human happiness which is the ultimate end it is not enough to have merely any kind of intelligible knowledge; there must be divine knowledge, as an ultimate end, to terminate the natural desire. So, the ultimate end of man is the knowledge of God."

absence of recourse to a distinctly philosophical analysis of God. Here
Aquinas suggests, however, that there do exist natural or ordinary apprehensions of what it means to speak of "God," basic ideas derived from
ordinary experience of the nature of the world. These are notions available
to all mature human persons, irregardless of their philosophical sophistica-
tion. In other words, there are ordinary ways in which the *causal knowledge of God* can be derived (or intuited imperfectly) by all rational persons.
Aquinas alludes to such ordinary, pre-philosophical knowledge in various
places, in terms that are explicitly causal. Three such examples may briefly
be mentioned in order to give clear examples of what might be called
somewhat improperly "a posteriori intuitions" of the existence of God.

First, Aquinas discusses the intellectual apprehension of degrees of
goodness. Human beings encounter a diversity of goods and a hierarchy of
goods, such that the question of what is of greater intrinsic significance is
naturally proposed to us. What should I live for? The search for happiness
through the love of authentic (and inauthentic) goods gives rise to consideration of the metaphysical *question* of a sovereign and transcendent good
that is the source of all others. The point is made clearly in *ScG* I, c. 11:

> Man naturally knows God in the same way as he naturally desires
> God. Now, man naturally desires God in so far as he naturally desires
> beatitude, which is a certain likeness of the divine goodness. On this
> basis, it is not necessary that God considered in himself be naturally
> known to man, but only a likeness of God. It remains, therefore, that
> man is to reach the knowledge of God through reasoning by way of
> the likenesses of God found in his effects.

In other words, the desire for happiness can offer the possibility of conceiving of God (through a likeness to creatures) as a supreme good. This
conception does not entail a "quidditative" grasp of what God is. Nor can
it substitute itself for the rational certitude that God exists that is acquired
by the work of philosophical demonstration. Nevertheless, the latter
reflection can build upon the former intuition.

Second, there is an order that characterizes the events of the world of
nature around us. Simultaneously, there is a gratuity to this order, which
seemingly did not have to be as it is (as evidenced by the fact that nature
is subject to chance events). This naturally raises the question of why there
is such order within the world, and whether it is derived from a transcendent source. By an analogy drawn from art, one can conceive of God as
the artistic source of the order of the world. This is to conceive of God in
terms that are intellectual, as the wisdom that fashioned the world.[101]

---

[101] Aquinas uses this comparison in his discourse on the articles of the Creed (*Credo*,
a. 1) specifically so as to appeal to ordinary persons, not specialists in philosophy.

Third, the contingency of material substances that come into and go out of existence demonstrates the radical historicity of physical beings. This in turn raises the question of whether all that exists is subject to temporal change. Is there a transcendent being that is not subject to the flux of time and becoming, and that does not undergo corruption or substantial change? If such a being or beings exist, then we must ascribe to them some form of ontological necessity.[102]

In each of these cases (considered here only illustratively and tangentially) the mind may grasp intuitively something of the causal interdependencies and essential limitations that characterize the beings we experience. Such thought naturally propels us toward the question of a primary, non-dependent, and non-limited source and origin of the world that is intelligent and good. In other words, such ideas make the question of the existence of God a natural one, with deeply personal and ontological overtones. This occurs, however, through a posteriori reflection on experience, and conceives of God only indirectly, in terms of the world we know, and simultaneously as a mystery that transcends the ordinary scope of our knowledge. Such reflection is a substitute neither for philosophical argumentation nor for supernatural faith in divine revelation. However, it serves as a kind of natural disposition to the former and support (or "place of contact") for the latter.

Conclusion

The goal of this chapter was to sketch out an order of argumentation (or to designate an intellectual path) that runs from omega to alpha, from creatures to God, passing along discernibly distinct but interrelated stages, and tied in one way or another to the authentic metaphysical thought of Aquinas. This allows us to reappropriate a form of argument that appeals to metaphysical structures, compositions, and causal dependencies in realities we experience, so as to pass by way of a posteriori demonstration to the necessary affirmation of the existence of God. This account does not commit one to any kind of pre-theoretical, conceptual understanding or

---

[102] *In Ioan.*, prologue, 4: "[Some in times past] came to a knowledge of God from his eternity. They saw that whatever was in things was changeable, and that the more noble something is in the grades of being, so much the less it has of mutability. For example, the lower bodies are mutable both as to their substance and place, while heavenly bodies, which are more noble, are immutable in substance and change only with respect to place. We can clearly conclude from this that the first principle of all things, which is supreme and more noble, is changeless and eternal." For a similar reflection, see *Comp. Theol.*, c. 3. The inferential sense of a transcendent ontological cause of contingent beings remains valid, even if the imagistic cosmology of the example is outdated.

intuition of God, and is not aprioristic in nature. It does not possess, therefore, the essential characteristics of ontotheological reasoning as understood in the Kantian tradition. Furthermore, it does not depend per se, that is to say in its logical presuppositions, upon the immediate appeal to divine revelation or Christian theology. However, by its distinctly philosophical consideration of the real distinction, it allows one to understand all secondary beings as derivative from God, as a primary, uniquely transcendent source. Consequently, it also allows one to speak *philosophically* of a metaphysics of *creation*, that is to say, of creatures who receive the entirety of their existence from God.

Under a first aspect (reasoning toward the existence of God) this reflection passes *in via inventionis* from creatures to God, coming to understand the necessity of the latter in light of the former. Here one is seeking to approach the first principle intellectually, and this way of discovery has been the primary concern of this chapter. Under a second aspect, however, one can then attempt to consider all creatures in light of God. Such reflection passes *in via judicii* from God to creatures, judging all things in relation to their ultimate source and first principle. The first form of thought ascends toward the absolute, while the second descends from him to consider all else in its relation to God. It is under both of these inseparable aspects of reflection that philosophical thought for Aquinas takes on the characteristic of wisdom, or *sapientia*. Both in considering God indirectly through the medium of his creaturely effects and in judging all things in light of their primal cause, the mind attains to a kind of ultimate perspective. Furthermore, in knowing something of God philosophically, and in knowing that the human person resembles God intellectually, reason also comes to know itself in a more profound way. For seen in this light, the human being can be understood to be *made for* intellectual knowledge of the divine, for the aspiration to the primary truth of God himself. Evidence of this intrinsic purpose emerges, then, from rational argumentation concerning God. Yet this argumentation affects decidedly our understanding of why the human person exists. It is with this sapiential perspective on God and rational creatures that I will be concerned in the final chapter of this book.

8

Analogia Sapientiae

I N THE INTRODUCTION of this book I noted that both Aristotle and Thomas Aquinas claim that there exists a philosophical knowledge of God that is genuinely sapiential, by which one may attain an indirect but real natural knowledge of God, and consider all secondary realities, and especially human beings, in light of God. They also both claim that this form of knowledge is the teleological end of human persons, in which human reason attains its natural summit. In modernity, however, the aspiration to such wisdom has been questioned in at least two influential ways. The Kantian objection argues that such knowledge is necessarily aprioristic, and does not lead to an authentic knowledge of the transcendence of God. Rather, natural theology is the immanentist construction of the transcendental subject, by which a human being seeks to obtain an organized knowledge of sense experience. An older theological objection, stemming from Luther and reappropriated by Barth and, in a sense, Heidegger, claims that the search for the knowledge of God through metaphysical, natural theology acts to impede a true openness to the authentic knowledge of God offered by Christian revelation. Heidegger in particular seems to suggest that any metaphysical argument for the existence of God would implicitly seek to imprison our genuinely religious knowledge of God within an aprioristic system.[1]

---

[1] Interpretations of Luther, Barth, and Heidegger on the subject of natural knowledge of God are of course quite complex. Witness in this respect, the contrasting interpretations of Barth's doctrine of analogy by Hans Urs von Balthasar, trans. E. Oakes, *The Theology of Karl Barth* (San Francisco: Ignatius, 1992), and Bruce McCormack, *Karl Barth's Critically Realistic Dialectical Theology* (Oxford: Clarendon Press, 1995). For the influence of Luther and Barth upon the young Heidegger, see S. J. McGrath, *The Early Heidegger & Medieval Philosophy*, chapter 1.

The primary claim of this book has been that there is a natural knowledge of God accessible to human persons that is not based either upon aprioristic philosophical conceptions of God, nor upon aprioristic commitments of Christian faith. Furthermore, this natural theological knowledge is a principal manifestation of the deep, human tendency toward God enrooted in the spiritual faculties of intellect and will. In the first seven chapters of this book, I have explored—in a historical, critical, and finally, constructive way—the parameters and order of a genuinely a posteriori approach to God by way of natural, metaphysical reasoning. Concretely, then, I have sought to demonstrate that in the case of Thomistic metaphysical reasoning, the Kantian objection to natural theology does not apply. Human beings are capable by nature of obtaining genuine knowledge of the existence of God through human reasoning.

Even if this is the case, however, there still remain delicate questions concerning the character of this natural, human tendency toward God. For on the one hand, if the Kantian claim is that we can attain to no certain knowledge of God in himself, Thomistic metaphysics posits that we can obtain true positive knowledge of God. However, on the other side of the spectrum, the theological objection mentioned above states that all pretensions to natural knowledge of God in fact inevitably project human conceptions onto the divine problematically, obscuring or marring the true disclosures of God that come by way of revelation. Against such perspectives, the Thomist tradition insists that an authentic, metaphysical knowledge of God is indirect, apophatic, and radically incomplete. Therefore this knowledge itself calls for a deeper completion that can come about only by way of grace. It illustrates the fact that the human subject is intrinsically open, and not closed, to the higher knowledge of God that is the effect of divine revelation. Furthermore, the classical Thomistic claim is that the identification of a philosophical approach to God *is needed even within theology* if we are to manifest this intrinsic, natural ordering of the subject toward the knowledge of God, such that the authentic revelation of God in Christ is not understood as something wholly *extrinsic* to human nature.[2]

---

[2] Not only Aquinas but also the subsequent Dominican commentary tradition perpetually insisted upon the *philosophical* identification of a potential "point of contact" between nature and grace (due to the natural inclination of the human person toward God), and also upon the fact that the grace of the beatific vision is not wholly extrinsic or disproportioned to human nature. See, for example, *ScG* III, c. 54: "The divine substance is not beyond the capacity of the created intellect in such a way that it is altogether foreign to it, as sound is from the object of vision, or as immaterial substance is from sense power; in fact, the divine substance is the first intelligible object and the principle of all intellectual cognition. But it is beyond the capacity of the created intellect, in the sense that it exceeds its power; just as sensible objects of extreme character are beyond the capacity of sense power. . . . So, a

The problem arises then, of how to rightly affirm that human beings are naturally capable of, or ordered toward, the sapiential knowledge of God. In what sense are human beings capable of an analogical and indirect (a posteriori) knowledge of God that is truly positive? In what sense is this knowledge necessarily incomplete, or characterized by an all-encompassing apophaticism? How do these two facets (positive and negative dimensions of analogical knowledge of God) respectively contribute to our *philosophical* understanding of the human person as a being naturally ordered toward the knowledge of God, yet as simultaneously open to the possibility of grace and redemption?[3]

In order to answer these questions in a balanced way, a series of modern Thomistic thinkers have stressed the apophatic dimensions of Aquinas's monotheistic thought, thereby seeking to avoid both the Scylla of an agnostic philosophical epistemology and the Charybdis of an overly ambitious philosophical discourse concerning God that would claim to know the nature of God intuitively, or conceptually.[4] A philosophical and Thomistic emphasis on our knowledge *that* God exists, and our simultaneously radical ignorance of *what* God is, demonstrates the profound compatibility between Thomistic natural theology, and the claims of Christian divine revelation. Revelation is the answer of who or what God is, responding to the void in our knowledge of God that philosophy helps

---

created intellect needs to be strengthened by a divine light in order that it may be able to see the divine essence." This viewpoint is maintained by such commentators as Sylvester of Ferrara and John of St. Thomas. For a recent defense of Cajetan that interprets his teaching in a similar light against the commonplace charge of grace/nature extrinsicism, see Ralph McInerny, *Praeambula Fidei*, 69–90. For a helpful examination of the debates concerning "grace extrinsicism" in modern theology see Harm Goris, "Steering Clear of Charybdis: Some Distinctions for Avoiding 'Grace Extrinsicism' in Aquinas," *Nova et Vetera* (English edition) 5, no. 1 (2007): 67–80.

[3] I am speaking here of an ontological and natural openness that characterizes the human person as a rational being, and not of an active moral disposition, or voluntary desire. In fallen human beings, the natural disposition toward God can be (in part) thwarted, ignored, or frustrated in the concrete exercise of human acts, as I emphasize below.

[4] For Thomistic authors emphasizing this aspect of Aquinas's thought, see, for example, A.-D. Sertillanges, *Le christianisme et les philosophes* (Paris: Aubier, 1939), 1: 268–73; Gilson, *Le Thomisme*, 5th edition, 150–59; *The Elements of Christian Philosophy*, 104–35; Victor Preller, *Divine Science and the Science of God: A Reformulation of Thomas Aquinas* (Princeton: Princeton University Press, 1967), 266–71; David Burrell, *Aquinas: God and Action* (Notre Dame: University of Notre Dame Press, 1979), 12–41; Herbert McCabe, *God Matters* (London: Continuum, 1987), 2–9, 39–51; Turner, *Faith, Reason and the Existence of God*. I will return to the last text below. For a helpful survey and analysis of this strand of Thomistic interpretation, see Gregory Rocca, *Speaking the Incomprehensible God*, 27–48.

us to identify. This position seems comprehensive, insofar as it seeks to be a multi-sided response to the above-mentioned difficulties. However, this interpretive tendency has also given rise to an interpretive quandary concerning Aquinas's own thought, the apophatic dimensions of his metaphysical reflections on God, and the repercussions of these discussions for human anthropology.[5] For if the human person is naturally ordered toward the truth of God, and is therefore made for divine wisdom, then this teleological dimension of the person must be rendered perceptible by and through some kind of positive knowledge of God. We can in no way be inclined naturally to the knowledge of God as a final end if we can know nothing of his existence, goodness, and perfection. In consequence, excessively apophatic interpretations of Aquinas risk to render this sapiential dimension of the human person nearly indecipherable, or so paradoxical as to be almost unintelligible. However, on the other hand, if the understanding of positive knowledge of God that is given by metaphysics is to remain intrinsically open to revelation, then it must be able *from within its own parameters as rational knowledge* to conceive of *both* its intrinsic aspiration toward God *and* its radical imperfection.

In this chapter, then, I will explore three aspects of this sapiential knowledge of God: (1) the analogical consideration of God derived from creatures not as a negative theology, but as an ultimately positive knowledge, composed of a negative moment, a *via negationis*; (2) the analogical, positive knowledge of God as himself subsistent wisdom or personal truth; and (3) the understanding of the human person seen in light of God as a

---

5 Most famously, Jacques Maritain argued against the positions of Sertillanges in *Les Degrés du Savoir* (1932), Annexe III, "Ce Que Dieu Est," that philosophy acquires a genuinely positive knowledge of God, albeit analogically and indirectly. In a similar vein, see Jean-Hervé Nicolas, *Dieu connu comme inconnu, Essai d'une critique de la connaissance théologique* (Paris: Desclée de Brouwer, 1966); Charles Journet, *Connaissance et inconnaissance de Dieu* (Paris: Desclée de Brouwer, 1969). These approaches are all marked, however, by the Cajetanian interpretation of Thomistic analogy that was criticized in chapters 1 and 5, as well as Maritain's somewhat peculiar interpretation of an analogical "intuition of being," that risks to smuggle God into the transcendental range of knowing. As Humbrecht points out (*Théologie Négative et Noms Divins chez Saint Thomas d'Aquin*, 34n1), Maritain's treatment of the positive knowledge of God in this treatise is problematic, as he affirms simultaneously therein that God is intelligible for human beings *sub ratione entis primi*, while affirming that God stands outside the field of *ens commune*. The latter claim is certainly true. However, for Aquinas the intelligible range of the *ratio entis* and the ontological range of *ens commune* are coextensive. God is known only as the *cause* of common being, but not as a "member" (i.e., *sub ratione*). As I shall discuss below, then, the genuine articulation of a positive knowledge of God must rest, for Aquinas, upon his particular understanding of the *ad alterum* analogy between God and creatures.

being that is naturally open to, or ordered toward, divine wisdom. The final argument of this chapter posits, therefore, conclusions of Thomistic philosophy that overlap significantly with Christian theology: because the human being is capable of a real but indirect—and therefore imperfect—knowledge of God, so also the human person is naturally disposed toward, and open to, the mystery of God that is given in revelation. Because revelation is not derivable from metaphysical knowledge of God, it remains extrinsic to and transcendent of human nature. However, because it responds to the deepest human inclination toward truth, authentic revelation also fulfills gratuitously the deepest intrinsic teleological dimension of the human person. There is an analogical similitude, then, between God's wisdom as manifest in his works of nature and his wisdom as manifest in the works of grace.

Negative Theology, and the Real Distinction between Essence and Existence

In discussing analogical consideration of God derived from creatures, I will not seek to revisit the manifold, complex elements of Aquinas's understanding of the analogical knowledge of God as they have been treated—very competently—in recent studies.[6] Instead, I will simply discuss briefly Aquinas's understanding of the analogy between creatures and God as an analogy *ad alterum* in his mature thought. Herein, as a way of approaching the interpretive quandaries concerning Aquinas's own theories, I will emphasize the role the Aristotelianism of Aquinas plays in his interpretation of Dionysius the Areopagite's apophaticism. As I have argued in previous chapters, the Aristotelian causal analysis is central to Aquinas's metaphysics, so here I will discuss how causal knowledge of God as pure actuality renders analogical divine names of God possible in the first place. Simultaneously, I will argue that because God is known as pure actuality, the identity of God transcends all conceptual comprehension. In differentiation from some interpretations of Aquinas's thought that are excessively apophatic, my argument will be that the causal and analogical

---

6 See for example John Wippel, *The Metaphysical Thought of Thomas Aquinas*, 501–75, and the insightful study of Rudi Te Velde, *Aquinas on God*, esp. 65–147. Gregory Rocca's *Speaking the Incomprehensible God* and Thierry-Dominique Humbrecht's *Théologie Négative et Noms Divins chez Saint Thomas d'Aquin* stand out as two expert studies that have recently reexamined the question of knowledge of God in Aquinas in a comprehensive way. Humbrecht's detailed comparison of Albert's and Aquinas's commentaries on *The Divine Names* of Dionysius (350–478), as well as his nearly exhaustive survey of Aquinas's texts on divine names, and negative and positive knowledge of God (85–320; 479–508; 637–730), offer numerous points of reference for any future contribution to the debate.

knowledge of God in Aquinas is the source of an ultimately positive, if indirect, knowledge of the one God, yet one leaving us open to further knowledge of God, by grace.

The majority of interpreters of Aquinas agree that his mature positions on the subject of the analogical knowledge of God are most clearly formulated in the *Summa theologiae* I, question 13.[7] Here, particularly in article 5, he treats of our capacity to speak of the likeness between the created world and God that is a result of the resemblances between effects and their transcendent, primary cause. It is because all created being depends upon God causally for its existence and perfections that it must in some way resemble him as the source from which it is derived.[8] Therefore, *in light of* the demonstrative knowledge of God that results from a metaphysical argumentation for the existence of God, one may rightfully seek to identify certain transcendent perfections, or attributes, that pre-exist in God in a surpassing or more perfect fashion than they do in creatures. Our language for such perfections can be drawn only from creatures, and therefore will be imperfect as to its "mode of signification." However, we may speak truthfully of God through such language.[9] It is in this sense that Aquinas speaks of "divine names" for God.

---

[7] See also, *ScG* I, c. 30–36; *De potentia Dei,* q. 7, esp. aa. 5–7. Humbrecht has shown that Aquinas held firmly to a non-univocal, analogical knowledge of God throughout his life, but that his mature positions are best reflected in these later writings in response to the radical apophaticism of Maimonides, against which he insisted on a real middle way between univocity theory and pure equivocity in the predication of divine names. See, especially, *Théologie Négative et Noms Divins,* 65–67, 554–56, 773–75; as well as Ysabel de Andia, "*Remotio–negatio.* L'évolution du vocabulaire de saint Thomas touchant la voie négative," *AHDLMA* 68 (2001): 45–71.

[8] *ST* I, q. 13, aa. 1, 2, 3, 5. A. 5: "Whatever is said of God and creatures, is said according to the relation of a creature to God as its principle and cause, wherein all perfections of things pre-exist excellently. Now this mode of community of idea is a mean between pure equivocation and simple univocation. For in analogies the idea is not, as it is in univocals, one and the same, yet it is not totally diverse as in equivocals; But a term which is thus used in multiple senses signifies various proportions to some one thing. Thus "healthy" applied to urine signifies the sign of animal health, and applied to medicine signifies the cause of the same health." See also *ScG* I, c. 29.

[9] *ST* I, q. 13, a. 3: "Our knowledge of God is derived from the perfections which flow from him to creatures, which perfections are in God in a more eminent way than in creatures. Now our intellect apprehends them as they are in creatures, and as it apprehends them it signifies them by names. Therefore as to the names applied to God, there are two things to be considered—viz., the perfections which they signify, such as goodness, life and the like, and their mode of signification. As regards what is signified by these names, they belong properly to God, and more properly than they belong to creatures, and are applied primarily to him. But as regards their mode

As I have discussed in chapter 3, Aquinas purposefully eschews the use of an analogy *multa ad unum* in order to discuss this form of analogical thinking, insofar as recourse to this type of analogy would risk to construe both God and creatures as participating in a common characteristic or attribute, such as "being," in two distinct modes, say as finite and infinite. Rather, he understands this comparison as an analogy *ad alterum*, containing only two terms, in which one (the creature) is used to signify analogically the other (God) by imperfect comparison. *Because it exists due to God,* the creature in its participated being, goodness, unity, and so on, reflects indirectly something of what God is in himself.[10] In other words, Aquinas introduces an analysis of ontological causal dependence into the heart of his theory of analogical predication as pertaining to God. Because creatures depend causally upon God directly for their being, they also may be a route by which to ascend intellectually toward a consideration of the perfections that must necessarily characterize God as Creator. Because they participate in his perfections, they reflect something of what he must be in himself.[11]

---

of signification, they do not properly and strictly apply to God; for their mode of signification applies to creatures."

[10] In *ST* I, q. 13, a. 5, Aquinas clearly distinguishes between a *multa ad unum* and an *ad alterum* use of analogy, rejecting the former and invoking the latter to speak about creature-to-God analogical discourse: "Now names are thus used [analogically] in two ways: either according as *many things are proportioned to one*, thus for example 'healthy' is predicated of medicine and urine in relation and in proportion to health of a body, of which the former is the sign and the latter the cause; or according as *one thing is proportionate to another*, thus 'healthy' is said of medicine and animal, since medicine *is the cause of health* in the animal body. And in this way some things are said of God and creatures analogically, and not in a purely equivocal nor in a purely univocal sense. For we can name God only from creatures" (emphasis added). Evidently, Aquinas is refusing the idea that God and creatures might both be considered instantiations of "being," in the way a cause and effect are both understood as "healthy" in the first example. Instead, the "being" or "goodness" of the effect (the creature) allows us to affirm something analogically of God, yet imperfectly, as "toward" the undisclosed cause from which all things proceed.

[11] In *ST* I, q. 13, Aquinas does not explicitly develop the connection between participation theory and analogy. However, it is certainly valid to infer from his extended thought that the basis for analogical predication is not only creative causality, but also the participatory structure of created reality, according to which God is the transcendent efficient and exemplary cause of all that is. See on this front the helpful reflections of Te Velde, *Aquinas on God*, chapters 4–5, where he follows an extensive analysis of *ST* I, q. 13, on analogy with an extensive analysis of *ST* I, q. 44, a. 1, on creation and participation, showing the logical connections between these facets of Aquinas's thought. On causality as the principle of resemblance, and therefore, analogy, see the study of John Wippel, "Saint Thomas on our Knowledge of God and the Axiom that Every Agent Produces Something Like Itself," in *Metaphysical Themes in Thomas Aquinas* 2, 152–71.

Aquinas's own theory of analogical knowledge of God is, of course, influenced by a diversity of medieval and ancient sources: Aristotle, Augustine, Dionysius and John Damascene, Proclus and Avicenna, as well as Albert the Great.[12] Furthermore, these influences are in turn qualified by Aquinas's own unique interpretation of the metaphysics of the real distinction between *esse* and essence, with its corresponding influence upon his understanding of participated being.[13] One way of explaining analogy, therefore, is to focus almost exclusively on the real distinction. God is the cause of all that exists, insofar as it exists. The real distinction in creatures is the central point at which we discern their absolute dependence upon God, and therefore accordingly is the key locus at which to begin any discussion of analogical and apophatic discourse concerning God. All that exists bears some similitude to its transcendent, uncreated cause. In this case the participated existence (*esse*) of creatures indicates the transcendent cause of existence that is God by way of an ontological similitude or resemblance. Therefore, God can be signified analogically by recourse to the notion of *esse* as one who subsists in himself necessarily, as *Ipsum esse subsistens.*[14]

In the early twentieth century, however, this seemingly plausible thesis was radicalized, beginning with the French Dominican A.-D. Sertillanges, and later rearticulated (more moderately) by Étienne Gilson.[15] For these Thomists, *positive* knowledge of God is derived almost exclusively through

---

[12] See the survey of influences by Humbrecht, *Théologie Négative et Noms Divins*, 38–106.

[13] I have mentioned the importance of the real distinction for Aquinas's metaphysical thought generally at numerous points above. For a helpful, and quite balanced, reflection on its importance with respect to the analogical knowledge of God, see Bernard Montagnes, *La doctrine de l'analogie de l'Etre d'après saint Thomas d'Aquin*, chapter 2. Montagnes's treatment of the "hierarchy of *esse*" (God as the transcendent efficient cause of existence in creatures) does not ignore the equally important "hierarchy of essences," (God's essence as the transcendent exemplar of all created natures), which in turn indicates the perfection of the transcendent essence of God.

[14] Indeed, in *ST* I, q. 13, a. 11, Aquinas asks whether the name "He Who Is" is the most proper name of God, and goes on to say that it is because "it does not signify form, but simply existence itself. Hence since the existence of God is his essence itself, which can be said of no other, it is clear that among other names this one specially denominates God, for everything is denominated by its form."

[15] In addition to Sertillanges's *Le Christianisme et les philosophes*, mentioned above, his commentary on Aquinas's *ST* I, q. 13 (A.-D. Sertillanges, "Renseignments techniques," in *Somme Théologique, Dieu*, vol. 2 [Paris: Revue des Jeunes, 1926], 371–407, esp. 383ff.), was of great influence. Maritain responded polemically to the latter text in *Les Degrés du Savoir*, and this debate, in turn, had an effect upon the thinking of Gilson (*Le Thomisme, Elements of Christian Philosophy*) who sided (in a nuanced way) with Sertillanges.

the medium of *existence*, while the consideration of created *essences* yields an almost exclusively *negative* knowledge of God. Apophaticism must recall that while God is the cause of creatures who *exist* (which therefore resemble him in their *esse*), these creatures are also finite in nature. They are *composed* of existence and essence, such that their natures participate in being uniquely due to the causal activity of God. Accordingly, since God is the unique source of all existence in created beings, and is existence itself, he can be signified analogically by means of *esse*. However, because God transcends absolutely all of the essences or natural kinds of the created existents that depend upon him, he may not be signified by predications stemming from the determinate natures of created beings.[16] That is to say, from the analogical perspective, he may not be indicated by means of any concept derived from created essences. According to the radical formulation of this position by Sertillanges at the beginning of the last century, this means that God is existence "without essence, or without nature."[17] Or, in the words of Anton Pegis, a disciple of Gilson, who was influenced by both him and Sertillanges,

---

[16] This position is clearly articulated by Sertillanges in *Le Christianisme et les philosophes*, 1:268–73; See likewise Gilson, *Elements of Christian Philosophy*, 108–35, where despite many nuances, Gilson approaches at points a position nearly identical with Sertillanges. 134: "In our attempt to describe God by removing from Him what is proper to the being of creatures, we must give up essence in order to reach the open sea of pure actual existence, but we must also keep the notion of essence present to the mind so as not to leave it without any object. This we do when, to the question, where do we find God? We simply answer, beyond essence. By establishing himself in the definite negation of posited essence, the theologian realizes that he is placing God above that which is deepest in the only kind of reality he knows. At that moment, the theologian is not beyond being; on the contrary, he is beyond essence, at the very core of being." One has the right to ask whether such a statement has a real basis in Aquinas's thought. For example, *ST* I, q. 3, aa. 3 and 4(!), as well as q. 13, a. 8, clearly affirm a capacity to speak conceptually about the nature and essence of God, through analogies derived from creatures. I will return to this below.

[17] In *Le Christianisme et les philosophes*, 268–72, Sertillanges goes as far as to say that "God has no nature. . . . Saint Thomas formally affirms this in the *De Ente et Essentia*, c. 6, that God has no essence." When it comes to God, he claims, Aquinas practices an absolute "agnosticism of definition. . . . Goodness, wisdom, power and other [such attributes], Aquinas did not hesitate to affirm 'Non sunt in Deo.'" "The 'unknowable' is his unique name. Consequently, the divine attributes . . . in their multiplicity and mode of representation, do not represent anything else than the names of creatures." More mild echoes of this perspective appear in Gilson as well; see *Elements of Christian Philosophy*, 118–19. As Humbrecht points out (*Théologie Négative et Noms Divins*, 66), the claim that "God has no essential attributes" stems from Maimonides, in *Guide for the Perplexed* I, c. 5. Aquinas, meanwhile, clearly rejected such a minimalist account of the natural knowledge of God, in purposeful contradistinction to the position of Maimonides.

"When St. Thomas said that God was utterly unknown, what was he saying but that man should seek the divine transcendence by a total unknowing?"[18]

In recent English-speaking Thomism, this more radically apophatic reading of Aquinas has been further developed by Herbert McCabe, and subsequently by Denys Turner.[19] Because of his perceptive and eloquent treatment of the subject, Turner's views merit prolonged study and consideration.[20] In this context, however, I wish to mention only three important intellectual options he takes, each of which accentuates the apophatic or purely negative character of our knowledge of God, as understood by Aquinas. I will then respond to this interpretation by a series of considerations that I think oblige one to understand Aquinas's apophaticism differently, by taking into account other elements of his metaphysical thought.

Turner's justification of a radically apophatic reading of Aquinas springs from his understanding of caused existence as created dependence, and the causal character of the significations of natural theological discourse. The ground or basis for his reading of Aquinas on analogical predication from creatures to God springs from his notion of *esse*, and his notion of *esse* is closely aligned with his consideration of *creation*, that is to say, with the radical giving of existence to all things by God.[21]

The discovery of the real distinction between essence and existence in creatures begins for Turner from a consideration of the gratuity of being in

---

[18] Anton Pegis, *"Penitus Manet Ignotum," Medieval Studies* 27 (1965): 226, as cited by Gregory Rocca, *Speaking the Incomprehensible God*, 27.

[19] I am alluding in particular to the two above-mentioned works, Herbert McCabe's *God Matters*, and Denys Turner's *Faith, Reason and the Existence of God*. McCabe acknowledges his profound debt to Gilson on p. 1 of his book, and refers to him implicitly in subsequent chapters pertaining to the negative knowledge of God (esp. 40–46). Turner's work, in turn, is clearly inspired in part by the arguments of McCabe, as I will show.

[20] I would not wish my critical comments of this author to be misconstrued, as I think his work *Faith, Reason and the Existence of God* is truly excellent on a multiplicity of fronts.

[21] For Turner's analysis of *esse*, particularly as related to creation and the existence of God, see *Faith, Reason and the Existence of God*, 38–47, 169–90, 233–47. Turner himself specifies on 209, n. 24, that he considers the question of the existence of God synonymous with the question of creation *ex nihilo*, of why the world exists at all, and on 178–79 makes clear that his concept of *esse* is fundamentally determined by an analysis of creation *ex nihilo*. He refers here in turn to McCabe's work, who posits a similar nexus of ideas in *God Matters*, 40–46, 59–60. 40 and 43: "Aquinas's Five Ways, as I read them, are sketches for five arguments to show that a certain kind of *question* about our world and ourselves is valid: 'Why the world, instead of nothing at all?' This is a question, in Aquinas's jargon, about the *esse* of things, their being over against nothing, not just their being over against some alternative or over against potentiality. . . . *Esse* in Aquinas's jargon belongs to the doctrine of creation,

all things.[22] All that we experience can be conceived of in light of the possibility that it not exist at all. Therefore we can pose a fundamental metaphysical question: "Why is there something rather than nothing?" This latter question is not to be understood (we are told) in either Leibnizian or Heideggerian terms, but rather as the consideration of existents we experience against the backdrop of *their radical capacity for nonbeing*. It is because we *can* envisage *there being nothing* that the beings we do experience must be seen in their radical gratuity, or non-necessity.[23] By the same measure, such beings can be understood as natures that can exist or not exist, natures that *receive existence gratuitously*. Therefore, they can be conceived of simultaneously as *created*, that is to say, as being or existing, over and against nothingness, by no cause of their own, but in dependence upon some more primal, absolutely unique source of existence. They are beings in which there is a real distinction between essence and existence, while the being that is at their origin is not such a being.[24] Consequently, the question of why there is something rather than nothing allows the problem of creation to emerge philosophically, and simultaneously that of

---

of which Aristotle had no notion at all. . . . He does not, as Aquinas does, ask the Jewish question, the question of *esse*, of the existence of things not over against potentiality but over against nothing."

[22] *Faith, Reason and the Existence of God*, 177–79.

[23] Ibid., 226–47. 245: "But finally, what are we to say about the ultimately odd question: 'What if *nothing at all* existed?'—or, in other words: 'Is the world as such contingent?' The answer to this question has to be that the world—everything that exists—is absolutely, in every possible respect, and awesomely contingent; but that it is contingent in a purely 'existential' way in that it is from this contingency that we derive our primitive notion of 'existence' itself, what Thomas calls *esse*. And we can see the nature of this radical contingency from the fact that the answer to the question 'Why anything?' could not be provided by anything counting as, in the ordinary sense, an 'explanation' by reference to antecedent states of affairs. . . . We get at the notion of existence, *esse*, in its proper sense, precisely as that which stands against there being nothing at all. . . . It is, therefore, the centrality of this *esse* to Thomas's metaphysics which places the 'Why anything?' question at the centre of his arguments for the existence of God. For it is this *esse*'s standing in absolute, unmediated, contrast with nothing at all which gets to the contingent heart of creation, and to the heart of the sense in which creation is contingent."

[24] Ibid., 178–79: "The 'real distinction' between *esse* and *essentia* holds for Thomas only as of *created esse*. . . . What you predicate when you predicate *esse* of a creature and strictly *as created* is that it stands against—that is to say, in contradictory opposition to—there being nothing at all; for that is what it is for a creature to be created: it is for it 'to be' in that sense which contrasts with there being nothing whatsoever. . . . It follows from this that we do not grasp fully the *esse* of a creature until we have shown that it is created. That is to say, what reveals the nature of created *esse* is precisely the same as what shows God to exist *as* the Creator of *esse*."

the existence of God. Recourse to the necessary being of God is the only way to explain sufficiently the existence of a world that might not be, a world in which nothingness might precede existence.[25]

Second, therefore, creatures do testify to God analogically by way of their causal dependencies in the order of existence, and by this same measure, permit reflection on the divine names (analogically derived predications for God). Yet, they do so even while impeding us to predicate essential attributes, since the essences or natural features of creatures we experience are not indicative per se of the transcendent existence of God. These essences are, after all, radically contingent: in them, nothingness precedes being, and unlike God, they could have not existed. In their finitude, then, they are utterly inadequate at signifying "what" God is in himself.[26] For in the latter, there can be no composition of finite essence and participated existence. God in his simplicity transcends all positive "essential" characterizations.[27] Consequently, no finite essence given existence is adequate to signify the incomprehensible essence of God.

Third, therefore, Turner follows David Burrell in distinguishing between positive analogical characteristics of God and his merely "formal features" or negatively derived characteristics.[28] The former are names that can be derived from God's being the source of all existence, positive terms

---

[25] Ibid., 242: "The question 'Why is there anything rather than nothing?' [is] fundamental both to the argument-strategy of the 'five ways' as proofs and to Thomas's conception of God as Creator. For it is a question which gets us to the point of seeing the world as created; that is to say, as standing in that relation of absolute contingency to there being nothing at all which constitutes the 'act of existence,' *esse*. It is for this reason that the question leads us to the point at which we know that we should have to say of what answers to it, that it itself is *esse* without qualification—*ipsum esse subsistens*. . . . Once you admit the question, you are already a theist."

[26] Ibid., 183–86.

[27] Ibid., 185–86: "Of course, we could not know what it means to say that God is 'pure act,' *ipsum esse subsistens*. . . . In fact, the incomprehensibility of the statement 'God is *ipsum esse subsistens*' is not an *aporia* reductive of Thomas's theological metaphysics to absurdity. It is, on the contrary, a precise theological statement, intended to mark out with maximum clarity and precision the *locus* of the divine incomprehensibility, the *ratio Dei*, the most fundamental of the 'formal features' of God. . . . Since it is far from being the case that describing God as 'pure act' gives us some firm purchase on the divine nature, one may go so far as to say that talking about God thus is already a kind of failed speech, a 'babble'; for to pretend to remain in full command of the meaning of such words through any self-evidently meaningful extension of their ordinary senses is idolatrously reductive of theological language."

[28] Ibid., 40–42, 186. The distinction is taken from David Burrell, "Distinguishing God from the World," *Language, Meaning and God: Essays in Honour of Herbert McCabe, O.P.*, ed. Brian Davies (London: Geoffrey Chapman, 1987), 77.

such as goodness and perfection that are coextensive in some way with existence. The latter, meanwhile, are names signifying negative transcendence, and act as linguistic determinations of the divine ineffability. They include features such as simplicity and eternity.[29] Here, Turner appeals to Aquinas's famous affirmation that we might know by natural reason that God exists, and what God is not, but not what God is.[30] Consequently, "you do not know what God is. But all the same, there is a job to be done of determining whether the 'unknowability' you may have got to in your contemplation of the world is in truth the divine unknowability, the divine 'otherness.'. . . For the penultimate unknowability of creatures is always less than God's ultimate incomprehensibility."[31] Furthermore, for Turner, the positive significations of God (such as goodness and perfection) are in fact affirmed of God even while themselves being subject to an ultimate apophatic qualification: they are affirmed as being in God, yet as something utterly unknown. Here a double negation is intended. We know that to say God is *not* good, or perfect, is false (i.e., *not* the case). And consequently, God *is* truly good, and perfect. But as to what God's perfection or goodness is, we have no conception. His positive attributes are enshrouded in incomprehensibility.[32] They are approached through negations of affirmations of imperfections attributed to God, such that they stand at the edges of what we might proclaim intelligibly by means of a coherent philosophical grammar. Our positive discourse concerning God terminates in a mystery of unknowing.

---

[29] *Faith, Reason and the Existence of God*, 41: "Nothing is easier, to begin with, than to see that, in [Aquinas's] discussion of the divine simplicity in [*ST* I] question 3, what is demonstrated is not some comprehensible divine attribute, some affirmation which marks out God from everything else, but some marker of what constitutes the divine incomprehensibility, as distinct from the incomprehensibility of everything else. It is helpful, in this connection, to take note of David Burrell's distinction between those names of God which denote substantive 'attributes,' such as 'goodness,' 'beauty,' 'justice' and 'mercy' and so forth, and those names of God which denote what he calls 'formal features'—among which he numbers 'simplicity' and 'eternity.' Whereas the 'attributes' predicate of God, on whatever logical grounds justify such predications, terms predicable of creatures, the 'formal features' 'concern our manner of locating the subject for characterization, and hence belong to a stage prior to considering attributes as such.'" The last citation is from the above-mentioned text of Burrell.

[30] *ST* I, q. 3, prologue.

[31] *Faith, Reason and the Existence of God*, 42.

[32] Ibid., 186: "But if we do not know what 'pure act' means anyway, in the sense that we possess some concept of it, then it follows that we know no better what 'wholly perfect' or 'good *simpliciter*' means than we know what 'pure act' means, except that they must be true of God, which is enough *to know that their contradictories are false*" (emphasis added).

Turner's writing contains many nuances to which this succinct presentation cannot do sufficient justice, and his interpretation of Aquinas is quite profound, as were those of McCabe, Gilson, and Sertillanges that preceded him. Each gives great respect to the ineffability of the divine essence and the reality of divine transcendence. Meanwhile, this radically apophatic conception of God is articulated by Turner in direct contrast to what he takes to be ontotheological conceptions of deity so as to circumvent entirely the Kantian criticisms of Enlightenment theism. And in his analysis of Aquinas as a non-ontotheological thinker, he gives argumentative credence to many of the themes that I have tried to articulate in this book. Nevertheless, one might pose some reasonable criticisms of the account of apophaticism to which this form of Thomistic interpretation gives rise. Here I will limit myself to three brief considerations, followed by reflections of my own on the subject.

First, there is the question of the starting point of this approach to analogical language for God. The decision to make the created dependency of *esse* virtually the unique determinate for the consideration of divine names contains within it a latent difficulty. For by designating this dimension of created reality as the center for consideration of potential analogates (and non-analogates) to God, one excludes a priori the recourse to what in this book has been termed the progressive *via inventionis* of causal analysis in creatures. An analysis of the complexity of the causal composition of creatures in terms of form and matter, substance and accident, as well as substantial act versus teleological operation, must necessarily precede a consideration of created *esse* and essence, if the latter notions are to be appropriately employed in order to speak about God analogically.[33] In fact, what we see Aquinas doing in *ST* I, q. 3 (the *locus classicus* of apophatic thought to which Turner continually refers) clearly presupposes something like this. There, he reflects on the simplicity of God by undertaking the systematic negation of a series of compositions that characterize created reality. These compositions are presupposed as having been previously identified *prior to* the demonstrations of the existence of God (in *ST* I, q. 2, a. 3), and are now employed *in light of* those demonstrations as a way of understanding God's simplicity and pure actuality. Here, then, Aquinas distinguishes in creatures act and potentiality,[34] form

---

[33] It is noteworthy in this respect that McCabe (*God Matters*, 43, cited above) *opposes* the knowledge of being as act and potency with the knowledge of being as *esse* vs. nothingness, claiming that the former pertains (for Aristotle) to generation, while the latter pertains (for Aquinas) to creation *ex nihilo*. This dichotomizing schema (which in turn affects Turner's thought) is unnecessary, and as I have tried to show in the previous chapter, does not represent well Aquinas's own harmonization of the metaphysics of *esse*, of act and potentiality, and of substantial generation.

[34] *ST* I, q. 3, a. 1.

and matter,[35] nature and individuality,[36] and substance and accident,[37] *in addition to* essence and existence.[38] He simultaneously denies these compositions in God. Underlying such reflection is a commitment to a deeply Aristotelian vision of reality that in turn allows one to construe a *positive* understanding of God's divine simplicity. I will return to this point below.

Second, just as Turner does not consider other forms of caused composition in creatures as indicative (by way of negation) of the divine simplicity, so he does not have recourse to them in order to explain the real distinction between existence and essence. The real distinction is not explained in terms of previously established causes such as form and matter, substance and operation, potentiality and actuality (as I have attempted to do in the previous chapter). Instead, it is envisaged in light of the notion of the sheer act of finite existence over and against the *possibility of nothingness*. This is the case because in fact Turner (not unlike Gilson) conceives of the distinction between *esse* and essence primarily in terms of divine *creation*, invoking the latter act as the explanation of why there is something rather than nothing. But if one is to make the question "why is there something rather than nothing" the question by which one discovers created *esse*, then in fact *esse* appears only in light of the consideration of nothingness. And nothingness, as such, is a mentally construed hypothesis (a pure possibility) that does not obtain in our world, and that has never been experienced. The argument from contingency in Aquinas (at least as I have interpreted it in the previous chapter, based upon *Summa contra Gentiles* I, 15) is best understood as an argument from the real potentiality in individual material beings to not exist (their potentiality to not be), necessitating in turn extrinsic causes for each, and ultimately (because of the impossibility of an infinite series) a transcendent, primary cause who exists necessarily. An argument from nothingness, however, is an argument from sheer logical possibility, construed intentionally in the human mind. In this case, existence becomes intelligible only through the prior consideration of a possible world, a world in which there would be nothing. The former approach begins from the contingency of individuals, and reasons by causal series to something that transcends them. The latter consideration treats the logical possibility of nothingness as the medium through which we conceive of the creation of all things.[39]

---

[35] *ST* I, q. 3, a. 2.

[36] *ST* I, q. 3, a. 3.

[37] *ST* I, q. 3, a. 6.

[38] *ST* I, q. 3, a. 4.

[39] Turner himself insists on the distinction of the two approaches, citing approvingly a statement of McCabe (*God Matters*, 59), "As Herbert McCabe says, when speaking of God as 'the source of *esse*,' we are speaking of 'the being of the thing not just overagainst a world-without-it, but overagainst *nothing*, not even 'logical space' "

In a certain sense, then, this approach inverts the order of investigation envisaged by Aquinas, which begins from the real existence of beings we experience, and their perfections, but also from their causal compositions (as beings composed of substance and accidents, act and potency, essence and existence) that signify in turn their causal dependencies in the order of being. The latter dependencies then lead us to the necessary affirmation of God as one who completely transcends the world of dependent existents, and is pure actuality. According to the a posteriori approach I have sketched out in chapter 7, no concept of "creation" is presupposed. Only in light of the discovery of the existence of God, and an adequate reflection on his transcendent freedom as pure actuality, can we then theorize adequately what it means metaphysically for God to create, and consider the possibility of God's not having created the world at all (i.e., of there being nothing). At this point, it is reasonable to question: since God was *not* compelled to create the world, what does the free gift of creation reveal concerning God's goodness and wisdom? In other words, "why is there something rather than nothing" is a metaphysical question rightly asked after the discovery of the existence of God, and is primarily concerned with God's *nature and intentions* (God's goodness and providential design), and not with the existence of God.[40] Turner and McCabe, like Gilson before them, introduce a properly theological perspective into the order of metaphysical argumentation prematurely.

Third, Aquinas makes use of analogies drawn from *diverse* compositions one finds in creatures (not merely the *esse*/essence distinction) to attribute to God in his simplicity what is complex in creatures. This commits one to

---

(*Faith, Reason and the Existence of God*, 178). According to McCabe, the possibility for this conception comes from the revelation of the biblical narrative, and not Greek philosophy (*God Matters*, 43). Does this understanding not substitute as a first principle of philosophy a theologically revealed "logical possibility" (that God might not have created anything)? The same question emerges with regard to the rational demonstration of the existence of God: it can be construed as an ultimate explanation for all things only against the backdrop of the logical possibility of nothingness.

[40] Aquinas understands the reason for creation *philosophically* in light of God's goodness, in *ScG* III, chapters 16–21. However, elsewhere he deepens this viewpoint *theologically*, by understanding the goodness of creation as an expression of Trinitarian love, and the desire of God to share his divine life with spiritual creatures by grace. This is illustrated most profoundly in the *ST* I, where he treats creation and created dependence (*ST* I, q. 44–45) only *after* an extensive consideration of the simplicity and personal hypostases of the triune God, and *an analysis of the divine missions* of the Word and Holy Spirit (q. 43) by which God wishes to inhabit rational creatures by grace. The latter missions are the ultimate reasons for the creation and therefore the ultimate answer (which only revelation can give) as to "why there exists something rather than nothing."

understanding the simplicity of God's pure actuality under a multiplicity of conceptual angles. For example, because human beings are both form and matter, there is a differentiation in them between their nature ("man") and their material individuality ("Socrates"). However, because this distinction does not obtain in God, he is not formless or without individuality, but *both* form *and* individual. The two exist *without real distinction* in God.[41] Likewise, Aquinas signifies God as "operation,"[42] "quality,"[43] "substance,"[44] "individual,"[45] "existence,"[46] and as "form,"[47] and "essence,"[48] while still maintaining the divine simplicity. In other words, the multiple dimensions that are composite in creatures (form/material individual; substance/qualitative operation; existence/essence) are attributed by Aquinas to the pure actuality of God, even while he maintains that they exist in God without complexity. Why does Aquinas undertake this order of reflection? Immediate recourse to the *esse*/essence distinction, the analogy of *esse*, and the corresponding rejection of the adequateness of any created essence to the divine essence does not allow us to answer this question. It does not seem to admit sufficiently, therefore, the complexity of Aquinas's procedure. In fact, the answer is that Aquinas is presupposing an Aristotelian-inspired causal analysis of creatures, and this analysis allows him to demarcate in creatures multiple composite dimensions. These dimensions in turn provide a diversity of notions by which the divine nature might be signified analogically. However, due to the incomprehensible simplicity of

---

[41] This is the point of *ST* I, q. 3, a. 3.

[42] *ST* I, q. 13, a. 8: "Because therefore God is not known to us in his nature, but is made known to us from his operations or effects, we can name him from these. . . . Hence this name 'God' is a name of operation so far as relates to the source of its meaning."

[43] *ST* I, q. 13, a. 1, ad 3: "To signify substance with quality is to signify the *suppositum* with a nature or determined form in which it subsists. Hence, as some things are said of God in a concrete sense, to signify his subsistence and perfection, so likewise nouns are applied to God signifying substance with quality."

[44] *ST* I, q. 13, a. 11, ad 1: "The name 'He Who Is,' is the name of God more properly than this name 'God,' as regards its source, namely, existence. . . . But as regards the object intended by the name, this name 'God' is more proper, as it is imposed to signify the divine nature; and still more proper is the Tetragrammaton [YHWH], imposed to signify the substance of God itself, incommunicable and, if one may so speak, singular."

[45] *ST* I, q. 13, a. 9.

[46] *ST* I, q. 13, a. 11.

[47] *ST* I, q. 3, a. 2.

[48] *ST* I, q. 13, a. 2, ad 3: "We cannot know the essence of God in this life, as he really is in himself; but we know him accordingly as he is represented in the perfections of his creatures; and thus the names imposed by us signify him in that manner only."

the divine nature, each such notion must be rethought analogically so as to speak rightly (if necessarily inadequately) of the mystery of God.

In what follows then, I would like to present succinctly some observations concerning the causal character of Aquinas's interpretation of analogical knowledge of God, and in doing so would like to emphasize ways in which the progressive analysis of causal composition (the *via inventionis*) of previous chapters might permit one to qualify one's interpretation of the negative knowledge of God in Aquinas's thought.

Causality, Apophaticism, and Analogy

In his treatment of the nature of God in the *Summa theologiae*, Aquinas both follows and inverts the order of Aristotle's *Posterior Analytics* with regard to the notion of scientific knowledge. For whereas Aristotle had claimed that scientific understanding presupposes that we first know *that something is*, and subsequently ask *what the thing is*,[49] Aquinas claims that we first ascertain *that God exists*, but subsequently seek to understand *not what* God is, but rather *what God is not*.[50] And in this way, he maintains the notion of an Aristotelian scientific, causal approach to understanding God, even while safeguarding against any appeal to a quidditative knowledge of what God is, formulated in terms of species and genre. This kind of thinking is impossible even for merely heuristic reasons (i.e., in order to begin thinking about God). Instead, we can formulate a unified notion of God *indirectly* based upon his effects: God is the provident Creator and cause of all that exists. For this reason, Aquinas substitutes for any conceptual definition of God a thematic appeal to Dionysius the Areopagite's threefold via taken from *On the Divine Names*.[51] God is known *per viam*

---

[49] *Posterior Analytics* II, 7, 92b5–12: "For it is necessary for anyone who knows what a man or anything else is to know too *that* it is."

[50] *ST* I, q. 3, prologue: "When the existence of a thing has been ascertained there remains the further question of the manner of its existence, in order that we may know its essence. Now, because we cannot know what God is, but rather what he is not, we have no means for considering how God is, but rather how he is not." See the insightful analysis of this issue by Te Velde, *Aquinas on God*, 72–77, who takes issue with the reading of this text as uniquely negative in kind, and emphasizes the continuity with Aristotelian method. Having shown *that* God exists in *ST* I, q. 2, Aquinas now asks *what* God is. 73: "The Aristotelian model of the search for the definition needs thus to be transformed and in a certain sense adapted to the singular case of the divine essence, which does not fall under any genus and which therefore cannot be positively identified in its essence through a categorical analysis of its essential constitution. The alternative way of identifying the essence of God must therefore be indirectly and negatively with reference to the categorical structure of material reality as such."

[51] The basic text of Dionysius is *De divinis nominibus*, c. 7, 3.

causalitatis, as the transcendent cause of creatures. Because creatures must in some way resemble their cause as his effects, therefore, certain attributes of creatures may be ascribed to God in a transcendent, analogical way. However, due to God's utterly ineffable and transcendent manner of existing, these attributes must be thought *per viam negationis*, or *remotionis*, that is to say, by negating or removing from them all that pertains necessarily to creaturely imperfection. Finally, *per viam eminentiae*, these analogical ascriptions given to God may be thought to exist in him in an all-surpassing, preeminent way, not found in any creaturely form.

> From the knowledge of sensible things, the whole power of God cannot be known; nor therefore can his essence be seen. But because they are his effects and depend upon their cause, we can be led from them so far as to know of God whether he exists, and to know of him *what must necessarily belong to him, as the first cause of all things, exceeding all things caused by him*. Hence we know of his relationship with creatures in so far as he is *the cause* of them all; also that creatures *differ from him*, inasmuch as he is *not* in any way part of what is caused by him; and that creatures are not removed from him *by reason of any defect on his part*, but *because he superexceeds them all*.[52]

So for example, if creatures are created by God as good, then their goodness reflects analogically something of the subsistent goodness of God himself. However, the goodness of God cannot be characterized by the limiting imperfections that characterize (both ontological and moral) goodness in creatures. Therefore, while goodness exists in God, or while God *is* preeminently good, his goodness is of an utterly surpassing and ineffable kind, utterly distinct from that of creatures.[53] According to this way of thinking, creatures in their goodness do resemble God analogically as the effects of the Creator resemble their cause, toward whom (*ad alterum*) they point, even while being infinitely inferior to him. Therefore, while they allow us to signify positively what he is essentially (subsistent goodness), they do not provide us with a conceptual grasp of his essence, nor any direct understanding of what his goodness is.[54] The latter can be designated or signified only by recourse to a mode of discourse drawn from creatures, and employed imperfectly to signify the reality of the incomprehensible essence of God.[55]

---

[52] *ST* I, q. 12, a. 12 (emphasis added; translation slightly modified). Note that just after this text Aquinas proceeds to clarify (in q. 13) the analogical character of the knowledge this way of thinking permits. For similar texts, employing the triple *viae*, see *ScG* I, c. 30; *In de Div. Nom.*, c. 7, lec. 4; *De potentia Dei*, q. 7, a. 5, ad 2.

[53] *ST* I, q. 6, a. 2.

[54] *ST* I, q. 13, a. 6.

[55] *ST* I, q. 13, aa. 3 and 6.

A plethora of very helpful studies exist on the topic of Aquinas's treatment of the triple *viae* and the analogical knowledge of God they provide. For the purposes of my argument here, I wish only to emphasize three noteworthy features of this process of reasoning, each of which points toward the *positive* significance of the knowledge of God attained through philosophical reason. After this, I will discuss the positive analogical ascription of wisdom to God as a divine name.

The first point I wish to emphasize is that although Aquinas's interpretation of the analogical knowledge of God is characterized by recourse to the Neoplatonic axioms of Dionysius, this latter set of reflections is also recast in the image of an Aristotelian methodology. It is because a prior causal analysis of composite being exists that the intrinsic ontological limitations and dependencies of finite beings emerge as an object of scientific, that is to say, causal consideration. According to this procedure of reflection, positive knowledge of being is foundational, and contextualizes all appeal to apophatic modes of signification.

The foundational, epistemic priority of positive to negative knowledge is first of all a general truth for Aquinas. Following Aristotle, he insists that every negation is in fact a mental act or intention predicated upon the prior admission of something existent, and therefore (epistemically) positive and affirmative. We may negate the existence of something or characteristics of a certain kind, only because we always, already have some prior, positive knowledge of beings, upon which we base our understandings of what is (and is not) the case. Every negation, therefore, implies some kind of prior affirmation.[56] St. Thomas specifically applies this basic noetic principle to the problem of negative knowledge of God: whatever is negated of God presupposes some positive knowledge, including positive knowledge of God's existence. Writing about the divine names in contradistinction to Maimonides, he states:

---

56 *ELPH* I, 8, commenting upon *De Interpretatione*, c. 5, 17a8–9: "The first enunciation is the affirmation, next is the negation." Aquinas says that there are three reasons for the priority of the affirmation with respect to the negation: (1) the affirmation is more simple, and is a condition for the negation, which negates a positive term; (2) the composition of concepts that is constitutive of the affirmation is prior to the division of concepts, which constitutes the negation; (3) with respect to the thing signified, the affirmation signifies existence (*esse*), which is ontologically prior to nonbeing (*non esse*), just as a habitus is naturally prior to its privation. In other words, truth is predicated upon what exists, such that knowledge depends upon the priority of being in act, while negation can occur only with reference to what exists in act, and consequently, with respect to an affirmation. See Humbrecht's analysis of the primacy of affirmation over negation in this text by Aquinas in *Théologie Négative et Noms Divins*, 168–85, esp. 181.

The idea of negation is always based upon an affirmation: as evinced by the fact that every negative proposition is proved by an affirmative: wherefore unless the human mind knew something positively about God, it would be unable to deny anything about him. And it would know nothing if nothing that it affirmed about God were positively verified about him. Hence following Dionysius [*Divine Names*, c. 12], we must hold that these terms signify the divine essence, albeit defectively and imperfectly.[57]

This means that, according to Aquinas, the logical presupposition for *any* negative or apophatic theological reflection concerning God is the prior knowledge of three things: (1) existence in creatures, (2) the existence of God that is derived from creatures, and (3) the necessity of the ascription of some perfections of creatures to God (in an analogical fashion) as the primary cause. Simply put, the similitude between creatures and God established by the *via causalitatis* precedes, contextualizes, and gives warrant to the *via negationis*.

Second, then, the mental negations by which one removes from one's ascriptions to God any significations denoting imperfection are themselves only a *moment within* the reflection on God as the primary cause of the world, and as preeminently perfect in an incomprehensible way. Such negations allow one to approach some understanding of the transcendence of God, who cannot be understood to exist in any kind of continuity with creatures as if he were one in a series of finite, participated beings. He therefore transcends all modes of signification derived from creatures. Yet even negative reflection on the pure actuality of God not only presupposes awareness of divine causality, and therefore the positive resemblance of created effect to uncreated cause, but also *negates the limitations* that are proper to the modes of being that are characteristic of creatures. By negating these non-perfections (effectively a kind of negation of a negation), the mind makes more precise the *affirmation* of the supereminent characteristics of the one God, and thus qualifies apophatically the epistemological mode of its own knowledge of God.[58] Such thinking, however, is meant to carry us forward toward a term that is utterly positive, yet transcendent of

---

57 *De potentia Dei*, q. 7, a. 5. See the analysis of this text by Te Velde, *Aquinas on God*, 74; Humbrecht, *Théologie Négative et Noms Divins*, 151–68.

58 In the words of Humbrecht, *Théologie Négative et Noms Divins*, 778: "In this domain, 'negative theology' designates something that is materially absent, and which is in fact misnamed. Theology as such is discourse concerning God, philosophical or theological, and does not include a 'species' differentiated by the negation. . . . Strictly speaking, it is not theology that is negative but one of its modes [of discourse]. The negation is a 'way'. . . . Its role is to remove from God all that which is not proper to him in himself."

participated, finite being. Correspondingly, Aquinas makes perfectly clear that despite its imperfect, indirect character (lacking all *quidditative* knowledge of the divine essence), our naming of God signifies truly *what God* is *substantially in himself.*[59]

Last of all, the so-called negative perfections of God (which Turner and Burrell call "formal features"), such as simplicity, eternity, infinity, immutability, and impassibility, are in fact employed in order to qualify our truly positive designations that pertain to God's preeminence as primary cause. The reason for this is that although these divine names are formulated largely by way of negation (i.e., for God to be simple is for him to *not* be composed of a real distinction between existence and essence, substance and accident, etc.), nevertheless, the *premise* of such negations is the *affirmation* of the pure actuality of God, and the unique perfection of the latter. In fact, because God is known through a causal analysis and by means of the primacy of actuality over potentiality, therefore he is the primary cause of creatures and pure actuality. But if this is the case, then the imperfections that characterize the causal composition of creatures do not characterize God, and therefore must not be ascribed to him if we are to take seriously his *positive* perfection. To remove composition, finitude, alteration, or suffering from God, therefore, is to say something of his positive preeminence in its transcendence. Consequently, divine names such as simplicity, infinity, immutability, and impassibility are employed in true judgments concerning God *as he is in himself.* For

---

[59] One sees this most clearly in *ST* I, q. 13, a. 2, where, writing against Maimonides, Aquinas states that names can be applied to God *substantialiter*: "These names [such as goodness and wisdom] signify the divine substance, and are predicated substantially of God, although they fall short of a full representation of him. . . . For these names express God insofar as our intellects know him. Now since our intellect knows God from creatures, it knows him as far as creatures represent him. Now God prepossesses in himself all the perfections of creatures, being himself simply and universally perfect. Hence every creature represents him, and is like him so far as it possesses some perfection; yet it represents him not as something of the same species or genus, but as the excelling principle of whose form the effects fall short, although they derive some kind of likeness thereto. . . . So when we say, 'God is good,' the meaning is not, 'God is the cause of goodness,' or 'God is not evil,' but the meaning is, 'whatever good we attribute to creatures, preexists in God,' and in a more excellent and higher way. Hence it does not follow that God is good, because he causes goodness but rather on the contrary, he causes goodness in things because he is good." In q. 13, a. 12, asking if affirmative propositions can be formed about God, Aquinas states, "God as considered in himself is altogether one and simple, yet our intellect knows him by different conceptions because it cannot see him as he is in himself. Nevertheless, although it understands him under different conceptions, it knows that *one and the same simple object corresponds to its conceptions.*"

example, God who is source of all other (composite) beings is indeed truly simple in his very being, due to the perfection of his pure actuality. Divine simplicity, therefore, characterizes in some irreducible sense the positive perfection of God's transcendent existence, goodness, and love, such that these latter divine names cannot be reflected upon adequately without reference to the former.[60]

In saying this, we need not take anything away from what Turner and others rightly insist upon concerning the radically imperfect mode by which we ascribe positive names to God. The divine essence remains incomprehensible. Because we know God analogically from creatures, we therefore ascribe perfections to him in terms drawn from creatures. The reality signified is truly God, but the mode of signification for this form of knowledge depends so profoundly upon creaturely understanding that we are simultaneously obliged to affirm that we do not know "what" these perfections are as they exist in God.[61] Consequently, our way of knowing

---

[60] Aquinas affirms as much explicitly in *ST* I, q. 13, a. 4: "But our intellect, since it knows God from creatures, in order to understand God, forms conceptions proportional to the perfections flowing from God to creatures, which perfections pre-exist in God *unitedly and simply*, whereas in creatures they are received, divided, and multiplied." Evidently, Aquinas thinks that unity and simplicity truly characterize the divine essence as it is in itself, even if we clarify the content of these names by means of the *via negationis*. An indisputable evidence of this stems from the fact that divine simplicity was considered from the Patristic age to the time of Aquinas a tenet of *theological dogma* as well as metaphysics, codified by the Fourth Lateran Council in 1215 (Denz. 428), as pertinent to the condemnation of the Trinitarian theology of Joachim of Fiore. Consequently, Aquinas in *ST* I, q. 3, is establishing the metaphysical truth of a doctrine of faith that will in turn qualify what he says about the unique essence of the Father, Son, and Holy Spirit (in qq. 27–31). Put quite simply, if we cannot speak *positively* of the simplicity of the divine essence (albeit indirectly), then the articulation of Trinitarian theology (for example: "the Father generates the Son as possessing in himself the plenitude of the divine essence") is radically undermined. Similar things could be said concerning divine impassability, which characterizes the perfection of God's act of being as divine love. See on these points, Gilles Emery, "The Immutability of the God of Love and the Problem of Language Concerning the 'Suffering of God,'" in *Divine Impassibility and the Mystery of Human Suffering*, ed. J. Keating and T. J. White (Grand Rapids: Eerdmans, 2009), and *The Trinitarian Theology of Saint Thomas Aquinas*, trans. F. Murphy (Oxford: Oxford University Press, 2007), 128–50.

[61] As Humbrecht states quite helpfully: "In effect, to say that God is the cause of beauty because he is himself beautiful is not to have comprehended the essence of divine beauty. To affirm the cause is not to see the cause and to affirm the eminence of this cause is not to represent it intellectually. The truth of the proposition surpasses the comprehensive extent of one's discourse. Concerning God, we know neither his essence nor even his being, but we know (and that by his effects) that the proposition 'God exists' or 'God is beautiful' is true. It is not because God is not

God remains imperfect, and even radically so, even as it aspires naturally to the positive knowledge of what God is in himself, or rather, precisely because it does. The human person is naturally ordered toward the wisdom of God as an intellectual creature, yet remains simultaneously open to God's as-yet-uncomprehended mystery. A human being is ontologically capable, therefore, of receiving authentic divine self-revelation as the extrinsic and gratuitous fulfillment of his or her intrinsic natural desire for knowledge of God.

Analogia Sapientiae: God as the Subsistent Wisdom That Is the Origin of the World

In the first part of the *Summa theologiae*, Aquinas discusses eight attributes of God (simplicity, perfection, goodness, infinity, omnipresence, immutability, eternity, and unity), and seven immanent operative perfections (God's knowledge or truth, life, will, love, justice, mercy, and power). Any comprehensive Thomistic consideration of wisdom in God, therefore, would need to concern itself with the distinctly metaphysical signification of each of these attributes and the ways each of them must necessarily qualify one's understanding of the wisdom of God. My goal here, however, is to indicate briefly only some central ways in which one might rightly characterize the wisdom of God analogically: in terms of (1) simplicity, (2) perfection, (3) truth, and (4) love. The first two of these are "substantive" attributes of God, while the latter two are "operative."[62] Due to Aquinas's analysis of divine simplicity (which I will discuss below), however, these two "sets" of attributes are in fact one in God, and are identical with God's divine wisdom as well. By considering each of the four in relation to wisdom, then, I wish to suggest at the term of this *via inventionis*, or way of inquiry into the knowledge of God, how we can say that God is wise. Correspondingly, this permits one to affirm, from a Thomistic point of view, that the mind aspires

---

understood that he is not attained, just as it is not because he is not represented intellectually that he is not signified" (*Théologie Négative et Noms Divins*, 780).

[62] This is the order of inquiry Aquinas himself follows in the *ST*, moving from the analogical consideration of the "substance" or essence of God (qq. 3–13), to the question of the immanent operations of God (qq. 14–21), before moving on to consider God as a principle of extrinsic effects (qq. 22–26). See the explanation of this in the prologues to questions 14 and 22. *ST* I, q. 14, prologue: "Having considered what belongs to the divine substance, we have now to treat of God's operation. And since one kind of operation is immanent, and another kind of operation proceeds to the exterior effect, we treat first of knowledge and of will . . . and afterwards of the power of God." Evidently, this structure of reasoning reproduces Aristotelian divisions of being in act from *Metaphysics* Θ, which were studied in chapter 2, above.

naturally to wisdom, that is to say, to the truth concerning God as he is in himself. At the same time, I wish to consider in what way our knowledge of the wisdom of God is deeply incomplete, or imperfect, and therefore, in what sense the mind aspires naturally to a more perfect knowledge of God than it can accomplish by its own powers. This will allow me to terminate, in the last part of the chapter, with metaphysical reflections on the human being as a being naturally open to the mystery of God.

As I have mentioned above, in *Summa theologiae* I, q. 3, Aquinas discusses the simplicity of God by means of a series of negations, in which he removes from the consideration of God any of the imperfections characteristic of composition (or ontological complexity) in creatures. The presupposition of this procedure is that God is pure actuality. Therefore, what is multiple in creatures is somehow one and simple in God. For example, in God there is no body, or material potentiality, subject to actualization by another.[63] Therefore, in contrast to material beings, there is no distinction in God between his nature (as, for example, in our case: "man") and his individuality as a subject ("Socrates"). This is because God is not a form/matter composite, but is immaterial and completely unique in kind (rather than one within a natural series).[64] God, then, in his individual uniqueness is his deity.[65] Nor is there a distinction in God between his essence and his existence, since he is the cause of existence in all others, and possesses existence by nature, such that he is his existence.[66] For this same reason, he cannot be signified by any predicamental genus, as he would then be identified with only one kind of being, or region of being, and would not be himself the transcendent cause of all beings.[67] In God who is pure actuality and subsistent existence, there are no accidents: all that exists in God is essential to his nature, and identical with his very act of being.[68] God, then, is altogether simple. By this same measure, he cannot enter into composition with creatures, but is their altogether transcendent source.[69] Consequently, he is also absolutely omnipresent to all things, more intimate to them than they are to themselves, even while remaining utterly distinct from, and in no way identical to, them.[70] In this transcendence, he remains for us utterly incomprehensible.

To affirm that God is wisdom, then, is to affirm that his wisdom is identical with his simplicity and pure actuality. This means that his wisdom

---

63 *ST* I, q. 3, a. 1.
64 *ST* I, q. 3, a. 2.
65 *ST* I, q. 3, a. 3.
66 *ST* I, q. 3, a. 4.
67 *ST* I, q. 3, a. 5.
68 *ST* I, q. 3, a. 6.
69 *ST* I, q. 3, a. 7.
70 *ST* I, q. 3, a. 8; q. 8, a. 1.

is not characterized by the potencies of a material body. It is altogether immaterial. Furthermore, it is unique in kind (or essence), being utterly distinct from that wisdom pertaining to any other intellectual nature (for example, that of "composite forms" such as human beings or "separate forms" such as angels).[71] This wisdom *is* God's own essence *and* his subsistent existence (which are one only in God).[72] It cannot be designated by any genus of philosophical predication, but is beyond all the forms of our intra-worldly manner of knowing. Because it is pure actuality, the wisdom of God is not an "accident" of his substance (a quality), but rather, God is subsistent wisdom.[73] This wisdom does not enter into composition with creatures, but is the transcendent cause of all that exists, and is more intimate to creatures than they are to themselves.[74] All the while, divine wisdom remains essentially distinct from the created order and in itself is incomprehensible to us.

The perfection of the divine essence of God is articulated by Aquinas in terms of the pure actuality of God as well.[75] Perfection in realities we experience stems most especially from their teleological operations that are derived in turn from their accidental operational powers.[76] Just as Aristotle understood the pure actuality of God as something transcending the distinction between substantial being and accidental perfecting operations, so too Aquinas understands the pure actuality of God as "containing" in a transcendent sense the actuality of subsistence as well as the perfection that is characteristic of teleological operations.[77] However, in God there is no composition. Therefore, operational perfection in him takes on a uniquely substantial mode. God is his perfecting operation, and consequently, is substantially perfect.[78] Furthermore, as God is the efficient cause of all creatures, the perfections of the latter preexist in him in a preeminent way,

---

[71] *ST* I, q. 12, a. 2.

[72] *ST* I, q. 13, a. 5: "By the term 'wise' applied to a man, we signify some perfection distinct from a man's essence, and distinct from his power and existence . . . whereas when we apply it to God, we do not mean to signify anything distinct from his essence, or power, or existence. Thus also this term 'wise' applied to man in some degree circumscribes and comprehends the thing signified; whereas this is not the case when it is applied to God; but it leaves the thing signified as uncomprehended, and as exceeding the signification of the name."

[73] *ST* I, q. 3, a. 6, ad 1.

[74] *ST* I, q. 9, a. 1, ad 2.

[75] *ST* I, q. 4, a. 1.

[76] *ST* I, q. 5, aa. 1 and 4.

[77] *ScG* I, c. 28: "Again, each thing is perfect according as it is in act, and imperfect according as it is in potency and lacking act. Hence, that which is in no way in potency, but is pure act, must be most perfect. Such, however, is God. God is, therefore, most perfect."

[78] *ST* I, q. 4, a. 2, ad 1.

yet without any of the defects or limitations that are characteristic of creatures.[79] In this way, God is sovereignly good, since he is the cause of the (substantial and operational) perfections of goodness in creatures, and contains in himself the goodness of pure actuality, while remaining free of the limitations of ontological and moral goodness in creatures.[80]

For God to exist and to be actively operative are identical, and in this way he is also perfect. With respect to wisdom, this means that the immaterial operation of wisdom in God is something identical with his very nature or essence. God is his act of wisdom.[81] Because he is also pure actuality, this wisdom is the transcendent origin of all creatures and therefore contains in itself in preeminent fashion all of the existing perfection found in the latter, including that of their goodness.[82] The wisdom of God, then, knows no intrinsic imperfection or diminution, but is itself sovereignly good. Again, this intrinsic perfection remains in itself utterly transcendent and unknown to us.

This consideration of the simplicity and perfection of the divine wisdom of God leaves us with the firm conclusion that in God wisdom is subsistent and identical with God's very essence. Therefore, if we wish to understand in some way *how* God is subsistent wisdom, we will wish to consider the immanent life of God as *sapientia*. However, as mentioned above, Aquinas suggests that to do so we must consider God by analogical comparison with the immanent vital operations of intellect and will in rational creatures. These operations are characterized by acts of knowledge (in which the mind knows

---

79 *ST* I, q. 4, a. 2: "Since God is the first effective cause of things, the perfections of all things must pre-exist in God in a more eminent way."

80 *ST* I, q. 6, a. 1: "To be good belongs pre-eminently to God. For a thing is good according as to its desirableness. Now everything seeks after its own perfection; and the perfection and form of an effect consist in a certain likeness to the agent, since every agent makes its like; and hence the agent itself is desirable and has the nature of the good. For the very thing which is desirable in it is the participation of its likeness. Therefore, since God is the first effective cause of all things, it is manifest that the aspect of good and of desirableness belong to him."

81 *ST* I, q. 4, ad 3: "Dionysius says [*The Divine Names*, c. 5] that, although existence is more perfect than life, and life than wisdom, if they are considered as distinguished in idea; nevertheless, a living thing is more perfect than what merely exists, because living things also exist and intelligent things both exist and live. Although therefore existence does not include life and wisdom, because that which participates in existence need not participate in every mode of existence; nevertheless God's existence includes in itself life and wisdom, because nothing of the perfection of being can be wanting to him who is subsisting being itself."

82 *ST* I, q. 9, a. 1, ad 2: "Wisdom . . . diffuses its likeness even to the outermost of things; for nothing can exist which does not proceed from the divine wisdom by way of some kind of imitation, as from the first effective and formal principle; as also works of art proceed from the wisdom of the artist."

truthfully), and love (or voluntary appetite). Divine *sapientia*, then, may be understood analogically through a consideration of God's truth and love.

Truth, according to Aquinas, is a property of the intellect by which its knowledge of a reality is adequate to that reality. It entails a relation: our thought is true when what we think corresponds to reality. Truth, then, is primarily in the intellect as a form of knowledge, but relates to what the known thing is in itself.[83] Of course, the mind of a human being is progressively qualified by the acquisition of all kinds of truths, amidst a complex life of human reasoning. Truth in the human intellect, then, takes place through the medium of concepts and judgments, which refer in turn (truly or falsely) to real things or persons. In God, however, truth, or intellectual knowledge, cannot be accidental, or acquired through a progressive actuation of intellectual potentiality. Rather, God's act of knowing is subsistent and is pure actuality.[84] Furthermore, God is not qualified intellectually by the relation to another reality, by which he might become a more adequate kind of knower, and upon which he depends. He does not know himself through a complex medium, that is to say, through the finite and accidental world of human conceptuality, and images, or through angelic *species*. Rather, God is simultaneously (1) the object of his very act of knowing, (2) the medium through which he knows his own divine essence, and (3) the act of knowing.[85] In this way, he is subsistent contemplation, or "thought thinking itself," to use the expression of Aristotle, embraced by Aquinas.[86]

---

[83] *ST* I, q. 16, a. 1: "Since the true is in the intellect in so far as it is conformed to the object understood, the aspect of the true [*ratio veri*] must needs pass from the intellect to the object understood, so that also the thing understood is said to be true in so far as it has some relation to the intellect." See also the basic text on the transcendentals, *De ver.*, q. 1, a. 1, and the helpful study of truth in Aquinas by Jan Aertsen, *Medieval Philosophy and the Transcendentals*, 243–89.

[84] *ST* I, q. 14, a. 2.

[85] See the intricate argumentation of *ST* I, q. 14, aa. 3 and 4. After having claimed that (a) God's intellect is his substance and (b) it is pure actuality, such that the divine act of understanding cannot be qualified from the exterior, and moved from potency to act, Aquinas reasons thus (a. 4): "To understand is not an act passing to anything extrinsic, for it remains in the operator as his own act and perfection; as existence is the perfection of the one existing: just as existence follows on the form, so in like manner to understand follows on the intelligible species. Now in God there is no form which is something other than his existence. . . . Hence as his essence itself is also his intelligible species, it necessarily follows that his act of understanding must be his essence and his existence. *Thus it follows from all the foregoing that in God, intellect, and the object understood, and the intelligible species, and his act of understanding are entirely one and the same. Hence, when God is said to be understanding, no kind of multiplicity is attached to his substance*" (emphasis added).

[86] *Metaphysics* Λ, 9, 1074b15–34. Aquinas refers to this passage at the beginning of the article just cited (*ST* I, q. 14, a. 4), such that his comments there are clearly an

For St. Thomas, then, the fact that God is wisdom denotes in part that God can be signified analogically as a pure act of contemplation. Because God is self-contemplating, and possesses in himself the perfect comprehension of his divine essence, wisdom in its most proper sense is the knowledge that God has of himself.[87] God is in himself personal truth.[88] However, this does not mean that God is somehow noetically solipsistic, or unable to comprehend creatures. On the contrary, since God is pure actuality, his wisdom is also the source of the being which all creatures receive from him and in which they participate. Therefore, *precisely because* God alone knows the perfect plenitude of being that is his divine essence (his subsistent wisdom), he in turn knows all that derives from himself.[89] As contemplative wisdom, God knows the created order through the medium of his divine essence without having to "exit" from himself, learn from another, or undergo any progressive noetic amelioration through dependence upon another. This independence is not the result of an isolating egotism on God's part, as it would be in a created person. To think this way is to fail to realize the incomprehensible transcendence of God, his pure actuality, and the reality of his creative causality that derives only from his own free initiative. On the contrary, it is only because God is so radically independent

---

attempt to interpret the *noesis noeseos* formula respectfully in light of his own metaphysics.

[87] "Augustine says, 'In God to be is the same as to be wise.' But to be wise is the same thing as to understand. Therefore in God to be is the same thing as to understand. But God's existence is his substance. Therefore, the act of God's intellect is his substance" (*ST* I, q. 14, a. 4, with respect to *De Trin.* VII, c. 2).

[88] *ST* I, q. 16, a. 5: "Truth is found in the intellect according as it apprehends a thing as it is; and in things according as they have being conformable to an intellect. This is to the greatest degree found in God. For his being is not only conformed to his intellect, but it is the very act of his intellect. And his act of understanding is the measure and cause of every other being and of every other intellect, and he himself is his own existence and act of understanding. Whence it follows not only that truth is in him, but that he is truth itself, and the sovereign and first truth."

[89] *ST* I, q. 14, a. 5: "Since the divine power extends to other things by the very fact that it is the first effective cause of all things . . . God must necessarily know things other than himself. And this appears still more plainly if we add that the very existence of the first cause, God, is his own act of understanding. Hence whatever effects pre-exist in God, as in the first cause, must be in his act of understanding, and all things must be in him according to an intelligible mode." See, similarly, *ScG* I, c. 48–49; *In Meta.*, XII, lec. 11. Aquinas is adopting here a classic interpretation of Aristotle's theology initiated by Themistius and further developed by Avicenna. God in his simplicity knows things other than himself through the medium of own essence, and as the cause of all other beings. See Georges Vajda, "Notes d'Avicenne sur la 'Théologie d'Aristote,'" *Revue Thomiste* 51 (1951): 346–406.

that creatures can be given being, and can remain in existence *through God's self-knowledge*, and thus can be so perfectly known in all that they *are*. The autonomy of God's self-contemplation with respect to creatures is the ground and basis for God's capacity to give existence freely by his wisdom, that is, to create and govern creatures *in* wisdom, yet through a knowing love that is absolutely free.

Spiritual love, for Aquinas, is a movement of the will toward a good that is desired for its own sake.[90] What is good, here, is understood in metaphysical terms. "The good is that which all desire."[91] This phrase is cited by Aquinas and interpreted as signifying the goodness of being.[92] Human beings, for example, are good due to their very existence, their nature and qualities, and their actions. To love another human person, then, entails the desire for his or her good (that he or she survive and flourish), and the aspiration to some kind of communal life (however proximate or remote) with the person loved.[93] To become more perfect through love requires that we acknowledge the intrinsic goodness of other persons, and that in loving them, we develop our capacity to act on behalf of their good, and to act with them in view of the common good. This requires in turn the giving of ourselves through the medium of virtuous acts. In human persons, then, love can potentially undergo a progressive growth and development, a passage from potentiality to actuality, expressed by means of the moral and religious virtues.[94]

God, however, due to his absolute perfection, possesses in himself ineffable goodness.[95] He does not become good through another. Furthermore, in differentiation from every creature, God knows himself as this goodness comprehensively and, consequently, can love himself in all that he is, infinitely.[96] Love in God is not accidental but substantial. He is love in all he is.[97] What has been said for God as the operative act of contemplation, or truthful knowledge, is also true for God as love. Just as he is

---

[90] *ST* I, q. 20, a. 1.

[91] Aristotle, *Nic. Ethics* I, 1, 1094a3.

[92] In *ST* I, q. 5, a. 1.

[93] *ST* I, q. 20, a. 1, ad 3: "An act of love always tends towards two things; to the good that one wills and to the person for whom one wills it."

[94] For a sustained treatment of Aquinas's analysis of love (including his influences from Aristotle, Augustine, and Dionysius), see Michael Sherwin, *By Knowledge and By Love* (Washington, DC: The Catholic University of America Press, 2005), esp. 63–118.

[95] *ST* I, q. 6, aa. 2–3.

[96] *ScG* I, c. 74.

[97] *ScG* I, c. 73; *ST* I, q. 20, a. 1, ad 3: "So love is called the unitive force, even in God, yet without implying composition; for the good that he wills for himself is no other than himself, who is good by his essence."

knowledge and knows himself, so also he is love and loves himself. God is his act of loving, and as such, both knows and loves his own divine essence and goodness.[98] All else is both known and loved in and through the knowledge and love that God has of himself.

We might conclude this brief reflection on divine wisdom, then, by noting that it is because God's wisdom is loving that he gives being to creatures. He does so, however, only as one who is sovereignly free. Because of the pure actuality of the loving wisdom of God, God can create not because of a compulsion, or through an inclination to become more perfect, but by pure gratuity, and as a sheer gift.[99] While we love created persons because they are good, with respect to God we must say the inverse. Creatures are good because God loves them.

> Now it has been shown above (q. 19, a. 4) that God's will is the cause of all things. It must needs be, therefore, that a thing has existence, or any kind of good, only inasmuch as it is willed by God. To every existing thing, then, God wills some good. Hence, since to love anything is nothing else than to will good to that thing, it is manifest that God loves everything that exists. Yet not as we love. Because since our will is not the cause of the goodness of things, but is moved by it as by its object, our love, whereby we will good to anything, is not the cause of its goodness; but conversely, its goodness, whether real or imaginary, calls forth our love, by which we will that it should preserve the good it has, and receive besides the good it has not, and to this end we direct our actions: whereas the love of God infuses and creates goodness.[100]

This love for creation derives more originally from the love God has for his own divine essence, a love existing eternally as a dimension of his own sapiential contemplation. Because God knows of his own goodness and loves it, so also he can will to create freely finite beings as an expression of this love, so that the latter might participate (however imperfectly) in his own goodness and perfection.[101] Only if we believe in a God who is love

---

[98] Aquinas understands this as the reason for the supreme happiness, or beatitude, of God in *ST* I, q. 26, aa. 1–2.

[99] In *ST* I, q. 19, a. 2, Aquinas argues that the self-communication of divine goodness, through the act of creation and the gift of grace, is befitting on account of God's pure actuality and supreme goodness. However, in aa. 3–5, he clarifies why on account of this same pure actuality and supreme perfection, God's act of creation cannot be necessary. (The latter idea amounts to a metaphysical impossibility.)

[100] *ST* I, q. 20, a. 2.

[101] In *ST* I, q. 6, a. 4, Aquinas qualifies this statement in an Aristotelian fashion. After criticizing the Platonic theory of forms he writes: "Everything is therefore called good from the divine goodness, as from the first exemplary, effective and

as pure actuality can we also believe in creation as a radically unnecessary free act. Only if creation is an uncoerced free act can we in turn understand created existence as a true gift. Consequently, only then can we believe that the existence of creatures is undergirded by an omnipresent, and omniscient, but truly incomprehensible love.

Sapientia and the Final End of Man

I have stated above that the principal two modern objections to natural theology are (1) the philosophical claim that by recourse to it we may derive no knowledge of God that is not based upon some kind of a priori intuition (a problematic ontotheology), and (2) the theological claim that our attempts to derive such natural knowledge necessarily render obscure our need for divine revelation. However, in the account of analogical knowledge of God that I have given above, both of these dangers have been avoided. The positive statements concerning the wisdom of God are based upon a posteriori demonstrations of God's existence as pure actuality and the analogical manner of thinking to which it gives rise, rather than an aprioristic account of God's identity, or a (dialectically posited) refusal of all positive knowledge of God. However, this claim should not be allowed to obscure the fact that such knowledge is made through the dark veil—not of faith—but of indirect and inferential reason. We may say that God is wise, and something of what God's wisdom is, in its simplicity, perfection, truthfulness, and love. However, we do not know "what" the wisdom of God that created the world is in itself. We do not perceive it in an immediate way, nor can we define it conceptually in a quidditative fashion. Aquinas goes so far as to say that if creatures resemble God's wisdom through their being caused by him, God does not for that reason resemble creatures.[102] Therefore, the knowledge acquired by this form of philosophical reflection does not proceed from the premise that no further knowledge of God is possible or desirable. In fact, it would serve philosophically to establish the contrary of both these insinuations.

As a consequence, the aspiration to knowledge of God in human persons leaves us before a twofold conclusion as concerns human nature.[103]

---

final principle of all goodness. Nevertheless, everything is called good by reason of the similitude of the divine goodness belonging to it, which is formally its own goodness, whereby it is denominated good."

[102] *ST* I, q. 4, a. 3, ad 4.

[103] A number of comments may be in order here for readers who may consider the following paragraphs from a Christian theological perspective. First, it should be kept in mind that I am claiming here only to offer reflections upon nature philosophically (derived from common human experience and the natural powers of reason) rather than theologically (by appeal to divine revelation). As Hans Urs Von

On the one hand, we are naturally structured such that we are intellectually inclined to seek to know God. Based upon the knowledge we can acquire of the existence of God, we can acquire an understanding of what we are made for, and in doing so attain an imperfect but real spiritual happiness. On the other hand, even the most developed natural knowledge of God is of such an imperfect character that the mystery of God in himself remains utterly beyond our experience and comprehension. The knowledge and felicity such an approach provides remains on some level unsatisfying. However, *because* we can acquire an indirect, imperfect knowledge of God, *consequently*, we can *also* desire naturally even to know God as he is in himself, that is to say, by an immediate, more perfect knowledge. Therefore we may naturally desire what we cannot achieve by our own powers. From a *philosophical* point of view, then, we can conclude that only a new initiative of divine self-revelation (what in fact Christian theology calls the grace of

Balthasar has rightly pointed out, a Christian can reflect upon nature in distinctly philosophical and theological ways, such that the principles and conclusions of each perspective are complementary and mutually influential to one another, but not identical (*The Theology of Karl Barth*, 273). I take it that Aquinas does this regularly. Second, and most importantly, I am making claims about the *structure* of human nature per se, and *not* about its *concrete historical state*, under the destructive effects of sin, and the healing effects of grace. In other words, I am presuming that there are capacities proper to human nature that do not need grace in order to exist, and that the capacity to know God and even to desire God as one's true final end is one of these. However, in the concrete historical state of fallen and redeemed humanity, such capacities *in order to be exercised properly, or perhaps at all*, may well stand in need of the healing and corrective effects of grace and revelation. Therefore, it is possible that the Thomistic philosophical understanding of human persons I am appealing to might never have come into being concretely outside of a culture in which receptivity to divine revelation existed, and due to the workings of grace. Nevertheless, it is a distinctly *philosophical* understanding, based upon natural powers. There can remain a distinct kind of natural happiness (albeit a very imperfect one) derived from the philosophical consideration of God, even within the realm of faith. Third, even if (according to Aquinas) non-Christians have attained to some true knowledge of God—sometimes through philosophical reflection—this knowledge was frequently admixed with errors, and led to forms of religious practice that were inimical to the true Christian worship of God (*In Ioan.* XVII, lec. 2, 2195; lec. 6, 2265). In our fallen state, according to Aquinas's anti-Pelagian writing, a *natural* love of God above all things is impossible without grace (*ST* I–II, q. 109, aa. 1–4). This means that in the concrete historical order, in order to recognize God as one's true final end *even naturally*, some kind of *supernatural* grace of God (that itself implies—but is not limited to—the gift of supernatural faith) is necessary. Last, it should go without saying that the natural knowledge of and desire for God are in no way a substitute (according to Aquinas or Catholic doctrine) for the activity of justifying faith, informed by charity, and the revealed knowledge of God that accompanies this faith (*ST* I–II, q. 109, aa. 5–10). The latter alone leads to salvation. Our wounded natural capacity for God, therefore, can *in no way* procure for us the gift of justification or salvation.

the beatific vision) can fulfill *entirely*—yet gratuitously—our own deepest wellsprings of desire for the truth.[104]

In conclusion of this chapter I will note briefly, then, three characteristics of human, philosophical wisdom understood in light of our consideration of God's wisdom (*in via judicii*, considering the effect in light of its cause). First, human knowledge of God is a participated wisdom, tending toward the truth and love of God himself. By its very nature it is capable of giving ultimate teleological meaning to all other human intellectual sciences and ethical pursuits, even while respecting the integrity of each of the latter. Second, this wisdom opens from within, toward the desire for a yet more perfect knowledge of God, thus signaling as a metaphysical truth that human beings are capable by nature of the desire to see God. Third, the philosophical consideration of the natural desire for God allows us to better understand authentic divine revelation in Christ as a gratuitous gift that transcends the range of all human natural capacities or expectations, yet simultaneously fulfills by superabundance the intrinsic aspirations of the human person.

The first point follows from a consideration of human reason in light of divine reason. Because human beings are spiritual animals, being in themselves rational and free, they bear within themselves an intrinsic similitude of divine wisdom through their operations of knowledge and voluntary love. We should therefore understand human aspirations to truth and love analogically after the paradigm of a transcendent model, or divine exemplar. While God is necessarily wise and loving in his ineffable

---

[104] In saying these things I am of course touching upon the famous controversy over the question of Henri de Lubac's interpretation of Aquinas, represented principally in *Surnaturel* and *Le mystère du surnaturel* (Paris: Aubier, 1965). It is not my intention here, however, to discuss any aspect of this controversy, which is for the most part a *distinctly theological* and historical one. De Lubac claims at points that there exists in human beings a "natural desire for the supernatural" or for the beatitude promised by divine grace, in Christ. For an important critical appraisal of De Lubac's work, see Lawrence Feingold's *The Natural Desire to See God according to St. Thomas Aquinas and His Interpreters* (Dissertation, Rome, 2001). I will, however, touch upon the controversy peripherally by speaking from a *philosophical* point of view about what kinds of conclusions one might arrive at based upon the intrinsic structure of Aquinas's metaphysical reasoning. In what sense does the created spirit naturally desire to know God, and why? The viewpoint I am offering does in fact align quite closely with the theological positions of some who have written on the "surnaturel" controversy, especially the French Dominican Marie-Joseph Le Guillou ("Surnaturel," *Revue des Sciences Philosophiques et Théologiques* 34 [1950]: 226–43), as well as the more recent study of Georges Cottier, *Le Désir de Dieu; Sur Les Traces de Saint Thomas* (Paris: Parole et Silence, 2002). For a helpful theological treatment of the issue that discusses the position of these authors, see Reinhard Hütter, *Desiring God: The Natural Desire for the Vision of God according to Thomas Aquinas, an Essay in Catholic Theology* (Naples, FL: Sapientia Press, forthcoming).

essence, we may become wise and loving by means of a progressive acquisition of intellectual and moral virtues. The latter are, in us, "accidental"
properties that qualify what we are teleologically but do not alter us substantially. However, whereas God has the knowledge and love of *himself* as
his final end, the human person is most perfect through the pursuit of the
knowledge and love *of God.* Because the human person is open to the universal good, and the universal truth about things, he or she is also capable
by nature of aspiring to the knowledge of the cause of all being and goodness, God himself. Articulating this viewpoint in terms of the biblical
notion of human beings as made in the image of God, Aquinas writes:

> Since man is said to be to the image of God by reason of his intellec-
> tual nature, he is the most perfectly like God according to that in
> which he can best imitate God in his intellectual nature. Now the
> intellectual nature imitates God chiefly in this, that God understands
> and loves himself. Wherefore we see that the image of God is in man
> in three ways. First, inasmuch as man possesses *a natural aptitude* for
> understanding and loving God; and this aptitude consists *in the very
> nature of the mind,* which is common to all men. Secondly, inasmuch
> as man actually or habitually knows and loves God, though imper
> fectly; and this image consists in the conformity of grace. Thirdly,
> inasmuch as man knows and love God perfectly; and this image con-
> sists in the likeness of glory.[105]

Such an explicit affirmation of the *distinctly natural* range of human knowledge ("a natural aptitude") within the context of a properly *theological* discussion is striking. It shows that Aquinas in his theological writing presupposes
a subjacent metaphysical vision of the human person's natural capacity for
God. The created intellect necessarily has a teleological inclination toward
God as a *natural final end* that perfects the human person. And if the human
being is naturally capable of perceiving such knowledge as an end, then he or
she can also choose to purposefully organize the conclusions of the lesser or
lower sciences of human reason in light of the knowledge of God.[106] He or
she can also (in principle) subordinate prudentially the pursuit of all practical ends to the consideration of the supreme goodness of God.[107] Consequently, from a Thomistic point of view, all speculative sciences and practical

---

[105] *ST* I–II, q. 93, a. 4 (emphasis added).
[106] *ScG* I, c. 1: "The name of the absolutely wise man is reserved for him whose consideration is directed [not to any particular end, but] to the end of the universe,
which is also the origin of the universe. That is why, according to the Philosopher
[*A*, 1, 981b28], it belongs to the wise man to consider the highest causes."
[107] As I have alluded to above, Aquinas affirms unambiguously in *ST* I–II, q. 109, a. 3,
that human beings are capable by their natural power of a natural love of God

activities are in some way capable of participating in human philosophical wisdom, just as human philosophical wisdom is itself a finite participation in the ordering wisdom of God.[108]

What is significant about this view is that it suggests that man's natural aspiration toward God is in no way extrinsic to *any* basic human activity of knowledge and love. Rather, any and all of the lesser forms of knowledge and practical activity that characterize human culture are potentially subject to a *distinctly philosophical* unification from above, through the discernment that all things come from God and that the rational creature is naturally capable of a certain kind of return toward God. The understanding of creatures in light of God (wisdom in its descending dimension, or *via judicii*) therefore places in perspective the ultimate role of all other forms of human knowledge and action, supplying the latter not with their own proper objects (since the object of each science or practical activity is unique), but giving these, rather, their most ultimate meaning, and ethical purpose.[109] Furthermore, if this natural

---

above all created things. However, he also makes clear that in the fallen state of man, this natural capacity cannot be rightly developed and exercised without the activity of redemptive grace. Yet, within the concrete historical economy of grace, a distinctly natural form of thinking about the final end of the human person may be "rediscovered," and may rightly identify God as the natural final end of human acts, even philosophically.

[108] *ST* I–II, q. 66, a. 5: "The greatness of a virtue, as to its species, is taken from its object. Now the object of wisdom surpasses the objects of all the intellectual virtues: because wisdom considers the supreme cause, which is God, as stated at the beginning of the *Metaphysics*. And since it is by the cause that we judge of an effect, and by the higher cause that we judge of the lower effects, hence it is that wisdom exercises judgment over all the other intellectual virtues [including practical prudence], directs them all, and is the architect of them all."

[109] Aquinas speaks of this "judgment" of wisdom in *ST* I–II, q. 57, a. 2, c., and ad 1: "Wisdom considers the highest causes . . . wherefore it rightly judges all things and sets them in order, because there can be no perfect and universal judgment that is not based upon the first." It is important to note, however, that for both Aristotle and Aquinas, every science treats a given object, and cannot be supplanted by another (even higher) discipline, just as say, a metaphysician could not, by virtue of his metaphysical science, judge directly the merits of the (very good) genetic and paleological evidence for the evolution of organic species. For that he or she would have to study the biological evidence. "But in regard to that which is last in this or that genus of knowable matter, it is science [*scientia*] that perfects the intellect. Wherefore according to the different kinds of knowable matter, there are different habits of scientific knowledge; whereas there is but one wisdom." Philosophical wisdom alone treats the highest causes and principles of all things. Therefore, it judges all other sciences, not only by defending their first principles (the first principles of metaphysical realism discussed in chapter 7), but also by judging their conclusions in light of the first cause and supreme good, God. Metaphysical theology, for example,

aspiration toward wisdom is in fact "assumed and fulfilled" by the higher wisdom of revelation, then there need not be any extrinsic relationship between the human aspiration toward the Trinitarian God made possible by grace and the realm of natural knowledge and practical action. Rather, the former order of grace can assume the operations of human action teleologically, by virtue of the sapiential dimension of the person, his or her natural locus of orientation toward God.[110]

Second, this natural knowledge of God is characterized by a passage from effects to a transcendent cause, and in this sense is a mediated, indirect knowledge, which remains deeply imperfect. However, this same knowledge by its very nature alerts us to the truth that there is a primary origin and giver of existence *who is not known immediately.* By consequence, in its very structure such indirect and imperfect knowledge can give rise to the *natural* desire to know the principal cause of all that is *in a non-mediated* and *direct* way. That is to say, metaphysical theology makes possible the *philosophical* justification of the natural human desire to know God as he is in himself.[111] Aquinas insists upon this point in multiple texts where he defends by arguments of *philosophical reason* the possibility of the beatific vision. In doing so he argues that because the human person is capable of natural knowledge of God based upon effects, he or she may know of the existence of a transcendent cause. However:

---

might permit one to consider the ontological presuppositions of evolution: i.e., the ways in which God's creative agency maintains in being and governs the evolution of living species, or what evolution can tell us, or cannot tell us, about natural kinds.

[110] Aquinas discusses the higher *sapientia of sacra doctrina* in *ST* I, q. 1, aa. 5 and 6, and makes clear (q. 1, a. 5, ad 2) that theological reflection both can and should make use of the legitimate conclusions and processes of philosophical, scientific, moral reasoning that are derived from natural human reflection. It does so without itself proving their conclusions (a. 6, ad 2), but rather by judging of them in light of ultimate revealed truths. Aquinas's doctrine of the infused virtues as graces that orient natural human virtues toward supernatural ends also reposes upon the presupposition of a higher wisdom of grace that assumes a lower structure of nature intrinsically capable of being ordered toward God. (See, for example, *ST* I–II, q. 63, a. 3.)

[111] I am affirming here a *natural* desire to know the first cause immediately, as distinct from either a natural or supernatural desire specified by a supernatural object, i.e., desire for the beatific vision due to the explicit recognition of the truth of the Catholic faith, etc. This need not mean that in man's concrete fallen state such a natural desire to know God might ever be *elicited* in an effective way without the instigation of grace. That is a distinct question, concerning the need for grace in fallen human beings that they might regain the power to act virtuously, according to their own natural capacities. Independently of the question of *whether* a person might acquire the virtue of philosophical wisdom independently of the activity of grace (or was ever meant to, if human beings were created in a state of grace originally), the object, capacity, and end of such a virtue are natural.

> So great is the desire for knowledge within us that, once we appre-
> hend an effect, we wish to know its cause. Moreover, after we have
> gained some knowledge of the circumstances investing a thing, our
> desire is not satisfied until we penetrate to its essence. Therefore our
> natural desire for knowledge cannot come to rest within us until we
> know the first cause, and that not in any way, but in its very essence.
> This first cause is God. Consequently, the ultimate end of an intel-
> lectual creature is the vision of God in his essence. [112]

Controversy exists over whether passages such as this one affirm a natural
inclination toward the supernatural grace of beatitude (the position of De
Lubac), or rather a natural tendency in the human intellect to desire the
immediate knowledge of the first truth (the classical Dominican position).
My own view is the latter. However, at least one thing remains incontrovert-
ible. Because the mind is capable of knowing God as a transcendent, but
undisclosed, cause, it is also naturally capable of desiring to know God as he
is in himself. And in this way, natural knowledge of God leads to a terminus
that is both a kind of natural perfection and an intrinsically incomplete act.
That is to say, we can achieve imperfect happiness through the natural
knowledge of God. For in knowing the effects (and the cause through the
effects), the human person attains to a kind of wisdom (the knowledge of
the primary cause of being). Yet by the same measure, this person also
wishes to know the cause *in itself*, that is to say, the *essence* of the cause. [113]

   This leads us to the third and final point. If human beings are naturally
open to God's own life and mystery, then they are ontologically capable of
receiving from God a grace-filled accomplishment that their own nature
does not necessitate or exact. However, authentic divine revelation, if it orients the human person toward a more intimate knowledge of God, is not
something purely extrinsic to the nature of the human person either. The
latter point follows from all that has been said above. Because we are capable
of a kind of elicited or explicit sapiential, positive knowledge of God *that is
imperfect*, so too are we capable of recognizing ourselves as beings who both
know and desire God, but who do not know God as we desire. Therefore,

---

[112] *Comp. Theol.*, c. 104. Employing this same argument in *ST* I, q. 12, a. 1, Aquinas
makes clear that he considers it an argument from natural reason. See also *De ver.*,
q. 8, a. 1; *ScG* III, c. 51, 54, 57; *In Ioan.*, c. 1, lec. 11.

[113] Aquinas claims that the imperfect knowledge of God accorded by philosophical
wisdom does give to the human soul a certain kind of natural happiness or felicity, albeit one which is "imperfect." In this sense he can speak of a twofold end of
the human being: to imperfect beatitude through natural, philosophical contemplation and to perfect beatitude through the supernatural grace of the beatific
vision by which we may see the essence of God. See on this *Expos. de Trin.*, q. 6,
a. 4, ad 3; *ScG* I, c. 2; *ST* I–II, q. 3, a. 6, and Te Velde, *Aquinas on God*, 155–60.

the human person is in some real sense *philosophically* comprehensible as a being who might potentially transcend itself through a living encounter with God effectuated by the mystery of grace.[114] The order of wisdom is not only an analogical order "on the way down" toward inferior sciences that it can order toward God. It is also an analogical science "on the way up" toward the claims of divine revelation and the Christian encounter with the mystery of God. Philosophy at its extreme edges, in other words, gives warrant to the eschatological aspirations of Christian revelation and makes the latter rationally intelligible under certain aspects.[115]

If philosophical wisdom demonstrates man's natural openness to the mystery of God, then, it also can affect our theological understanding of the work of grace in the human person. The revelation of God in Christ is given to human beings by the grace of faith, but this faith does have a point of contact in human nature wherein the grace of faith elicits a graced response to God. Clearly it is *both* our natural openness to God *and* the consciousness of its intrinsic limitations that render us capable of receiving the grace of God. Without the former, the complementarity of grace and nature would not be possible. If there is not an ontologically presupposed point of contact for grace within nature (a natural structure in us at least capable of tending toward God teleologically under grace), then grace cannot act upon our intrinsic personal life, actions, and desires as intellectual and voluntary agents. If nature cannot recognize its own intrinsic limitations, however, then it cannot cooperate with the reception of grace as a gift, and the distinction between grace and nature will become indecipherable for it. Therefore, if the pursuit of philosophical wisdom is *in no way* a sufficient or necessary condition for the graced recognition of divine revelation as such (Eph 2:8: "For it is by grace that you have been saved through faith"), nevertheless, it does help us see "after the fact'—that is to say, *within* Christian theological interpretation—how our created human nature is truly capable of a graced state of being. The aspiration to such wisdom is not a form of "epistemological works righteousness."[116] And why should it be any more than the labor of Christian theology (which is after all an epistemological work), of which it can form an integrated, if distinguishable, part? Nor is it a *theologia gloriae*, a theology of glory. For as

---

[114] My underlying presupposition, taken from M. J. Le Guillou, is that the natural tendency in us toward imperfect beatitude is an ontological condition in the creature for the possibility of the communication of divine beatitude by grace. Because we may aspire naturally to the perfect knowledge of God, the grace of the vision fulfills an intrinsic dimension of ourselves gratuitously. Both forms of "beatitude" are gifts of God that may complement each other, then, though the latter is infinitely greater than the former.

[115] See the arguments to this effect by Aquinas in *ScG* III, c. 147.

[116] The phrase is that of Robert Jenson.

Aquinas insists upon so forcefully and profoundly, the glory of God remains hidden and utterly incomprehensible to the natural light of human reason. In fact, it would be better to say the inverse: metaphysical apophaticism intensifies our recognition of the transcendence of God, and correspondingly makes us acutely aware of the limitations of our human knowledge. Within the life of grace, the deepened philosophical understanding of this aspect of our human condition is consistent with and disposes us to a deeper recognition of the gift of redemption. It should thereby make more evident to us the supreme goodness of the initiative of God who gave us in his freedom—and through no merit of our own, but rather despite ourselves—to "behold the glory of the Lord" (2 Cor 3:18). And this not by our own efforts, but by grace alone, through the Trinitarian life of Christ, crucified and glorified.

A

Philosophical Wisdom and the Final End of Man

Thomas Aquinas and the Paradigm of Nature-Grace Orthodoxy

The two most influential paradigms in modern theology concerning the relationship of grace to nature are at opposite extremes of the spectrum, and yet the extremes touch in their criticism of Thomism as it is exposited in the classical Dominican tradition.

On the one hand, there is the influential view of Karl Barth, whose radical vision of the extrinsic transcendence of grace to nature was paired with an equally radical—some would say dialectical—disavowal of any predisposition or potential inclination in human nature for the gift of divine life. On the other hand, there is the vision of Henri de Lubac in his *Surnaturel*, which charts the idea of an inclination toward the supernatural inscribed in the human spirit from its creation, such that we are always and everywhere animated by a latent natural desire for the gratuitous gift of supernatural beatitude, the vision of God. One paradigm sees in man no natural point of contact (*Anknüpfungspunkt*) upon which grace might act to elevate him beyond his own natural capacities (such that grace must itself create in human nature the very conditions for its own reception).[1] The other sees in man's natural capacities an innate—we might say inherent—inclination toward divine life, a life that is provided by grace alone, such that man is an enigma or paradox of natural desiring for that which grace alone can disclose and resolve.[2]

Originally published as "Imperfect Happiness and the Final End of Man: Thomas Aquinas and the Paradigm of Nature-Grace Orthodoxy," *The Thomist* 78 (2014): 247–89. Reprinted by permission.

[1] See Karl Barth, *Church Dogmatics* 1/1, trans. G. W. Bromiley (London and New York: T&T Clark, 2003), 27–36.

[2] Henri de Lubac, *Surnaturel: Études historiques* (Paris: Aubier, 1946), 231–60, 433–34; "Duplex hominis beatitudo (Saint Thomas, I-II, q. 62, a. 1)," *Recherches de science religieuse* 35

There are nuances to the positions that both Barth and de Lubac developed on these matters over the course of their careers. Both paradigms maintain important forms of opposition to the classical Dominican tradition, however, and not least because of the Aristotelian character of its interpretation of Aquinas on the matter of the final end of man. The Barthian paradigm perceives with distrust the attempt by Thomists to demonstrate a natural openness to God by way of the philosophical ascent to God through metaphysical analysis of created being and through a corresponding reflection on the natural final end of man as made in some real way for the contemplation and love of God.[3] The other paradigm sees this same metaphysics and anthropology as, if not theologically illicit, then at least as potentially misleading, particularly as interpreted by figures such as Thomas de Vio Cajetan, Sylvester of Ferrara, and Domingo Báñez.[4] The reason for this is that it risks formulating the notion of an autonomous human nature, knowledge of God, and natural beatitude that have their own rational integrity in distinction from (and therefore over and against) a uniquely supernatural explanation of the final end of man (the grace of the beatific vision) that alone explains the deeper meaning of the structure of human nature.[5] By contrast, de Lubac is famous for claiming that human nature is ultimately unintelligible and existentially inexplicable except in reference to grace.[6] He contrasts Ca-

---

(1948): 290–99; *The Mystery of the Supernatural*, trans. Rosemary Sheed (New York: Herder and Herder, 1998), 55–56, 140–66.

3 On Barth's mistrust of the analogy of being as the "invention of the anti-Christ," see *Church Dogmatics* 1/1, xiii, 40–42, 69, 119–20, 239–40; see also Bruce L. McCormack, "Karl Barth's Version of an 'Analogy of Being': A Dialectical No and Yes to Roman Catholicism," in *The Analogy of Being: Invention of the Anti-Christ or the Wisdom of God?*, ed. Thomas Joseph White (Grand Rapids, MI: Eerdmans, 2010), 88–144; Bruce L. McCormack, *Karl Barth's Critically Realistic Dialectical Theology: Its Genesis and Development, 1909–1936* (New York: Oxford University Press, 1995).

4 See, for example, de Lubac, *Surnaturel*, 153–54, 174–75, 437; *Mystery of the Supernatural*, 68–74, 157–59, 194. One can identify common themes in texts of Dominican commentators on Aquinas such as Cajetan's commentary on *ST* I, q. 78, a. 1, n. 5 (Leonine ed., 5:252); *ST* I-II, q. 3, a. 8 (Leonine ed., 6:36); Sylvester of Ferrara's commentary on *ScG* III, c. 51 (Leonine ed., 14:140–43); Domingo Báñez, *Scholastica commentaria in primam partem*, q. 12, a. 1 (Valencia: Biblioteca de Tomistas Españoles, 1934), 248–51. Despite the nuances between these diverse thinkers, the conceptual continuity between them on this topic offers enough unity to form what might be called a theological "tradition," followed in turn by subsequent Thomist commentators. De Lubac himself presupposes the existence of a conceptual continuity between these diverse authors, with whom he takes issue.

5 See, for instance, de Lubac, *Surnaturel*, 101–28, 226–92.

6 De Lubac, *Mystery of the Supernatural*, 54–55: "For this desire [for supernatural beatitude] is not some 'accident' in me. It does not result from some peculiarity, possibly alterable, of my individual being, or from some historical contingency whose effects are more or less transitory. *A fortiori* it does not in any sense depend upon my deliberate will. It is in me as a result of my belonging to humanity as it is, that humanity which is, as we say, 'called.' For God's call is constitutive. My finality, which is expressed by this desire, is inscribed upon my very being as

jetan the Aristotelian with Aquinas on this point. Cajetan argued—following Aristotle—that every nature is inclined to a proportionate natural end, while Aquinas saw that our human nature is naturally ordered toward the formally supernatural as such.[7] It follows from Aquinas's viewpoint that human beings cannot come to know their natural end by means of philosophical analysis or argument, but only through the medium of divine revelation, because it is a supernatural mystery.[8]

We might note here the extreme difference between these two positions. While one side condemns the tradition of Aristotelian-inspired anthropology for its excess of ambition regarding natural knowledge and love of God, the other side condemns it for its inherent deficit or lack, as the natural inclination is seen to be ordered only to a naturally proportionate end and not to supernatural beatitude as such. One side argues that the Thomistic tradition cannot account sufficiently for the *extrinsic* transcendence of grace to nature, while the other side claims that it does not account sufficiently for the *intrinsic* directedness of nature to grace. What these two specifically opposed extremes share by way of a common genus of presupposition is a conviction that the classical Thomistic tradition fails to safeguard a balanced sense of grace-nature extrinsicism and nature-grace intrinsicism.

In this appendix, I argue that both these approaches have failed to perceive the balance and integrity of the Thomistic grace-nature paradigm, and that its unique strength can be identified by way of the points of emphasis these other traditions seek themselves to safeguard, each in mutual opposition to the other. That is to say, Barthians attempt rightly to uphold the transcendence and gratuity of grace vis-à-vis all natural dispositions or inclinations in human persons, while de Lubacians rightly wish to underscore the deeply congruent rapport of nature's inner aspirations and the teleological promptings of grace, sealed within one concrete economic provi-

---

it has been put into this universe by God." Note that the call of grace is constitutive of human nature in concrete human history.

[7] Ibid., 154–59.

[8] Ibid., 208–9: "But is the desire for the beatific vision really, in its full nature and force, able to be known by reason alone? This I do not believe.... I want to remain firmly within theology. I am not trying to establish a philosophical thesis, but to study a dogmatic thesis and all that it implies.... I do not say that the knowledge gained by reason of a natural desire, outside any context of faith, 'proves strictly that we are called to the beatific vision,' and that therefore we can naturally attain 'the certainty that we have been created for that end'; on the contrary I say that the knowledge that is revealed to us of that calling, which makes us certain of that end, leads us to recognize within ourselves the existence and nature of that desire." Note the claim here that the final natural end of man is the beatific vision as such, and therefore it cannot be known except by way of divine revelation. As Lawrence Feingold has noted (*The Natural Desire to See God According to St. Thomas Aquinas and His Interpreters* [Naples, FL: Sapientia Press, 2010], 307–9), de Lubac had changed his position on this point, arguing earlier in *Surnaturel* (467–69 n. D) that the supernatural end of the human person was in some sense philosophically demonstrable. I return to the significance of this issue below.

dence of God with respect to spiritual creatures. Both appeal to divergent extremes of Augustinian notions of grace: the sheer gratuity of salvation with regard to any human effort versus the theme of the restless heart that can only be healed and saved by grace. But both of these respective truths need to be corrected in correlation to each other and are capable of being harmonized precisely by recourse to a certain kind of *philosophical* reading of Aquinas regarding the final end of man.

In order to analyze and argue for this point of view, I focus in particular upon Aquinas's interpretation of Aristotelian contemplation of God via natural causes as a form of "imperfect natural happiness." I argue that by his treatment of the philosophical demonstrability of the imperfection of this form of happiness, Aquinas makes clear two corresponding points. First, the natural desire for the vision of God is a rational, philosophical desire and is distinct from the hope for the beatific vision inspired by infused theological virtues, but *just for this reason*, the latter grace is not extrinsic to the former natural disposition and desire. Here Aristotelianism allows Aquinas to avoid a pure grace-nature extrinsicism of the kind de Lubacians can rightly criticize in Barthians. Second, yet for this very reason (i.e., because a teleological openness to God is inscribed in our nature), the pursuit of our natural end is not indicative of any natural inclination toward the formally supernatural as such. Grace remains entirely transcendent of our natural powers, innate inclinations, and proportionate ends. Here Aristotelianism allows Aquinas to avoid a pure grace-nature intrinsicism of the kind Barthians might rightly be concerned about in the writings of de Lubac. Thomism is not an eccentric form of Catholic theological teaching with respect to the paradigm of grace-nature orthodoxy. Rather, this form of Aristotelian-influenced Christianity is also deeply Augustinian: it stands at the core of the tradition and best articulates its diverse tensions in a congruent unity.

Aquinas on Imperfect Happiness and Aristotelian-Inspired Christianity

What precisely Aristotle understands to be the perfect happiness proper to human nature is among the most historically contested topics of ancient philosophy, subject to a subtle variety of interpretations.[9] Nevertheless, despite all the interpretive

---

9 Denis J. M. Bradley offers a helpful introduction to the scope of interpictive problems of Aristotle on the subject of happiness in *Aquinas on the Twofold Human Good* (Washington, DC: The Catholic University of America Press, 1997), 369–423. See also Carlo Natali, *The Wisdom of Aristotle* (Albany: State University of New York Press, 2001), who offers a helpful survey of contemporary literature. A classic interpretation that remains pertinent may be found in René Antoine Gauthier and Jean Yves Jolif, *L'Éthique à Nicomaque: Introduction, traduction et commentaire* (Louvain: Publications Universitaires de Louvain; Paris: Éditions Béatrice-Nauwelaerts, 1959), 1:26–88; 2:848–66, 873–99. For interpretations of Aristotle that stress the potential continuity between Aristotle's own affirmations and Aquinas's Aristotelianism, see Ralph McInerny, *Ethica Thomistica: The Moral Philosophy of Thomas Aquinas* (Washington, DC: The Catholic University of America Press, 1997), 12–34; Kevin Flan-

ambiguities, Aristotle in the *Nicomachean Ethics* (Book 10) clearly identifies philosophical contemplation as the greatest source of happiness for the rational being that
man is and interprets this happiness as the act of the highest human virtue, that of
wisdom (Book 6; see also *Metaphysics* 1 and 12).[10] It is for this virtue that the moral and political virtues exist, and it is by it that human beings are turned toward the
consideration of the highest truth, namely, that pertaining to the perennial reality
of God and the separate substances. Consequently, happiness, for Aristotle, consists
not only of an activity that we should desire for its own sake (the act of knowledge
that comes by way of contemplation) but in an activity tending toward that which is
most true and sovereignly good: the goodness of God himself. Happiness therefore
has both a subjective element in the person who is happy and an objective element
stemming from the beatifying reality that the person loves. It is something within us
that characterizes the immanent operation of reason, but it is necessarily directed to
something that transcends us that is the noblest ontological reality itself.[11]

   There are at least three distinct goals that Aquinas has in mind when he comments upon Aristotle on this subject. First, he wishes to acknowledge the delineation

---

nery, "Can an Aristotelian Consider Himself a Friend of God?" in *Virtue's End: God in the
Moral Philosophy of Aristotle and Aquinas*, ed. Fulvio Di Blasi, Joshua P. Hochschild, and Jef-
fery Langan (South Bend, IN: St. Augustine's Press, 2008), 1–12.

10 *Nicomachean Ethics* 10.7.1177a11-1178a8. "If happiness is activity in accordance with excellence [virtue], it is reasonable that it should be in accordance with the highest excellence; and
this will be that of the best thing in us. Whether it be intellect or something else that is this element which is thought to be our natural ruler and guide and to take thought of things noble
and divine, whether it be itself also divine or only the most divine element in us, the activity of
this in accordance with its proper excellence will be complete happiness. This activity is contemplative" (1177a11-18). Note the allusion to the contemplation of the divine as the highest
good of man. Aristotle interprets such speculative wisdom as the highest virtue in *Nicomachean Ethics* 6.7.1141a9-1141b22. Similarly, in *Metaphysics* 1.1-2, wisdom is identified with the
speculative knowledge of the highest causes and principles, namely, God and the separate substances. Aristotle returns to this viewpoint at the end of his inquiries, in *Metaphysics* 12.7 and 9,
where he treats of the life of God as pure actuality and subsistent contemplation. The intellectual life of God is thus analogous to but also different from the act of human speculative understanding. See, for instance, *Metaphysics* 12.7.1072b24-30: "If, then, God is always in that good
state in which we sometimes are, this compels our wonder; and if in a better this compels it yet
more. And God *is* in a better state. And life also belongs to God; for the actuality of thought
is life, and God is that actuality; and God's essential actuality is life most good and eternal. We
say therefore that God is a living being, eternal, most good, so that life and duration continuous
and eternal belong to God; for this *is* God." Translations of Aristotle are taken from *The Complete Works of Aristotle*, ed. Jonathan Barnes (Princeton, NJ: Princeton University Press, 1995).

11 On these points I follow the interpretations of Sir David Ross (*Aristotle* [London: Meu-
then; New York: Barnes & Noble, 1966], 232–34), which are seemingly Christianizing but
also eminently defensible. See, more recently, Aryeh Kosman, "Metaphysics Λ, 9: Divine
Thought," in *Aristotle's* Metaphysics *Lambda*, ed. Michael Frede and David Charles (Oxford:
Clarendon Press, 2000), 307–26, esp. 308–12.

of Aristotle's own arguments, as they are inherent to the logical progression of the Stagirite's reasoning, beginning from his own first principles. This form of analysis is most expressly evidenced in Aquinas's commentary on the *Nicomachean Ethics*, but it is also adopted for his own argumentative use in many other settings, where Aristotelian arguments are employed with the presupposition that they have an integrity and lucidity of their own with an enduring import.[12]

Second, Aquinas is concerned to show by way of his own reformulation of these arguments the truth of what Aristotle teaches, that the human being is naturally inclined to seek a given form of perfection and end that is proper to his rational nature, and that this end is in some sense indicative of the kind of nature that the human being possesses—a human nature capable of happiness through the contemplation of God.[13] Certainly, Aquinas follows Aristotle in arguing that there is a distinctly natural, philosophical wisdom proper to man that is the highest accomplishment of his human nature, whereby he can attain a unique form of happiness or beatitude that is superior to that achieved by way of the moral virtues, but which presupposes the latter as its base and foundation of support.[14] Philosophical wisdom and the happiness that accompanies it are not illusory and do reveal to us something profound about the inner character or essence of what it is to be human, something far from trivial and that holds true not only for non-Christians who lack explicit revelation of God but also for Christians who, though children of God, also remain by nature rational human beings.[15] In fact, one could rightly argue that, because of the grace they receive, Christians are more likely to uncover philosophically this natural potency for God that Aristotle himself rightly but only imperfectly identified.[16]

God in this scenario is not understood in a strictly Aristotelian fashion, howev-

---

12 For Aquinas's analysis of Aristotle's notions of happiness and contemplation, see most notably *In I Ethic.*, lec. 9–18 (Marietti ed., 103–223); *In X Ethic.*, lec. 9–12 (Marietti ed., 2065–125): "the highest of human activities is contemplation of truth; and this is evident from the two reasons by which we judge the excellence of activity. First, on the part of the faculty that is the principle of the activity. This activity is obviously the highest, as the intellect is the best element in us. Second, on the part of the object determining the species of the activity. Here too this activity is the highest because, among the objects that can be known, the suprasensible—especially the divine—are the highest. And so it is in the contemplation of these objects that the perfect happiness of man consists" (*In X Ethic.*, lec. 10 [Marietti ed., 2087], trans. C. I. Litzinger, O.P. [Chicago: Henry Regnery Press, 1964]). Aquinas has recourse to the arguments found in these and other texts of Aristotle in the *Summa contra Gentiles* and the *Summa theologiae*, a point to which I return below.

13 The idea is underscored especially clearly in *ScG* III, c. 37. See also *ST* I-II, q. 3, aa. 3–4; II-II, q. 180, a. 4.

14 See *ST* I-II, q. 3, a. 5, which in turn references arguments from *Nic. Ethics* 10.7 and 8.

15 *ST* I-II, q. 3, a. 6. Aquinas analogously also speaks about the natural contemplation of God in angels in *ST* I, q. 56, a. 3.

16 Consider in this regard the suggestive texts of *ScG* I, cc. 4–5; *ST* I, q. 1, a. 1; and *In Ioan.* 17, lec. 2 (Marietti ed., 2195); lec. 6 (Marietti ed., 2265).

er, but also according to the tradition of classical patristic and medieval Christian monotheism. Aquinas imports much of what Aristotle demonstrates metaphysically regarding God while also expanding and altering the arguments in light of his own distinctive metaphysics of creation and creative analogical reflection on the names or attributes of God.[17] Furthermore, it is certainly the case that the separate substances are not understood in an identical way in the two authors, as Aquinas reinterprets the doctrine of the contemplation of the living prime movers in light of the Christian doctrine of the angels, who are now understood in light of the metaphysics of the real distinction between *esse* and essence, the metaphysical composition that is the congenital sign of their creation from nothing.[18] Philosophical wisdom as a natural virtue exists for Aquinas, assuredly in continuity with that of Aristotle but reformulated within a Christian epoch and interior to a development of philosophy that is harmonious with Christian revelation.

Third, Aquinas reinterprets Aristotle's notion of the natural human happiness that is attained by way of philosophical contemplation of God. He does so in light of his Christian and Augustinian understanding of the grace of the beatific vision of God as the ultimate final end of man, a final end that transcends the limited happiness that human nature can procure for itself.[19] He therefore argues on the one hand that the happiness procured by natural contemplation of God is something real, and that it is proper to man.[20] On the other hand, he argues that as genuine as this form of happiness is, it is nonetheless constitutionally imperfect and open from within to a yet greater or more perfect completion, by way of the vision of God.[21] The reason

---

17 See the helpful, subtle analyses of the Christian reinterpretation of Aristotle in Aquinas's metaphysics by Aimé Forest, *La structure métaphysique du concret* (Paris: Vrin, 1931), esp. 133–66; and by Jan A. Aertsen, *Nature and Creature: Thomas Aquinas' Way of Thought* (Leiden and New York: Brill, 1987).

18 The point is made forcefully in *ST* I, q. 3, a. 4, and *ST* I, q. 50, a. 2, ad 3. See the remarks on Aquinas's angelology in relation to Aristotle's theories of separate substances in Leo Elders, "St. Thomas Aquinas' Commentary on the *Metaphysics* of Aristotle," in *Autour de St. Thomas d'Aquin* (Paris: FAC Éditions, 1987), 134–38.

19 *ST* I-II, q. 3, a. 2, ad 4; I-II, q. 3, a. 8.

20 *ST* I-II, q. 3, a. 6, corp. and ad 1.

21 *ST* I-II, q. 3, a. 5: "the last and perfect happiness, which we await in the life to come, consists entirely in contemplation. But imperfect happiness, such as can be had here, consists first and principally in contemplation, but secondarily in an operation of the practical intellect directing human actions and passions, as stated in *Nicomachean Ethics* X, 7, 8." *ST* I-II, q. 3, a. 6: "man's happiness is two-fold, one perfect, the other imperfect. And by perfect happiness we are to understand that which attains to the true notion of happiness; and by imperfect happiness that which does not attain thereto, but partakes of some particular likeness of happiness.... Accordingly perfect happiness cannot consist essentially in the consideration of speculative sciences ... the entire consideration of the speculative sciences cannot extend farther than knowledge of sensibles can lead. Now man's final happiness, which is his final perfection, cannot consist in the knowledge of sensibles.... Consequently it follows that man's happiness cannot consist in the

for this is that the soul of man is naturally animated by a desire for a yet more perfect knowledge of God, a desire even, if possible, to see the essence of God immediately.[22]

Here is where the complexity enters, in the form of a series of questions that have received varying answers over the years. Does the natural desire for the vision of the essence of God as Aquinas understands it necessarily imply in the rational soul of man an innate inclination toward or orientation to the supernatural grace of the beatific vision? Or does it correspond instead to a natural desire for unmediated knowledge of the first truth that is proper to man's rational faculties? And therefore is it something *philosophically* discernible in prescinding from the consideration of the work of grace as such? Correspondingly, in arguing for the relative perfection of natural contemplative happiness and its relative imperfection in light of the desire to see God, does Aquinas seek to analyze contemplative happiness by means of philosophical arguments as such, or is his analysis of imperfect natural happiness formally constituted by theological reflection?

Answers to these questions depend in part upon how one reads de Lubac's claims. There are good reasons to see in his arguments the affirmation of an innate natural inclination toward the grace of supernatural beatitude as such.[23] If this is the case, and if Aquinas is interpreted in accord with de Lubac, then Aquinas's arguments regarding the final end of man and the imperfection of natural happiness pertain to the consideration of a theological mystery as such, one understood or known of only because of divine revelation, and which must remain transcendent of the natural powers of human reason.

Like Scotus, Toletus, and Soto before him, de Lubac understands there to be an innate natural inclination for the beatific vision inscribed in man, but one he can only know about by grace (thus understanding the teleological structure of his own nature fully only in light of divine revelation).[24] The nature of the human being is in

---

consideration of speculative sciences. However, just as in sensible forms there is a participation of the higher substances, so the consideration of speculative sciences is a certain participation of true and perfect happiness." Translations of the *Summa theologiae* are taken from *Summa Theologica*, trans. English Dominican Province (New York: Benziger Brothers, 1920; reprint, 1947).

[22] *ST* I-II, q. 3, a. 8: "If the human intellect, knowing the essence of some created effect, knows no more of God than *that He is*, the perfection of that intellect does not yet reach simply the First Cause, but there remains in it the natural desire to seek the cause. Wherefore it is not yet perfectly happy. Consequently, for perfect happiness the intellect needs to reach the very essence of the First Cause. And thus it will have its perfection through union with God as with that object, in which alone man's happiness consists."

[23] De Lubac, *Mystery of the Supernatural*, 55: "My finality, which is expressed by this desire, is inscribed upon my very being as it has been put into this universe by God.... In other words, the real problem, if problem it is, involves the being whose finality is 'already,' if one can say so, wholly supernatural—for such is the case with us." Ibid., 76: "Upon this being he has given me, God has imprinted a supernatural finality; he has made to be heard within my nature a call to see him."

[24] For a helpful study of the history of this position, see Feingold, *Natural Desire to See God*,

this respect an unintelligible paradox decrypted only by revelation in Christ.[25] Denis Bradley, in keeping with de Lubac's perspective, therefore argues that the critique Aquinas makes, of Aristotelian natural happiness as "imperfect," is itself a merely dialectical argument regarding the limits of any non-Christian, naturalistic conception of human ends.[26] What emerges from this treatment of the question is a kind of Blondelian reading of Aquinas: philosophy operates apologetically under the influence of theology, to show itself open from within to the specific aims of a higher science, that of divine revelation.[27] The *méthode d'immanence* of Blondel was employed

---

esp. chaps. 4, 10, and 14. De Lubac insists on the alignment of his views with the historical positions of Scotus, Soto, and Toletus, as his numerous citations of their positions in both *Surnaturel* and *Mystery of the Supernatural* make clear.

25 De Lubac, *Mystery of the Supernatural*, 167: "We are creatures, and have been given the promise that we shall see God. The desire to see him is in us, it constitutes us, and yet it comes to us as a completely free gift. Such paradoxes should not surprise us, for they arise in every mystery; they are the hallmark of a truth that is beyond our depth." De Lubac is making a twofold claim here: (1) that we cannot be fulfilled in the innate tendencies of our natural inclinations except by a supernatural good and (2) that we cannot know this about ourselves except through faith in the supernatural revelation of Christianity. It follows that our deepest *natural* constitution and inclination are not discernible or ultimately intelligible except in light of faith and divine revelation. Were there natural arguments for this uniquely supernatural end, there would be the possibility of a purely rational demonstration of a revealed mystery, an idea that, as noted above, de Lubac unambiguously disavows in his later work.

26 Bradley, *Aquinas on the Twofold Human Good*, 395–404, 424–81. The radicality of Bradley's views fully emerges at the end of the book (ibid., 514–34). "Is Aquinas's argument for the endlessness [i.e., purposelessness] of human nature philosophically cogent? The Thomistic argument is 'dialectical': it begins with an Aristotelian tenet about nature, that a nature must be able to attain its proper end and satisfaction, but it demonstrates that, in fact, human nature cannot reach its own ultimate perfection or completion in any naturally attainable end. The conclusion of the Thomistic argument is not that man actually has a supernatural end but that human nature has no ultimately satisfying natural end and that unless a supernatural end (the vision of God) is possible and can be achieved men are creatures made 'in vain.' Human nature, so Aquinas reasons, has no satisfying end and, in that sense, no ultimate natural end; it is, in other words, naturally 'endless'" (ibid., 520).

27 The argument is particularly pronounced in Blondel's thesis from 1893. See Maurice Blondel, *Action (1893): Essay on a Critique of Life and a Science of Practice*, trans. O. Blanchette (Notre Dame, IN: University of Notre Dame Press, 2007), 357: "Absolutely impossible and absolutely necessary for man, that is properly the notion of the supernatural. Man's action goes beyond man; and all the effort of his reason is to see that he cannot, that he must not restrict himself to it [i.e., natural reason]. A deeply felt expectation of an unknown messiah; a baptism of desire, which human science lacks the power to evoke, because this need is itself a gift. Science can show its necessity; it cannot give it birth. Indeed, if we have to found a real society and cooperate with God, how could we presume to succeed in doing so without recognizing that God remains the sovereign master of his gift and of his operation? A necessary admission, but one that ceases to be efficacious, if we do not call on the unknown mediator or if we close ourselves off from the revealed savior." Note that this conclusion is offered as the term of a philosophical argument.

to demonstrate that certain philosophical questions, when pursued loyally, can only be answered theologically, and even reveal the hidden presence of grace evoking in philosophical reason an implicit search for the supernatural. At that point, as both Reginald Garrigou-Lagrange and John Milbank have rightly noted (with differing value judgments), the distinction of the natural and the supernatural begins to break down because there is no more specifically *natural* ultimate term of the human intellect.[28] The natural question of human happiness is philosophically unresolvable and terminates only when that same question attains specifically theological forms of information. It is in becoming theology, we might say, that philosophical ethics attains some kind of resolution from its inherent restlessness and constitutional irresolution.

But is this true? One way of treating the question is to return to Aquinas's treatments of natural contemplation of God as a form of imperfect happiness in the *Summa contra Gentiles*. By making a few precise observations, we can offer an alternative and more classical interpretation of the question.

---

28 See John Milbank, *The Suspended Middle: Henri de Lubac and the Debate Concerning the Supernatural* (Grand Rapids, MI: Eerdmans, 2005); Réginald Garrigou-Lagrange, *De Revelatione* (Paris: J. Gabalda; Rome: F. Ferrari, 1921), 1:125–32. Interestingly, twenty-five years before *Surnaturel* was published, Garrigou-Lagrange restates the position of Blondel in terms that closely mirror later positions of de Lubac. "The new Apologists answer: our aspiration toward the supernatural order is not found in our nature as such, abstractly considered, but in man as he is established de facto and in the concrete with an orientation toward a supernatural end. For man in this world is not in a merely natural state but—even if he does not possess habitual grace or supernatural faith—he is preceded by and stirred up by actual grace that he might turn toward God the author of salvation. Nor is it necessary that the aspiration toward Christianity be perceived in one's consciousness as properly supernatural in reference to his end. It suffices that we be conscious of our incapacity to fulfill the higher desires of the soul, and that we recognize that the fulfillment of these aspirations is found in Christianity. We can experience this restlessness according to the statement of St. Augustine, 'our hearts are restless until they rest in thee.'" "Respondent novi Apologetae: aspiratio nostra ad ordinem supernaturalem non invenitur in nostra natura secundum se et abstracte considerata, sed in homine qualis de facto et in concreto conditus est cum ordinatione ad finem supernaturalem. Nunc enim homo non est in statu mere naturali, sed, etiam si non habeat gratiam habitualem nec fidem supernaturalem, praevenitur et excitatur a gratia actuali ut sese convertat ad Deum auctorem salutis. Nec necesse est aspirationem ad Christianismum conscientia percipi ut proprie supernaturalis est suo fine, sufficit ut simus conscii *incapacitatis* nostrae ad superiores tendentias animae implendas, et ut agnoscamus satisfactionem harum aspirationum in Christianismo inveniri. Possumus nostram inquietudinem experiri secundum illud S. Augustini: 'Irrequietum est cor nostrum donec requiescat in te'" (Garrigou-Lagrange, *De Revelatione*, 1:130). This resembles the affirmation of de Lubac that human nature only ever exists in a historical economy of grace in such a way that the human being is constituted in his or her "concrete" historical nature as ordered toward the supernatural end of grace. See de Lubac, *Mystery of the Supernatural*, 54–56, 76.

A Philosophical Treatment of Imperfect and Perfect Happiness

In *Summa contra Gentiles* III, chapter 24, Aquinas begins what is undoubtedly his most protracted treatment of human beatitude and the final end of human existence, "That to understand God is the final end of every intellectual substance."[29] This chapter prepares the reader for Aquinas's treatment of happiness, as he goes on in chapters 26–36 to identify what ultimate human happiness does not consist of (pleasures of the flesh, honor, glory, riches, power, the goods of the body, the moral and artistic virtues, even the virtue of prudence). All of this is antecedent to his treatment of contemplation as happiness in chapter 37, where he argues that "the ultimate felicity of man consists in the contemplation of God." He then in chapters 38–63 conducts an extensive treatment of what, ultimately, the most perfect contemplation of God consists of, approximately half of which deals with the grace of the beatific vision as the ultimate source of human happiness (chapters 51–63). For our purposes, it is essential to focus not only on chapter 37, but also chapter 39 ("That human felicity does not consist in the knowledge of God gained through demonstration") and chapter 48 ("That man's ultimate felicity does not come in this life"), for here we see Aquinas's "Aristotelianism" in its most overt form, employed at the service of his Christian Augustinian conception of the final end of man.

In chapter 37, Aquinas argues that the ultimate felicity of man consists of the contemplation of God. He employs a procedure of argument that is taken from Aristotle. He first notes that the inferior goods (wealth, pleasure, honor, and moral virtue and prudence) cannot account of themselves for the happiness of man. That which does is something proper to the human person as such: the contemplation of the truth. "Indeed, this is the only operation of man which is proper to him, and in this he shares nothing in common with the other animals" (paragraph 2). Therefore it is that to which all other goods and acts of virtue are ultimately oriented. Why is this? Speculative knowledge alone can make use of the other inferior, "relative" ends that are proper to our nature while directing them to their ultimate term (paragraphs 3 and 7). It has a directive and assimilative capacity that alone can subordinate *all that is in* the human person to that which is *most specific to* the human person.[30]

As Aristotle also argues, this is a form of life that allows man to resemble in the

---

[29] English translations of *ScG* III are taken from *Summa contra Gentiles*, trans. Vernon J. Bourke (Notre Dame, IN: University of Notre Dame Press, 2001).

[30] *ScG* III, c. 37, para. 7: "In fact, all other human operations seem to be ordered to this one, as to an end. For, there is needed for the perfection of contemplation a soundness of body, to which all the products of art that are necessary for life are directed. Also required are freedom from the disturbances of the passions—this achieved through the moral virtues and prudence—and freedom from external disorders, to which the whole program of government in civil life is directed. And so, if they are rightly considered, all human functions may be seen to subserve the contemplation of truth." The argument resembles the reasoning of Aristotle in *Nic. Ethics* 10.7.1177b1-26.

highest part of himself that which is noblest in the order of being as such: God and the separate substances (paragraphs 4 and 5).[31] Likewise, because this is the most interior of activities, it is that which is least subject to the whims of external fate and threat from loss of external goods (paragraph 6).[32] Lastly, the contemplation of the truth in question provides happiness arising from the truth that is contemplated:

> it is not possible for man's ultimate felicity to consist in the contemplation which depends on the understanding of principles [i.e., the habit of understanding], for that is very imperfect.... nor does it lie in the area of the sciences which deal with lower things, because felicity should lie in the working of the intellect in relation to the noblest objects of understanding. So, the conclusion remains that man's ultimate felicity consists in the contemplation of wisdom, [and] only in the contemplation of God.[33]

Whether these arguments work or not depends in some sense upon the arguments that have preceded them: the idea that human happiness is a kind of activity,[34] that it is an operation of an intellectual substance,[35] that various forms of operations can be excluded as providing ultimate happiness,[36] and so forth. Furthermore, there are anthropological claims that have been argued for in *Summa contra Gentiles* II that are seemingly presupposed: that there are in human persons spiritual faculties of intellect and free will that imply an immateriality of form and which are therefore incorruptible as spiritual faculties,[37] and that these are ordered toward the true and the good and are capable of seeking the first truth and the absolute good.[38] The order in which the claims are made is controversial, as is the validity of some of the arguments made along the way. Whatever we make of all these claims and their order, however, there can be little doubt that the arguments Aquinas is employing in this chapter are of Aristotelian provenance. Clearly, in fact, almost all of them are found in virtually identical form in Books I, VI, and X of the *Nicomachean Ethics*, where Aristotle discusses the activity of happiness, the virtue of wisdom, and the final end of contemplation, respectively. What is more, the same arguments can be identified in Aquinas's own commentary on the *Nicomachean Ethics*, precisely at these points.[39] In arguing that the natural, final end of man is the happiness attained through the virtue of wisdom—that is, through the contemplation of God by way of natural knowledge of God—Aquinas is arguing philosophically as a medieval Aristotelian, or in light of what he takes to be the truth that stems from perennially valid Aristotelian philosophical principles.

---

31 See the similar reasoning of *Nic. Ethics* 10.7.1177b27-1178a8.

32 See the similar reasoning of *Nic. Ethics* 10.8.1178a9-1178b7.

33 Paragraphs 8 and 9. Cf. *Nic. Ethics* 10.7.1177a15; *Metaphysics* 12.7.1072b25-26.

34 *ScG* III, c. 26.   35 *ScG* III, c. 25.

36 *ScG* III, cc. 27–36.   37 *ScG* II, c. 79.

38 See, for example, the theories of created intellect in Aquinas's reflections on what is common to men and angels in *ScG* II, c. 91.

39 See *In I Ethic.*, lec. 10, on happiness as an activity of man; *In VI Ethic.*, lec. 5 and 6, on wisdom as speculative knowledge of divine things and the highest science; and *In X Ethic.*, lec. 9–13, on contemplation as the highest form of happiness.

This is all said with respect to the relative *perfection* of natural happiness. What about its relative *imperfection*? Aquinas will argue for the insufficiency of the happiness procured by natural knowledge for human beings in chapters 39 and 48 of Book III. Here in particular, Aquinas's genuine creativity as a medieval philosophical developer of Aristotelian thought begins to shine through in acute ways. He self-consciously employs arguments or observations of Aristotle from the *Metaphysics* and the *Ethics* regarding the inherent instability and limitations of the felicity procured by natural knowledge of God in such a way as to move beyond the explicit arguments employed by Aristotle himself. In other words, Aquinas is seeking to analyze in Aristotelian terms the limits of the natural happiness of any created intellect so as to make room philosophically, so to speak, for the perfection of happiness that is granted by the beatific vision alone, which he will treat in chapters 51–63.[40]

In chapter 39, we find Aquinas arguing for the imperfection of human happiness procured from the knowledge of God attained "by way of demonstration" (i.e., through the philosophical virtue of wisdom). The seven arguments he enunciates all have to do in some way with the inevitable potency for perfect knowledge in human reason that remains nonactualized or inoperative, even once philosophical demonstrative knowledge of God and his attributes has been attained. The first argument is based upon the very form of the knowledge of God attained through philosophical demonstrations. Following Aristotle, Aquinas argues that this knowledge employs a posteriori forms of demonstration: it begins from effects that we know directly in or-

---

40 The philosophical character of Aquinas's arguments on this topic is emphasized helpfully by Adriano Oliva in "La contemplation des philosophes selon Thomas d'Aquin," *Revue des sciences philosophiques et théologiques* 96 (2012): 585–662, esp. 631–41. Oliva's erudite and important essay demonstrates conclusively by a thorough analysis of numerous texts that Aquinas affirmed unambiguously the existence of a philosophical contemplation of God, which is naturally perfective of the human intellect. Furthermore, Oliva argues convincingly that the text of *ScG* III, c. 48, has a philosophical character, even if the argument is used eventually to demonstrate the fittingness of the philosopher's receptivity to supernatural revelation. The historical context is that of the dialogue between the theologians and the faculty of arts at the University of Paris, with Aquinas attempting to refute Averroist interpretations of Aristotle while trying to show that philosophical argument at its summit, by its own lights and principles, can detect reasons for being open to the mystery of divine revelation. *Sacra doctrina* is respectful, then, of the integral reflections of sound philosophy and can assimilate the latter without violence to the integrity of philosophy as a discipline. "The 'philosophical' doctrine elaborated by Aquinas presupposes that reason *by means of creatures* might aim toward the contemplation of God [in himself] and that it can attain even to the affirmation that such contemplation [of God *in se*] is possible, but above all this philosophical contemplation implies that the first cause should fittingly reveal itself and unite itself to the creature" (ibid., 639–40). Oliva's interpretation of the natural desire for God in Aquinas contrasts in various respects with the one offered in this essay. Oliva does avidly defend de Lubac's interpretation of Aquinas on this topic. Nevertheless, because he underscores strongly the *philosophical mode of demonstration* in Aquinas's argument, Oliva seems to me to differ significantly from de Lubac.

der to infer the necessary existence of a transcendent cause of those effects, one that we do not know directly.[41] But in this case we can say only *that* God is and *what* God is not, as he is not like the effects that depend upon him:

> we reach a proper knowledge of a thing not only through affirmations but also through negations.... But there is a difference between these two modes of proper knowledge: through affirmations, when we have a proper knowledge of a thing, we know *what* the thing is, and how it is separated from others; but through negations, when we have a proper knowledge of a thing, we know *that* it is distinct from other things, yet what it is remains unknown. Now this is the proper knowledge that we have of God through demonstrations. Of course, this is not sufficient for the ultimate felicity of man.[42]

Aquinas gives a list of names of God that are based primarily upon negative knowledge by comparison with creatures: He is "immutable, eternal, incorporeal, altogether simple, one," and so on.[43] Here Aquinas's Dionysian apophaticism is undergirded by his Aristotelian approach to the knowledge of the divine. Owing to its indirect and mediated character, the knowledge we have of God in this life is primarily negative in character. But in this case, because this knowledge is so deeply imperfect and radically indirect, the happiness it procures, while real, is also fundamentally incomplete. Such knowledge leaves the potential of the intellect for beatifying knowledge of God only imperfectly actuated.

The other arguments employed in chapter 39 are congruent with the former one: the knowledge of God attained by means of demonstration is difficult, and most men are unable to attain it in the course of their lives (paragraph 2). The history of thought shows that different philosophers discover different truths about the divine. Thus any one thinker's understanding should be seen to remain in potency to a further perfection (paragraph 3).[44] Such knowledge can coexist with a mixture of errors and with other forms of unhappiness, and is consequently imperfect (paragraph 4). This form of knowledge, because of its difficulty, is tinged with uncertainties of various sorts indicative of an imperfect form of knowledge (paragraph 5). It is a form of

---

41 This is the point Aquinas is famous for making later on in *ST* I, q. 2, aa. 1–2, regarding the "demonstrative arguments" for the existence of God, where he distinguishes his own approach from that of Anselm's ontological argument. Aquinas's demonstrations seek to move from created effects to their hidden cause (God), while Anselm argues that one can infer the very necessity of the existence of God from the conceptual definition of God (a view Aquinas rejects). See on this point Rudi te Velde, *Aquinas on God* (Aldershot, UK: Ashgate, 2006), 37–48.

42 *ScG* III, c. 39, para. 1.

43 Ibid.

44 *ScG* III, c. 39, para. 3: "But this sort of knowledge of God, acquired by way of demonstration, still remains in potency to something further to be learned about God, or to the same knowledge possessed in a higher way, for later men have endeavored to add something pertinent to divine knowledge to the things which they found in the heritage of their predecessors. Therefore, such knowledge is not identical with ultimate felicity."

knowledge that leaves us still hoping (restlessly) for yet greater knowledge and consequently is imperfect (paragraph 6). Knowledge through habitual consideration of various objects, such as is inevitable to human nature in this life, is necessarily of such a kind as to leave a spiritual well of nonactualized potency in remainder, so long as we are considering one object alone and not another that we could be considering alternatively. Therefore the forms of knowledge we enjoy in this life by means of abstraction and habitual rational reflection, however noble, simply cannot actualize all the potency of the intellect as such (paragraph 7).[45]

In chapter 48, Aquinas argues that man's ultimate felicity does not come about in this life. Again he employs Aristotelian arguments in view of trans-Aristotelian ends. The chapter contains several arguments, but a number of them in particular appeal directly to observations from Aristotle himself in order to argue that the imperfect happiness of this life cannot be considered the most ultimate resting place of the natural desire for the contemplation of God. The first of these (in paragraph 3) appeals to Book I of the *Nicomachean Ethics* (1.10.1100b5). Aristotle notes that an initially evident characteristic of happiness would seem to be its stability and rest, and the fact that it is impervious to potential turns of bad fortune. But as Aquinas notes, no contemplative happiness procured by this life, however perfect, is entirely impervious to the sadness stemming from bad fortune. Second (in paragraph 4), Aquinas appeals to Book X of the *Nicomachean Ethics* (10.7.1177a11), where Aristotle claims that happiness consists of perfect operation in accord with the highest virtue. As Aquinas notes, however, the virtue of speculative wisdom is attained only at the term of a long ascent, with great difficulty, and lasts only for the short time of one's older age in life. Therefore it is not a perfect—that is, enduring and stable—form of happiness. Third, Aristotle observes in Book II of the *Nicomachean Ethics* (2.6.1106b24) that even in the virtuous man there is at times the passionate impulse that causes him to overstep the mean of virtue. In noting this (paragraph 5), Aquinas is making an implicit reference to the truth of the fallen character of human existence and to the inevitability of occasional grave sin even in the virtuous pagan, if that person be without the implicit recourse to the help of grace.[46] But serious sin, in

---

45 *ScG* III, c. 39, para. 7: "Now, our intellect is in potency to all intelligible objects, such as was explained in Book II (c. 47). But two intelligible objects can exist simultaneously in the possible intellect, by way of the first act which is science, though perhaps not by way of the second act which is consideration. It is evident from this that the entire potency of the possible intellect can be reduced to act at one time [in principle]. So, this is required for its ultimate end which is felicity. But the aforesaid knowledge of God which can be acquired through demonstration does not do this, since, even when we possess it, we still remain ignorant of many things. Therefore, such knowledge of God is not sufficient for ultimate felicity."

46 See in particular *ST* I-II, q. 109, a. 8: "Whether man without grace can avoid sin?" On the notion of pagan virtue in Aquinas, see the exchange between Brian J. Shanley, "Aquinas on Pagan Virtue," *The Thomist* 63 (1999): 553–77; and Thomas M. Osborne Jr., "The Augustinianism of Thomas Aquinas's Moral Theory," *The Thomist* 67 (2003): 279–305.

however noble a soul, is necessarily a cause of sadness, and so Aristotle himself phil-osophically alludes to the precariousness of happiness in every human being in this world, including those who strive to be virtuous.

Fourth, Aquinas offers an argument (in paragraph 9) that he articulates else-where and that he presumes to be taken directly from Book I of the *Nicomachean Ethics* (1.10.1101a14-20). Aristotle there argues that human beings only attain hap-piness by way of internal virtues, but in dependence upon certain external goods that support a life of virtue. Even if we live in amenable circumstances at a particular time, this stability is relative and depends upon precarious external circumstances. As the future unfolds, there is the possibility of bad fortune undermining our human hap-piness. So, even in the midst of the speculative contemplation of the highest realities and our practice of ennobling moral virtues, an inherent fragility remains endemic to the human situation. Consequently, the highest contemplative happiness that nature affords is attained by human persons only imperfectly, and in a less perfect way than in the higher intelligences, namely, God and the separate substances. According to Aquinas, this is why Aristotle says that human persons can attain some form of hap-piness, but only *in their manner as men*: imperfect in comparison to the immaterial realities they seek to imitate.[47]

Interestingly, Aquinas speaks both here (in paragraph 9) and in the *Summa theo-logiae* (I-II, q. 3, a. 6) of the natural virtue of wisdom as an imperfect "participation" in the beatitude of heaven. Aristotle generally eschews participation language because he associates this language with that of the forms of Plato.[48] But Aquinas is seeing right-ly that Aristotle himself saw philosophically that there must exist a more perfect form of contemplative happiness in the higher life of God and the separate substances, one that we seek to imitate and that we gravitate toward in natural contemplation of God.[49]

We can complete these observations by noting briefly one more Aristotelian form of argumentation, employed by Aquinas in chapter 50, where he argues "that the natural desire of separate substances does not come to rest in the natural knowl-

---

[47] *Nic. Ethics* 1.10.1101a14-20: "Why then should we not say that he is happy who is active in conformity with complete excellence and is sufficiently equipped with external goods, not for some chance period but throughout a complete life? ... Certainly the future is obscure to us, [and yet] happiness, we claim, is an end and something in every way final. If so, we shall call blessed those among living men in whom these conditions are, and are to be, fulfilled—but blessed *men*." *ScG* III, c. 48, para. 9: "For, in regard to the full understanding of truth, men can attain it only through enquiry, and they are utterly deficient in regard to objects which are most intelligible in their nature.... And so, felicity in its perfect character cannot be present in men, but they may participate somewhat in it, even in this life.... Hence [Aris-totle] in *Nic. Ethics* I, where he asks whether misfortunes take away happiness, having shown that felicity consists in the works of virtue which seem to be most enduring in this life ... concludes that those men for whom such perfection in this life is possible are happy as *men*, as if they had not attained felicity absolutely, but merely in human fashion."

[48] See Aristotle's criticisms of the Platonic theory of forms in *Nic. Ethics* 1.6; *Metaphysics* 12.3-5.

[49] See on this point Oliva, "La contemplation des philosophes selon Thomas d'Aquin," 638–39.

edge which they have of God." Here (in paragraphs 3 and 4) he employs arguments for the imperfection of natural knowledge in any creaturely intellect. These arguments are drawn from Aristotle's *Metaphysics* (1.2.982b12) and his *Posterior Analytics* (2.1.89b22). The first argument given here is based on the observation from the text in the *Metaphysics* that all men desire by nature to know, and that they seek knowledge of causes. In other words, the work of creaturely intellectual life is to explore causes, passing from effects to the origination of those effects.

Therefore, the desire to know, which is naturally implanted in all intellectual substances, does not rest until, after they have come to know the substances of the effects, they also know the substance of the cause. The fact then, that separate substances know that God is the cause of all things whose substances they see, does not mean that natural desire comes to rest in them, unless they also see the substance of God Himself. (paragraph 3)

The second argument recasts this observation in terms of the text from the *Posterior Analytics*. Here Aristotle places in pairs the four basic scientific questions that characterize human inquiry. Aristotle pairs asking "whether something is the case" (factually) with the question of "why it exists." Likewise, the question of "if something in particular exists" is related to asking "what that something is." If something is the case, we ask why it is so. If something exists, we ask what it is. Aquinas goes on to comment:

Now, we observe that those who see *that something is so* naturally desire to know *why*. So, too, those acquainted with the fact *that something exists* naturally desire to know *what this thing is*, and this is to understand its substance. Therefore, the natural desire to know does not rest in that knowledge of God whereby we know merely *that He is*. (paragraph 4)

Rather, our intellect aspires naturally by virtue of the fact that it knows that God exists, to know what he is—to see him as he is in himself.

In both these arguments from chapter 50, the Augustinian theme of the inherent restlessness of the natural desire of the created intellect is given an Aristotelian philosophical articulation.[50] The inherent (we might say intrinsic) inclination of the intellect for the immediate knowledge of God is rooted in the natural desire to know the cause, not only through the mediation of the effects of the cause, but also in itself. This inclination is manifested through an express desire of human nature, one that springs naturally from the knowledge of God that is proper to angelic and human natures. The imperfect character of our natural knowledge of God, then, is not only a certain kind of beatitude that truly does perfect human nature. It is also precisely because of its relative perfection, and therefore corresponding imperfection as an end, the necessary occasion for the rendering explicit of a desire for a yet higher perfection of knowledge. This higher end is indeed one that nature cannot procure

---

50 The theme of the restless heart in Augustine can be interpreted in two ways: in relation to the dynamic natural tendency of reason to seek the knowledge of the first cause, and in terms of the operations of the human soul under the effects of infused grace. Here I consider only the first idea, in accord with Aquinas's clearly philosophical manner of argumentation in *ScG* III.

for itself.[51] Therefore the natural desire for the immediate knowledge of God is inscribed in us by nature insofar as we are innately ordered toward the search for the truth about causes and are capable of indirect, mediated knowledge of the first cause. For this same reason we are capable of an inefficacious desire for a knowledge of God that is immediate, one that surpasses our human powers and that our native capacities cannot procure. That is to say, we are naturally capable of the desire to see God.

A Theological Treatment of Imperfect and Perfect Happiness

Despite the suspicions one might have to the contrary, there can be little question that the form of argumentation employed by Aquinas in the abovementioned chapters of Book III of the *Summa contra Gentiles* is in fact philosophical and rational in nature and not one that is derived directly or immediately from revealed first principles as such, nor from Christian theology. Apart from the internal logic of the arguments themselves (which are based upon Aristotelian principles), this is evident from the context in which they are employed. It is true that the arguments presume the awareness of the givens of revealed faith. But Aquinas frames such arguments not to clarify views of dogmatic theology per se, but to show from principles of Aristotelian natural reason that various rational (properly philosophical) objections to the Christian revelation of the beatific vision are themselves philosophically untenable.[52] These objections sprang from the Latin Averroism of Aquinas's time, a form of rationalist Aristotelianism that sought to oppose the natural final end of man to his purported Christian end, to oppose Aristotelian ethics and Augustinian teleology. So it is often thought that Siger of Brabant and Boethius of Dacia, in particular, argued that human happiness consists of a natural union of the human philosopher with the agent intellect of the separate substances and God: effectively a kind of natural philosophical contemplation of the separate substances. This Averroist stance was eventually criticized in the Parisian condemnations of Aristotelian rationalism in 1277.[53]

---

51 Aquinas offers quite clear arguments to this effect in *ScG* III, c. 52: "That no created substance can, by its own natural power, attain the vision of God in his essence."

52 Writing on this section of *ScG* III, Oliva remarks, "It is important to note that the arguments which ground the reasoning of Thomas are borrowed explicitly from the Philosopher, as if to underscore that he conceives of his reasoning as a coherent extension of the Aristotelian doctrine." "La contemplation des philosophes selon Thomas d'Aquin," 636.

53 See Dag Nikolaus Hasse, "Influence of Arabic and Islamic Philosophy on the Latin West," in *The Stanford Encyclopedia of Philosophy*, ed. Edward N. Zalta, http://plato.stanford.edu/entries/arabic-islamic-influence/: "In 1277, several philosophical theses concerning human happiness and the good life were condemned: that happiness is to be had in this life and not in another (art. 176), that there is no better state (of life) than studying philosophy (art. 40). These articles are apparently directed at masters of arts at the university of Paris, among them Siger of Brabant and Boethius of Dacia. As we know from fragments of Siger's treatise *On Happiness* (*De felicitate*), he embraces Averroes' thesis that all intellects are made blessed through the conjunction with the active intellect. In Siger's interpretation, human beings

It is clear that Aquinas is arguing against just such a position *Summa contra Gentiles* III, chapters 41–45.[54]

How does Aquinas treat this question, meanwhile, in an unambiguously theological context? In other words, does he employ the Aristotelian philosophical arguments we have been studying above within a specifically doctrinal theological context, and if so, why? Toward this end, we should consider briefly two related texts in the *Summa theologiae*. The first of these is question 12, article 1, of the *Prima pars*, where Aquinas considers philosophical objections to the possibility of the vision of God in a specifically theological context. The second is question 3, article 6, of the *Prima secundae*, where Aquinas considers the imperfect character of natural contemplative happiness in comparison with the beatific vision that is promised in faith.

The first text (*ST* I, q. 12, a. 1) asks "Whether any created intellect can see the essence of God." The objections that Aquinas notes stem in large part from reasonable claims regarding the transcendence of God with respect to the human intellect. God is infinite (obj. 2), surpasses the intelligibility of all created existents (obj. 3), and thus surpasses the proportionate range of human understanding that is native to the creaturely intellect of man (obj. 4). The arguments are not unreasonable. Aquinas responds with two arguments, the first of which is theological (based upon the premises of faith in divine revelation) and the second philosophical. The first is based upon the *auctoritas* of the *sed contra* in the article: "We shall see him as He is" (1 Jn 2:2). Revelation teaches us that, by the grace of Christ's paschal mystery, we are called to the vision of God. Commenting on this, Aquinas explains that the pure actuality of God is what is most intelligible in itself, even if this superabundant intelligibility naturally tran-

---

in such a state think God by an intellection which is God himself. There are many indications that Siger was convinced that the knowledge of the separate substances and thus the attaining of human happiness is possible in this life. Boethius of Dacia is also convinced that human happiness can be reached in this life, which is a happiness proportioned to human capacities, whereas the highest kind of happiness as such is reserved to the afterlife (in his treatise *De summo bono*). Boethius appears to be inspired by Arabic theories of intellectual ascension, but does not endorse a theory of conjunction, as does Siger. His conviction that the philosopher's life is the only true life echoes the very self-confident and elitist stance taken by the major Arabic philosophers."

54 On Latin Averroism at the time of Aquinas, see Fernand Van Steenberghen, *Introduction à l'étude de la philosophie medievale* (Louvain: Publication Universitaires; Paris: Beatrice-Nauwelaerts, 1974), 531–54. See more recently Jörn Müller, "*Duplex beatitude*: Aristotle's Legacy and Aquinas' Conception of Human Happiness," in *Aquinas and the Nicomachean Ethics* (Cambridge: Cambridge University Press, 2013), 52–71. Müller shows how Aquinas wishes to interpret Aristotle to show philosophically that any happiness afforded by indirect knowledge of God, while real, is imperfect, and therefore inherently open to the perfect happiness made possible by the supernatural grace of vision. He does so not only in contrast to Averroist positions, but also in part in contrast to the reading of the *Nicomachean Ethics* offered by Albert the Great, who did not seek to identify in Aristotle a rational foundation for the argument that man has a natural desire to see the essence of God.

scends the native power of understanding of every created intellect. Yet the human intellect is created to seek to understand what is most intelligible in itself and to acquire
beatitude or happiness through the stable possession of knowledge of this object.

Consequently, if the human intellect is ordered toward happiness by way of the
knowledge of God (which revelation says it is), then this same intellect would lack
some inherent actuation and perfection of happiness were it not to come to see God
face to face. Therefore, theologically, it is fitting to understand the beatific vision as
the supernatural end of man.

Aquinas goes on to say that the objections of this article are also contrary to reason, however, and he repeats an argument similar to that seen in the *Summa contra
Gentiles* (*ScG* III, c. 50, paragraphs 3 and 4), based upon the *Metaphysics* (1.2) and
the *Posterior Analytics* (2.1):

> For there resides in every man a natural desire to know the cause of any effect which he sees;
> and thence arises wonder in men. But if the intellect of the rational creature could not reach so
> far as to the first cause of things, the natural desire would remain void.

What is Aquinas saying here? Clearly, he is referring to philosophical premises,
as he says himself, and yet at the same time he is arguing in view of a theological revealed truth, represented by the citation of the First Letter of John in the *sed contra*.
Is he attempting to prove by natural reason a doctrine of faith—one that we are giv-
en to know uniquely by revelation? Does he really think that philosophical reason
can demonstrate the existence of a revealed mystery? This seems unlikely, because
he is quite clear about the fact that the mystery of the Trinity cannot be known by
any effort of unaided natural reason, and the vision of the Holy Trinity does in fact
constitute the final supernatural end of man.[55] Consequently, it seems that one of
two possibilities must obtain in this case. (1) A theologian reflecting upon the revealed truth of the beatific vision of the Holy Trinity is employing a philosophical
argument in order to show (from the standpoint of natural reason) the *mere possibility* of a theologically revealed truth. (2) A philosophical argument is being made
that shows the *rational fittingness* or *natural plausibility* of a theological article of
faith, but does not demonstrate conclusively the reality of that object (which can be
known only through faith). In the end, it seems to me likely that Aquinas is assuming

---

55 Most notably, Aquinas is explicit about the fact that the principles of revealed faith can only
be known by way of divine revelation (*ST* I, q. 1, a. 2); that the mystery of the Trinity, which
is the deifying mystery of the vision of God, is utterly unknown to natural human reason (*ST*
I, q. 32, a. 1); and that the inclination to the supernatural vision of God is not innate to the
human person, but rather that this vision is something "neither eye has seen nor ear heard,"
and thus transcends our native human conceptions (*ST* I-II, q. 62, a. 3). It bears mentioning
that this stress on the transcendence of supernatural mystery to all forms of natural knowledge and rational demonstration was underscored vividly in the First Vatican Council (*Dei
Filius*, 1870) against the tenets of nineteenth-century Catholic "rationalism," which sought
to argue, beginning from natural premises, for the demonstrative rationality of belief in the
mysteries of the faith.

both of these truths: a philosophical argument can be employed to argue that an object of faith made known by way of divine revelation is something that is, philosophically speaking, not metaphysically impossible but rather existentially appropriate.

Based on these considerations, we can conclude with certitude two things. First, Aquinas is here employing philosophy in the service of a principle of *sacra doctrina* as he provides for in question 1, article 5, of the *Prima pars*, where he argues that philosophy can serve as a subordinate science to theological faith, allowing the latter to partake of the intelligibility of the conclusions of the former.[56] Just as when Aquinas offers philosophical arguments for the nature of the soul in the context of his theological treatise on the original creation of man and woman, so here he is making use of philosophical argument in the context of a specifically theological treatment of the final end of man.[57] Second, the philosophical argument in question, *in this context*, can only be considered an argument of *fittingness* and not a rational demonstration.[58] The human person naturally desires to know the first cause immediately. Reason can show the potential openness of the human intellect to completion through the perfect happiness of the grace of the beatific vision. It cannot demonstrate the existence of this grace and this final end by arguments of natural reason alone. In fact, such a grace is, strictly speaking, not even intelligible in its essence except by virtue of supernatural faith because, as a mystery, its character eludes the understanding of natural reason considered within the limits of its innate boundaries and possibilities of understanding.

If this is the case, then the arguments in Book III, chapter 50, of the *Summa contra Gentiles* and question 12, article 1, of the *Prima pars*—though identical in structure philosophically speaking—can be interpreted in two very different ways. In the former text, philosophy is being employed to show a natural desire to know God immediately, not a natural desire for the object of supernatural faith as such. The argument is to be considered rigorously demonstrative. This would especially make sense were Aquinas writing against the philosophical claims of Averroism in order to defend the potential harmony of the truths of faith and natural reason.[59] In the latter

---

56 *ST* I, q. 1, a. 5, ad 2: "This science (*sacra doctrina*) can in a sense depend upon the philosophical sciences, not as though it stood in need of them, but only in order to make its teaching clearer."

57 *ST* I, qq. 75–79.

58 This is the interpretation of Aquinas given by the classical Dominican commentatorial tradition, which takes into account what he says about the revealed character of the supernatural end of man in texts such as *ST* I-II, q. 62, a. 3. The faith is congruent with demonstrations of reason, but the truths of the faith are not derivative from rational arguments. See, for example, Sylvester of Ferrara's commentary on *ScG* III, c. 51, n. III (Leonine ed., 14:141), in which he discusses the argument in *ST* I, q. 12, a. 1; and Báñez, *Scholastica commentaria in primam partem*, q. 12, a. 1 (Valencia ed., 249), who argues that *ScG* III, c. 50, presents philosophical arguments that man naturally desires to see God were this somehow possible, but does not of course seek to demonstrate a natural human capacity to attain effectively to the beatific vision.

59 See Müller, "*Duplex beatitude*," 67–69, who interprets the argument in a similar sense.

text, the same demonstrative argument is being used not as a way of demonstrating the existence of the revealed supernatural end of man, but as an argument of fittingness showing that this end revealed in Christ is not something alien or contrary to, but rather in harmony with, the natural aspirations of the human person, albeit on a higher plane made possible only by grace.

A complementary form of reasoning is found in question 3, article 6, of the *Prima secundae*, a text that presents a suitable place to conclude our consideration of Aquinas's teaching on imperfect happiness. Here Aquinas is considering what happiness, or beatitude, is from a theological point of view, and in article 6 asks specifically "Whether man's happiness consists in the consideration of the speculative sciences." That is to say, does it consist in the exercise of the Aristotelian virtue of wisdom, the activity of the natural contemplation of God?

Aquinas rehearses several of the arguments we saw above in Book III of the *Summa contra Gentiles*. First he alludes to a previous discussion (*ST* I-II, q. 3, a. 2, ad 4) of the imperfect character of human happiness in this life, making the point that the contemplation of God that is available to human reason is frail and can only be exercised periodically, rather than in an enduring and ever-present way. He goes on to make the point that all natural knowledge of God obtained in this life is derived from sensible realities and does not permit an immediate knowledge of God in himself. Therefore it stirs up in us a desire for knowledge of something that we cannot attain perfectly. Such knowledge stems from a natural desire for God that only grace can fulfill.[60] Yet Aquinas does go on to conclude that this natural knowledge of God by means of indirect contemplation of God through his effects *does* constitute an imperfect form of beatitude, one that is a true "participation" in the more perfect happiness of the blessed, albeit in a uniquely natural and limited way: "just as in sensible forms there is a participation of the higher substances, so the consideration of speculative sciences is a certain participation of true and perfect happiness." A gloss on this idea is found in article 2, response to the fourth objection, where Aquinas makes clear that there are analogous forms of happiness:

Since happiness signifies some final perfection; according as various things capable of happiness can attain to various degrees of perfection, so must there be various meanings applied to happiness.... Wherefore the Philosopher, in placing man's happiness in this life (*Nic. Ethics* I, 10), says that it is imperfect and after a long discussion, concludes: "We call men happy, but only as men." But God has promised us perfect happiness, when we shall be "as the angels ... in heaven (Mt 22:30)."

---

60 *ST* I-II, q. 3, a. 6: "Now the first principles of the speculative sciences are received through the senses, as the Philosopher clearly states at the beginning of the *Metaphysics* (I, 1), and at the end of the *Posterior Analytics* (II, 15). Wherefore the entire consideration of the speculative sciences cannot extend farther than knowledge of sensibles can lead.... Now it has been shown that man cannot acquire through sensibles the [immediate] knowledge of separate substances, which are above the human intellect. Consequently, it follows that man's happiness cannot consist in the consideration of the speculative sciences."

The key point is that Aquinas does acknowledge an authentic perfection in the happiness accorded by the natural knowledge of God. That happiness can be known even philosophically and rationally to be imperfect (as the philosopher himself admits). Consequently, this same philosophical sense of the yet greater perfectibility of man can be employed theologically to show, by an argument of fittingness, that the theological promise of the vision of God is not only not absurd but also that, if real, it pertains to the greatest possible good available to man. Reason does not prove the existence of the supernatural vision of God, which is known only by grace, but the revelation of the perfect happiness of the vision does speak to the deepest desires of the human heart for happiness through contemplative knowledge of God, even immediate knowledge, and it surpasses those desires even as it fulfills them.

Unlike Blondel, Aquinas has succeeded in maintaining the distinction and integrity of the philosophical order as distinct from the theological. Philosophical contemplation provides a genuine form of beatitude that pertains to human reason and that is not reducible to a moment within an apologetics in view of theology or Christian ethics. And yet this relative beatitude is imperfect and inherently open from within to a further completion. Thus Aquinas has also avoided an extrinsicism that would employ philosophy against the claims of Christian Augustinian teleology (as with Siger of Brabant and Boethius of Dacia) or that would appeal to Christian theology against any claims to a philosophical knowledge of the natural structure and end of man (as found in Barth). Rather, philosophical reasoning, while not identical with theological understanding, does show by various signs that the revealed claims of theology are not only not unreasonable, but also genuinely attractive to what is most rational in us, even as they surpass natural reason.

Can we speak here, then, of philosophical contemplation of God as an imperfect end? Aquinas does not usually employ this language and typically reserves the notion of the final end only for the immediate knowledge of God. (See, however, *ST* I-II, q. 62, a. 3, where he does clearly speak of imperfect beatitude as the "connatural end" of man.) But even if we do concede this linguistic point, Aquinas does discuss this imperfect beatitude in teleological terms, and of course it is only because there is a relatively consistent beatitude accessible to natural human reason that the final end of immediate knowledge of God even becomes philosophically accessible to natural human reason. Consequently, the perspective of Aquinas is balanced on a clear but delicate edge: if we affirm too one-sidedly a merely natural end that is *not* constituted by the immediate knowledge of God (but "merely" by an indirect philosophical contemplation of God), we lose sight of the intrinsic natural orientation of the human spirit toward God in himself. If we emphasize the latter inclination exclusively, so as to emphasize man's natural desire for the vision of God, then we will be obliged to deny that indirect philosophical contemplation of God is a truly teleological form of beatitude. In doing so, however, we will be obliged to negate the philosophical and rational intelligibility of the claim that the immediate knowledge of God constitutes the final end of man, as this claim can only be made based on the premise of the real but imperfect beatitude accorded by natural contemplation.

Navigating between the Extremes: Neither Intrinsicism nor Extrinsicism

In the previous two sections, I delineated how Aquinas, in two of his main works, clearly interprets Aristotle's understanding of natural happiness in such a way as to show the inherent openness of the human person to the beatific vision by grace. The intrinsic ordering of the human person toward contemplation of God—and even the immediate vision of God—does not amount to a natural inclination toward supernatural grace as such. In fact, Aquinas explicitly disavows the idea that there exists in the intellectual creature an innate inclination of the intellect toward the grace of faith or the *lumen gloriae*:

> the theological virtues direct man to supernatural happiness in the same way as *by the natural inclination man is directed to his connatural end*. Now the latter happens in respect of two things. First, in respect of the reason or intellect, insofar as it contains the first universal principles which are known to us by the natural light of the intellect, and which are reason's starting-point, both in speculative and in practical matters. Secondly, through the rectitude of the will which tends naturally to good as defined by reason. But these two fall short of the order of supernatural happiness, according to 1 Corinthians 2:9: "The eye hath not seen, nor ear heard, neither hath it entered into the heart of man, what things God hath prepared for them that love Him." Consequently in respect of both the above things man needed to receive in addition something supernatural to direct him to a supernatural end. First, as regards the intellect, man receives certain supernatural principles, which are held by means of a Divine light: these are the articles of faith, about which is faith. Secondly, the will is directed to this end, both as to that end as something attainable—and this pertains to hope—and as to a certain spiritual union, whereby the will is, so to speak, transformed into that end—and this belongs to charity. *For the appetite of a thing is moved and tends towards its connatural end naturally; and this movement is due to a certain conformity of the thing with its end.*[61]

One can observe right away the anti-Pelagian tenor of this argument. The human intellect is not naturally oriented toward the supernatural faith, which alone gives us knowledge that the vision of the Holy Trinity is the final end of man. The human will is not naturally inclined to the revealed object of supernatural faith. For all of this, the infused virtues of faith, hope, and love must be given.

One would be ill advised to treat such a text as merely a conceptual outlier or eccentric addition to Aquinas's normative thought. On the contrary, the anti-Pelagian tenor of his mature theology is thematic and profound. Most notably, Aquinas insists that the theological virtues give the spiritual faculties of the intellect and will new "species" or "objects" of knowledge and love.[62] Consequently, the object known and desired

---

[61] *ST* I-II, q. 62, a. 3; emphasis added.

[62] *ST* I-II, q. 62, a. 2: "habits are specifically distinct from one another in respect of the formal

by the supernatural inclination of the will toward the beatific vision (in faith) simply cannot be the same object willed by the philosophical or natural desire to see God. The subject may be identical (God in himself), but the formal object by or through which the reality is desired is utterly distinct.

It follows that there are infused moral virtues that accompany the infused theological virtues and that elevate the ordinary exercise of the cardinal virtues (prudence, justice, fortitude, temperance), so that these may now attain the formal objects of the theological virtues as such:

Effects must be proportionate to their causes and principles. Now all virtues, intellectual and moral, that are acquired by our actions, arise from certain natural principles pre-existing in us, as above stated (I-II, q. 51, a. 1): instead of which natural principles, God bestows on us the theological virtues, whereby we are directed to a supernatural end, as stated (I-II, q. 62, a. 1). Wherefore we need to receive from God other habits corresponding, in due proportion, to the theological virtues, which habits are to the theological virtues, what the moral and intellectual virtues are to the natural principles of virtue.[63]

This distinctively Thomistic thesis (which was not universally accepted and was typically questioned by several great Franciscan thinkers) would make little sense at all were the spiritual faculties of man "always, already" naturally inclined toward the formally supernatural objects of faith, hope, and love as such.[64]

We see another reflection of this concern in Aquinas's treatment of grace (in question 110 of the *Prima secundae*) as a quality of the soul that is not merely reducible to the infusion of new habitual virtues.[65] Grace must be something "deeper" in the soul than a set of new habits. Why? Because grace cannot simply qualify the

---

difference of their objects. Now the object of the theological virtues is God Himself, Who is the last end of all, as surpassing the knowledge of our reason. On the other hand, the object of the intellectual and moral virtues is something comprehensible to human reason. Wherefore the theological virtues are specifically distinct from the moral and intellectual virtues." See also *ST* I-II, q. 54, a. 2, corp. and ad 1, to which Aquinas refers in this article and which I have cited here. He is categorical about the fact that supernatural virtues have formal objects that specify them, and that our natural powers may not attain these objects by their own powers.

63 *ST* I-II, q. 63, a. 3.

64 Duns Scotus argues that, strictly speaking, God could give a subject the theological virtues without the accompanying infused moral virtues. See on this point, for example, *Questiones in III Sententiarum* d. 36, unica, esp. n. 28; *Ordinatio* III, suppl., d. 36, a. 3. See the helpful commentary on this point by Allan B. Wolter, *Duns Scotus on the Will and Morality* (Washington, DC: The Catholic University of America Press, 1986), 90–91. Such a viewpoint seems to contrast necessarily with that of Aquinas. Analogously, Duns Scotus and William of Ockham both argue in different ways that God could in principle dispense a person even from the necessity of infused virtues as a precondition for salvation. See the pertinent remarks on this subject by Thomas Williams in "Scotus on Virtue," in *The Cambridge Companion to Duns Scotus*, ed. T. Williams (Cambridge: Cambridge University Press, 2003), esp. 365–66.

65 *ST* I-II, q. 110, a. 2.

teleological orientation of preexisting spiritual powers. These powers are not naturally inclined in and of themselves toward formally supernatural ends. Consequently,
grace must act from "deeper within" the human subject, elevating the spiritual powers toward formally supernatural ends, and this new inclination is something prior
to the "mere" infusion of new supernatural habits into the preexisting inclinations of
natural powers. Grace, then, is a quality infused into the essence of the soul, one that
serves as the ontological condition for the possibility of infused virtue.[66] If, by contrast, the soul's faculties were already naturally inclined toward the formally supernatural objects of faith, hope, and love as such, it would not be necessary that grace
operate at this "level" of the human person. Instead, it could simply heal and perfect
the faculties in keeping with their own natural orientations or inclinations, and there
would be no need to elevate them from within toward a new supernatural object.

Given this Thomistic emphasis on the necessity of grace to orient the soul toward the *lumen gloriae*, it is also not surprising that Aquinas should insist that the
natural faculties and powers, such as those of the intellect and will, can only tend
toward ends that are proportionate to their own natures, ends that their natures can
attain by their proper created powers.

The reason and will are naturally directed to God, inasmuch as He is the beginning and end of
nature, but in proportion to nature. But the reason and will, according to their nature, are not
sufficiently directed to Him in so far as He is the object of supernatural happiness.[67]

Supernatural beatitude as known and desired by grace is a good that remains
wholly disproportionate to the natural powers and inclinations proper to intellectual
creatures. Aquinas is quite explicit about this:

*Now no act of anything whatsoever is divinely ordained to anything exceeding the proportion of
the powers which are the principles of its act*; for it is a law of Divine providence that nothing
shall act beyond its powers. *Now everlasting life is a good exceeding the proportion of created nature*; since it exceeds its knowledge and desire, according to 1 Corinthians 2:9: "Eye hath not
seen, nor ear heard, neither hath it entered into the heart of man." And hence it is that no created nature is a sufficient principle of an act meritorious of eternal life, unless there is added a
supernatural gift, which we call grace.[68]

One can note from such observations that there is a serious conceptual price
to pay for conforming Aquinas's texts too hastily to a reading that insists abruptly
upon there being in his thought the affirmation of a "natural desire for the supernatural." One could lose sight completely of the thematic, multidimensional character
of Aquinas's anti-Pelagian teaching regarding the way that grace specifies and elevates

---

[66] See *ST* I-II, q. 110, aa. 3–4.
[67] *ST* I-II, q. 62, a. 1, ad 3. For other examples of this often invoked principle of Aquinas, see,
likewise, *De ver.*, q. 14, a. 2; q. 22, a. 5; *ST* I-II, q. 15, a. 4; q. 25, a. 2.
[68] *ST* I-II, q. 114, a. 2; emphasis added.

the spiritual faculties of man by means of new and distinctly supernatural objects and inclinations.[69]

But if all that I am saying here is true, does this not conflict with what I argued above in the previous section? After all, the human being has a natural desire to see God immediately. Is this not a natural desire for the supernatural? We should note that Aquinas underscores two affirmations that are in no way incompatible: (1) the human soul has a natural desire to see God immediately, one that is even philosophically demonstrable, and (2) the human soul is in no way naturally inclined to the supernatural object of faith as such, an object of knowledge that orients the soul toward the supernatural vision of the Holy Trinity.

The first of these affirmations is admittedly quite nuanced. The natural inclination toward contemplation of the truth about God *indirectly* derived from creatures does allow the intellect to desire naturally and rationally by its own powers a yet more immediate knowledge of God. In this regard Aquinas speaks differently of "inclinations" as contrasted with "desires." Our inclinations remain proportionate to our human nature. Our desires, however, which stem from our natural inclinations, can attain those realities that we cannot procure by our own power. It is in this sense that we can understand Aquinas's clear affirmation that there is inscribed in the human intellect an innate desire to see God.[70] The desire to see God is an expression

---

69 Note how significantly the affirmations of Aquinas that we have been considering differ from de Lubac's claims about his thought in *Surnaturel*, 451–52 (regarding *ST* I, q. 23, a. 2): "St. Thomas speaks here in general of two sorts of ends: one which is entirely beyond the proportion of all created nature and which consists in the divine vision, the other which is proportionate to the nature and its powers. He does not say that man, or that the rational creature has a two-fold finality. His doctrine … is … that 'natural' things have an end of the second sort, interior to nature, while spiritual beings have an end of the second kind, beyond all nature" (my translation). De Lubac is claiming that Aquinas's talk of proportionate inclinations does not apply to spiritual realities, but only to natural ones. It is true that Aquinas speaks more commonly (almost exclusively) of a twofold "beatitude," not a twofold "end." But he does affirm that the supernatural object of faith is utterly transcendent of the proportionate end of human nature. Furthermore, Aquinas never contrasts the spirit and nature in the way that de Lubac proposes. Rather, it is simply natural for the human intellect to desire to see God immediately. This natural desire is not identical to a proportionate inclination to the formally supernatural as such. It is this last point that de Lubac's defenders typically fail to see.

70 *De Virtutibus*, q. 1, a. 10: "But just as man acquires his first perfection, that is, his soul, by the action of God, so too he has his ultimate perfection, which is his perfect happiness, immediately from God, and rests in it. Indeed this is obvious from the fact that man's natural desire cannot rest in anything save in God alone. For it is innate in man that he be moved by a desire to go on from what has been caused and inquire into causes, nor does this desire rest until it arrives at the first cause, which is God." "Ita et ultimam suam perfectionem, quae est perfecta hominis felicitas, immediate habet a Deo, et in ipso quiescit: quod quidem ex hoc patet quod naturale hominis desiderium in ullo alio quietari potest, nisi in solo Deo. *Innatum est enim*

of our deepest human inclination to know the truth about the first cause, and at the same time, this desire clearly reaches out beyond what is in our proportionate power to accomplish or achieve. It is not, however, a desire for the formal object of supernatural beatitude as such, which can only be obtained by grace.[71]

Later Thomistic Scholastics like Sylvester of Ferrara and Domingo Báñez would refer to this desire as "an elicited desire to see God."[72] Once the human intellect attains to the elicited (explicit) knowledge of the existence of a transcendent cause (God) through God's effects, it is natural that the mind should still wish (were it possible) to know that cause directly and immediately. Therefore there is a natural desire to see God that arises at the term of the human philosophical quest for the ultimate explanation of reality. But that desire is inscribed in our human nature not in reference to the supernatural as such (formally specified by grace), but rather in reference to the truth about the first cause and final end of all things (formally specified by the natural search for causes). It is for this reason that such commentators also speak of the natural desire to see God as *conditional*. It is true that the human spirit remains fundamentally unfulfilled as regards its own final end if the human intellect does not come to see God. Consequently, it would be most good to know who or what God is in some immediate way, were that possible. But an absolute, resolute hope of seeing God face to face is only possible supernaturally, by grace, once we come to know by faith in divine revelation that such a possibility has really been accorded to us.[73]

One may legitimately contest the language of "elicited desire" and of the "conditional" character of our innate tendency to want to see God immediately. Clearly, this terminology as such is not present in Aquinas's texts, and it does evolve within

---

homini ut ex causatis desiderio quodam moveatur ad inquirendum causas; nec quiescit istud desiderium quousque perventum fuerit ad primam causam, quae Deus est" (emphasis added). *Disputed Questions on Virtue*, trans. Ralph McInerny (South Bend, IN: St. Augustine's Press, 1999).

71 *ST* I-II, q. 62, aa. 1–3.

72 Thomistic commentators classically speak of an "elicited desire" to know God immediately that is stimulated by limited natural knowledge of God as the first cause, and of the "conditional" or "inefficacious" character of this more ultimate desire. I am alluding to the interpretation of Aquinas on the "natural desire to see God" that is characteristic of the Dominican commentatorial tradition (Cajetan, Sylvester of Ferrara, Báñez, and others). On the development of this tradition and the textual foundations for its interpretations, see Feingold, *Natural Desire to See God*, chaps. 8–9, 11–12.

73 *ST* II-II, q. 17, a. 2: "the hope of which we speak now, attains God by leaning on His help in order to obtain the hoped for good. Now an effect must be proportionate to its cause. Wherefore the good which we ought to hope for from God properly and chiefly is the infinite good, which is proportionate to the power of our divine helper, since it belongs to an infinite power to lead anyone to an infinite good. Such a good is eternal life, which consists in the enjoyment of God Himself." This passage displays unambiguous theoretical unity with *ST* I-II, q. 62, a. 1, emphasizing the need for grace precisely because of the limited capacities of natural proportionate inclinations.

the context of subsequent disputes between Thomists and Scotists. Aquinas does not himself speak of the natural desire to see God in these terms. Nevertheless, what is noteworthy is that Aquinas does believe there is a rational basis for arguing philosophically that the human intellect desires naturally to see God immediately. Furthermore, this argument is developed through the medium of an appeal to the imperfect, express knowledge of God attained by natural contemplation, and which itself indicates the natural desire for a yet more complete knowledge of God. One may speak of this awakened desire (indicative of an innate tendency) in terms other than that of elicited desire.[74] But one can readily understand what this term seeks to express: the human being is awakened by knowledge of God to a tendency in himself that nature provides but cannot fulfill, and, at the same time, this tendency is not an inclination toward the supernatural mystery of Christ, formally revealed as such. The latter grace comes gratuitously to act upon the intrinsic desire of the human person in a way that simultaneously fulfills and utterly transcends the innate tendencies of the human heart.

If this vision of Aquinas is correct, as I have argued on the basis of his philosophical analysis of human happiness, then it follows that, *pace* both Barth and de Lubac, a positive Thomistic reading of Aristotle cannot rightly be accused of being either one-sidedly extrinsicist or intrinsicist. Clearly the former is not the case. The natural desire for the vision of God, as Aquinas defends it philosophically (in texts such as *ScG* III, c. 50, and *ST* I, q. 12, a. 1), is a rationally intelligible desire and is therefore necessarily utterly distinct from the hope for the beatific vision inspired by infused theological virtues. But, *just for this reason*, the grace of the vision is not purely extrinsic to the natural disposition and desire. If we return to Aquinas's reasoning, the argument is simple. We can truly know *something* of the primary cause of creation through his effects (the creatures we experience immediately), and therefore natural contemplation of God is possible. Because God is the most intelligible and sovereignly good of all realities, knowledge of him even by way of the mediation of his effects constitutes a genuine form of happiness, however imperfect. So this knowledge is a certain kind of final end for the human person. Precisely because this knowledge is achieved only through the mediation of effects, however, it is imperfect and therefore inchoately suggests the possibility of a higher fulfillment to be desired. In other words, the

---

74 Oliva, "La contemplation des philosophes selon Thomas d'Aquin," 647–49, offers trenchant criticism of the notion of an "elicited desire" to see God as something alien to Aquinas's own views, insisting instead on the innate character of the natural desire to see God in the created human spirit. Oliva does affirm, however, that the innate inclination toward the vision of God becomes manifest through the rational (philosophical) desire to know the first cause. That is precisely why this desire can be analyzed by means of rational argument, as Oliva insists. Consequently, there is a natural mediate knowledge that expresses or manifests in more explicit terms a deeper innate tendency to wish to know the complete truth about God perfectly. Yet none of this should commit us to a natural inclination toward supernatural objects of revelation as such, or a natural desire for the graced knowledge and love of the Holy Trinity per se.

natural desire to see God, or to know God intellectually in himself, is rooted not in an innate inclination for the supernatural, but in an innate natural inclination to seek the truth through explicit and perfect knowledge of causes.[75] This inclination to wish to know God in himself is rooted in us structurally (merely naturally), and therefore the grace that invites us to come to know God immediately by vision is not something wholly alien to our human nature. Karl Barth is famous for claiming in his debates with Emil Brunner regarding natural theology that there is no natural point of contact in the soul wherein grace is received and to which the righteousness of faith is not wholly alien and other.[76] God gratuitously gives grace independently of any natural inclination toward God.[77] On this point, it does seem clear that Aquinas's Aristotelianism contrasts with the views of Barth. One might suggest that Barth's Kantian anthropological presuppositions are not entirely different in this respect from the rationalism of Siger of Brabant.[78] The extremes of antirevelatory rationalism and dialectical revelatory actualism share something profound in common, something to which Aquinas's Aristotelian realism offers us an alternative. His philosophy allows him to avoid a pure grace-nature extrinsicism of the kind de Lubacians might criticize rightly in Barthians and in philosophical rationalists alike.

Yet at the same time, for this very reason (because a natural openness to the possibility of the supernatural is inscribed in our nature), our natural end is not indicative of any natural inclination toward the supernatural as such. Grace remains entirely transcendent of our natural powers, innate inclinations, and proportionate ends. Yet without the natural capacity to know God and the corresponding capacity to desire the felicity of perfect happiness, the grace-inspired supernatural hope of seeing God would itself be wholly unnatural and alien to human nature. No grace could substitute itself or supplement per se for such a natural absence, and indeed the aims of grace would be in this case necessarily opposed to those of nature. Therefore this natural, philosophically identifiable dimension of human nature is the ontological presupposition for the possibility of an economy of grace ordered toward the *lumen gloriae*, or the vision of God. Here Aristotelianism allows Aquinas to avoid a pure grace-nature intrinsicism of the kind Barthians might rightly be concerned about in the theology of de Lubac. It also suggests a deeper irony, however: in the absence of a rigorous anthropology of Aristotelian natural teleology, de Lubac's theology fails to articulate the true grounds for a legitimate integralism or intrinsicism. By risking

---

75 Aquinas, *In I Ethic.*, lec. 2: "Naturale desiderium nihil aliud est quam *inclinatio inhaerens rebus ex ordinatione primi moventis,* quae non potest esse supervacua" (emphasis added).

76 See, for example, Barth, *Church Dogmatics* 1/1, 27–36, 41.

77 Ibid., 238–42. Grace comes to human nature in such a way as to create the conditions for its own reception *sans appui* in human nature as we find it in its fallen state. This gift is radically alien and makes the analogy or likeness to God in us possible only because of the work of grace itself and in differentiation to all that is natural in us as such.

78 On the influence of Kantian epistemology on Barth's theology, see McCormack, *Karl Barth's Critically Realistic Dialectical Theology,* 43–49, 129–30, 155–62, 218–26, 245–62.

the collapse of the natural and supernatural orders into one another, or by not distinguishing them adequately, de Lubac's theology risks running the same ultimate course as that of Barth. There is no natural point of contact, no natural term of human reason, having its own integrity and structure, to which grace addresses itself and that is elevated by grace.[79] Instead, man has *either* a uniquely supernatural destiny *or* a destiny of *natura pura*.[80] A dialectic of either/or reminiscent of Jansenism is inscribed into the heart of the human being. The world is either all for grace or disordered by the turn toward nature alone without grace.

This viewpoint is clearly dissimilar from that of Aquinas, who states that human beings ought to love God above all things naturally, and that this distinctly natural order toward God is distinct from, but also the structural (not temporal) presupposition for the gift of charity.[81] Were this not the case, then the mystery of charity as a grace given to human beings that they might love God above all things would be unnatural, alien, and violent to human nature.[82] The orders of natural and supernatural love are not identical with one another, but neither are they in any way extrinsic to one another. Likewise, the ordering toward contemplative happiness that is natural to man is not identical with the inclination to the beatific vision that is an effect of grace, and cannot procure it as such. But the latter gift of grace is not given in such a way as to remain wholly extrinsic to the natural desire for knowledge of the truth, and especially to the "philosophical" natural desire for the immediate knowledge of God. This natural inclination and desire cannot procure the grace-inspired inclination toward, and hope for, the beatific vision as such. But the latter gift elevates and fulfills a preexisting teleological structure in man. Because of this irreducible duality and simultaneous profound harmony, an authentic Christian culture can and must maintain a vital interest in natural speculative knowledge of God, even while habitually placing such knowledge in the service of Christian life and theological contemplation.

---

79 See the criticism to this effect by Steven A. Long in his *Natura Pura: On the Recovery of Nature in the Doctrine of Grace* (New York: Fordham University Press, 2010), chap. 1. I have offered analogous reflections in "The 'Pure Nature' of Christology: Human Nature and *Gaudium et Spes* 22," *Nova et Vetera* (English ed.) 8 (2010): 283–322.

80 This is why de Lubac insists continually on the *concrete* and *historical* economic state of man as fallen and addressed by grace, in order to defend the idea that the supernatural end of man is his unique end, and that therefore he does not exist in a state of pure nature! Man's natural intellectual activity is ultimately specified by the object of faith as such (leading eventually to the vision), or so one might conjecture, given the nature of the defense being made. See, for example, *Mystery of the Supernatural*, 54–56.

81 *ST* I-II, q. 109, a. 3.

82 *ST* I, q. 60, a. 5: "Since God is the universal good, and under this good both man and angel and all creatures are comprised, because every creature in regard to its entire being naturally belongs to God, it follows that from natural love angel and man alike love God before themselves and with a greater love. Otherwise, if either of them loved self more than God, it would follow that natural love would be perverse, and that it would not be perfected but destroyed by charity."

Conclusion: Aquinas's Christian Aristotelianism and Augustinian Orthodoxy

I have argued that the natural desire for the vision of God is a rational, philosophical desire that arises from man's reaching an imperfect beatitude of the natural contemplation of God and as an outcropping of that beatitude. Therefore (1) when grace promises us a yet higher beatitude of seeing God face to face, it does not act extrinsically to our natural end, and (2) nature is not intrinsically ordered toward the objects of supernatural revelation as such but is surpassed by the higher order of divine life even as it is fulfilled by it. Both arguments make the same point in two distinct ways.

Against Barth and with de Lubac, there exists a natural point of contact in us such that grace is not alien to human nature and can lead human nature without violence through the ascent upward into the supernatural life of God. It does so in profound accord with nature's own highest inclinations and through an accomplishment of those aspirations that nature cannot realize for itself. Aristotelian philosophy thus vindicates Augustinian theology. An Aristotelian sense of the imperfection of natural happiness disposes us to see the ways that the restless heart of man in the economy of God's grace can be elevated to find its most perfect rest only in the supernatural life of God.

Against de Lubac and with Barth, grace is something wholly transcendent of our human nature, to which ordinary human reasoning and willing are not innately and naturally inclined or proportioned. One might say instead that there is an analogy between the natural end (which implies the desire to see God immediately) and the formal object of revelation (which elicits theological hope in the vision of the Holy Trinity) without an identification of the two. Beatified human beings thus remain forever mere creatures who are structurally incapable of any intrinsic possibility of self-divinization, and the work of salvation in us always stems from the ontologically prior, entirely free initiative of God. An Aristotelian philosophical realism regarding the imperfection of human natural capacities for happiness redounds to a deepened Augustinian sense of the sheer gratuity of grace and supernatural beatitude, a life beyond what any human eye has seen, ear has heard, or heart imagined. Seen as the nuanced and coherent encounter of these two truths, Aquinas's Aristotelian Christianity appears for what it is: not an eccentric teaching located at the periphery of Catholic doctrine regarding nature and grace, but rather a form of theology that stands at the core of the Catholic tradition and articulates its diverse elements in a sufficiently intricate, unified way, with a normative value that is irreplaceable and a doctrinal integrity that is unsurpassed.

B

Divine Names

Introduction

In the age of high scholasticism, the summit of philosophical thought was seen to reside in the demonstrative knowledge that we might have of God, and in the speculative contemplation of the attributes of God: properties such as divine simplicity, perfection, goodness, immutability, eternity, and so forth. This medieval vision of philosophy presumes of course that we might derive knowledge of God from creatures, positive knowledge that is both demonstrative and in a sense contemplative. But is this claim true? Do creatures bear any relation of similitude to God, from which we might perceive truths about God himself? If so, *in what way* do the ontological characteristics of creatures (their perfections and limitations) allow us, or not allow us, to speak of what God is and of what God is not? From creatures, how can philosophy offer names for God? As a way of entering into the question, I consider briefly the basic answer offered by Aquinas and some objections to that solution, setting the stage for thinking more deeply about how we might name God philosophically.

In the *Summa theologiae*, Aquinas broaches this topic quite early on, in question 4, article 3 (where he asks, "Whether any creature can be like God?").[1] There he makes a fundamental distinction between what he elsewhere terms "univocal agents" and "non-univocal" or "equivocal" agents.[2] Let us be clear: we are speaking here of

---

Originally published as "Monotheistic Rationality and Divine Names: Why Aquinas' Analogy Theory Transcends Both Theoretical Agnosticism and Conceptual Anthropomorphism," in *God*, ed. Anselm Ramelow (Munich: Philosophia Verlag, 2013), 31–70. Reprinted by permission.

[1] All English citations from the *Summa theologiae* are taken from English Dominicans, trans., *Summa Theologica* (New York: Benziger, 1947).

[2] This precise terminology is employed in *Summa contra Gentiles* I, cc. 29, 31, but the same conceptual analysis and examples used there are presented again here, and later in *ST* I, q. 13, a. 2, to articulate how we analogically speak of God. See the analysis of this conceptual distinction in Aquinas by Norman Kretzmann, *The Metaphysics of Theism: Aquinas's Natural Theology in* Summa Contra Gentiles *I* (Oxford: Clarendon Press, 1997), 147–57.

univocity and equivocity as something that pertains not only to our logical designations about reality (how we name reality), but also as something proper to the reality itself, characterizing the being of things. Univocal agents, for Aquinas, are those who transmit that form or essence of being that they themselves possess to the realities they act upon. Their very natures are transmitted to the other: so a parent communicates human life to his or her child, and both the parent and the child possess the same (essentially identical) human nature. Both are equally human, univocally speaking.

By contrast, the light and warmth of the sun do not make the creatures of the earth to be sunlight or to partake as such of the processes of fusion reaction that are characteristic of the nature of a star. They do, however, transmit effects of the sun, from which there accrues a certain likeness between the light and warmth of the earth and that of the sun itself. This is an equivocal agency because the two realities remain distinct in species or nature. And so it would be equivocal to say that the earth is a sun (because the two are not of the same species), but we can, Aquinas says, attribute a likeness of genus to the two entities, invoking a commonly shared quality: the earth and the sun are both warm bodies, albeit of specifically different kinds and to differing degrees, but in a common genus.

But God is not a generic kind of reality among others, a being among other beings, as we will have occasion to return to later. So how might we speak of him? Here Aquinas posits a famous theorem: "If there is an agent not contained in any *genus*, its effects will still more distantly reproduce the form of the agent, not that is, so as to participate in the likeness of the agent's form according to the same *specific or generic* formality, but only according to some sort of analogy; as existence is common to all. In this way all created things so far as they are beings, are like God, as the first and universal principle of all being … God is essential being, whereas other things are beings by participation."[3] So, for St. Thomas, the philosopher is capable of the rational consideration of the attributes of God by recourse to a process of analogical naming.

Historically, there are positions that take Aquinas's understanding of the analogical naming of God to be problematic by way of mutually opposed extremes. For some, his theory of naming God is too weak and fails to offer a sufficiently strong sense of names that can carry over from creatures to God in "precisely the same sense," that is, univocally. We need univocal predication to safeguard true knowledge of God. This is the view of Duns Scotus, and today it is championed by some analytic philosophers of religion, such as, perhaps most notably, Richard Swinburne.[4] In his

---

3 *ST* I, q. 3, a. 4, corp. and ad 3.
4 See the articulation of this view, for example, in John Duns Scotus, *Opus Oxeniense* I, d. 3, a. 1. On the Scotist doctrine of univocal predication of divine attributes more generally, see Olivier Boulnois, *l'Être et représentation: Une généalogie de la métaphysique moderne à l'époque de Duns Scot* (Paris: Presses Universitaires de France, 1999), and "La destruction de l'analogie et l'instauration de la métaphysique," in *Sur la connaissance de Dieu et l'univocité de l'étant*, (Paris: Presses Universitaires de France, 1988), 11–81; Richard Cross, *Duns Scotus* (Oxford: Oxford University Press, 1999), 33–39, and *Duns Scotus on God* (Aldershot and Burlington:

book *The Coherence of Theism*, Swinburne offers a univocalist account of God's attributes in which he ascribes to God such properties as beliefs, real relations to creatures, existence in time, and being a "substance," presumably in a larger genus with other substances.[5] These are all ascriptions Thomists find anthropomorphic. For others, meanwhile, Aquinas's theory of analogical naming is too strong or too ambitious and fails to acknowledge the radical limitations of all our attempts to describe or prescribe notions for the divine, even when an analogical distance is acknowledged. The radical equivocity of all our names for God recalls to us the truth of the unspeakable and incomprehensible transcendence of God: the divine darkness. This is the view of Heidegger, who builds upon the Kantian prohibition of classical arguments for the existence of God and who labels such scholastic thinking "ontotheology."[6] Today, Jean Luc Marion most eloquently represents this view. He appeals to Dionysius the Areopagite's radical apophaticism in order to develop a phenomenological ontology of divine love, and of the consideration of the creation as gift.[7] Marion wishes to approach the mystery of God by means of the philosophical mystery of the goodness and "givenness" of reality, without recourse to causal argumentation derived from a metaphysical consideration of the being of things.[8] Marion gives a rhetorically potent label to this latter form of reflection, especially when it seeks to speak of God: that of "conceptual idolatry."[9] And in his early work, Marion suggests this ascription could be given even to the work of Aquinas himself.[10]

In the face of these criticisms, the fundamental question is simple, Is Aquinas's account of the analogical naming of God true, and is it helpful to us today in seeking

---

Ashgate, 2005), 251–54. Richard Swinburne appeals to and interprets Scotus in order to articulate aspects of his own theory of religious language, especially in *The Coherence of Theism*, rev. ed. (Oxford: Clarendon Press, 2010), chap. 5. There are further qualifications and applications of the doctrine in *Revelation* (Oxford: Clarendon Press, 1992), chap. 3, and *The Christian God* (Oxford: Clarendon Press, 1994), chap. 7.

5 See, for example, Swinburne, *Coherence of Theism*, chaps. 10 and 12.

6 See, in particular, Martin Heidegger, "The Onto-theo-logical Constitution of Metaphysics," in *Identity and Difference*, trans. J. Staumbaugh (New York: Harper and Row, 1969), 42–74. The notion of ontotheology in the work of Immanuel Kant appears most importantly in *Critique of Pure Reason* II, III, 7.

7 See, for example, Jean Luc Marion, *The Idol and the Distance*, trans. T. A. Carlson (New York: Fordham University Press, 2001); *God without Being*, trans. T. A. Carlson (Chicago and London: University of Chicago Press, 1991); *Being Given: Toward a Phenomenology of Givenness*, trans. J. L. Kosky (Stanford, CA: Stanford University Press, 2002).

8 See *God without Being,* chap. 6; *Being Given,* Books III–V.

9 On this idea, see Jean Luc Marion, "De la 'mort de Dieu' au noms divines: L'itinéraire théologique de la métaphysique," in *l'Être et Dieu*, ed. D. Bourg (Paris: Cerf, 1986), 113.

10 Marion, *God without Being*, 29–32, 73–83, underscores both difficulties and promising possibilities in Aquinas's analogical approach to metaphysical thinking about God. Aquinas is not seen to escape entirely from the dangers of ontotheology. Subsequently, however, he argues that Aquinas's thought does not represent a species of ontotheological thinking. See Jean-Luc Marion, "Saint Thomas d'Aquin et l'onto-théo-logie," *Revue Thomiste* 95 (1995): 31–66.

to talk about the mystery of God philosophically? In what follows I briefly consider the topic from five distinct but interrelated viewpoints that follow upon one another by logical succession. To consider Aquinas's procedure of divine naming, I discuss his "analogical" appropriations of Aristotle, Proclus, and Maimonides. The first section considers the use St. Thomas makes of Aristotle for what Bernard Montagnes terms "predicamental"—here referred to as "horizontal analogy"—or analogical significations of being to diverse modes of *created* being. Meanwhile, Aquinas's use of Proclus in the second section allows us to consider the background of a theory of "transcendental analogy," or significations *posed of God*, derived from creatures.[11] The consideration of Aquinas's critique of Maimonides on divine naming in the third section allows us to see how these forms of analogical signifying steer away from any radically apophatic or even agnostic approach to the divine. What, then, is divine naming as an analogical procedure? This is considered in the fourth section. Last, in the fifth section, I discuss how analogical naming of God is intrinsically open (but in qualified ways only) to the use of attributions of names based on divine revelation (as in Christian Trinitarian theology) as well as metaphorical terms for God (which are frequent in the biblical tradition). The divine names are complementary to human metaphorical speaking about God and to the mystery of divine revelation regarding the inner life of God. These succinct considerations allow us to conclude by thinking about the Judeo-Christian tradition and the philosophical rationality of offering divine names for God.

The Analogy of Being in Creatures

Let us begin by thinking about the origins of the theory of the transcendentals, as it first began to emerge in Aristotle's thought. Aristotle famously differed with Plato regarding the nature of the good, or whether the good has a form in which all other goods participate. In the *Republic*, Plato had offered a theory of the latter: of the good as a transcendent essence or form—an Idea—from which all other realities derive their intrinsic goodness.[12] Aristotle, with his well-known phrase "Plato and the truth I love both but the truth more," parted company with Plato in *Nicomachean Ethics* I, chapter 6, and provided an alternative understanding of the good not as a form, but as a reality or property said analogically by proportionality across a spectrum of categories, or predicamental modes of being.[13] That is to say, realism regard-

---

11   On the distinction of predicamental and transcendental analogy in Aquinas, see Bernard Montagnes, *La doctrine de l'analogie de l'être d'après Saint Thomas d'Aquin* (Louvain: Publications Universitaires; Paris: Béatrice-Nauwelaerts, 1963); Cornelio Fabro, *Participation et causalité selon saint Thomas d'Aquin* (Paris-Louvain: Publications Universitaires de Louvain, 1961).

12   Plato, *Republic* VI, 505a2-507b10; 511b3–e; 533b–c; 541a.

13   Aristotle, *Nic. Ethics* I, 6, 1196b24–26, 27–28: "But of honor, wisdom, and pleasure, just in respect of their goodness, the accounts are distinct and diverse, the good, therefore, is not

ing our immediate experiences provides us with evidence of a complex world, Aristotle's diverse categorical modes of being, in which there are irreducibly diverse genera of beings: substances, their natures, quantities, qualities, relations, habits, actions, passions, times, places, environments, positions.[14] None of these categories are finally and utterly reducible to one another, whether ontologically, logically, experientially, or linguistically. Our ordinary language and phenomenological experiences implicitly suggest a diversity of "folds" to reality that the intellect can then trace conceptually. But the good is said of all these categories, not in a specifically or generically unified way (as in the case of a form), but only in an analogical way, according to proportion. A is to B as C is to D.[15] A good *time* to play American football is different from a good *place* to do so. The *substantial* goodness of a human person insofar as he or she exists is distinct from his or her moral goodness (based on *operative* actions or qualities). (A human being who does great wrong is good in his substantive being, but not in his moral life.) An appropriate *quantity* of wine is distinct from an appropriate *quality*. A good *sweater* is distinct from a good *parent*, and so on. The good is said in many ways, because the goodness of the things themselves is realized according to a spectrum of similitudes, or in analogical fashion.

When Aquinas takes up this idea from Aristotle, he explicitly relates it to his understanding of the analogical significations of not only of the good but also of being, truth, and unity.[16] These notions, often referred to as transcendentals, are called such

---

something common answering to one Idea … Are goods one, then, by being derived from one good or by all contributing to one good, or are they rather one by analogy?" All translations of Aristotle are taken from J. Barnes, ed., *The Complete Works of Aristotle*, 2 vols. (Princeton, NJ: Princeton University Press, 1884).

14 Aristotle appeals to the ontologically primary character of the categorical modes of being in multiple places in his corpus. See, for example, *Categories*, *Physics*, Book I; *Metaphysics*, Books IV and V.

15 Aristotle, *Nic. Ethics* I, 6, 1196a23–29: "Further, since things are said to be good in as many ways as they are said to be (for things are called good both in the category of substance, as God and reason, and in quality, e.g. the virtues, and in quantity, e.g. that which is moderate, and in relation, e.g. the useful, and in time, e.g. the right opportunity, and in place, e.g. the right locality and the like), clearly the good cannot be something universally present in all cases and single; for then it would not have been predicated in all the categories but in one only."

16 Aquinas, *In I Ethic.*, lec. 6, n. 80: "To understand [Aristotle's criticisms of Plato's Idea of the Good] we must know that Plato held the 'ideal' to be the 'ratio' or nature and essence of all things that partake of the idea. It follows from this that there cannot be one idea of things not having a common nature. *But the various categories do not have one common nature, for nothing is predicated of them univocally. Now good, like being with which it is convertible, is found in every category.* Thus the *quiddity or substance*, God, in whom there is no evil, is called good; the intellect, which is always true, is called good. In *quality* good is predicated of virtue, which makes its possessor good; in *quantity*, of the mean, which is the good in everything subject to measure. In *relation*, good is predicated of the useful which is good relative

because they span or transcend multiple categories, and so each of them can only be denoted in analogical ways. So the being of a substance (such as being human) is distinct from the being of a property like a quality (such as being musical). The unity of an operation (such as sight) is different from the unity of a place (such as the parking lot). Truth statements that concern relations ("that is his father") are different from truth statements that concern passions ("he is currently undergoing surgery"). In short, the transcendental notions are both grounded in the multiplicity of the ontological character of reality and are said analogically of that reality.[17]

The upswing of this fact is twofold. First, for Aquinas, it follows necessarily not just for God but even for ordinary realities that surround us, that there are certain nontrivial features of these realities that we *cannot* speak of in purely univocal terms, and to do so would represent a serious misunderstanding of the structure of reality as well as the logic of realistic predication.[18] As Cajetan rightly noted against Scotus, the significations of the good for Aquinas take on their common meaning, or offer a readily identifiable common core only in an analogically unified way: transcendental notions (such as goodness or being) are intrinsically analogical notions, not univocal ones.[19] Goodness, for St. Thomas, can be defined in a unified fashion as that perfection of finality or actuation by which a thing or property becomes in some way appetible or desirable. For we desire the good.[20] But ontologically, the realization of this perfection takes on different forms and only appears mysteriously in and through a diversity of forms: the perfection of a degree of human love simply is formally distinct from the perfection of the art of playing the violin: a good friend, a good violinist. To try to reduce this commonality to a generic form is to rob the no-

---

to a proper end. In *time*, it is predicated of the opportune; and in *place* of a location suitable for walking, as in a summerhouse. *The same may be said of the other categories.* It is clear, therefore that there is not some one good that is the idea or the common 'ratio' of all goods. Otherwise good would not be found in every category but in one alone." Emphasis added. Translation by C. I. Lintzinger, *Commentary on the Nicomachean Ethics* (Chicago: Henry Regnery, 1964). This text resonates with the basic text of Aquinas on the transcendentals as such; *De ver.*, q. 1, a. 1.

17 For further evidence of this view in Aquinas, see his *In IV Meta.*, lec. 2; *In XII Meta.*, lec. 4.

18 For the logically adjacent criticisms of the Platonic forms in Aquinas, see *De ver.*, q. 10, a. 6; *ScG* II, c. 26; III, c. 24, 69; *In Div. Nom.* V, lec. 2.

19 See the study of Cajetan's critique of Scotus on this point by Joshua Hochschild, *The Semantics of Analogy: Rereading Cajetan's* De Nominum Analogia (Notre Dame, IN: Notre Dame University Press, 2010). Hochschild makes the point I am emphasizing ontologically in semantic terms: "Cajetan's analysis of what a proportionally unified concept entails for the rest of logic confirms the importance of context, and the necessary role of judgment, in the use and interpretation of analogical terms. Cajetan, apparently unlike some of his contemporaries, does not hold that words have fixed semantic properties independently of their role in sentences; rather they must be understood and analyzed in light of propositional and inferential context" (174).

20 See *ST* I, q. 5, a. 1; *De ver.*, q. 21, a. 1. Aquinas appeals for his definition of the good in the first of these texts to Aristotle's *Nic. Ethics* I, 1, 1094a3.

tion of the good of its intrinsic flexibility and to obscure the perception of the irreducibly ontologically complex realization of the good.

Second, we can already conclude, even from talking about intraworldly realizations of being or of the good, that God cannot be signified univocally, or under the
sign of a common form shared with creatures, no matter how carefully qualified. For,
as Aquinas notes in the *Summa contra Gentiles* I, 32, if the goodness of God could be
signified—for instance, in univocal continuity with goodness as it is realized in this
world—then goodness would have a formal constitution. It would be a species of
thing, or something specific common to a multiplicity of realities. But if it were a giv-
en species or genus, then it would not be applicable to all the other genera or species
of beings, but only to one.[21] Meanwhile, however, God is not in any one genus of being, for if he were, he would be a subsidiary member of the larger collection of beings
who participate in the being common to all creatures, and would not be the author
of every genus of existent realities.[22] Therefore, just because God exists as the author
of all created being, and of all genera of beings, he cannot partake univocally of a specific or generic attribute in common with other similar kinds of realities.

Likewise, if goodness did pertain to God univocally, it would be applicable to
other realities only metaphorically. Why? Because God alone would be good and
other realities would be so only equivocally speaking, as in a Manichean vision of reality. In other words, because of his essentially unique, univocal possession of goodness, such goodness would be incommunicable to others who do not share in the
divine essence. Or the inverse: some species of created reality known to be good univocally could alone be designated as the good, and God could only be said to be so
equivocally in comparison with that reality. It is as if we were to say that only the lion
is specifically good and everything else is good insofar as it resembles the lion. So
God or Mother Theresa or one's best friend may be said to be good insofar as they are
like the lion. But to say that God is a lion is a metaphor, as there are features of the

---

[21] See *ScG*, I, c. 32, paras. 2 and 4: "An effect that does not receive a form specifically the same
as that through which the agent acts cannot receive according to a univocal predication the
name arising from that form. Thus, the heat generated by the sun and the sun itself are not
called univocally hot. Now, the forms of the things God has made do not measure up to a
specific likeness of the divine power; for the things that God has made receive in a divided
and particular way that which in Him is found in a simple and universal way. It is evident,
then, that nothing can be said univocally of God and other things ... Moreover, whatever is
predicated of many things univocally is either a genus, a species, a difference, an accident, or
a property. But, as we have shown, nothing is predicated of God as a genus or a difference;
and thus neither is anything predicated as a definition, nor likewise as a species, which is constituted of genus and difference. Nor, as we have shown, can there be any accident in God,
and therefore nothing is predicated of Him either as an accident or a property, since property
belongs to the genus of accidents. It remains, then, that nothing is predicated univocally of
God and other things." Translation by A. Pegis, *Summa contra Gentiles* I (Garden City, NY:
Doubleday, 1955).

[22] See *ScG* I, c. 25, paras. 1–3.

essence of being a lion that cannot be attributed to God. For example, God—as the cause of every genus of being—is himself without matter or dependence upon physical causality of any kind. This differentiates him from an animal such as a lion. But just as the lion's nature is not capable of signifying God per se, so neither could goodness, if it were identified with any particular created essence. In the case of the lion, the differentiation from the divine essence is most easily demarcated by appeal to the matter of the being in question. In the case of other creatures, however, some form of complexity would intervene that would inevitably and essentially differentiate that being from God. This is the case even in spiritual creatures such as human beings or angels (presuming the latter exist) because in these beings there is still a difference between the nature of the reality and its existence: the things that exist as creatures do not exist by virtue of their very nature or essence. Rather, they are given being or receive their being from others.[23] But in the case of God, such is not the case. The existence of God is identical with his essence.[24] He thus surpasses every genus of creaturely being and therefore cannot be termed through the univocal appeal of the former in order to signify what he is.

The irony is that by beginning with the insistence on univocity in order to maintain continuity between our creaturely significations and God, we end up with an implicit turn toward radical equivocity that makes it impossible to signify God except by way of creaturely anthropomorphism. This can occur in a metaphorical way when God is depicted problematically in terms of the material forms of things in this world. It can occur in a more metaphysically sophisticated way by employing what are essentially human spiritual modes of being to designate God, without accounting for the transcendent alterity of the divine attributes and the analogical significations of these names, when used rightly of God. And so we end up like Richard Swinburne, ascribing to God changing beliefs, or existence in time, or a host of other anthropomorphic properties. Is this not something akin to what Marion deems "conceptual idolatry"? Univocal name-giving readily begets equivocity theory as a reaction. In reality, however, univocity theorists, to the extent that they avoid this form of problematic thinking, make implicit use of purely analogical concepts to discuss the divine names, at least insofar as they speak truthfully of God.

The Analogy of Being and God

Up to this point we have considered the ways that transcendental properties or names such as being or goodness are ascribed analogically across the horizontal trajectory, so to speak, of intracreaturely reality, that is, the categorical modes of being in this world. But there is another, more ultimate, sense in which they must be said analogically as well, of the first cause of creation. In the passage from creatures to God, there

---

[23] Aquinas, *De Ente et Essentia* IV–V.
[24] *ST* I, q. 3, a. 4; *ScG* I, c. 22.

is a use of analogy that Montagnes and others have termed "transcendental analogy." As a way of understanding this form of thinking, it is useful to consider briefly Aquinas's criticisms of Neoplatonist divine naming, and the way he interprets Proclus's *Book of Causes* as well as Dionysius's *Divine Names* in light of these criticisms.

In relating his understanding of divine names to the work of Proclus in the *Book of Causes*, Aquinas wishes to refute any notion that God is simply to be identified with the common being or goodness that stands at the heart of reality. In doing so, he makes clear his rejection of Neoplatonist emanationist schemas, which posit an underlying unity between the world and God (or seem to). God is not the common being that stands at the heart of reality and in which everything else participates "formally," so to speak.[25] To think this way is possible only if one confuses our intellectual abstract notion of being or of the good with a formal content in reality itself, an error of Plato perpetuated by his disciples.[26] Rather, what one must rightly do is appeal to the notion of God as the transcendent and unique *author* of the common being and goodness of created reality. It is this idea—which he finds in Proclus—that he does appreciatively receive from the Neoplatonic heritage: God alone subsists of himself, and in his simplicity is identical with his own existence and goodness.[27] By contrast, all created reality participates in existence and goodness that it receives from God, and does so only insofar as God is the cause and origin of all that proceeds from him. Consider in this respect Aquinas's commentary on proposition 4 in the *Book of Causes*: "The first of created things is being, and no created thing is before it." St. Thomas interprets it by recourse to Proposition 138: "Of all the principles which participate in the divine character, the first and highest is being."

Now what is common to all the distinct intelligences is first created being. Regarding this he presents the following proposition: *The first of created things is being, and there is nothing else created before it.* Proclus also asserts this in Proposition 138 of his book, in these words: "Being is the first and supreme of all that participate what is properly divine" and of the deified … Dionysius did away with the order of [Platonic Ideas], maintaining the same order as the Platonists in the perfections that other things participate from one principle, which is God. Hence in Chapter 4 of *On the Divine Names* he ranks the name of good in God as the first of all the divine names and shows that its participation extends even to non-being, understanding by non-being prime matter…. But among the other perfections from God that things participate,

25 See the commentary in *In de Causis*, lec. 3, 4, 24.
26 *In de Causis*, lec. 6; *In de Div. Nom* V, lec. 2; *ScG* I, 26; *De sub. sep.*, cc. 1 and 6.
27 *In de Causis*, lec. 21: "Now he proves that God is firstly and maximally simple, by reason of unity: for God is most greatly one since he is the first unity just as he is also the first goodness; and simplicity pertains to the definition of unity. For that which is one, not aggregated from many is called 'simple.' Whence God, insofar as he is firstly and maximally one, he is also firstly and maximally simple" (Elizabeth Anne Collins-Smith, trans., unpublished dissertation, University of Texas at Austin, 1991). Compare Aquinas's similar language in his own treatment of divine simplicity in *ST* I, q. 3, a. 7.

he puts being first. For he says this in Chapter 5 of *On the Divine Names*: "Being is placed before the other participations" of God "and being in itself is more ancient than the being of *per se* life, than the being of *per se* wisdom, and than the being of *per se* divine similitude."[28]

Consequently, Aquinas says, there results a similitude or analogy in the order of being between creatures and God that is derivative from this unique "transcendent" form of causality, a form of causality that is proper to God alone. God alone creates all that exists, and so it resembles him, but only analogically, as an entirely unique kind of cause.[29]

How, then, should we speak about the analogy between creatures and God? Here is the key to divine naming, the process that undergirds our speculative contemplation of the divine attributes. On this central point, Aquinas appropriates the thought of Dionysius the Areopagite and employs the latter cautiously to interpret Proclus's ideas about divine causality in a distinctly Christian monotheistic way.[30]

Aquinas argues that just because there is a unique, analogical, causal resemblance that stems from creation, so the human mind may ascend from the perfections found in creatures to the analogical consideration of the attributes of God. This form of thinking, however, must be threefold. First, because creatures exist and are good and so forth, God can be said to exist and be good analogically, *per viam causalitatis*, by way of causality. Insofar as God is the cause of creatures, their perfections must resemble him. If they have being or are good, then he must have being and be good, yet in a more perfect way, as the cause is greater than the effects. Second, however, we must just as soon affirm negatively (*per viam remotionis* or *negationis*) that God is not existent or good in the way creatures are, and so his divine essence is incomprehensible and unknown. We name him in darkness, for the cause utterly transcends the effects. Lastly, we also can and must affirm that God is existent and good *per viam eminentiae*, by way of preeminence, for whatever the unknown and unknowable existence and goodness of God are, they are superabundant and exceed in perfection anything we can or do know in this world.[31]

---

28 *Commentary on the Book of Causes*, proposition 4. Vincent A. Guagliardo, Charles R. Hess, and Richard C. Taylor, trans., *Commentary on the Book of Causes* (Washington, DC: The Catholic University of America Press, 1996).

29 See the similar doctrine of *ST* I, q. 13, a. 2.

30 See the discussion of this issue by Jan Aertsen, *Medieval Philosophy and the Transcendentals: The Case of Thomas Aquinas* (Leiden: Brill, 1996), 165–70.

31 See *ST* I, q. 12, a. 12. "Our natural knowledge begins from sense. Hence our natural knowledge can go as far as it can be led by sensible things. But our mind cannot be led by sense so far as to see the essence of God; because the sensible effects of God do not equal the power of God as their cause. Hence from the knowledge of sensible things the whole power of God cannot be known; nor therefore can His essence be seen. But because they are His effects and depend on their cause, we can be led from them so far as to know of God 'whether He exists,' and to know of Him what must necessarily belong to Him, as the first cause of all things, exceeding all things caused by Him. Hence we know of His relationship with creatures in so

Notice two things about this procedure. First, it elicits from the intelligence a constructive response of philosophical reason regarding the project of divine naming that is both rational and nuanced, which terminates in a positive form of knowledge. The mind is invited to affirm of God certain perfections that it must in turn also qualify negatively, as well as supereminently. But these qualifications build upon and perfect a fundamentally kataphatic or positive set of significations.[32] God truly is simple, good, wise, eternal, immutable, and so on. In saying such things, we speak truly of God. The life of the intellect is thus carried over in darkness, as it were, toward a light that is hidden yet whose hidden richness and intellectual attraction is divined through the search for the truth about our ontological origins. Against Swinburne, this model of divine naming is both analogical and adequate: it speaks coherently and truly of God as he is in himself, without falling into the anthropomorphisms of univocity.

Second, this procedure seems to place our conceptual gaze upon God at a two-fold distantiation from anything like the "conceptual idolatry" that Marion would seek to ward off. For on the one hand, even "univocal perfections" that we attribute to human beings, such as wisdom, cannot be attributed to God in the way categorical properties are attributed to other persons: for God is not wise by way of a quality that is attributed to his substance (as in a human person), but owing to his simplicity, God simply is his wisdom.[33] This means, however, that to say that God is wise is absolutely true, but it is also in some real sense incomprehensible.[34] That God is wise is something we know to be the case, but what the divine wisdom is itself remains unknown.[35] The mind rests in a positive intellectual judgment, albeit indirect and analogical, of something that pertains truly to God. God is wise, and the mind can rest in this truth. But this is also a rest as in darkness.

Criticisms of Radical Apophaticism

Aquinas's articulation of the divine names of God gives adequate sense to the utter transcendence of God. But does this same procedure veer too inordinately toward the equivocations of agnosticism? To consider the question, let us compare aspects of Aquinas's thought on divine naming with that of Maimonides, who died just a generation before Aquinas began teaching. Like Aquinas, Maimonides offers only a posteriori arguments for the existence of God. He is wary of any direct ideational intuitions of the divine as we find in Anslem's ontological argument. Rather, he seeks to derive from the transient and finite entities of the world we perceive, con-

---

far as He is the cause of them all; also that creatures differ from Him, inasmuch as He is not in any way part of what is caused by Him; and that creatures are not removed from Him by reason of any defect on His part, but because He super-exceeds them all." The basic text of Dionysius from which the threefold *viae* are taken is *De divinis nominibus*, c. 7, 3.

32 *ST* I, q. 13, aa. 2–3, 6, 11.   33 *ST* I, q. 3, a. 6; q. 13, a. 2.

34 *ST* I, q. 3, prol.; q. 13, a. 3.   35 *ST* I, q. 12, aa. 1 and 12; q. 13, a. 6.

sidered as effects, knowledge of the necessary existence of a transcendent cause of the world that exists without ontological change or limitation of power.[36] Nevertheless, for Maimonides, such argumentation is not intended to terminate in any form of positive contemplation or consideration of the attributes or names of God, but only in what we might call a radically apophatic form of equivocity: God cannot be named from this world except negatively.[37] Famously, Maimonides claims that divine names can be taken in two ways. First, they may signify not what God is in himself, but only likenesses of effects derived from God with effects produced by creatures. So to say, for instance, that God is wise is to say that God is the cause of beings that are themselves wise, and that he acts through his effects as does one who is wise. This does not entail that we might properly attribute to God wisdom in and of himself, however. Maimonides affirms the opposite. Second, to attribute to God a name is to affirm only that the negation of that name cannot be ascribed to God. So to say that God is living, for example, is only to say that we cannot ascribe to God the mode of being proper to nonliving things.

While Maimonides does clearly affirm some form of speculative, demonstrative knowledge of God, his philosophy foreshadows in certain respects that of Immanuel Kant. Our demonstrations of the existence of God amount to something akin to a heuristic exercise in rehearsing the possibility of meaning in the universe. But they allow us to say nothing of God in himself. The potential idolatry of the gentile philosophers is displaced by a practical study of the moral law: a turn toward the primacy of practical intellect in the wake of speculative apophaticism. This is one way to read Kant and Maimonides in light of one another (by way of a Kantian intensification of Maimonidian apophaticism). Such a reading is of some influence among modern Orthodox Jewish intellectuals deeply influenced by Kant's treatment of the religious limitations of speculative reason, figures such as Joseph Soloveichik and David Novak.[38]

Aquinas offers a number of points of response to Maimonides's arguments. His simplest and strongest argument states that if all our language concerning God were simply and utterly equivocal, we would be incapable of saying anything about God at all, whether positive or negative, even by way of demonstration: "all our knowl-

---

[36] See *Guide for the Perplexed* II, c.1.

[37] *Guide for the Perplexed* I, cc. 52–59.

[38] Soloveichik was trained in Neo-Kantian theory under Herman Cohen and criticized the causal metaphysics of Maimonides from this perspective, reinterpreting Talmudic observances in light of Kantian anthropology. The speculative antinomies of our inherent "agnosticism" thus open the path to resolution of acute existential human questions only by means of religious faith. Soloveichik locates the resolution of the mystery of being human in the observances of the Torah. See his *The Halakhic Mind* (New York: Free Press, 1986), esp. 92–97; and *Halakhic Man* (Philadelphia: Jewish Publication Society, 1983), esp. 128–37. For the thinking of David Novak on this subject, see, in particular, *The Natural Law in Judaism* (Cambridge: Cambridge University Press, 2008), and *Talking with Christians: Musings of a Jewish Theologian* (Grand Rapids, MI: Eerdmans, 2005).

edge of God is taken from creatures, so that if there were agreement in name alone, we would know nothing of God save some empty words with nothing to underwrite them. It would also follow that all the demonstrations concerning God advanced by the philosophers would be sophistical. For example, if it were said that whatever is in potency is reduced to act by a being in act, and from this it were concluded that God is being in act, since all things are brought into existence by him, there would be a fallacy of equivocation."[39] Because we cannot say truly that God is pure act.

Likewise, if God is spoken of from his effects only by comparison with the effects of creatures and not in himself, then we may say God is fire in that he cleanses us like fire cleanses physically, or that he is wise because he creates order just as wise persons are the source of order in human dealings. But this criterion is so thin that it allows us to equate the application of terms such as fire and wisdom to God with equal and undifferentiated validity. In short, if Maimonides is correct, there is no differentiation possible between rigorously analogical names for God—such as divine simplicity, goodness, wisdom, and so forth—and merely metaphorical names—such as fire, lion, or husband.[40]

Again, if there were no difference between saying that "God is alive" and saying that "God is not a nonliving thing," then there would be no difference between saying "God is alive" and saying that "God is a lion." For a lion is not a nonliving thing. The differentiations between God and creatures must be identified not only through the elaboration of purely negative differences, but also through the articulation of positive differentiations within creatures and between creatures and God.[41]

Aquinas's responses to Maimonides predict in interesting ways consequences of radical equivocity theory. They show prefigurations of the kind of postmodernist forms of divine naming we see arise in the wake of Kant and Heidegger: if we relegate the project of divine naming to the purely equivocal, the philosophical rationality of the Judeo-Christian tradition necessarily becomes unstructured. Our discourse about God loses its grounding in our more proximate and logically prior forms of explanation and demonstration. Consequently, we can no longer justify sufficiently what we say of God philosophically and why. Speculative reason consequently has little to contribute regarding what we might or might not say regarding God. The process of divine naming thus descends into a field where metaphor and analogy stand shoulder to shoulder and become indifferentiated. Two possibilities then emerge. One is that divine naming becomes an exercise in an insufficiently structured form of intuitive description, merging images, univocal names, and analogies, all jumbled together, without sufficient discrimination or rigorous justification. We arguably see this in the writings on the divine in the late Heidegger, in Mari-

---

[39] *De Potentia Dei*, q. 7, a. 7. Ralph McInerny, trans., *Thomas Aquinas: Selected Writings* (London: Penguin Books, 1998). See likewise *ScG* I, c. 33.

[40] *De Potentia Dei*, q. 7, a. 5.

[41] *De Potentia Dei*, q. 7, a. 5.

on's philosophy of God, and in the theology of thinkers like Barth and Balthasar. The other possibility is that divine naming is interpreted as the rhetorical exercise of the author, a sophistical and arbitrary imposition of discourse by the will to power. So then the name of God has to be the subject of a never-ending deconstructionist critique that seeks to explain whether certain metaphors or names are oppressive or liberating in given cultural and political contexts. This is the intellectual backdrop to the religious pluralist and feminist forms of critical skepticism with regard to the classical monotheistic tradition that are prevalent in contemporary religious studies departments. How to adjudicate between either of these options is, it seems to me, impossible, unless we first solve the speculative problem that lies behind their mutual development.

Leave it to say that when divine naming is rightly oriented, no matter by how many important apophatic qualifications, it is necessarily also always analogical in orientation. The knowledge of what God is not is in some way grounded in and pre-supposes some form of kataphatic or positive knowledge of God by way of causal si-militudes, insofar as God is the creative author of the reality from which we begin to know him and name him.

A last but not unimportant comparison of Aquinas and Maimonides should be mentioned with regard to the divine name given in Exodus 3:14–15. The name of God in his singularity given in Exodus 3:15 (*YHWH*) is uttered under the euphe-mism of *Kyrios* in the Greek Septuagint, and "Lord" in English. It seems to be inter-preted in meaning or explicated by Exodus itself in 3:14 with the theological gloss "I am He who is," or perhaps "I will be who I will be." Aquinas follows Maimonides (*Guide for the Perplexed* 1.60–62), as well as Origen and Jerome, in distinguishing between *YHWH* (from Ex 3:15) and "I am He who is" (Ex 3:14) as distinct divine names. Nevertheless, Aquinas also interprets the names as inseparable and mutually related.[42] In his metaphysical exegesis in *ST* I, q. 13, a. 9, and a. 11, ad 1, he identifies the Tetragrammaton as the divine name that signifies the incommunicability of the divine nature in its individuality, just as a singular name signifies the incommunica-bility of the individual human being (like "Paul" or "Rebecca"). This contrasts with the name "God," which signifies the nature (a. 8), and the name "He who is," which signifies the uniqueness of the perfection of God as *Ipsum esse subsistens*: subsistent being in itself (a. 11). Although these signifying terms are diverse, their multiplic-ity is derived from our human manner of knowing God based upon terms drawn from creatures, creatures that are themselves complex. For, as *ST* I, q. 3 (esp. aa. 3–4), has already made clear, while in material creatures there is a real distinction between individuality and nature, as well as between essence and existence, there is no real distinction in God between either nature and individual, or essence and existence. Therefore, while we may rightly designate God in various senses (as existence, deity,

---

42 See Armand Maurer, "St. Thomas on the Sacred Name 'Tetragrammaton,'" *Mediaeval Studies* 34 (1972): 275–86.

or individual) under these terms, in their ultimate ontological ground, they signify he who is absolutely simple. By consequence, the multiplicity of terms can be seen only as complementary and interrelated, within a larger biblical and metaphysical framework of apophatic and kataphatic approaches to naming God. In short, when we say God is he who is, or is the divine nature—or is this singular personal God: the Lord—we are saying three different things and signifying God in three different ways: as existence itself, as he who has the divine nature, and in his personal singularity. But these three are in God himself, truly one.

The point of this particular reflection, however, is to underscore that Aquinas thinks that the philosopher *qua* philosopher can identify a certain analogy even for the naming of God in his singular personal individuality. That is, the philosopher can at least conceive of the possibility of giving a personal name to God, as we give the name "Paul" or "Rebecca" to another. At the same time, however, precisely because of the apophatic and indirect form of our natural knowledge and naming of God, the awareness or knowledge of who God is personally in himself is inaccessible to us.[43] Consequently, while we can speak, with Maimonides, of the so-called philosophical mystery of the individual name of God, or his personal identity, this is something that is not naturally disclosed to us. We stand naturally upon a precipice of darkness, looking out into the divine possibility: the possibility that God should, from the other side of the gulf of unknowing, address us personally, as a "Thou": as he did to Moses in the desert, as "I am He who is." And as he did to all humanity in the human flesh of Christ, the God-man. As Jesus says in the Gospel of St. John, invoking the divine name, "For when you have lifted me up [upon the Cross], then you will know that I am" (Jn 8:28). Sinai and Golgotha speak the divine name to us in a new and henceforth unknown way, to communicate to us the singularity and identity of he who is, and of he who approaches us personally, through the encounter of revelation. But even within the realm of philosophical divine naming alone, we do have a certain analogy from which to "anticipate" this pure possibility of reason: that of the personal disclosure of God's individual singularity, in and through experiential contact.

Offering Divine Names

What, then, is divine naming as an analogical procedure? How does Aquinas himself employ words and concepts to signify the divine? We have looked at various examples above. In various texts, however, Aquinas focuses specifically upon the theoretical issue of how divine naming takes place through analogical significations of the divine nature. And here he famously gives two diverse and potentially competing answers to the question. The first is from *De veritate* q. 2, a. 11 (ca. 1256), while the second is from *Summa theologiae* I, q. 13, a. 5 (ca. 1266). In the first text, Aquinas de-

---

43 Cf. *ST* I, q. 12.

velops the idea of an "analogy of proportionality" between creatures and God. This form of analogy implies a likeness between the properties of two things, without implying any necessary causal relation between the two things. So, for instance, we can see that the human eye perceives and that analogically speaking the human mind perceives. Yet this need not imply that the sensate powers of physical sight depend upon mental insight, or vice versa. Correspondingly, one might speak of human wisdom, or of divine wisdom, and in doing so one is speaking analogically by proportionality. There is something in common between creaturely wisdom and the wisdom of God, but the latter is also different from and unlike human understanding. The divine wisdom, meanwhile, has in itself no "real relation" to human wisdom, meaning that it has no ontological relativity to human creaturely modes of being. The divine wisdom of God is not determined in its very existence in any way by causal dependence upon creatures, nor is it to be grouped in any way within a common genus of wisdom that might conceptually circumscribe modes of wisdom both finite and infinite. The analogy of proportionality is meant to safeguard the absolute transcendence and alterity of God with respect to creatures.

In the later text (*ST* I, q. 13, a. 5), Aquinas characterizes the analogy between creatures and God by what he terms an analogy of attribution *ad alterum*: the analogy between the Creator as cause and his creaturely effects. Here the order of thinking starts from the side of creatures: we approach the mystery of God philosophically only by beginning with the creaturely realities we experience immediately. The arguments for the existence of God are a posteriori demonstrations, by which we argue from the inherent ontological dependencies we see in creatures (in their "chains" of mutual interdependence and contingency) to the necessary existence of a transcendent, creative cause.[44] Because creatures exist, God must exist. The cause is known only through its effects (indirectly and a posteriori), but it is also thus truly known, however imperfectly.

It follows from all this that we can posit necessarily a similitude between the effects and the cause, because every created effect must in some way resemble its transcendent cause.[45] Consequently, all created effects are *related* to their transcendent cause, and their properties can be traced back to him by way of this causal similitude and this corresponding relational dependency. The "analogy of attribution" between creatures and God is therefore not one that refers to God linguistically as an analogate term within a broader set, as if God were a species of being within a larger ge-

---

44 On the demonstrations for the existence of God in Thomas Aquinas, see Edward Feser, *Aquinas* (Oxford: Oneworld Press, 2009); John Wippel, *The Metaphysical Thought of Thomas Aquinas* (Washington, DC: The Catholic University of America Press, 2000); Rudi te Velde, *Aquinas on God* (Aldershot: Ashgate, 2006).

45 On this principle in Aquinas, see John Wippel, "Thomas Aquinas on Our Knowledge of God and the Axiom That Every Agent Produces Something Like Itself," in *Metaphysical Themes in Thomas Aquinas II* (Washington, DC: The Catholic University of America Press, 2007), 152–71.

nus, or a mere member of *ens commune*, one present in the total set of created beings.
Rather, the analogical names we derive from creation for the sovereign and transcendent Creator all refer to him as in darkness, as to that lodestar from which all things
proceed, and in whom all perfections must be present in simplicity and perfect actuation, but who himself rests above the modes of being of mere finite effects. God can
be spoken of using terms derived from creatures (through a process of refinement or
purification), and so words like "simplicity," "perfection," "goodness," "eternity," "wisdom," and so on can be attributed to him, based on the relation between creatures
and God. But what God's very perfection or goodness or wisdom is is something that
remains inscrutable and incomprehensible. We speak the truth of God, but as at the
summit (or in the abyss) of a philosophical "mystery" that is grounded in rational deliberation but also rationally indissoluble.

Many modern commentators on Aquinas have posited that these two texts are
basically opposed on some level, and denote mutually incompatible approaches to the
offering of divine names.[46] The earlier Aquinas sought to underscore the primacy of
the Aristotelian "analogy of proportionality," while the later Aquinas focused upon
a more Platonic form of analogical thinking (analogy of attribution *ad alterum*) that
saw all beings as derived from (participating in) the transcendent gift of being from
God. Aquinas the Aristotelian cedes (in part at least) to Aquinas the Neoplatonist.
This genealogical reading of Aquinas has its intellectual attractions, but it also seems
to overstate implausibly the developmental aspect of Aquinas's metaphysical thinking over the course of ten years. More fundamentally, it certainly seems possible to
read the two texts as basically compatible with one another. On this reading, each underscores a distinct aspect of the process of analogical naming of God: the reality of
inherent similitude of attributes and the causal dependency upon or relationality of
creatures toward the Creator. On this reading, the analogy of attribution is that which
underscores the radical dependence of all creatures upon God: just as they depend
upon him for their very being in act (*actus essendi*), so also God is utterly transcendent
of the creaturely realm, and in him the act of being is identical with his very essence.
He does not receive existence or being in act from others but is himself the unique giver of the gift of creation. So God is simultaneously present in all his creation, but also
hidden, as the cause is discerned obscurely within the effects that are incapable ontologically of representing him adequately. That being said, however, when we turn to
speak of what God is in himself, independently of creatures and from before the dawn
of creation, we must also acknowledge that he has inherent perfections that are to be
attributed to him by virtue of his very nature. If we say, for instance, that God is wise,
or good, or simple, or eternal, we speak truly of that which God is in himself. And so
the analogy of proportionality (A is to B as C is to D) underscores not relational dependence and similitude of effects that depend upon the cause, but the inherent likeness of creatures to God *by way of attributes found analogously in each*. The qualities of

---

46 Most influentially, Montagnes, *La doctrine de l'analogie*.

wisdom found in human beings are in some way inherent to them, just as the substantial wisdom of God is inherent to God and identical with God's very essence. So God truly is wise, and Socrates is truly wise, in two differentiated ways.

One form of analogy (attribution) helps us to safeguard causal dependency and therefore to underscore the transcendence of God. It serves as a caution against univocity, and if we lose sight of it, we risk falling into the dangers of an overly optimistic kataphaticism. The wisdom of God and the wisdom of Socrates may be known truly under a common analogical concept, but that concept needs to be differentiated internally by the rigors of apophatic purification. The distance between the two wisdoms is one that is underscored by remembrance of the unique character of the *actus essendi* of God: God is his wisdom and gives existence to all other beings, and by that measure he remains incomprehensible and intellectually incircumscribable. The other form of analogy (proportionality) safeguards the capacity of analogy to name the intrinsic properties or attributes of God, and serves as a caution against equivocity and radical apophaticism. The cause is not comprehended in its effects, but divine naming may signify the inherent deity of God, however imperfectly and indirectly. Not only is God truly wise, good, simple, and so on, but God is all these things in an incomprehensible form of perfection that exceeds that of being found in creatures. Divine naming is therefore not an agnostic procedure, but speaks under the veil of darkness into the very life of God.

Philosophical Wisdom and Divine Revelation

The view of analogical names for God that we have been considering is based in fact upon claims of natural reason, whether those claims are universally accepted or not. But this admission leaves open the question of knowledge of God by way of divine revelation. Or does it? Does the theory of analogical naming as I have presented it leave room open to the grace of divine revelation? Or is such theory opposed implicitly to the real possibilities of human religion and divine revelation, such that once it is developed to its logical conclusion, reason may no longer become truly receptive to biblical thinking? In this case it would be a kind of "religion within the limits of analogical reason." And certain Reformed and Lutheran critics (such as Karl Barth and Eberhard Jüngel) have argued in diverse ways that this is the case for Aquinas's thought.[47] We should consider how the analogical naming of God is intrinsically open (but in qualified ways only) to the attributions of names based on divine revelation, as one finds in Christian Trinitarian theology. And also (but distinctly!), how does it permit but also qualify the use of metaphorical terms for God, as is frequent in the biblical tradition?

The first question is not about biblical *metaphors*, but rather about *proper analo-*

---

[47] On the criticisms of Barth and Jüngel, see Thomas Joseph White, "How Barth Got Aquinas Wrong: A Reply to Archie J. Spencer on Causality and Christocentrism," *Nova et Vetera* (English ed.) 7, no. 1 (2009): 241–70.

gies that are specific to divine revelation alone, and not proper to philosophical theology. What are some examples? The two most evident that stem from Christian claims of divine revelation are those that denote Jesus of Nazareth as the Son of God and as the Word (taking the latter in the conceptual sense of *logos, verbum*, not in the sensible sense of the spoken word) of God. It is evident that the patristic and scholastic theological tradition took these divine names to be known only through divine revelation, but also to be something other than mere metaphors. That is to say, orthodox Christian doctrine affirms that there is a real distinction of persons in the Most Holy Trinity, such that the eternal Son of God is intemporally begotten of the Father, as the *Logos* of the Father. The analogies of Son and Word here are correlative and in a sense mutually correcting.[48] The analogy of generation implies a real begetting and a real distinction of persons that is constitutive of the very life of God. The analogy of the *Logos* implies that the begetting is wholly immaterial and purely spiritual. Because the begetting in question is nonmaterial, it cannot be represented or even conceived merely in terms of temporal becoming and the historical development of physical bodies. Rather, it must be thought out along the lines of the inner image of God that we find in the spiritual soul of human beings: in terms of the procession of conceptual thought and spiritual wisdom from the subject of the human person. As the human concept is secreted immaterially from the human intellect, through the medium of abstraction, so analogously, the eternal *Logos* proceeds from the Father immaterially. However, because there is a begetting of distinct persons in God, the immaterial procession in God is totally different from the procession of a concept from the mind of a single person. The Son is truly distinct from the Father personally, even as his *Logos* or eternal truth. Furthermore, human thoughts are merely the changing contingent properties of the human subject (accidents of a substance, and ontologically flimsy accidents at that), while the *Logos* is not a characteristic or accidental property of the Father, but possesses in himself the very being and incomprehensible essence of the Father. He is substantially identical with the Father in essence, "God from God, light from light, true God from true God," as the Nicene Creed states. All that is in the Father is in his eternally begotten *Logos*, the Son, who with the Father and the Holy Spirit simply *is* the one God.

One has no reason to know about the inner Trinitarian life of God, apart from the encounter with divine revelation in the person of Christ. And so, correspondingly, if one does have reason to believe in this mystery, it is in virtue of the grace of supernatural faith and not apart from it. But is such belief consonant with the vision of analogical divine names that has been described above, or is it not? From a Thomist point of view, it most certainly is and this affirmation of harmony should be accepted from the beginning as a theological first principle. Supernatural faith and human reason (when each is rightly understood, in and through an unending historical process of mutual purification) do not contradict and may be accepted as presenting distinct but compatible and

---

[48] *ST* I, q. 27, aa. 1–2; q. 34, a. 2.

interrelated truths.[49] On this view, if the exponent of Christian doctrine is to hold that Jesus Christ is both God and man, and is the person of the *Logos* made flesh (Jn 1:14), then he must also hold that Jesus, insofar as he is God, is one in being with the Father (Jn 1:1–3). But if this same Christian thinker is also committed to the kind of robust philosophical account of God to which I have alluded above, then there is also the necessity to qualify or understand the divinity of Christ in light of the divine names that are appropriately given to the one God, in keeping with philosophical reason. Actually, this is said too abruptly, as the scriptural revelation itself gives approbation to a host of divine names that might "overlap" with those articulated in philosophy. In the Bible, after all, God is revealed as being unique and one, sovereignly good, wise, eternal, alive, omnipresent, himself love, just, and so forth. To think about these names is therefore not only to think of God philosophically. Rather, philosophical reflection can come to the aid of theological reflection as a "subordinate science," as a way to seek further clarity and depth of understanding of what divine revelation has already given. Consequently, we might say that sacred theology can seek rightly to understand as deeply as possible not only the truth that the Father, Son, and Holy Spirit are one in being, and yet distinct persons, but also that the divine essence of the Father, Son, and Holy Spirit is itself simple, perfect, good, eternal, infinite, one, life itself, and so on.

In this view, what is not permitted is that we might import univocal conceptions of deity into the life of the divine persons such that philosophical irrationalities are introduced into Trinitarian doctrine. It is perfectly and necessarily true to say that philosophical reason cannot demonstrate nor disprove the existence of the Holy Trinity, for natural reason by its own powers simply cannot attain the divine essence directly, but only names God indirectly from creatures. It thus cannot demonstrate nor disprove that God is essentially a Trinity of persons. For philosophy attaining even to its summit, "what" God is in himself immediately remains veiled. But it is true to say that philosophical reason can detect and diagnose serious philosophical irrationalities when they are introduced into theological reasoning, and can by that same measure seek to safeguard not only the prerogatives of enlightened reason, but also the prerogatives of a sound Christian doctrine of God. If, for example, a narrative of kenotic historical development is introduced into the life of God, such that the Son is differentiated from the Father personally and "formally" in and through his historical existence in time as human, then the temporality of history is introduced into the very constitution of the life of God and the distinction of the Trinitarian persons. By this same measure, however, the unity and the transcendence of God as Creator both risk to be undermined by what, following Marion, we might call another *distinctly theological* species of conceptual idolatry. In this case, the mystery of God's wholly other incomprehensibility is obscured artificially.[50] Philosophy also has

---

[49] This is the view of the First Vatican Council, *Dei Filius* (1870).

[50] This argument is presented in more detail in Thomas Joseph White, "Kenoticism and the Divinity of Christ Crucified," *The Thomist* 75, no. 1 (2011): 1–42.

a necessary role *within* theology that ennobles that theology while also respecting the primacy of the principles of faith that it serves. A healthy philosophical reason aids in the protection of human religious thinking from intellectually problematic forms of anthropomorphism, and from intraworldly projective schemes of conceptuality transferred problematically onto the life of God. Philosophy helps us "keep [ourselves] from idols" (1 Jn 5:21). It also helps us see how a truly profound presentation of Trinitarian faith, that takes divine transcendence seriously, may speak to the profound longing of human reason to have a deeper understanding of the inner life of God. Just as philosophy trails off into the sublime unknowing of the immanent essence of God and only approaches God in darkness, so also the revelation of the Trinity, truly received in supernatural faith, "answers" structurally to the natural desire to know the first cause of created reality.[51] In this way, revelation truly unveils the mystery of God, not in philosophical terms alone, but in the new luminous light and deep obscurity of faith. If that faith is presented in philosophically informed ways, it shows the deep solidarity between our natural aspiration to know the names of God by the pathways of metaphysical reflection and ascent and the supernatural gift of knowledge of the inner life of God by way of the revelation in Christ and the descent of the living God into human flesh and history.

In light of the first topic of revealed analogies, we can more succinctly consider the issue of metaphor. Aquinas notes rightly at the beginning of the *Summa theologiae* that biblical theology is immersed in metaphorical expressions for God and his provident activities.[52] Does the analogical study of the divine names rule out the use of such ascriptions? Clearly not: consideration of the love of God is not opposed to the consideration of God's jealousy. Think of parallels: justice and anger, divine power and the warring arm of God, the life of God and God as a vine who gives sustenance to Israel, the just and merciful decisions of God and the portrait of God as turning his face away or toward us. The real question is not whether the two modes of signification are compatible. In fact, what was said above about the potential for a philosophical, conceptual idolatry would apply here all the more intensively: without analogical thinking of the divine names, the use of metaphors could quickly become insufficiently intellectually structured. God could be envisaged only under the idioms of matter, a veritable "ontic being among beings," in the worst of the Heideggerian senses of that prescription. A naïve literalism can therefore also be fraught with the dangers of a naïve idolatry.

Rather, the real question is: If one does possess both natural and supernatural ascriptions of divine names that are proper and not metaphorical (such as divine simplicity, goodness, unity, but also Sonship, *Logos*, etc.), *then why might there be any need for metaphorical ascriptions at all?* What in fact do they contribute to the rest?

One initial and evident answer is that they condescend to our ordinary human ways of coming to understand any subject matter (including God) through the medium of the sensible and of representational images and symbols. Thinking of God under

---

51 *ST* I, q. 12, a. 1. 52 *ST* I, q. 1, a. 9.

the images of his physical world, through the poetry of divine revelation, is not antiphilosophical or antitheological. On the contrary, this manner of proceeding is integral to and compatible with the human way we think in general about all the things that we consider. Indeed, it is true to say this in a variety of disciplines: the modern sciences, ordinary philosophical analysis, contemporary ethical argument, and political and legal theory. All of these disciplines make great use of metaphors, and it is inevitable that one should grasp an intelligible subject matter through this irreducibly human way of representing reality. To do less would be inhuman, and God comes to human beings through the medium of human knowledge and culture. In doing so, he sanctifies and elevates linguistic metaphorical modes of knowing and signifying to a new plane (in biblical revelation), but in a way that is consistent with our natural way of being.

Likewise, we can also say that metaphors touch upon the embers of the human heart in ways that ennoble and speak more deeply to human affectivity and so to the wholistic composite of the human subject, as both body and soul, mind and symbol, passions and rationality. Metaphorical knowledge illustrates or symbolizes actively, so to speak, the life of grace working among human beings, making the goodness and reality of God *tangible* in ways that mere conceptuality alone could not do adequately. In this sense, the metaphorical incarnation of the scriptures is itself a preparation for and foreshadowing of the ontological incarnation of God in human flesh, and the presence of the activity of God in the sacramental liturgy of the Catholic faith.

The more subtle issue, however, pertains to the richness of symbols, precisely as a form of intellection, for metaphorical knowledge is sometimes more crude than knowledge that is uniquely conceptual. Yet it is also capable of suggesting a plenitude of conceptual depth and plurality in a way that merely conceptual thought is not. To say that Christ is a source of divine grace is itself consonant with the teaching of John 15:5: "I am the Vine and you are the branches." For Christ is the source of divine life, both by virtue of his divinity and through the medium of his human nature, through which he freely gives grace to human beings.[53] It is incomplete, however, to say this alone about the image of the vine. For this image also simultaneously represents something about the way God works progressively in creatures (like viniculture), from within (like sap), and in multiple ways (in a diversity of branches). It suggests by analogy with the growth of plant life on a spiritual plane that God is the resplendent, uncreated wisdom who is the source of the progressive divine illumination of the human mind, that he is the uncreated life of charity who is the inspiration of the movements of growth in charity in the human heart. It suggests that God acts in view of the growth of virtue of human beings, even in view of their redemption (the fruit of the vine), which opens up the question of the final state of the soul after death, and that of the final state of the "vine" of human history. In short, the metaphor, which is often very basic or very material, is also simultaneously suggestive of a depth and wealth of theological conceptuality.

---

53 *ST* III, q. 8, a. 1.

We can finish with a thought regarding the philosophical and theological comparison of religions. The poetic heritage of the Western theological canon (from, say, the Bible to John of the Cross) should be studied simply out of respect for the mature designs of human art and rationality, if for no other reason. But it also serves as a basis for dialogue with the poetic traditions of the Rig Veda, the Buddhist canon of sermons, Confucian philosophy of the political significance of ritual, and Daoist philosophy of nature. The metaphorical and poetic dimension of Scripture serves as a necessary partner to the high speculation of the Judeo-Christian tradition (e.g., in scholastic theology), which has built so extensively upon the foundation of scriptural names of God. But it also can serve as a medium for interaction with the poetic but also highly speculative forms of reflection found in other traditions, often conducted through the medium of their own symbolic and representational modes of expression. Such symbolic thinking often accompanies the more distinctly "philosophical" ontological and ethical analysis one finds in a diversity of human religious traditions.

Therefore the theological study of divine names and the genuine openness to intellectual universality are not rightly juxtaposed or contrasted, but are in fact deeply interrelated. The capacity to understand all things in light of God invites the mind to a more universal horizon, and makes possible the hope of a true intellectual unity, so that the quest for universal truth is not one that occurs in vain or against the backdrop of the void. The deepest capacity to accept and admire the distinction and qualities of the variety of creatures can be found within the aspiration to the knowledge of God. This knowledge invites one to a profound form of respect and gradual, responsible critical judgment regarding the integral values and truths present in the patrimonies of human religious and philosophical reflection.

Conclusion

What might we conclude from these arguments? First, that the analogical use of language is grounded in our ordinary linguistic practices and analysis of commonplace entities. Speaking analogically about the existence, unity, and goodness of created realities entails a process of conceptual unlearning and relearning of the range of meanings of various terms, so as to come to an analogically unified grasp of the ontological complexity of reality. Second, the causality of God is unlike any other, such that when we speak of God, we are necessarily obliged to qualify our language at various removes and by a relatively ornate process of speculative reflection, so that we might speak of God rightly and well. And even when we do so, when we do signify God in what he is, we do so noncomprehensively and apophatically, as speaking of a mystery that infinitely surpasses us, even as it is in some real sense intellectually accessible to us. Third, the philosophical articulation of names for God need not be the arbitrary imposition of a pseudo-rational rhetoric nor a mere exercise of intellectual false hope. On the contrary, the speculative impulse to seek to understand something of God is the noblest aspiration of the human intellect, and is the "place" that our mind might also naturally encounter the philosophical *question* (itself philosophically un-answerable) of the possibility of divine self-disclosure, that is, of divine revelation. That divine revelation itself, meanwhile, elicits the use of a healthy and sound philosophical form of reflection, such that ontological thinking should exist even within the practice of theological reasoning itself. Lastly, however, philosophical and theological traditions do well to enrich themselves by a deep immersion in the poetic and metaphorical traditions of the Bible, as well as the broader traditions of human literature and religious reflection.

The perspective of this chapter is of course set at odds with the tendencies of the contemporary university, which is structured culturally in view of the values of pragmatic liberal pluralism and the axiomatic acceptance of rational heterogeneity. However, the attempt to underscore the existential centrality of knowledge of God is perhaps more pertinent to that same university than might initially be evident. For, historically, the rational search for understanding about God was at the center of the university and gave inward rational unity or teleological orientation to the whole edifice of scientific learning. I am referring to the vision of the medieval university at its origins, but we might apply this classical insight to the heart of the contemporary world by a kind of inversion. What happens when we take away the reference point of God as an object of human investigation? Surely the postmodern fracturing of the distinct scientific discourses in contemporary academic culture is in part related to this noteworthy philosophical absence. Might one not be so bold as to suggest a correspondence between the forgetfulness of philosophical theology and the obscurity of the unity of modern learning?

Of course, what is provocatively said here of philosophical theology might perhaps be stated with even more certainty with regard to philosophy tout court. For it is above all philosophy that gives unity to all other forms of knowledge and brings them all into one ultimate form of organized discourse, and without this, the universality of the university is endangered. But can philosophy really do this without talking about God? According to Aquinas, we know created realities first in our natural order of understanding, but we understand them best only in light of the attributes of God, the first principle and final end of all things. In his light alone do we grasp the meaning of all lesser, created lights. Modern secularized philosophy departments are busy working to protect themselves from the aggressive claims of neuroscience on the one hand, and the relativizing hermeneutical stances of postmodern literature on the other. Philosophy is often seen as trying to reassert its right to exist or its relevance, as it stands between the Charybdis of empiricist reductionism and the Scylla of rationalist relativism. But the way of reassertion of philosophy's irreducible splendor and unifying role even in the heart of the contemporary academy comes in part through the reassertion of philosophy's capacity to seek God, and to speak rationally and truthfully about God. This gives ultimate light to the unity of all natural learning. In this task, the multiform reflections of Thomas Aquinas on the analogical naming of God are an inestimable resource, and one of perennial value.

APPENDIX C

On the Nature of Christian Philosophy

A Response to Critics

I would like first to thank Fr. Burrell and Drs. Healy and Schindler for their attentive reading and extremely thoughtful responses to my book, a work that does not merit the careful attention that they have given to it. Each of them offers both appreciation and critique on a subject that is itself important: the nature of philosophical theology. In what follows I do not seek to respond comprehensively to the many and intricate themes elaborated in the previous three essays. Instead, I take three controversial topics or themes—each of which recurs in more than one of these essays—and respond to them in turn. The idea is not to try to elaborate a final word on the topic under consideration, but to advance the conversation in substantive ways. I treat, then, briefly the following: (1) creation and the philosophical order of discovery versus the order of sapiential judgment, (2) Cajetan and the analogical naming of God, and (3) the topic of Christian philosophy. In responding to these varied (and in some ways opposed) criticisms of *Wisdom in the Face of Modernity*, I hope to offer some clarifications more generally of what I take to be the nature of Christian philosophy.

Creation: Philosophical Order of Discovery and Sapiential Judgment

A central argument of this book is that metaphysical argumentation—especially when treating that of God and the idea of "creation"—must give careful attention to the distinction between the order of progressive discovery of the principles of metaphysics (*via inventionis*) and the ultimate order of judgment regarding those principles, in light of what is most ultimate (judgment *in via judicii*). For example, it is one

"Engaging the Thomistic Tradition and Contemporary Culture Simultaneously: A Response to Burrell, Healy, and Schindler," *Nova et Vetera* (English ed.) 10, no. 2 (2012): 605–23, was originally published as a response to essays by David B. Burrell, D. C. Schindler, and Nicholas J. Healy Jr. in *Nova et Vetera* (English ed.) 10, no. 2 (2012): 531–604. D. C. Schindler's essay was also published in chapter 9 of *The Catholicity of Reason* (Grand Rapids, MI: Eerdmans, 2013). This response is reprinted by permission.

thing to argue progressively (1) that the human being comes to know conceptually by virtue of the power of the agent intellect; (2) that this power for universal abstraction implies that there is a faculty of the soul (intellect) that is immaterial; (3) that this immateriality of the faculty of the intellect implies also that the soul is in some way itself subsistently immaterial and incorruptible; and then (4) to see, in light of metaphysical argumentations for the existence of God as the universal author of created being, that the spiritual soul of the human being must be created immediately by God in the body of the newly conceived human being, without the intermediary of human parents. This is an abbreviated version of a progressive "ascent" toward discovery *in via inventionis*. It is another thing, however, to see the same principles in light of what is ultimate, *in via judicii*, in light of the wisdom of God the Creator, as one can best come to know this wisdom through the work of philosophy. In light of the creation of the soul by God, for instance, who is himself subsistent intellect and wisdom, one can judge that the human soul has intellectual powers as a created imitation of God's own uncreated light and by a certain form of participation in God's exemplary act of knowing. One can judge that knowledge in an intellectual human creature is only a "proper accident" or property of the subsistent person, whereas in God, intellect and subsistence just are in some unfathomable way identical. (God is his wisdom.) Likewise, we can consider from this perspective that even the first act of human knowledge (the simplest, most seemingly "banal" abstract knowledge of the medium-sized dry goods around us) is already a participation (however faint) in the eternal truth of God, and that the dynamic ordering of the human person toward the search for the truth about things in the world is itself already sustained in being by God in view of the possibility of a yet greater encounter with the truth about God. In other words, the knowledge of God is "prefigured" in a certain sense in every other act of ordinary knowledge, as our human potency for the truth is progressively unveiled and its inner tendency toward God becomes more manifest. Nevertheless, *in via inventionis*, this ultimate perspective of seeing the intellectual tendency of the mind toward God is not evident. The judgment "from the top down" that sees the work of the mind in light of God cannot be smuggled in from the beginning *as a logical premise of philosophical demonstration itself*. This would amount to an illicit, artificial hijacking of the integral work of the philosophical endeavor. Rather, this more ultimate perspective comes only at the *term* of the order of investigation and discovery, and as its most sublime, profound, and even in a sense "mysterious" result. In light of the metaphysical discovery of God, everything that has previously been known has to be reevaluated anew, because God is the transcendent cause of all that is.

David Burrell on the one hand and Nicholas Healy and D. C. Schindler on the other differ by extremes when it comes to this general thesis regarding the order of discovery as distinct from the order of final judgment. They differ by extremes, however, because of a common concern that they share: intellectual discomfort with a certain Aristotelian interpretation of Aquinas. For his part, Burrell has defended a conception of Aquinas's philosophical theology that leans heavily upon the initial importance of *monotheistic faith* as a catalyst for medieval thinking about God.[1] He alludes in his critique, therefore, to his ambivalence about the idea of a philosophical demonstration of creation that might depend in some real sense upon Aristotelian metaphysical premises. On this reading, creation is not so much something to be *demonstrated* for Aquinas, as it is something to be presumed ("prephilosophically" in faith) and then *explicated* grammatically and metaphysically. Aquinas's philosophical theology can be seen in one sense as a carefully determined linguistic study in what we can and cannot say regarding the truths of monotheistic faith in the Creator, from the side of mere human reason. The language of metaphysics in Aquinas thus serves to manifest the truth of the Creator and to protect us from betraying the transcendence of the God of revelation. This antirationalist vision of human reason intends to underscore where the soul's authentic source of mystical transformation lies: not in rationalist demonstrations, but through experience of the energies of grace and divine love.

Healy and Schindler, meanwhile, are worried that the Aristotelian-Thomistic account I have offered delivers not too much but far *too little* to human reason *philosophically*. They claim especially that there must be some form of aprioristic knowledge of God that undergirds the rational search for God "from the beginning." Likewise, both Healy and Schindler underscore that there are elements of Aquinas's metaphysics of being that we must "always, already" somehow know from the start, or that at any rate cannot be made to fit squarely within an Aristotelian approach to progressive metaphysical discovery. Among these are the participated character of being, an initial intuitive grasp of the transcendentals, and the "intensive" notion of *esse* that Aquinas creatively adapted from Neoplatonic sources. Why do they insist so much on aprioristic knowledge? Here in fact they are implicitly appealing, through Hans Urs von Balthasar's rereading of the history of philosophy, to the importance of Maurice Blondel: all knowledge we gain—even through our initial desire for truth in ordinary life—is always, already an anticipation of the desire for the immediate vision of the truth of God himself.[2] So the ultimate term of human knowing (even in its supernatural mode) is in some sense anticipated "pretheoretically" in the initial impulses of human *intellectus* (i.e., in basic human insights into ordinary reality). Every act of knowing is an anticipation of the fullness of the knowledge of God, and

---

[1] See the statements to this effect in Burrell's "Analogy, Creation, and Theological Language," in *The Theology of Thomas Aquinas*, ed. Rik Van Nieuwenhove and Joseph Wawrykow (Notre Dame, IN: University of Notre Dame Press, 2005), 77–98, esp. 78, and the argument in David Burrell, CSC, *Aquinas: God and Action* (Notre Dame, IN: University of Notre Dame Press, 1979), 3, 12–13, 135–45.

[2] See in particular the argument of Maurice Blondel, *L'Action: Essai d'une critique de la vie et d'une science de la pratique* (Paris: Alcan, 1893). Apriorist conceptions of knowledge of God are also espoused in *L'Être et les êtres: Essai d'ontologie concrete et intégrale* (Paris: Alcan, 1935).

every act of desire for the truth is an unexplicated intimation of the possibility of the beatific vision.[3] Whereas Burrell would like to assign the tasks of human reason a more moderate horizon of exercise, in respect for the transcendence of divine revelation, Healy and Schindler seem to wish to assign to reason "from the start" a strong set of protheological or protosupernatural impulses. Both views seek to negotiate the relations of faith and reason in such a way as to demonstrate the integral cooperation of the two, but they do so from somewhat competing angles. What these two viewpoints share, however, is an ambivalence about the role played by an Aristotelian doctrine of gradual discovery, especially as it is applied within a Thomistic metaphysics to the truth of creation. For one side (Burrell), the insistence is upon what faith must give from the start, which Aristotle could not have arrived at himself, and which Aquinas did not come to unaided by revelation. For the other side (Healy and Schindler), the truth of revelation is also genetically primal, but philosophical dimensions of the human person also always, already correspond to and anticipate this gift in the form of aprioristic tendencies toward knowledge of God the Creator. The innate teleological end of nature is the world of grace.

What might we say to these two extremes? Briefly, three things. First, it is true that for Aquinas and Aristotle alike, not *all* knowledge per se is attained a posteriori. Following Aristotle, Aquinas argues in his commentary on the *Posterior Analytics* (Book I, lec. 1) that precisely in order to make rational arguments about anything one must first know something else by way of simple apprehensions that precede reasoning.[4] In Thomistic terms, *intellectus* (apprehension/insight) of basic truths gives the epistemological prerequisite for *ratio* or rational argumentation. Were this not the case, we would fall into the error of thinking we had to prove everything we know demonstratively, which is absurd.[5] But what do we know prior to all argumentation? Aquinas himself specifically speaks about the categorial modes of being

---

3   The idea that human natural desire tends implicitly toward the aspiration to the grace of the vision of God is of course a core theme of Blondel's *L'Action*.

4   See *Post. Anal.* I, 1, 71a. Aquinas's commentary on this text touches immediately upon the issue at hand: "Now Plato maintained that science is not caused by syllogisms, but by the impression of ideal forms in our souls. He also said that the material forms in natural things flow from these ideal forms, so that these material forms participate in some way in forms separated from matter. From this if follows that natural agents do not cause the forms of inferior things; all they do is prepare matter to participate in separated forms. Similarly, study and practice do not cause science in us; all they do is remove impediments to scientific knowledge, and restore as it were, a remembrance of things that we know naturally by the impression of separated forms. Aristotle held a contrary view on both points. He maintained that natural forms are made actual by forms existing in matter, i.e., by the forms of natural agents, and, similarly, that science is made actual in us through some kind of pre-existing knowledge. This implies that science results from a syllogism of some kind of argument. For when we argue, we proceed from one thing to another." Thomas Aquinas, *Commentary on Aristotle's* Posterior Analytics, trans. R. Berquist (South Bend, IN: Dumb Ox Books, 2007).

5   See *Post. Anal.* I, 3, 72b5–9, and Aquinas's *ELP*, I, lec. 7.

(substances, with their various essential natures, quantities, qualities, relations, habits, etc.) as the ontological ground from which we take our initial apprehensions of the reality and that we implicitly name in ordinary language.[6] This knowledge is imperfect, however, and needs to develop through progressive analysis of reality. It is for this reason that a theoretical and rational study of metaphysical principles and causes must be developed.[7]

Second, if human beings do advance intellectually only through rational consideration, analysis, and progressive insight (which is the case), then there has to be a progressive study of the principles of being, running from such features of reality as substances and their properties, to potentiality for being versus being in actuality, to existence as distinct from essence, and the consideration of more ultimate themes: participated being and how we see the "transcendental" features of being (unity, goodness, truth, beauty) in light of the created character of being. Evidently, major Thomistic scholars have argued for decades about the precise order in which these diverse principles might be most coherently and convincingly assembled and presented within a progressive scientific study of being. Some (like John Wippel and W. Norris Clarke) begin with participation. Others (like Étienne Gilson, Cornelius Fabro, and Leon Elders) begin with the real distinction between essence and existence or the transcendentals. Others (like Ralph McInerny and Benedict Ashley) start with form and matter (and the philosophy of nature more generally). Others (like Reginald Garrigou-Lagrange, Lawrence Dewan, and myself) begin with substance and accidents and the act/potency distinction. Naturally, not everyone can stand in equally stolid company. But regardless of the diversity of views in such a domain (and all joking aside), the truth is that all the various practitioners of this discipline agree that *all* of these diverse principles and themes are in fact constitutive dimensions of the science of metaphysics, that they are *interrelated* and *must be shown to be so* in any integral presentation of Thomistic ontology. The study of such principles (in whatever precise order that is deemed most adequate) thus seeks to

---

6 *ELP*, prologue.

7 See *ELP* I, lec. 3. Responding to Plato's problem in the *Meno* of the slave boy who can infer geometrical truths, Aquinas writes, "Learning, properly speaking, is the coming-to-be of science in us. But that which comes to be, prior to its coming to be, was not being in the full sense. In one sense it was being, and in another sense it was non-being, i.e., it was being in potency and non-being in act. To come to be is to be brought from potency to act. What we learn, therefore, is neither fully known beforehand, as Plato thought, nor is it altogether unknown.... What we learn was known potentially or virtually in universal principles which were foreknown. But if we understand knowledge (*scientia*) in its proper sense as actual knowledge, then what we learn was *not* foreknown. To learn, therefore, is to be brought from potential or virtual knowledge to knowledge which is proper and actual." Aquinas goes on in *ELP* I, lec. 4, to note how Aristotle shows that the progress of scientific understanding takes place through the knowledge of causes and the demonstrative reasoning that accompanies such knowledge. To illustrate the thesis, he gives explicit examples from passages in the *Metaphysics* of Aristotle regarding the science of being.

explicate the initial *intellectus* regarding the structure of being, allowing it to move out into a deeper rational *scientia*, or scientific understanding of the structure of the real. It is precisely this deeper scientific form of study that permits in turn a yet more ultimate set of considerations regarding the demonstrative knowledge of the existence of God, and the philosophical consideration of creation.

Last, whatever one might say as a non-Thomist, the fact of the matter is that Aquinas, pace Bonaventure, does not think the ontological argument (based upon aprioristic knowledge of God) is a viable or realistic option. Blondel and Aquinas part company on this score.[8] Meanwhile, Aquinas does think that creation (defined as the understanding of the total ontological dependence of creatures upon the first cause for the reception of their very being) is demonstrable by natural reason.[9] He even clearly states that he thinks philosophers such as Plato, Aristotle, and Proclus did attain some form of explicit philosophical awareness of the truth of creation, strictly conceived.[10] Aquinas affirms that there is a uniquely a posteriori form of demonstrative philosophical knowledge of creation as such, and he aims to show this in multiple texts, not least in the second book of the *Summa contra Gentiles*.[11] Consequently, it is clear that he does think that (1) there is a distinctly philosophical scientific order of knowledge that leads progressively to the understanding of creation; (2) this order of discovery does not depend upon faith as such for the reception of its own *intrinsic* principles as a *philosophical* argument; and (3) this form of philosophical discovery allows us to judge all things sapientially in light of God, seeing him in a more ultimate stage of rational reflection as the author of all that exists, so that we can reread all that exists in the light of God's creative activity and wisdom.

Of course there is such a thing as *pre*philosophical or *pre*demonstrative natural knowledge of God in human beings. Aquinas argues in *Summa contra Gentiles* III that all human beings are capable of forming an imperfect metaphysical understanding of the existence of God, based on their ordinary experiences of the created or-

---

8 Blondel presents a version of the ontological argument for the existence of God in *L'Action*, 339–50, as a core idea of that work. Aquinas argues in a contrary sense; see *ST* I, q. 2, a. 1, ad 1 and 2. On Aquinas's rejection of Bonventure's use of the ontological argument, see the recent study by Anna Bonta Moreland, *Known by Nature: Thomas Aquinas on Natural Knowledge of God* (New York: Crossroad, 2010), 147–48.

9 Aquinas says this in the most evident fashion in *ScG* I, c. 9, paras. 2–4, and the affirmation there is supported in turn by the basic outline and arguments of *ScG* II.

10 For texts of Aquinas on Plato and Aristotle, see Mark Johnson, "Did St. Thomas Attribute a Doctrine of Creation to Aristotle?" *New Scholasticism* 63 (1989): 129–55, and Lawrence Dewan, "Thomas Aquinas, Creation and Two Historians," *Laval théologique et philosophique* 50 (1994): 363–87. Aquinas discusses the philosophical doctrine of creation in Proclus in *In de Causis*, commenting on proposition 4: "The first of created things is being, and no created thing is before it." See on this point Jan Aertsen, *Medieval Philosophy and the Transcendentals: The Case of Thomas Aquinas* (Leiden: Brill, 1996), 166–70.

11 Regarding the uniquely a posteriori character of our knowledge of God the Creator, see the unequivocal claims in *ScG* I, cc. 10–11. Likewise, see *ST* I, q. 2, a. 1, ad 1 and 2.

der.[12] Young children can be inducted into a deep sense of the reality of God and his providence. Yet all this is distinct from an aprioristic intuition that precedes (or merely coincides with) the mind's encounter with sensate realities. As has been stated above, such knowledge claims to be prephilosophical and virtually preexperiential. The problem with putting too much of the work of knowledge of God "upfront," in aprioristic intuitivism, is that this risks the collapse of the order of discovery and sapiential judgment into one another, substituting for reasoned argumentation a more poetical, intuitive, and associative form of thought.[13] Rich and seemingly religious as such thought may be, it can have two unfortunate effects: it can block a metaphysical science of being from developing as such (i.e., a disciplined and progressive structure of reflection instead of intuition alone) and, more importantly, it can obscure the grounds or ultimate reasons for the judgment of wisdom itself. By initially trying overly to sacralize ordinary human intuition artificially, we might paradoxically render opaque how the study of ordinary things leads us eventually to the sure demonstrative awareness (in philosophical terms) that even the initial and ordinary forms of knowledge we have are (from the beginning) a true participation in the knowledge that God has of himself. A progressive order of discovery and an ultimate and more sublime form of ordering judgment in light of God are interrelated forms of knowledge, and so the refusal of the former can easily undermine the practice of the latter. The immanent and transcendent poles of God's presence to reason are not to be opposed to one another, of course, but the grasp of their simultaneous reality occurs *for us* according to a certain order.

Cajetan and the Analogical Naming of God

A second topic pertains to analogical naming of God. Here again the critiques diverge, along lines in accord with the former topic. David Burrell is concerned that my account of divine names is overly burdened by a simplistic and artificial dualism of "positive" or "affirmative" names (such as goodness, wisdom, etc.) versus "negative" names (simplicity, infinity). Furthermore, he is not convinced that *ST* I, qq. 3–11,

---

12 See in particular *ScG* III, c. 38.

13 Consider in this respect a citation from Blondel, *L'Action*, 435–36: "There is, then, no object whose reality can be conceived and affirmed without our having embraced in an act of thought the total series, without our actually submitting ourselves to the exigencies of the alternative it imposes on us, in a word, without passing through the point where there shines forth the truth of the Being who illumines every reason and before which every will must take a stand. We have the idea of an objective reality; we affirm the reality of objects. But to do so we must implicitly pose the problem of our destiny and subordinate to an option all that we are and all that is for us. We do not reach being and beings, save by passing through this alternative; depending on the way we decide, the sense of being is inevitably changed. The knowledge of being implicates the necessity of the option; being in knowledge is not before but after the freedom of choice." J. M. Somerville, trans., as cited in Henri Bouillard, SJ, *Blondel and Christianity* (Washington, DC: Corpus Books, 1969), 110.

even constitutes a treatment of divine names at all, and that it may be better characterized as an exercise in identifying formal features of our language as it comes to signify what God is—and, truth be told, more precisely what God is not. He worries that my account of analogical naming claims to deliver more than it can by way of a kataphatic aspiration to signify what God is in himself. He is also concerned that it seeks to do this wrongly, or with insufficient attention to the linguistic forms of Aquinas's discussions of knowledge of God. Schindler, meanwhile, finds the discussion of analogy in the book helpful but wonders whether there is enough continuity safeguarded between creaturely significations and those terms taken from creatures that are employed to signify the reality of God. To simplify drastically, while Burrell worries that the account I offer might aspire to too much by way of the practice of naming God, Schindler worries that it might deliver too little. One is concerned about an absence of apophaticism and the other an excess of apophaticism. Or so it seems to me.

Rather than attempt to respond directly to these concerns, I will present briefly an expansion on the perspective offered in this book, by way of an appeal to analogy theory in Thomas de Vio Cajetan's reading of Aquinas. Cajetan makes two distinctions regarding analogy that are pertinent to the discussion under question (both of which have been pointed out to me by Joshua Hochschild); I think these distinctions might serve as a kind of indirect but substantive response to the opposed concerns of Burrell and Schindler.

First, in his treatise on analogy *De Nominum Analogia* (from 1498), when speaking about analogy of attribution, Cajetan distinguishes between "formal" and "material" considerations of this analogy.[14] Formally (in itself per se), the analogy of attribution involves the denomination of secondary analogates by reference to something extrinsic, the primary analogate. So a medicine might be called "healthy" analogically because the medicine is the cause of something extrinsic to it, namely, the health in the animal. Both the medicine and the animal can be called "healthy," yet health is formally present only in one (the animal) and not the other (the medicine). (We do not inquire into the declining or recovering health of a medicine.) "Materially," however, it may happen that a secondary analogate might in fact share in the same formality or property that is found in the primary analogate. Cajetan gives the examples of being and goodness: an accident can be called a being on account of its relation to substance, which is a being more properly, just as the cause of the being of the accident is the being of the substance. And yet both the substance and the accident truly "exist," albeit in analogically similar ways—accidents do have their own appropriate degree of being, although being is more in the substance than it is in the acci-

---

14 Cajetan, *De Nominum Analogia* II, c. 11. See the particularly helpful study of Joshua Hochschild, *The Semantics of Analogy: Rereading Cajetan's De Nominum Analogia* (Notre Dame, IN: University of Notre Dame Press, 2010). In what follows, I am greatly indebted to comments from and conversations with Professor Hochschild.

dent. It is an open question for Cajetan, given an individual case, whether the formal features of our analogical language are being employed to designate accurately (or to "map onto") *real ontological similitudes in the reality itself.* But Aquinas is clear that in the case of our terms used to signify God, this is precisely what we are doing: taking terms derived from creaturely existents and purifying them of all significations that would be deceptive in order to signify (however imperfectly) something of God that is true in itself.[15] Aquinas follows Aristotle in arguing that every grammatical statement we make is either an affirmation (i.e., positive) or a negation, and so when we speak of God, we necessarily speak in affirmations or negations. There are no other options.[16] The point here, however, is twofold: first, even if positive and negative terms are lodged formally in our language, "materially" the language of God is meant to denote, well, God. And so it is not strange but actually correct to take the exercise of *ST* I, qq. 3–11, to be about the naming of God, precisely through the complex web of semantic indications to which David Burrell gives such splendid and brilliant attention in his book *Aquinas: God and Action.* Second, as Aristotle teaches in the *Posterior Analytics*, and as Aquinas *explicitly* appeals to in his theory of discourse concerning God, every negative judgment we make implies dependence upon some prior and more fundamental positive judgment.[17] To say "John is not here" presupposes some more primal understanding of where "here" is, who "John" is, and so on. Likewise, to denote the divine simplicity, infinity, eternity, and so forth negatively is not only to affirm what God is not, but also to presuppose kataphatic, nonapprehensive knowledge of what God is: pure actuality, perfection, subsistent goodness, subsistent wisdom, and the like. The negative names therefore not only presuppose but also color or qualify in important ways our use of the affirmative or positive names of God.[18] They invite us to consider more truthfully the Creator in his transcendence as utterly differentiated from all creatures, and they allow us to denote his corresponding incomprehensibility.

Cajetan makes a second distinction in his commentary on *ST* I, q. 13, a. 6, that is quite pertinent to this discussion as well.[19] There he notes that the four term-analogy "of proper proportionality" (*A* is to *B* as *C* is to *D*) allows one to compare terms or items without necessarily implying a relation of causal dependence between them.[20] This is a point Aquinas makes in *De ver.*, q. 2, a. 11. To employ an example from St. Thomas, sight is to the eye as understanding is to the intellect. But the act of see-

---

[15] *ST* I, q. 13, a. 2.

[16] *ELP* I, lec. 39.

[17] *ELP* I, lec. 39, n. 8, and lec. 40, n. 1. In his *De potentia Dei*, q. 7, a. 5, Aquinas explicitly applies this idea to the question of divine naming within the context of his discussion of the exaggerated apophaticism of Maimonides.

[18] See *ScG* I, c. 14, para. 3; *De potentia Dei*, q. 9, a. 7.

[19] *Sancti Thomae Aquinatis opera omnia.* Leonine ed., vol. IV, 151–52.

[20] Cajetan, Commentary on *ST* I, q. 13, a. 6, IV.

ing is not the cause of the act of understanding, nor vice versa.[21] What *is* signified by this form of analogy, however, is the intrinsic formal resemblance between two things. So eyes do formally see as actions, and intelligence understands. This form of analogy most carefully safeguards the intrinsic form or resemblance between two beings as *each existing intrinsically* in two distinct ways.[22] Meanwhile, analogy of attribution (*B* is analogous to *A* because *B* is somehow related to *A*) may more readily denote something that proper proportionality does not, because the relation of *B* to *A* may be a causal one, and we know that an effect can be understood as an imitation or participation in the cause.[23] The point Cajetan makes here in regard to *ST* I, q. 13, aa. 5–6, is that Aquinas employs the analogy of attribution to discuss how we can name God from creatures, because he is concerned to show how we can derive names from creaturely effects that can truly designate the transcendent cause, who is the Creator. And yet, in doing so, we are not "assimilating" God conceptually to the prison of our understanding of creaturely modes of being. Why not? Precisely because the attribution of the term *is* analogical: it respects the absolute differentiation between Creator and creature, and the corresponding incomprehensibility of the mystery of God. This differentiation is safeguarded by our realization that God is *ipsum esse subsistens*. He is infinitely perfect and therefore has no composition of created, participated *esse* such that he might be denoted under the auspices of creaturely forms.

If we stopped at this point, we might have enough to counter the concerns of Schindler, simply by insisting that the analogy of attribution does adequately allow us to signify something of what God is in himself, from creatures, without recourse on our part to any a priori knowledge of God. Analogy of attribution thus allows us to signify because its correct use is based upon a knowledge of God derived from his created effects, through metaphysical argumentation.

And yet it was a concern of Cajetan (in dialogue with Scotists) to safeguard the fact that the significations of goodness, wisdom, existence, and so on really do in some way carry over analogically into the designation of the hidden, inner life of God. Here he notes, arguably rightly, that the analogy of attribution that Aquinas employs to name God (in the *Summa contra Gentiles* and the *Summa theologiae*) does itself also presuppose in turn a use of the analogy of proper proportionality. For formally the analogy of attribution is employed to signify extrinsic causality and participation, while formally the analogy of proper proportionality is employed to signify how things are both intrinsically alike and unlike (by diverse affirmations qualified with negations). And so here the two "formal features" of analogy can be

---

21 The example is discussed helpfully by Joshua P. Hochschild, "Analogy in Logic, Metaphysics and Theology: Did St. Thomas Change His Mind about Proportionality?" *The Thomist* 77 (2013): 531–58.

22 Commentary on *ST* I, q. 13, a. 6, IV. See the similar argument in *De Nom. Analogia* III, 29, on the different significations of analogies of attribution and proportionality.

23 Commentary on *ST* I, q. 13, a. 6, IX, XII.

said to converge on the same matter. Attribution taken individually can be employed to signify a *causal* relationship between secondary and primary analogates. Proportionality taken individually can be employed to signify the way in which one analogate may resemble another *intrinsically*. Only if both are employed together, however, can we signify that creatures resemble what God is in himself *intrinsically*, yet they do so only imperfectly, through the means of a causal resemblance, as effects reflecting their transcendent source. God is recognized first and foremost only as a hidden cause of creatures that are his effects, and yet the effects must resemble the cause ontologically in some way. Consequently, we can use both forms of analogy together to emphasize simultaneously both extrinsic causality and intrinsic resemblance, respectively. Attribution is the epistemological ground for the articulation of the creature-Creator analogy, while proportionality brings it to perfection. For example, we may say that God, who is denominated "good" by analogy of attribution as the cause of creaturely goodness, also contains in himself, as cause, an intrinsic superior goodness in which created goodness participates, and so he is also denominated "good" by analogy of proportionality. The two analogies together help to capture the intrinsic likeness of creatures to God (*per viam causalitatis*) as well as the radical otherness of divine goodness from all creaturely finite goodness (*per viam remotionis*), and so also to maintain that the incomprehensible goodness of God, which remains utterly in darkness to our natural human reason, is supereminent to that of all creatures (*per viam eminentiae*). *Because* this relationship of causality is formally extrinsic but also implies a relationship of likeness, the use of the analogy of attribution not only lays the groundwork for respecting the transcendent alterity of God, it also invites us to use proper proportionality to consider the likeness amidst utter difference that creatures have, even to the unknown God.[24]

It seems to me that this interpretation of Aquinas offered by Cajetan satisfies, or at least offers substantive responses to, the twin and opposed concerns of Burrell and Schindler.

Christian Philosophy

Finally, Healy and Schindler are concerned about my orthodoxy as regards the Catholic teaching magisterium. In citing selected texts from papal writings, they hope to signal that we live in a post–Neoscholastic Church, and that there is the danger in my book of the idea of a philosophy "separated" from the influences of faith. I am skeptical about the claim that the Catholic magisterium or the modern popes would resent the renewal of Aristotelian-Thomistic studies today, nor do I think that one is required (by the canons of a sound hermeneutic of the Second Vatican Council) to believe that a radical break has occurred with regard to the Church's long-standing

---

[24] For a similar argument, see F. X. Maquart, *Elementa Philosphiae* (Paris: Andreas Blot, 1938), 2:35–42.

recommendation of the study of Thomistic philosophy. But let us leave this issue to one side. The more substantive question to address in this context is Schindler's claim that the Thomistic approach the book outlines represents a kind of "epistemological Semipelagianism," a philosophy that would seek to approach God apart from or in purposeful ignorance of key resources of faith and theology as gainsays to the tasks of philosophy.[25] What are the influences of theology upon the objects and actions of philosophy? Or, more succinctly, what do we mean by "Christian philosophy"?

The term "Semipelagianism" has its origins in the late sixteenth century. It was employed in the Lutheran *Book of Concord*, and subsequently by Dominicans and Augustinians, in disputes with the Society of Jesus regarding Luis Molina's *Concordia* and throughout the subsequent *De Auxiliis* controversy. The term was employed then and has been used since that time, in particular, to denote the perceived theological errors of the monastic communities of southern Gaul in the fifth century, with whom Prosper of Aquitaine debated in defense of Augustine's mature doctrine of grace. Dominicans and others feared that these errors were repeating themselves (in a different but similar form) in the teachings of Molina. Employed in this way, Semipelagianism denotes pejoratively a particular account of the relationship between grace and free will in ethical actions. Whereas Pelagianism denotes the idea that natural human acts of the will can lead to righteousness before God and salvation (apart from grace), Semipelagianism denotes the idea that the human free will can dispose itself either to integral natural righteousness or even to the merit of grace independently of or apart from the prevenient work of grace. On this account, even if salvation is by grace alone (pace Pelagianism), the reparation of nature and its dispositions for grace can occur morally in the human will (to some extent at least) independently of grace (pace Augustinianism).

In speaking of epistemological Semipelagianism, Schindler is purposefully making an interesting analogical comparison, suggesting that a certain form of Thomistic rational theology would seek to acquire an integral form of wholeness, either as a predisposition to or in autonomous independence from the world of grace, theology, and faith.

It is important to realize that it was not only Dominicans and Augustinians who classically employed the term "Semipelagian" to characterize their theological opponents. The followers of Michael Baius and Cornelius Jansen also employed the term to characterize the ideas of Dominicans as well as Jesuits. And here the term acquired a different meaning, for while it is a fully legitimate concern to insist upon the intimately interrelated domains of grace and nature, supernatural faith and philosophy, it is also an important concern to insist on their real distinction. And it is the absence of a true distinction of grace and nature in the thought of Baius that initially

---

25 This criticism echoes in some respects the one that is found among Protestant critics of Thomism. Robert Jenson is known to have employed an almost identical term for Thomistic natural theology: "epistemological works righteousness."

caused him to come under censor from Pope St. Pius V.[26] Baius, like the Jansenists who came after him, in truth believed the distinction between nature and grace to be in a certain respect a result of the fall of man.[27] Consequently, the true nature of the human free will of man could be identified only within actions of charity.[28] Supernatural and natural converged into one "form" of charity, such that nature and grace were seemingly difficult to distinguish formally. When Rome condemned this idea, the response that was subsequently given by the followers of Baius to the Scholastics was that they were "Semipelagian" for their insistence on the clear distinction of the realms of nature and grace.[29] In truth, we need to avoid two extremes: on the one hand, epistemological Semipelagianism, which would fail to identify the profound ways that philosophy and theology are called upon to interact and mutually affect one another, and on the other hand, epistemological Baianism, which would risk to collapse all philosophy into the world of theology, so that all seeming philosophical and ontological reflection is in some way "always, already" implicitly either Christology (Barth) or theological anthropology (arguably Rahner and the late Przywara as well).[30] The First Vatican Council (in *Dei Filius*) rightly insisted on the distinction of principles and objects of study in the dual orders of natural and supernatural knowledge against the danger of a confusion. The Second Vatican Council (e.g., in *Gaudium et Spes*) emphasized the historical interrelations of grace and nature, faith and reason, especially in addressing the concrete existential questions of the human condition. Our task is to read Vatican I and Vatican II on this question, not in opposition to each other, but within the context of a hermeneutic of profound continuity. In that way the two documents enrich each other. In fact, that is the direction that has been charted by Pope John Paul II's encyclical *Fides et Ratio* (1998).[31] Whether Henri de Lubac and Hans Urs von Balthasar adequately navigated within the territory between the two problematic extremes is of course disputable, but that they sought to do so is clear. Modern Thomism, however, has most certainly sought out an appropriate theological balance in this domain and has done so in promising ways.

---

26 See the condemned propositions from the 1567 bull *Ex omnibus afflictionibus*, in Denzinger, 15th ed., nn. 1001–1080.

27 Denziger, 1004, 1007.

28 Denziger, 1016, 1020, 1025, 1027.

29 This issue eventually entered into the magisterium, as the Jansenist Augustinians began to reject under this name certain scholastic formulations of the doctrine of grace. See the fourth and fifth condemned propositions drawn from the *Augustinus* of Jansenius (Denzinger, 2001–2007): "(4) It is semi-Pelagian to say prevenient grace can be resisted or accepted by the human will. (5) It is semi-Pelagian to say that Christ died for everyone."

30 On the later doctrine of Erich Przywara, see Kenneth Oakes, "The Cross and the *Analogia Entis* in Erich Przywara," in *The Analogy of Being: Invention of the Anti-Christ or the Wisdom of God?* ed. Thomas Joseph White, (Grand Rapids, MI: Eerdmans, 2010), 147–71; see also Richard Schenk, "Analogy as the *discrimen naturae et gratiae*: Thomism and Ecumenical Learning," in White, *Analogy of Being*, 172–91.

31 I am thinking here in particular of *Fides et Ratio*, §75–79.

To consider briefly the topic of "Christian philosophy," we can make two distinctions, both of which stem from the thinking of Jacques Maritain (in his reading of St. Thomas) and both of which are present in the encyclical *Fides et Ratio*.[32] The first of these is the distinction between the *objective* mutual influences of theological faith upon philosophical reason (and vice versa) as compared to the mutual *subjective* influences. The objects of faith influence philosophical reason when a truth of divine revelation and sacred theology invites human reason to the consideration of a deeper understanding of the structure of reality, and does so in ways that can affect reflection, not only theologically as such but also within the domain, so to speak, of philosophy as such. The process can work in the other direction too, as when philosophical ideas affect the way we explicate or approach our theological understanding of divinely revealed mysteries. So, for example, historically, Christian *theological* reflection upon the mystery of the divine persons (including the mystery of the hypostatic union) has stimulated a deeper metaphysical and *philosophical* reflection upon human personhood in general. But also, simultaneously, a deeper philosophical reflection on human personhood (as we find, say, in Aquinas) has affected the ways theologians conceive of the mystery of the Triune persons in analogical distinction to created persons. Similar reflections could be offered regarding topics such as the metaphysics of the one God, creation, the natural law, the ethics of marriage, and so on.

Subjective influences, by contrast, correspond not to the respective objects of philosophy and sacred theology (and their inevitable influence upon each other), but to the broader ways that grace (or its rejection or absence) affects the subject who carries out philosophical study as such—or the ways that grace (or its rejection or absence) affects philosophical culture over time more generally, within the existential mesh of history. Here the key issue is how the presence of grace conditions the development of the intellect not directly (e.g., through the objects of revelation being considered) but indirectly in and through the effects of grace on other faculties, such as the will (principally) as well as the passions. Grace gives the spiritual heart and the emotional and sensate dimensions of the human person a deeper inclination and zeal to study even certain natural topics (such as those pertaining to God, the soul, or the status of objective moral claims). The absence or refusal of grace can incline the will away from whole traditions of philosophy as well as particular philosophical topics. A culture of banalization of the human person through technology, materialism, sensualism, and addiction can form generations of persons in which there occurs a certain typical ha-

---

32 See in particular the analysis of the concept of "Christian philosophy" by Jacques Maritain in *De la philosophie chrétienne* (1932) and *Science et Sagesse* (1935), in his *Oeuvres Completes*, vols. 5 and 6 (Fribourg and Paris: Éditions Universitaires de Fribourg et Éditions St. Paul, 1982 and 1984). What I articulate below is highly indebted to him, but also to Georges Cottier, in his book *Les chemins de la raison: Questions d'épistémologie théologique et philosophique* (Paris: Parole et Silence, 1997). One cannot help but notice both that the language in Cottier's book on Christian philosophy is heavily indebted to Maritain, and that it is virtually identical in various places with the language of *Fides et Ratio*, §75–79.

bituation of the passions and a corresponding secular set of intellectual pursuits and interests. By such a process, the culture itself becomes seemingly impervious to deeper philosophical and moral truths. Therefore there exists in the human person a natural *structure* objectively capable of potentially discovering profound philosophical truths about the human person. Subjectively, however, this structure remains inert or unactualized, thwarted existentially by the cultural and historical as well as personal conditions in which the person or a particular society might try to philosophize.

This last idea brings us to a second Thomistic distinction one can make between the *order of specification* and the *concrete exercise* of that order. Aquinas introduces this distinction in *De Malo*, q. 6, and *ST* I–II, q. 9, a. 1 (as well as other texts), in order to discuss the dual primacy of the will and the intellect. The intellect has a primacy over the will in the order of specification, because what we know formally specifies our act of desiring or willing, and we can love only what we first know. The will, however, has a primacy in the concrete exercise of the life of the mind, because the will moves the intellect to consider this or that object and to focus on this or that discipline or interest. Maritain (and the encyclical *Fides et Ratio* after him) employs Aquinas's distinction slightly differently in order to treat the question of Christian philosophy.[33] This treatment builds upon and expands the use of the previous distinction (objective and subjective mutual influences).

In the order of specification, philosophy and theology are both characterized by distinct objects: they are specifically distinct subject matters that give rise to distinguishable disciplines of study and thought.[34] The sapiential discipline of *sacra doctrina* is formally distinct from that of philosophy, and each science has its own first principles and final ends of reflection. (This was the concern of *Dei Filius* at Vatican I.) Consequently, *Fides et Ratio* insists on the idea of an "autonomy" of specification when it comes to philosophy, which does not receive its first principles or final ends from supernaturally revealed faith as such.[35] Meanwhile, in its concrete exercise, philosophy is subject in a profound way to Christian influences, both objectively (through the consideration of objects of divine revelation, even from a philosophical point of view) and subjectively (through the effects of grace upon human persons and their cultures), within the existential mesh of human history.[36] Consequently, we can

---

[33] See *Fides et Ratio*, §§16, 43, 45, 48, 67, 75, 76, 100. See the study of this aspect of the encyclical by Jean-Miguel Garrigues, "Autonomie Spécifique et Ouverture Personelle de la Raison à la Foi," *Nova et Vetera* (French ed.) 73, no. 4 (1998): 95–106.

[34] *Fides et Ratio*, §76.

[35] *Fides et Ratio*, §75: "Moreover, the demand for a valid autonomy of thought should be respected even when theological discourse makes use of philosophical concepts and arguments. Indeed, to argue according to rigorous rational criteria is to guarantee that the results attained are universally valid. This also confirms the principle that grace does not destroy nature but perfects it: the assent of faith, engaging the intellect and will, does not destroy but perfects the free will of each believer who deep within welcomes what has been revealed."

[36] *Fides et Ratio*, §76.

speak of philosophy as being a distinctly natural discipline in the order of specification, wholly distinguishable from the mystery of divine revelation and from grace as
such. To fail to do so is to fall into epistemological Baianism. But we must also insist
upon the fact that philosophy is always subject in its concrete exercise to the effects
of grace present in a culture or in particular human persons, or to the rejection and
absence of such grace. To fail to do so is to fall into epistemological Semipelagianism.

Philosophy has a true autonomy of specification vis-à-vis theology, but not an
autonomy in its concrete exercise or historical mode of being. We should rightly insist on a distinction of orders, but not a separation or absence of mutual influence.
This is true also of natural theology: it is something structurally possible for human
nature, but in its concrete exercise it will be highly conditioned by the presence of
divine revelation, both with regard to the consideration of certain "objective" dimensions of the study (e.g., as historically in the metaphysical consideration of divine
unity, omnipotence, and omniscience) and in the subjective dispositions it meets in
those who might pursue its study (or fail to) in any given age, cultural setting, or in
the course of one's own personal history.

Schindler and Healy are concerned that the resurgence of a certain kind of Aristotelian Thomism might insist too strongly on the first trait (autonomy) while failing
in various ways to allow for and acknowledge the role of grace in the concrete history
of human philosophizing. In some circumstances, this problematic tendency might
well arise. But let me conclude by noting two counterpoints that must be considered
equally when thinking about the renewal of natural theology within the context of
"Christian philosophy." First, the orders of theological faith and human philosophical reason, while distinguishable, are not intended to be separated but tend inherently under grace toward greater and greater mutual interaction and, in a qualified way,
toward mutual influence. They also tend, *precisely insofar as they mutually influence
each other*, to become each more themselves in terms of their own inner tendencies
and capacities. The person of faith becomes more aware over time of the primacy and
distinctness of the supernatural with respect to the natural, but the philosophical believer also becomes equally aware over time of the integrity or dignity of philosophical argument as such, according to its own inner structure and teleological orientation, in distinction from theological understanding and argumentation. This does
not mean one's philosophy is less dependent upon influences from theology or that
it has less influence over the way theology is conducted. Just the opposite is implied:
a greater sense of the dignity and gratuity of divine revelation can make philosophy
more docile to influences received from faith. And a greater sense of the integrity of
genuine philosophical discovery can greatly enrich theology in its rightful assimilation of philosophical concepts and ideas, in view of uniquely theological ends.

Second, and last, grace presupposes nature in such a way that a culture of grace
(and a forteriori a culture of healthy theology) requires a culture of knowledge of
nature and of philosophical learning. It is not absurd that one might be concerned

about an excessively rationalistic Neoscholasticism. But it is equally important to avoid a culture of theological fideism that has no sufficient grounding in the philosophical knowledge of nature, classical virtue theory, natural law, philosophical understanding of modern science and cosmology, or, above all, philosophical ways of speaking truthfully about God. For a theology that can no longer speak of God metaphysically is no theology at all and will inevitably become (despite whatever kinds of Christocentric intentions are present) a mere narrative theology or, in spite of everything, a mere "theological anthropology." It is precisely to ensure a genuinely Christian philosophy (i.e., a philosophy that is ultimately theocentric in orientation, capable of cooperating with divine revelation) that we need also to be attentive to the integrity of philosophy according to its own inner structure and form of development. This is particularly true with regard to natural theology, which allows human beings to speak rightly and well of God in his incomprehensible transcendence, his immanence to creation, and his sapiential wisdom, which governs all creatures. To do this in Catholic theology today, there is a need for renewal of the study of the metaphysics of Aquinas, his treatment of the "names" of the one God, and his profound philosophical reflection about the structure of human persons and of reality more generally. This form of renewed Thomistic thinking need not cut us off from the deepest forms of conversation with our contemporaries. On the contrary: if it is done rightly, it can help facilitate conversation at a level of profundity and effectiveness that few other intellectual resources in the Catholic tradition have the power to do.

Bibliography

Works by Thomas Aquinas

Collationes super Credo in Deum. Paris: Nouvelles Editions Latines, 1969.

Compendium theologiae ad fratrem Reginaldum socium suum carissimum. Vol. 42 of *Sancti Thomae de Aquino opera omnia*. Leonine Edition. Rome: Editori di San Tommaso, 1979.

De aeternitate mundi, contra murmurantes. In *Opuscula Omnia*, vol. 1, edited by P. Mandonnet. Paris: P. Lethielleux, 1927.

De ente et essentia. In *Opuscula Philosophica*, vol. 1, edited by R. Spiazzi. Turin and Rome: Marietti, 1950.

De malo. Vol. 23 of *Sancti Thomae de Aquino opera omnia*. Leonine Edition. Rome: Editori di San Tommaso, 1979.

De potentia Dei. Edited by P. M. Pession. In *Quaestiones disputatae*, edited by Raymundus Spiazzi, vol. 2. Turin and Rome: Marietti, 1965.

De spiritualibus creaturis. Edited by M. Calcaterra and T. S. Centi. In *Quaestiones disputatae*, edited by R. Spiazzi, vol. 2. Turin and Rome: Marietti, 1965.

De substantiis separatis. Vol. 40 of *Sancti Thomae de Aquino opera omnia*. Leonine Edition. Rome: Editori di San Tommaso, 1969.

De veritate. Vol. 22, pts. 1–3, of *Sancti Thomae de Aquino opera omnia*. Leonine Edition. Rome: Editori di San Tommaso, 1975–1976.

Expositio libri Peryermenias. Vol. 1, pt. 1, of *Sancti Thomae de Aquino opera omnia*. Leonine Edition. Rome: Editori di San Tommaso, 1882.

Expositio libri Posteriorum. Vol. 1, pt. 2, of *Sancti Thomae de Aquino opera omnia*. Leonine Edition. Rome: Editori di San Tommaso, 1882.

Expositio super librum Boethii de Trinitate. Vol. 50 of *Sancti Thomae de Aquino opera omnia*. Leonine Edition. Rome: Editori di San Tommaso, 1992.

In duodecim libros Metaphysicorum Aristotelis expositio. Edited by M. R. Cathala and R. M. Spiazzi. Turin and Rome: Marietti, 1964.

In librum beati Dionysii de divinis nominibus expositio. Edited by Ceslaus Pera. Turin and Rome: Marietti, 1950.

In librum de causis expositio. In *Opuscula Omnia,* vol. 1, edited by P. Mandonnet. Paris: P. Lethielleux, 1927.

In octo libros Physicorum Aristotelis expositio. Edited by P. M. Maggiòlo. Turin and Rome: Marietti, 1965.

Scriptum super libros Sententiarum magistri Petri Lombardi episcopi Parisiensis. Vols. 1–2, edited by P. Mandonnet. Paris: P. Lethielleux, 1929. Vols. 3–4, edited by M. Moos. Paris: P. Lethielleux, 1933–1947.

Sententia libri Ethicorum. Vol. 47 of *Sancti Thomae de Aquino opera omnia.* Leonine Edition. Rome: Editori di San Tommaso, 1969.

Summa contra Gentiles. Vols. 13–15 of *Sancti Thomae Aquinatis opera omnia.* Leonine Edition. Rome: R. Garroni, 1918–1930.

Super Boetium de Hebdomadibus. In *Opuscula Omnia,* vol. 1, edited by P. Mandonnet. Paris: P. Lethielleux, 1927.

Super Epistolam ad Romanos. Vol. 1 of *Super Epistolas S. Pauli,* edited by R. Cai. Turin and Rome: Marietti, 1953.

Summa theologiae. Vols. 4–12 of *Sancti Thomae Aquinatis opera omnia.* Leonine Edition. Rome, 1888–1906.

Translations of Works by Thomas Aquinas

Commentary on Aristotle's Metaphysics. Translated by J. P. Rowan. Notre Dame, IN: Dumb Ox Books, 1995.

Commentary on Aristotle's Physics. Translated by J. P. Rowan. Notre Dame, IN: Dumb Ox Books, 1999.

Commentary on the Book of Causes. Translated by V. Guagliardo, C. Hess, and R. Taylor. Washington, DC: The Catholic University of America Press, 1996.

Commentary on the Gospel of St. John I. Translated by J. Weisheipl. Albany, NY: Magi, 1980.

Commentary on the Nicomachean Ethics. Translated by C. I. Lintzinger. Chicago: Henry Regnery, 1964.

Compendium of Theology. Translated by C. Vollert. London: B. Herder, 1955.

Faith, Reason and Theology. Translated by A. Maurer. Toronto: PIMS, 1987.

On the Power of God. Translated by English Dominican Province. Westminster, MD: Newman, 1952.

Summa contra Gentiles I. Translated by A. Pegis. Garden City, NY: Doubleday, 1955.

Summa contra Gentiles II. Vols. 1 and 2. Translated by J. Anderson. Garden City, NY: Doubleday, 1956.

Summa contra Gentiles III. Vols. 1 and 2. Translated by V. J. Burke. Garden City, NY: Doubleday, 1956.

Summa theologica. Translated by English Dominican Province, 1920. New York: Benzinger Brothers, 1947.

Thomas Aquinas: Selected Writings. Translated by R. McInerny. London: Penguin Books, 1998.

Truth. Translated by R. Schmidt. Chicago: Henry Regnery, 1954.

Classical and Medieval Works

Aristotle. *The Complete Works of Aristotle.* The Revised Oxford Translation. 2 vols. Edited by J. Barnes. Princeton: Princeton University Press, 1984.

Augustine. *Opera Omnia.* Edited by D. A. B. Caillau. Paris: Éditions Pau Mellier, 1842.

Avicenna. *Avicenna latinus, Liber de philosophia prima sive scientia divina.* 3 vols. Edited by S. Van Riet. Leyden and Louvain: Brill and Éditions Peeters, 1977–1983.

Bonaventure. *Opera Omnia.* Quarracchi: Collegii S. Bonaventurae, 1882–1902.

———. *Works of St. Bonaventure.* Vol. 2. Edited by P. Boehmer and Z. Hayes. New York: Franciscan Institute Publication, 2002.

John of St. Thomas. *Cursus Philosophicus.* Paris: Vivès, 1883.

Luther, Martin. *Luther's Works.* Edited by J. Pelikan (vols. 1–30) and H. Lehmann (vols. 31–55). Philadelphia: Fortress Press, 1955–.

Plato. *Complete Works.* Edited by J. M. Cooper and D. S. Hutchinson. Indianapolis and Cambridge: Hackett Publishing, 1997.

Plotinus. *Enneads.* Translated by S. MacKenna. London: Penguin, 1991.

Scotus, John Duns. *Opera Omnia.* Vatican City: Typis Polyglottis Vaticanis, 1950–1993.

Suarez, Francisco. *Opera Omnia.* Paris: Vivès, 1856–1877.

Modern Works

Aertsen, Jan. *Medieval Philosophy and the Transcendentals.* Leiden: Brill, 1996.

———. *Nature and Creature.* Leiden: Brill, 1988.

Andia, Ysabel de. "*Remotio–negatio.* L'évolution du vocabulaire de saint Thomas touchant la voie négative." *AHDLMA* 68 (2001): 45–71.

Anscombe, Elizabeth. "Causality and Determination." In *Causation,* edited by E. Sosa and M. Tooley, 88–104. Oxford: Oxford University Press, 1993.

Appold, Kenneth. *Orthodoxie als Konsensbildung: Das theologische Disputationswesen an der Universität Wittenberg zwischen 1570 und 1710.* Beitrage zur historischen Theologie. Tübingen: Mohr Siebeck, 2004.

Ariew, Roger. "Descartes and Scholasticism: The Intellectual Background of Descartes' Thought." In *The Cambridge Companion to Descartes,* edited by J. Cottingham, 58–90. Cambridge: Cambridge University Press, 1992.

Ashley, Benedict. "The River Forest School and the Philosophy of Nature Today." In *Philosophy and the God of Abraham,* edited by R. James Long, 1–16. Toronto: Pontifical Institute of Medieval Studies, 1991.

————. *The Way toward Wisdom*. Notre Dame: Notre Dame University Press, 2006.

Aubenque, Pierre. *Le Problème de l'Être chez Aristote*. Paris: Presses Universitaires de France, 1972.

————. "Étienne Gilson et la Question de l'Être," in *Étienne Gilson et Nous*. Paris: J. Vrin, 1980, 79–92.

Balmes, Marc. *Peri Hermeneias: Essai de réflexion, du point du vue de la philosophie première, sur le problème de l'interprétation*. Fribourg: Éditions Universitaires de Fribourg, 1984.

Balthasar, Hans Urs Von. *Cordula oder der Ernstfall*. Einsiedeln: Johannes, 1966.

————. *The Moment of Christian Witness*. Translated by R. Beckley. San Francisco: Ignatius, 1994.

————. *The Theology of Karl Barth*. Translated by E. Oakes. San Francisco: Ignatius, 1992.

Barth, Karl. *Church Dogmatics* I, 1. Translated by G. W. Bromiley and T. F. Torrance. London and New York: T&T Clark, 2004.

Bastit, Michel. "Etiologie et Théologie." In *Essais sur la Théologie d'Aristote*, edited by M. Bastit and J. Follon, 51–68. Louvain: Éditions Peeters, 1998.

————. *Les Principes des Choses en Ontologie Médiévale*. Bordeaux: Éditions Bière, 1997.

————. *Le Quatre Causes De L'Être Selon La Philosophie Première D'Aristote*. Louvain: Éditions Peeters, 2002.

————. "La Science Théologique d'Aristote." *Revue Thomiste* 93 (1993): 26–49.

————. "Le Thomisme est–il un Aristotélisme?" *Revue Thomiste* 101 (2001): 101–16.

Berti, Enrico. "De qui est fin le moteur immobile?" In *Essais sur la Théologie d'Aristote*, edited by M. Bastit and J. Follon, 5–28. Louvain: Éditions Peeters, 1998.

————. "Multiplicity and Unity of Being in Aristotle." *Aristotelian Society* 101, no. 2 (2001): 185–207.

————. "Reconsidérations sur l'Intellection de 'Indivisibles' selon Aristotle, *De Anima* III, 6." In *Corps et Âme*, edited by R. Dherbey, 391–404. Paris: J. Vrin, 1996.

————. "Unmoved Mover(s) as Efficient Cause(s) in *Metaphysics* L, 6." In *Aristotle's Metaphysics Lambda*, edited by M. Frede and D. Charles, 181–206. Oxford: Clarendon Press, 2000.

Betz, John. "Beyond the Sublime: The Aesthetics of the Analogy of Being." *Modern Theology* 21, no. 3 and 22, no. 1 (2005 and 2006): 367–411 and 1–50.

Blondel, Maurice. *L'Action*. In *Oeuvres Completes*, vol. 1. Paris: Presses Universitaires de France, 1995.

————. *L'Être et les tres*. Paris: Librarie Felix Alcan, 1935.

Bodéüs, Richard. *Aristote et la théologie des vivants immortels*. Paris: St. Laurent, 1992.

Bonino, Serge–Thomas. "Pluralisme et théologisme." *Revue Thomiste* 94 (1994): 530–53.

Boulnois, Olivier. *l'Être et représentation.* Paris: Presses Universitaires de France, 1999.

———. "La destruction de l'analogie et l'instauration de la métaphysique." In *Sur la connaissance de Dieu et l'univocité de l'étant,* texts of John Duns Scotus, 11–81. Paris: Presses Universitaires de France, 1988.

———. "Quand commence l'onto-théo-logie? Aristote, Thomas d'Aquin et Duns Scot." *Revue Thomiste* 95 (1995): 85–108.

Bradley, Denis. *Aquinas on the Twofold Human Good.* Washington, DC: The Catholic University of America Press, 1997.

———. "Rahner's *Spirit in the World*: Aquinas or Hegel?" *Thomist* 41 (1977): 167–99.

———. "Transcendental Critique and Realist Metaphysics." *Thomist* 39 (1975): 631–67.

Brock, Stephen. "Harmonizing Plato and Aristotle on *Esse*: Thomas Aquinas and the *De hebdomadibus.*" *Nova et Vetera* (English edition) 5, no. 3 (2007): 465–94.

———. "On Whether Aquinas's Ipsum Esse Is 'Platonism.'" *Review of Metaphysics* 60 (2006): 723–57.

Brunner, Emil. *The Christian Doctrine of God.* Translated by O. Wyon. Philadelphia: Westminster, 1950.

Burrell, David. *Aquinas: God and Action.* Notre Dame: University of Notre Dame Press, 1979.

———. "Distinguishing God from the World," *Language, Meaning and God: Essays in Honour of Herbert McCabe, O.P.* Edited by B. Davies. London: Geoffrey Chapman, 1987.

———. *Freedom and Creation in Three Traditions.* Notre Dame: University of Notre Dame Press, 1993.

Carraud, Vincent. *Causa sive ratio: La raison de la cause, de Suarez à Leibniz.* Paris: Presses Universitaires de France, 2002.

Chene, Dennis Des. *Physiologia: Natural Philosophy in Late Aristotelian and Cartesian Thought.* Ithaca and London: Cornell University Press, 1996.

Clarke, William N. *Explorations in Metaphysics.* Notre Dame: University of Notre Dame Press, 1994.

———. *Person and Being.* Milwaukee: Marquette University Press, 1993.

———. *The Philosophical Approach to God: a Neo-Thomist Perspective.* Winston-Salem, NC: Wake Forest University Press, 1979.

Colin, Pierre. *L'Audace et le Soupçon: la crise du modernisme dans le catholicisme français 1893–1914.* Paris: Desclée de Brouwer, 1997.

Come, Arnold B. *Kierkegaard as Humanist; Discovering My Self.* Montreal: McGill-Queen's University Press, 1995.

Cottier, George. *Le Désir de Dieu; Sur Les Traces de Saint Thomas.* Paris: Parole et Silence, 2002.

————. *Les Chemins de la Raison*. Paris: Parole et Sagesse, 1997.

————. "Thomisme et modernité." In *Saint Thomas au XXe Siècle*, edited by S. Bonino, 352–61. Paris: Éditions St.-Paul, 1994.

Couloubaritsis, Lambros. *La Physique d'Aristote*. Bruxelles: Éditions Ousia, 1997.

Courtine, Jean-François. *Inventio analogiae Métaphysique et ontothéologie*. Paris: J. Vrin, 2005.

————. "Métaphysique et ontothéologie." In *La Métaphysique: son histoire, sa critique, ses enjeux*, edited by J.-M. Narbonne and L. Langlois. Paris and Quebec: J. Vrin and Les Presses de l'Université de Laval, 2000.

————. *Suarez et le système de la métaphysique*. Paris: Presses Universitaires de France, 1990.

Cross, Richard, *Duns Scotus*. Oxford: Oxford University Press, 1999.

————. *Duns Scotus on God*. Aldershot and Burlington: Ashgate, 2005.

————. "Where the Angels Fear to Tread: Duns Scotus and Radical Orthodoxy." *Antonianum* 76, no. 1 (2001): 7–41.

Dalferth, Ingolf. *Theology and Philosophy*. Oxford: Blackwell, 1988.

Descartes, René. *Méditations Métaphysiques*. Paris: J. Vrin, 1978.

Dewan, Lawrence. "Aristotelian Features of the Order of Presentation in St. Thomas Aquinas' *Summa theologiae, Prima pars*, qq. 3–11." In *Philosophy and the God of Abraham*, edited by R. James Long. Toronto: Pontifical Institute of Medieval Studies, 1991.

————. "Aristotle as a Source for St. Thomas' Doctrine of *esse*." www.nd.edu/ Departments/Maritain/ti00/schedule.htm.

————. *Form and Being: Studies in Thomistic Metaphysics*. Washington, DC: The Catholic University of America Press, 2006.

————. "Jacques Maritain, St. Thomas, and the Birth of Metaphysics." *Études Maritainiennes/Maritain Studies* 13 (1997): 3–18.

————. "Thomas Aquinas, Creation and Two Historians." *Laval théologique et philosophique* 50, no. 2 (1994): 363–87.

Dieter, Theodor. *Der junge Luther und Aristoteles; Eine historisch-systematische Untersuchung zum Verhältnis von Theologie und Philosophie*. Berlin and New York: De Gruyter, 2001.

Di Noia, J. A. "Karl Rahner." In *The Modern Theologians*, edited by D. F. Ford, 118–33. Oxford: Blackwells, 1997.

Donneaud, Henri, ed. "Correspondance Étienne Gilson–Michel Labourdette." *Revue Thomiste* 94 (1994): 479–529.

————. "Étienne Gilson et Maurice Blondel dans le Débat sur la Philosophie Chrétienne." *Revue Thomiste* 99 (1999): 497–516.

————. "La *Revue Thomiste* et la Crise Moderniste." In *Saint Thomas au XXe Siécle*, edited by S. Bonino, 76–94. Paris: Éditions St.-Paul, 1994.

————. "*Surnaturel* au crible du thomisme traditionnel." *Revue Thomiste* 101 (2001): 53–71.

Dumoulin, Bertrand, *Analyse Génétique de la Métaphysique d'Aristote*. Paris: Les Belles Lettres, 1986.

Dych, William V. *Karl Rahner*. Collegeville, MN: Liturgical Press, 1992.

Elders, Leo, "Aristote et l'objet de la métaphysique." In *Autour de Saint Thomas d'Aquin*, 147–66. Paris: FAC Éditions, 1987.

———. *Aristotle's Theology*. Assen: Van Gorcum, 1972.

———. "La connaissance de l'être et l'entrée en métaphysique." *Revue Thomiste* 80 (1980): 533–48.

———. "La Nature et l'Ordre Surnaturel." *Nova et Vetera* (French edition) 70, no. 1 (1995): 18–35.

———. "La premier principe de la vie intellective." *Revue Thomiste* 62 (1962): 571–86.

———. *La Théologie Philosophique de Saint Thomas d'Aquin*. Paris: Téqui, 1995.

———. "Le Rôle de la Philosophie en Théologie." *Nova et Vetera* (French edition) 72, no. 2 (1997): 34–68.

———. *The Metaphysics of Being of St. Thomas Aquinas in a Historical Perspective*. Leiden: Brill, 1993.

———. *The Philosophical Theology of Thomas Aquinas*. Leiden: Brill, 1993.

———. "St. Thomas Aquinas' Commentary on the *Metaphysics* of Aristotle." In *Autour de St. Thomas d'Aquin*, 123–46. Paris: FAC Éditions, 1987.

Emery, Gilles. "The Immutability of the God of Love and the Problem of Language Concerning the 'Suffering of God.'" In *Divine Impassibility and the Mystery of Human Suffering*, edited by J. Keating, and T. J. White. Grand Rapids: Eerdmans, 2009.

———. *The Trinitarian Theology of Saint Thomas Aquinas*. Translated by F. Murphy. Oxford: Oxford University Press, 2007.

Fabro, Cornelio. *Participation et causalité selon saint Thomas d'Aquin*. Paris-Louvain: Publications Universitaires de Louvain, 1961.

Feingold, Lawrence. *The Natural Desire to See God according to St. Thomas Aquinas and His Interpreters*. Dissertation, Rome, 2001.

Festugière, A. J. *Les Trois Protreptiques de Platon*. Paris: J. Vrin, 1973.

Floucat, Yves. "Enjeux et Actualité d'une Approche Thomiste de La Personne." *Revue Thomiste* 100 (2000): 384–407.

———. "Étienne Gilson et la métaphysique thomiste de l'acte d'être." *Revue Thomiste* 94 (1994): 360–95.

Forest, Aimé. *La Structure Métaphysique du Concret*. Paris: J. Vrin, 1931.

Fouilloux, Étienne. *Une Église en Quête de Liberté: la Pensée Catholique Française entre Modernisme et Vatican II, 1914–1962*. Paris: Desclée de Brouwer, 1998.

Freddoso, Alfred J. "Introduction." In Francisco Suarez, *On Creation, Conservation and Concurrence: Metaphysical Disputations, 20–22*. South Bend, IN: St. Augustine's Press, 2002.

Frede, Michael. *Essays in Ancient Philosophy*. Oxford: Clarendon Press, 1987.

———. "La Théorie Aristotélicienne de l'Intellect Agent." In *Corps et Âme*, edited by Romeyer Dherbey, 377–90. Paris: J. Vrin, 1996.

Garrigou-Lagrange, Reginald. *Dieu, Son Existence et Sa Nature*. Paris: Beauchesne, 1914.

———. *Le Sens du Mystère et le Clair-Obscur Intellectuel*. Paris: Desclée et Brouwer, 1934.

———. *Les Preuves de Dieu*. Paris: Beauchesne, 1910.

Garrigues, Jean-Miguel. "Autonomie Spécifique et Ouverture Personelle de la Raison à la Foi." *Nova et Vetera* (French edition) 98, no. 3 (1998): 95–106.

Geiger, Louis. *La Participation dans la Philosophie de S. Thomas d'Aquin*. Paris: J. Vrin, 1942.

———. *Philosophie et Spiritualité*. 2 vols. Paris: Cerf, 1963.

Gilson, Étienne. *Autour de St. Thomas*. Paris: J. Vrin, 1983.

———. *Being and Some Philosophers*. 2nd ed. Toronto: Pontifical Institute of Medieval Studies, 1952.

———. *Constantes Philosophiques de l'Être*. Paris: J. Vrin, 1983.

———. *Correspondance avec Jacques Maritain, 1923–1971*. Edited by G. Prouvost. Paris: J. Vrin, 1991.

———. *Elements of Christian Philosophy*. Garden City, NY: Doubleday, 1959.

———. *Études sur le rôle de la pensée médiéval dans la formation du système cartésien*. Paris: J. Vrin, 1984.

———. *Index Scholastico-cartésien*. Paris: Alcan, 1913.

———. *Introduction à la Philosophie Chrétienne*. Paris: J. Vrin, 1960.

———. *Jean Duns Scot, introduction à ses positions fondamentales*. Paris: J. Vrin, 1952.

———. *Le Thomisme*. 5th ed. Paris: J. Vrin, 1948.

———. *Le Thomisme*. 6th ed. Paris: J. Vrin, 1965.

———. *L'Être et l'Essence*. 2nd ed. Paris: J. Vrin, 1972.

———. *Réalisme Thomiste et Critique de la Connaissance*. Paris: J. Vrin, 1939.

———. *Thomism: The Philosophy of Thomas Aquinas*. 6th ed. Translated by L. Shook and A. Maurer. Toronto: PIMS, 1992.

———. *The Unity of Philosophical Experience*. New York: Scribner and Sons, 1937.

Goris, Harm. "Steering Clear of Charybdis: Some Distinctions for Avoiding 'Grace Extrinsicism' in Aquinas." *Nova et Vetera* (English edition) 5, no. 1 (2007): 67–80.

Gorman, Michael, and Jonathan J. Sanford, eds. *Categories Historical and Systematic Essays*. Washington, DC: The Catholic University of America Press, 2004.

Griffiths, Paul. "How Reason Goes Wrong: A Quasi-Augustinian Account of Error and Its Implications." In *Reason and the Reasons of Faith*, edited by P. Griffiths and R. Hütter, 145–59. New York and London: T&T Clark, 2005.

Haldane, J., and J. Smart, *Atheism and Theism*. Oxford: Blackwells, 1996.

Halper, Edward. "Aristotle on Knowledge of Nature." *Review of Metaphysics* 37 (1984): 811–35.

Hart, David Bentley. *The Beauty of the Infinite.* Grand Rapids: Eerdmans, 2003.

———. "No Shadow of Turning: On Divine Impassibility." *Pro Ecclesia* 11 (2002): 184–206.

———. "The Offering of Names: Metaphysics, Nihilism, and Analogy." In *Reason and the Reasons of Faith,* edited by P. Griffiths and R. Hütter, 255–94. New York and London: T&T Clark, 2005.

Hegel, G. W. F. *Lectures on the Philosophy of Religion.* Vol. 3. Translated by R. Brown, P. Hodgson, J. Stewart. Berkeley and Los Angeles: University of California Press, 1985.

Heidegger, Martin. *Being and Time.* Translated by J. Macquarrie and E. Robinson. Oxford: Blackwells, 2000.

———. *The Fundamental Concepts of Metaphysics: World, Finitude, Solitude.* Translated by W. McNeill and N. Walker. Bloomington: Indiana University Press, 2001.

———. *Hegel's Phenomenology of Spirit.* Translated by P. Emad and K. Maly. Bloomington: Indiana University Press, 1988.

———. *Identity and Difference.* Translated by J. Staumbaugh. New York: Harper and Row, 1969.

———. *Introduction to Metaphysics.* Translated by G. Fried and R. Polt. New Haven and London: Yale University Press, 2000.

Holtzer, Vincent. "Analogia Entis–Christologique et Penseé de l'Être chez Hans Urs von Balthasar." *Theophilyon* 4, no. 2 (1999): 463–512.

Humbrecht, Thierry-Dominique. *Théologie Négative et Noms Divins chez Saint Thomas d'Aquin.* Paris: J. Vrin, 2005.

Hütter, Reinhard. *Desiring God: The Natural Desire for the Vision of God according to Thomas Aquinas. An Essay in Catholic Theology.* Naples, FL: Sapientia Press, forthcoming.

———. "The Directedness of Reasoning and the Metaphysics of Creation." In *Reason and the Reasons of Faith,* edited by P. Griffiths and R. Hütter, 160–93. New York and London: T&T Clark, 2005.

Irwin, T. H. *Aristotle's First Principles.* Oxford: Clarendon Press, 1988.

Israel, Jonathan. *Radical Enlightenment.* Oxford: Oxford University Press, 2001.

Jaeger, Werner. *Aristotle: Fundamentals of the History of His Development.* Oxford: Clarendon Press, 1948.

Jenson, Robert. *Systematic Theology.* Vol. 1, *The Triune God.* Oxford: Oxford University Press, 1997.

Johnson, Mark. "Did St. Thomas Attribute a Doctrine of Creation to Aristotle?" *New Scholasticism* 63 (1989): 129–55.

Jordon, Mark. "The Grammar of *Esse*: Re-reading Thomas on the Transcendentals." *Thomist* 44 (1980): 1–26.

Journet, Charles. *Connaissance et inconnaissance de Dieu.* Paris: Desclée de Brouwer, 1969.

———. *Introduction à la Théologie.* Paris: Desclêe de Brouwer, 1947.

Jüngel, Eberhard. *God as the Mystery of the World.* Translated by D. Guder. Grand Rapids: Eerdmans, 1983.

Kahn, Charles. "Aristotle on Thinking." In *Essays on Aristotle's De Anima,* edited by M. Nussbaum and A. Rorty, 359–79. Oxford: Clarendon Press, 1992.

Kant, Immanuel. *Critique of Pure Reason.* Translated by N. Kemp Smith. London: Macmillan, 1990.

———. *The Metaphysics of Morals.* Translated by M. Gregor. Cambridge: Cambridge University Press, 1996.

———. *Prolegomena to Any Future Metaphysics.* Translated by P. Carus and J. Ellington. Indianapolis and Cambridge: Hackett Publishing, 1977.

———. *Religion within the Boundaries of Mere Reason.* Translated by A. Wood and G. Di Giovanni. Cambridge: Cambridge University Press, 1998.

Kasper, Walter. *Jesus the Christ.* Translated by V. Green. Tunbridge Wells, UK: Burns and Oates, 1993.

Kerr, Fergus. *Immortal Longings: Versions of Transcending Humanity.* London: SPCK, 1997.

Kisiel, Theodore. *The Genesis of Heidegger's Being in Time.* Berkeley and Los Angeles: University of California Press, 1993.

Knasas, John. *The Preface to Thomistic Metaphysics.* New York: Peter Lang, 1990.

———. "Transcendental Thomism and the Thomistic Texts." *Thomist* 54 (1990): 81–95.

Kockelmans, Joseph. *On the Truth of Being.* Bloomington: Indiana University Press, 1984.

Kosman, Aryeh. "The Activity of Being in Aristotle's *Metaphysics.*" In *Unity, Identity and Explanation in Aristotle's Metaphysics,* edited by T. Scaltsas, D. Charles, and M. L. Gill, 195–215. Oxford: Oxford University Press, 1994.

Kretzmann, Norman. *The Metaphysics of Creation.* Oxford: Clarendon Press, 1999.

———. *The Metaphysics of Theism.* Oxford: Clarendon Press, 1997.

Le Guillou, Marie-Joseph. "Surnaturel." *Revue des Sciences Philosophiques et Théologiques* 34 (1950): 226–43.

Lennox, James. "Plato's Unnatural Teleology." In *Platonic Investigations,* edited by D. O'Meara, 195–218. Washington, DC: The Catholic University of America Press, 1985.

Leo XIII. *Encyclical Letter Aeterni Patris.* Reprinted in English in vol. 1 of the *Summa theologica.* Westminster: Christian Classics, 1981.

Libera, Alain de. *La Philosophie Médievale.* Paris: Presses Universitaires de France, 1989.

Lloyd, G. E. R. "*Metaphysics Λ,* 8." In *Aristotle's Metaphysics Lambda,* edited by M. Frede and D. Charles, 245–74. Oxford: Clarendon Press, 2000.

Lonergan, Bernard. *Grace and Freedom.* In *The Collected Works of Bernard Lonergan,* vol. 1. Toronto: University of Toronto Press, 2000.

————. *Gratia Operans.* In *The Collected Works of Bernard Lonergan*, vol. 1. Toronto: University of Toronto Press, 2000.

————. *Insight.* New York: Harper and Row, 1978.

Loewenich, Walther von. *Luther's Theology of the Cross.* Belfast: Christian Journals, 1976.

Lubac, Henri de. *Le mystère du surnaturel.* Paris: Aubier, 1965.

————. *Surnaturel.* Paris: Éditions Montaigne, 1946.

MacDonald, Scott. "Aquinas' Parasitic Argument." *Medieval Philosophy and Theology* 1 (1991): 119–55.

MacIntyre, Alasdair. *Three Rival Versions of Moral Inquiry.* Notre Dame: University of Notre Dame Press, 1990.

Mandonnet, Pierre. *Review of Le Thomisme* by Étienne Gilson, 2nd ed. *Bulletin thomiste* 1 (1924): 133–36.

Mansion, Susan. *Le Jugement d'Existence Chez Aristote.* Louvain: Centre De Wulf-Mansion, 1976.

Maquart, F. X. "Aristote n'a-t-il affirmé qu'une distinction logique entre l'essence et l'existence?" *Revue Thomiste* 26 (1926): 62–72 and 267–76.

Maréchal, Joseph. *Le Point de Départ de la Métaphysique*, Cahier V. Paris: Librarie Félix Alcan, 1926.

————. *Point de Départ de la Métaphysique* V. 2nd ed. Paris: Desclée de Brouwer, 1949.

Marion, Jean-Luc. "De la 'mort de Dieu' au noms divines: l'itinéraire théologique de la métaphysique." In *l'Être et Dieu*, edited by D. Bourg, 103–32. Paris: Cerf, 1986.

————. "Saint Thomas d'Aquin et l'onto-théo-logie." *Revue Thomiste* 95 (1995): 31–66.

Maritain, Jacques. *Approches de Dieu.* In *Oeuvres Complètes*, vol. 10. Fribourg and Paris: Éditions Universitaires and Éditions St.-Paul, 1985.

————. *Approches sans Entraves.* In *Oeuvres Complètes*, vol. 13. Fribourg and Paris: Éditions Universitaires and Éditions St.-Paul, 1992.

————. *Court Traité de l'Existence et de l'Existant.* In *Oeuvres Complètes*, vol. 9. Fribourg and Paris: Éditions Universitaires and Éditions St.-Paul, 1990.

————. *De Bergson à Thomas d'Aquin.* In *Oeuvres Complètes*, vol. 8. Fribourg and Paris: Éditions Universitaires and Éditions St.-Paul, 1989.

————. *De la philosophie chrétienne.* In *Oeuvres Complètes*, vol. 5. Fribourg and Paris: Éditions Universitaires and Éditions St.-Paul, 1982.

————. *La Philosophie Bergsonienne.* In *Oeuvres Complètes*, vol. 1. Fribourg and Paris: Éditions Universitaires and Éditions St.-Paul, 1986.

————. *Les Degrés du Savoir.* Paris: Desclée de Brouwer, 1932.

————. *Les Degrés du Savoir.* In *Oeuvres Complètes*, vol. 4. Fribourg and Paris: Éditions Universitaires and Éditions St.-Paul, 1983.

————. *Sagesse.* In *Oeuvres Complètes*, vol. 9. Fribourg and Paris: Éditions Universitaires and Éditions St.-Paul, 1990.

————. *Science et Sagesse.* In *Oeuvres Complètes*, vol. 6. Fribourg and Paris: Éditions Universitaires and Éditions St.-Paul, 1984.

————. *Sept Leçons sur l'Être.* Paris: Téqui, 1933.

Markum, Richard. *Signs and Meanings.* Liverpool: Liverpool University Press, 1996.

Marshall, Bruce. "Faith and Reason Reconsidered: Aquinas and Luther on Deciding What Is True." *Thomist* 63 (1999): 1–48.

————. *Trinity and Truth.* Cambridge: Cambridge University Press, 2000.

Mascall, Eric. *Existence and Analogy.* London: Longmans, Green, 1949.

————. *He Who Is: A Study in Traditional Theism.* London: Longmans, Green, 1943.

————. *The Openness of Being.* London: Darton, Longman, and Todd, 1971.

————. *Words and Images: A Study in Theological Discourse.* London: Longmans, Green, 1957.

Maurer, Armand. *Being and Knowing.* Toronto: Pontifical Institute of Medieval Studies, 1990.

McCabe, Herbert. *God Matters.* London: Continuum, 1987.

McCormack, Bruce. *Karl Barth's Critically Realistic Dialectical Theology.* Oxford: Clarendon Press, 1995.

McGrath, S. J. *The Early Heidegger and Medieval Philosophy: Phenomenology for the Godforsaken.* Washington, DC: The Catholic University of America Press, 2006.

McInerny, Ralph. *Being and Predication.* Washington, DC: The Catholic University of America Press, 1986.

————. *Aquinas and Analogy.* Washington, DC: The Catholic University of America Press, 1996.

————. "Do Aristotelian Substances Exist?" *Sapientia* 44 (1999): 325–38.

————. *Praeambula Fidei: Thomism and the God of the Philosophers.* Washington, DC: The Catholic University of America Press, 2006.

McKirahan, Richard, Jr. *Principles and Proofs: Aristotle's Theory of Demonstrative Science.* Princeton: Princeton University Press, 1992.

Milbank, John. *The Suspended Middle: Henri de Lubac and the Debate Concerning the Supernatural.* Grand Rapids: Eerdmans, 2005.

Milbank, John, and Catherine Pickstock, eds. *Radical Orthodoxy.* New York and London: Routledge, 1999.

————. *Truth in Aquinas.* London and New York: Routledge University Press, 2001.

Montagnes, Bernard, *La doctrine de l'analogie de l'être aprés saint Thomas d'Aquin.* Louvain: Éditions Peeters, 1963.

Mournier, Emmanuel. *Le Personnalisme.* Paris: Presses Universitaires de la France, 1949.

Morerod, Charles. *Ecumenism and Philosophy: Philosophical Questions for a Renewal of Dialogue.* Naples, FL: Sapientia Press, 2006.

————. "Foi et Raison dans la Connaissance que Nous avons de Dieu." *Nova et Vetera* (French ed.) 73, no. 4 (1998): 113–38.

————. "La Relation entre les Religions selon John Hick." *Nova et Vetera* (French ed.) 75, no. 4 (2000): 35–62.

————. *Tradition et Unité des Chrétiens: Le Dogma Comme Condition de Possibilité de l'Oecuménisme.* Paris, France: Parole et Silence, 2005.

Muralt, André de. *Comment Dire l'Être.* Paris: J. Vrin, 1985.

————. *La Métaphysique du Phénomène.* Paris: J. Vrin, 1985.

Nicolas, Jean-Hervé. *Dieu connu comme inconnu, Essai d'une critique de la connaissance théologique.* Paris: Desclée de Brouwer, 1966.

O'Rourke, Fran. *Pseudo-Dionysius and the Metaphysics of Aquinas.* Leiden: Brill, 1992.

Owen, G. E. L. "Logic and Metaphysics in Some Earlier Works of Aristotle." In *Logic, Science, and Dialectic,* 180–99. Ithaca: Cornell University Press, 1986.

Owens, Joseph. *The Doctrine of Being in the Aristotelian Metaphysics.* Toronto: PIMS, 1978.

Peghaire, Julien. *Intellectus et Ratio selon St. Thomas d'Aquin.* Paris: J. Vrin, 1936.

Pegis, Anton. "St. Thomas and the Coherence of the Aristotelian Theology." *Medieval Studies* 35 (1973): 67–117.

Philippe, Marie-Dominique. *De l'Être à Dieu: De la philosophie première à la sagesse.* Vols. 1–3. Paris: Téqui, 1977.

————. "La Sagesse selon Aristote." *Nova et Vetera* (French ed.) 20, no. 4 (1945): 325–74.

————. *l'Être.* Vols. 1 and 2. Paris: Téqui, 1974.

Philipse, Herman. *Heidegger's Philosophy of Being.* Princeton: Princeton University Press, 1998.

Phillips, Wilfred G. "Rahner's Vorgriff." *Thomist* 56 (1992): 257–90.

Preller, Victor. *Divine Science and the Science of God: A Reformulation of Thomas Aquinas.* Princeton: Princeton University Press, 1967.

Prouvost, Géry. "Les relations entre philosophie et théologie chez É. Gilson et les thomistes contemporains." *Revue Thomiste* 94 (1994): 413–30.

————. *Thomas d'Aquin et les Thomismes.* Paris: Cerf, 1996.

Przywara, Erich. *Analogia Entis.* French translation by P. Secretan. Paris: Presses Universitaires de France, 1990.

Putallaz, Francois-Xavier. *Le Sens de la Réflexion chez Thomas d'Aquin.* Paris: J. Vrin, 1991.

Rabeau, Gaston. *Le Jugement d'Existence.* Paris: J. Vrin, 1938.

Rahner, Karl. *Foundations of Christian Faith.* London: Seabury, 1984.

————. *Geist in Welt: Zur Metaphysik der endlichen Erkenntnis bei Thomas von Aquin.* Innsbruck: F. Rauch, 1939.

————. *Hörer des Wortes.* German original, 1941. English translation by J. Donceel, *Hearer of the Word: Laying the Foundation for a Philosophy of Religion.* New York: Continuum, 1994.

————. *A Rahner Reader.* Edited by G. McCool. New York: Seabury, 1975.

————. *Spirit in the World.* Translated by W. Dych. London: Sheed and Ward, 1968.

————. *Theological Investigations* 3. London: Darton, Longman, and Todd, 1966.

————. *Theological Investigations* 4. London: Darton, Longman, and Todd, 1967.

Ramirez, Santiago. *De Gratia Dei.* Salamanca: Editorial San Esteban, 1992.

Reale, Giovanni. *The Concept of First Philosophy and the Unity of the Metaphysics of Aristotle.* Translated by J. Catan. Albany: State University of New York Press, 1980.

————. *Toward a New Interpretation of Plato.* Translated by J. Catan. Washington, DC: The Catholic University of America Press, 1997.

Riches, John, ed. *The Analogy of Beauty.* Edinburgh: T&T Clark, 1986.

Rolnick, Philip A. *Analogical Possibilities: How Words Refer to God.* Atlanta: Scholars Press, 1993.

Rocca, Gregory. *Speaking the Incomprehensible God: Thomas Aquinas on the Interplay of Positive and Negative Theology.* Washington, DC: The Catholic University of America Press, 2004.

Ross, W. D. *Aristotle's Metaphysics.* Oxford: Clarendon Press, 1924.

Sayre, Kenneth. *Plato's Late Ontology: A Riddle Resolved.* Princeton: Princeton University Press, 1983.

Scaltsas, Theodore. "Substantial Holism." In *Unity, Identity and Explanation in Aristotle's Metaphysics,* edited by T. Scaltsas, D. Charles, and M. L. Gill, 107–28. Oxford: Oxford University Press, 1994.

Scheler, Max. *Formalism in Ethics and Non-Formal Ethics of Values.* Translated by M. Frings and R. Funk. Evanston, IL: Northeastern University Press, 1973.

————. *Le Formalism en Ethique et l'Ethique Materièle des Valeurs.* Paris: Seuil, 1955.

Schönfeld, Martin. *The Philosophy of the Young Kant.* Oxford: Oxford University Press, 2000.

Sedley, David. "Metaphysics Λ, 10." In *Aristotle's Metaphysics Lambda,* edited by M. Frede and D. Charles, 327–50. Oxford: Clarendon Press, 2000.

Sertillanges, A.-D. *Le christianisme et les philosophes.* Paris: Aubier, 1939.

————. "Renseignments techniques." In *Somme Théologique, Dieu,* vol. 2, 371–407. Paris: Revue des Jeunes, 1926.

Shanley, Brian. "Divine Causation and Human Freedom in Aquinas." *American Catholic Philosophical Quarterly* 72, no. 1 (1998): 99–122.

Sherwin, Michael. *By Knowledge and By Love.* Washington, DC: The Catholic University of America Press, 2005.

Simmons, Edward. "The Thomistic Doctrine of the Three Degrees of Formal Abstraction." *Thomist* 22 (1959): 37–67.

Smalley, Beryl. *The Study of the Bible in the Middle Ages.* Notre Dame: University of Notre Dame Press, 1970.

Sondag, Gérard. *Duns Scot.* Paris: J. Vrin, 2005.

Spinoza, Benedict de. *Theological-Political Treatise.* Translated by M. Silverthorne and J. Israel. Cambridge: Cambridge University Press, 2007.

Stump, Eleonore. *Aquinas.* New York: Routledge, 2003.

Swinburne, Richard. *The Existence of God.* Oxford: Clarendon Press, 1991.

Tavussi, Michael. "Aquinas on Resolution in Metaphysics." *Thomist* 55 (1991): 199–227.

Te Velde, Rudi. *Aquinas on God.* Aldershot: Ashgate, 2006.

———. *Participation and Substantiality in Thomas Aquinas.* Leiden: Brill, 1995.

Torrance, Alan. "*Auditus Fidei*: Where and How does God Speak? Faith, Reason and the Question of Criteria." In *Reason and the Reasons of Faith*, edited by P. Griffiths and R. Hütter, 27–52. New York and London: T&T Clark, 2005.

Torrell, Jean-Pierre. "Nature et Grâce chez Thomas d'Aquin." *Revue Thomiste* 101 (2001): 167–202.

Turner, Denys. *Faith, Reason and the Existence of God.* Cambridge: Cambridge University Press, 2004.

Twetten, David. "Come distinguere realemente tra esse ed essenza in Tommaso d'Aquino: Qualche aiuto de Aristotele." In *Tommaso D'Aquino e l'oggetto della Metaphisica*, edited by Steven Brock, 149–92. Rome: Armando, 2004.

Vajda, Georges. "Notes d'Avicenne sur la 'Théologie d'Aristote.'" *Revue Thomiste* 51 (1951): 346–406.

Van Steenberghen, Fernand. *La Philosophie au XIIIe Siècle.* Louvain: Éditions Peeters, 1991.

———. *Le Problème de l'Existence de Dieu dans les Écrits de S. Thomas d'Aquin.* Louvain: Éditions de l'Institut Supérieur de Philosophie, 1980.

———. *Maître Siger de Brabant.* Louvain: Éditions Peeters, 1977.

Verbeke, Gerard. *D'Aristote à Thomas d'Aquin.* Louvain: Leuven University Press, 1990.

Vernier, J. M. *Théologie et Métaphysique de la Création chez St. Thomas d'Aquin.* Paris: Pierre Téqui, 1995.

Wéber, Eduard-Henri. *La Personne Humaine au XIIIe Siècle.* Paris: J. Vrin, 1991.

Weisheipl, James. *Friar Thomas d'Aquino.* Washington, DC: The Catholic University of America Press, 1974.

———. "The Meaning of *Sacra Doctrina* in *Summa Theologiae* I, q. 1." *Thomist* 38 (1974): 49–80.

———. *Nature and Motion in the Middle Ages*, edited by W. Carroll. Washington, DC: The Catholic University of America Press, 1985.

Wippel, James. *Metaphysical Themes in Thomas Aquinas.* Washington, DC: The Catholic University of America Press, 1984.

———. *Metaphysical Themes in Thomas Aquinas 2.* Washington, DC: The Catholic University of America Press, 2007.

———. *The Metaphysical Thought of Thomas Aquinas.* Washington, DC: The Catholic University of America Press, 2000.

Witt, Charlotte. *Substance and Essence in Aristotle.* Ithaca: Cornell University Press, 1989.

Wojtyla, Karol. *The Acting Person.* Translated by A. Potocki. Drodrect: D. Reidel Publishing, 1979.

_____. "La Personnalisme Thomiste." In *En Esprit et En Verité,* edited by G. Jarczyk. Paris: Le Centurion, 1980.

Wolterstorff, Nicolas. *John Locke and the Ethics of Belief.* Cambridge: Cambridge University Press, 1996.

Wundt, Max. *Die deutsche Schulmetaphysik des 17: Jahhunderts.* Tübingen: Mohr Siebeck, 1939.

Young, Julian. *Heidegger's Later Philosophy.* Cambridge: Cambridge University Press, 2002.

Zimmermann, Albert. *Ontologie oder Metaphysik?* Louvain: Peeters, 1998.

Reference Works

Decrees of the Ecumenical Councils. Translated by Norman Tanner. London and Washington, DC: Sheed and Ward and Georgetown University Press, 1990.

The Holy Bible, Revised Standard Version.

Index

abstractio formae, 136
abstractio totius, 136
abstraction
  Maritain's degrees of, 135–38,
    136*n*4
  Rahner on, 182–85, 196
accidental properties
  causality and, 127, 166–67, 222
  contingent beings and, 239
  metaphysical notions of, 211
  Rahner and, 194–95
  substance and, 161–63, 265
  Thomas and, 98
act of existence (*actus essendi*), 82
actuality
  Aristotle and, 54, 55, 59, 127,
    127*n*54
  being and, 51
  causal analysis of, 115–16, 158,
    159, 190
  esse/essence distinction and, 81,
    83, 85–86, 264–65
  of final cause, 41, 52, 53, 57
  of goodness, 42
  knowledge of existence of God and,
    235–45
  Maritain on, 153
  materiality and, 214
  metaphysical notions of, 211

  in movement, 45
  Rahner on, 194
  of substance, 55, 56, 60, 62, 162,
    222–25, 223*n*45
  Thomas and, 98, 127, 224*n*46,
    240*n*81
  transcendentals and, 163
ad alterum analogy
  esse/essence distinction and, 104,
    115
  Gilson and, 107, 120, 130
  knowledge of God and, 255, 257
  Maritain and, 134, 148
  in natural theology, 68, 202
  primary cause of being and, 165
  Thomas and, 90–91, 90*n*67,
    92*n*70, 97, 99, 225
  transcendentals and, 164
ad unum analogy of being, 20
Aertsen, Jan, 144, 161*n*53
Aeterni Patris, xxix, 6–9, 105
affirmative synthesis, 183
agent intellect, 43*n*40, 70*n*3, 122,
  176, 179, 181*n*27, 182, 184, 185,
  186, 188*n*41, 196. *See also* intellect
agnosticism, 7, 253
Albert the Great, 69*n*2
aliquid, 142, 142*n*18, 175*n*8